Wrapped-Up
FoxTrot

Other *FoxTrot* Books by Bill Amend

FoxTrot
Pass the Loot
Black Bart Says Draw
Eight Yards, Down and Out
Bury My Heart at Fun-Fun Mountain
Say Hello to Cactus Flats
May the Force Be with Us, Please
Take Us to Your Mall
The Return of the Lone Iguana
At Least This Place Sells T-shirts
Come Closer, Roger, There's a Mosquito on Your Nose
Welcome to Jasorassic Park
I'm Flying, Jack . . . I Mean, Roger
Think iFruity
Death by Field Trip
Encyclopedias Brown and White
His Code Name Was The Fox
Your Momma Thinks Square Roots Are Vegetables
Who's Up for Some Bonding?
Am I a Mutant or What!
Orlando Bloom Has Ruined Everything
My Hot Dog Went Out, Can I Have Another?
How Come I'm Always Luigi?
Houston, You Have a Problem
And When She Opened the Closet, All the Clothes Were Polyester

Anthologies

FoxTrot: The Works
FoxTrot *en masse*
Enormously FoxTrot
Wildly FoxTrot
FoxTrot Beyond a Doubt
Camp FoxTrot
Assorted FoxTrot
FoxTrot: Assembled with Care
FoxTrotius Maximus
Jam-Packed FoxTrot

Wrapped-Up FoxTrot

A Treasury with the Final Daily Strips

by Bill Amend

**Andrews McMeel
Publishing, LLC**

Kansas City

FoxTrot is distributed internationally by Universal Press Syndicate.

Wrapped-Up FoxTrot © 2009 by Bill Amend. All rights reserved. Printed in the United States of America. No part of this book may be used or reproduced in any manner whatsoever without written permission except in the case of reprints in the context of reviews. For information, write Andrews McMeel Publishing, LLC, an Andrews McMeel Universal company, 1130 Walnut Street, Kansas City, Missouri 64106.

09 10 11 12 13 BAM 10 9 8 7 6 5 4 3 2 1

ISBN-13: 978-0-7407-8158-2
ISBN-10: 0-7407-8158-8

Library of Congress Control Number: 2008942227

www.andrewsmcmeel.com
www.foxtrot.com

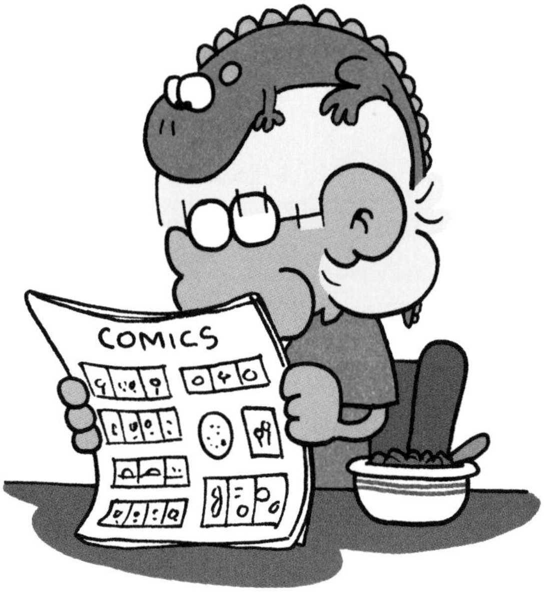
COMICS

DEDICATED WITH THANKS
TO MY READERS

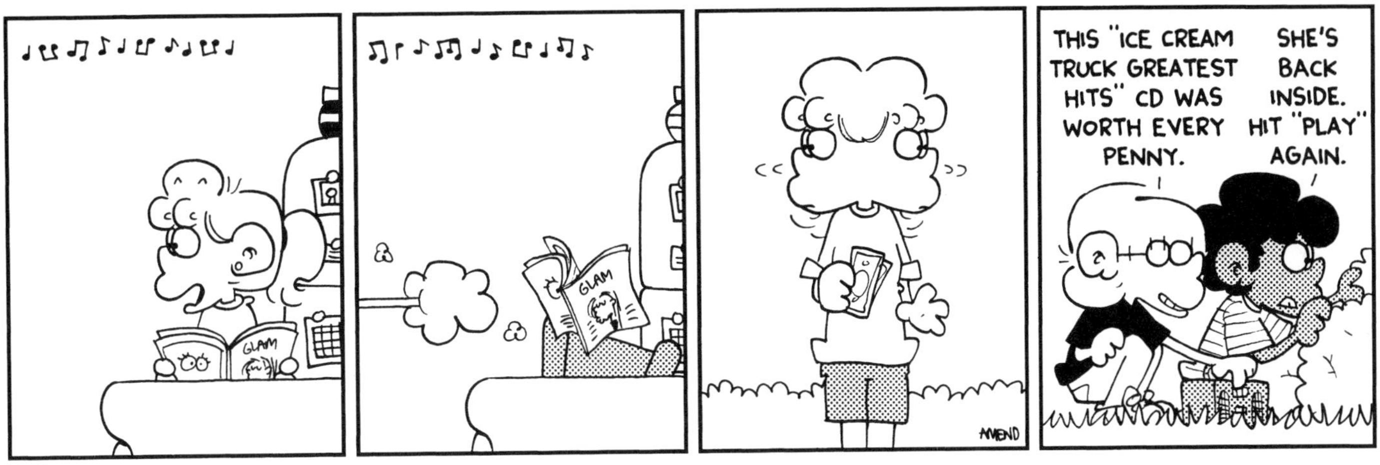
THIS "ICE CREAM TRUCK GREATEST HITS" CD WAS WORTH EVERY PENNY.
SHE'S BACK INSIDE. HIT "PLAY" AGAIN.

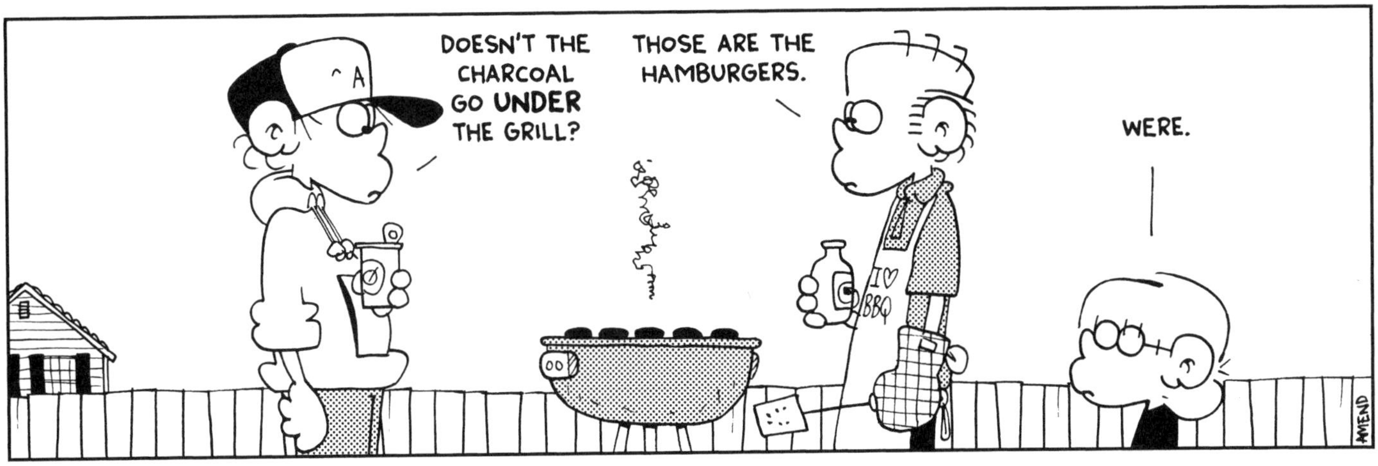
DOESN'T THE CHARCOAL GO **UNDER** THE GRILL?
THOSE ARE THE HAMBURGERS.
WERE.

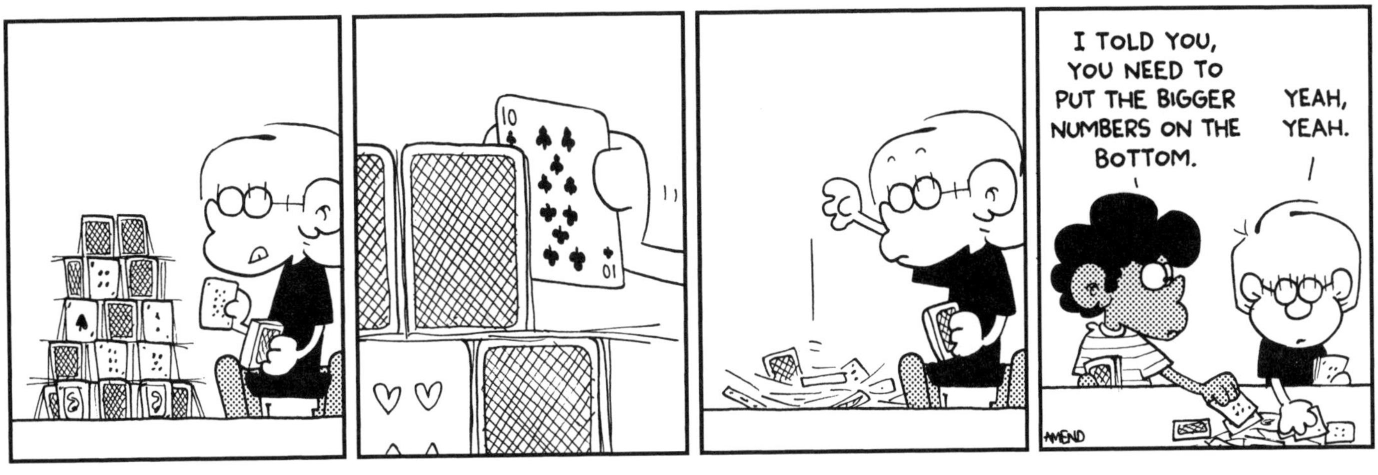
I TOLD YOU, YOU NEED TO PUT THE BIGGER NUMBERS ON THE BOTTOM.
YEAH, YEAH.

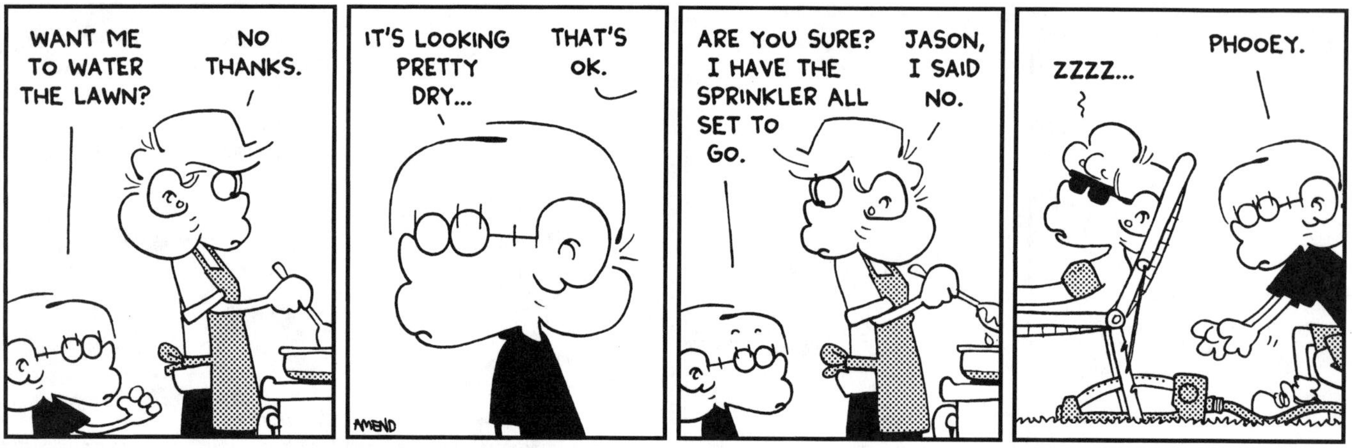
WANT ME TO WATER THE LAWN?
NO THANKS.
IT'S LOOKING PRETTY DRY...
THAT'S OK.
ARE YOU SURE? I HAVE THE SPRINKLER ALL SET TO GO.
JASON, I SAID NO.
ZZZZ...
PHOOEY.
AMEND

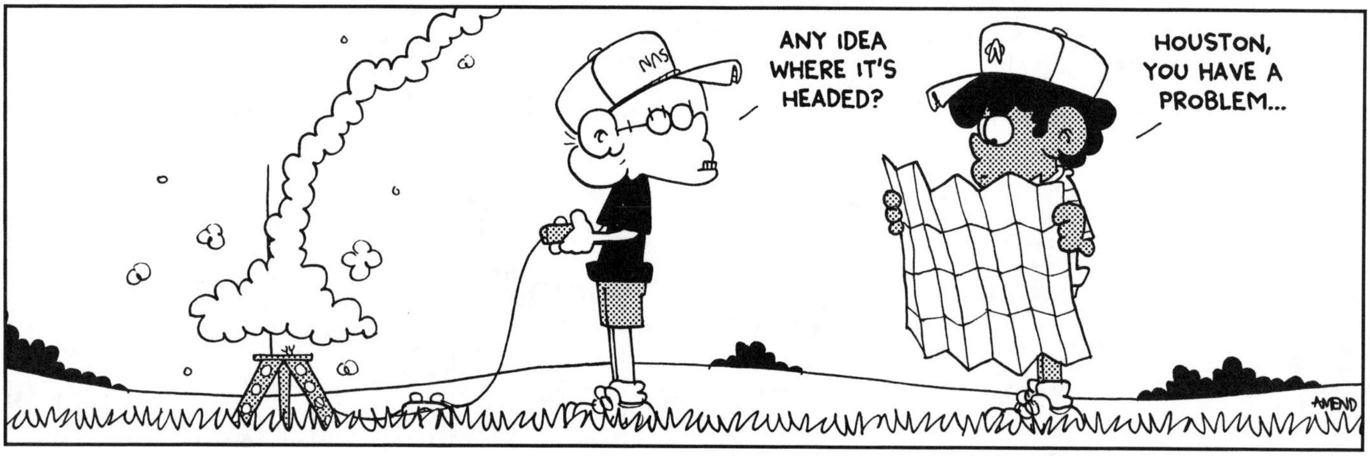
ANY IDEA WHERE IT'S HEADED?
HOUSTON, YOU HAVE A PROBLEM...
AMEND

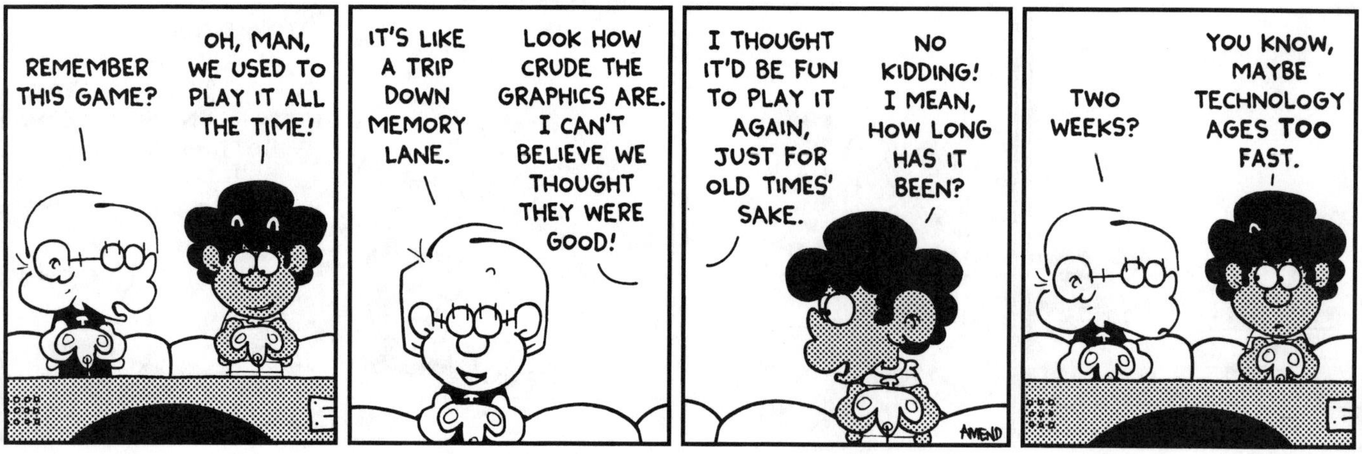
REMEMBER THIS GAME?
OH, MAN, WE USED TO PLAY IT ALL THE TIME!
IT'S LIKE A TRIP DOWN MEMORY LANE.
LOOK HOW CRUDE THE GRAPHICS ARE. I CAN'T BELIEVE WE THOUGHT THEY WERE GOOD!
I THOUGHT IT'D BE FUN TO PLAY IT AGAIN, JUST FOR OLD TIMES' SAKE.
NO KIDDING! I MEAN, HOW LONG HAS IT BEEN?
TWO WEEKS?
YOU KNOW, MAYBE TECHNOLOGY AGES TOO FAST.
AMEND

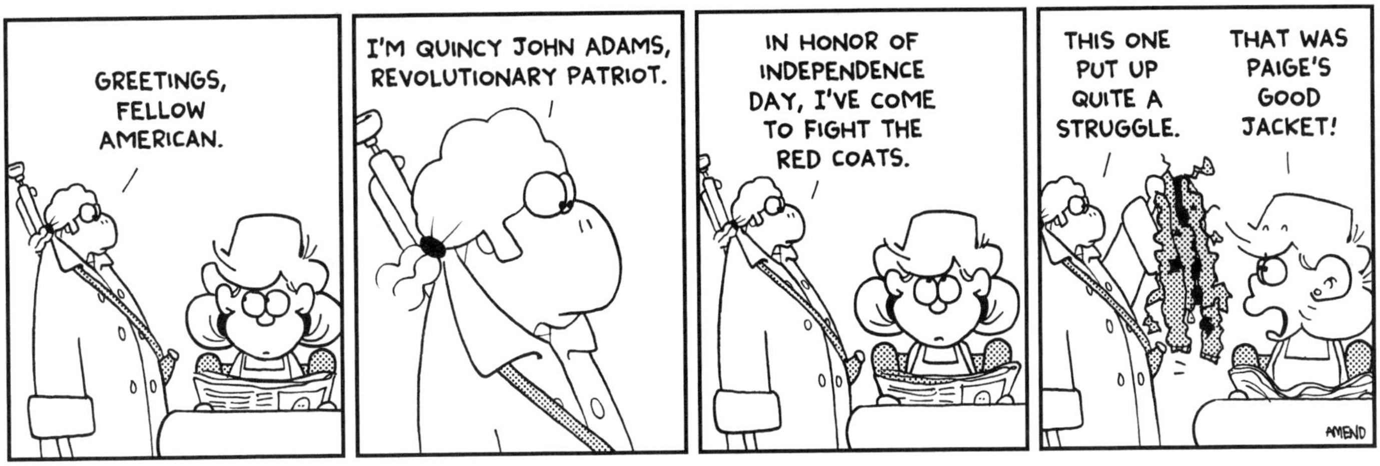
GREETINGS, FELLOW AMERICAN.
I'M QUINCY JOHN ADAMS, REVOLUTIONARY PATRIOT.
IN HONOR OF INDEPENDENCE DAY, I'VE COME TO FIGHT THE RED COATS.
THIS ONE PUT UP QUITE A STRUGGLE.
THAT WAS PAIGE'S GOOD JACKET!
AMEND

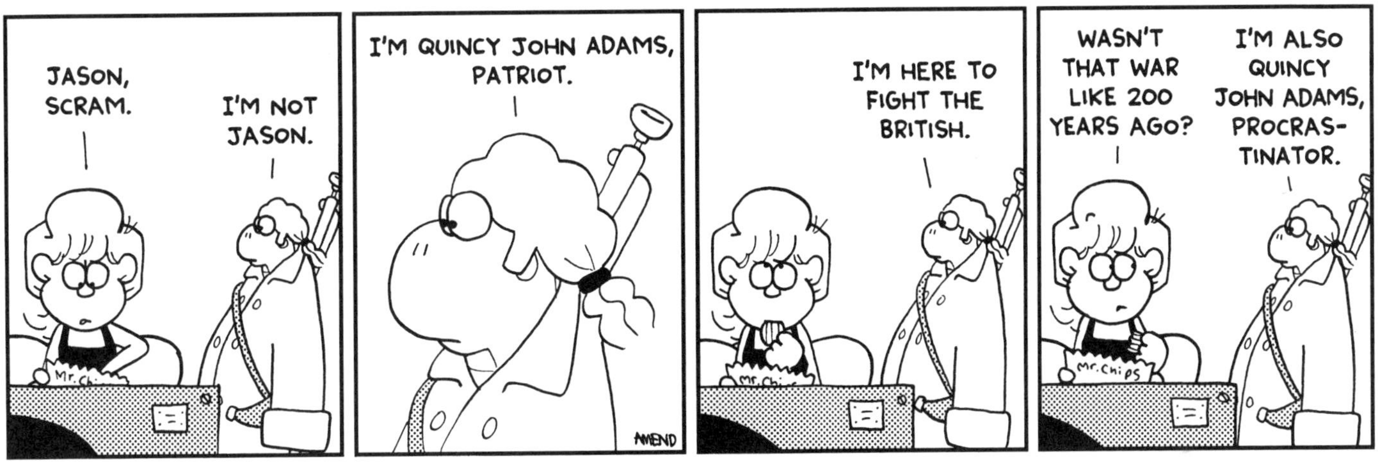
JASON, SCRAM.
I'M NOT JASON.
Mr. Chips
I'M QUINCY JOHN ADAMS, PATRIOT.
AMEND
I'M HERE TO FIGHT THE BRITISH.
WASN'T THAT WAR LIKE 200 YEARS AGO?
I'M ALSO QUINCY JOHN ADAMS, PROCRAS-TINATOR.
Mr. Chips

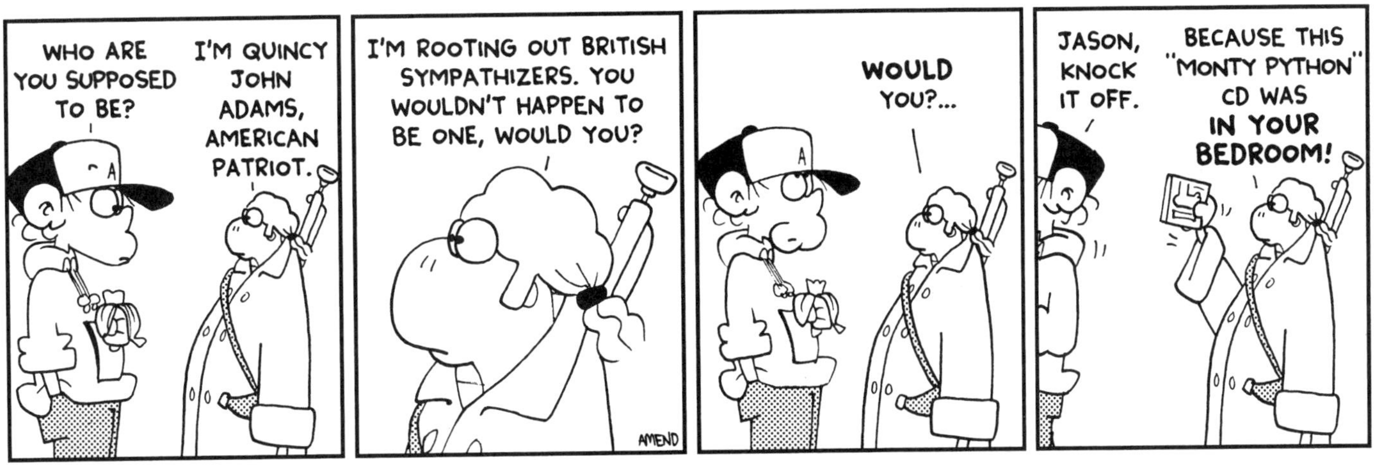
WHO ARE YOU SUPPOSED TO BE?
I'M QUINCY JOHN ADAMS, AMERICAN PATRIOT.
I'M ROOTING OUT BRITISH SYMPATHIZERS. YOU WOULDN'T HAPPEN TO BE ONE, WOULD YOU?
AMEND
WOULD YOU?...
JASON, KNOCK IT OFF.
BECAUSE THIS "MONTY PYTHON" CD WAS **IN YOUR BEDROOM!**

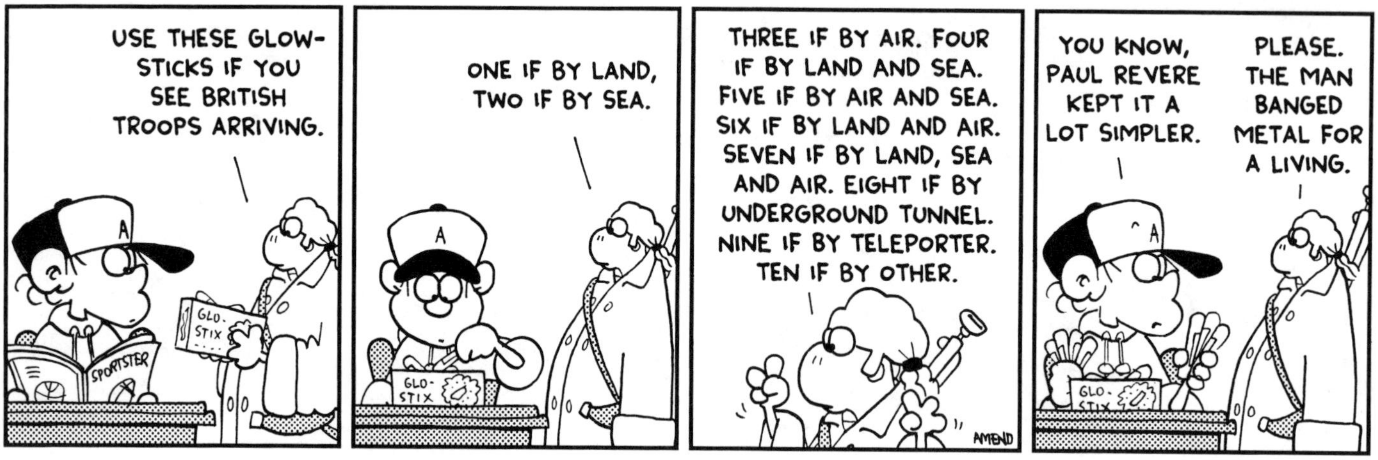
USE THESE GLOW-STICKS IF YOU SEE BRITISH TROOPS ARRIVING.
GLO-STIX
SPORTSTER
ONE IF BY LAND, TWO IF BY SEA.
GLO-STIX
THREE IF BY AIR. FOUR IF BY LAND AND SEA. FIVE IF BY AIR AND SEA. SIX IF BY LAND AND AIR. SEVEN IF BY LAND, SEA AND AIR. EIGHT IF BY UNDERGROUND TUNNEL. NINE IF BY TELEPORTER. TEN IF BY OTHER.
AMEND
YOU KNOW, PAUL REVERE KEPT IT A LOT SIMPLER.
PLEASE. THE MAN BANGED METAL FOR A LIVING.
GLO-STIX

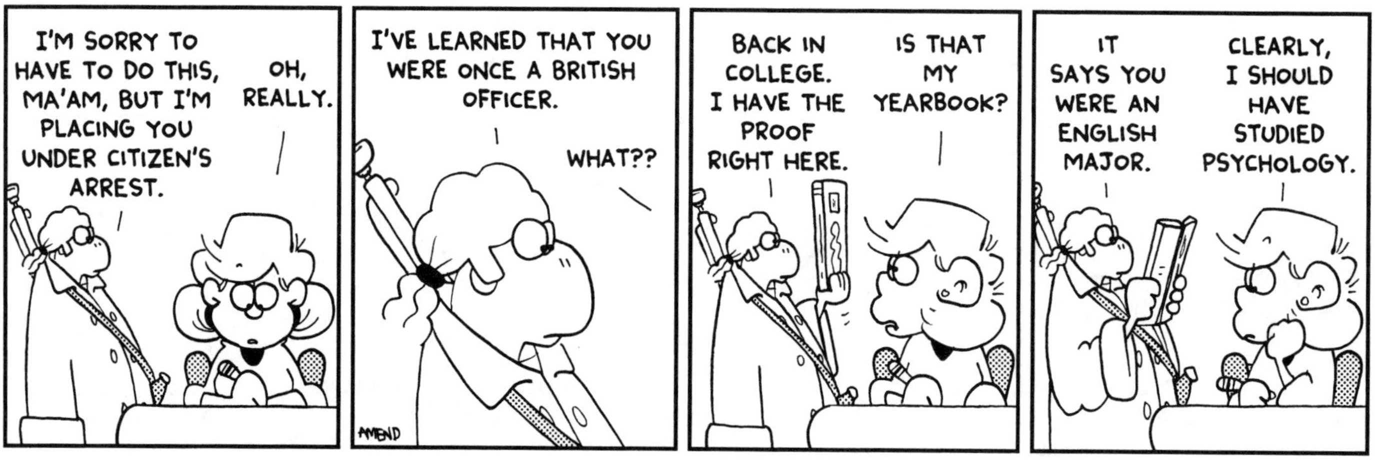
I'M SORRY TO HAVE TO DO THIS, MA'AM, BUT I'M PLACING YOU UNDER CITIZEN'S ARREST.
OH, REALLY.
I'VE LEARNED THAT YOU WERE ONCE A BRITISH OFFICER.
WHAT??
AMEND
BACK IN COLLEGE. I HAVE THE PROOF RIGHT HERE.
IS THAT MY YEARBOOK?
IT SAYS YOU WERE AN ENGLISH MAJOR.
CLEARLY, I SHOULD HAVE STUDIED PSYCHOLOGY.

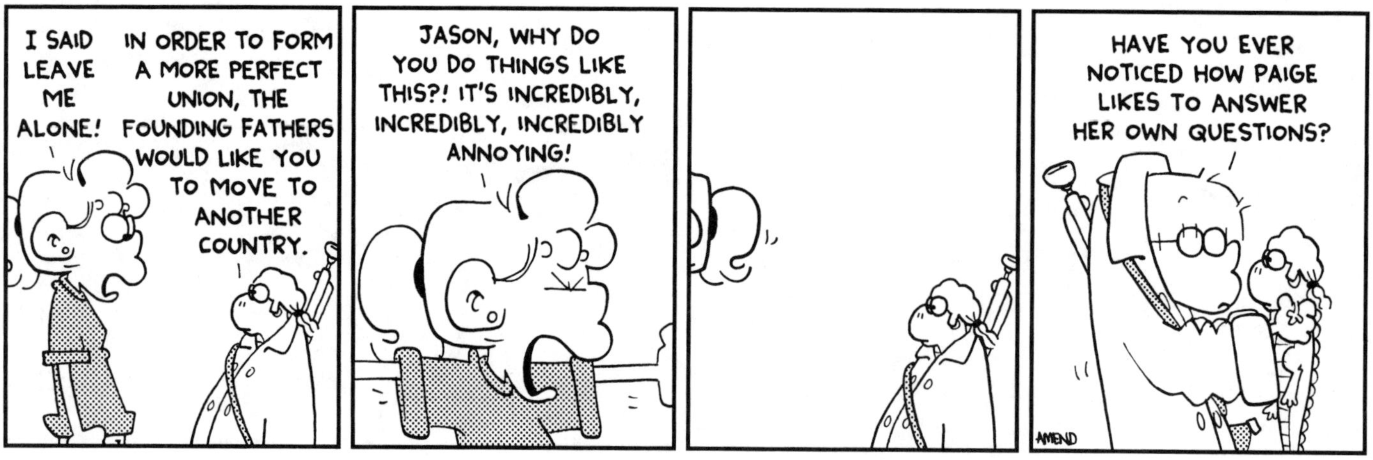
I SAID LEAVE ME ALONE!
IN ORDER TO FORM A MORE PERFECT UNION, THE FOUNDING FATHERS WOULD LIKE YOU TO MOVE TO ANOTHER COUNTRY.
JASON, WHY DO YOU DO THINGS LIKE THIS?! IT'S INCREDIBLY, INCREDIBLY, INCREDIBLY ANNOYING!
HAVE YOU EVER NOTICED HOW PAIGE LIKES TO ANSWER HER OWN QUESTIONS?
AMEND

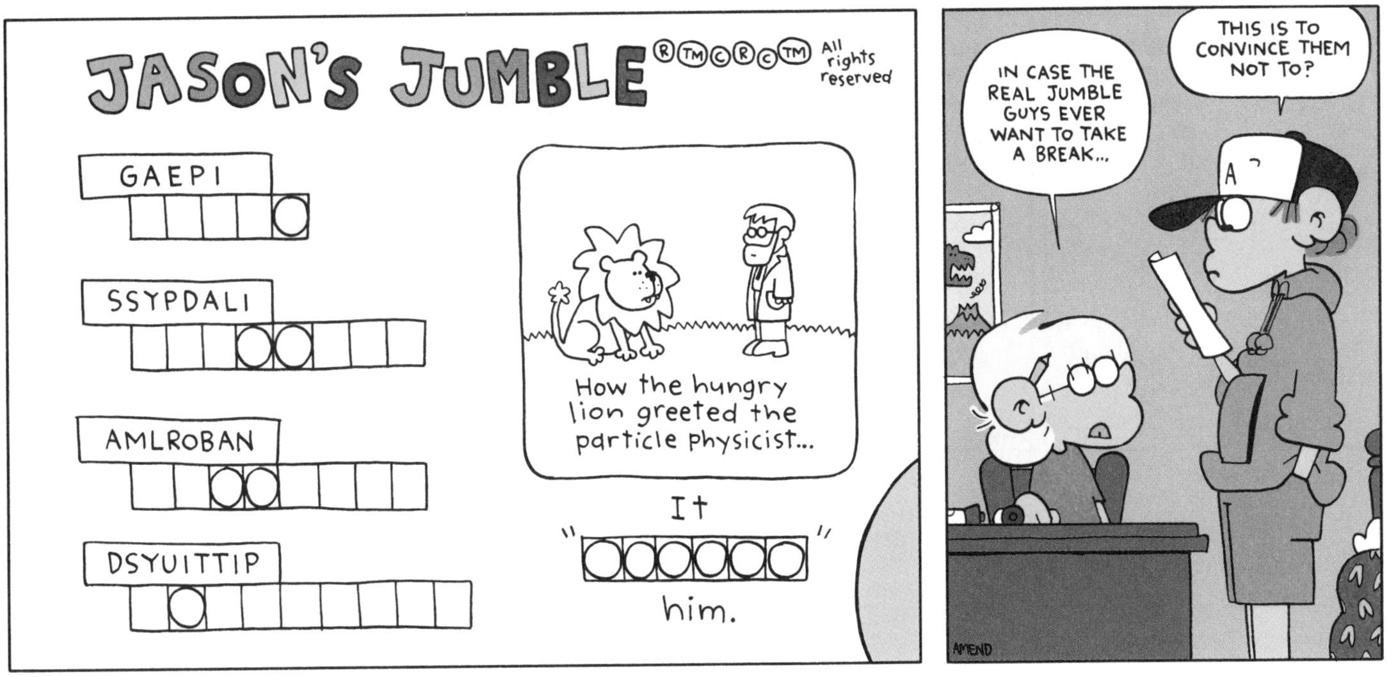
JASON'S JUMBLE ®™©®©™ All rights reserved
GAEPI
SSYPDALI
AMLROBAN
DSYUITTIP
How the hungry lion greeted the particle physicist...
It "" him.
IN CASE THE REAL JUMBLE GUYS EVER WANT TO TAKE A BREAK...
THIS IS TO CONVINCE THEM NOT TO?
AMEND

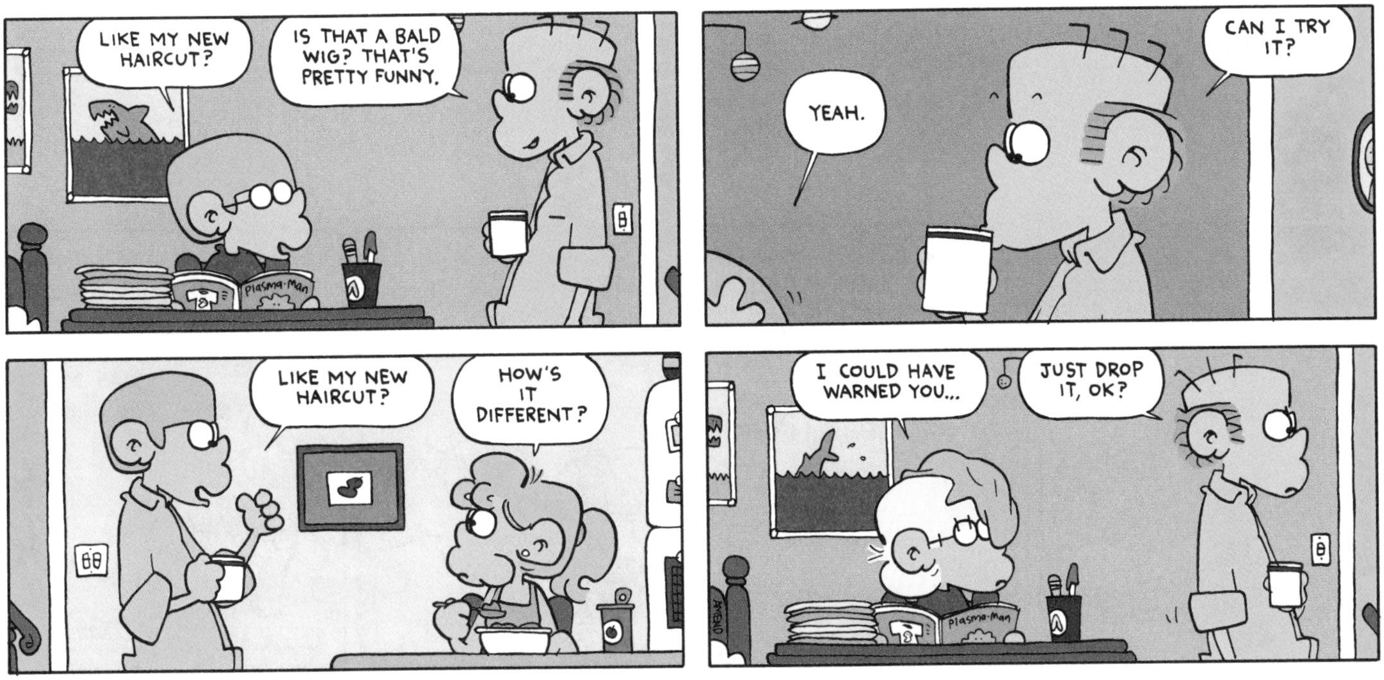
LIKE MY NEW HAIRCUT?
IS THAT A BALD WIG? THAT'S PRETTY FUNNY.
Plasma-Man
YEAH.
CAN I TRY IT?
LIKE MY NEW HAIRCUT?
HOW'S IT DIFFERENT?
I COULD HAVE WARNED YOU...
JUST DROP IT, OK?
Plasma-Man

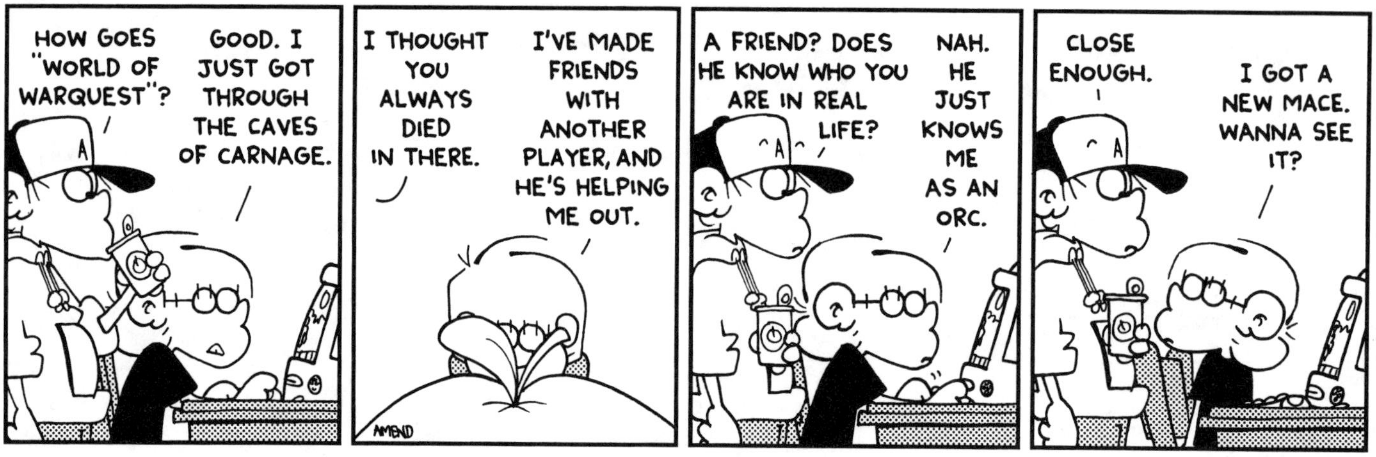
HOW GOES "WORLD OF WARQUEST"?
GOOD. I JUST GOT THROUGH THE CAVES OF CARNAGE.
I THOUGHT YOU ALWAYS DIED IN THERE.
I'VE MADE FRIENDS WITH ANOTHER PLAYER, AND HE'S HELPING ME OUT.
AMEND
A FRIEND? DOES HE KNOW WHO YOU ARE IN REAL LIFE?
NAH. HE JUST KNOWS ME AS AN ORC.
CLOSE ENOUGH.
I GOT A NEW MACE. WANNA SEE IT?

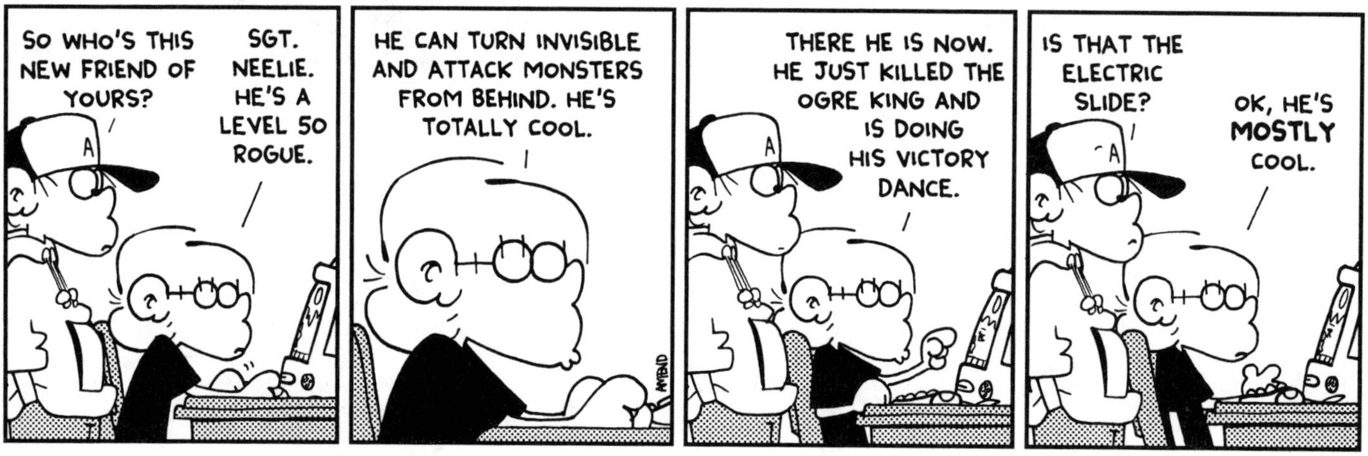
SO WHO'S THIS NEW FRIEND OF YOURS?
SGT. NEELIE. HE'S A LEVEL 50 ROGUE.
HE CAN TURN INVISIBLE AND ATTACK MONSTERS FROM BEHIND. HE'S TOTALLY COOL.
AMEND
THERE HE IS NOW. HE JUST KILLED THE OGRE KING AND IS DOING HIS VICTORY DANCE.
IS THAT THE ELECTRIC SLIDE?
OK, HE'S **MOSTLY** COOL.

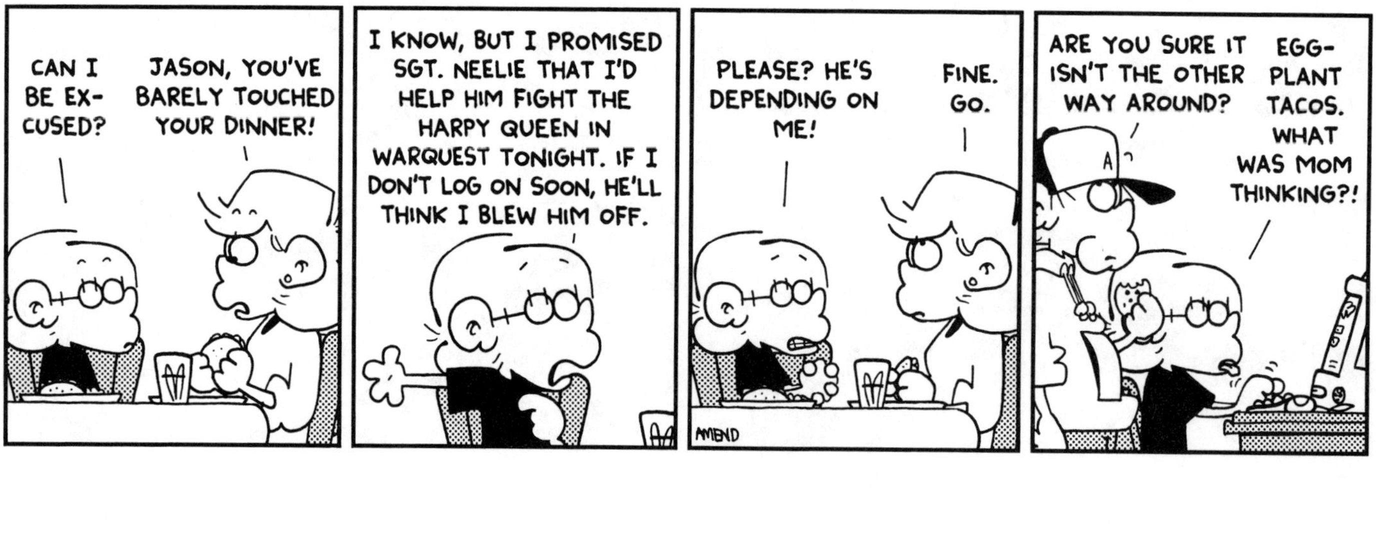
CAN I BE EX-CUSED?
JASON, YOU'VE BARELY TOUCHED YOUR DINNER!
I KNOW, BUT I PROMISED SGT. NEELIE THAT I'D HELP HIM FIGHT THE HARPY QUEEN IN WARQUEST TONIGHT. IF I DON'T LOG ON SOON, HE'LL THINK I BLEW HIM OFF.
PLEASE? HE'S DEPENDING ON ME!
FINE. GO.
AMEND
ARE YOU SURE IT ISN'T THE OTHER WAY AROUND?
EGG-PLANT TACOS. WHAT WAS MOM THINKING?!

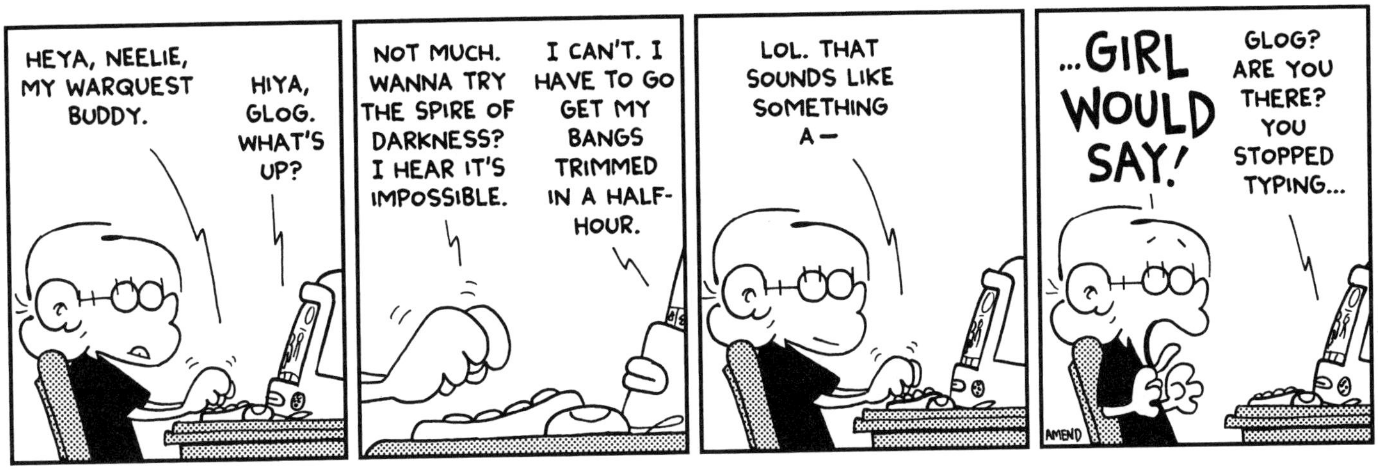
HEYA, NEELIE, MY WARQUEST BUDDY.
HIYA, GLOG. WHAT'S UP?
NOT MUCH. WANNA TRY THE SPIRE OF DARKNESS? I HEAR IT'S IMPOSSIBLE.
I CAN'T. I HAVE TO GO GET MY BANGS TRIMMED IN A HALF-HOUR.
LOL. THAT SOUNDS LIKE SOMETHING A—
...GIRL WOULD SAY!
GLOG? ARE YOU THERE? YOU STOPPED TYPING...
AMEND

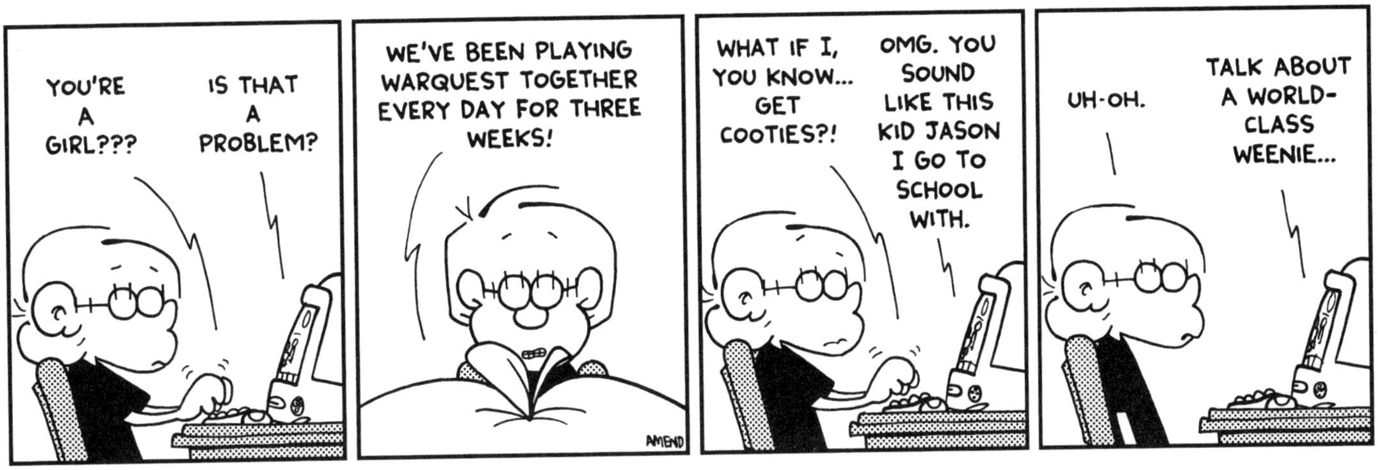
YOU'RE A GIRL???
IS THAT A PROBLEM?
WE'VE BEEN PLAYING WARQUEST TOGETHER EVERY DAY FOR THREE WEEKS!
AMEND
WHAT IF I, YOU KNOW... GET COOTIES?!
OMG. YOU SOUND LIKE THIS KID JASON I GO TO SCHOOL WITH.
UH-OH.
TALK ABOUT A WORLD-CLASS WEENIE...

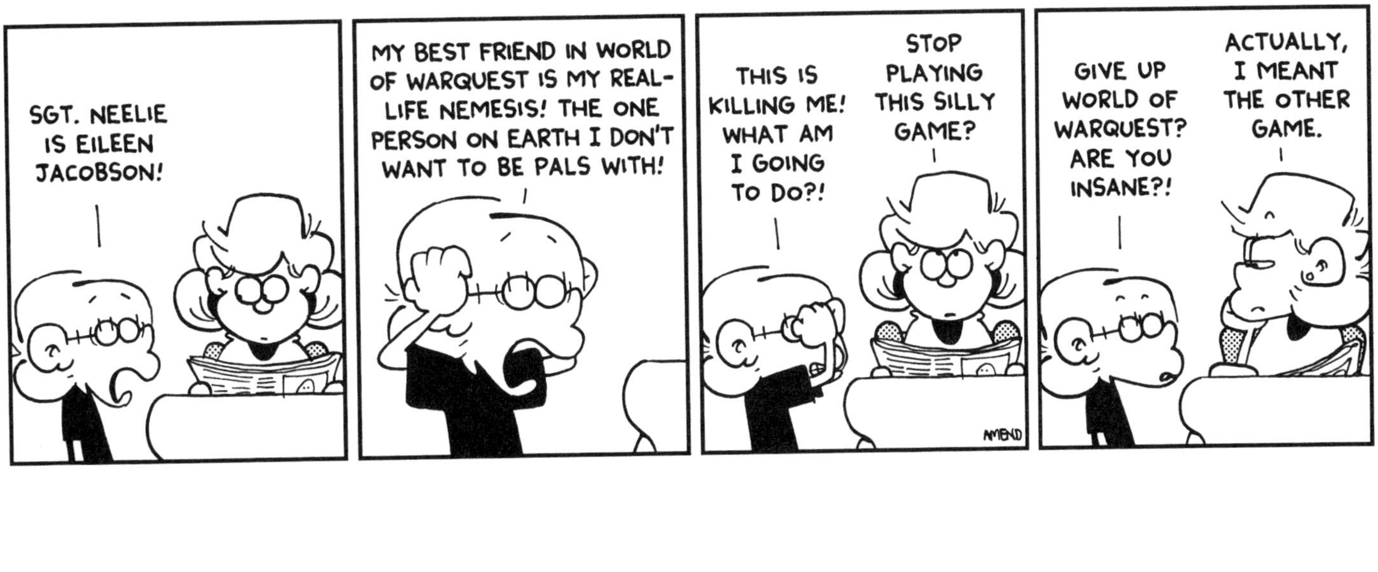
SGT. NEELIE IS EILEEN JACOBSON!
MY BEST FRIEND IN WORLD OF WARQUEST IS MY REAL-LIFE NEMESIS! THE ONE PERSON ON EARTH I DON'T WANT TO BE PALS WITH!
THIS IS KILLING ME! WHAT AM I GOING TO DO?!
STOP PLAYING THIS SILLY GAME?
AMEND
GIVE UP WORLD OF WARQUEST? ARE YOU INSANE?!
ACTUALLY, I MEANT THE OTHER GAME.

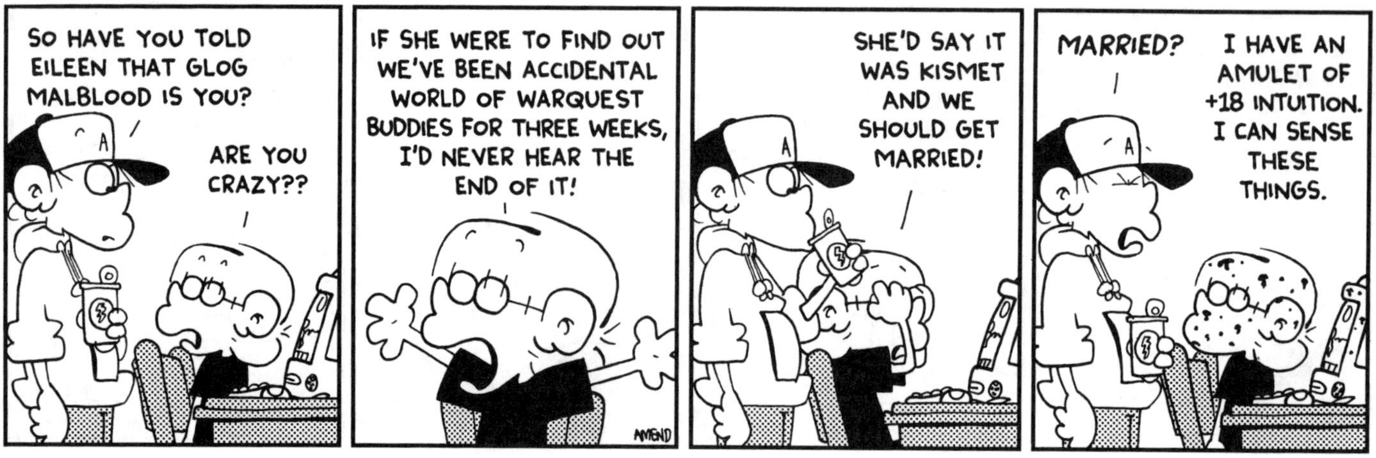
SO HAVE YOU TOLD EILEEN THAT GLOG MALBLOOD IS YOU?
ARE YOU CRAZY??
IF SHE WERE TO FIND OUT WE'VE BEEN ACCIDENTAL WORLD OF WARQUEST BUDDIES FOR THREE WEEKS, I'D NEVER HEAR THE END OF IT!
SHE'D SAY IT WAS KISMET AND WE SHOULD GET MARRIED!
MARRIED?
I HAVE AN AMULET OF +18 INTUITION. I CAN SENSE THESE THINGS.

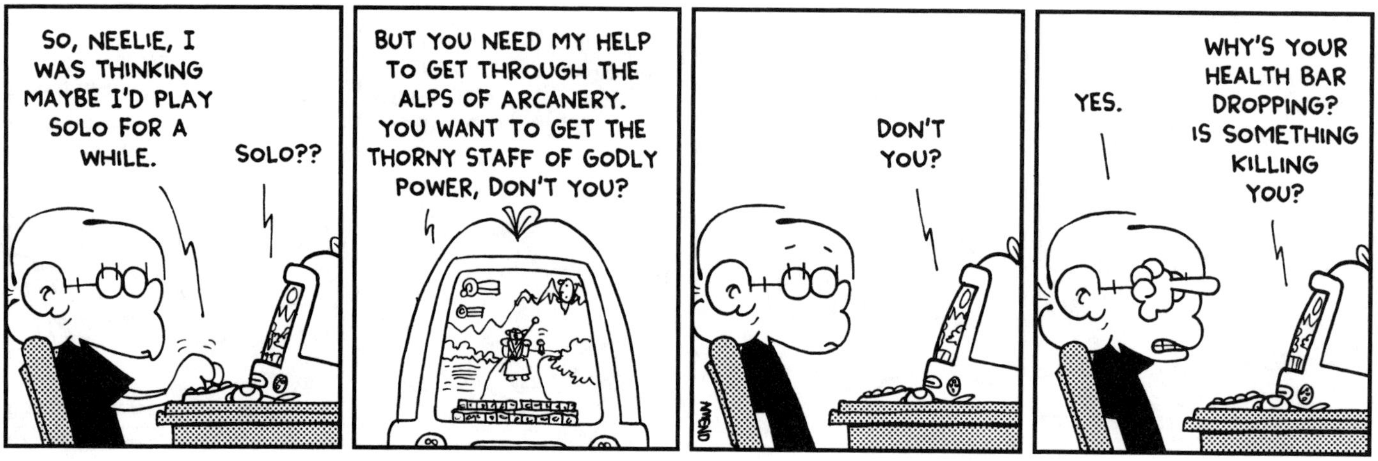
SO, NEELIE, I WAS THINKING MAYBE I'D PLAY SOLO FOR A WHILE.
SOLO??
BUT YOU NEED MY HELP TO GET THROUGH THE ALPS OF ARCANERY. YOU WANT TO GET THE THORNY STAFF OF GODLY POWER, DON'T YOU?
DON'T YOU?
YES.
WHY'S YOUR HEALTH BAR DROPPING? IS SOMETHING KILLING YOU?

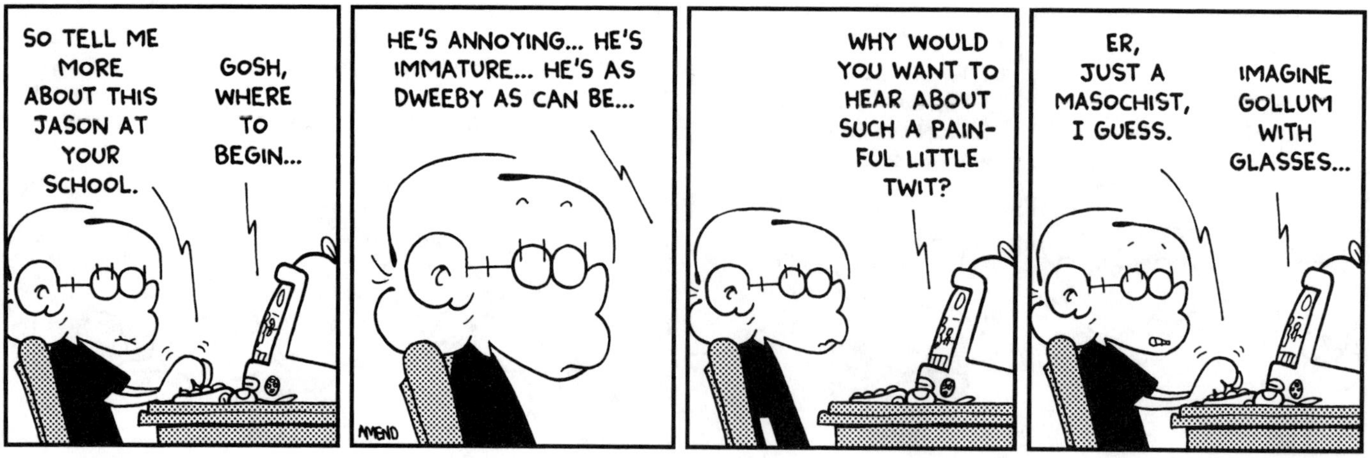
SO TELL ME MORE ABOUT THIS JASON AT YOUR SCHOOL.
GOSH, WHERE TO BEGIN...
HE'S ANNOYING... HE'S IMMATURE... HE'S AS DWEEBY AS CAN BE...
WHY WOULD YOU WANT TO HEAR ABOUT SUCH A PAIN-FUL LITTLE TWIT?
ER, JUST A MASOCHIST, I GUESS.
IMAGINE GOLLUM WITH GLASSES...

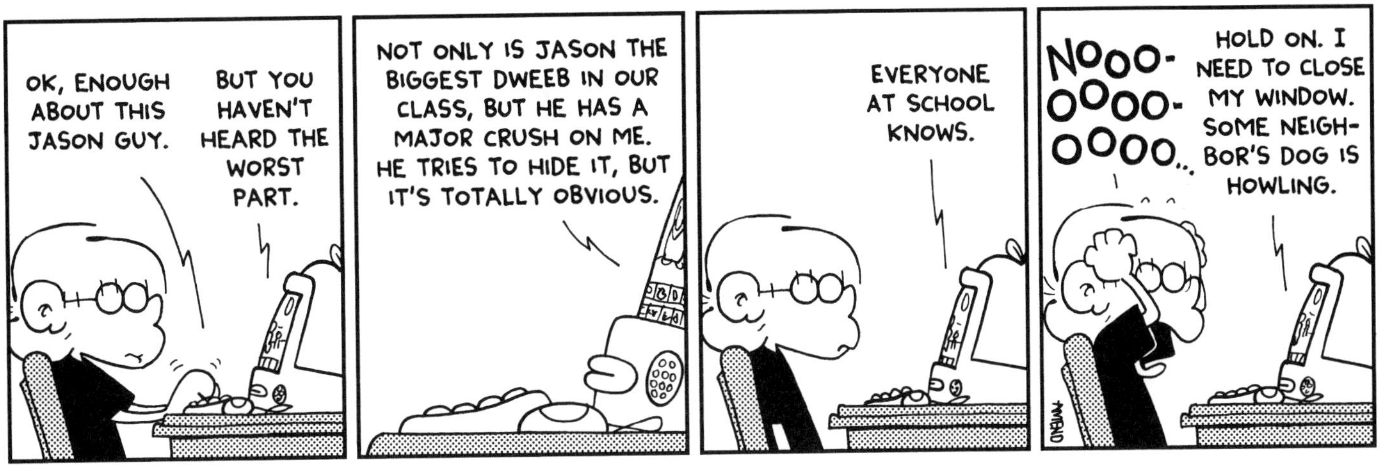
OK, ENOUGH ABOUT THIS JASON GUY.
BUT YOU HAVEN'T HEARD THE WORST PART.
NOT ONLY IS JASON THE BIGGEST DWEEB IN OUR CLASS, BUT HE HAS A MAJOR CRUSH ON ME. HE TRIES TO HIDE IT, BUT IT'S TOTALLY OBVIOUS.
EVERYONE AT SCHOOL KNOWS.
NOOO-OOOO-OOOO...
HOLD ON. I NEED TO CLOSE MY WINDOW. SOME NEIGH-BOR'S DOG IS HOWLING.

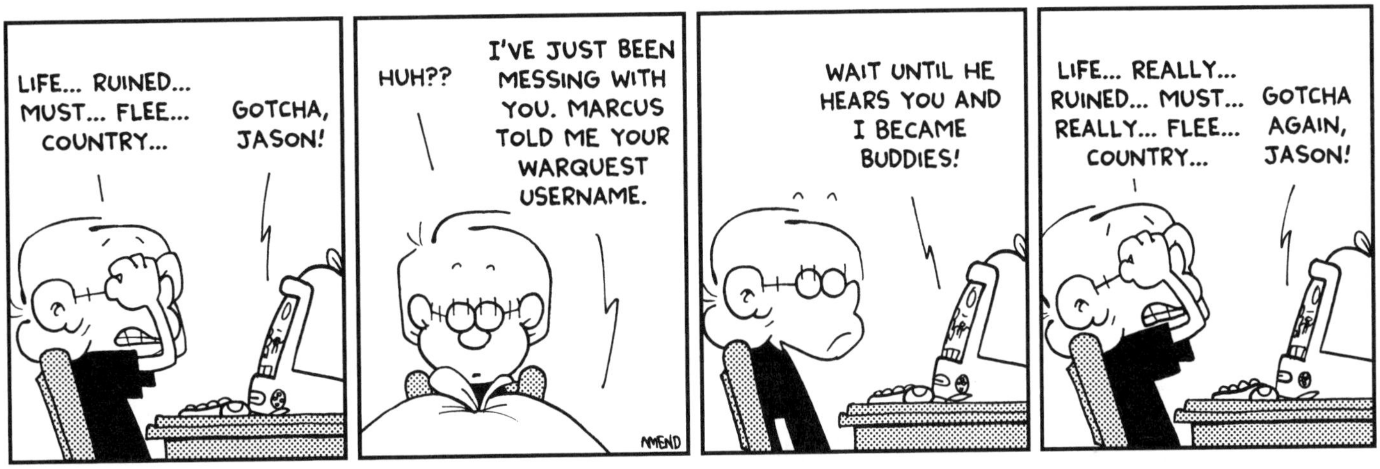
LIFE... RUINED... MUST... FLEE... COUNTRY...
GOTCHA, JASON!
HUH??
I'VE JUST BEEN MESSING WITH YOU. MARCUS TOLD ME YOUR WARQUEST USERNAME.
WAIT UNTIL HE HEARS YOU AND I BECAME BUDDIES!
LIFE... REALLY... RUINED... MUST... REALLY... FLEE... COUNTRY...
GOTCHA AGAIN, JASON!

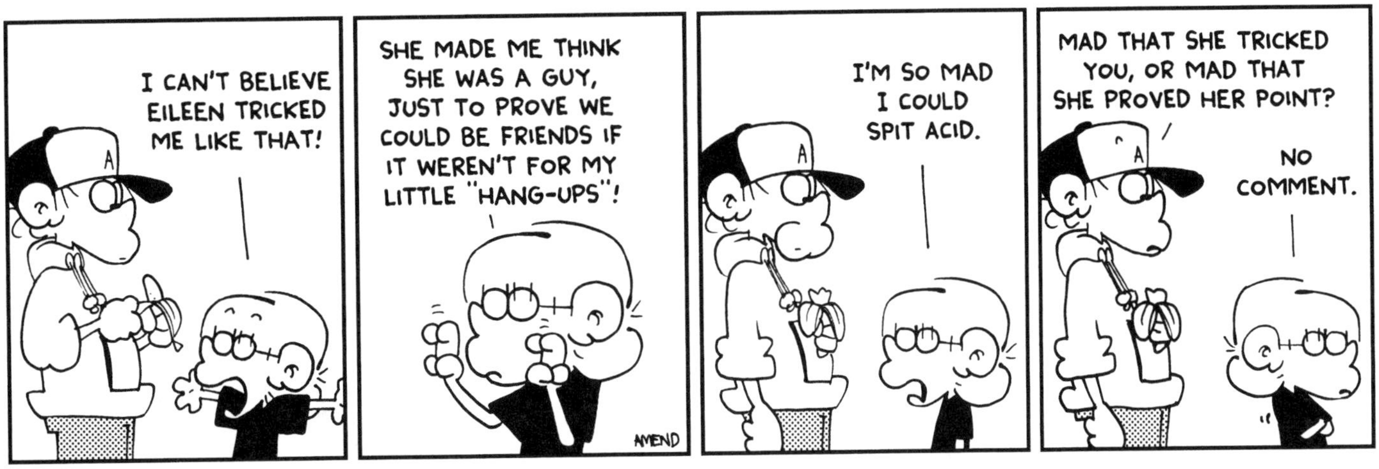
I CAN'T BELIEVE EILEEN TRICKED ME LIKE THAT!
SHE MADE ME THINK SHE WAS A GUY, JUST TO PROVE WE COULD BE FRIENDS IF IT WEREN'T FOR MY LITTLE "HANG-UPS"!
I'M SO MAD I COULD SPIT ACID.
MAD THAT SHE TRICKED YOU, OR MAD THAT SHE PROVED HER POINT?
NO COMMENT.

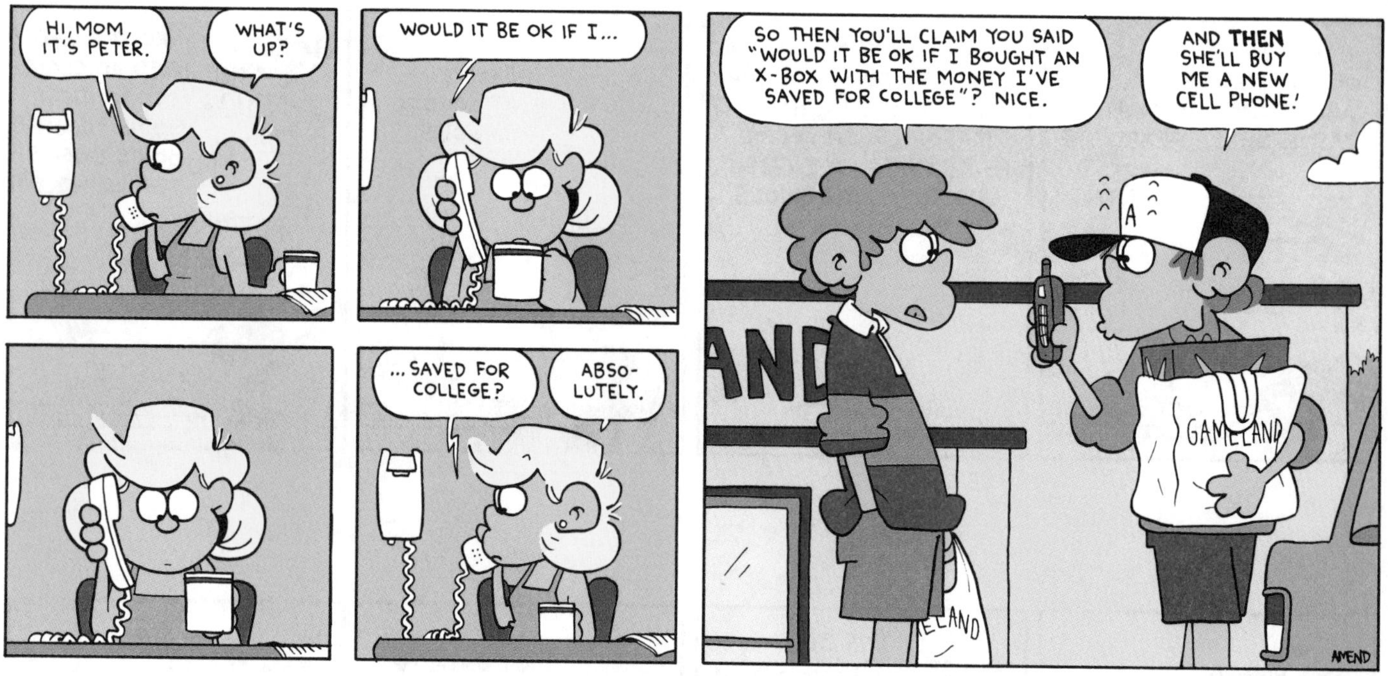
HI, MOM, IT'S PETER.
WHAT'S UP?
WOULD IT BE OK IF I...
...SAVED FOR COLLEGE?
ABSO-LUTELY.
SO THEN YOU'LL CLAIM YOU SAID "WOULD IT BE OK IF I BOUGHT AN X-BOX WITH THE MONEY I'VE SAVED FOR COLLEGE"? NICE.
AND THEN SHE'LL BUY ME A NEW CELL PHONE!
GAMELAND
AMEND

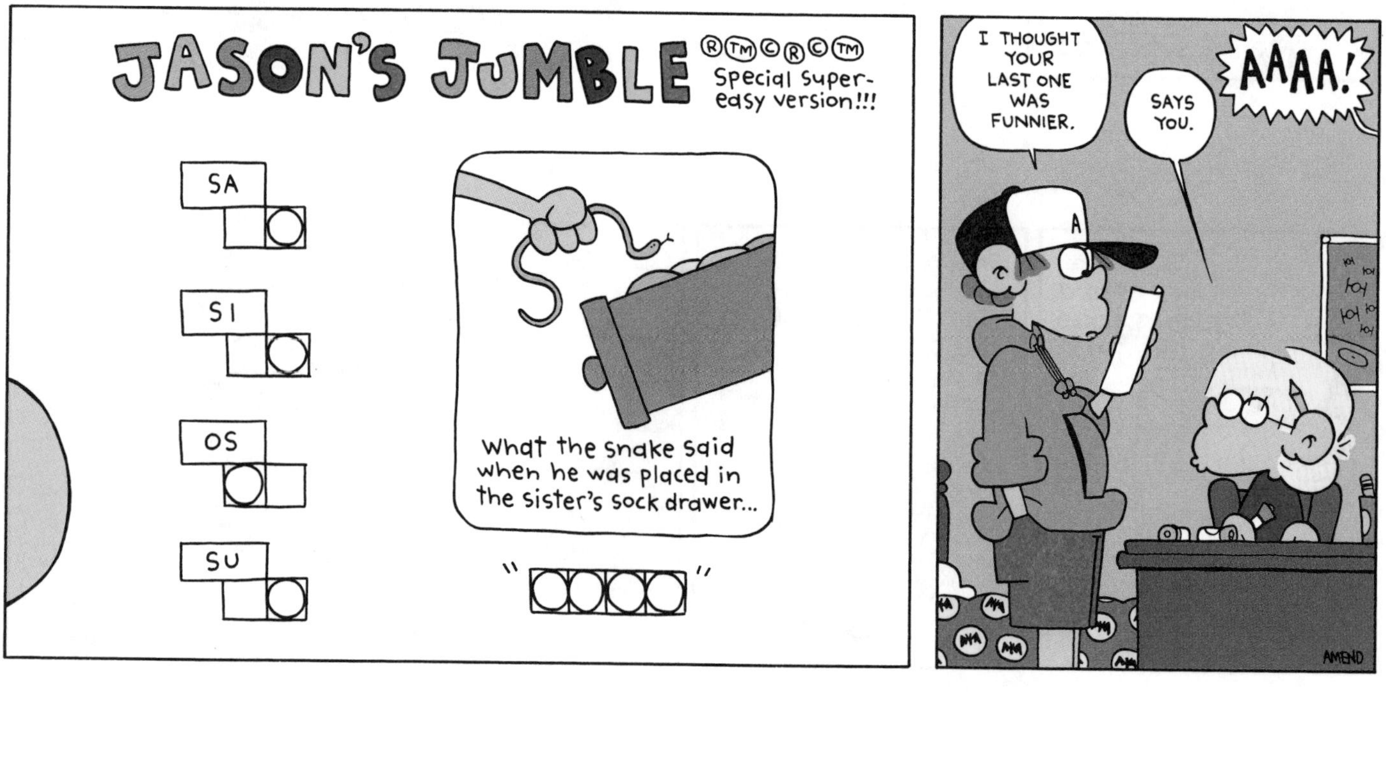
JASON'S JUMBLE ®™©®©™
Special super-easy version!!!
SA
SI
OS
SU
What the snake said when he was placed in the sister's sock drawer...
I THOUGHT YOUR LAST ONE WAS FUNNIER.
SAYS YOU.
AAAA!
AMEND

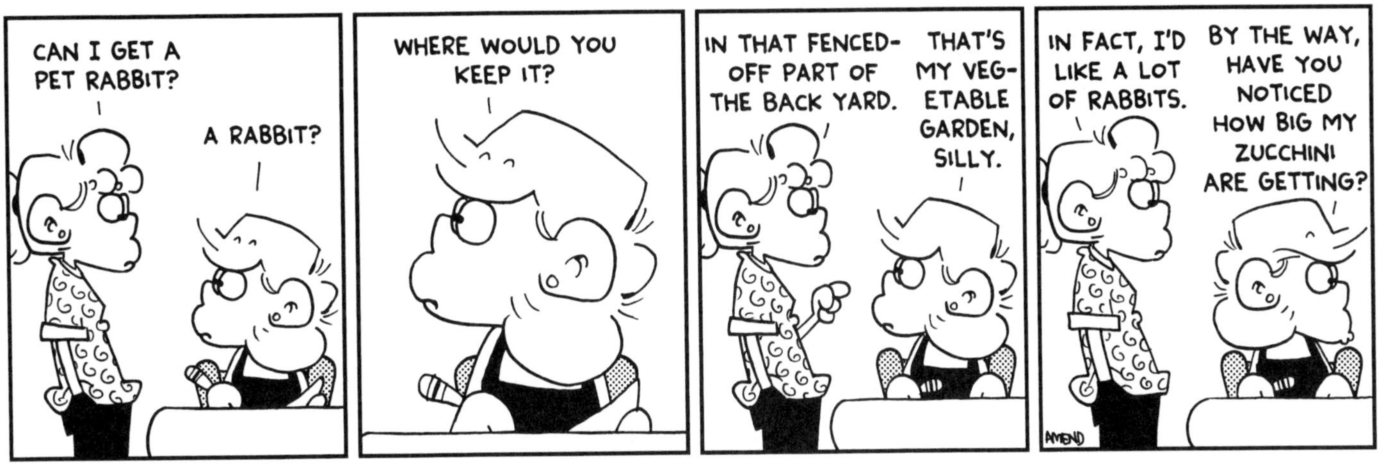
CAN I GET A PET RABBIT?
A RABBIT?
WHERE WOULD YOU KEEP IT?
IN THAT FENCED-OFF PART OF THE BACK YARD.
THAT'S MY VEG-ETABLE GARDEN, SILLY.
IN FACT, I'D LIKE A LOT OF RABBITS.
BY THE WAY, HAVE YOU NOTICED HOW BIG MY ZUCCHINI ARE GETTING?
AMEND

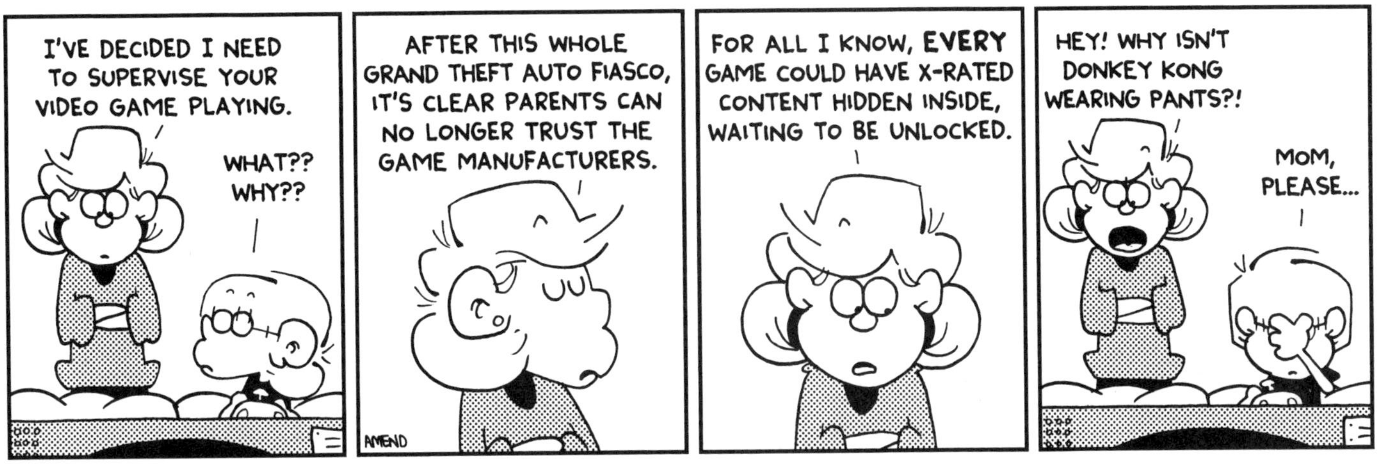
I'VE DECIDED I NEED TO SUPERVISE YOUR VIDEO GAME PLAYING.
WHAT?? WHY??
AFTER THIS WHOLE GRAND THEFT AUTO FIASCO, IT'S CLEAR PARENTS CAN NO LONGER TRUST THE GAME MANUFACTURERS.
AMEND
FOR ALL I KNOW, EVERY GAME COULD HAVE X-RATED CONTENT HIDDEN INSIDE, WAITING TO BE UNLOCKED.
HEY! WHY ISN'T DONKEY KONG WEARING PANTS?!
MOM, PLEASE...

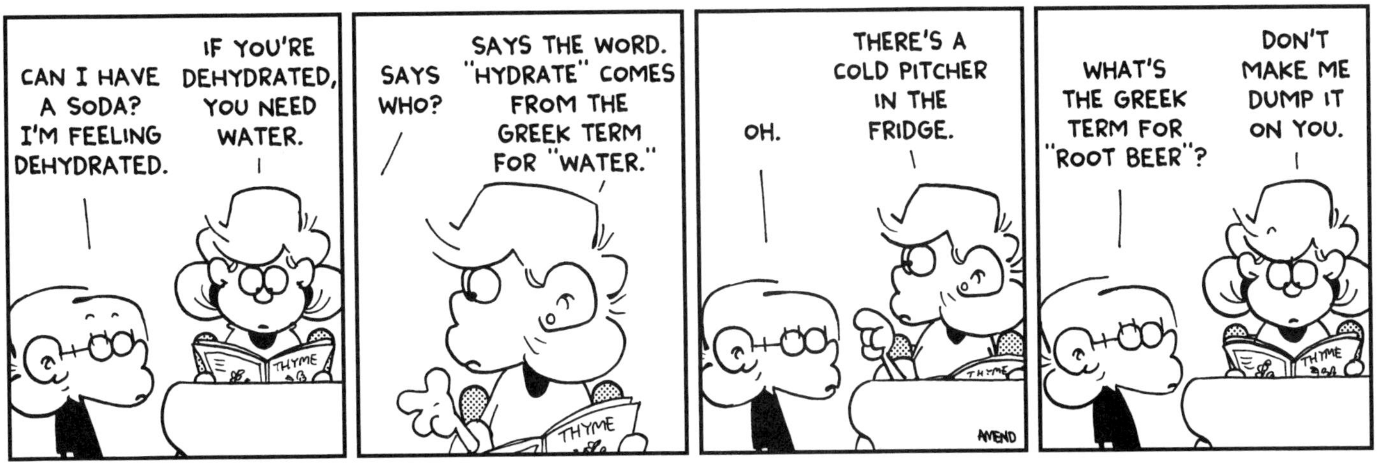
CAN I HAVE A SODA? I'M FEELING DEHYDRATED.
IF YOU'RE DEHYDRATED, YOU NEED WATER.
THYME
SAYS WHO?
SAYS THE WORD. "HYDRATE" COMES FROM THE GREEK TERM FOR "WATER."
THYME
OH.
THERE'S A COLD PITCHER IN THE FRIDGE.
THYME
AMEND
WHAT'S THE GREEK TERM FOR "ROOT BEER"?
DON'T MAKE ME DUMP IT ON YOU.
THYME

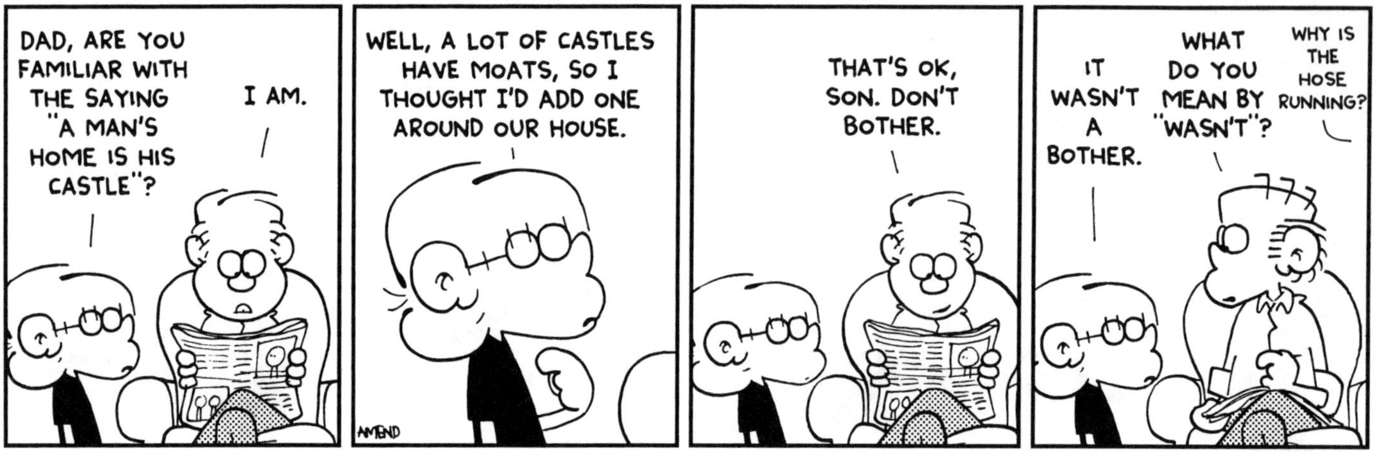
DAD, ARE YOU FAMILIAR WITH THE SAYING "A MAN'S HOME IS HIS CASTLE"?
I AM.
WELL, A LOT OF CASTLES HAVE MOATS, SO I THOUGHT I'D ADD ONE AROUND OUR HOUSE.
THAT'S OK, SON. DON'T BOTHER.
IT WASN'T A BOTHER.
WHAT DO YOU MEAN BY "WASN'T"?
WHY IS THE HOSE RUNNING?
AMEND

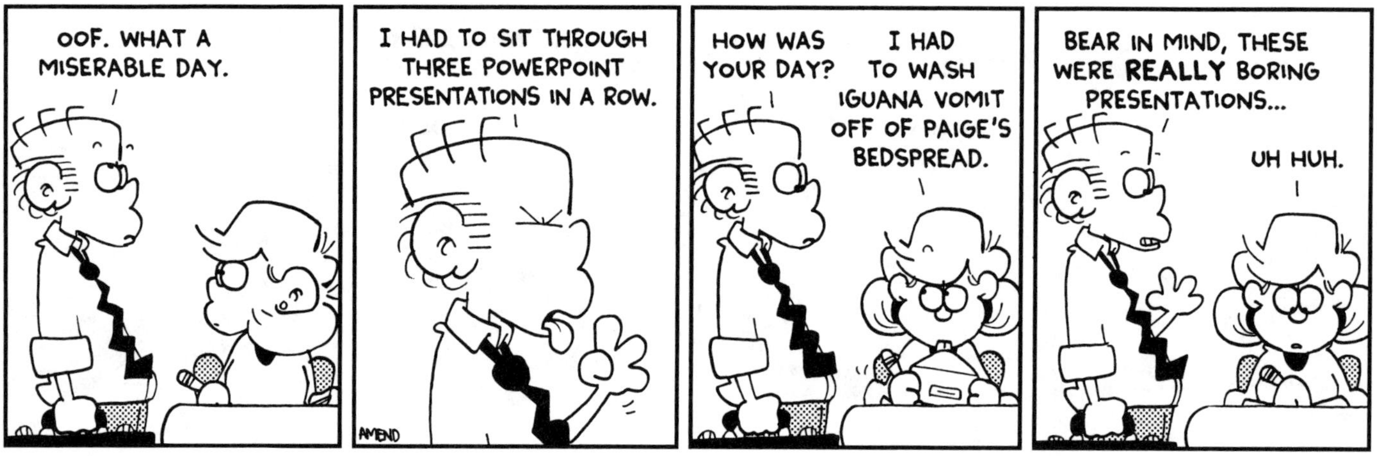
OOF. WHAT A MISERABLE DAY.
I HAD TO SIT THROUGH THREE POWERPOINT PRESENTATIONS IN A ROW.
HOW WAS YOUR DAY?
I HAD TO WASH IGUANA VOMIT OFF OF PAIGE'S BEDSPREAD.
BEAR IN MIND, THESE WERE REALLY BORING PRESENTATIONS...
UH HUH.
AMEND

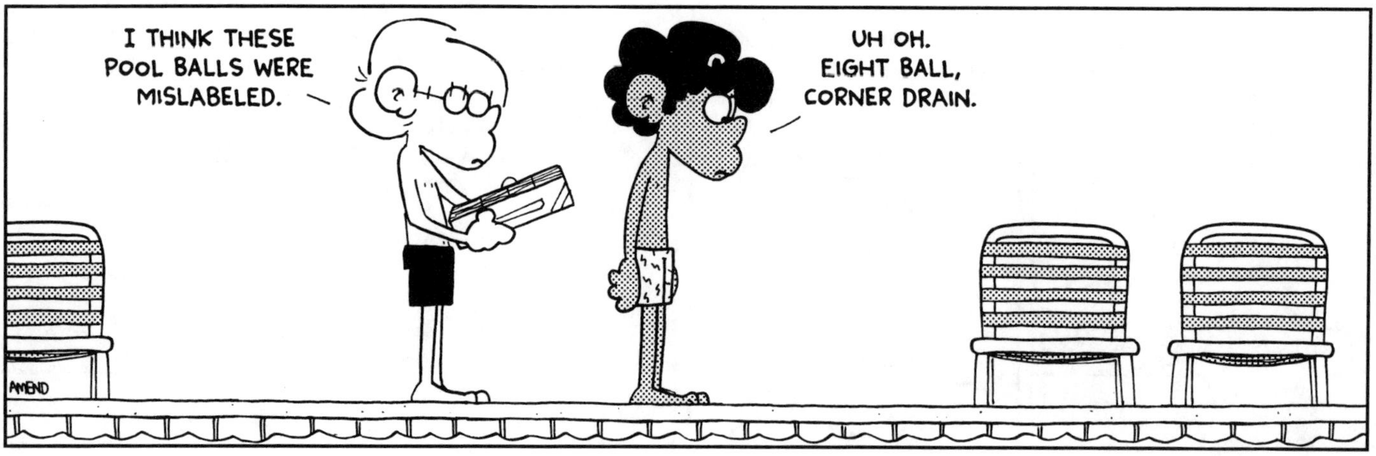
I THINK THESE POOL BALLS WERE MISLABELED.
UH OH. EIGHT BALL, CORNER DRAIN.
AMEND

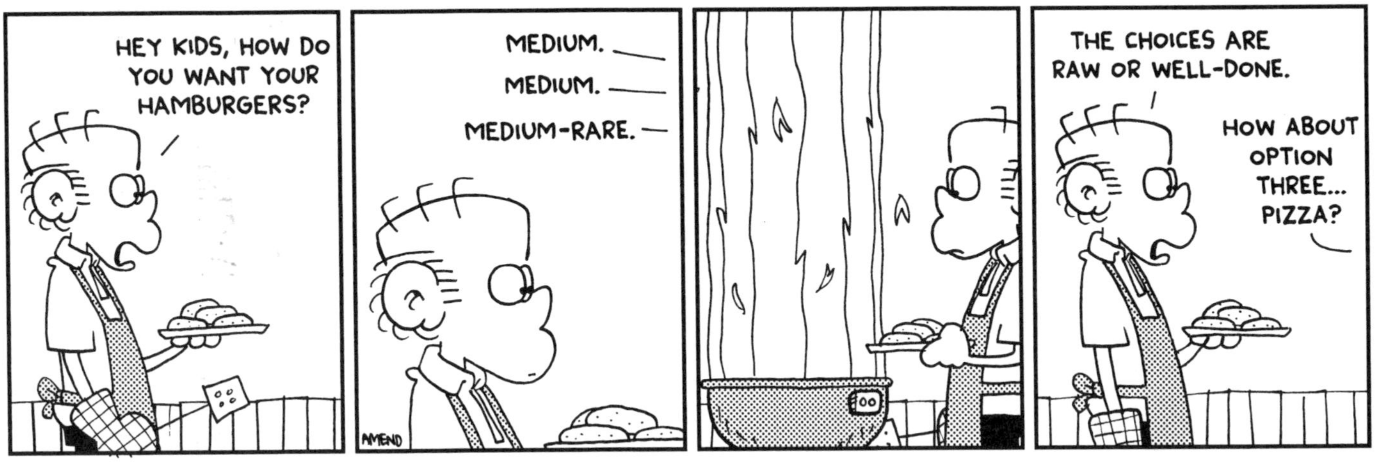
HEY KIDS, HOW DO YOU WANT YOUR HAMBURGERS?
MEDIUM.
MEDIUM.
MEDIUM-RARE.
THE CHOICES ARE RAW OR WELL-DONE.
HOW ABOUT OPTION THREE... PIZZA?

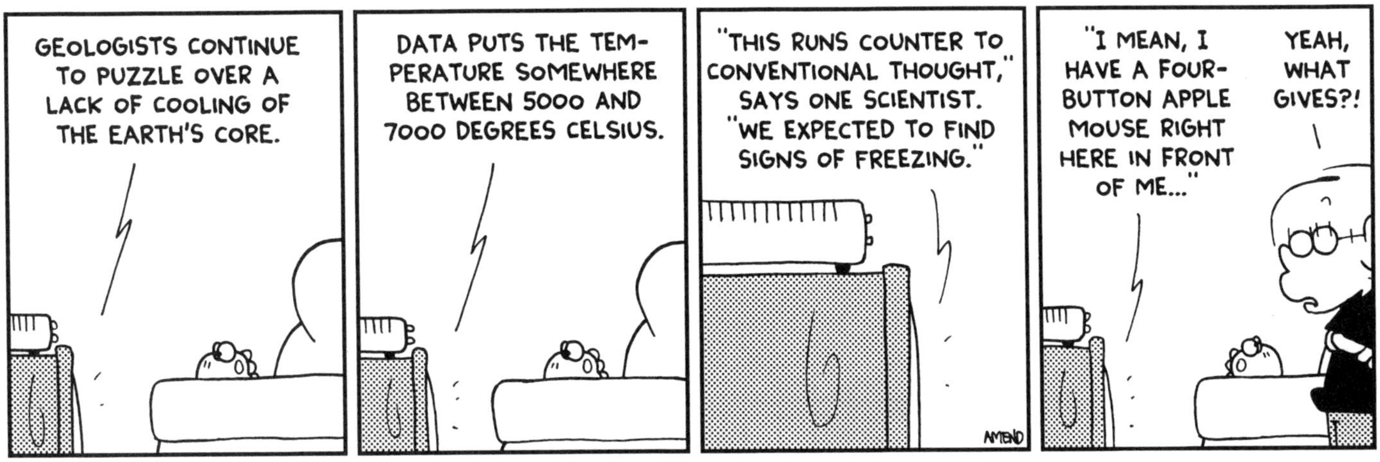
GEOLOGISTS CONTINUE TO PUZZLE OVER A LACK OF COOLING OF THE EARTH'S CORE.
DATA PUTS THE TEMPERATURE SOMEWHERE BETWEEN 5000 AND 7000 DEGREES CELSIUS.
"THIS RUNS COUNTER TO CONVENTIONAL THOUGHT," SAYS ONE SCIENTIST. "WE EXPECTED TO FIND SIGNS OF FREEZING."
"I MEAN, I HAVE A FOUR-BUTTON APPLE MOUSE RIGHT HERE IN FRONT OF ME..."
YEAH, WHAT GIVES?!

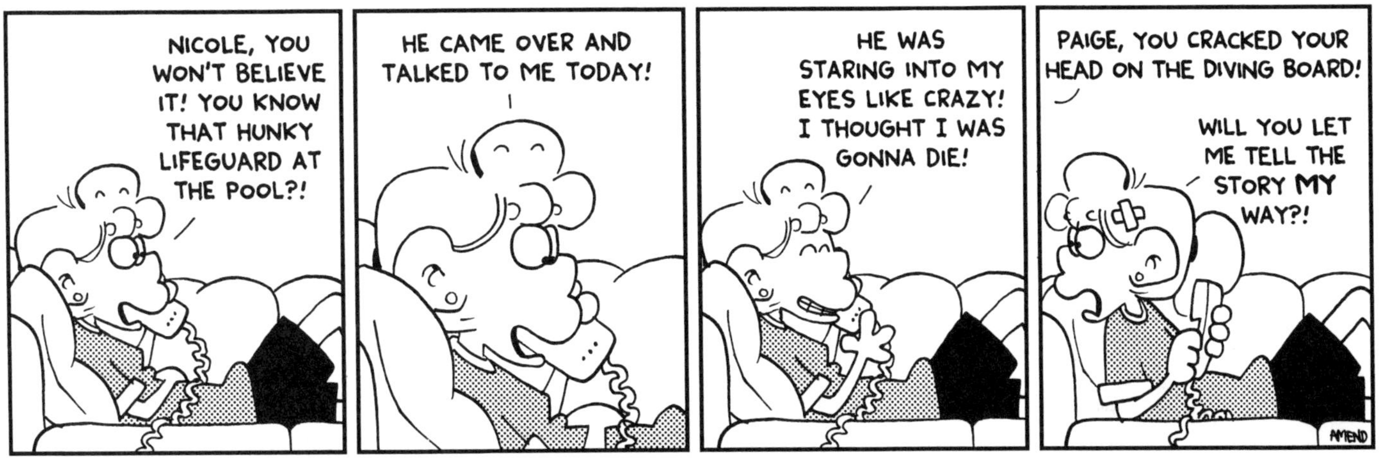
NICOLE, YOU WON'T BELIEVE IT! YOU KNOW THAT HUNKY LIFEGUARD AT THE POOL?!
HE CAME OVER AND TALKED TO ME TODAY!
HE WAS STARING INTO MY EYES LIKE CRAZY! I THOUGHT I WAS GONNA DIE!
PAIGE, YOU CRACKED YOUR HEAD ON THE DIVING BOARD!
WILL YOU LET ME TELL THE STORY **MY** WAY?!

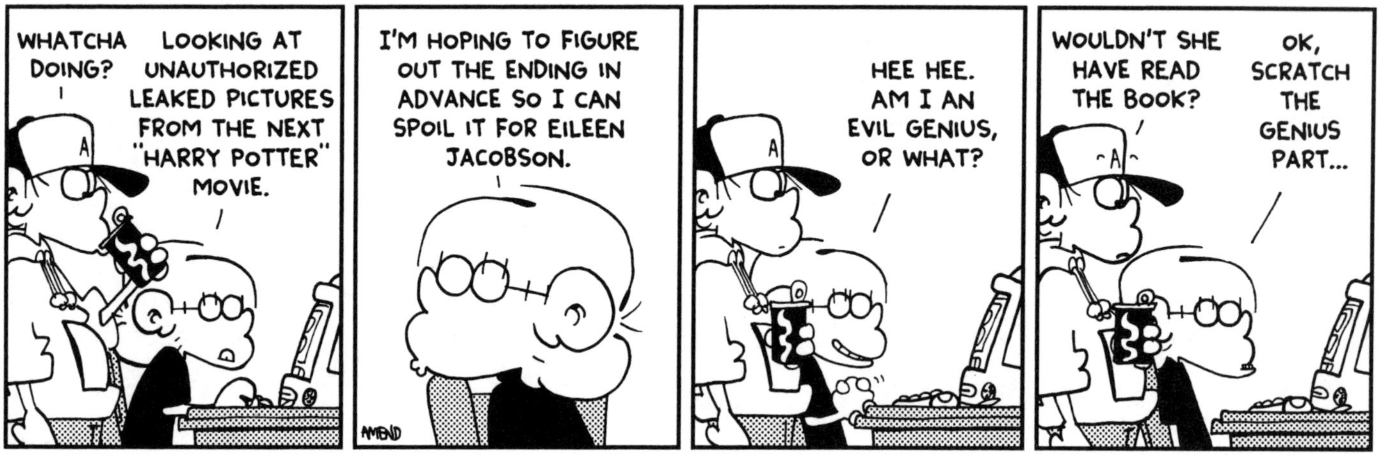
WHATCHA DOING?
LOOKING AT UNAUTHORIZED LEAKED PICTURES FROM THE NEXT "HARRY POTTER" MOVIE.
I'M HOPING TO FIGURE OUT THE ENDING IN ADVANCE SO I CAN SPOIL IT FOR EILEEN JACOBSON.
AMEND
HEE HEE. AM I AN EVIL GENIUS, OR WHAT?
WOULDN'T SHE HAVE READ THE BOOK?
OK, SCRATCH THE GENIUS PART...

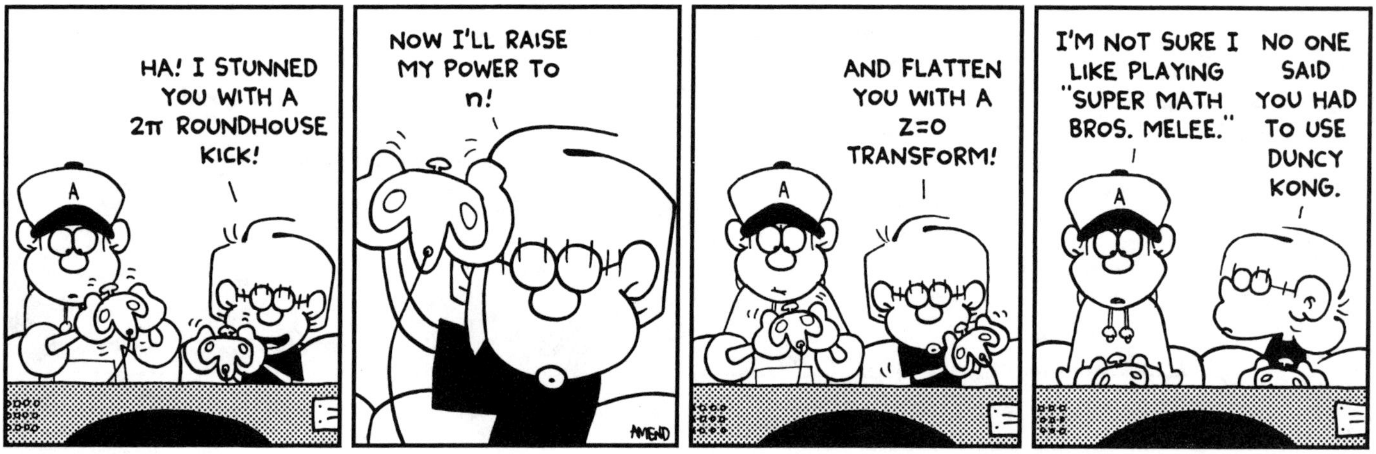
HA! I STUNNED YOU WITH A 2π ROUNDHOUSE KICK!
NOW I'LL RAISE MY POWER TO n!
AMEND
AND FLATTEN YOU WITH A Z=0 TRANSFORM!
I'M NOT SURE I LIKE PLAYING "SUPER MATH BROS. MELEE."
NO ONE SAID YOU HAD TO USE DUNCY KONG.

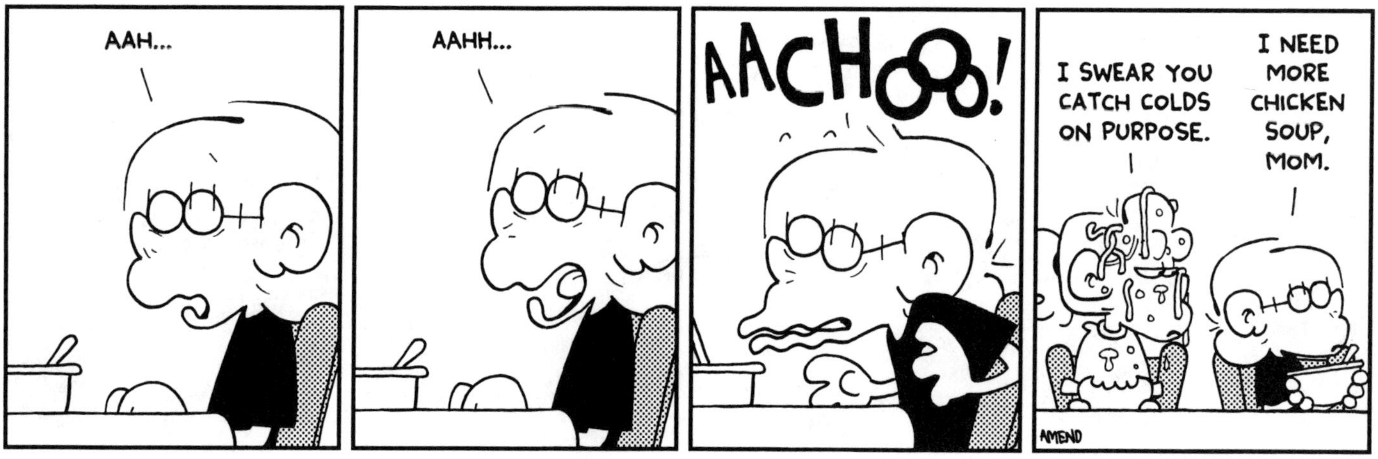
AAH...
AAHH...
AACHOOO!
I SWEAR YOU CATCH COLDS ON PURPOSE.
I NEED MORE CHICKEN SOUP, MOM.
AMEND

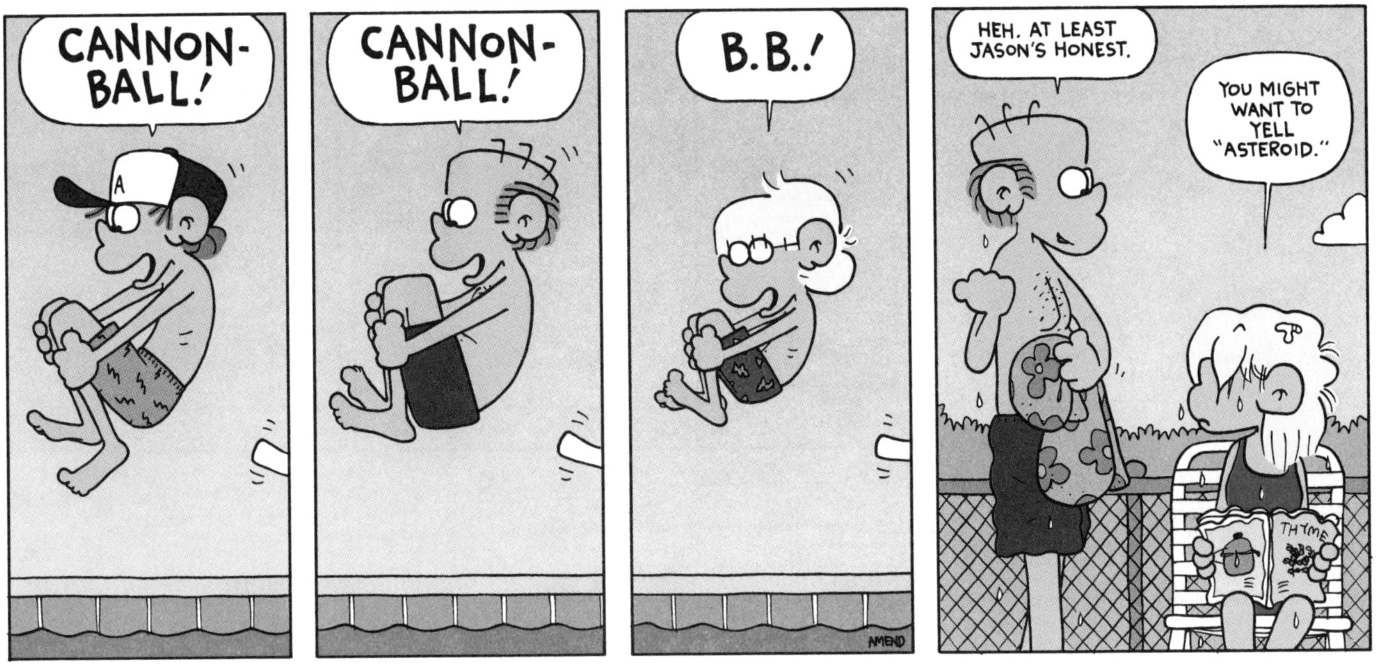
CANNON-BALL!
CANNON-BALL!
B.B.!
HEH. AT LEAST JASON'S HONEST.
YOU MIGHT WANT TO YELL "ASTEROID."
THYME
AMEND

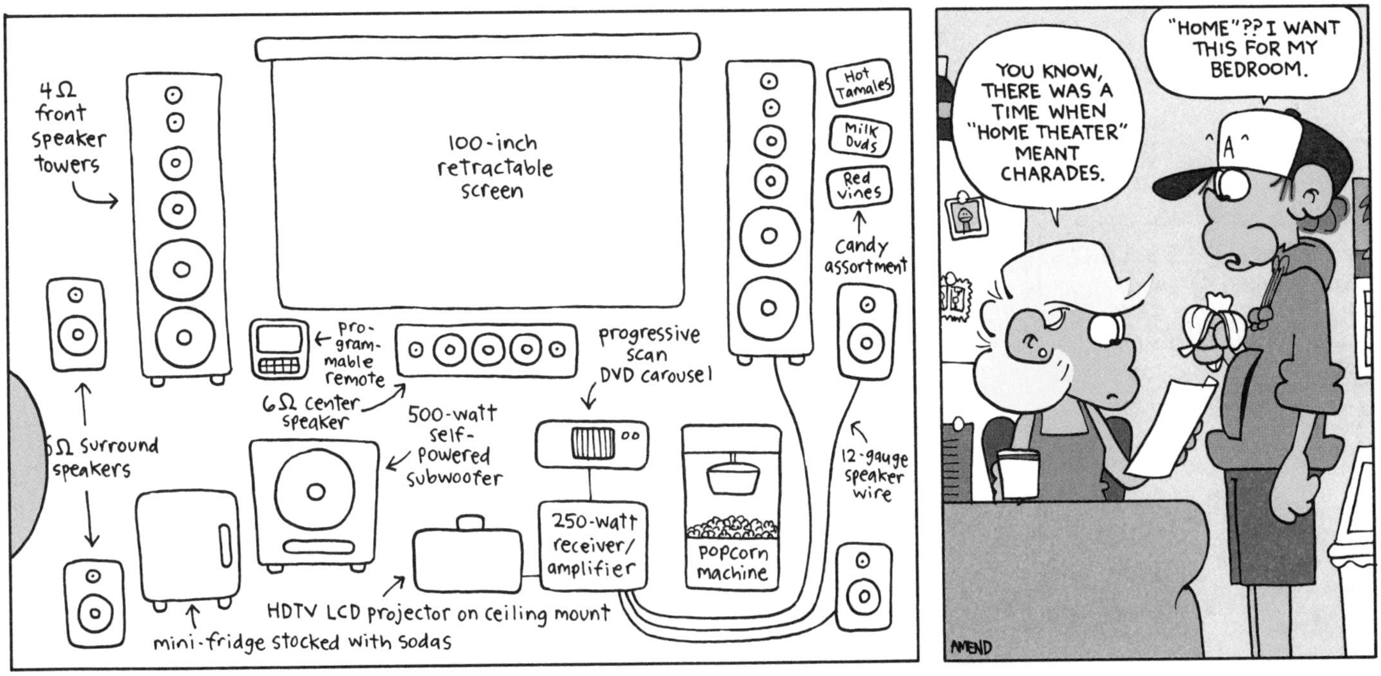
4Ω front speaker towers
100-inch retractable screen
Hot Tamales
Milk Duds
Red Vines
candy assortment
pro-gram-mable remote
progressive scan DVD carousel
6Ω center speaker
500-watt self-powered subwoofer
6Ω surround speakers
12-gauge speaker wire
250-watt receiver/amplifier
popcorn machine
HDTV LCD projector on ceiling mount
mini-fridge stocked with sodas
YOU KNOW, THERE WAS A TIME WHEN "HOME THEATER" MEANT CHARADES.
"HOME"?? I WANT THIS FOR MY BEDROOM.
AMEND

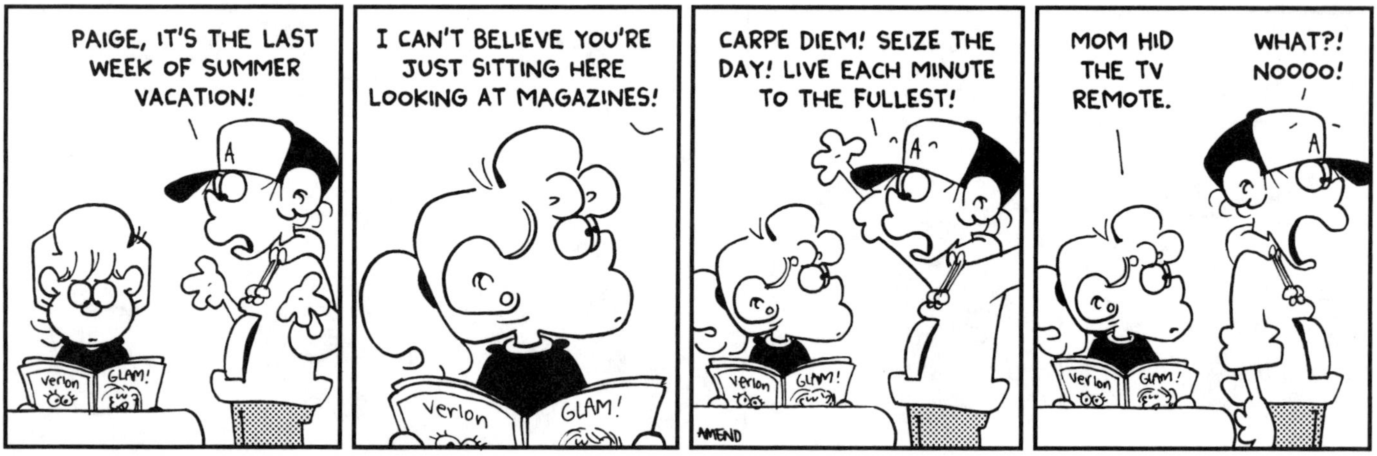
PAIGE, IT'S THE LAST WEEK OF SUMMER VACATION!
Verlon
GLAM!
I CAN'T BELIEVE YOU'RE JUST SITTING HERE LOOKING AT MAGAZINES!
CARPE DIEM! SEIZE THE DAY! LIVE EACH MINUTE TO THE FULLEST!
AMEND
MOM HID THE TV REMOTE.
WHAT?! NOOOO!

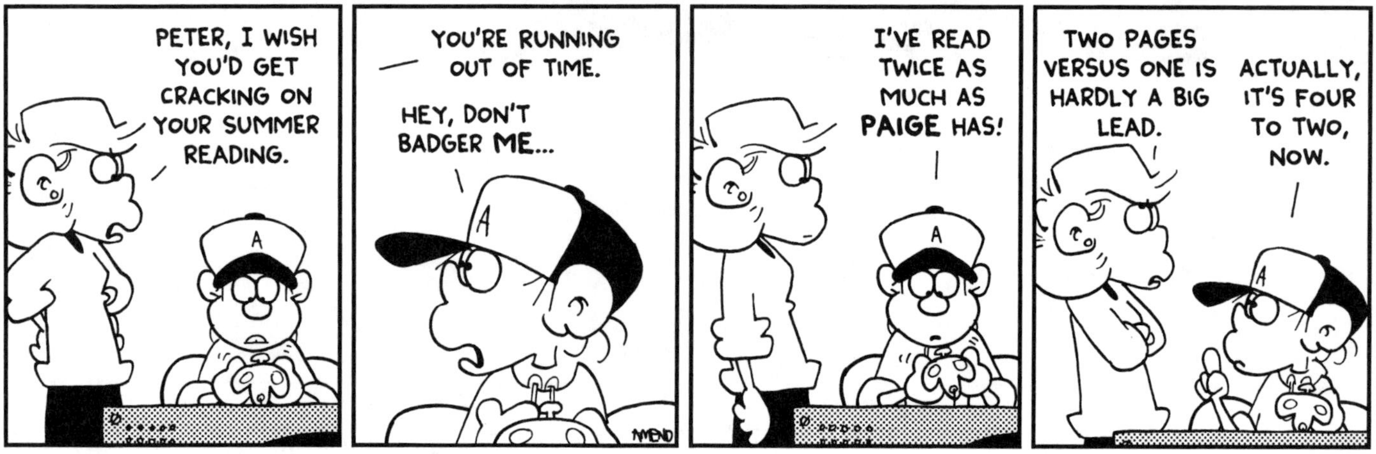
PETER, I WISH YOU'D GET CRACKING ON YOUR SUMMER READING.
YOU'RE RUNNING OUT OF TIME.
HEY, DON'T BADGER **ME**...
AMEND
I'VE READ TWICE AS MUCH AS **PAIGE** HAS!
TWO PAGES VERSUS ONE IS HARDLY A BIG LEAD.
ACTUALLY, IT'S FOUR TO TWO, NOW.

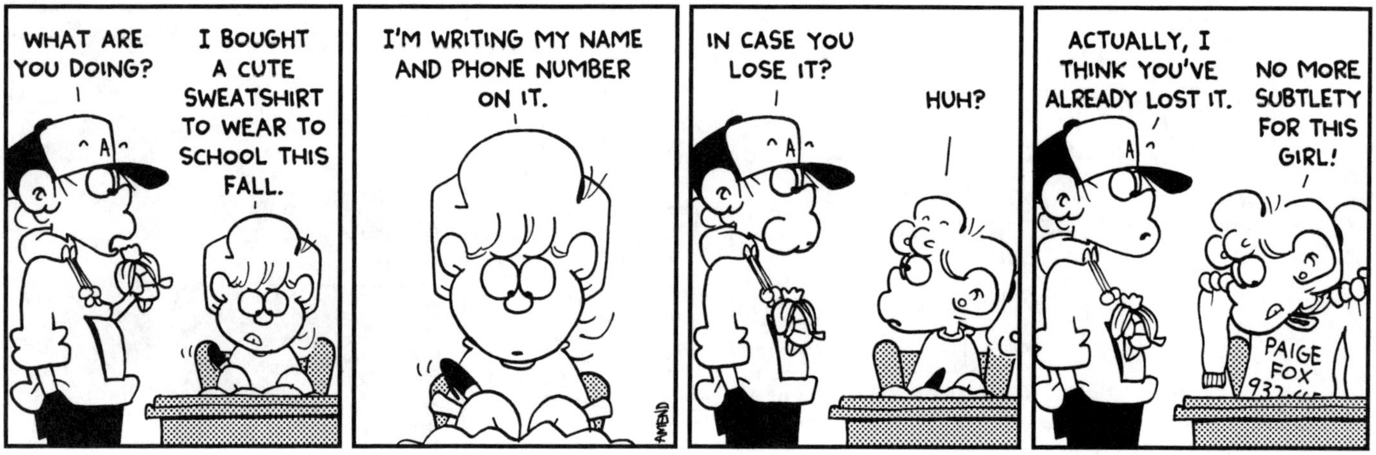
WHAT ARE YOU DOING?
I BOUGHT A CUTE SWEATSHIRT TO WEAR TO SCHOOL THIS FALL.
I'M WRITING MY NAME AND PHONE NUMBER ON IT.
AMEND
IN CASE YOU LOSE IT?
HUH?
ACTUALLY, I THINK YOU'VE ALREADY LOST IT.
NO MORE SUBTLETY FOR THIS GIRL!
PAIGE
FOX

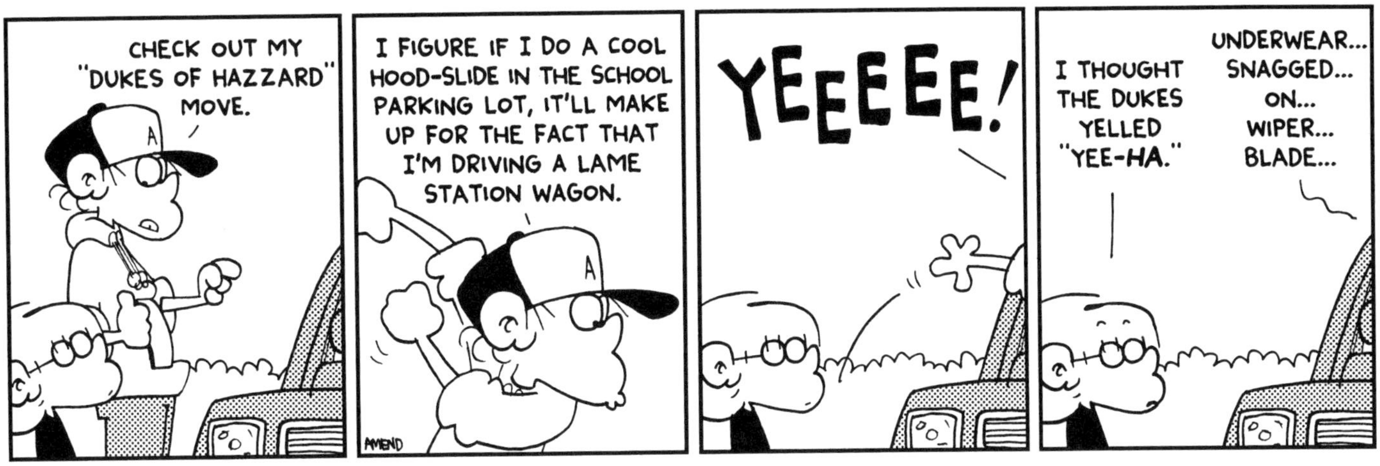
CHECK OUT MY "DUKES OF HAZZARD" MOVE.
I FIGURE IF I DO A COOL HOOD-SLIDE IN THE SCHOOL PARKING LOT, IT'LL MAKE UP FOR THE FACT THAT I'M DRIVING A LAME STATION WAGON.
AMEND
YEEEEE!
I THOUGHT THE DUKES YELLED "YEE-HA."
UNDERWEAR... SNAGGED... ON... WIPER... BLADE...

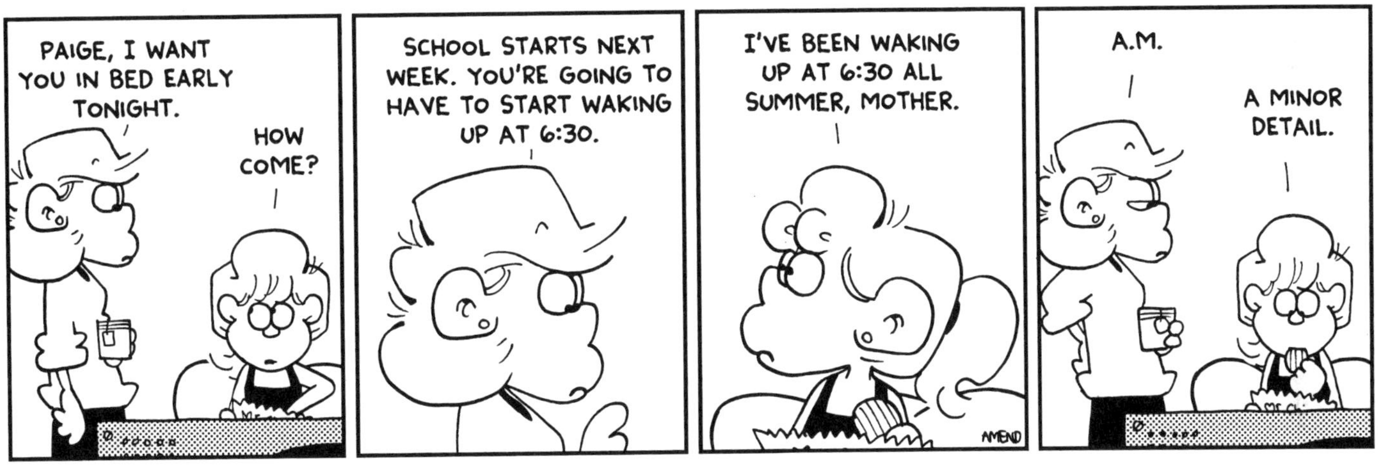
PAIGE, I WANT YOU IN BED EARLY TONIGHT.
HOW COME?
SCHOOL STARTS NEXT WEEK. YOU'RE GOING TO HAVE TO START WAKING UP AT 6:30.
I'VE BEEN WAKING UP AT 6:30 ALL SUMMER, MOTHER.
AMEND
A.M.
A MINOR DETAIL.

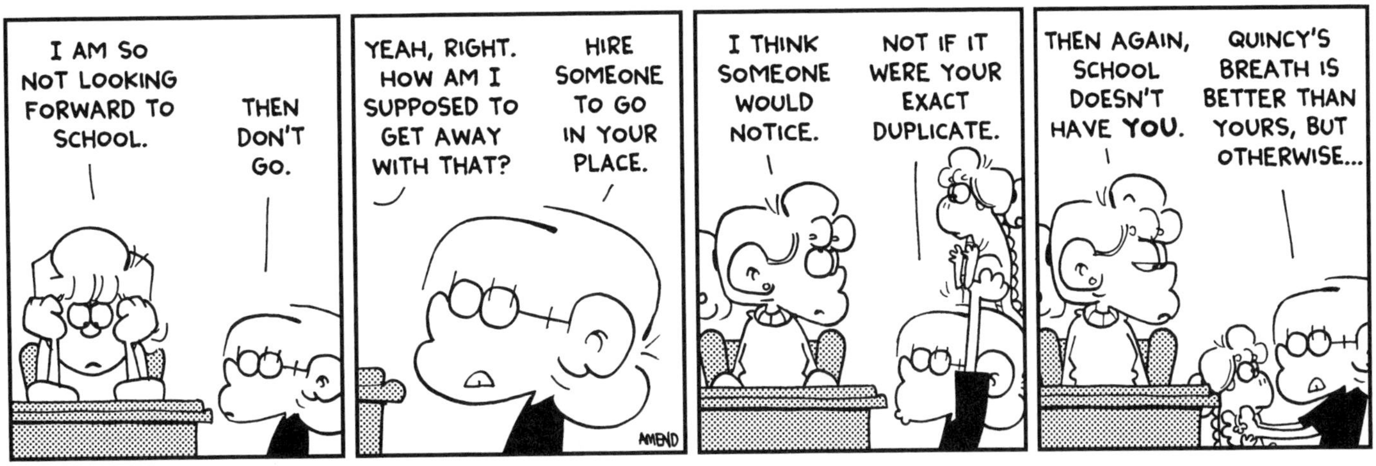
I AM SO NOT LOOKING FORWARD TO SCHOOL.
THEN DON'T GO.
YEAH, RIGHT. HOW AM I SUPPOSED TO GET AWAY WITH THAT?
HIRE SOMEONE TO GO IN YOUR PLACE.
AMEND
I THINK SOMEONE WOULD NOTICE.
NOT IF IT WERE YOUR EXACT DUPLICATE.
THEN AGAIN, SCHOOL DOESN'T HAVE YOU.
QUINCY'S BREATH IS BETTER THAN YOURS, BUT OTHERWISE...

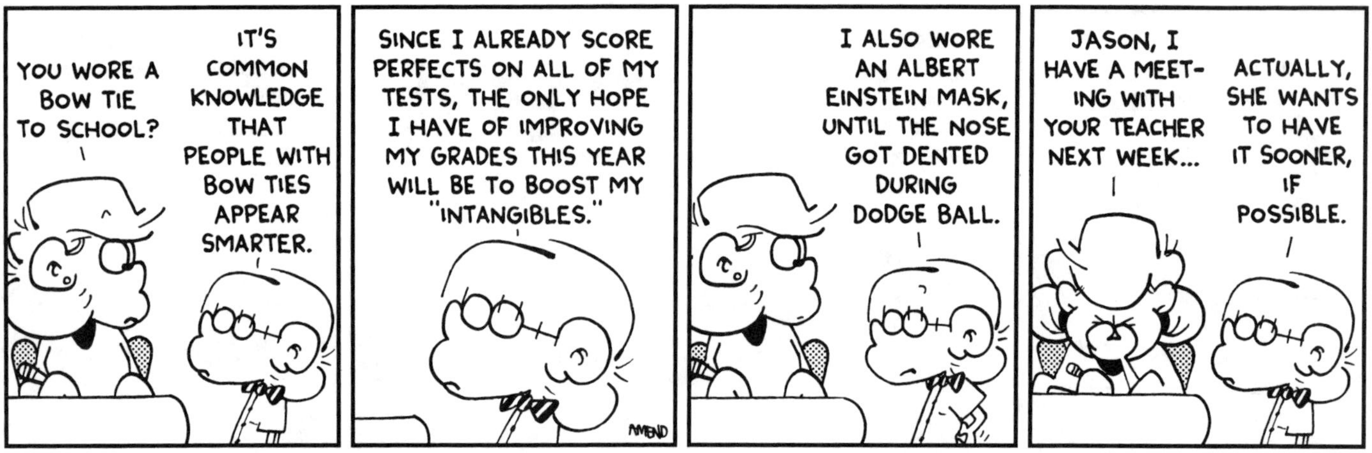
YOU WORE A BOW TIE TO SCHOOL?
IT'S COMMON KNOWLEDGE THAT PEOPLE WITH BOW TIES APPEAR SMARTER.
SINCE I ALREADY SCORE PERFECTS ON ALL OF MY TESTS, THE ONLY HOPE I HAVE OF IMPROVING MY GRADES THIS YEAR WILL BE TO BOOST MY "INTANGIBLES."
I ALSO WORE AN ALBERT EINSTEIN MASK, UNTIL THE NOSE GOT DENTED DURING DODGE BALL.
JASON, I HAVE A MEETING WITH YOUR TEACHER NEXT WEEK...
ACTUALLY, SHE WANTS TO HAVE IT SOONER, IF POSSIBLE.

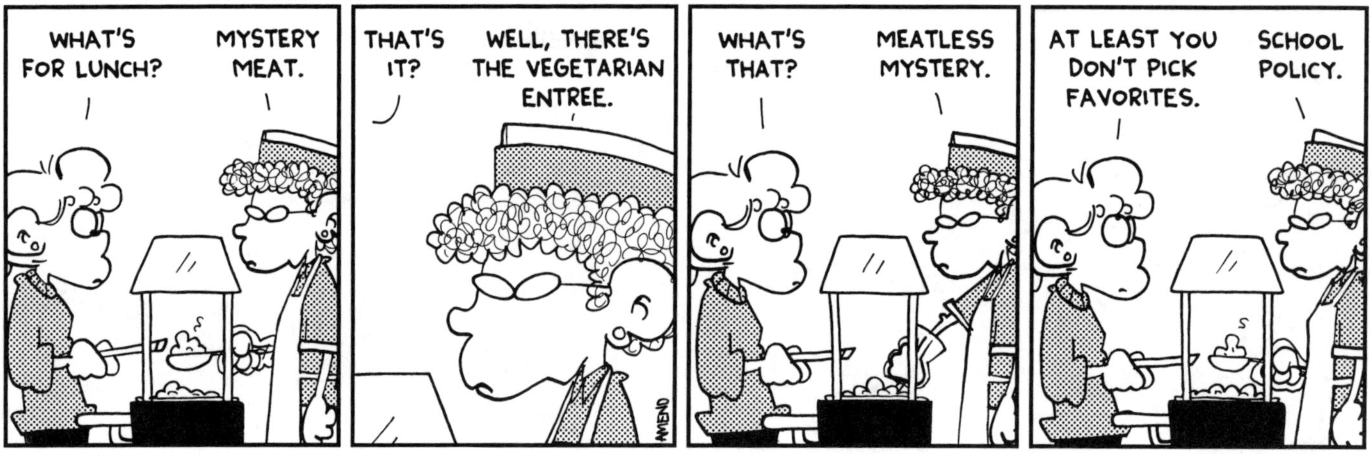
WHAT'S FOR LUNCH?
MYSTERY MEAT.
THAT'S IT?
WELL, THERE'S THE VEGETARIAN ENTREE.
WHAT'S THAT?
MEATLESS MYSTERY.
AT LEAST YOU DON'T PICK FAVORITES.
SCHOOL POLICY.

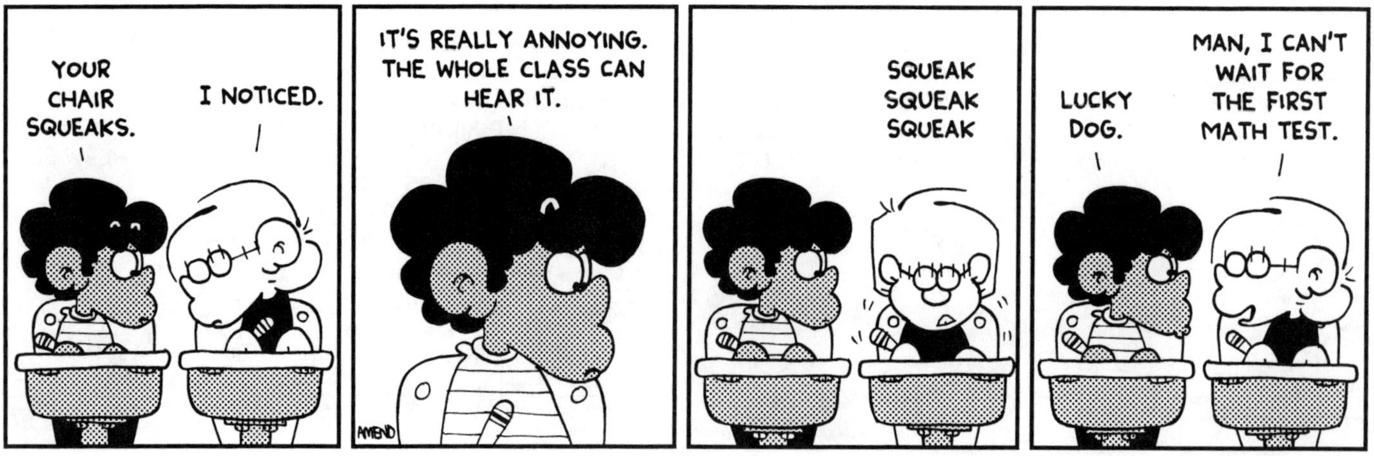
YOUR CHAIR SQUEAKS.
I NOTICED.
IT'S REALLY ANNOYING. THE WHOLE CLASS CAN HEAR IT.
SQUEAK SQUEAK SQUEAK
LUCKY DOG.
MAN, I CAN'T WAIT FOR THE FIRST MATH TEST.

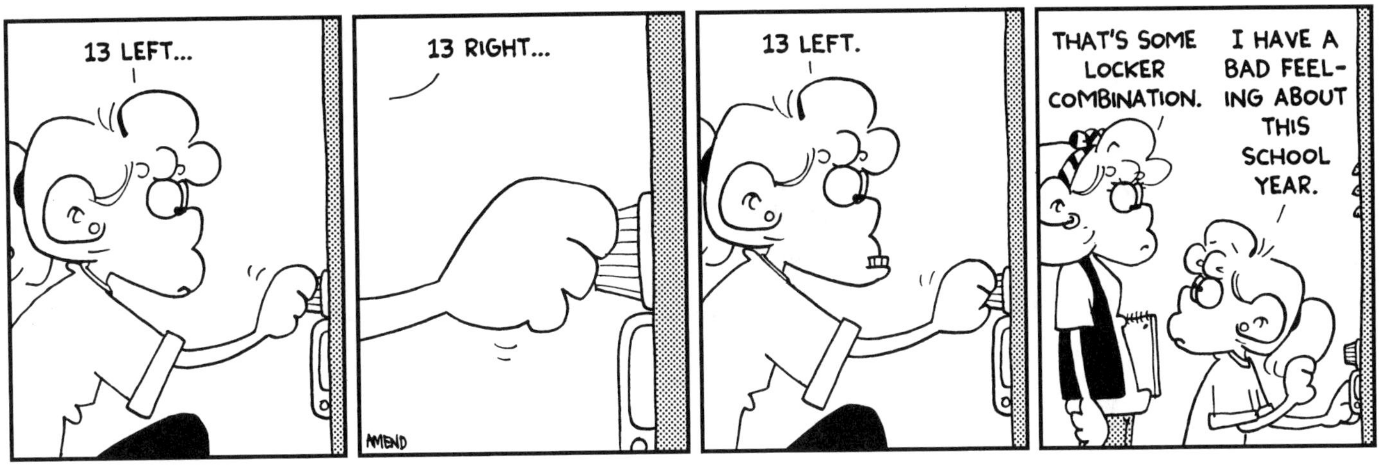
13 LEFT...
13 RIGHT...
13 LEFT.
THAT'S SOME LOCKER COMBINATION.
I HAVE A BAD FEEL-ING ABOUT THIS SCHOOL YEAR.
AMEND

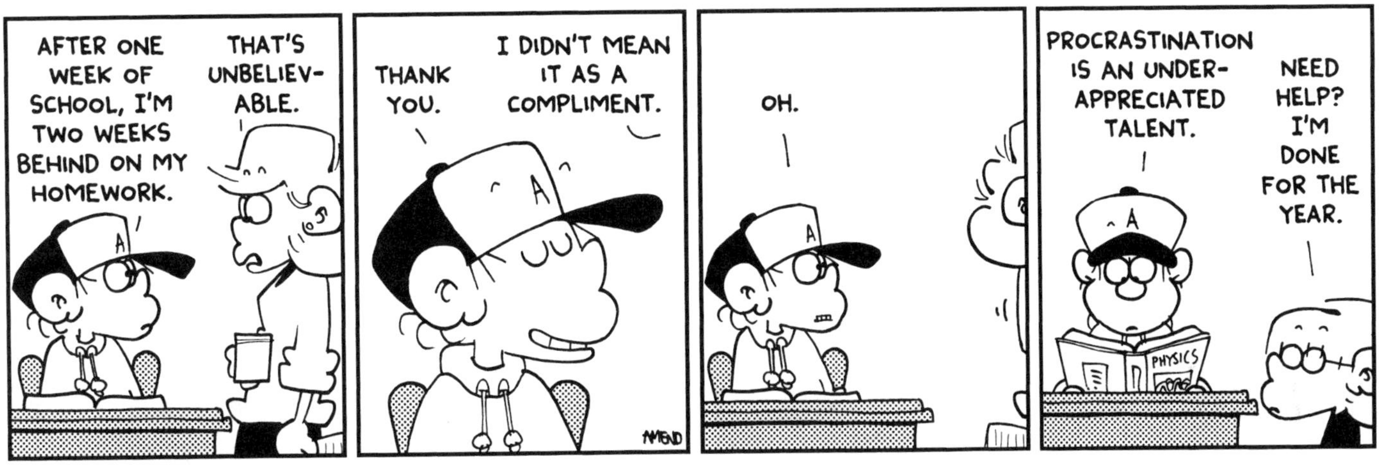
AFTER ONE WEEK OF SCHOOL, I'M TWO WEEKS BEHIND ON MY HOMEWORK.
THAT'S UNBELIEV-ABLE.
THANK YOU.
I DIDN'T MEAN IT AS A COMPLIMENT.
OH.
PROCRASTINATION IS AN UNDER-APPRECIATED TALENT.
NEED HELP? I'M DONE FOR THE YEAR.
PHYSICS
AMEND

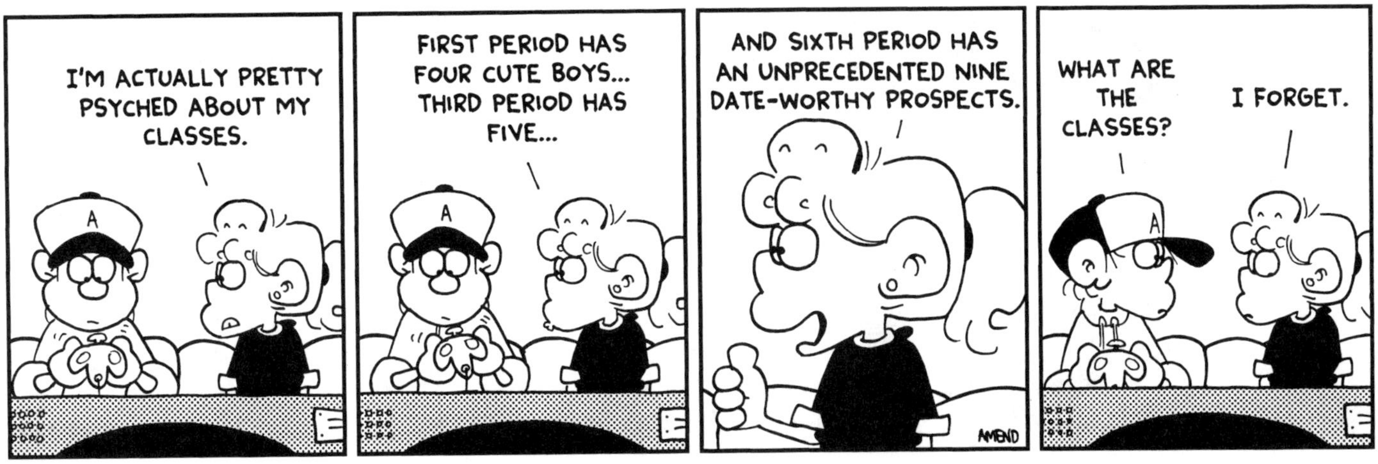
I'M ACTUALLY PRETTY PSYCHED ABOUT MY CLASSES.
FIRST PERIOD HAS FOUR CUTE BOYS... THIRD PERIOD HAS FIVE...
AND SIXTH PERIOD HAS AN UNPRECEDENTED NINE DATE-WORTHY PROSPECTS.
WHAT ARE THE CLASSES?
I FORGET.
AMEND

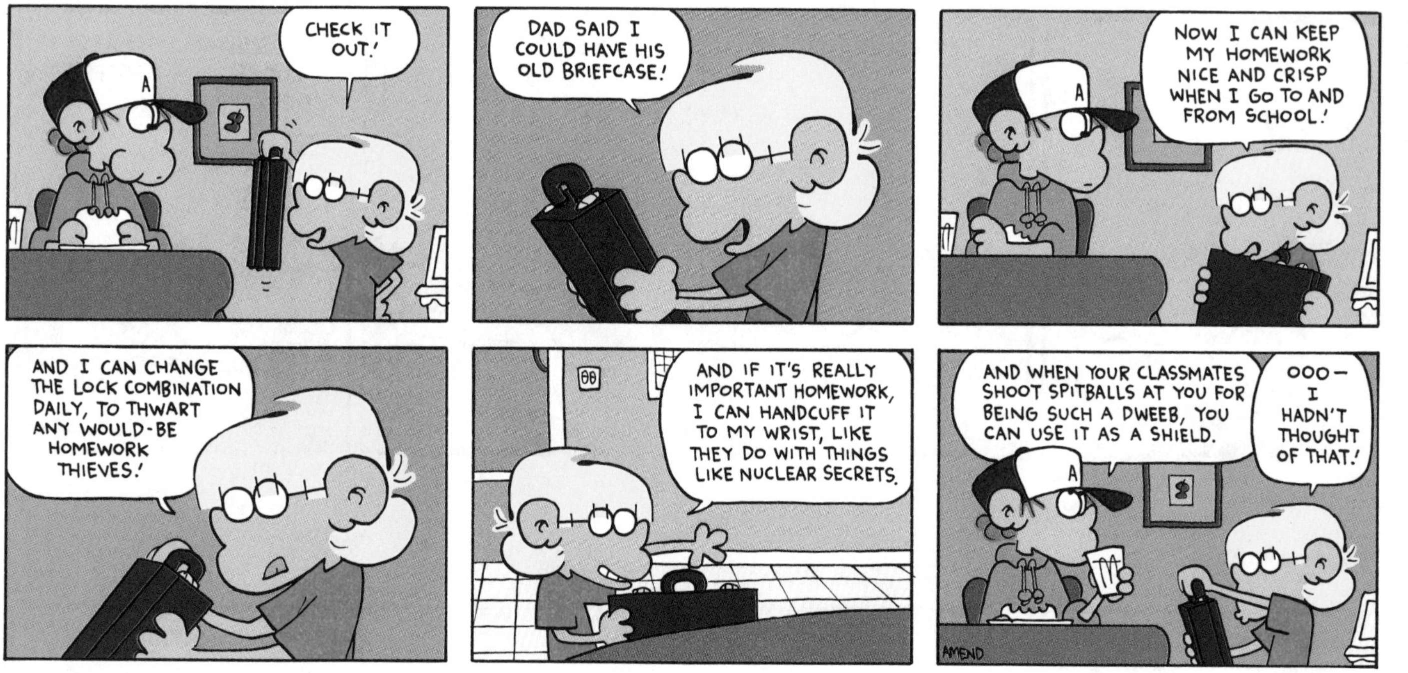
CHECK IT OUT!
DAD SAID I COULD HAVE HIS OLD BRIEFCASE!
NOW I CAN KEEP MY HOMEWORK NICE AND CRISP WHEN I GO TO AND FROM SCHOOL!
AND I CAN CHANGE THE LOCK COMBINATION DAILY, TO THWART ANY WOULD-BE HOMEWORK THIEVES!
AND IF IT'S REALLY IMPORTANT HOMEWORK, I CAN HANDCUFF IT TO MY WRIST, LIKE THEY DO WITH THINGS LIKE NUCLEAR SECRETS.
AND WHEN YOUR CLASSMATES SHOOT SPITBALLS AT YOU FOR BEING SUCH A DWEEB, YOU CAN USE IT AS A SHIELD.
OOO— I HADN'T THOUGHT OF THAT!
AMEND

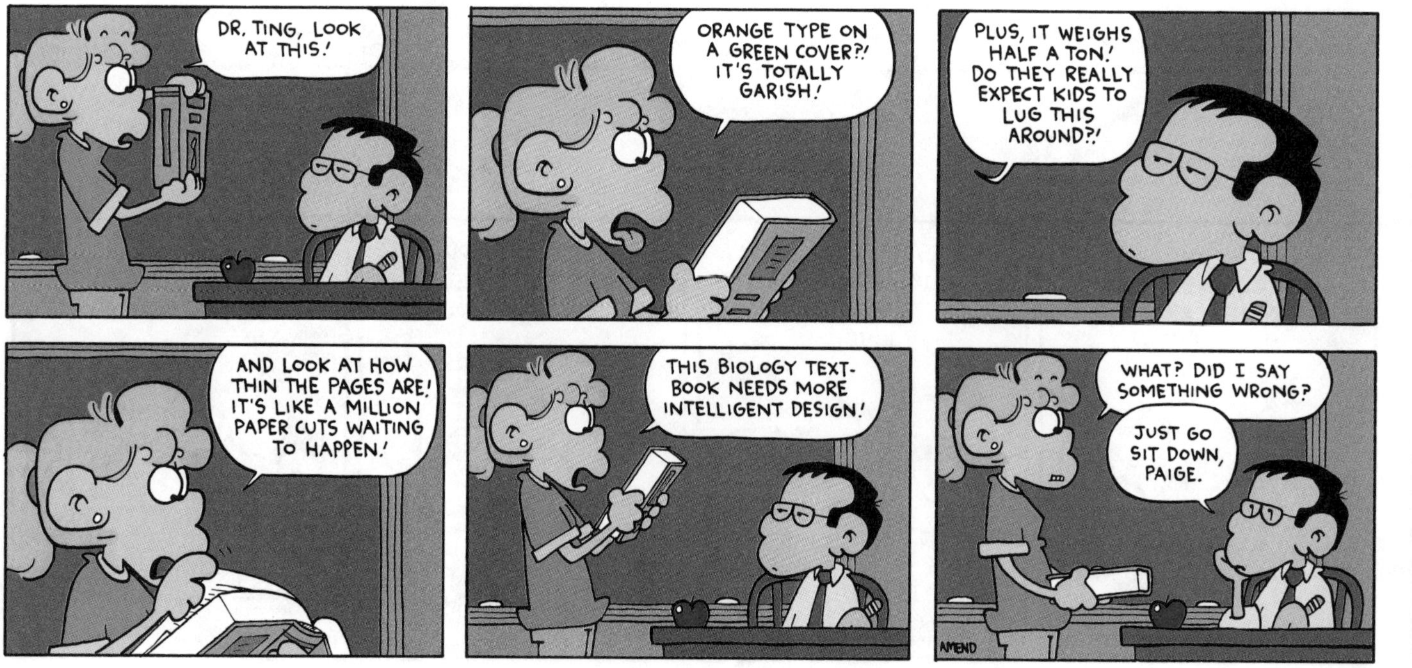
DR. TING, LOOK AT THIS!
ORANGE TYPE ON A GREEN COVER?! IT'S TOTALLY GARISH!
PLUS, IT WEIGHS HALF A TON! DO THEY REALLY EXPECT KIDS TO LUG THIS AROUND?!
AND LOOK AT HOW THIN THE PAGES ARE! IT'S LIKE A MILLION PAPER CUTS WAITING TO HAPPEN!
THIS BIOLOGY TEXTBOOK NEEDS MORE INTELLIGENT DESIGN!
WHAT? DID I SAY SOMETHING WRONG?
JUST GO SIT DOWN, PAIGE.
AMEND

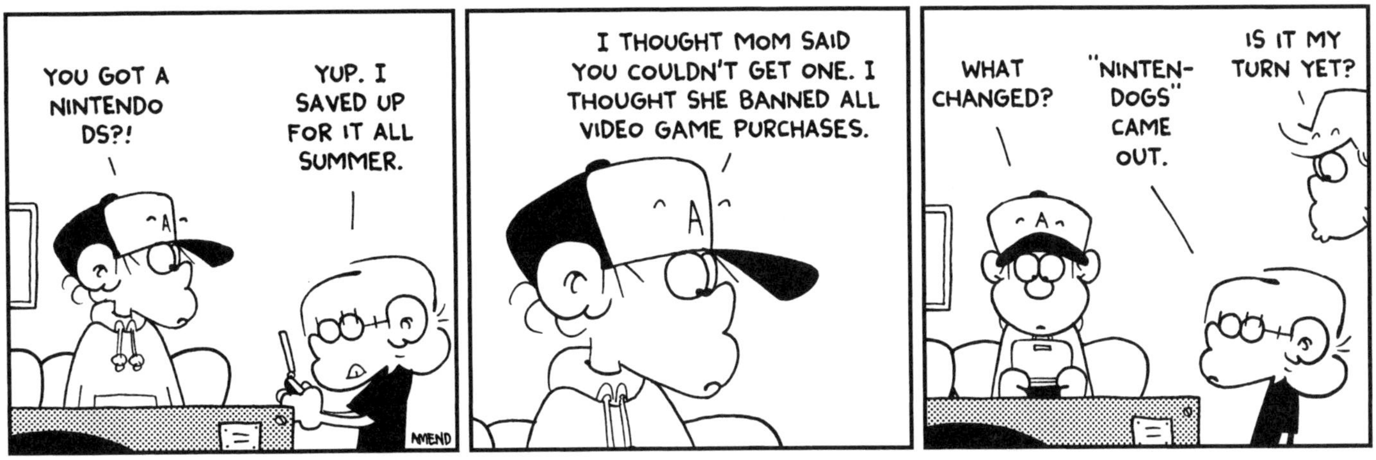
YOU GOT A NINTENDO DS?!
YUP. I SAVED UP FOR IT ALL SUMMER.
AMEND
I THOUGHT MOM SAID YOU COULDN'T GET ONE. I THOUGHT SHE BANNED ALL VIDEO GAME PURCHASES.
WHAT CHANGED?
"NINTEN-DOGS" CAME OUT.
IS IT MY TURN YET?

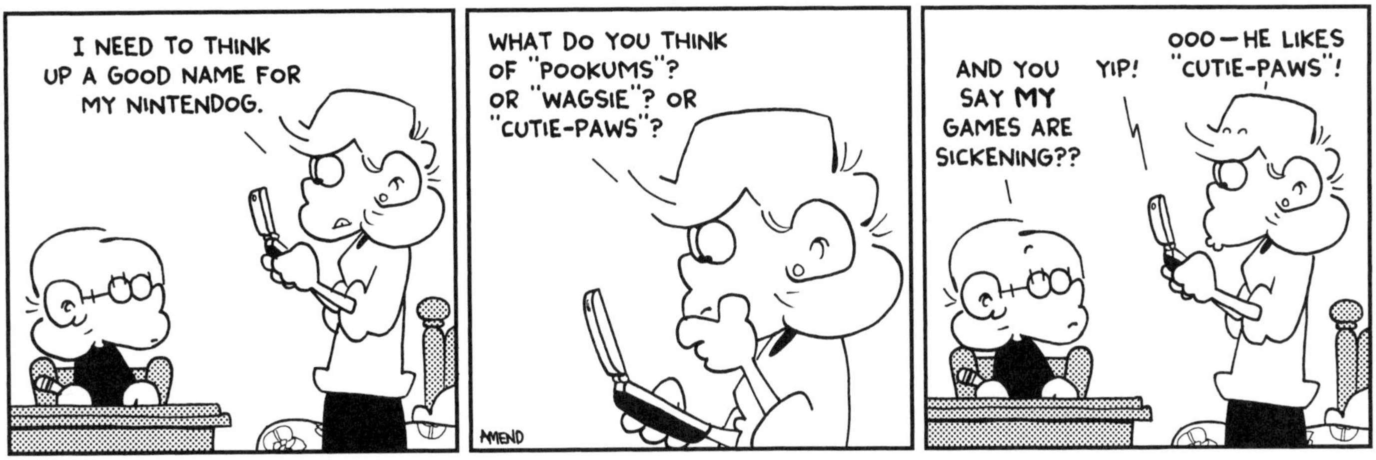
I NEED TO THINK UP A GOOD NAME FOR MY NINTENDOG.
WHAT DO YOU THINK OF "POOKUMS"? OR "WAGSIE"? OR "CUTIE-PAWS"?
AMEND
AND YOU SAY **MY** GAMES ARE SICKENING??
YIP!
OOO—HE LIKES "CUTIE-PAWS"!

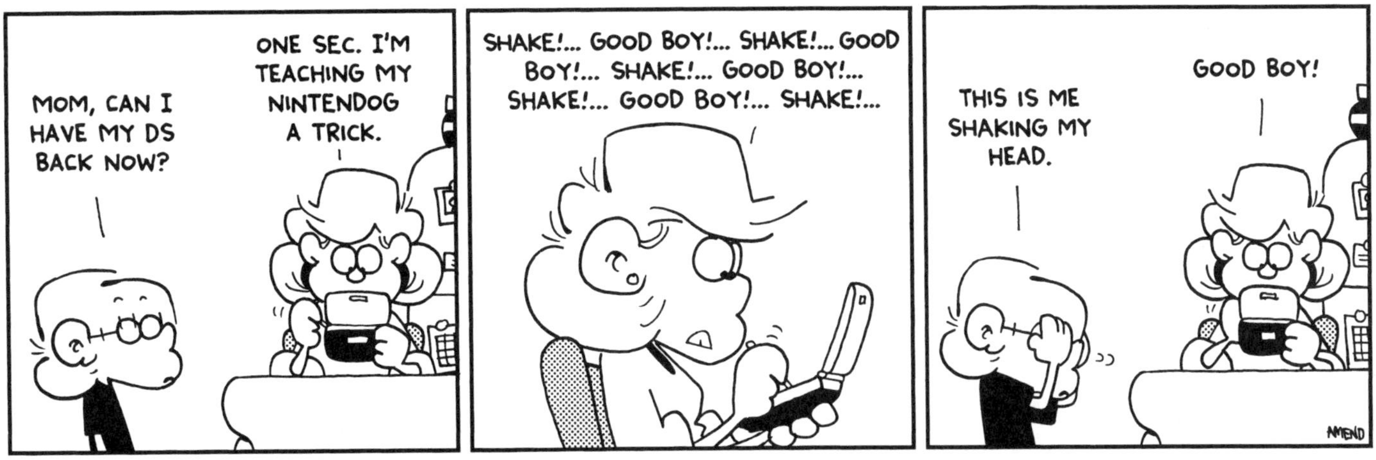
MOM, CAN I HAVE MY DS BACK NOW?
ONE SEC. I'M TEACHING MY NINTENDOG A TRICK.
SHAKE!... GOOD BOY!... SHAKE!... GOOD BOY!... SHAKE!... GOOD BOY!... SHAKE!... GOOD BOY!... SHAKE!...
THIS IS ME SHAKING MY HEAD.
GOOD BOY!
AMEND

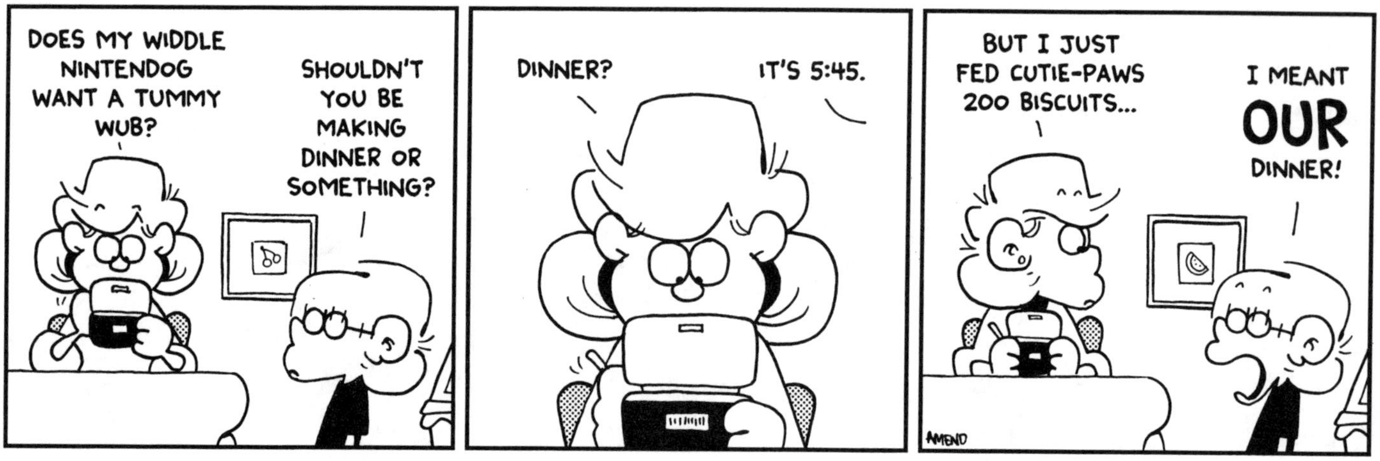
DOES MY WIDDLE NINTENDOG WANT A TUMMY WUB?
SHOULDN'T YOU BE MAKING DINNER OR SOMETHING?
DINNER?
IT'S 5:45.
BUT I JUST FED CUTIE-PAWS 200 BISCUITS...
I MEANT **OUR** DINNER!
AMEND

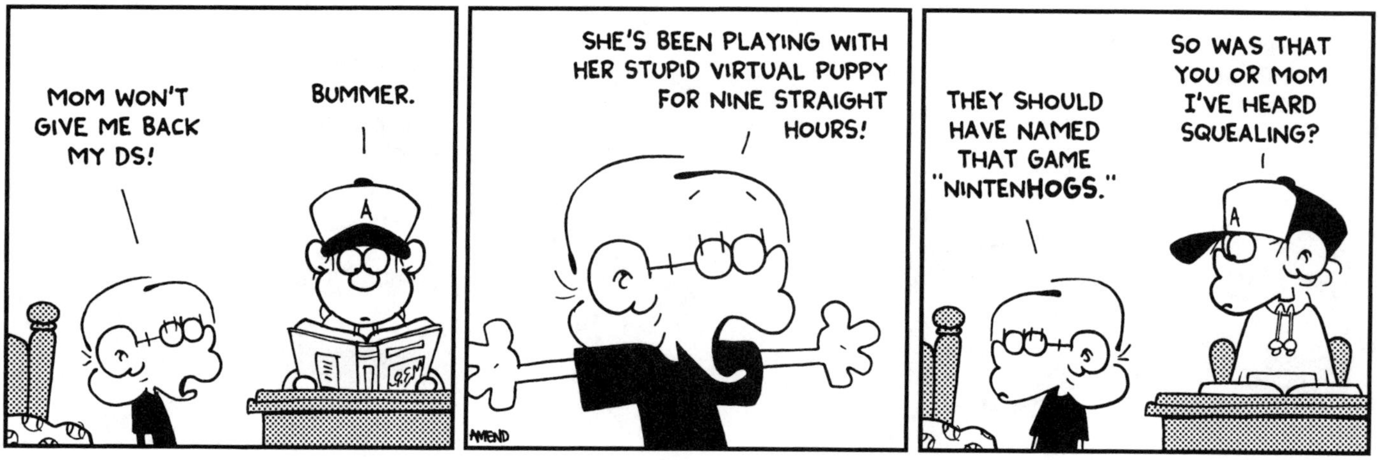
MOM WON'T GIVE ME BACK MY DS!
BUMMER.
SHE'S BEEN PLAYING WITH HER STUPID VIRTUAL PUPPY FOR NINE STRAIGHT HOURS!
AMEND
THEY SHOULD HAVE NAMED THAT GAME "NINTEN**HOGS**."
SO WAS THAT YOU OR MOM I'VE HEARD SQUEALING?

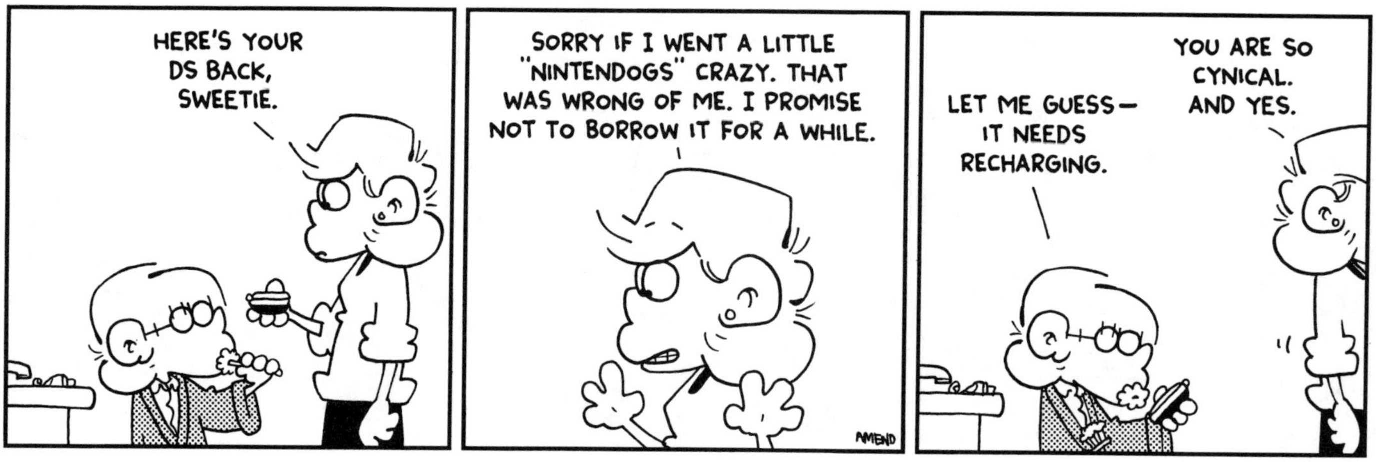
HERE'S YOUR DS BACK, SWEETIE.
SORRY IF I WENT A LITTLE "NINTENDOGS" CRAZY. THAT WAS WRONG OF ME. I PROMISE NOT TO BORROW IT FOR A WHILE.
AMEND
LET ME GUESS— IT NEEDS RECHARGING.
YOU ARE SO CYNICAL. AND YES.

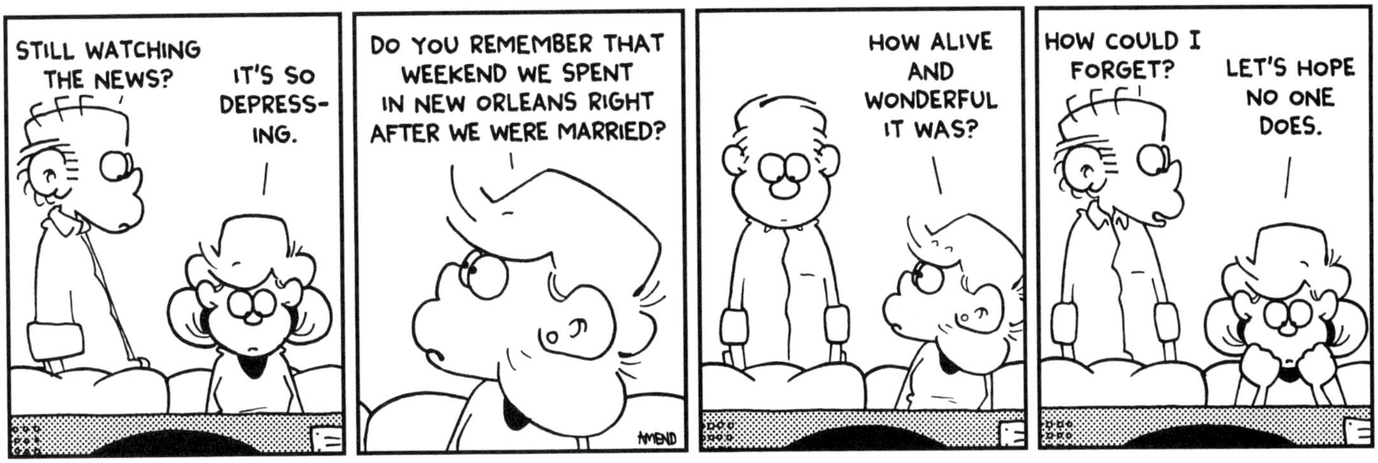
STILL WATCHING THE NEWS?
IT'S SO DEPRESS-ING.
DO YOU REMEMBER THAT WEEKEND WE SPENT IN NEW ORLEANS RIGHT AFTER WE WERE MARRIED?
HOW ALIVE AND WONDERFUL IT WAS?
HOW COULD I FORGET?
LET'S HOPE NO ONE DOES.
AMEND

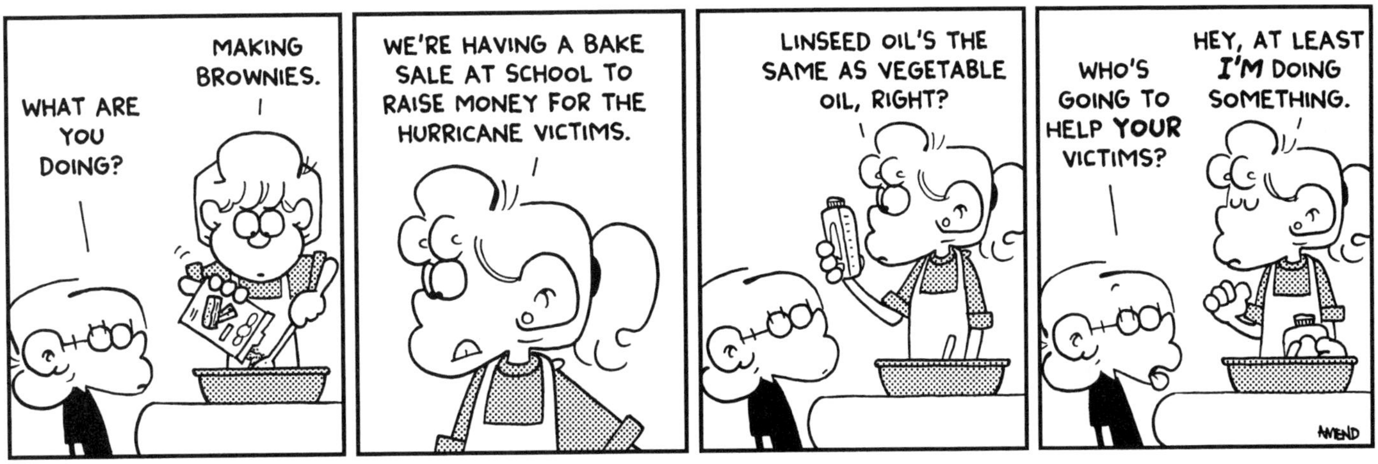
WHAT ARE YOU DOING?
MAKING BROWNIES.
WE'RE HAVING A BAKE SALE AT SCHOOL TO RAISE MONEY FOR THE HURRICANE VICTIMS.
LINSEED OIL'S THE SAME AS VEGETABLE OIL, RIGHT?
WHO'S GOING TO HELP YOUR VICTIMS?
HEY, AT LEAST I'M DOING SOMETHING.
AMEND

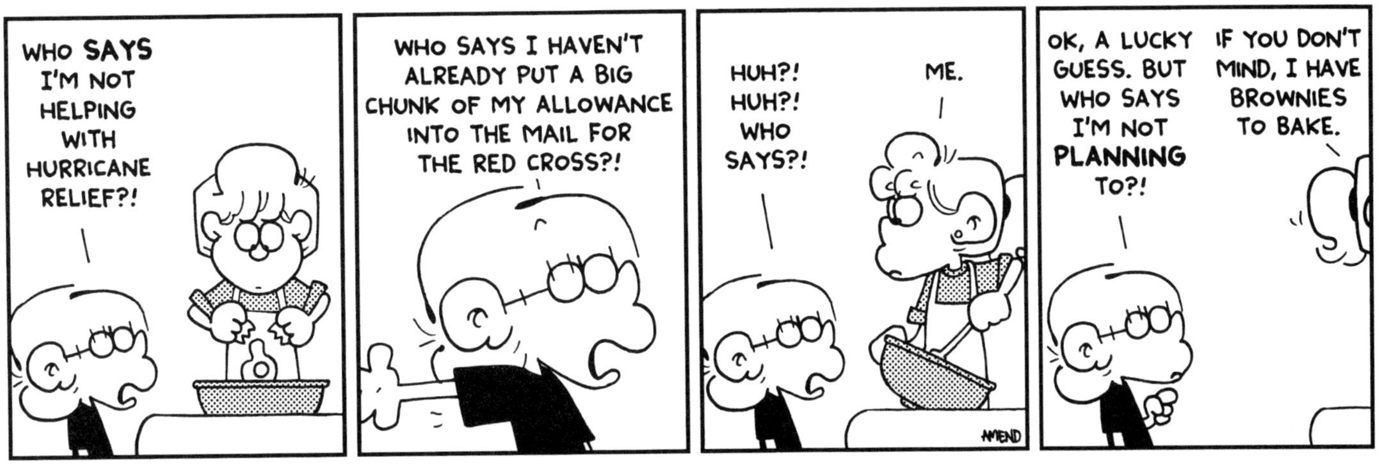
WHO SAYS I'M NOT HELPING WITH HURRICANE RELIEF?!
WHO SAYS I HAVEN'T ALREADY PUT A BIG CHUNK OF MY ALLOWANCE INTO THE MAIL FOR THE RED CROSS?!
HUH?! HUH?! WHO SAYS?!
ME.
AMEND
OK, A LUCKY GUESS. BUT WHO SAYS I'M NOT PLANNING TO?!
IF YOU DON'T MIND, I HAVE BROWNIES TO BAKE.

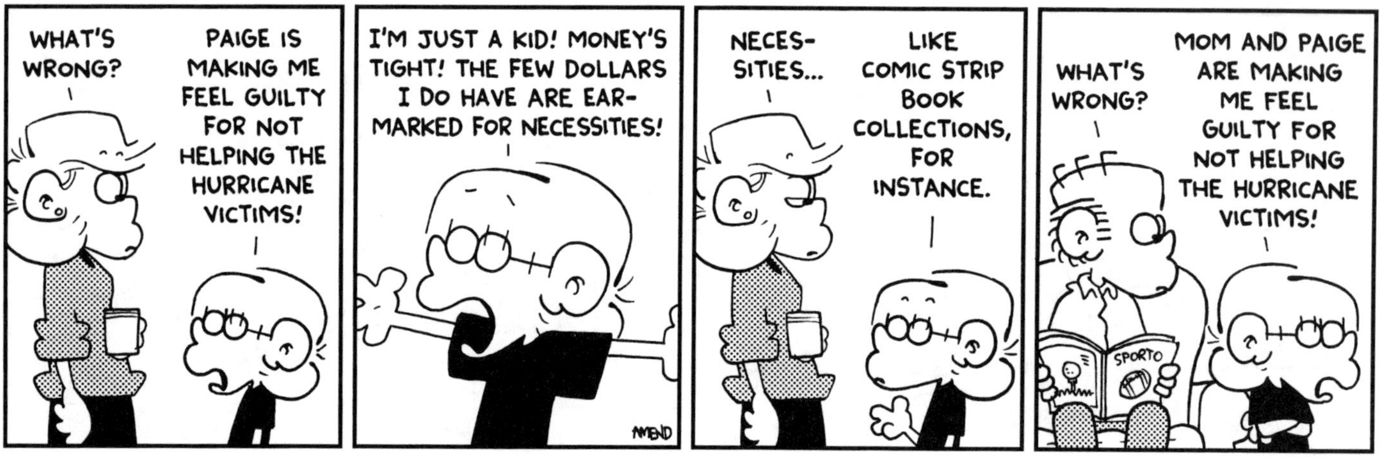
WHAT'S WRONG?
PAIGE IS MAKING ME FEEL GUILTY FOR NOT HELPING THE HURRICANE VICTIMS!
I'M JUST A KID! MONEY'S TIGHT! THE FEW DOLLARS I DO HAVE ARE EAR-MARKED FOR NECESSITIES!
AMEND
NECES-SITIES...
LIKE COMIC STRIP BOOK COLLECTIONS, FOR INSTANCE.
WHAT'S WRONG?
MOM AND PAIGE ARE MAKING ME FEEL GUILTY FOR NOT HELPING THE HURRICANE VICTIMS!
SPORTO

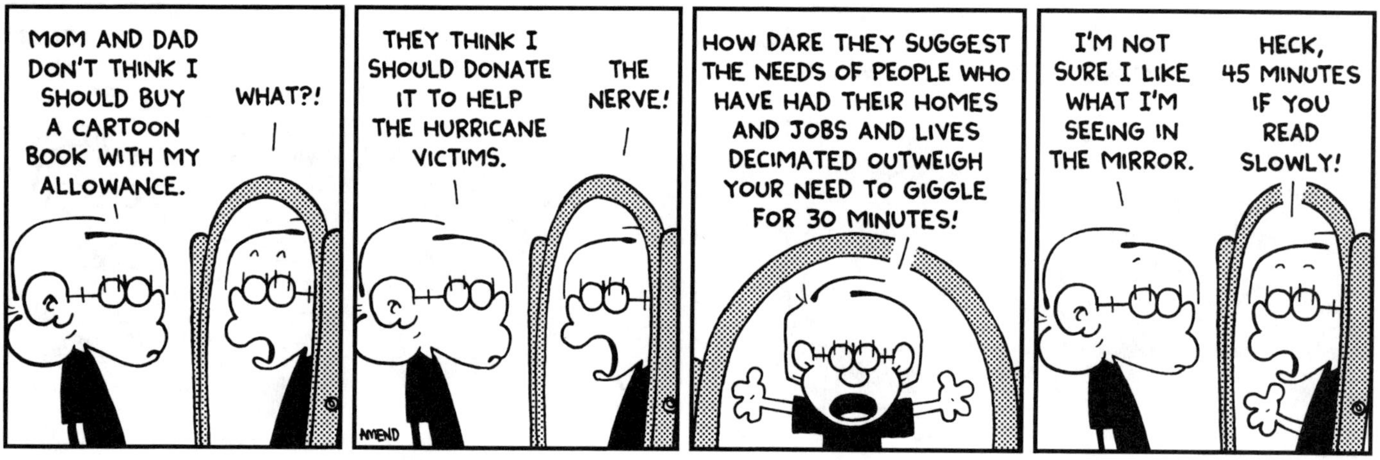
MOM AND DAD DON'T THINK I SHOULD BUY A CARTOON BOOK WITH MY ALLOWANCE.
WHAT?!
THEY THINK I SHOULD DONATE IT TO HELP THE HURRICANE VICTIMS.
THE NERVE!
AMEND
HOW DARE THEY SUGGEST THE NEEDS OF PEOPLE WHO HAVE HAD THEIR HOMES AND JOBS AND LIVES DECIMATED OUTWEIGH YOUR NEED TO GIGGLE FOR 30 MINUTES!
I'M NOT SURE I LIKE WHAT I'M SEEING IN THE MIRROR.
HECK, 45 MINUTES IF YOU READ SLOWLY!

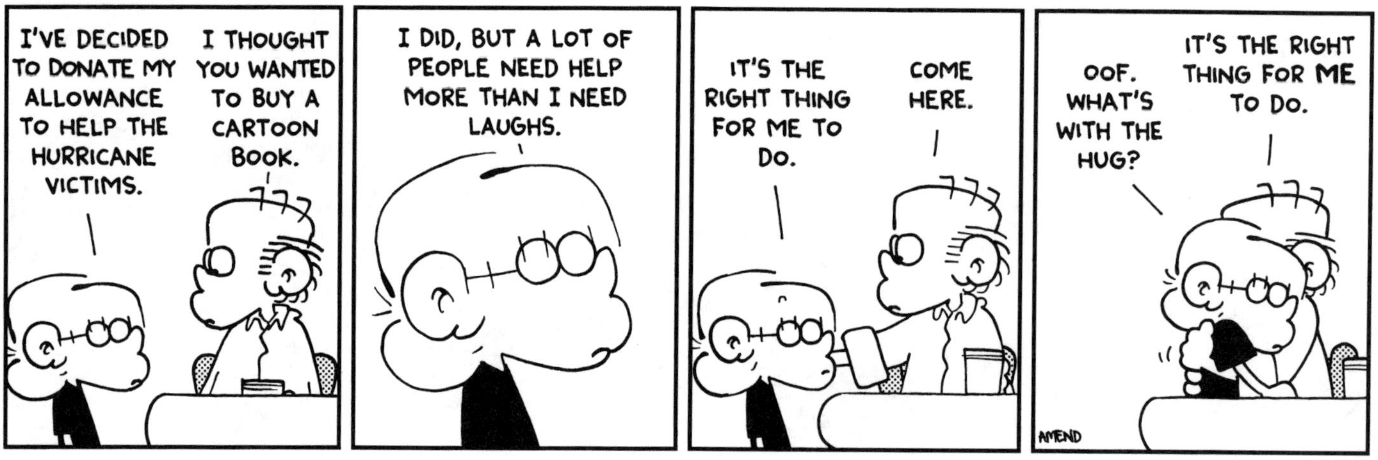
I'VE DECIDED TO DONATE MY ALLOWANCE TO HELP THE HURRICANE VICTIMS.
I THOUGHT YOU WANTED TO BUY A CARTOON BOOK.
I DID, BUT A LOT OF PEOPLE NEED HELP MORE THAN I NEED LAUGHS.
IT'S THE RIGHT THING FOR ME TO DO.
COME HERE.
OOF. WHAT'S WITH THE HUG?
IT'S THE RIGHT THING FOR ME TO DO.
AMEND

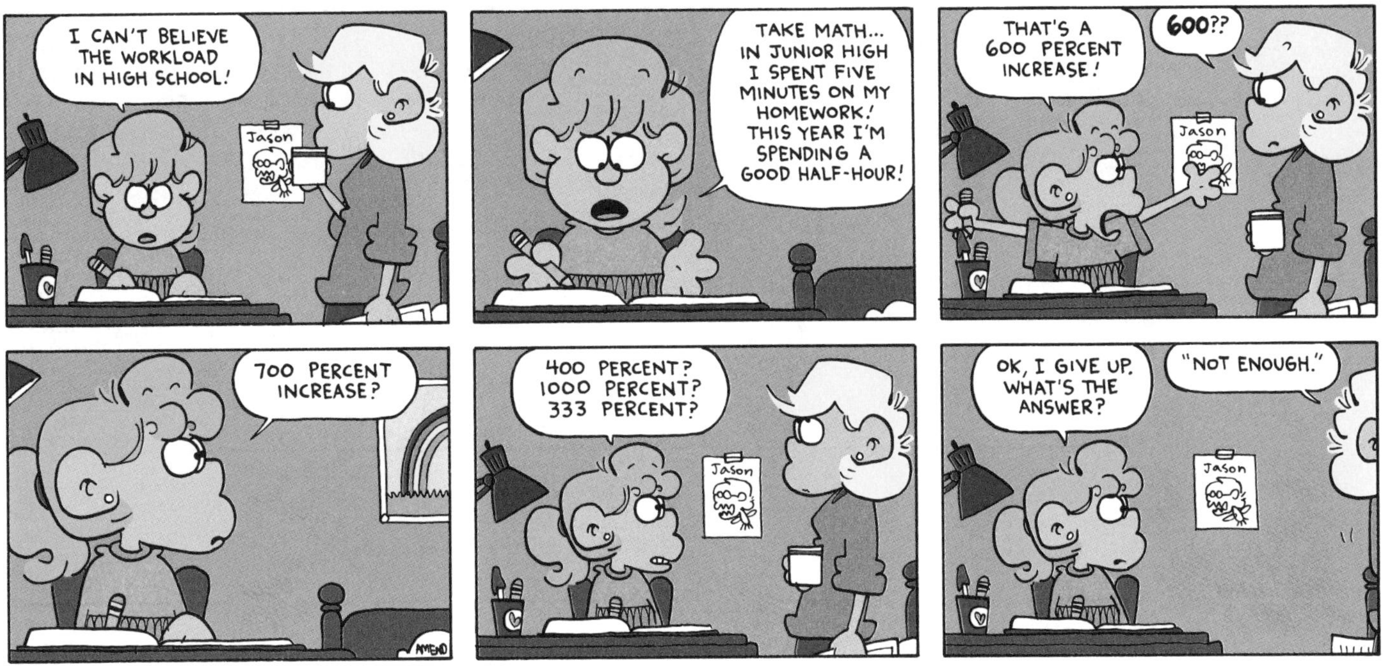
I CAN'T BELIEVE THE WORKLOAD IN HIGH SCHOOL!
Jason
TAKE MATH... IN JUNIOR HIGH I SPENT FIVE MINUTES ON MY HOMEWORK! THIS YEAR I'M SPENDING A GOOD HALF-HOUR!
THAT'S A 600 PERCENT INCREASE!
600??
Jason
700 PERCENT INCREASE?
400 PERCENT? 1000 PERCENT? 333 PERCENT?
Jason
OK, I GIVE UP. WHAT'S THE ANSWER?
"NOT ENOUGH."
Jason

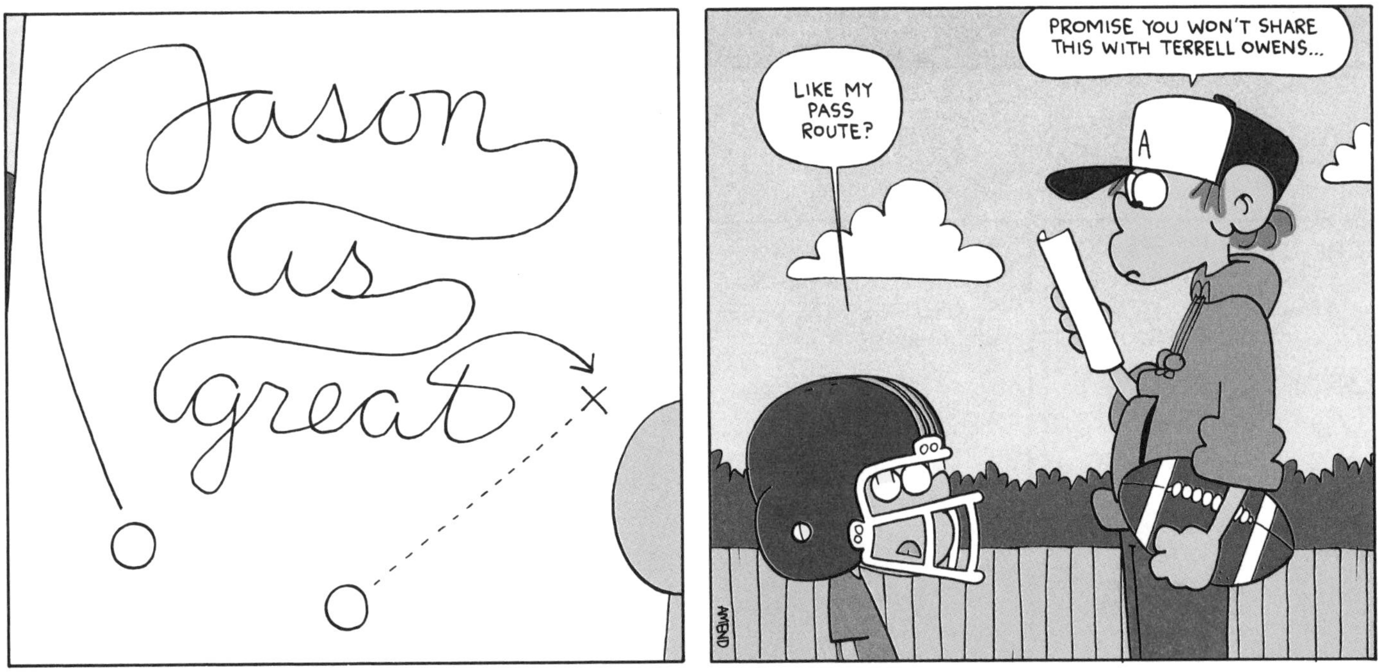
Jason as great
PROMISE YOU WON'T SHARE THIS WITH TERRELL OWENS...
LIKE MY PASS ROUTE?
A

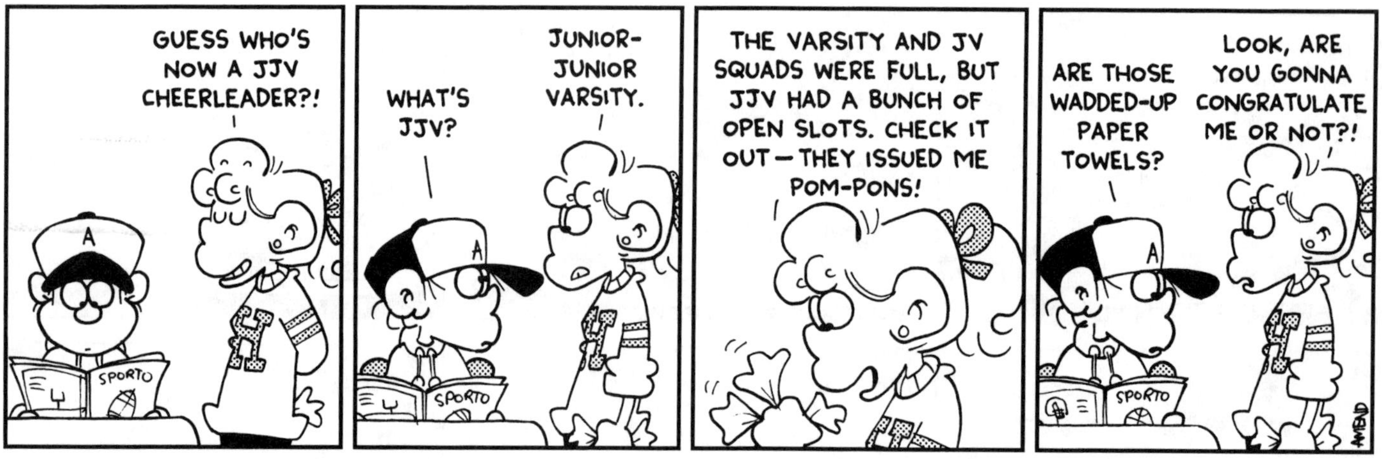
GUESS WHO'S NOW A JJV CHEERLEADER?!
WHAT'S JJV?
JUNIOR-JUNIOR VARSITY.
THE VARSITY AND JV SQUADS WERE FULL, BUT JJV HAD A BUNCH OF OPEN SLOTS. CHECK IT OUT—THEY ISSUED ME POM-PONS!
ARE THOSE WADDED-UP PAPER TOWELS?
LOOK, ARE YOU GONNA CONGRATULATE ME OR NOT?!

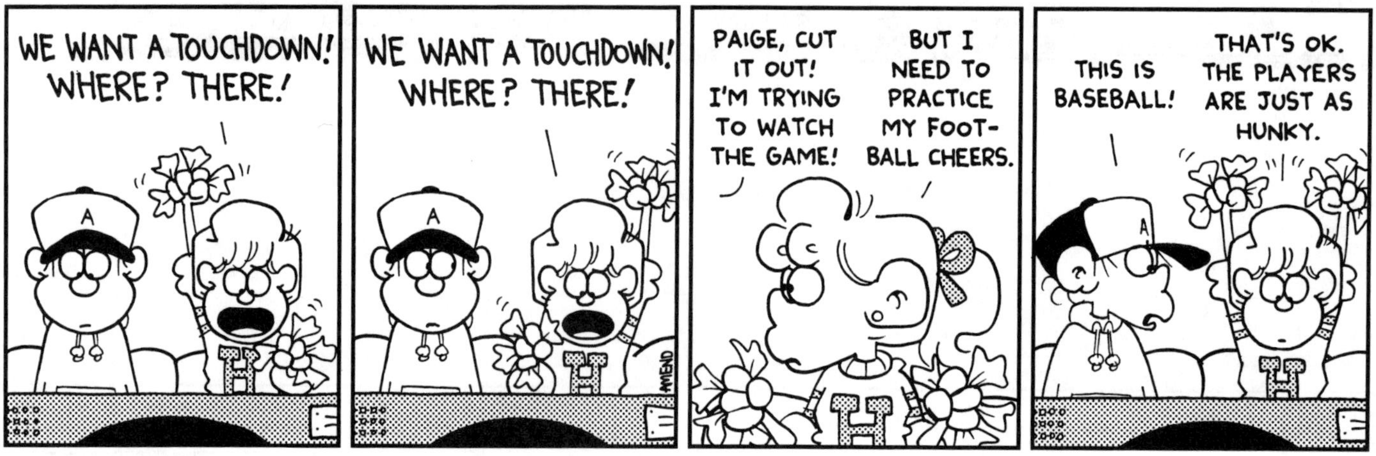
WE WANT A TOUCHDOWN! WHERE? THERE!
WE WANT A TOUCHDOWN! WHERE? THERE!
PAIGE, CUT IT OUT! I'M TRYING TO WATCH THE GAME!
BUT I NEED TO PRACTICE MY FOOT-BALL CHEERS.
THIS IS BASEBALL!
THAT'S OK. THE PLAYERS ARE JUST AS HUNKY.

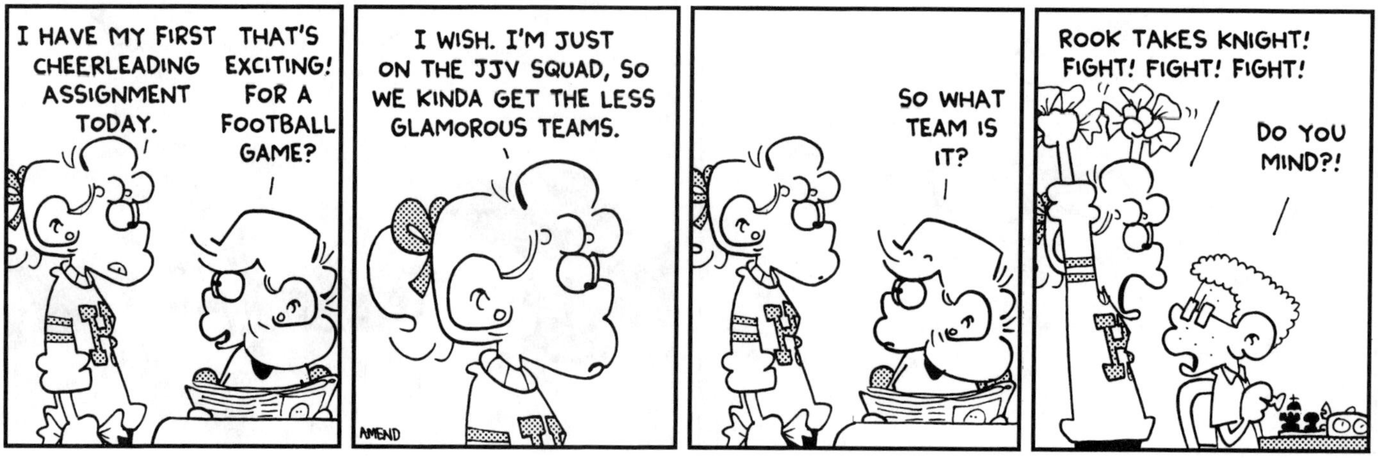
I HAVE MY FIRST CHEERLEADING ASSIGNMENT TODAY.
THAT'S EXCITING! FOR A FOOTBALL GAME?
I WISH. I'M JUST ON THE JJV SQUAD, SO WE KINDA GET THE LESS GLAMOROUS TEAMS.
SO WHAT TEAM IS IT?
ROOK TAKES KNIGHT! FIGHT! FIGHT! FIGHT!
DO YOU MIND?!

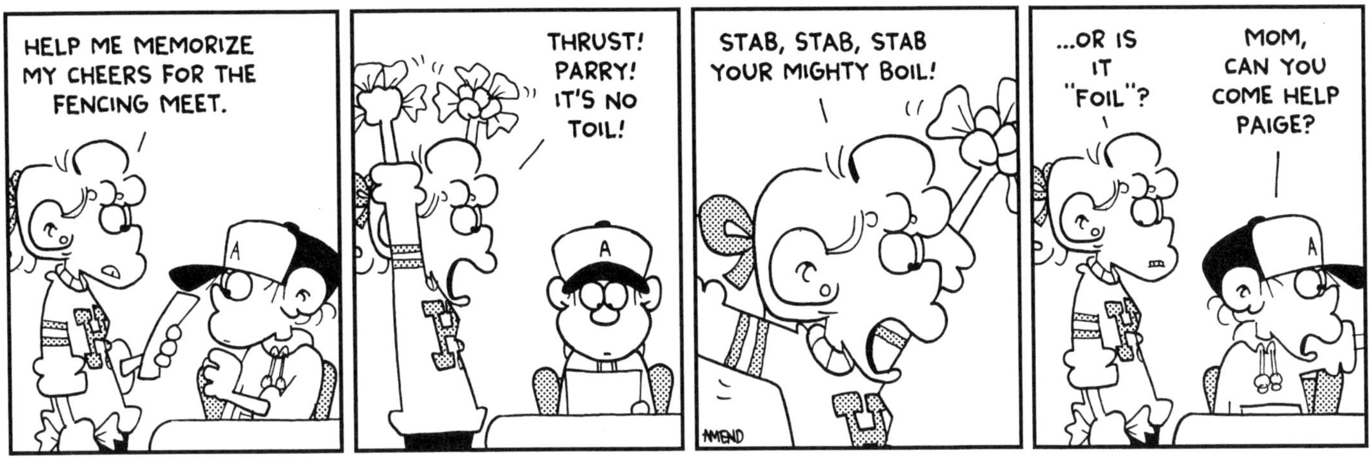
HELP ME MEMORIZE MY CHEERS FOR THE FENCING MEET.
THRUST! PARRY! IT'S NO TOIL!
STAB, STAB, STAB YOUR MIGHTY BOIL!
AMEND
...OR IS IT "FOIL"?
MOM, CAN YOU COME HELP PAIGE?

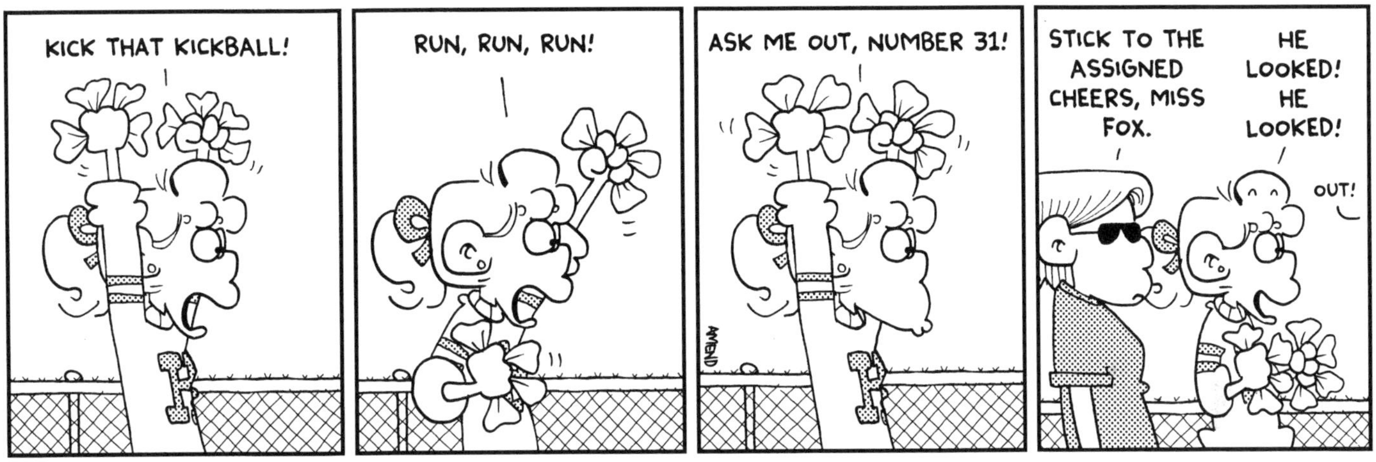
KICK THAT KICKBALL!
RUN, RUN, RUN!
AMEND
ASK ME OUT, NUMBER 31!
STICK TO THE ASSIGNED CHEERS, MISS FOX.
HE LOOKED! HE LOOKED!
OUT!

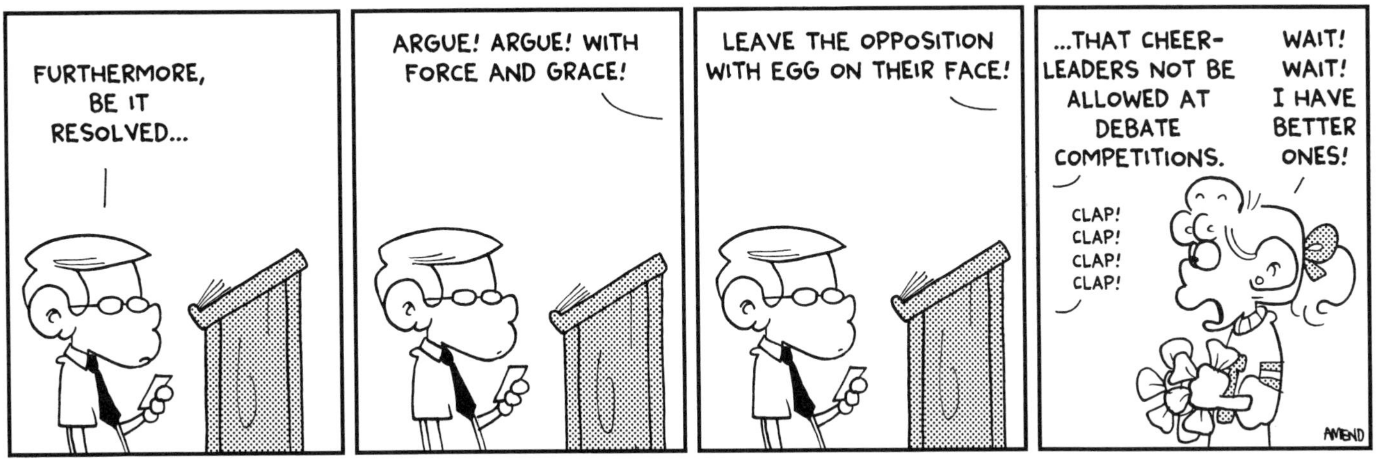
FURTHERMORE, BE IT RESOLVED...
ARGUE! ARGUE! WITH FORCE AND GRACE!
LEAVE THE OPPOSITION WITH EGG ON THEIR FACE!
...THAT CHEER-LEADERS NOT BE ALLOWED AT DEBATE COMPETITIONS.
CLAP! CLAP! CLAP! CLAP!
WAIT! WAIT! I HAVE BETTER ONES!
AMEND

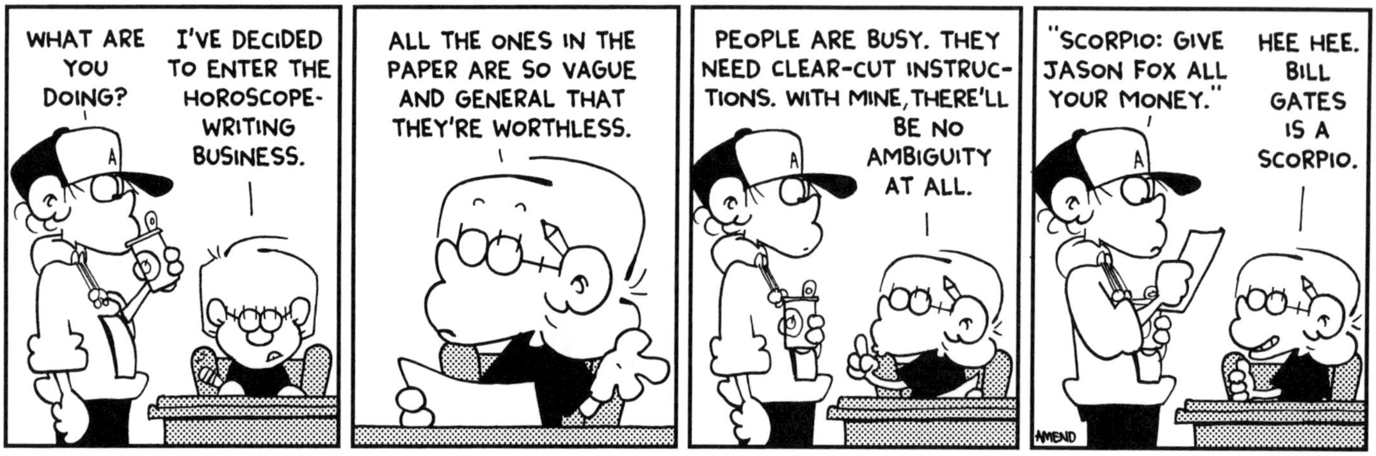
WHAT ARE YOU DOING?
I'VE DECIDED TO ENTER THE HOROSCOPE-WRITING BUSINESS.
ALL THE ONES IN THE PAPER ARE SO VAGUE AND GENERAL THAT THEY'RE WORTHLESS.
PEOPLE ARE BUSY. THEY NEED CLEAR-CUT INSTRUCTIONS. WITH MINE, THERE'LL BE NO AMBIGUITY AT ALL.
"SCORPIO: GIVE JASON FOX ALL YOUR MONEY."
HEE HEE. BILL GATES IS A SCORPIO.
AMEND

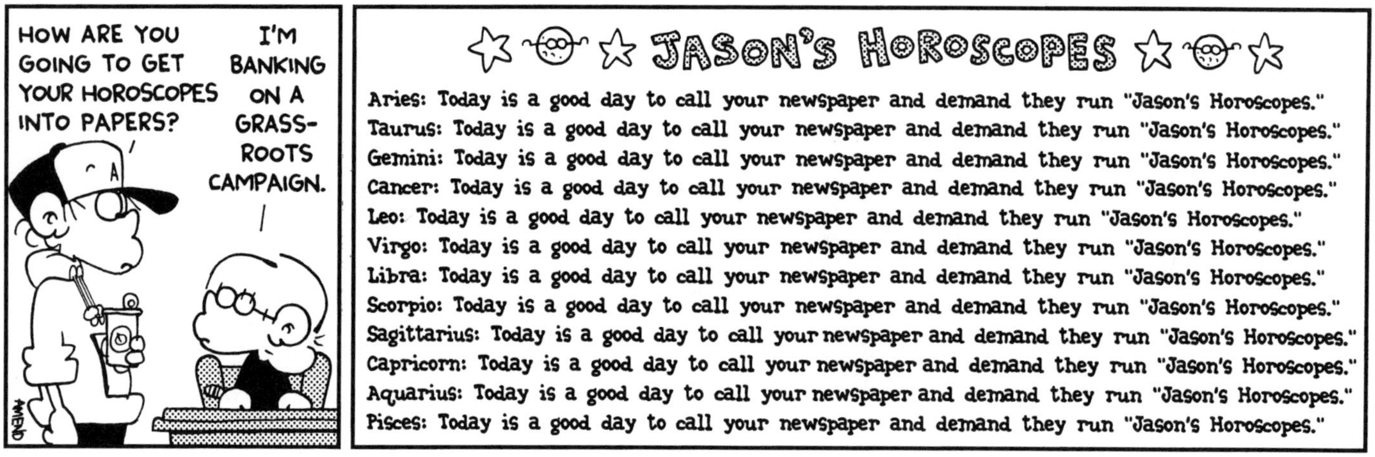
HOW ARE YOU GOING TO GET YOUR HOROSCOPES INTO PAPERS?
I'M BANKING ON A GRASS-ROOTS CAMPAIGN.
AMEND
JASON'S HOROSCOPES
Aries: Today is a good day to call your newspaper and demand they run "Jason's Horoscopes."
Taurus: Today is a good day to call your newspaper and demand they run "Jason's Horoscopes."
Gemini: Today is a good day to call your newspaper and demand they run "Jason's Horoscopes."
Cancer: Today is a good day to call your newspaper and demand they run "Jason's Horoscopes."
Leo: Today is a good day to call your newspaper and demand they run "Jason's Horoscopes."
Virgo: Today is a good day to call your newspaper and demand they run "Jason's Horoscopes."
Libra: Today is a good day to call your newspaper and demand they run "Jason's Horoscopes."
Scorpio: Today is a good day to call your newspaper and demand they run "Jason's Horoscopes."
Sagittarius: Today is a good day to call your newspaper and demand they run "Jason's Horoscopes."
Capricorn: Today is a good day to call your newspaper and demand they run "Jason's Horoscopes."
Aquarius: Today is a good day to call your newspaper and demand they run "Jason's Horoscopes."
Pisces: Today is a good day to call your newspaper and demand they run "Jason's Horoscopes."

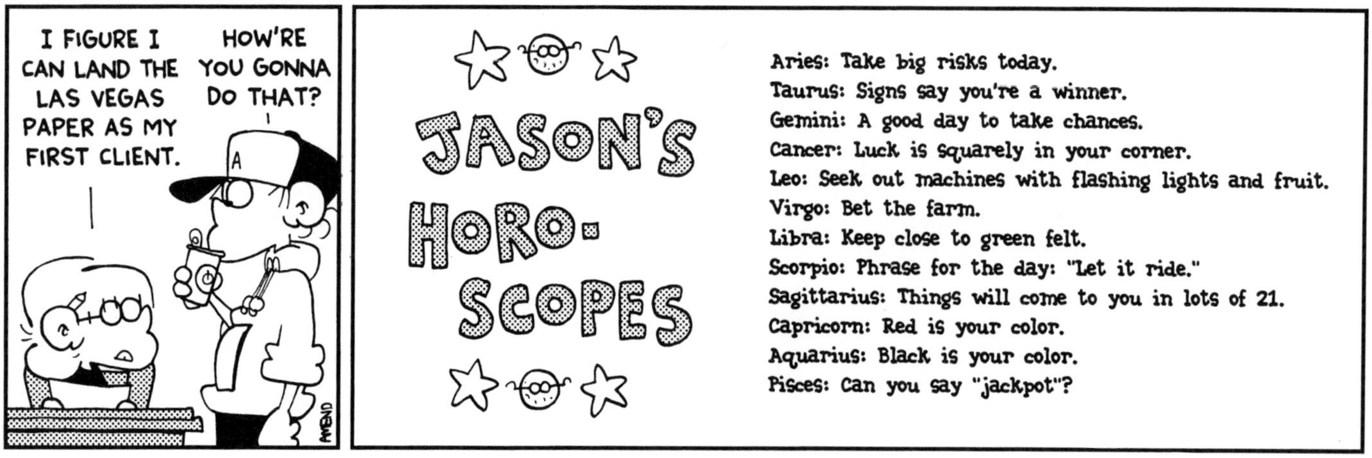
I FIGURE I CAN LAND THE LAS VEGAS PAPER AS MY FIRST CLIENT.
HOW'RE YOU GONNA DO THAT?
AMEND
JASON'S HORO-SCOPES
Aries: Take big risks today.
Taurus: Signs say you're a winner.
Gemini: A good day to take chances.
Cancer: Luck is squarely in your corner.
Leo: Seek out machines with flashing lights and fruit.
Virgo: Bet the farm.
Libra: Keep close to green felt.
Scorpio: Phrase for the day: "Let it ride."
Sagittarius: Things will come to you in lots of 21.
Capricorn: Red is your color.
Aquarius: Black is your color.
Pisces: Can you say "jackpot"?

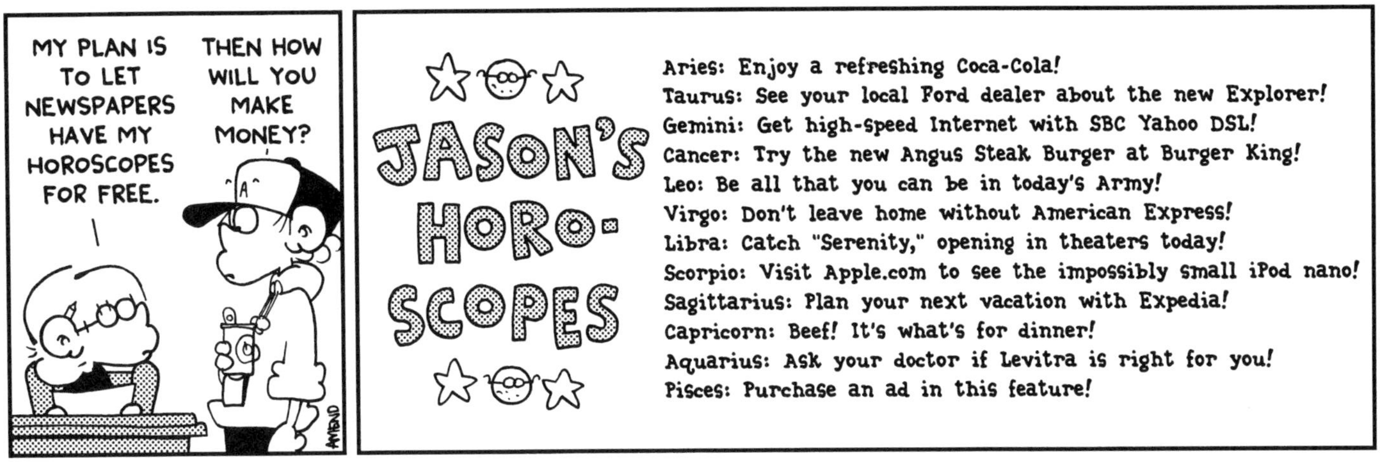
MY PLAN IS TO LET NEWSPAPERS HAVE MY HOROSCOPES FOR FREE.
THEN HOW WILL YOU MAKE MONEY?
JASON'S HORO-SCOPES
Aries: Enjoy a refreshing Coca-Cola!
Taurus: See your local Ford dealer about the new Explorer!
Gemini: Get high-speed Internet with SBC Yahoo DSL!
Cancer: Try the new Angus Steak Burger at Burger King!
Leo: Be all that you can be in today's Army!
Virgo: Don't leave home without American Express!
Libra: Catch "Serenity," opening in theaters today!
Scorpio: Visit Apple.com to see the impossibly small iPod nano!
Sagittarius: Plan your next vacation with Expedia!
Capricorn: Beef! It's what's for dinner!
Aquarius: Ask your doctor if Levitra is right for you!
Pisces: Purchase an ad in this feature!
AMEND

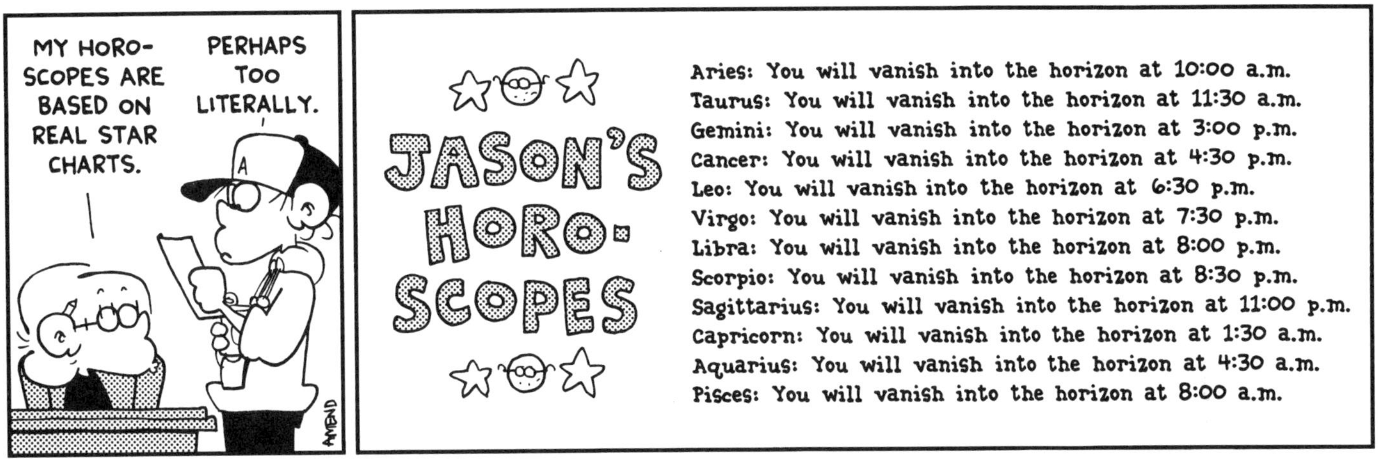
MY HORO-SCOPES ARE BASED ON REAL STAR CHARTS.
PERHAPS TOO LITERALLY.
JASON'S HORO-SCOPES
Aries: You will vanish into the horizon at 10:00 a.m.
Taurus: You will vanish into the horizon at 11:30 a.m.
Gemini: You will vanish into the horizon at 3:00 p.m.
Cancer: You will vanish into the horizon at 4:30 p.m.
Leo: You will vanish into the horizon at 6:30 p.m.
Virgo: You will vanish into the horizon at 7:30 p.m.
Libra: You will vanish into the horizon at 8:00 p.m.
Scorpio: You will vanish into the horizon at 8:30 p.m.
Sagittarius: You will vanish into the horizon at 11:00 p.m.
Capricorn: You will vanish into the horizon at 1:30 a.m.
Aquarius: You will vanish into the horizon at 4:30 a.m.
Pisces: You will vanish into the horizon at 8:00 a.m.
AMEND

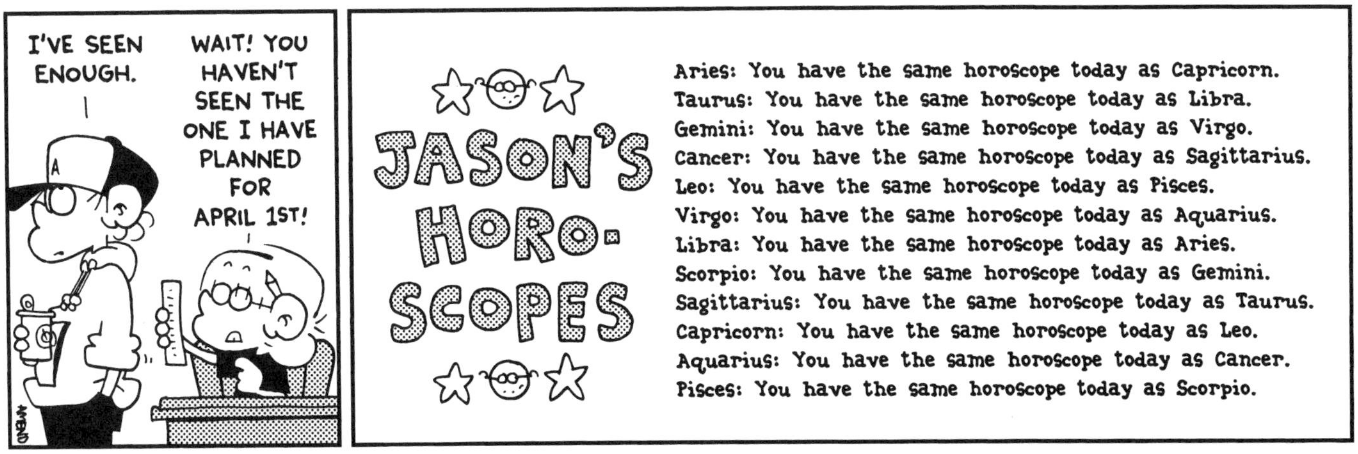
I'VE SEEN ENOUGH.
WAIT! YOU HAVEN'T SEEN THE ONE I HAVE PLANNED FOR APRIL 1ST!
JASON'S HORO-SCOPES
Aries: You have the same horoscope today as Capricorn.
Taurus: You have the same horoscope today as Libra.
Gemini: You have the same horoscope today as Virgo.
Cancer: You have the same horoscope today as Sagittarius.
Leo: You have the same horoscope today as Pisces.
Virgo: You have the same horoscope today as Aquarius.
Libra: You have the same horoscope today as Aries.
Scorpio: You have the same horoscope today as Gemini.
Sagittarius: You have the same horoscope today as Taurus.
Capricorn: You have the same horoscope today as Leo.
Aquarius: You have the same horoscope today as Cancer.
Pisces: You have the same horoscope today as Scorpio.
AMEND

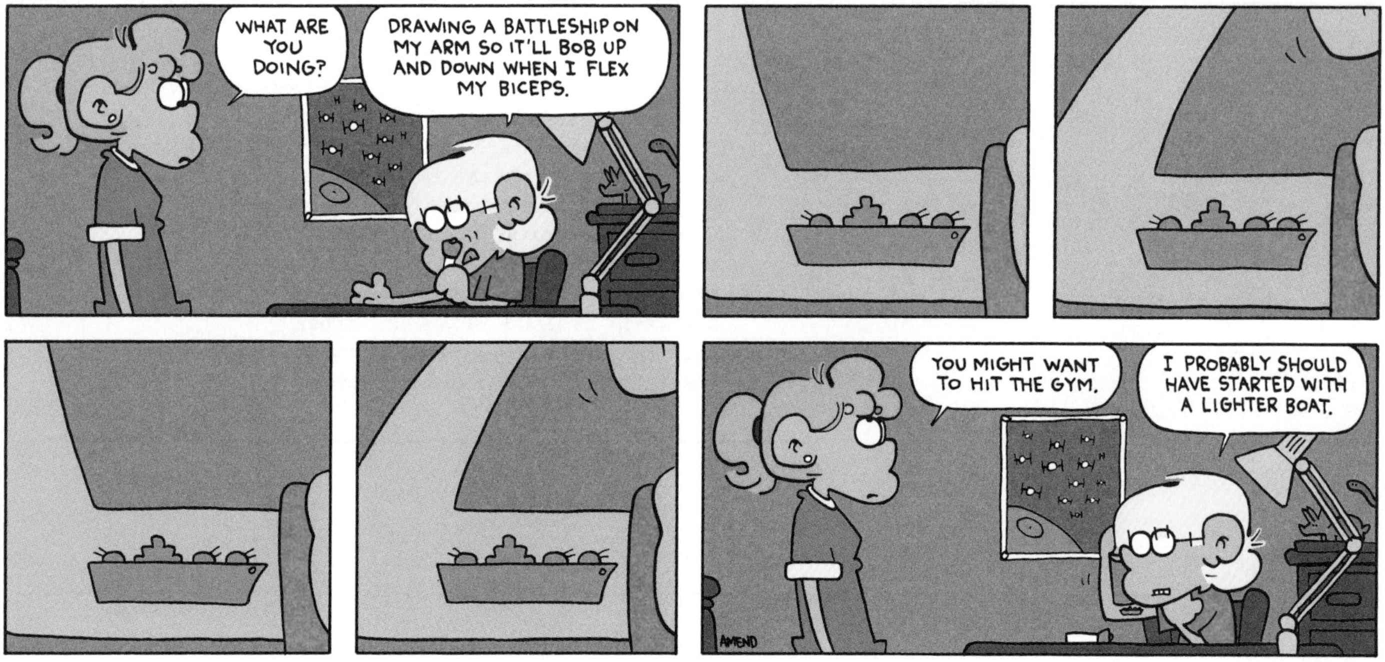
WHAT ARE YOU DOING?
DRAWING A BATTLESHIP ON MY ARM SO IT'LL BOB UP AND DOWN WHEN I FLEX MY BICEPS.
YOU MIGHT WANT TO HIT THE GYM.
I PROBABLY SHOULD HAVE STARTED WITH A LIGHTER BOAT.
AMEND

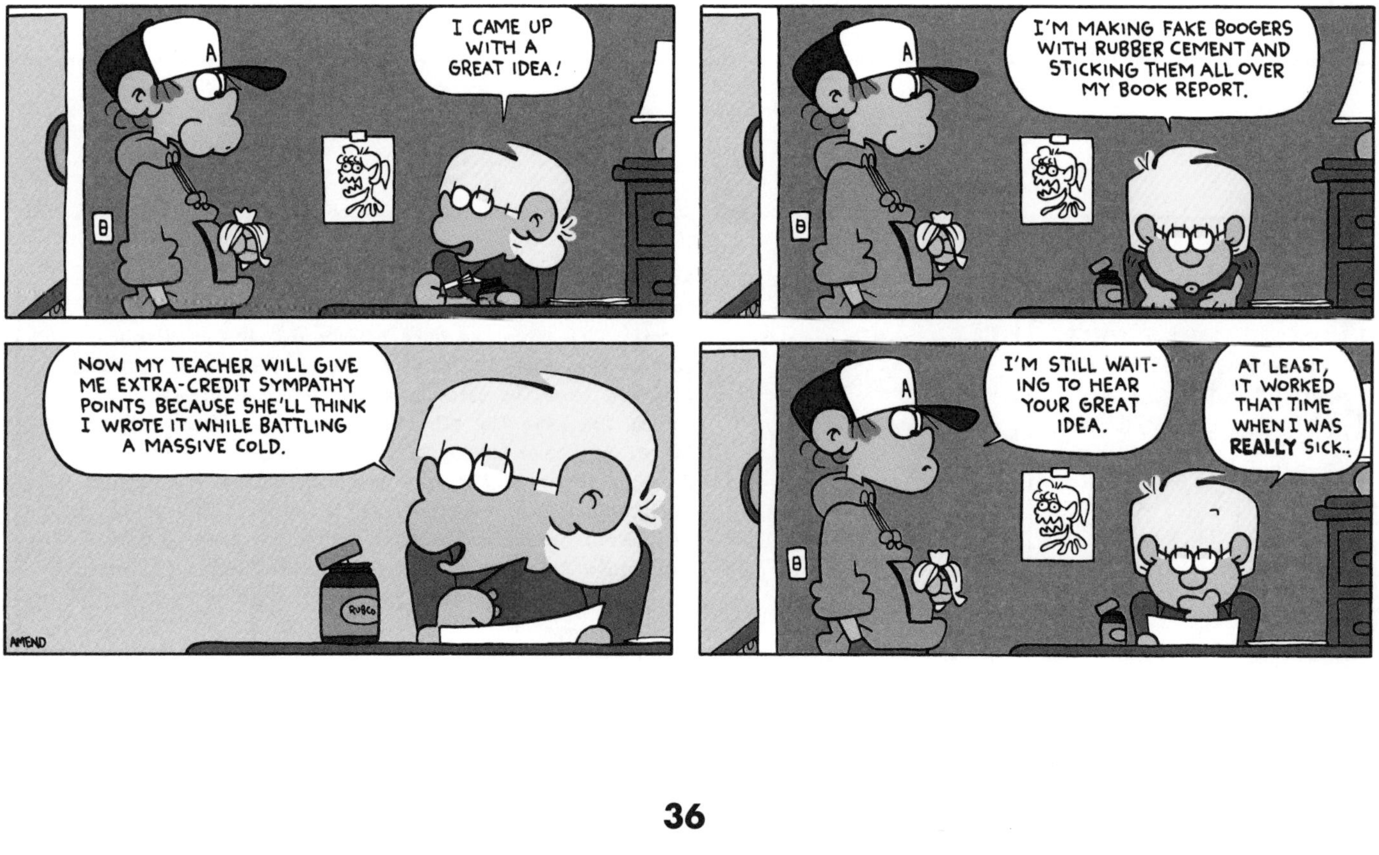
I CAME UP WITH A GREAT IDEA!
I'M MAKING FAKE BOOGERS WITH RUBBER CEMENT AND STICKING THEM ALL OVER MY BOOK REPORT.
NOW MY TEACHER WILL GIVE ME EXTRA-CREDIT SYMPATHY POINTS BECAUSE SHE'LL THINK I WROTE IT WHILE BATTLING A MASSIVE COLD.
RUBCO
AMEND
I'M STILL WAITING TO HEAR YOUR GREAT IDEA.
AT LEAST, IT WORKED THAT TIME WHEN I WAS **REALLY** SICK..

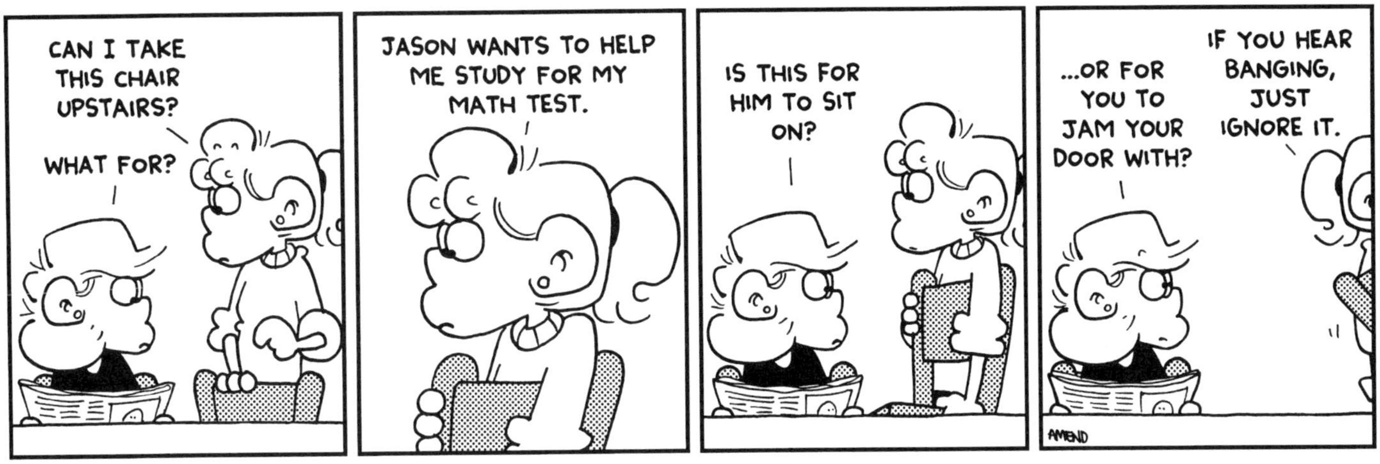
CAN I TAKE THIS CHAIR UPSTAIRS?
WHAT FOR?
JASON WANTS TO HELP ME STUDY FOR MY MATH TEST.
IS THIS FOR HIM TO SIT ON?
...OR FOR YOU TO JAM YOUR DOOR WITH?
IF YOU HEAR BANGING, JUST IGNORE IT.
AMEND

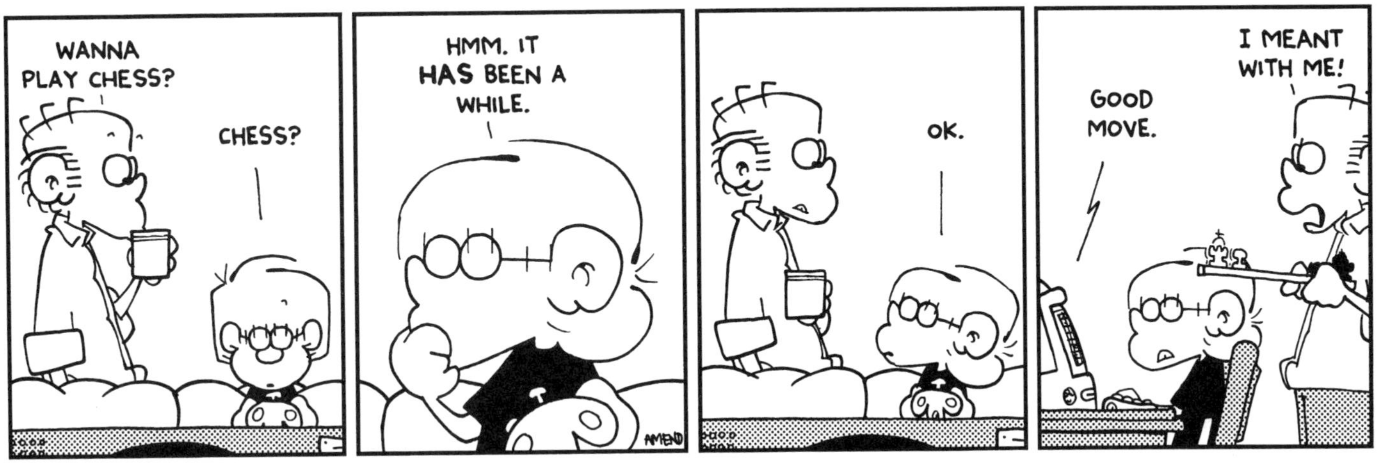
WANNA PLAY CHESS?
CHESS?
HMM. IT HAS BEEN A WHILE.
AMEND
OK.
GOOD MOVE.
I MEANT WITH ME!

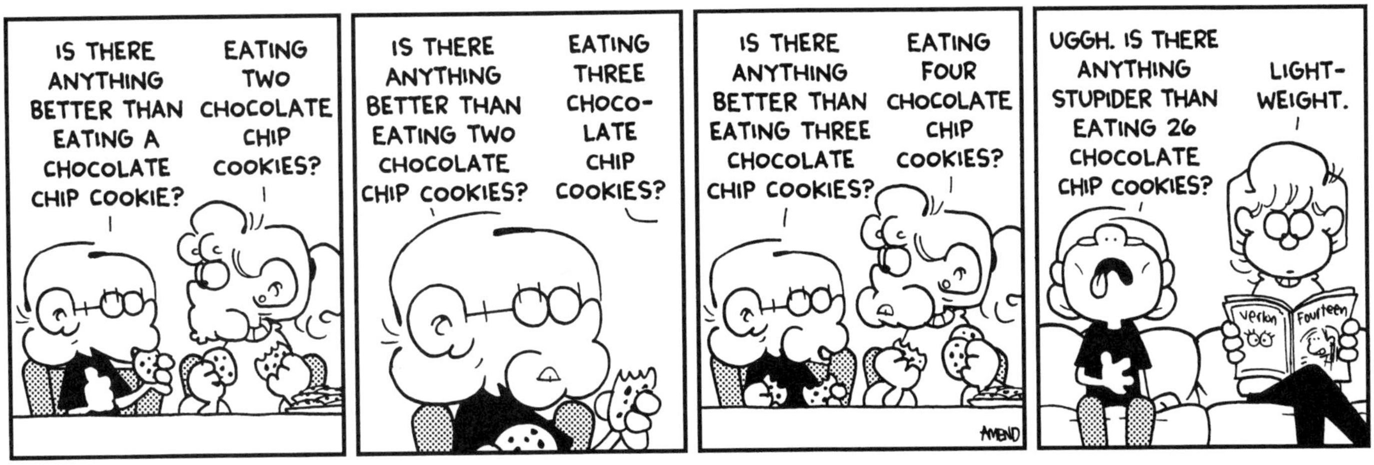
IS THERE ANYTHING BETTER THAN EATING A CHOCOLATE CHIP COOKIE?
EATING TWO CHOCOLATE CHIP COOKIES?
IS THERE ANYTHING BETTER THAN EATING TWO CHOCOLATE CHIP COOKIES?
EATING THREE CHOCO-LATE CHIP COOKIES?
IS THERE ANYTHING BETTER THAN EATING THREE CHOCOLATE CHIP COOKIES?
EATING FOUR CHOCOLATE CHIP COOKIES?
AMEND
UGGH. IS THERE ANYTHING STUPIDER THAN EATING 26 CHOCOLATE CHIP COOKIES?
LIGHT-WEIGHT.

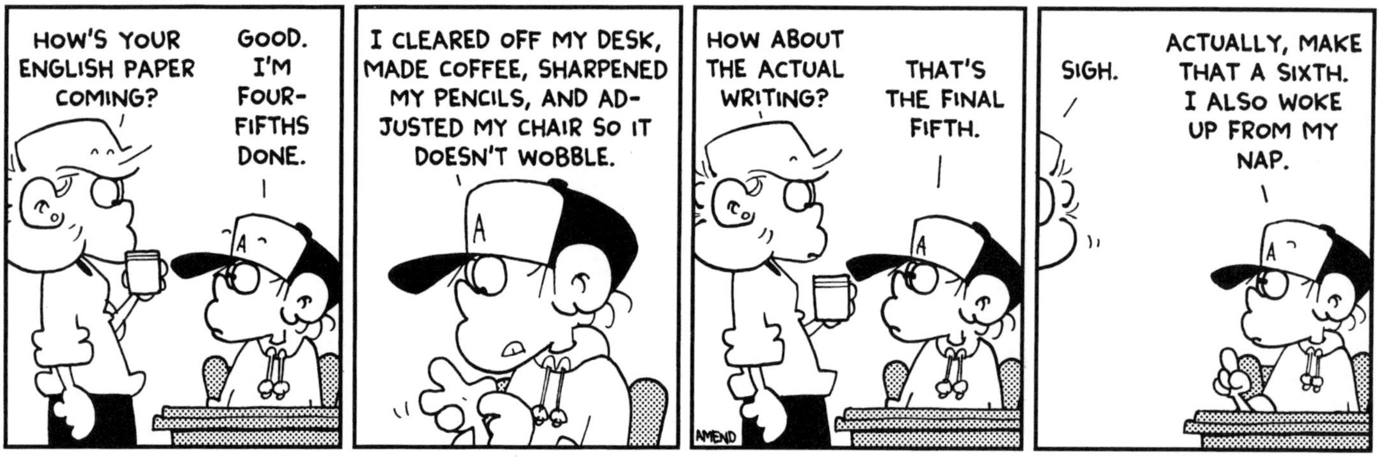
HOW'S YOUR ENGLISH PAPER COMING?
GOOD. I'M FOUR-FIFTHS DONE.
I CLEARED OFF MY DESK, MADE COFFEE, SHARPENED MY PENCILS, AND AD-JUSTED MY CHAIR SO IT DOESN'T WOBBLE.
HOW ABOUT THE ACTUAL WRITING?
THAT'S THE FINAL FIFTH.
SIGH.
ACTUALLY, MAKE THAT A SIXTH. I ALSO WOKE UP FROM MY NAP.
AMEND

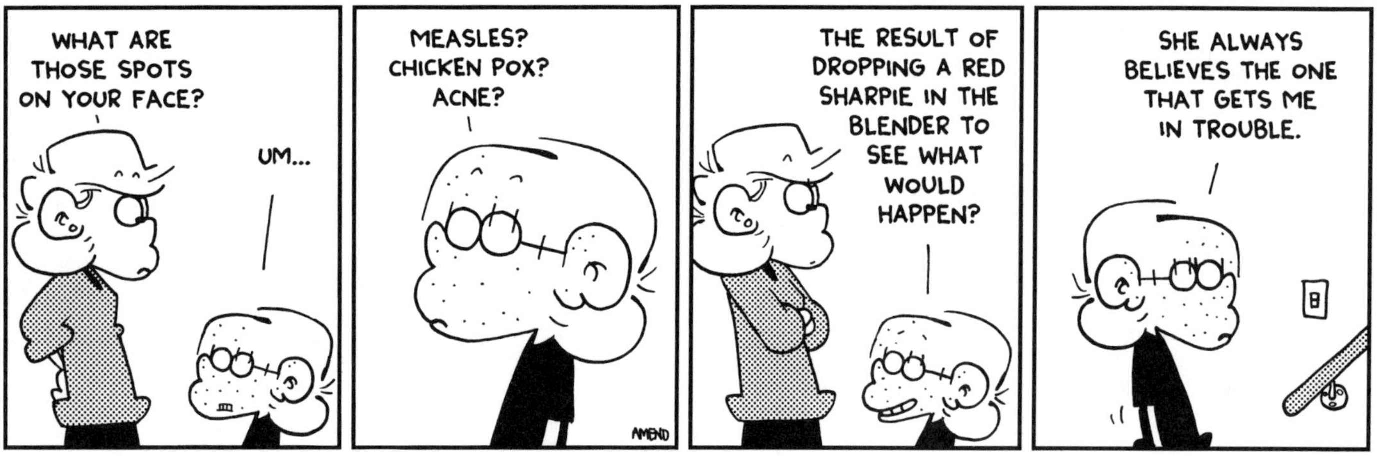
WHAT ARE THOSE SPOTS ON YOUR FACE?
UM...
MEASLES? CHICKEN POX? ACNE?
THE RESULT OF DROPPING A RED SHARPIE IN THE BLENDER TO SEE WHAT WOULD HAPPEN?
SHE ALWAYS BELIEVES THE ONE THAT GETS ME IN TROUBLE.
AMEND

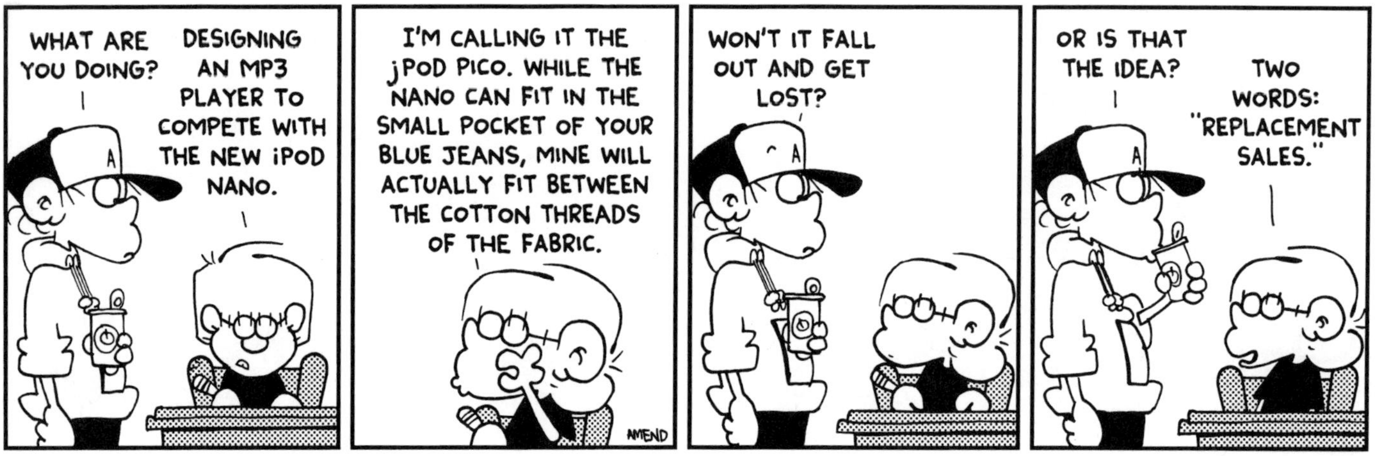
WHAT ARE YOU DOING?
DESIGNING AN MP3 PLAYER TO COMPETE WITH THE NEW iPOD NANO.
I'M CALLING IT THE jPOD PICO. WHILE THE NANO CAN FIT IN THE SMALL POCKET OF YOUR BLUE JEANS, MINE WILL ACTUALLY FIT BETWEEN THE COTTON THREADS OF THE FABRIC.
WON'T IT FALL OUT AND GET LOST?
OR IS THAT THE IDEA?
TWO WORDS: "REPLACEMENT SALES."
AMEND

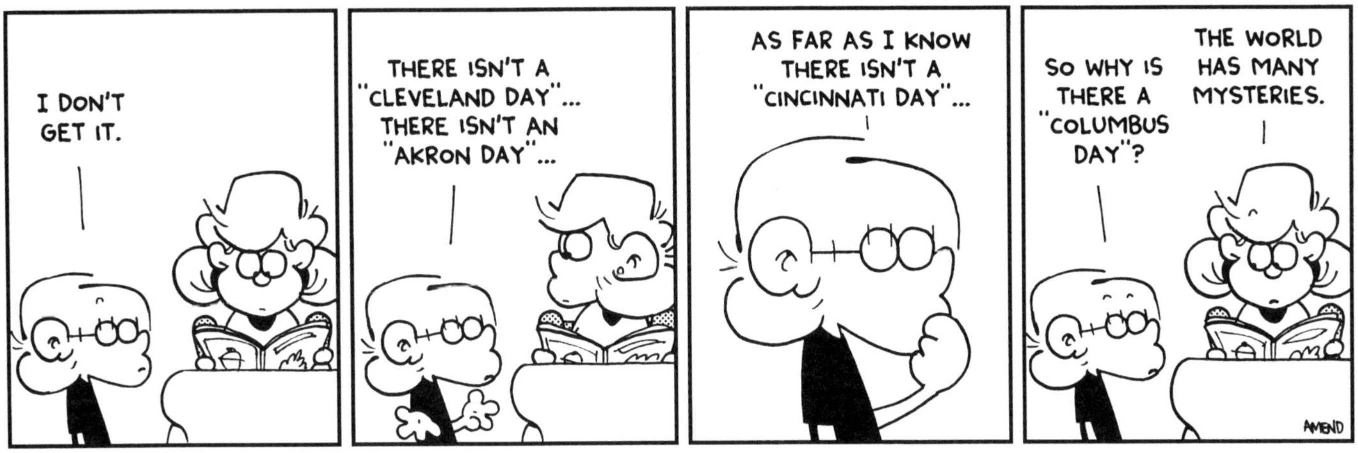
I DON'T GET IT.
THERE ISN'T A "CLEVELAND DAY"... THERE ISN'T AN "AKRON DAY"...
AS FAR AS I KNOW THERE ISN'T A "CINCINNATI DAY"...
SO WHY IS THERE A "COLUMBUS DAY"?
THE WORLD HAS MANY MYSTERIES.
AMEND

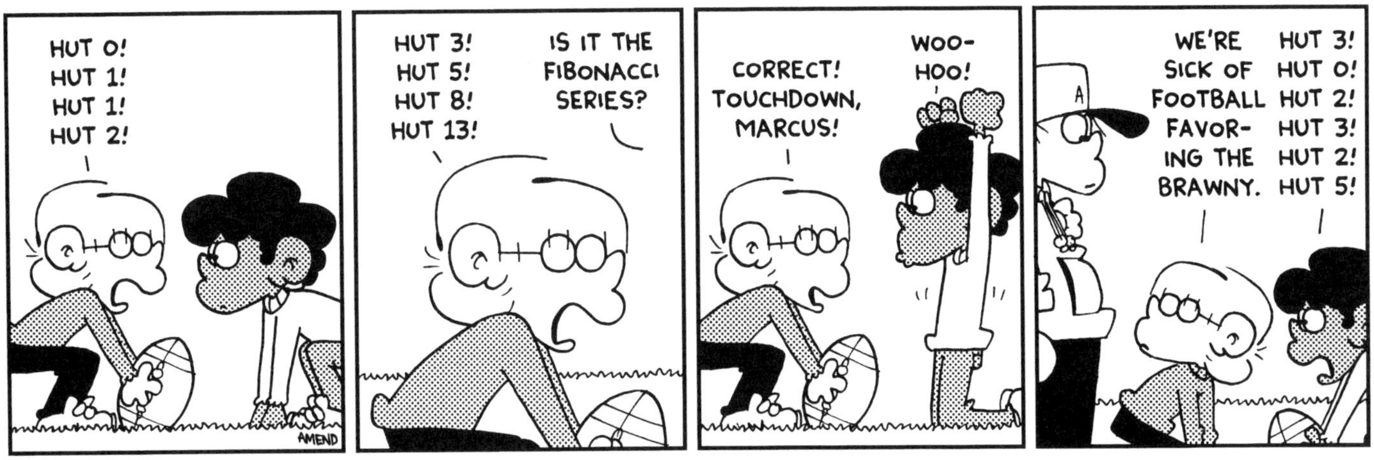
HUT 0! HUT 1! HUT 1! HUT 2!
AMEND
HUT 3! HUT 5! HUT 8! HUT 13!
IS IT THE FIBONACCI SERIES?
CORRECT! TOUCHDOWN, MARCUS!
WOO-HOO!
WE'RE SICK OF FOOTBALL FAVOR-ING THE BRAWNY.
HUT 3! HUT 0! HUT 2! HUT 3! HUT 2! HUT 5!

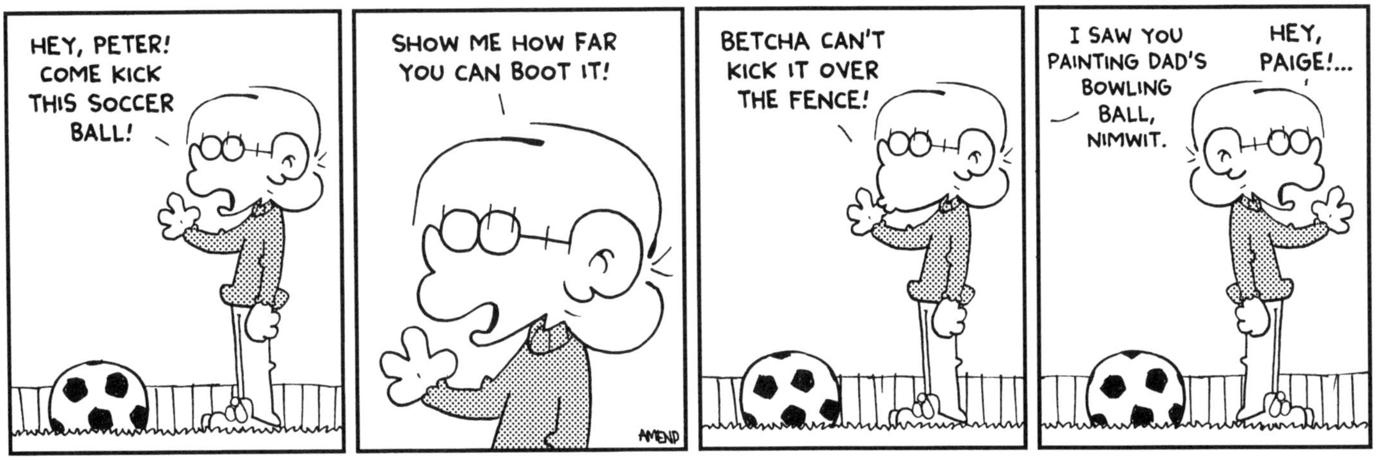
HEY, PETER! COME KICK THIS SOCCER BALL!
SHOW ME HOW FAR YOU CAN BOOT IT!
AMEND
BETCHA CAN'T KICK IT OVER THE FENCE!
I SAW YOU PAINTING DAD'S BOWLING BALL, NIMWIT.
HEY, PAIGE!...

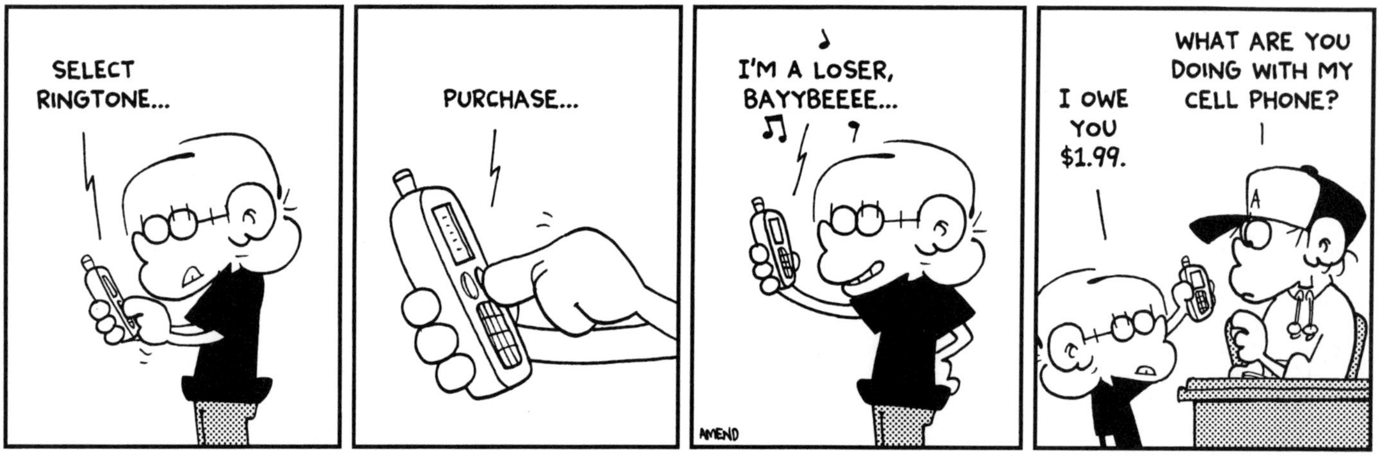
SELECT RINGTONE...
PURCHASE...
I'M A LOSER, BAYYBEEEE...
AMEND
I OWE YOU $1.99.
WHAT ARE YOU DOING WITH MY CELL PHONE?

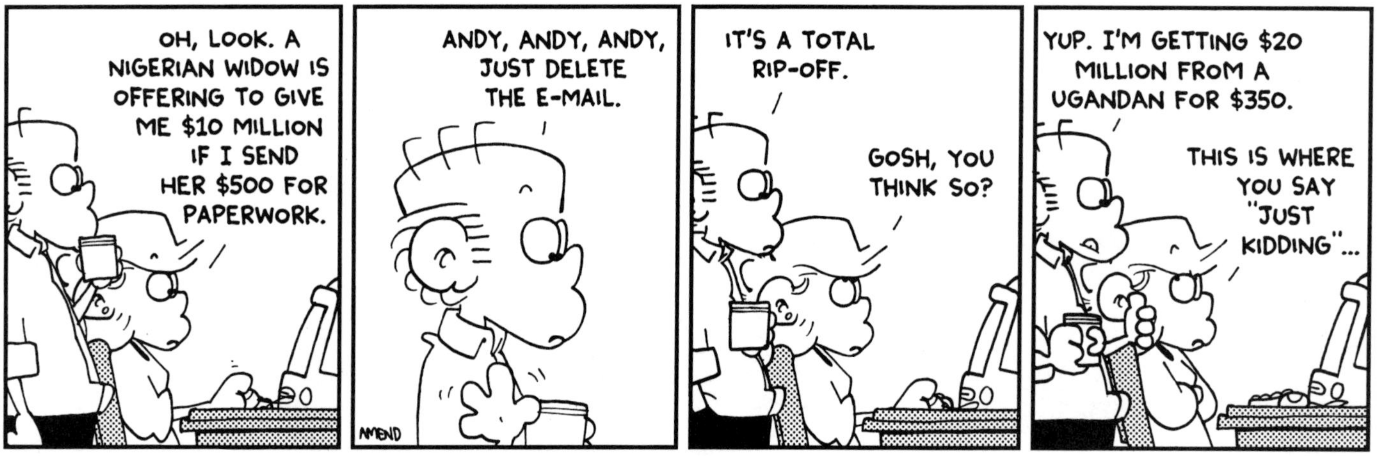
OH, LOOK. A NIGERIAN WIDOW IS OFFERING TO GIVE ME $10 MILLION IF I SEND HER $500 FOR PAPERWORK.
ANDY, ANDY, ANDY, JUST DELETE THE E-MAIL.
AMEND
IT'S A TOTAL RIP-OFF.
GOSH, YOU THINK SO?
YUP. I'M GETTING $20 MILLION FROM A UGANDAN FOR $350.
THIS IS WHERE YOU SAY "JUST KIDDING"...

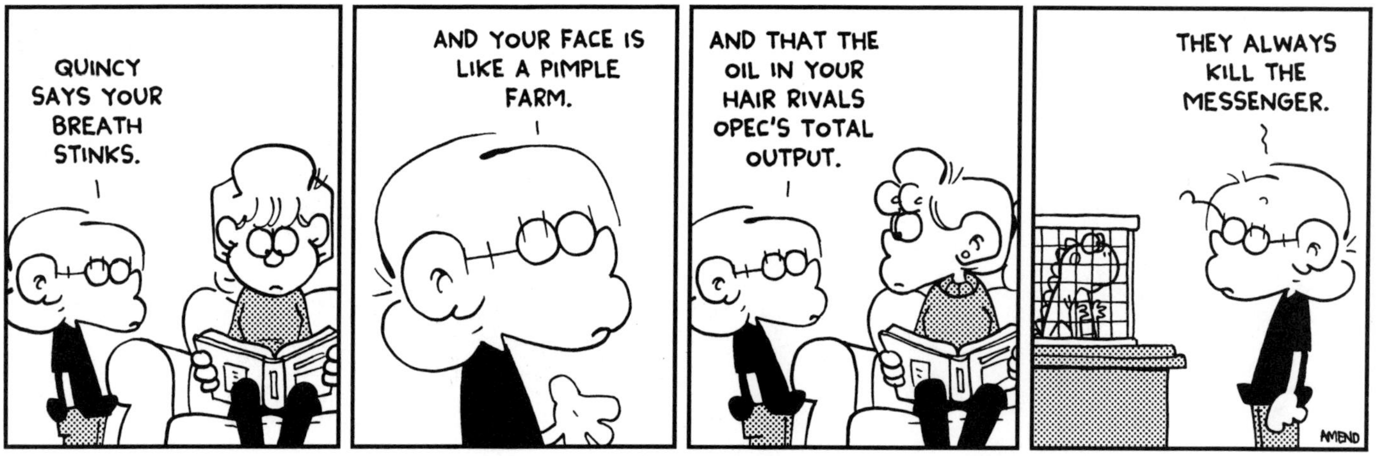
QUINCY SAYS YOUR BREATH STINKS.
AND YOUR FACE IS LIKE A PIMPLE FARM.
AND THAT THE OIL IN YOUR HAIR RIVALS OPEC'S TOTAL OUTPUT.
THEY ALWAYS KILL THE MESSENGER.
AMEND

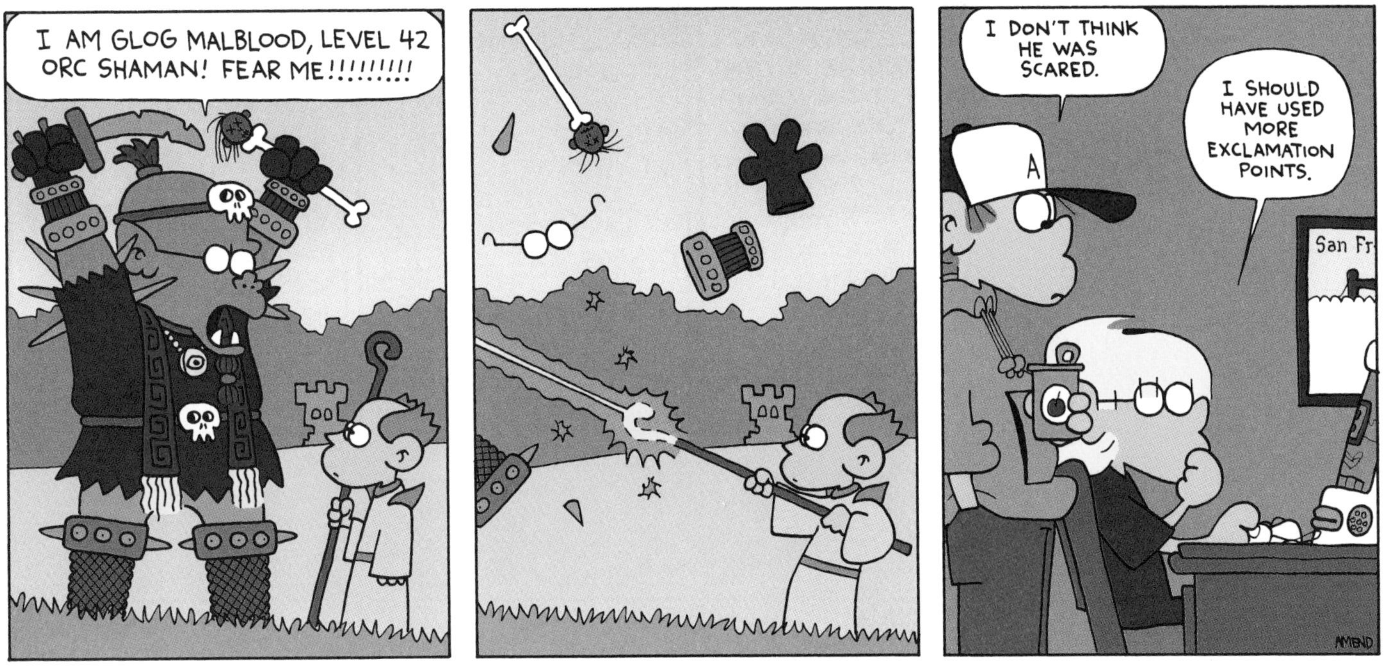
I AM GLOG MALBLOOD, LEVEL 42 ORC SHAMAN! FEAR ME!!!!!!!!!
I DON'T THINK HE WAS SCARED.
I SHOULD HAVE USED MORE EXCLAMATION POINTS.
AMEND

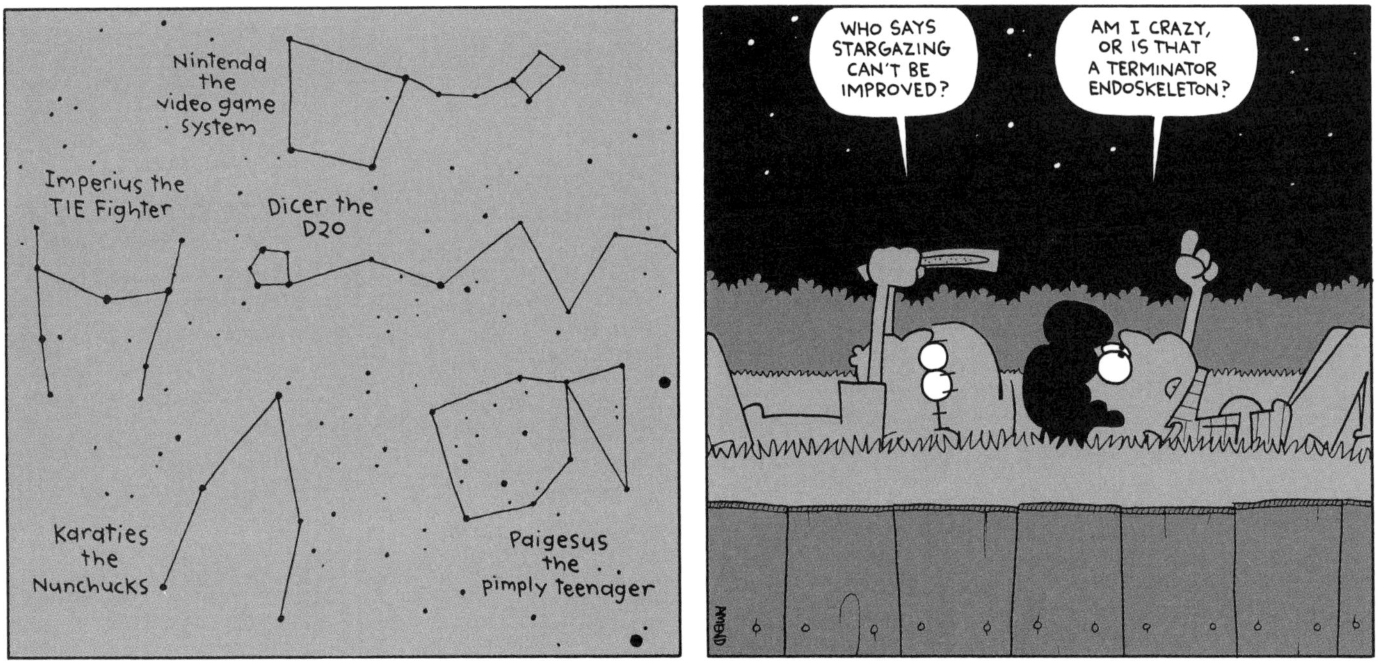
Nintendo the video game system
Imperius the TIE Fighter
Dicer the D20
Karaties the Nunchucks
Paigesus the pimply teenager
WHO SAYS STARGAZING CAN'T BE IMPROVED?
AM I CRAZY, OR IS THAT A TERMINATOR ENDOSKELETON?
AMEND

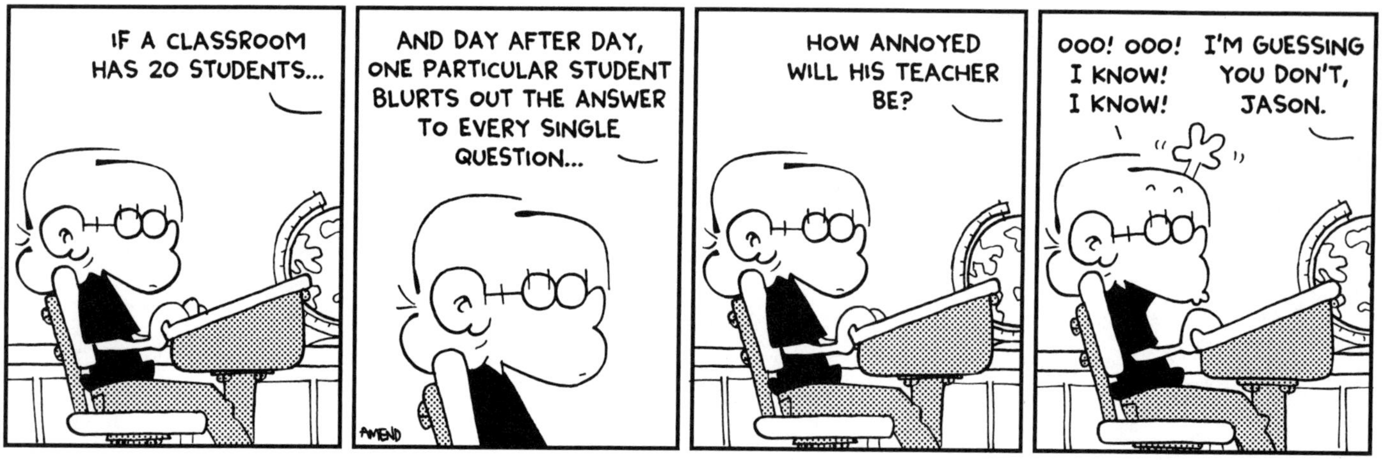
IF A CLASSROOM HAS 20 STUDENTS...
AND DAY AFTER DAY, ONE PARTICULAR STUDENT BLURTS OUT THE ANSWER TO EVERY SINGLE QUESTION...
HOW ANNOYED WILL HIS TEACHER BE?
OOO! OOO! I KNOW! I KNOW!
I'M GUESSING YOU DON'T, JASON.

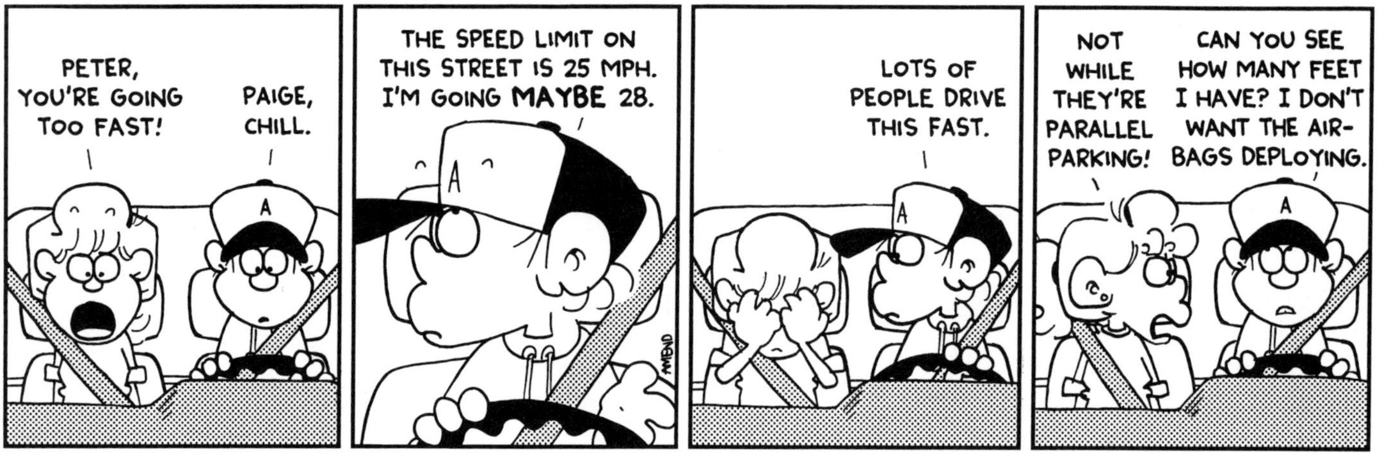
PETER, YOU'RE GOING TOO FAST!
PAIGE, CHILL.
THE SPEED LIMIT ON THIS STREET IS 25 MPH. I'M GOING MAYBE 28.
LOTS OF PEOPLE DRIVE THIS FAST.
NOT WHILE THEY'RE PARALLEL PARKING!
CAN YOU SEE HOW MANY FEET I HAVE? I DON'T WANT THE AIR-BAGS DEPLOYING.

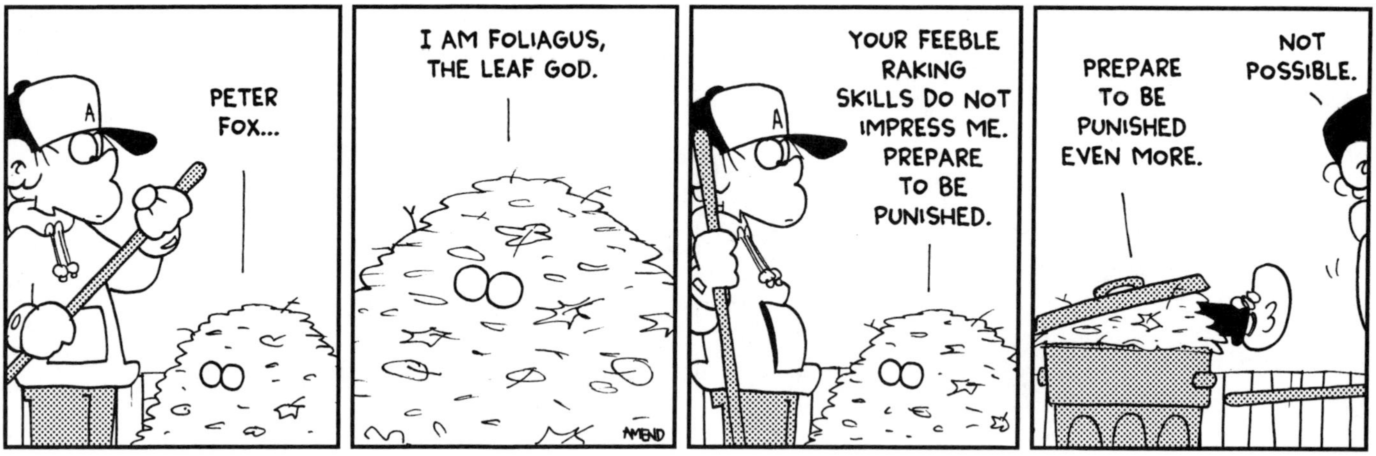
PETER FOX...
I AM FOLIAGUS, THE LEAF GOD.
YOUR FEEBLE RAKING SKILLS DO NOT IMPRESS ME. PREPARE TO BE PUNISHED.
PREPARE TO BE PUNISHED EVEN MORE.
NOT POSSIBLE.

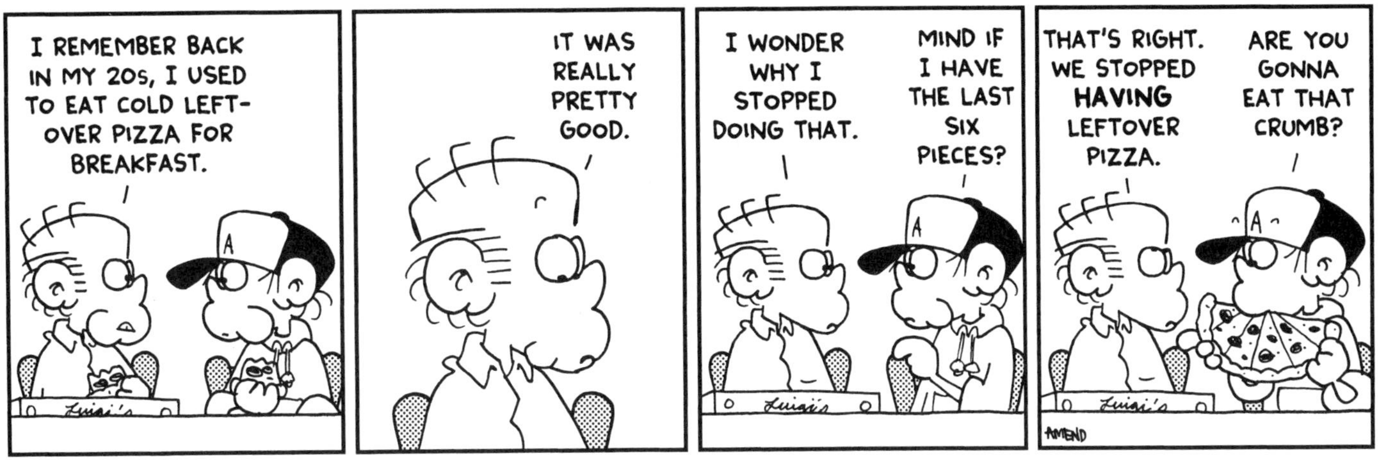
I REMEMBER BACK IN MY 20s, I USED TO EAT COLD LEFT-OVER PIZZA FOR BREAKFAST.
IT WAS REALLY PRETTY GOOD.
I WONDER WHY I STOPPED DOING THAT.
MIND IF I HAVE THE LAST SIX PIECES?
THAT'S RIGHT. WE STOPPED **HAVING** LEFTOVER PIZZA.
ARE YOU GONNA EAT THAT CRUMB?
AMEND

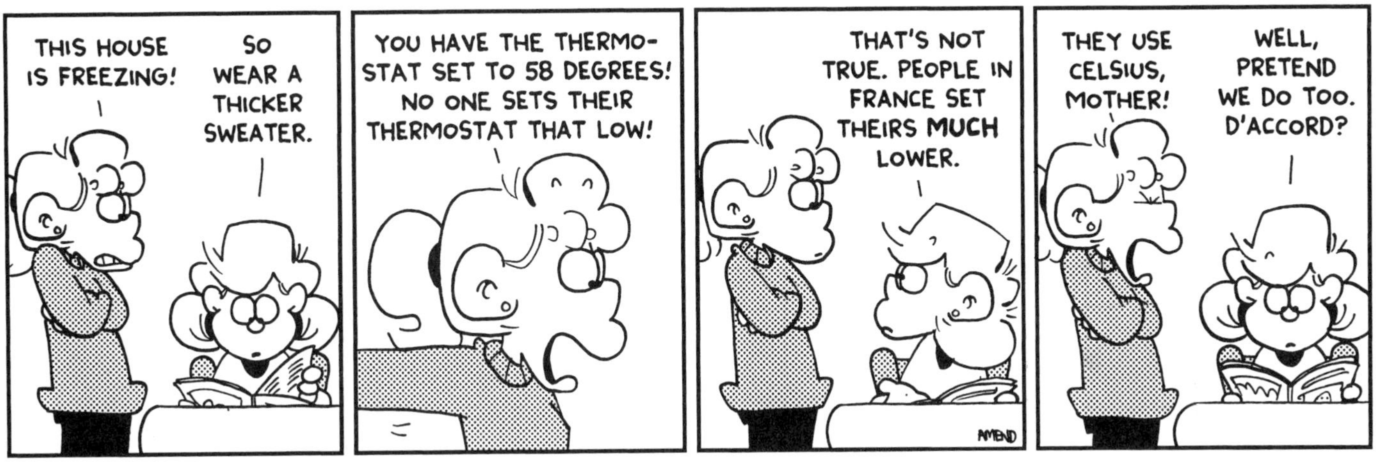
THIS HOUSE IS FREEZING!
SO WEAR A THICKER SWEATER.
YOU HAVE THE THERMO-STAT SET TO 58 DEGREES! NO ONE SETS THEIR THERMOSTAT THAT LOW!
THAT'S NOT TRUE. PEOPLE IN FRANCE SET THEIRS **MUCH** LOWER.
AMEND
THEY USE CELSIUS, MOTHER!
WELL, PRETEND WE DO TOO. D'ACCORD?

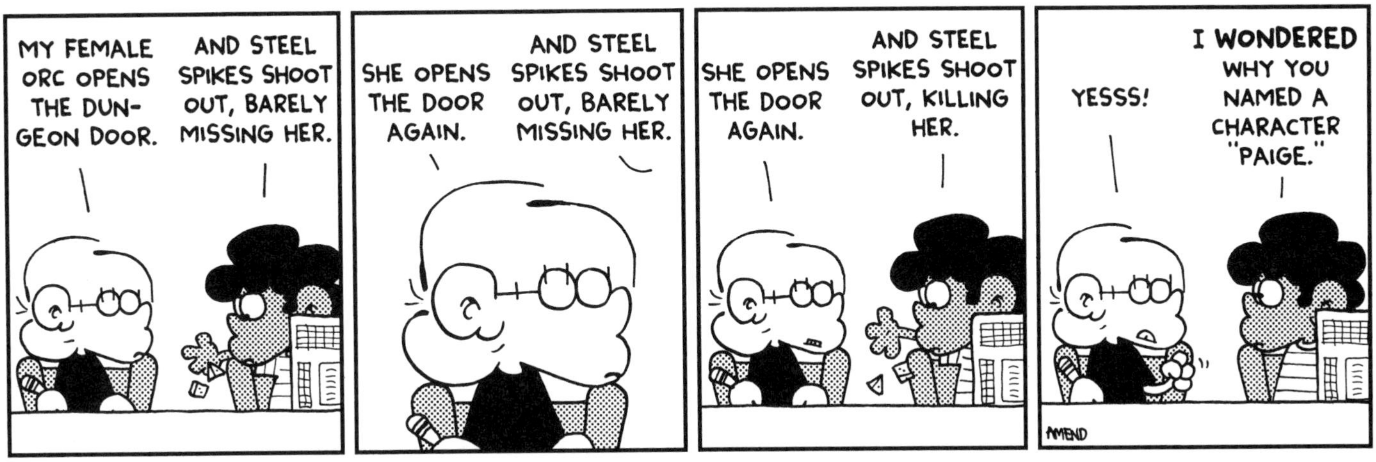
MY FEMALE ORC OPENS THE DUN-GEON DOOR.
AND STEEL SPIKES SHOOT OUT, BARELY MISSING HER.
SHE OPENS THE DOOR AGAIN.
AND STEEL SPIKES SHOOT OUT, BARELY MISSING HER.
SHE OPENS THE DOOR AGAIN.
AND STEEL SPIKES SHOOT OUT, KILLING HER.
YESSS!
I **WONDERED** WHY YOU NAMED A CHARACTER "PAIGE."
AMEND

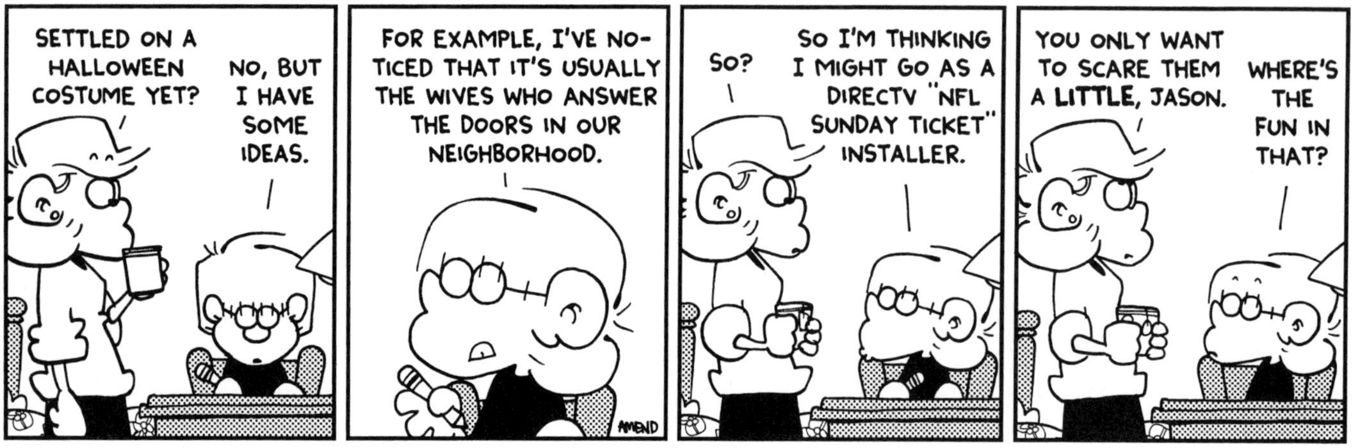
SETTLED ON A HALLOWEEN COSTUME YET?
NO, BUT I HAVE SOME IDEAS.
FOR EXAMPLE, I'VE NOTICED THAT IT'S USUALLY THE WIVES WHO ANSWER THE DOORS IN OUR NEIGHBORHOOD.
AMEND
SO?
SO I'M THINKING I MIGHT GO AS A DIRECTV "NFL SUNDAY TICKET" INSTALLER.
YOU ONLY WANT TO SCARE THEM A **LITTLE**, JASON.
WHERE'S THE FUN IN THAT?

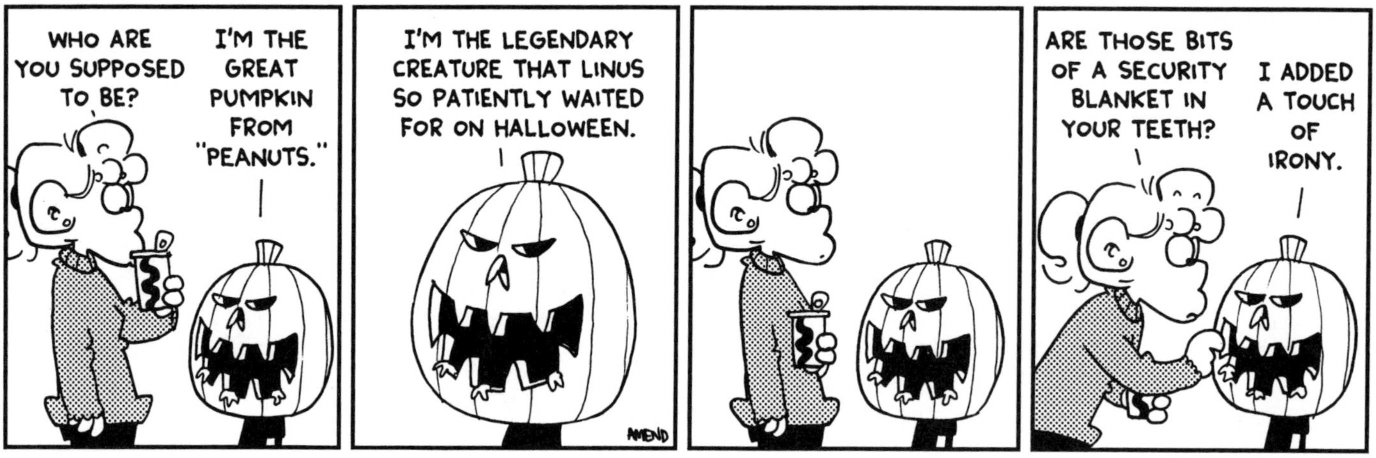
WHO ARE YOU SUPPOSED TO BE?
I'M THE GREAT PUMPKIN FROM "PEANUTS."
I'M THE LEGENDARY CREATURE THAT LINUS SO PATIENTLY WAITED FOR ON HALLOWEEN.
AMEND
ARE THOSE BITS OF A SECURITY BLANKET IN YOUR TEETH?
I ADDED A TOUCH OF IRONY.

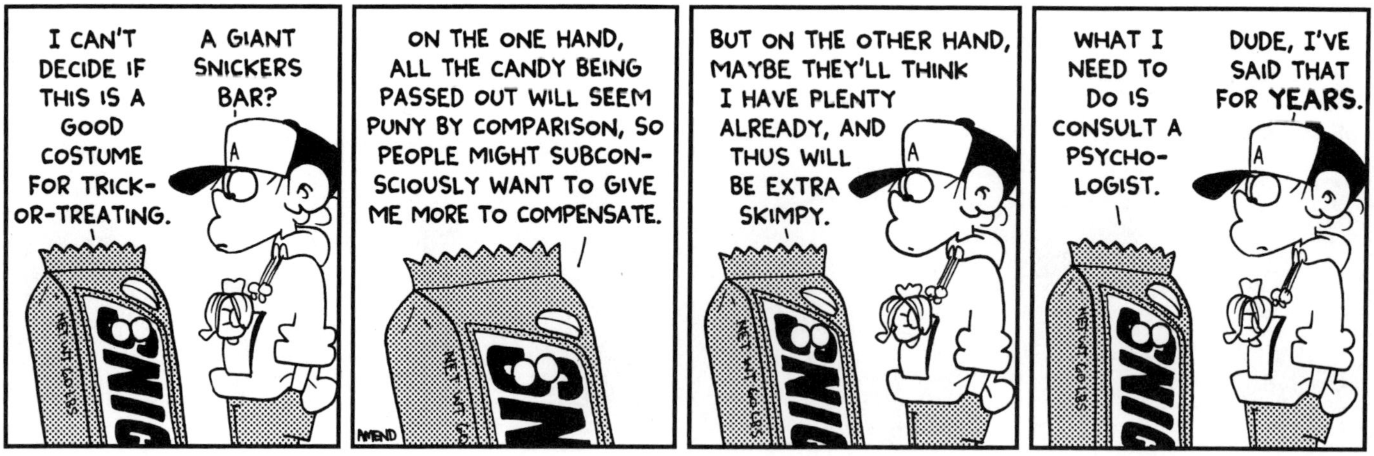
I CAN'T DECIDE IF THIS IS A GOOD COSTUME FOR TRICK-OR-TREATING.
A GIANT SNICKERS BAR?
ON THE ONE HAND, ALL THE CANDY BEING PASSED OUT WILL SEEM PUNY BY COMPARISON, SO PEOPLE MIGHT SUBCONSCIOUSLY WANT TO GIVE ME MORE TO COMPENSATE.
AMEND
BUT ON THE OTHER HAND, MAYBE THEY'LL THINK I HAVE PLENTY ALREADY, AND THUS WILL BE EXTRA SKIMPY.
WHAT I NEED TO DO IS CONSULT A PSYCHOLOGIST.
DUDE, I'VE SAID THAT FOR **YEARS**.

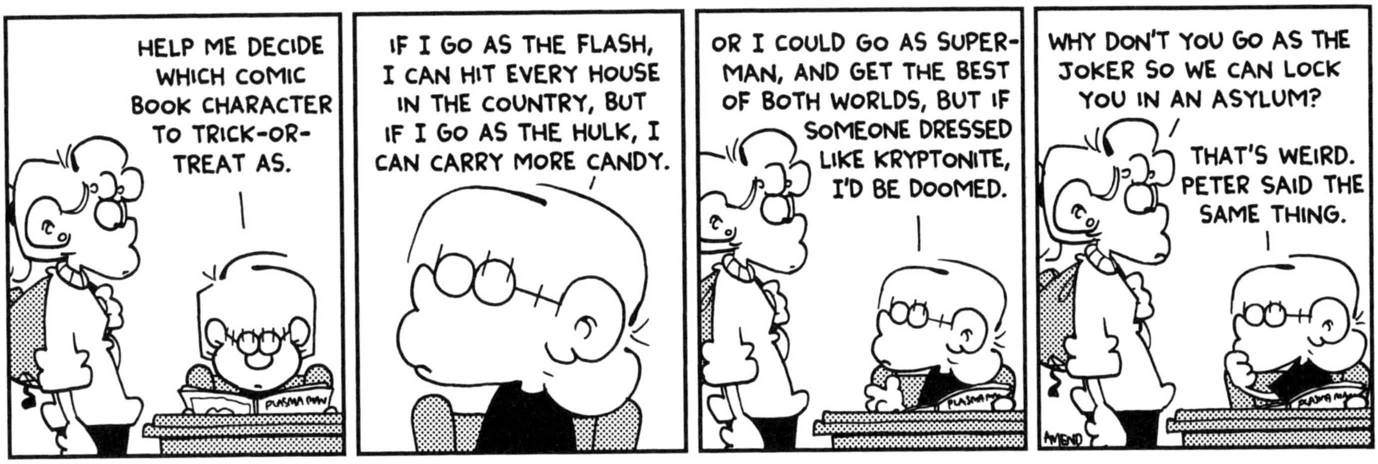
HELP ME DECIDE WHICH COMIC BOOK CHARACTER TO TRICK-OR-TREAT AS.
IF I GO AS THE FLASH, I CAN HIT EVERY HOUSE IN THE COUNTRY, BUT IF I GO AS THE HULK, I CAN CARRY MORE CANDY.
OR I COULD GO AS SUPER-MAN, AND GET THE BEST OF BOTH WORLDS, BUT IF SOMEONE DRESSED LIKE KRYPTONITE, I'D BE DOOMED.
WHY DON'T YOU GO AS THE JOKER SO WE CAN LOCK YOU IN AN ASYLUM?
THAT'S WEIRD. PETER SAID THE SAME THING.
AMEND

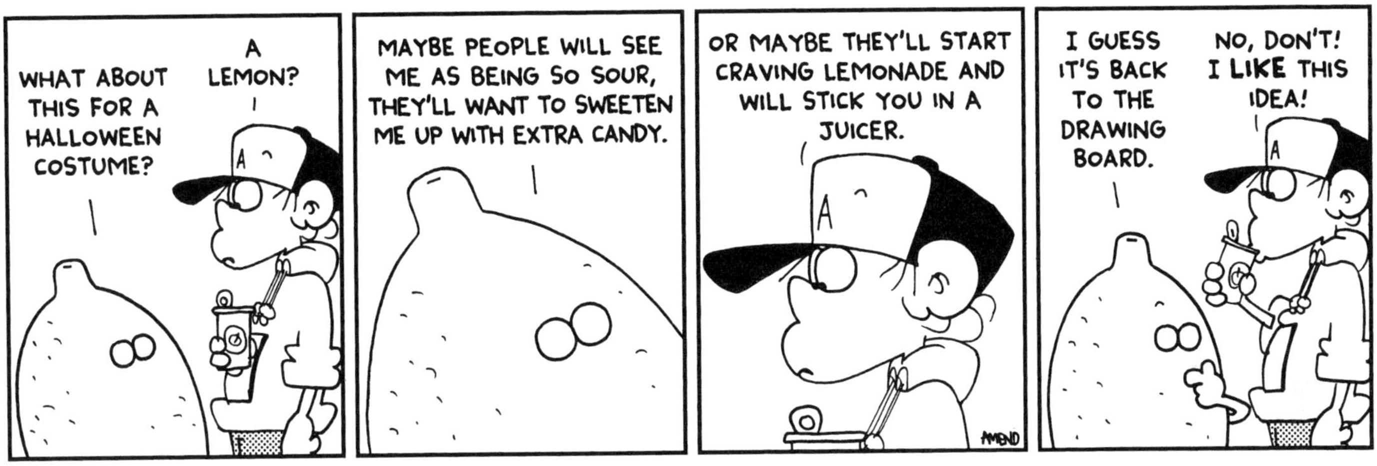
WHAT ABOUT THIS FOR A HALLOWEEN COSTUME?
A LEMON?
MAYBE PEOPLE WILL SEE ME AS BEING SO SOUR, THEY'LL WANT TO SWEETEN ME UP WITH EXTRA CANDY.
OR MAYBE THEY'LL START CRAVING LEMONADE AND WILL STICK YOU IN A JUICER.
AMEND
I GUESS IT'S BACK TO THE DRAWING BOARD.
NO, DON'T! I **LIKE** THIS IDEA!

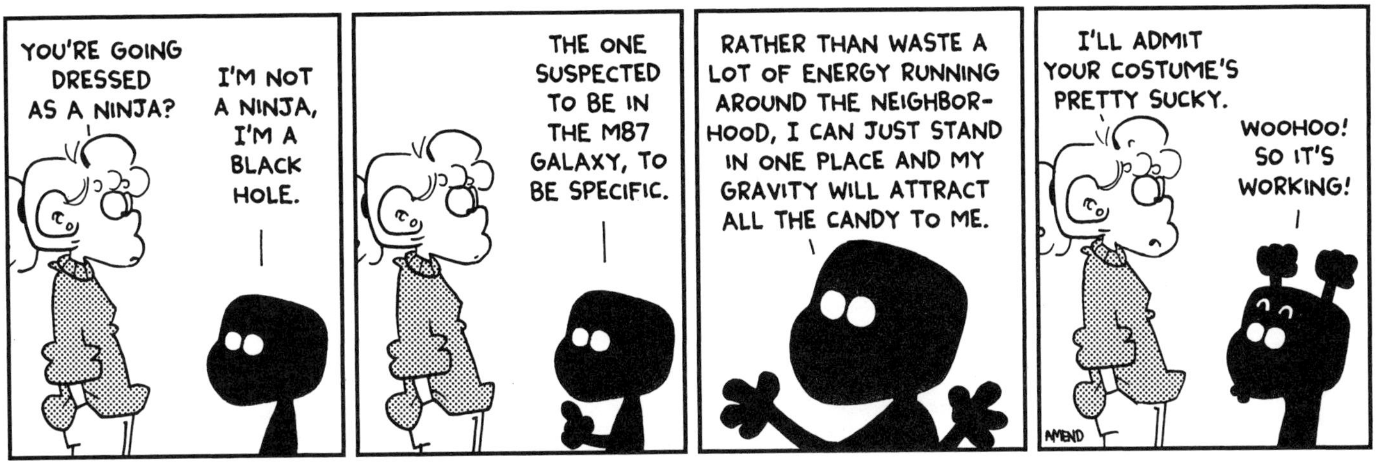
YOU'RE GOING DRESSED AS A NINJA?
I'M NOT A NINJA, I'M A BLACK HOLE.
THE ONE SUSPECTED TO BE IN THE M87 GALAXY, TO BE SPECIFIC.
RATHER THAN WASTE A LOT OF ENERGY RUNNING AROUND THE NEIGHBOR-HOOD, I CAN JUST STAND IN ONE PLACE AND MY GRAVITY WILL ATTRACT ALL THE CANDY TO ME.
I'LL ADMIT YOUR COSTUME'S PRETTY SUCKY.
WOOHOO! SO IT'S WORKING!
AMEND

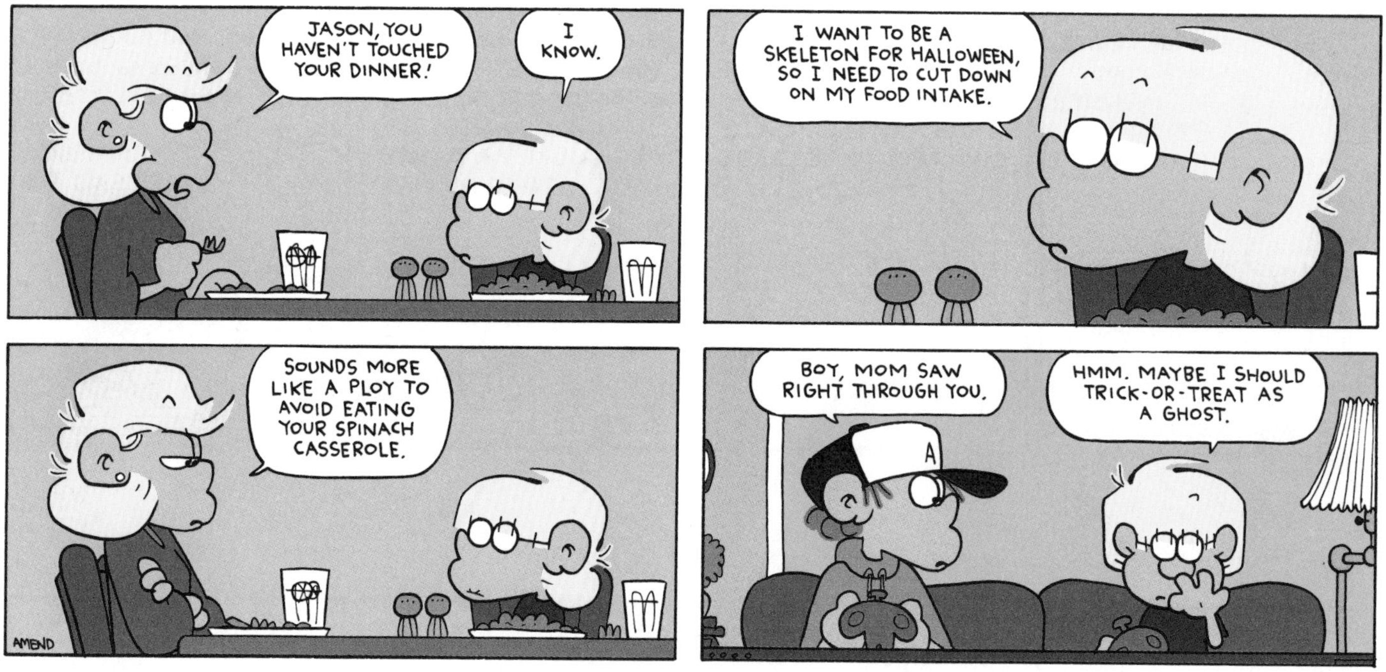
JASON, YOU HAVEN'T TOUCHED YOUR DINNER!
I KNOW.
I WANT TO BE A SKELETON FOR HALLOWEEN, SO I NEED TO CUT DOWN ON MY FOOD INTAKE.
SOUNDS MORE LIKE A PLOY TO AVOID EATING YOUR SPINACH CASSEROLE.
AMEND
BOY, MOM SAW RIGHT THROUGH YOU.
HMM. MAYBE I SHOULD TRICK-OR-TREAT AS A GHOST.

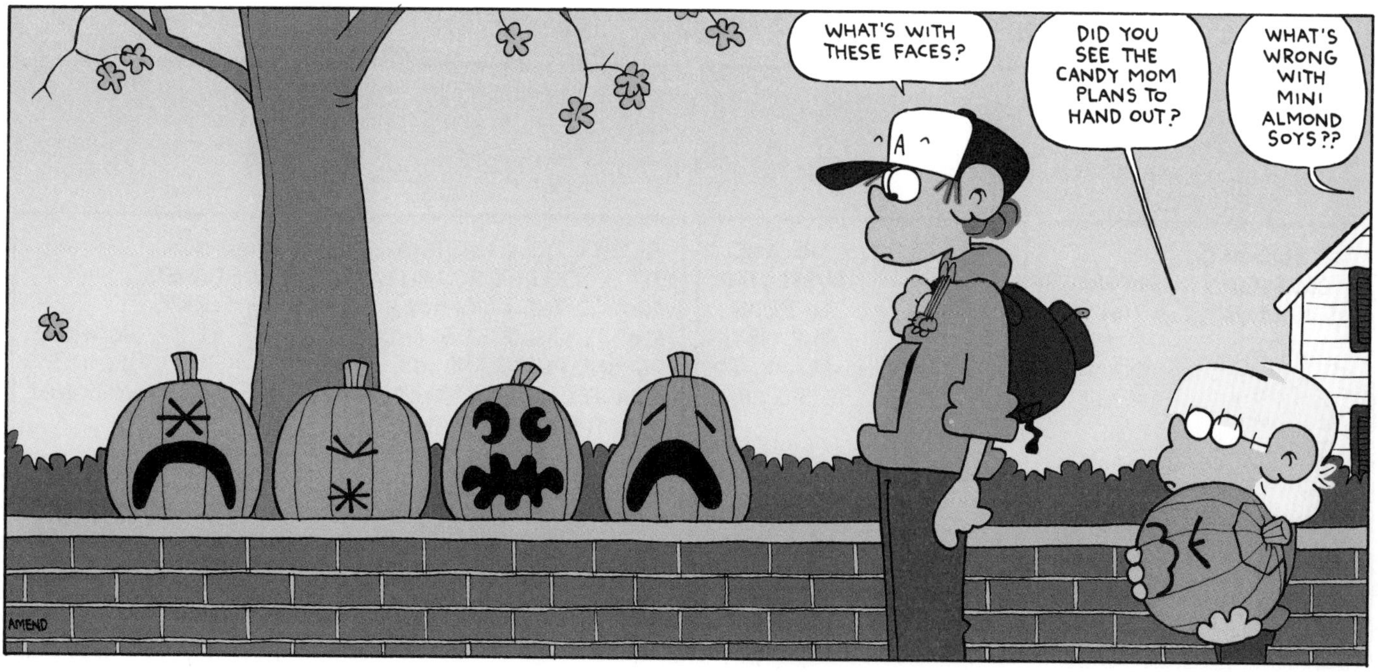
WHAT'S WITH THESE FACES?
DID YOU SEE THE CANDY MOM PLANS TO HAND OUT?
WHAT'S WRONG WITH MINI ALMOND SOYS??
AMEND

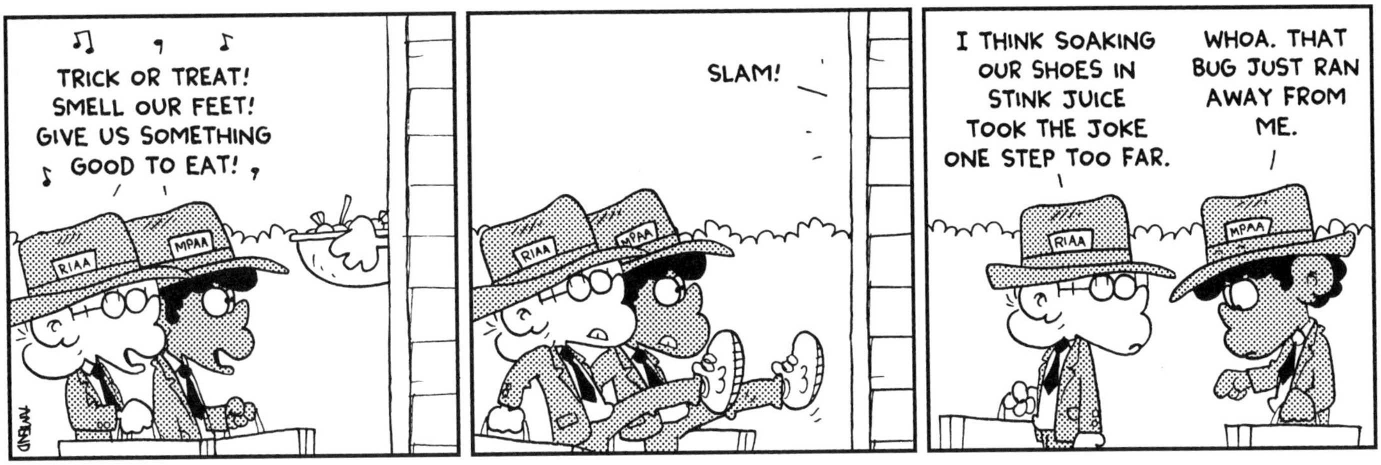
TRICK OR TREAT! SMELL OUR FEET! GIVE US SOMETHING GOOD TO EAT!
RIAA
MPAA
SLAM!
I THINK SOAKING OUR SHOES IN STINK JUICE TOOK THE JOKE ONE STEP TOO FAR.
WHOA. THAT BUG JUST RAN AWAY FROM ME.

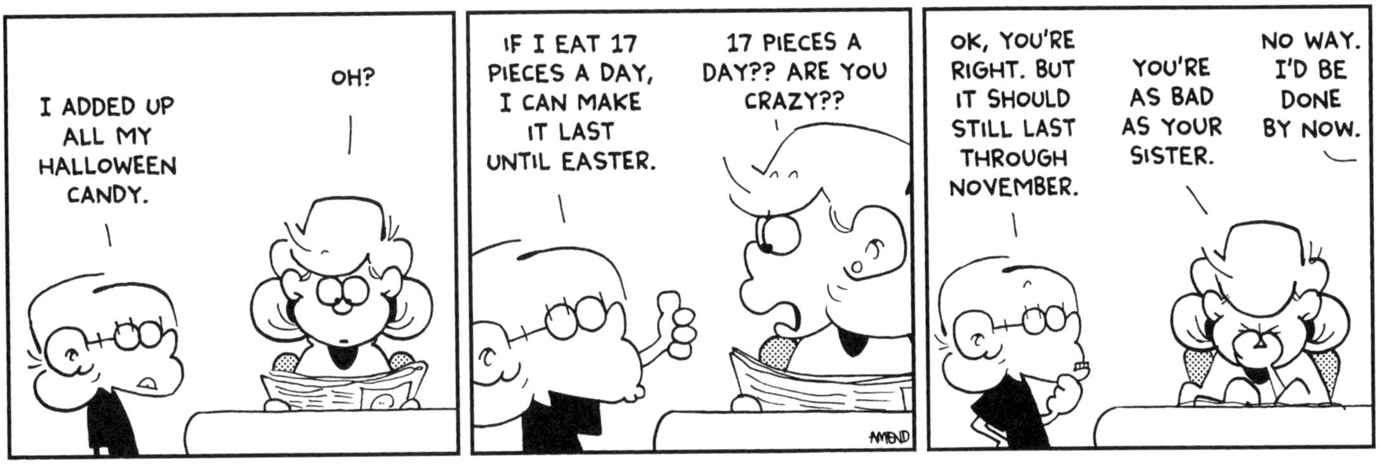
I ADDED UP ALL MY HALLOWEEN CANDY.
OH?
IF I EAT 17 PIECES A DAY, I CAN MAKE IT LAST UNTIL EASTER.
17 PIECES A DAY?? ARE YOU CRAZY??
AMEND
OK, YOU'RE RIGHT. BUT IT SHOULD STILL LAST THROUGH NOVEMBER.
YOU'RE AS BAD AS YOUR SISTER.
NO WAY. I'D BE DONE BY NOW.

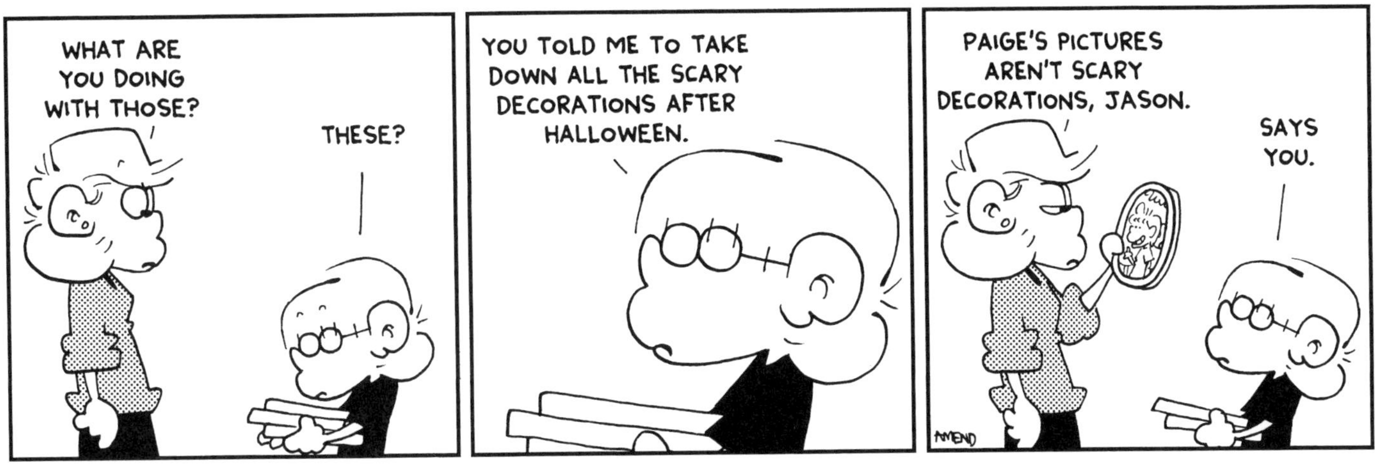
WHAT ARE YOU DOING WITH THOSE?
THESE?
YOU TOLD ME TO TAKE DOWN ALL THE SCARY DECORATIONS AFTER HALLOWEEN.
PAIGE'S PICTURES AREN'T SCARY DECORATIONS, JASON.
SAYS YOU.
AMEND

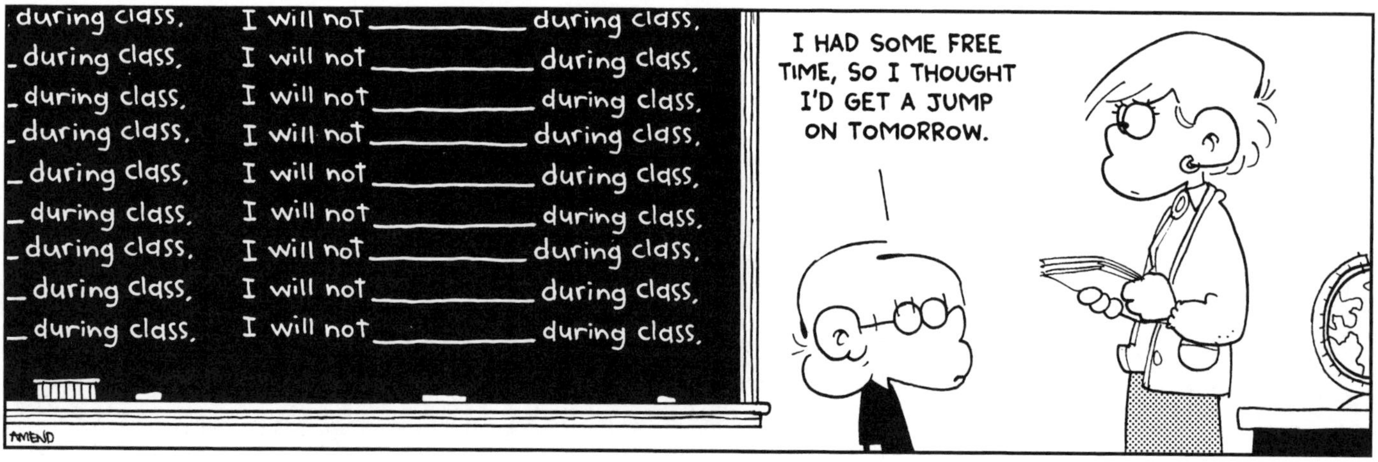
during class. I will not ______ during class.
during class. I will not ______ during class.
during class. I will not ______ during class.
during class. I will not ______ during class.
during class. I will not ______ during class.
during class. I will not ______ during class.
during class. I will not ______ during class.
during class. I will not ______ during class.
during class. I will not ______ during class.
I HAD SOME FREE TIME, SO I THOUGHT I'D GET A JUMP ON TOMORROW.
AMEND

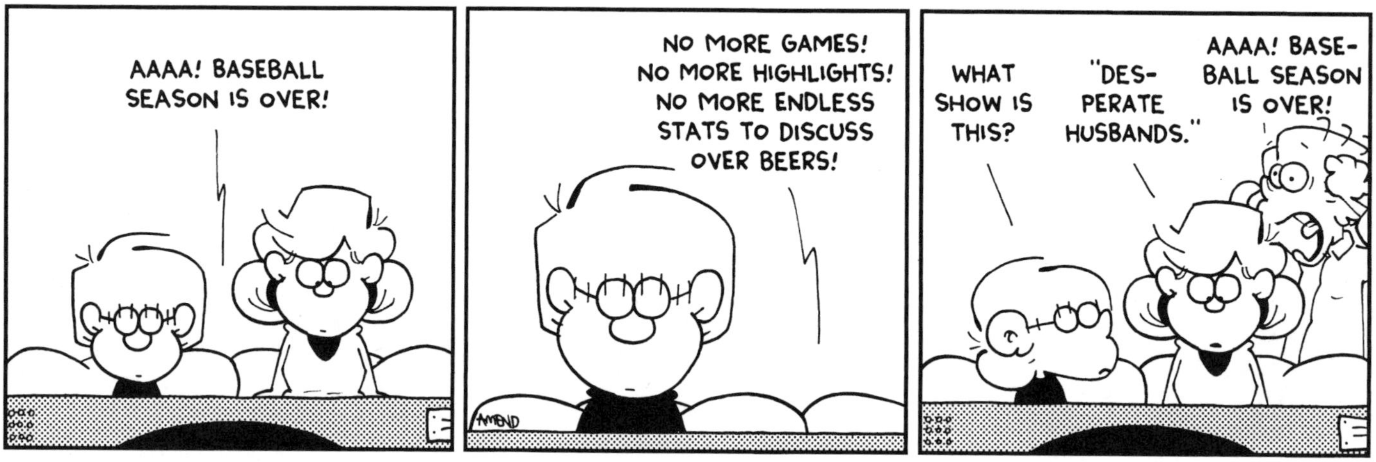
AAAA! BASEBALL SEASON IS OVER!
NO MORE GAMES! NO MORE HIGHLIGHTS! NO MORE ENDLESS STATS TO DISCUSS OVER BEERS!
WHAT SHOW IS THIS?
"DESPERATE HUSBANDS."
AAAA! BASEBALL SEASON IS OVER!
AMEND

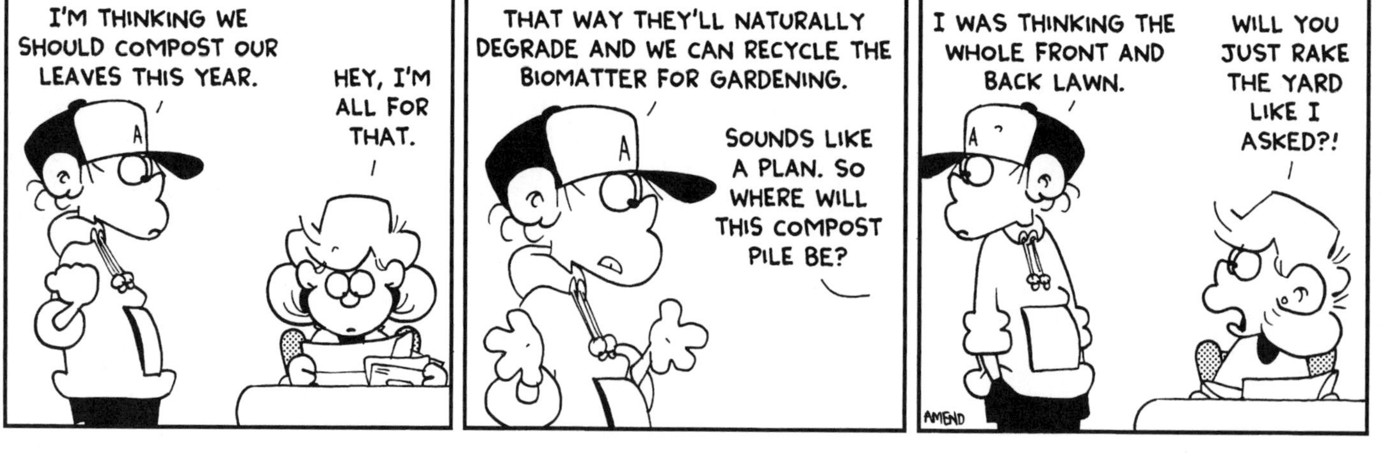
I'M THINKING WE SHOULD COMPOST OUR LEAVES THIS YEAR.
HEY, I'M ALL FOR THAT.
THAT WAY THEY'LL NATURALLY DEGRADE AND WE CAN RECYCLE THE BIOMATTER FOR GARDENING.
SOUNDS LIKE A PLAN. SO WHERE WILL THIS COMPOST PILE BE?
I WAS THINKING THE WHOLE FRONT AND BACK LAWN.
WILL YOU JUST RAKE THE YARD LIKE I ASKED?!
AMEND

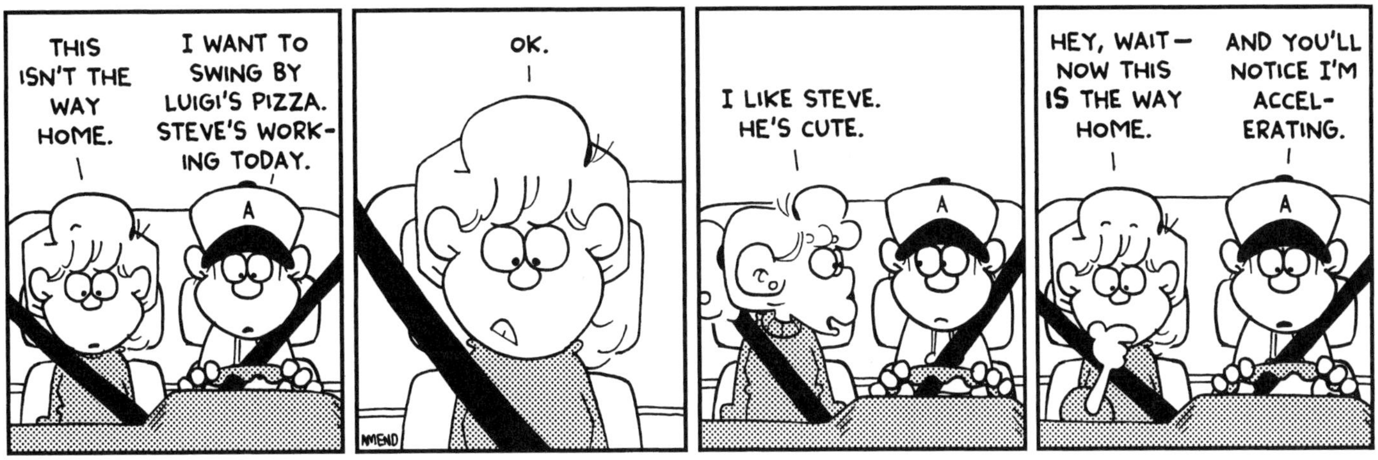
THIS ISN'T THE WAY HOME.
I WANT TO SWING BY LUIGI'S PIZZA. STEVE'S WORKING TODAY.
OK.
I LIKE STEVE. HE'S CUTE.
HEY, WAIT— NOW THIS IS THE WAY HOME.
AND YOU'LL NOTICE I'M ACCELERATING.
AMEND

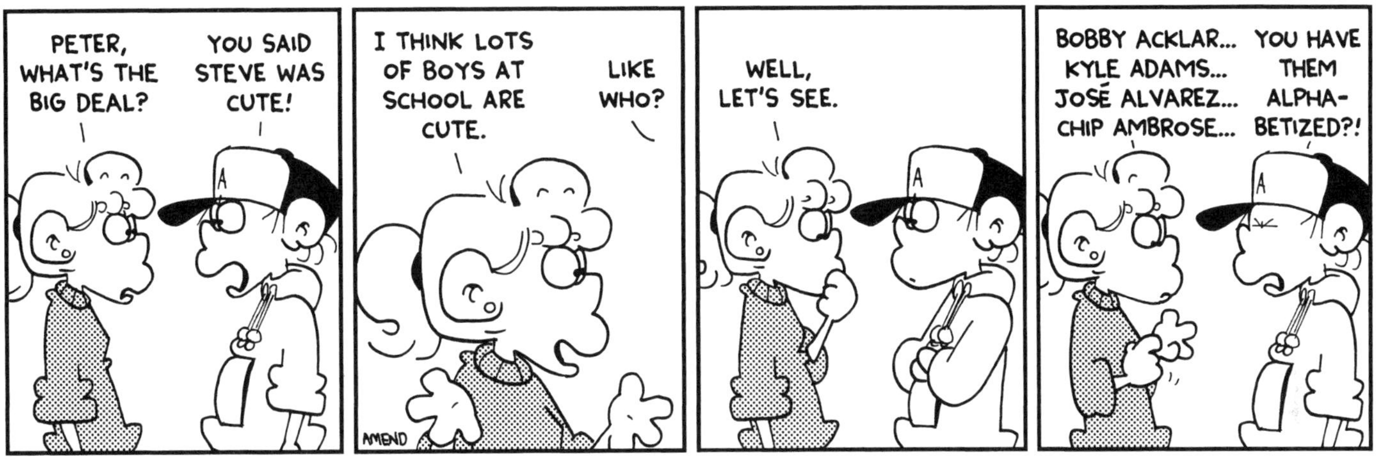
PETER, WHAT'S THE BIG DEAL?
YOU SAID STEVE WAS CUTE!
I THINK LOTS OF BOYS AT SCHOOL ARE CUTE.
LIKE WHO?
WELL, LET'S SEE.
BOBBY ACKLAR... KYLE ADAMS... JOSÉ ALVAREZ... CHIP AMBROSE...
YOU HAVE THEM ALPHABETIZED?!
AMEND

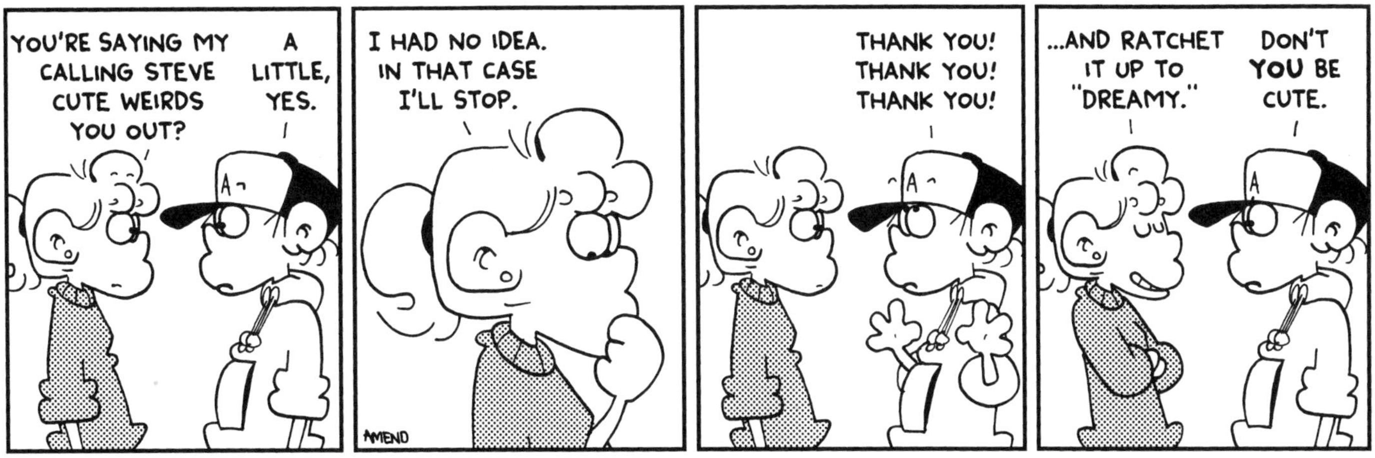
YOU'RE SAYING MY CALLING STEVE CUTE WEIRDS YOU OUT?
A LITTLE, YES.
I HAD NO IDEA. IN THAT CASE I'LL STOP.
THANK YOU! THANK YOU! THANK YOU!
...AND RATCHET IT UP TO "DREAMY."
DON'T YOU BE CUTE.
AMEND

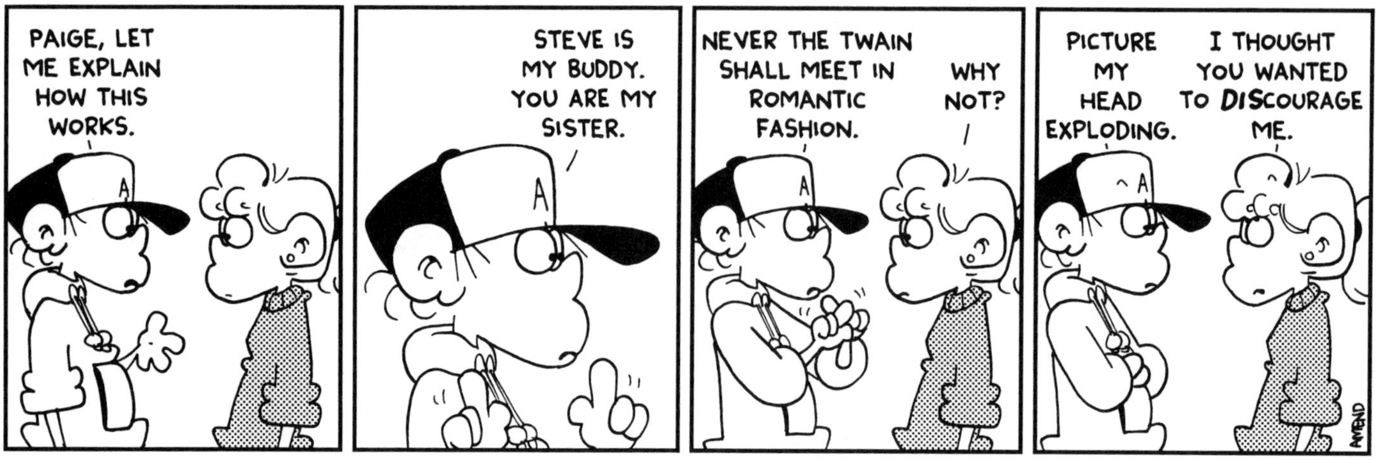
PAIGE, LET ME EXPLAIN HOW THIS WORKS.
STEVE IS MY BUDDY. YOU ARE MY SISTER.
NEVER THE TWAIN SHALL MEET IN ROMANTIC FASHION.
WHY NOT?
PICTURE MY HEAD EXPLODING.
I THOUGHT YOU WANTED TO *DIS*COURAGE ME.
AMEND

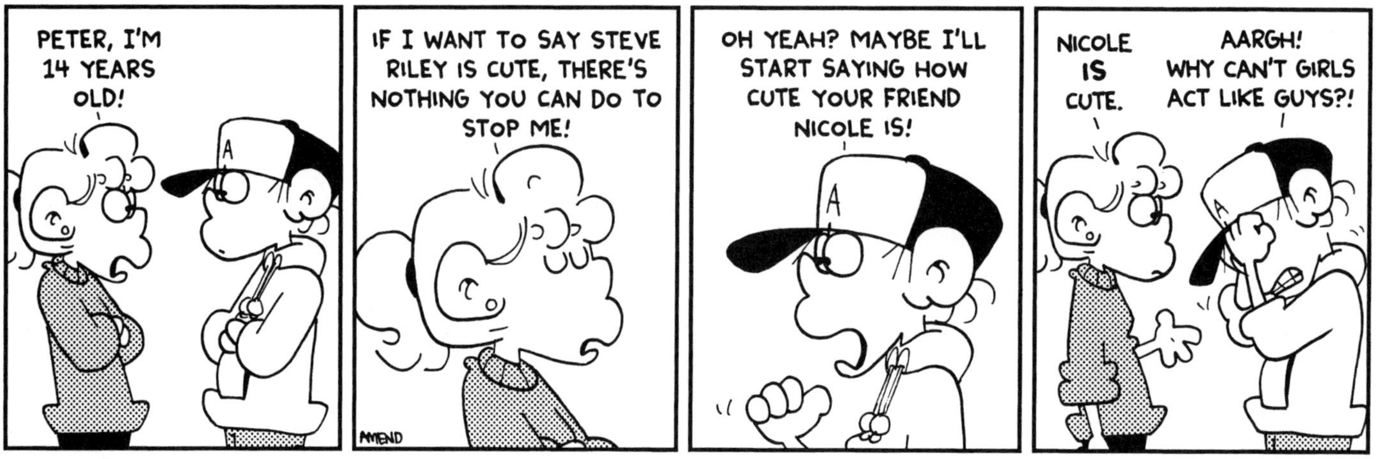
PETER, I'M 14 YEARS OLD!
IF I WANT TO SAY STEVE RILEY IS CUTE, THERE'S NOTHING YOU CAN DO TO STOP ME!
AMEND
OH YEAH? MAYBE I'LL START SAYING HOW CUTE YOUR FRIEND NICOLE IS!
NICOLE **IS** CUTE.
AARGH! WHY CAN'T GIRLS ACT LIKE GUYS?!

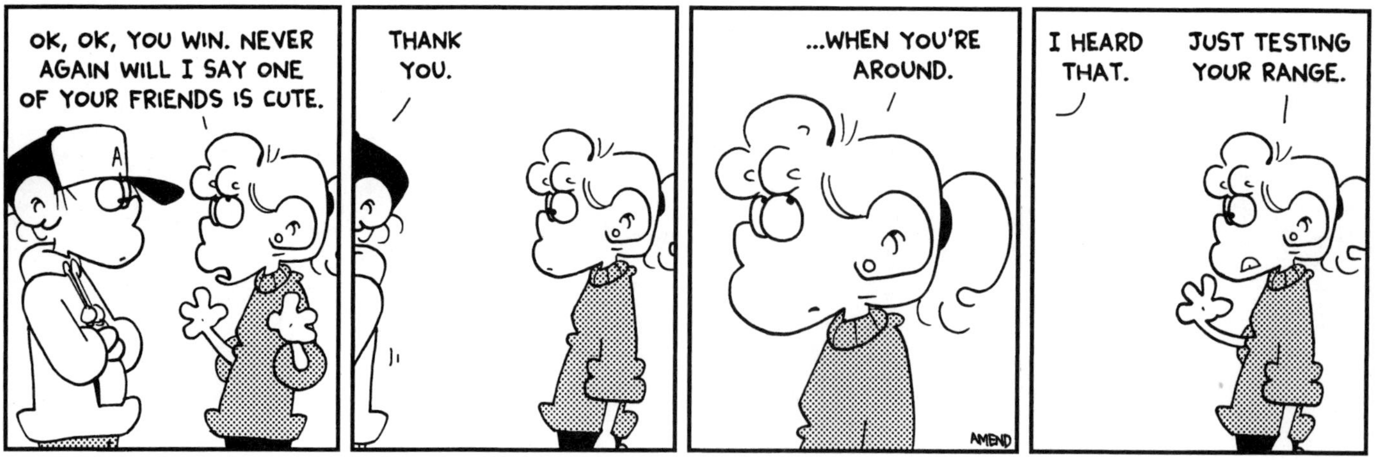
OK, OK, YOU WIN. NEVER AGAIN WILL I SAY ONE OF YOUR FRIENDS IS CUTE.
THANK YOU.
...WHEN YOU'RE AROUND.
AMEND
I HEARD THAT.
JUST TESTING YOUR RANGE.

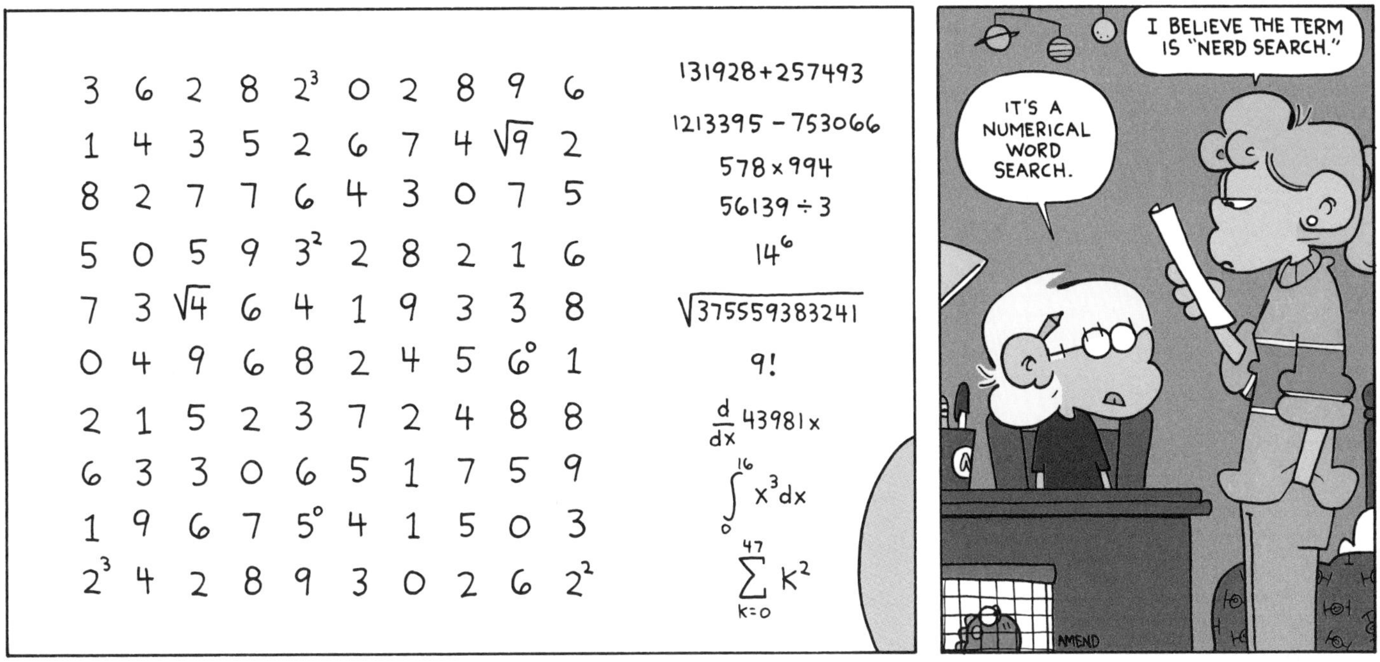

3 6 2 8 2^3 0 2 8 9 6
1 4 3 5 2 6 7 4 $\sqrt{9}$ 2
8 2 7 7 6 4 3 0 7 5
5 0 5 9 3^2 2 8 2 1 6
7 3 $\sqrt{4}$ 6 4 1 9 3 3 8
0 4 9 6 8 2 4 5 6^0 1
2 1 5 2 3 7 2 4 8 8
6 3 3 0 6 5 1 7 5 9
1 9 6 7 5^0 4 1 5 0 3
2^3 4 2 8 9 3 0 2 6 2^2
$131928+257493$
$1213395-753066$
578×994
$56139 \div 3$
14^6
$\sqrt{375559383241}$
$9!$
$\frac{d}{dx} 43981x$
$\int_0^{16} x^3 dx$
$\sum_{k=0}^{47} k^2$
IT'S A NUMERICAL WORD SEARCH.
I BELIEVE THE TERM IS "NERD SEARCH."
AMEND

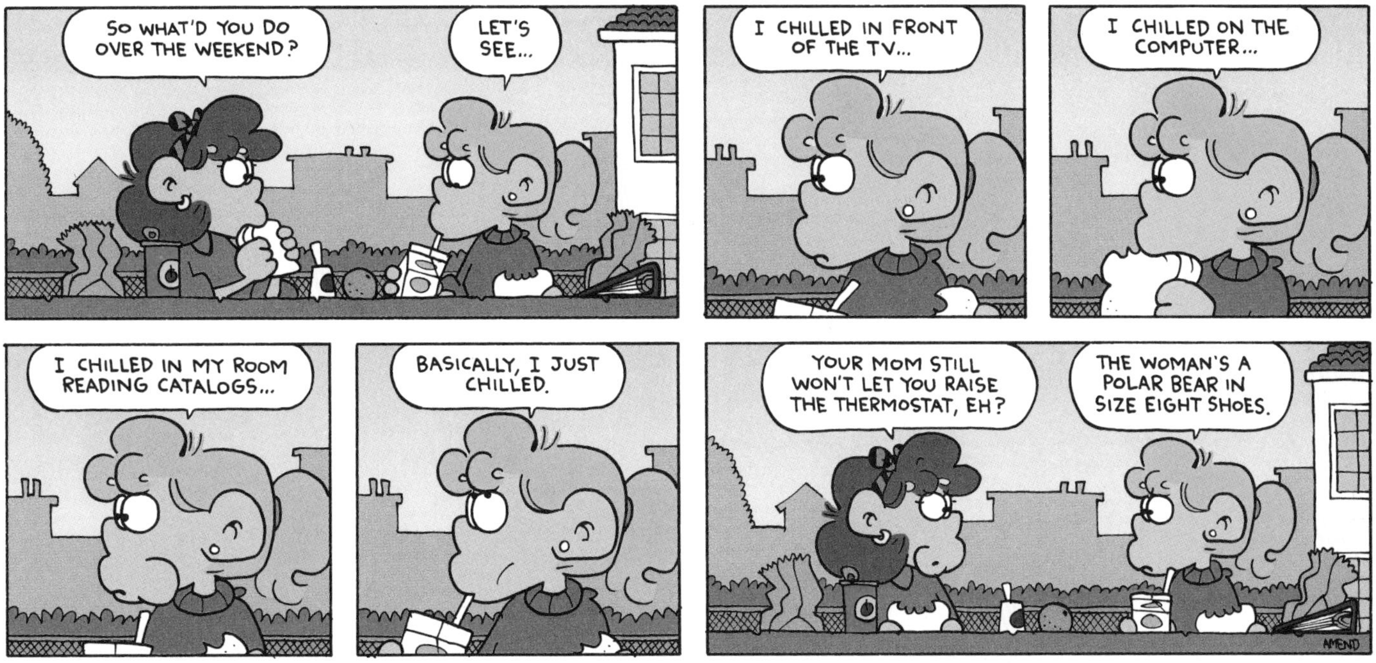

SO WHAT'D YOU DO OVER THE WEEKEND?
LET'S SEE...
I CHILLED IN FRONT OF THE TV...
I CHILLED ON THE COMPUTER...
I CHILLED IN MY ROOM READING CATALOGS...
BASICALLY, I JUST CHILLED.
YOUR MOM STILL WON'T LET YOU RAISE THE THERMOSTAT, EH?
THE WOMAN'S A POLAR BEAR IN SIZE EIGHT SHOES.
AMEND

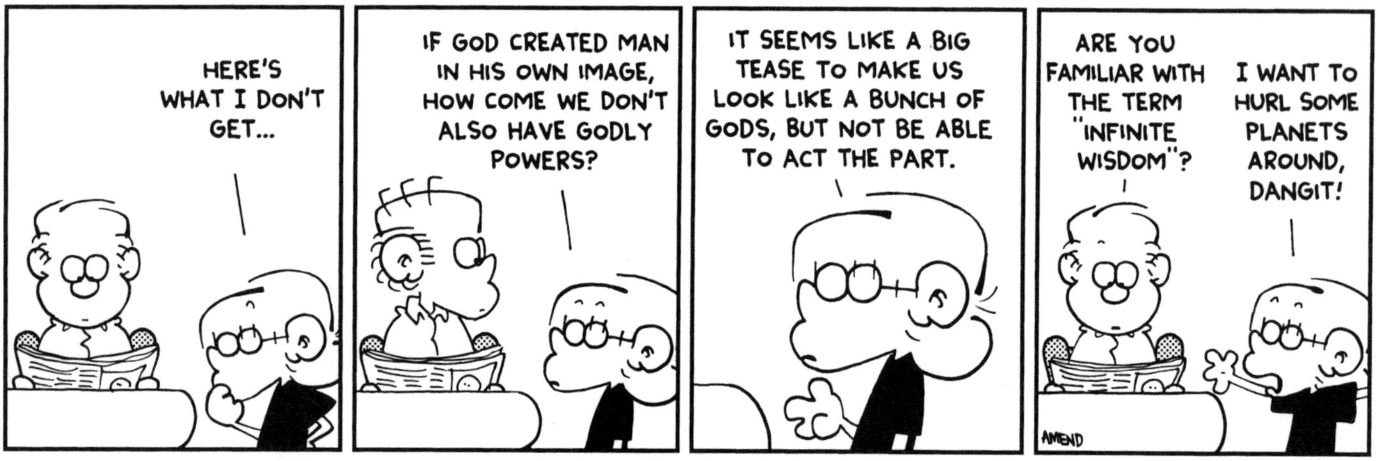
HERE'S WHAT I DON'T GET...
IF GOD CREATED MAN IN HIS OWN IMAGE, HOW COME WE DON'T ALSO HAVE GODLY POWERS?
IT SEEMS LIKE A BIG TEASE TO MAKE US LOOK LIKE A BUNCH OF GODS, BUT NOT BE ABLE TO ACT THE PART.
ARE YOU FAMILIAR WITH THE TERM "INFINITE WISDOM"?
I WANT TO HURL SOME PLANETS AROUND, DANGIT!
AMEND

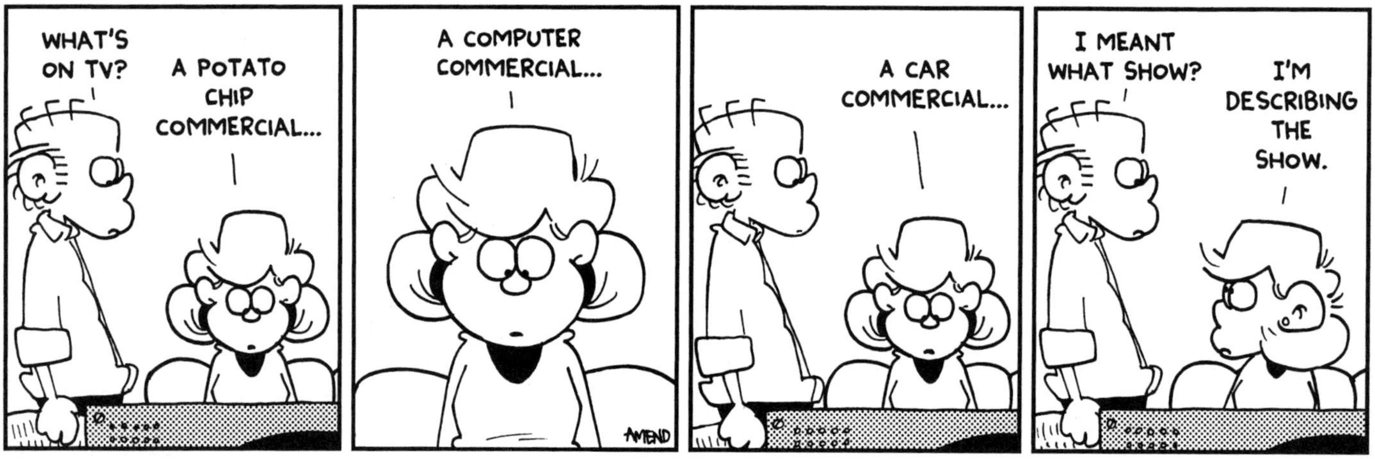
WHAT'S ON TV?
A POTATO CHIP COMMERCIAL...
A COMPUTER COMMERCIAL...
A CAR COMMERCIAL...
I MEANT WHAT SHOW?
I'M DESCRIBING THE SHOW.
AMEND

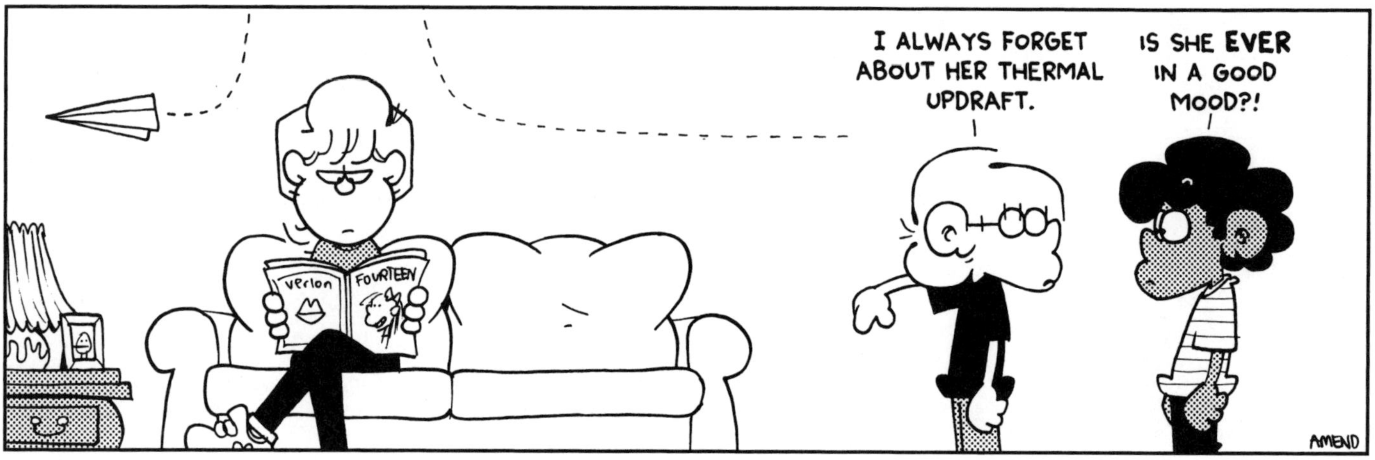
I ALWAYS FORGET ABOUT HER THERMAL UPDRAFT.
IS SHE **EVER** IN A GOOD MOOD?!
AMEND

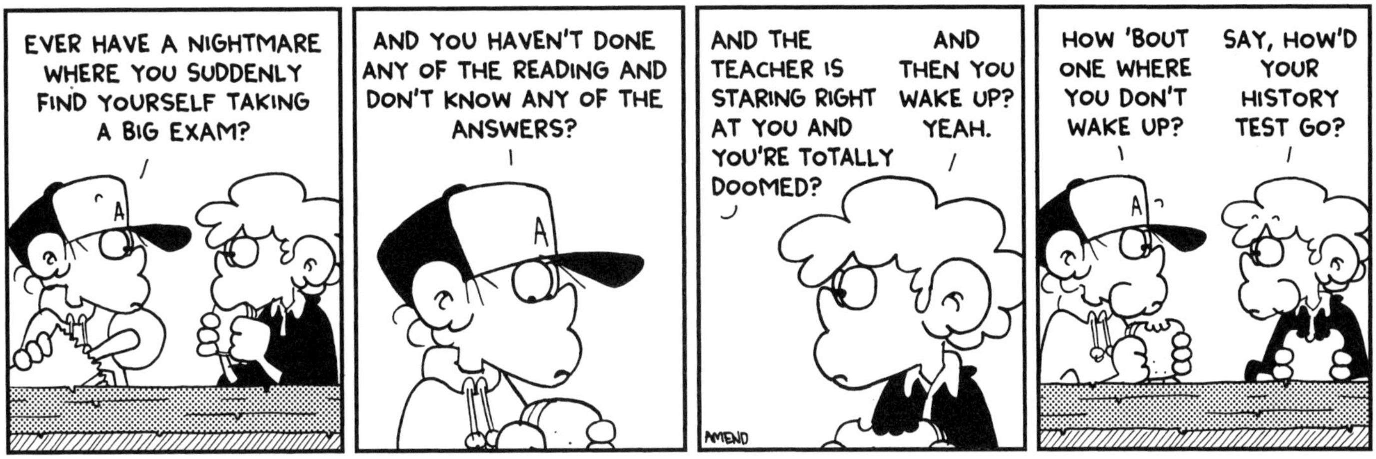
EVER HAVE A NIGHTMARE WHERE YOU SUDDENLY FIND YOURSELF TAKING A BIG EXAM?
AND YOU HAVEN'T DONE ANY OF THE READING AND DON'T KNOW ANY OF THE ANSWERS?
AND THE TEACHER IS STARING RIGHT AT YOU AND YOU'RE TOTALLY DOOMED?
AND THEN YOU WAKE UP? YEAH.
AMEND
HOW 'BOUT ONE WHERE YOU DON'T WAKE UP?
SAY, HOW'D YOUR HISTORY TEST GO?

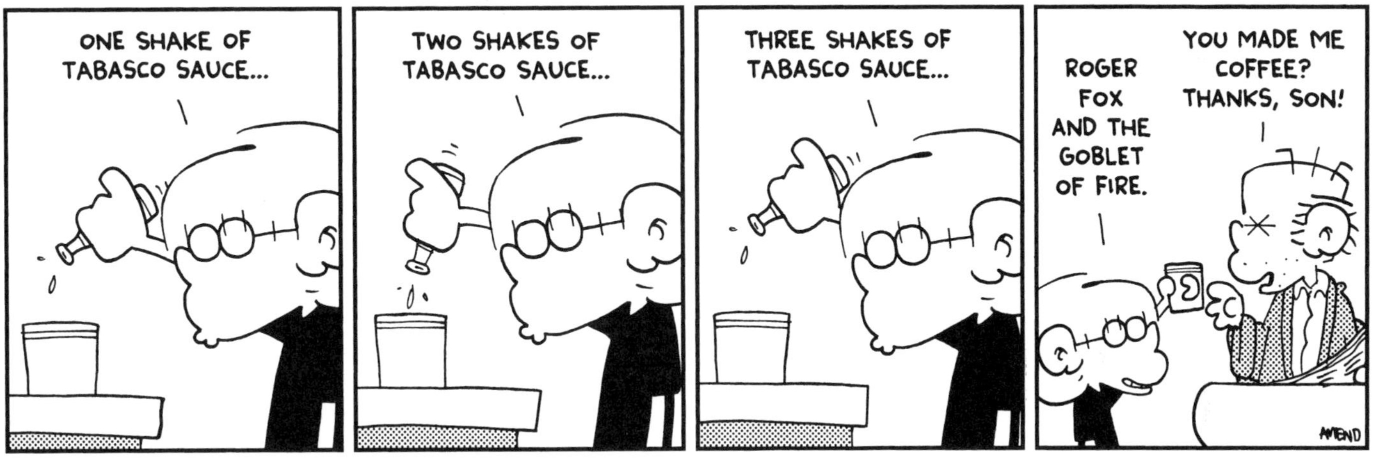
ONE SHAKE OF TABASCO SAUCE...
TWO SHAKES OF TABASCO SAUCE...
THREE SHAKES OF TABASCO SAUCE...
YOU MADE ME COFFEE? THANKS, SON!
ROGER FOX AND THE GOBLET OF FIRE.
AMEND

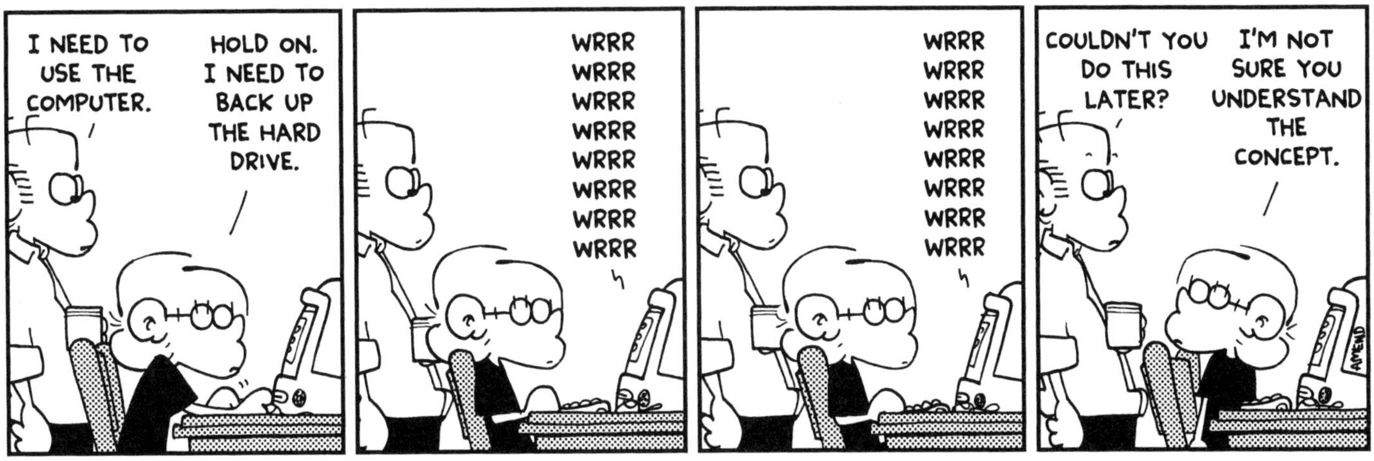
I NEED TO USE THE COMPUTER.
HOLD ON. I NEED TO BACK UP THE HARD DRIVE.
WRRR WRRR WRRR WRRR WRRR WRRR WRRR WRRR
WRRR WRRR WRRR WRRR WRRR WRRR WRRR WRRR
COULDN'T YOU DO THIS LATER?
I'M NOT SURE YOU UNDERSTAND THE CONCEPT.
AMEND

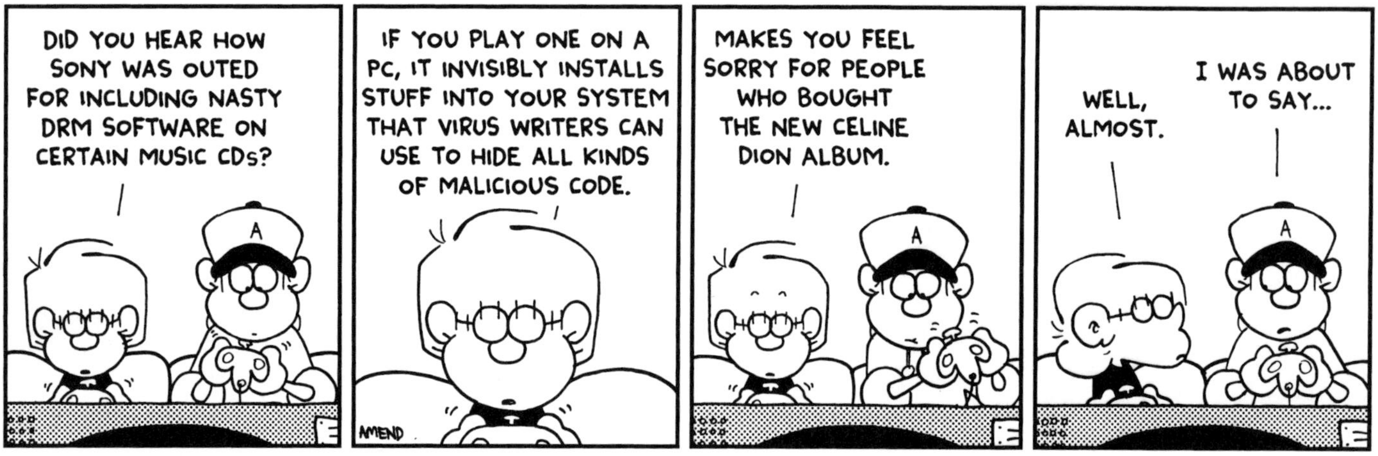
DID YOU HEAR HOW SONY WAS OUTED FOR INCLUDING NASTY DRM SOFTWARE ON CERTAIN MUSIC CDs?
IF YOU PLAY ONE ON A PC, IT INVISIBLY INSTALLS STUFF INTO YOUR SYSTEM THAT VIRUS WRITERS CAN USE TO HIDE ALL KINDS OF MALICIOUS CODE.
AMEND
MAKES YOU FEEL SORRY FOR PEOPLE WHO BOUGHT THE NEW CELINE DION ALBUM.
WELL, ALMOST.
I WAS ABOUT TO SAY...

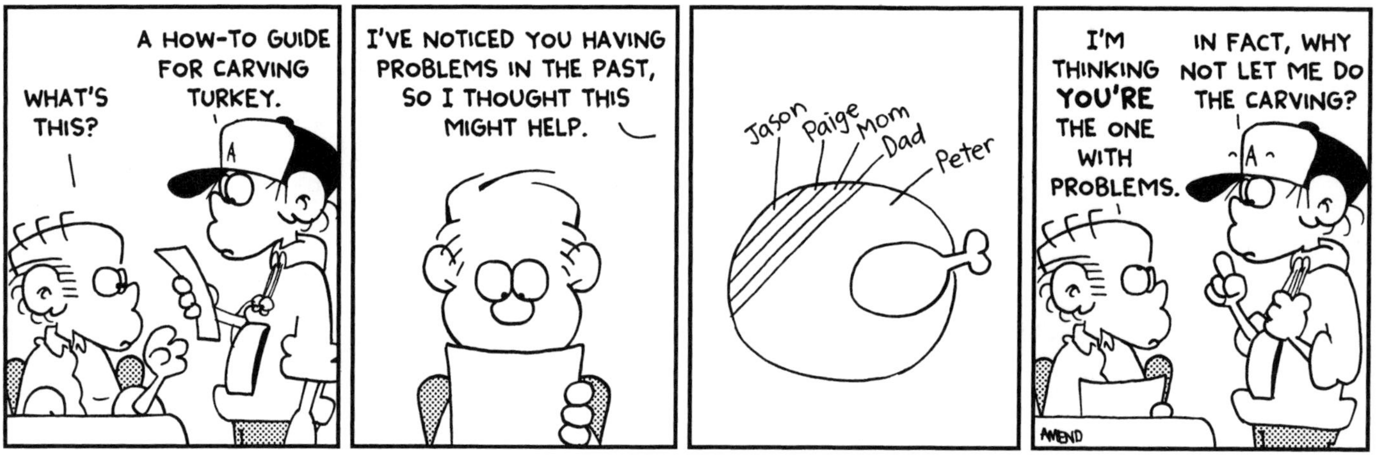
WHAT'S THIS?
A HOW-TO GUIDE FOR CARVING TURKEY.
I'VE NOTICED YOU HAVING PROBLEMS IN THE PAST, SO I THOUGHT THIS MIGHT HELP.
Jason
Paige
Mom
Dad
Peter
I'M THINKING **YOU'RE** THE ONE WITH PROBLEMS.
IN FACT, WHY NOT LET ME DO THE CARVING?
AMEND

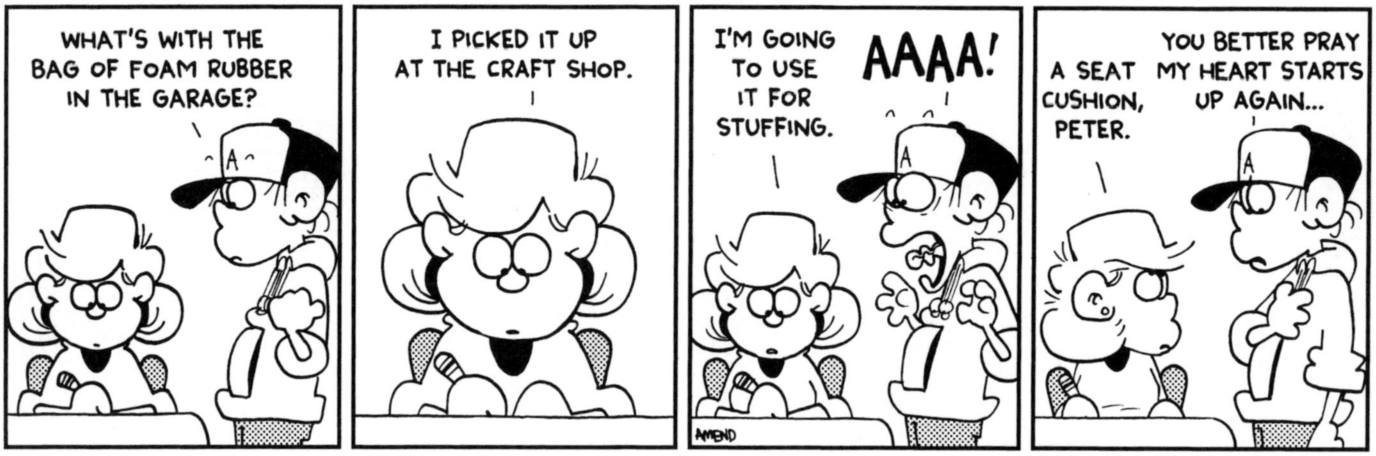
WHAT'S WITH THE BAG OF FOAM RUBBER IN THE GARAGE?
I PICKED IT UP AT THE CRAFT SHOP.
I'M GOING TO USE IT FOR STUFFING.
AAAA!
AMEND
A SEAT CUSHION, PETER.
YOU BETTER PRAY MY HEART STARTS UP AGAIN...

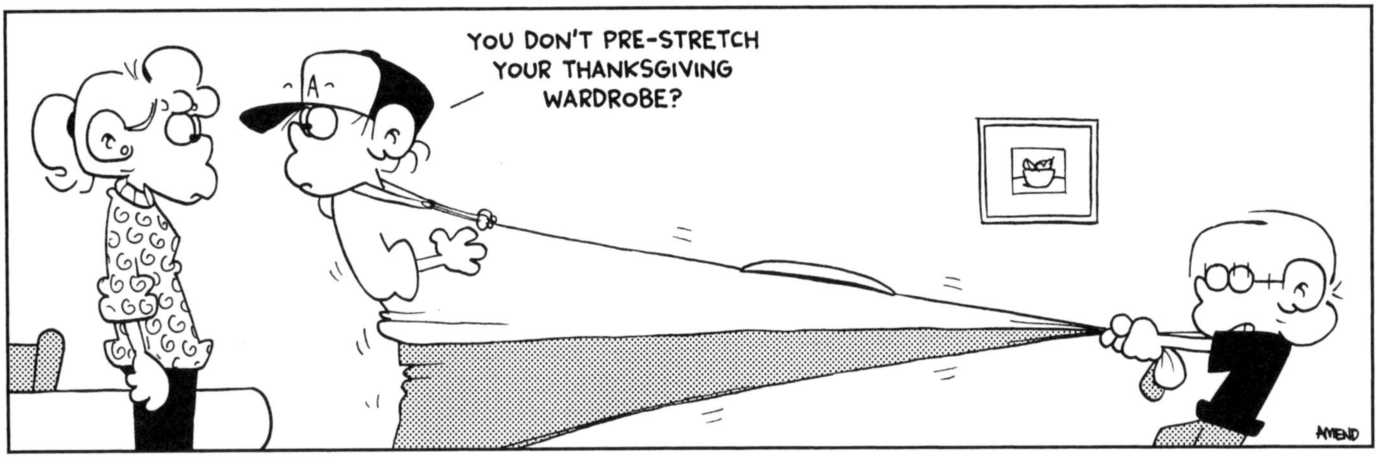
YOU DON'T PRE-STRETCH YOUR THANKSGIVING WARDROBE?

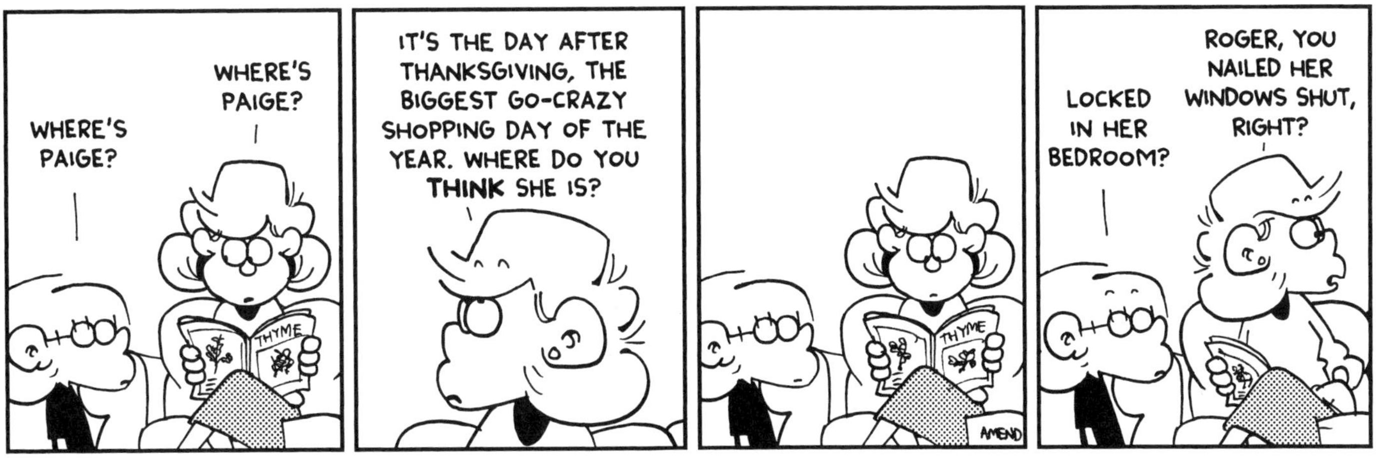
WHERE'S PAIGE?
WHERE'S PAIGE?
IT'S THE DAY AFTER THANKSGIVING, THE BIGGEST GO-CRAZY SHOPPING DAY OF THE YEAR. WHERE DO YOU **THINK** SHE IS?
LOCKED IN HER BEDROOM?
ROGER, YOU NAILED HER WINDOWS SHUT, RIGHT?

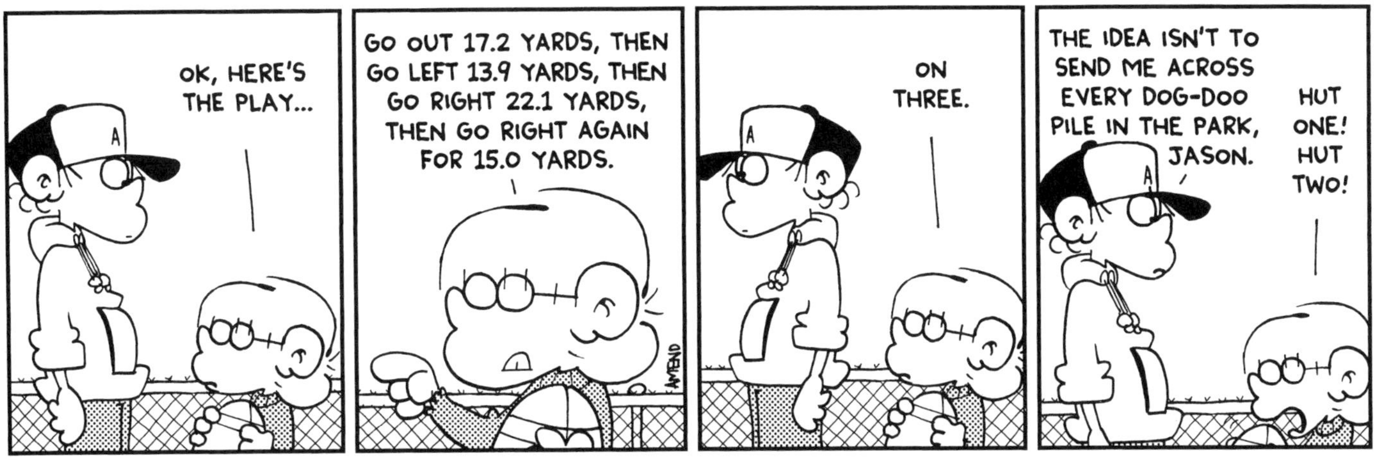
OK, HERE'S THE PLAY...
GO OUT 17.2 YARDS, THEN GO LEFT 13.9 YARDS, THEN GO RIGHT 22.1 YARDS, THEN GO RIGHT AGAIN FOR 15.0 YARDS.
ON THREE.
THE IDEA ISN'T TO SEND ME ACROSS EVERY DOG-DOO PILE IN THE PARK, JASON.
HUT ONE! HUT TWO!

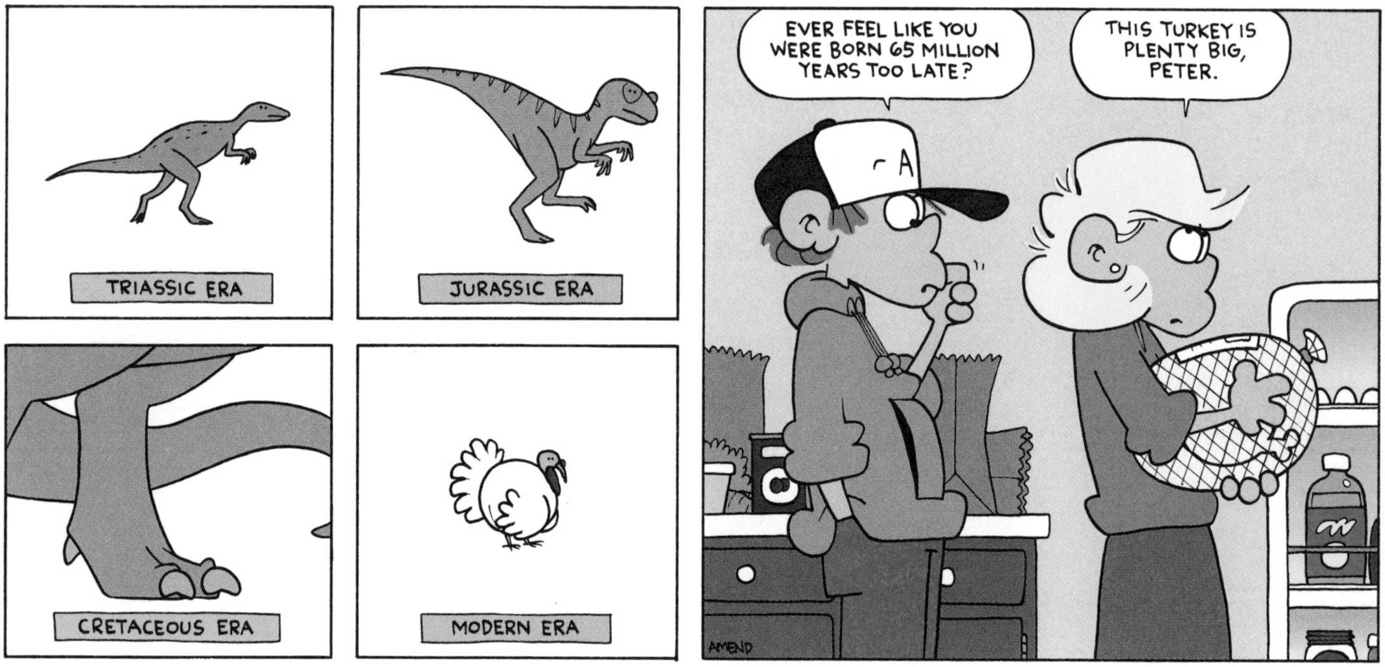
TRIASSIC ERA
JURASSIC ERA
CRETACEOUS ERA
MODERN ERA
EVER FEEL LIKE YOU WERE BORN 65 MILLION YEARS TOO LATE?
THIS TURKEY IS PLENTY BIG, PETER.
AMEND

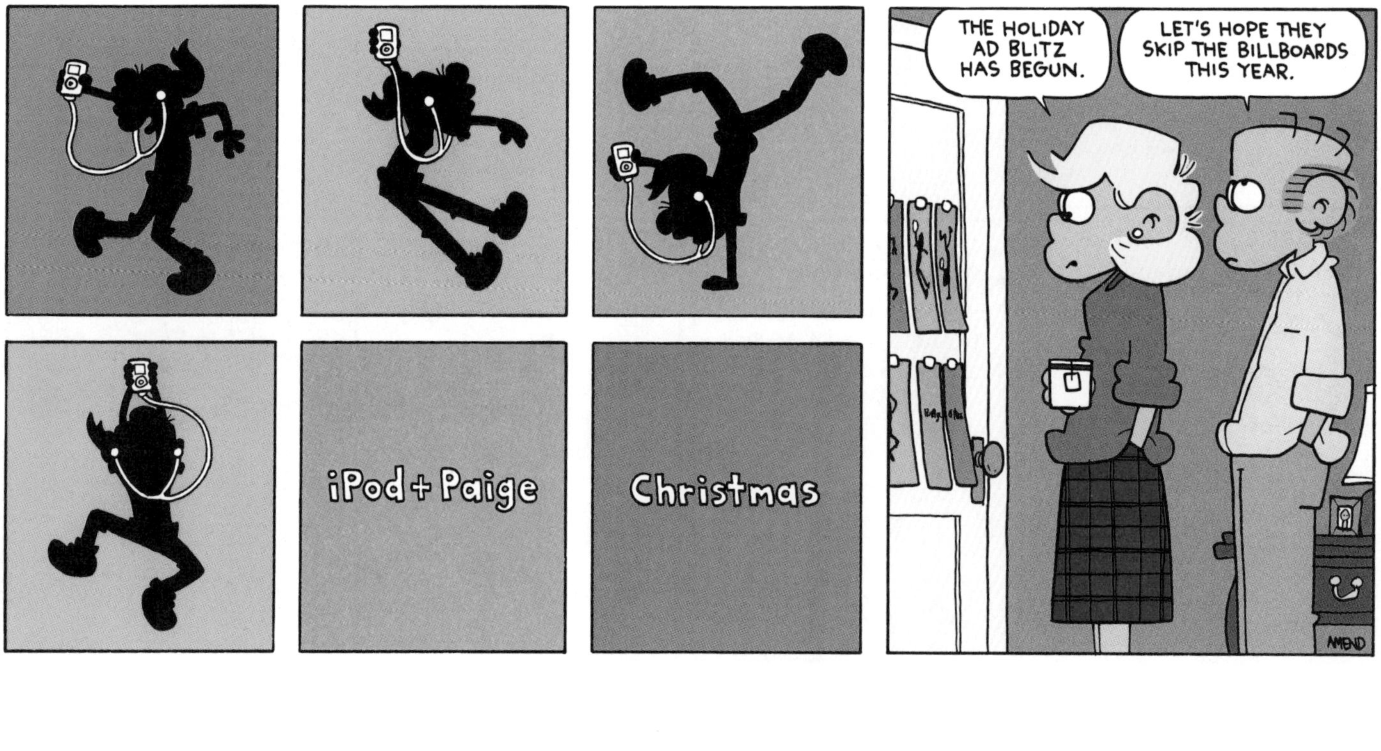
iPod + Paige
Christmas
THE HOLIDAY AD BLITZ HAS BEGUN.
LET'S HOPE THEY SKIP THE BILLBOARDS THIS YEAR.
AMEND

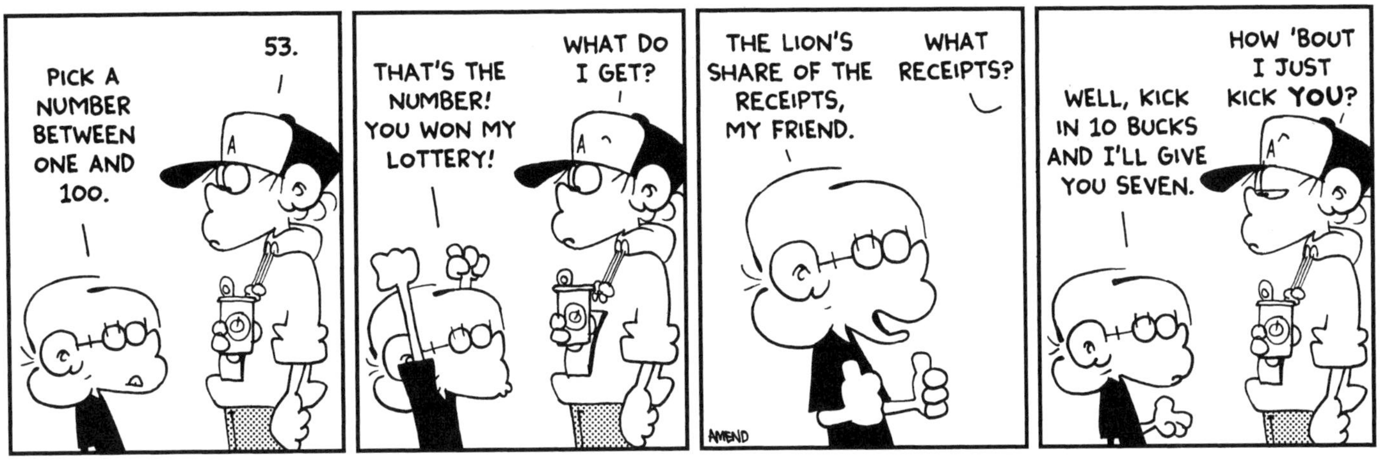
PICK A NUMBER BETWEEN ONE AND 100.
53.
THAT'S THE NUMBER! YOU WON MY LOTTERY!
WHAT DO I GET?
THE LION'S SHARE OF THE RECEIPTS, MY FRIEND.
WHAT RECEIPTS?
AMEND
WELL, KICK IN 10 BUCKS AND I'LL GIVE YOU SEVEN.
HOW 'BOUT I JUST KICK **YOU**?

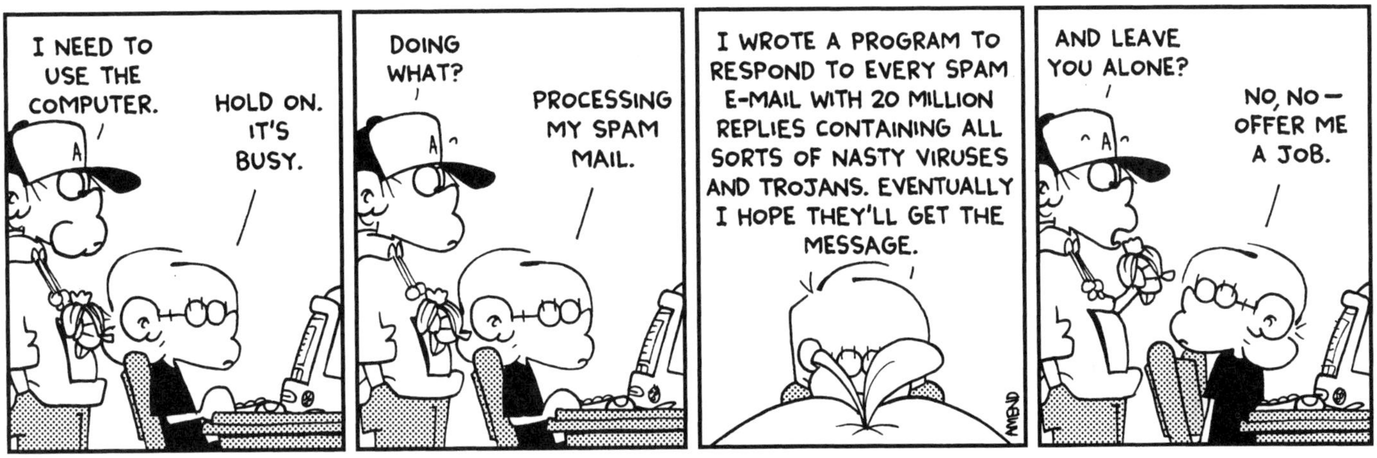
I NEED TO USE THE COMPUTER.
HOLD ON. IT'S BUSY.
DOING WHAT?
PROCESSING MY SPAM MAIL.
I WROTE A PROGRAM TO RESPOND TO EVERY SPAM E-MAIL WITH 20 MILLION REPLIES CONTAINING ALL SORTS OF NASTY VIRUSES AND TROJANS. EVENTUALLY I HOPE THEY'LL GET THE MESSAGE.
AMEND
AND LEAVE YOU ALONE?
NO, NO— OFFER ME A JOB.

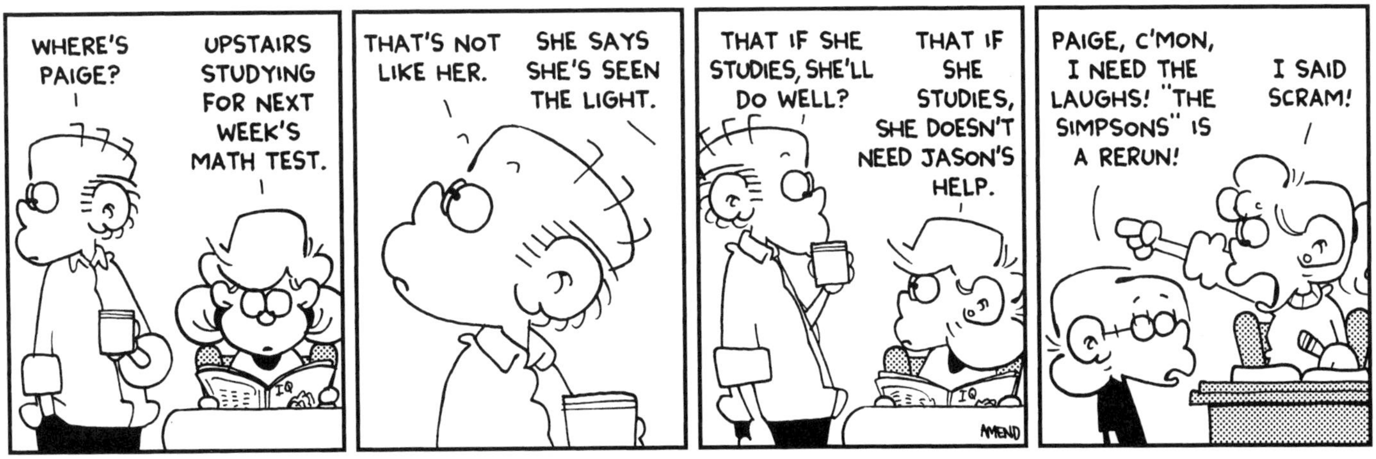
WHERE'S PAIGE?
UPSTAIRS STUDYING FOR NEXT WEEK'S MATH TEST.
IQ
THAT'S NOT LIKE HER.
SHE SAYS SHE'S SEEN THE LIGHT.
THAT IF SHE STUDIES, SHE'LL DO WELL?
THAT IF SHE STUDIES, SHE DOESN'T NEED JASON'S HELP.
IQ
AMEND
PAIGE, C'MON, I NEED THE LAUGHS! "THE SIMPSONS" IS A RERUN!
I SAID SCRAM!

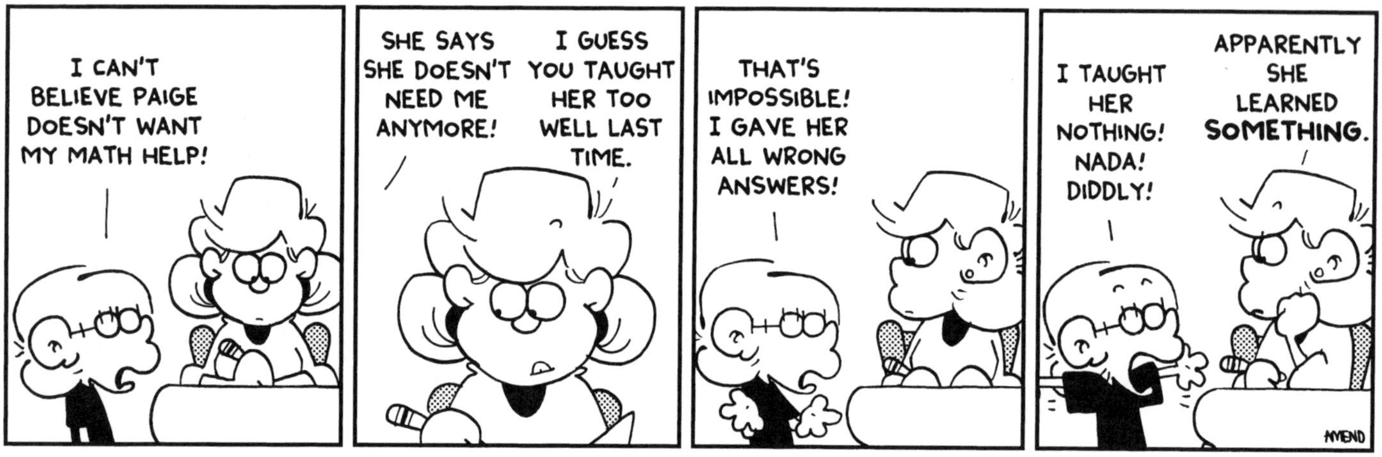
I CAN'T BELIEVE PAIGE DOESN'T WANT MY MATH HELP!
SHE SAYS SHE DOESN'T NEED ME ANYMORE!
I GUESS YOU TAUGHT HER TOO WELL LAST TIME.
THAT'S IMPOSSIBLE! I GAVE HER ALL WRONG ANSWERS!
I TAUGHT HER NOTHING! NADA! DIDDLY!
APPARENTLY SHE LEARNED SOMETHING.

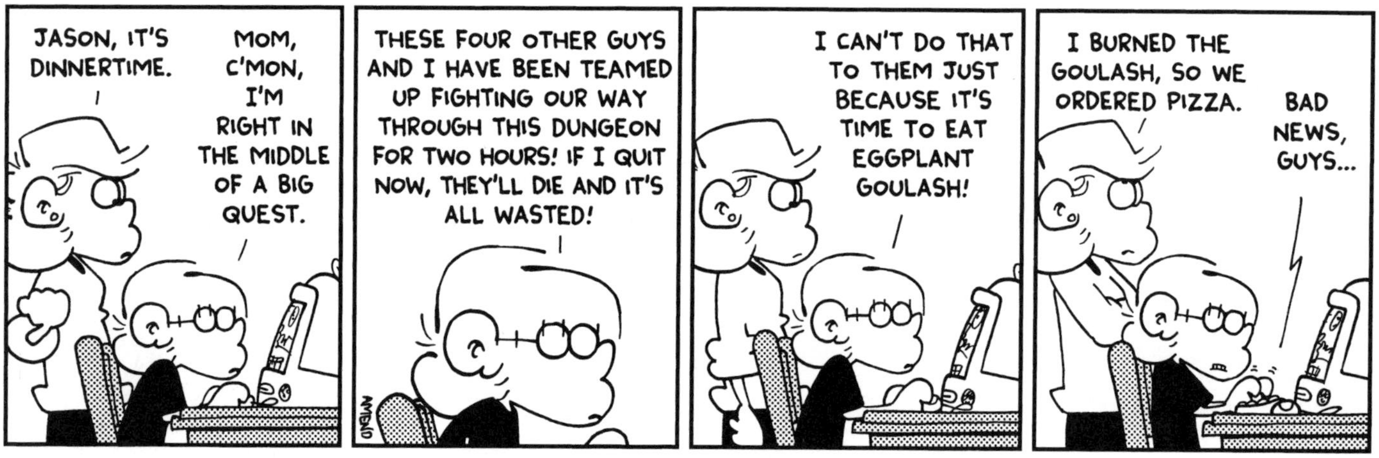
JASON, IT'S DINNERTIME.
MOM, C'MON, I'M RIGHT IN THE MIDDLE OF A BIG QUEST.
THESE FOUR OTHER GUYS AND I HAVE BEEN TEAMED UP FIGHTING OUR WAY THROUGH THIS DUNGEON FOR TWO HOURS! IF I QUIT NOW, THEY'LL DIE AND IT'S ALL WASTED!
I CAN'T DO THAT TO THEM JUST BECAUSE IT'S TIME TO EAT EGGPLANT GOULASH!
I BURNED THE GOULASH, SO WE ORDERED PIZZA.
BAD NEWS, GUYS...

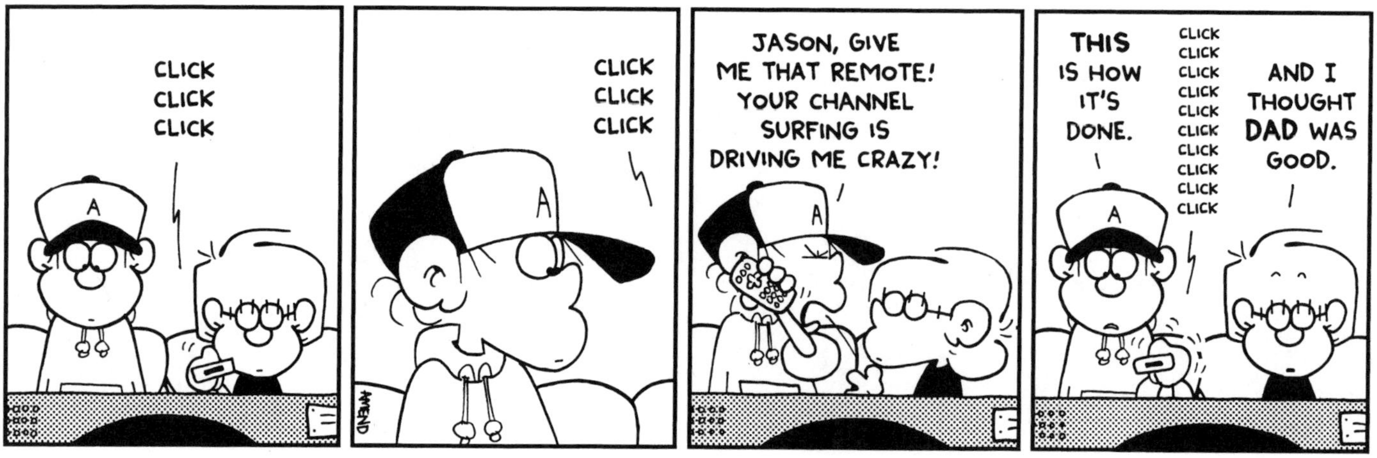
CLICK CLICK CLICK
CLICK CLICK CLICK
JASON, GIVE ME THAT REMOTE! YOUR CHANNEL SURFING IS DRIVING ME CRAZY!
THIS IS HOW IT'S DONE.
CLICK CLICK CLICK CLICK CLICK CLICK CLICK CLICK CLICK CLICK
AND I THOUGHT DAD WAS GOOD.

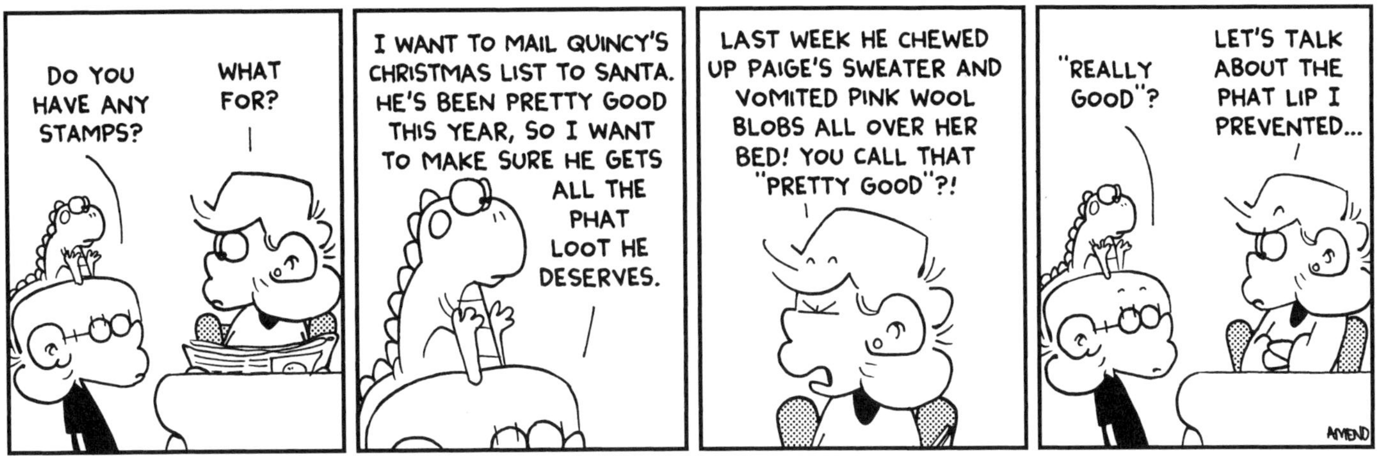
DO YOU HAVE ANY STAMPS?
WHAT FOR?
I WANT TO MAIL QUINCY'S CHRISTMAS LIST TO SANTA. HE'S BEEN PRETTY GOOD THIS YEAR, SO I WANT TO MAKE SURE HE GETS ALL THE PHAT LOOT HE DESERVES.
LAST WEEK HE CHEWED UP PAIGE'S SWEATER AND VOMITED PINK WOOL BLOBS ALL OVER HER BED! YOU CALL THAT "PRETTY GOOD"?!
"REALLY GOOD"?
LET'S TALK ABOUT THE PHAT LIP I PREVENTED...
AMEND

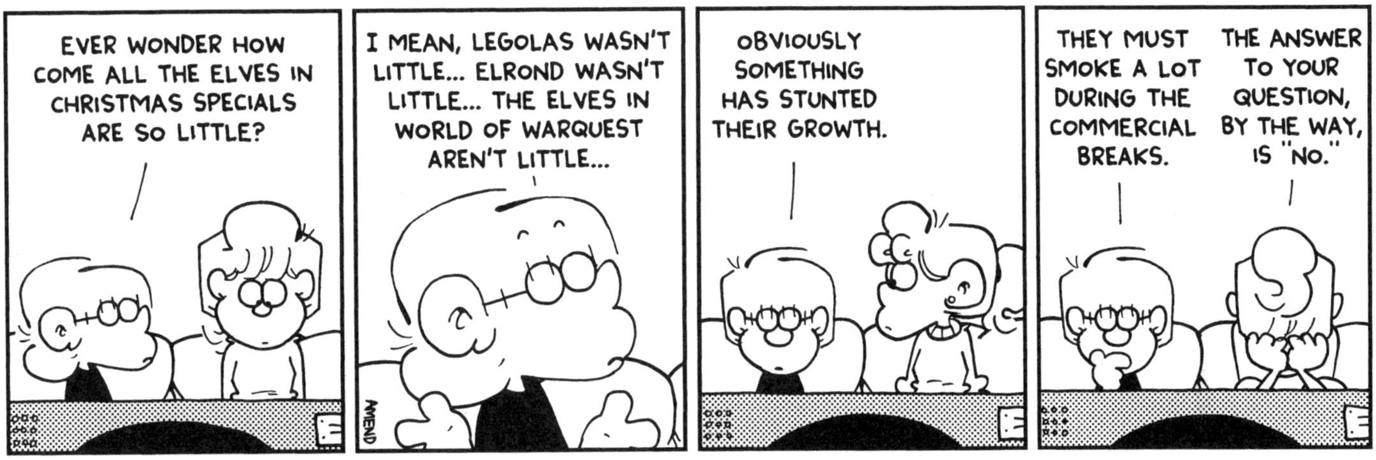
EVER WONDER HOW COME ALL THE ELVES IN CHRISTMAS SPECIALS ARE SO LITTLE?
I MEAN, LEGOLAS WASN'T LITTLE... ELROND WASN'T LITTLE... THE ELVES IN WORLD OF WARQUEST AREN'T LITTLE...
AMEND
OBVIOUSLY SOMETHING HAS STUNTED THEIR GROWTH.
THEY MUST SMOKE A LOT DURING THE COMMERCIAL BREAKS.
THE ANSWER TO YOUR QUESTION, BY THE WAY, IS "NO."

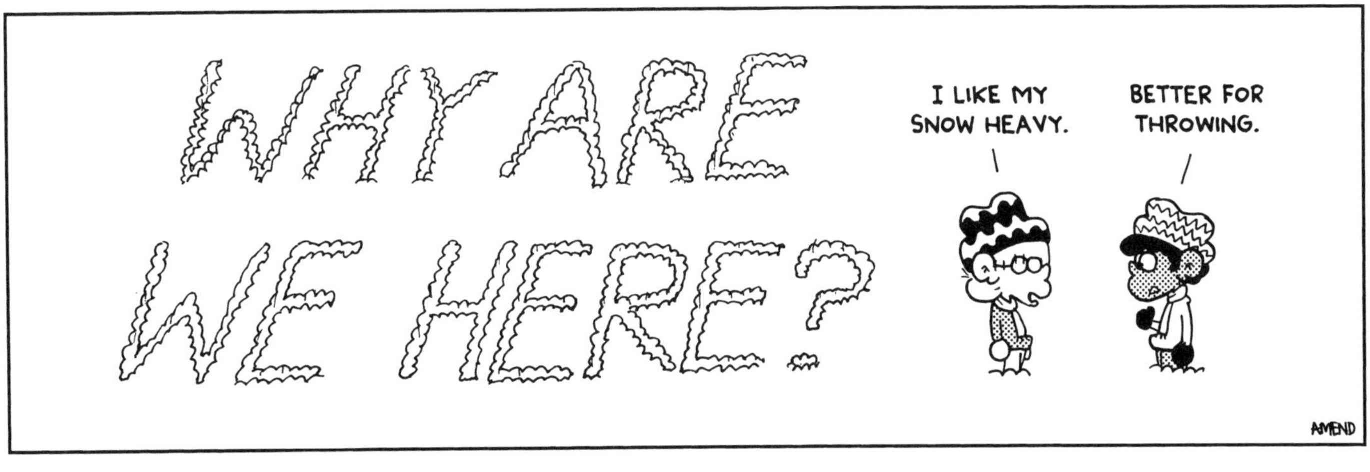
WHY ARE WE HERE?
I LIKE MY SNOW HEAVY.
BETTER FOR THROWING.
AMEND

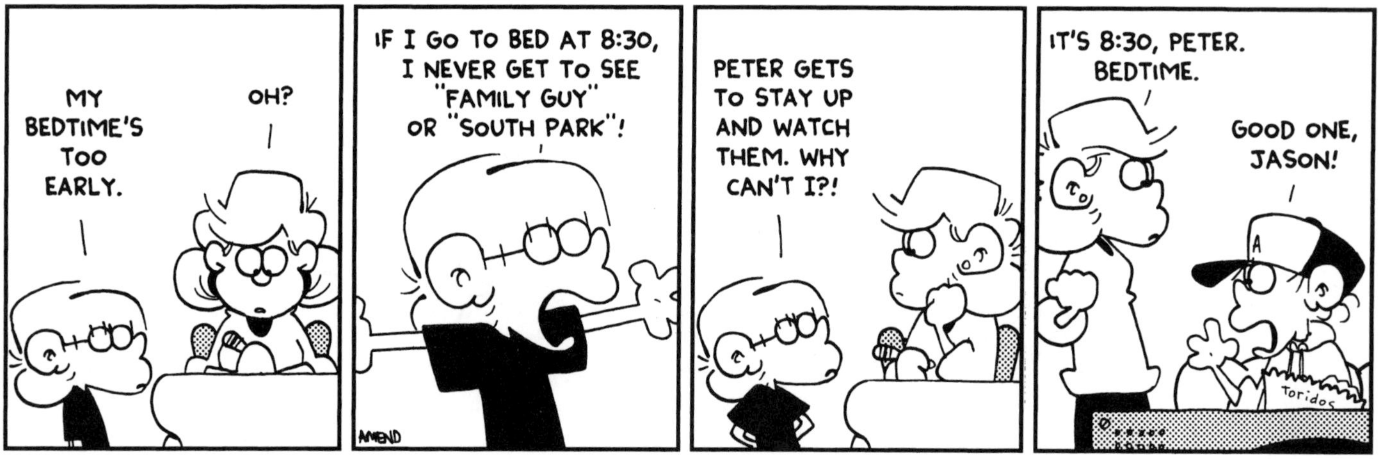
MY BEDTIME'S TOO EARLY.
OH?
IF I GO TO BED AT 8:30, I NEVER GET TO SEE "FAMILY GUY" OR "SOUTH PARK"!
PETER GETS TO STAY UP AND WATCH THEM. WHY CAN'T I?!
IT'S 8:30, PETER. BEDTIME.
GOOD ONE, JASON!
Toridos
AMEND

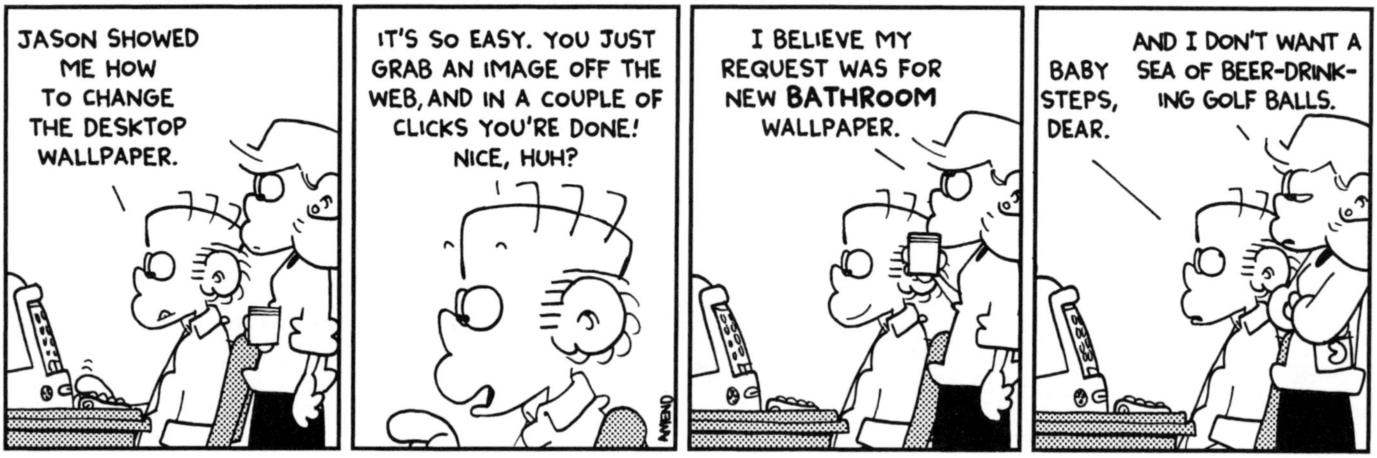
JASON SHOWED ME HOW TO CHANGE THE DESKTOP WALLPAPER.
IT'S SO EASY. YOU JUST GRAB AN IMAGE OFF THE WEB, AND IN A COUPLE OF CLICKS YOU'RE DONE! NICE, HUH?
I BELIEVE MY REQUEST WAS FOR NEW BATHROOM WALLPAPER.
BABY STEPS, DEAR.
AND I DON'T WANT A SEA OF BEER-DRINKING GOLF BALLS.
AMEND

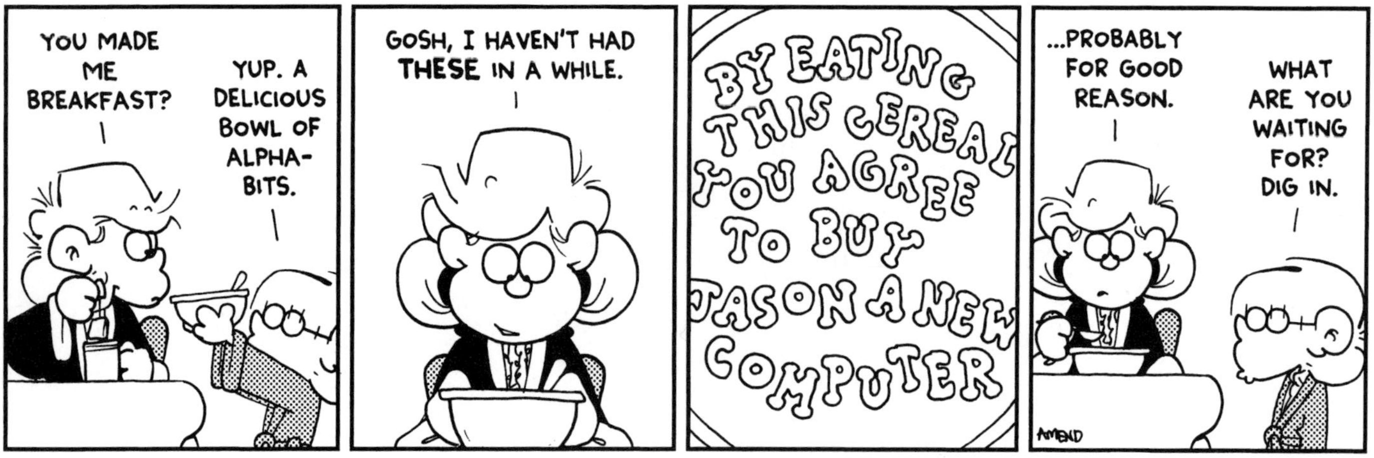
YOU MADE ME BREAKFAST?
YUP. A DELICIOUS BOWL OF ALPHA-BITS.
GOSH, I HAVEN'T HAD THESE IN A WHILE.
BY EATING THIS CEREAL YOU AGREE TO BUY JASON A NEW COMPUTER
...PROBABLY FOR GOOD REASON.
WHAT ARE YOU WAITING FOR? DIG IN.
AMEND

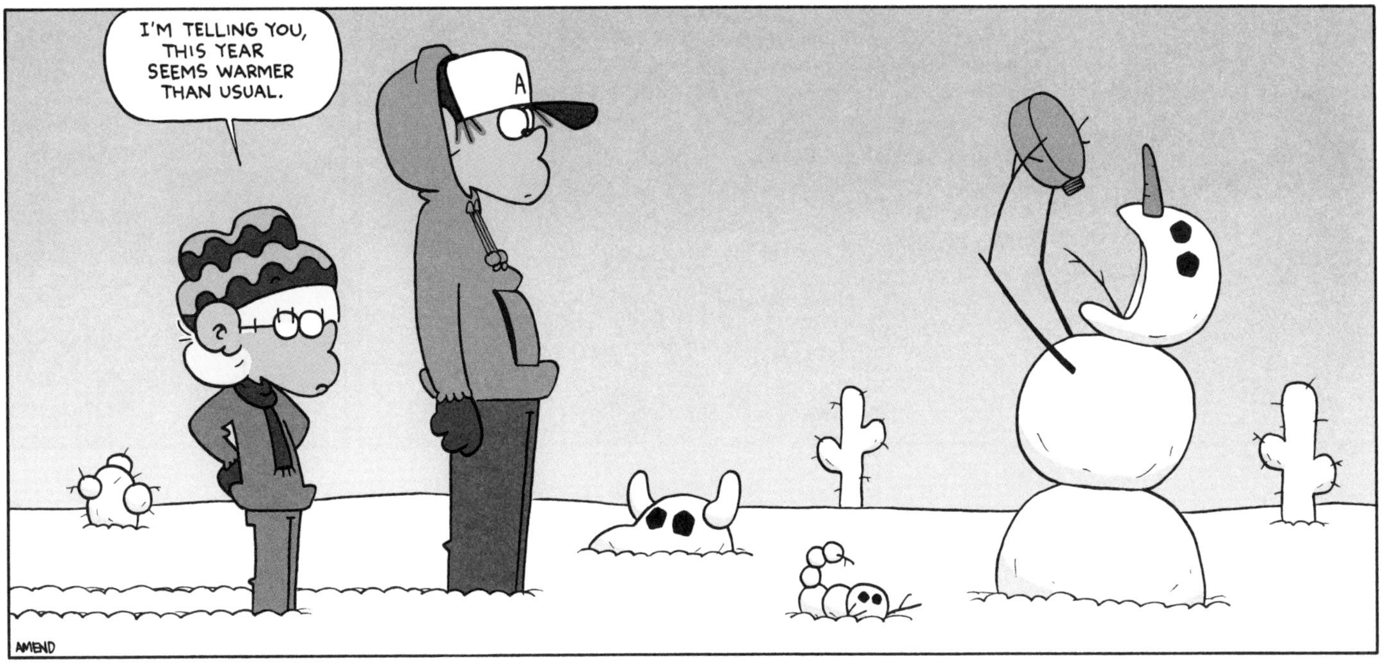
I'M TELLING YOU, THIS YEAR SEEMS WARMER THAN USUAL.
A
AMEND

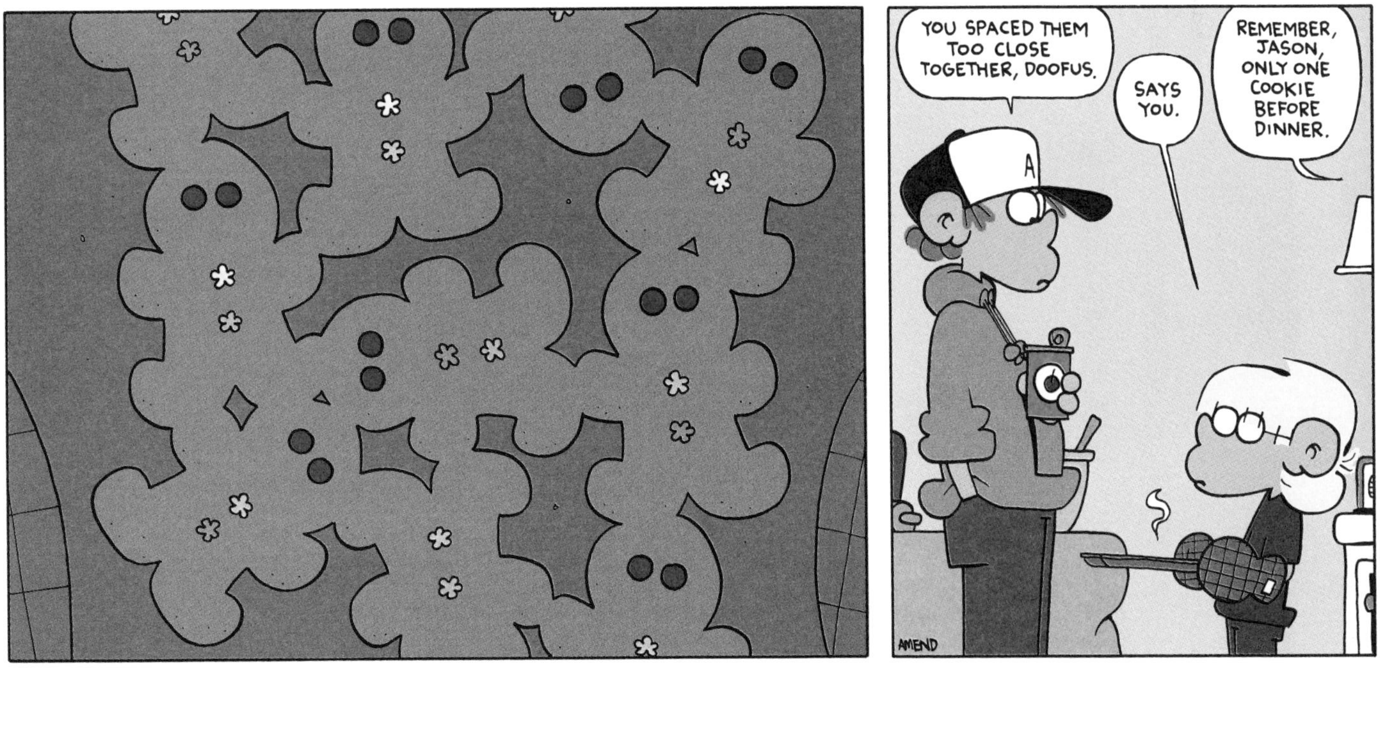
YOU SPACED THEM TOO CLOSE TOGETHER, DOOFUS.
SAYS YOU.
REMEMBER, JASON, ONLY ONE COOKIE BEFORE DINNER.
A
AMEND

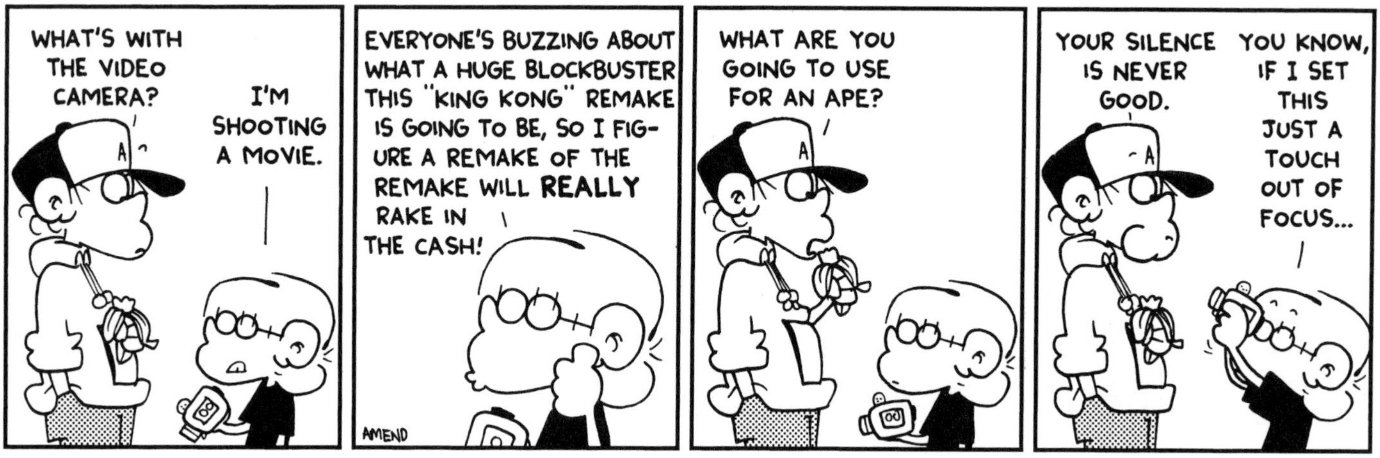
WHAT'S WITH THE VIDEO CAMERA?
I'M SHOOTING A MOVIE.
EVERYONE'S BUZZING ABOUT WHAT A HUGE BLOCKBUSTER THIS "KING KONG" REMAKE IS GOING TO BE, SO I FIGURE A REMAKE OF THE REMAKE WILL **REALLY** RAKE IN THE CASH!
AMEND
WHAT ARE YOU GOING TO USE FOR AN APE?
YOUR SILENCE IS NEVER GOOD.
YOU KNOW, IF I SET THIS JUST A TOUCH OUT OF FOCUS...

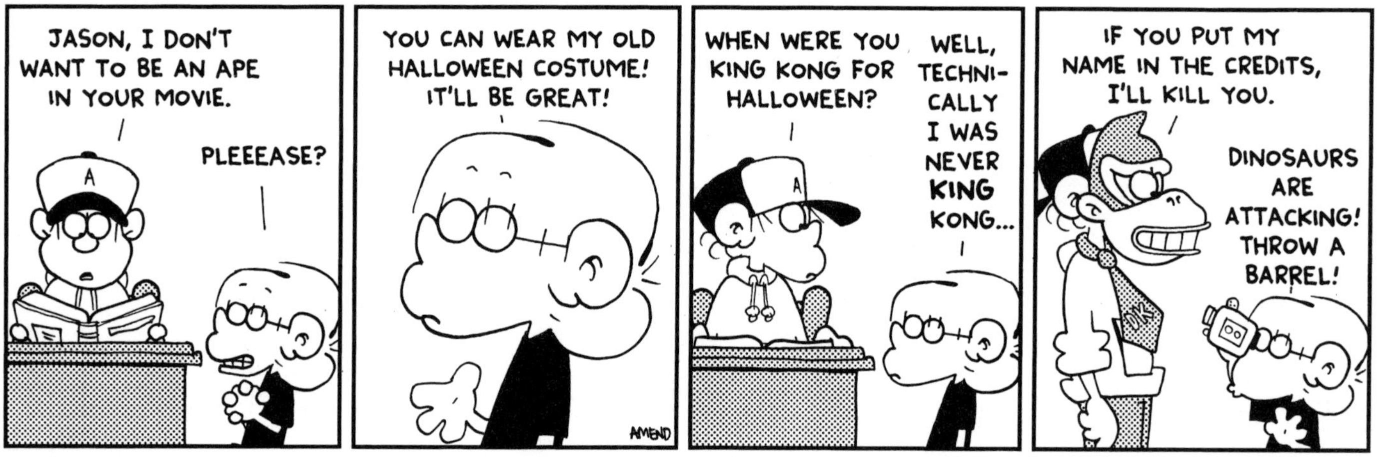
JASON, I DON'T WANT TO BE AN APE IN YOUR MOVIE.
PLEEEASE?
YOU CAN WEAR MY OLD HALLOWEEN COSTUME! IT'LL BE GREAT!
AMEND
WHEN WERE YOU KING KONG FOR HALLOWEEN?
WELL, TECHNICALLY I WAS NEVER **KING** KONG...
IF YOU PUT MY NAME IN THE CREDITS, I'LL KILL YOU.
DINOSAURS ARE ATTACKING! THROW A BARREL!

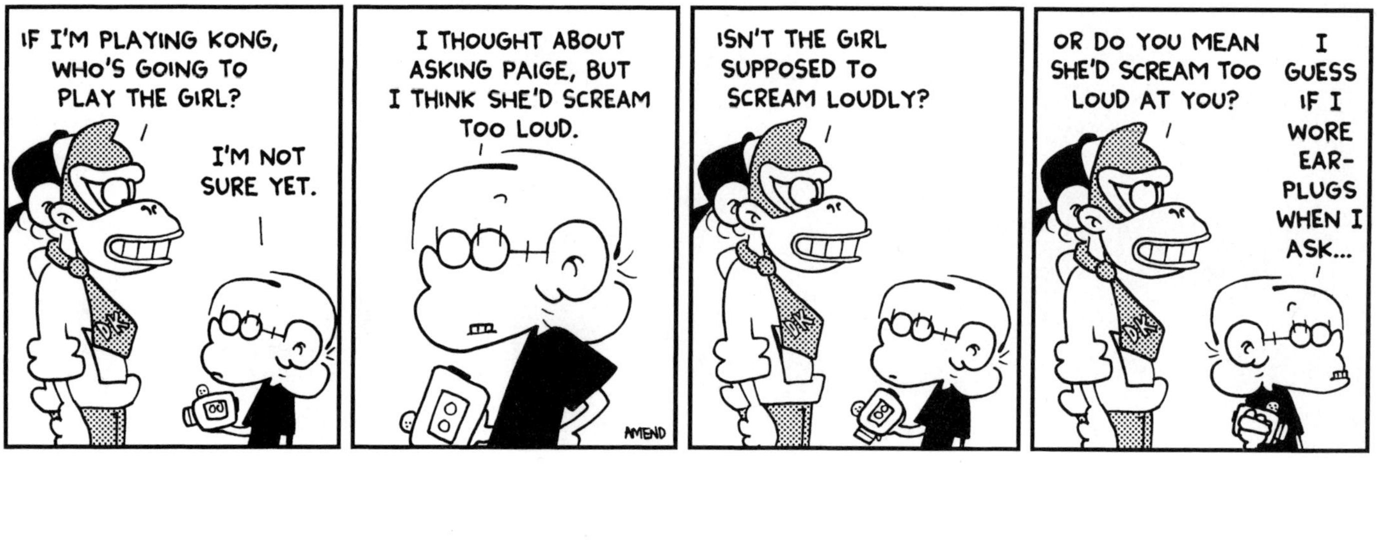
IF I'M PLAYING KONG, WHO'S GOING TO PLAY THE GIRL?
I'M NOT SURE YET.
I THOUGHT ABOUT ASKING PAIGE, BUT I THINK SHE'D SCREAM TOO LOUD.
AMEND
ISN'T THE GIRL SUPPOSED TO SCREAM LOUDLY?
OR DO YOU MEAN SHE'D SCREAM TOO LOUD AT YOU?
I GUESS IF I WORE EARPLUGS WHEN I ASK...

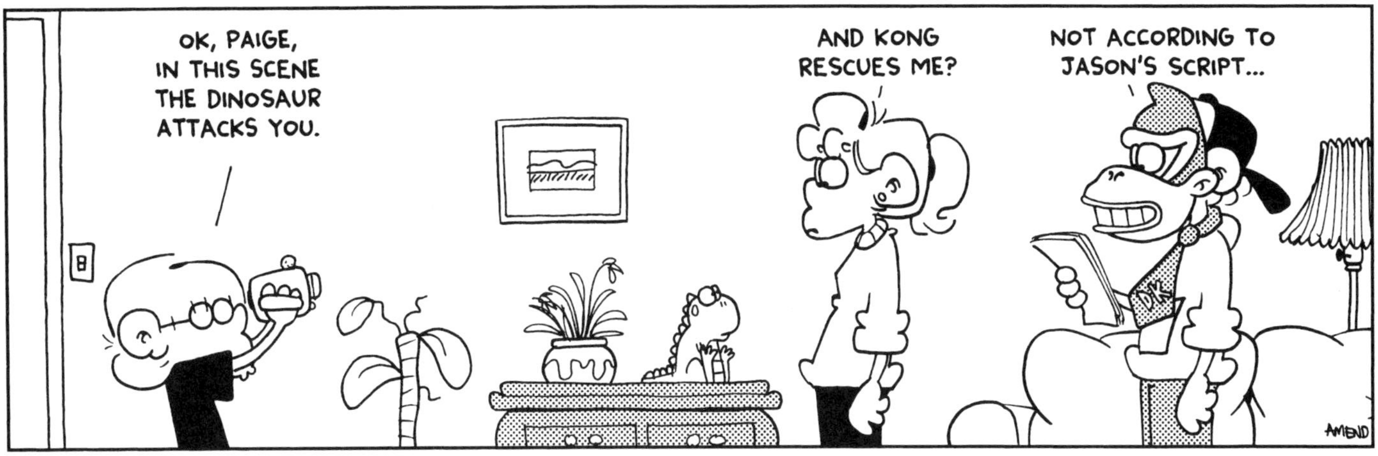
OK, PAIGE, IN THIS SCENE THE DINOSAUR ATTACKS YOU.
AND KONG RESCUES ME?
NOT ACCORDING TO JASON'S SCRIPT...
DK
AMEND

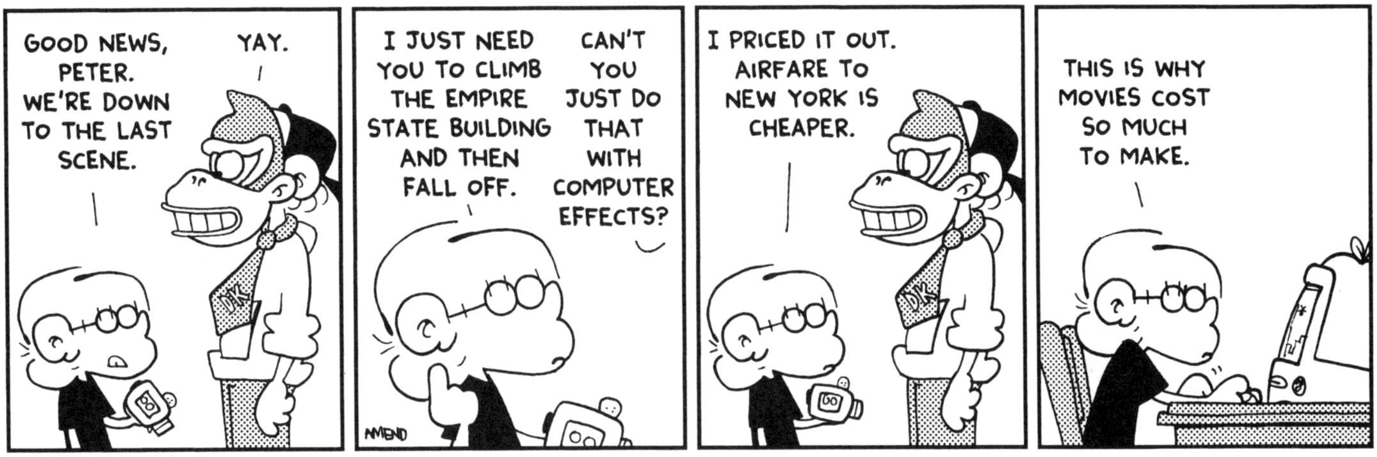
GOOD NEWS, PETER. WE'RE DOWN TO THE LAST SCENE.
YAY.
DK
I JUST NEED YOU TO CLIMB THE EMPIRE STATE BUILDING AND THEN FALL OFF.
CAN'T YOU JUST DO THAT WITH COMPUTER EFFECTS?
AMEND
I PRICED IT OUT. AIRFARE TO NEW YORK IS CHEAPER.
DK
THIS IS WHY MOVIES COST SO MUCH TO MAKE.

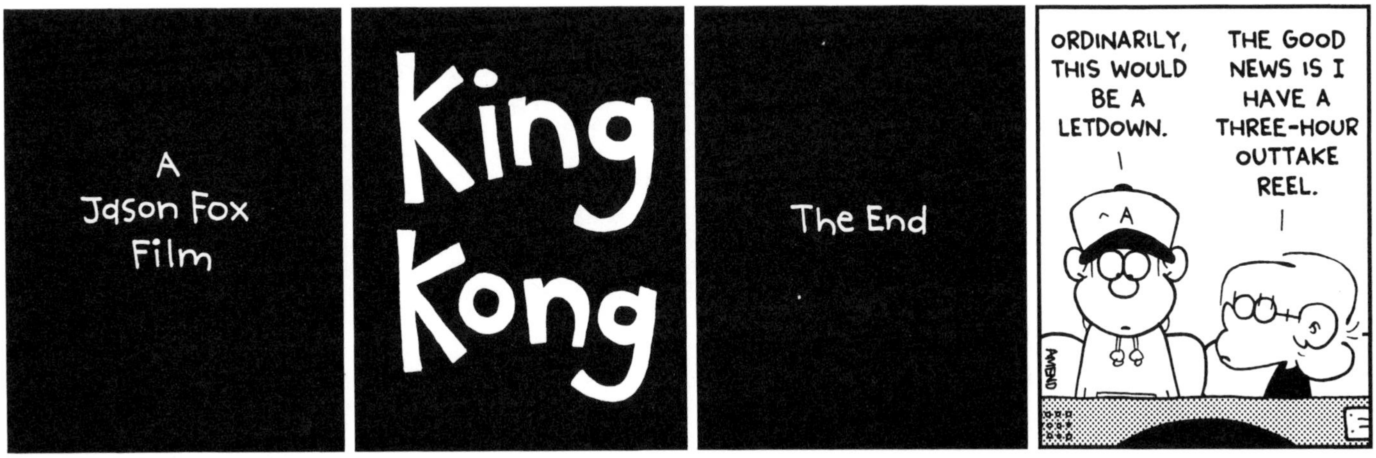
A
Jason Fox
Film
King
Kong
The End
ORDINARILY, THIS WOULD BE A LETDOWN.
THE GOOD NEWS IS I HAVE A THREE-HOUR OUTTAKE REEL.
A
AMEND

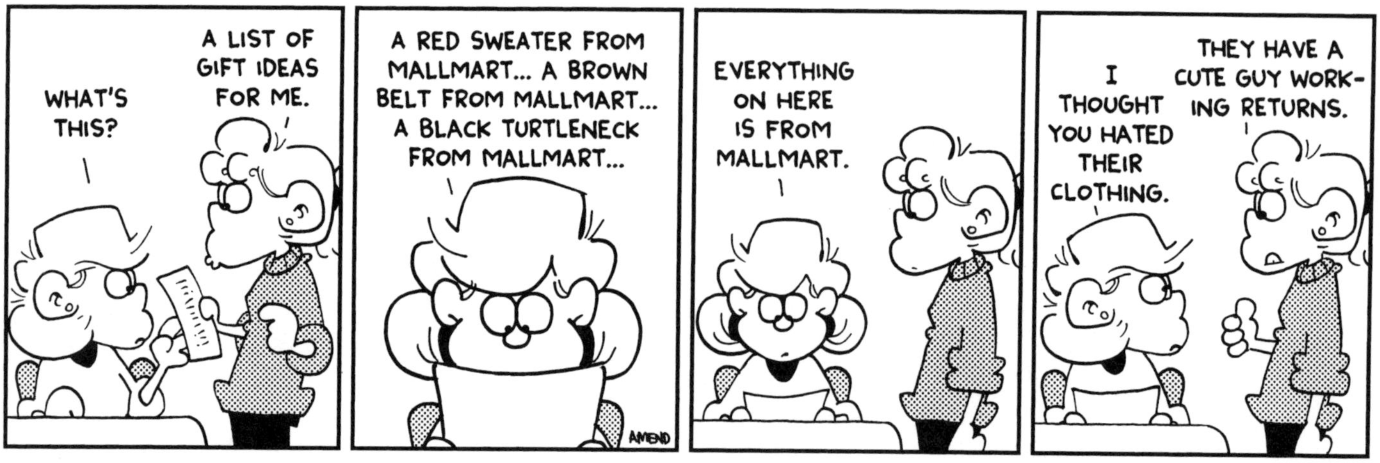
WHAT'S THIS?
A LIST OF GIFT IDEAS FOR ME.
A RED SWEATER FROM MALLMART... A BROWN BELT FROM MALLMART... A BLACK TURTLENECK FROM MALLMART...
AMEND
EVERYTHING ON HERE IS FROM MALLMART.
I THOUGHT YOU HATED THEIR CLOTHING.
THEY HAVE A CUTE GUY WORKING RETURNS.

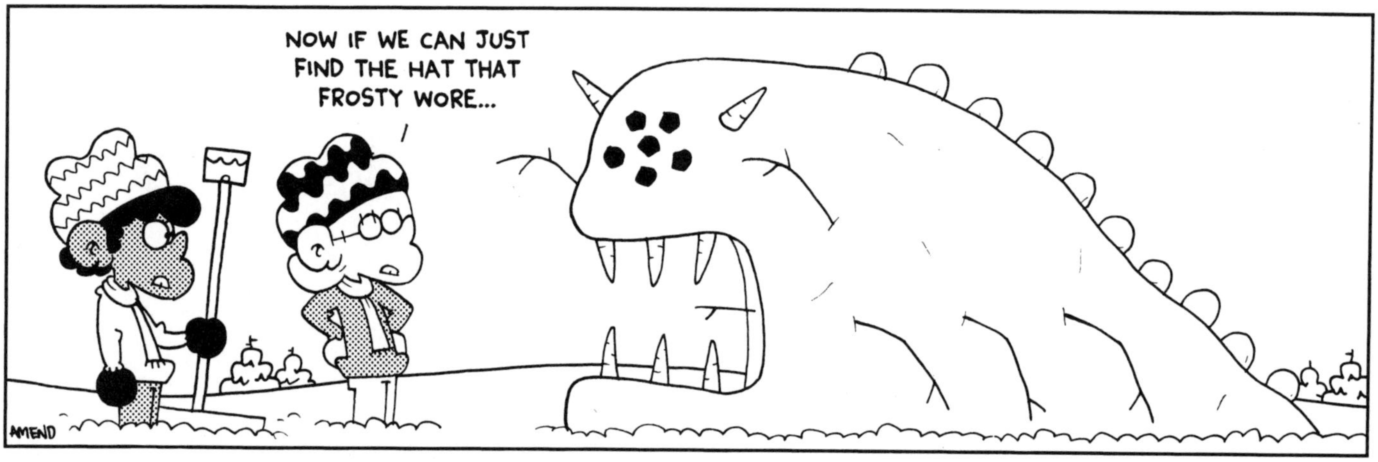
NOW IF WE CAN JUST FIND THE HAT THAT FROSTY WORE...
AMEND

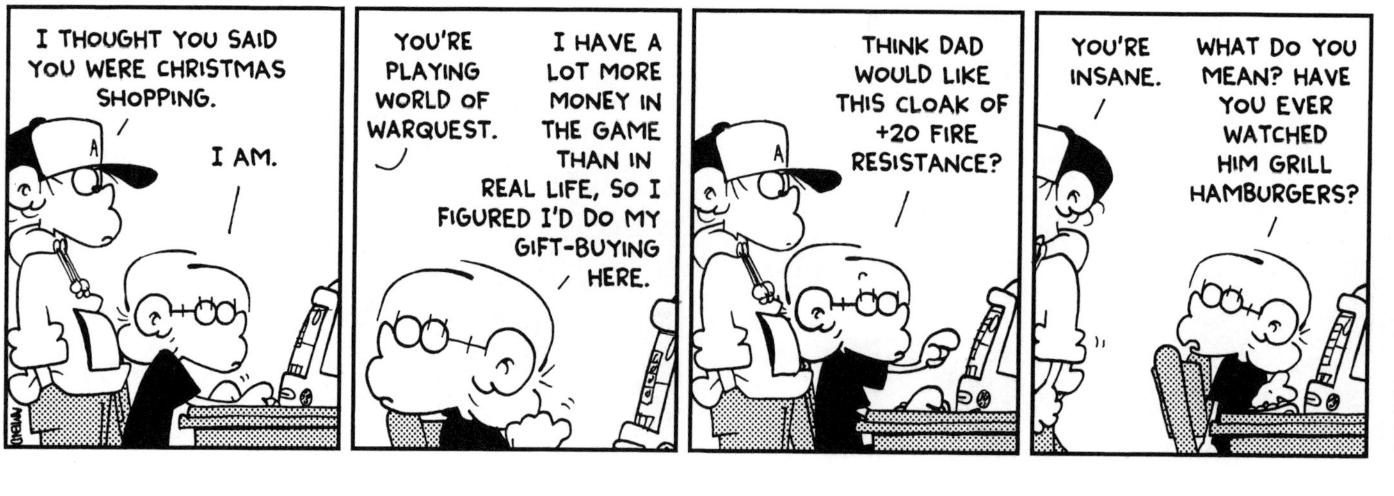
I THOUGHT YOU SAID YOU WERE CHRISTMAS SHOPPING.
I AM.
YOU'RE PLAYING WORLD OF WARQUEST.
I HAVE A LOT MORE MONEY IN THE GAME THAN IN REAL LIFE, SO I FIGURED I'D DO MY GIFT-BUYING HERE.
THINK DAD WOULD LIKE THIS CLOAK OF +20 FIRE RESISTANCE?
YOU'RE INSANE.
WHAT DO YOU MEAN? HAVE YOU EVER WATCHED HIM GRILL HAMBURGERS?

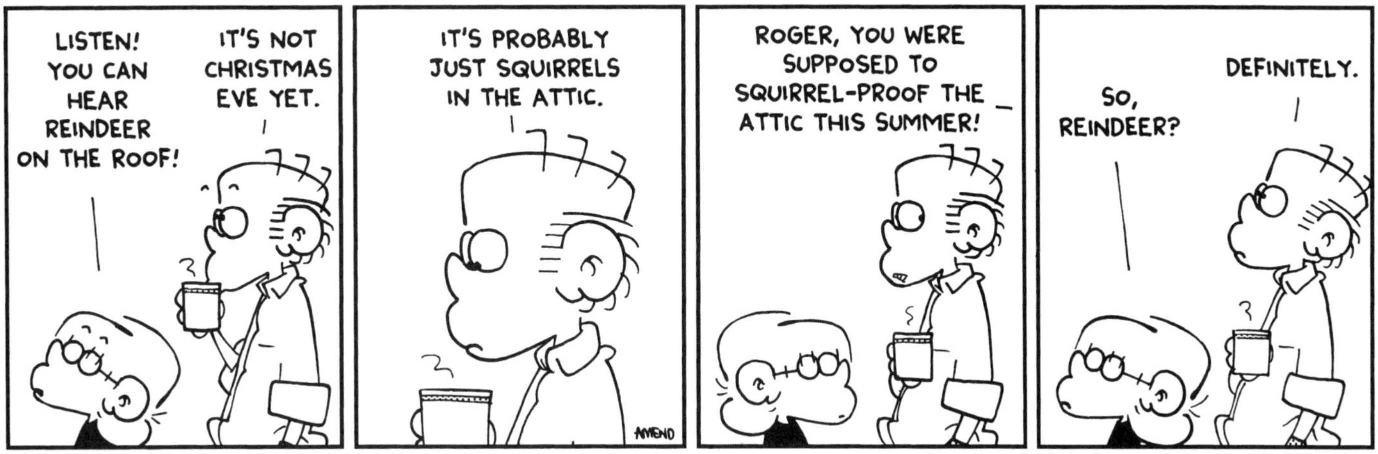
LISTEN! YOU CAN HEAR REINDEER ON THE ROOF!
IT'S NOT CHRISTMAS EVE YET.
IT'S PROBABLY JUST SQUIRRELS IN THE ATTIC.
AMEND
ROGER, YOU WERE SUPPOSED TO SQUIRREL-PROOF THE ATTIC THIS SUMMER!
SO, REINDEER?
DEFINITELY.

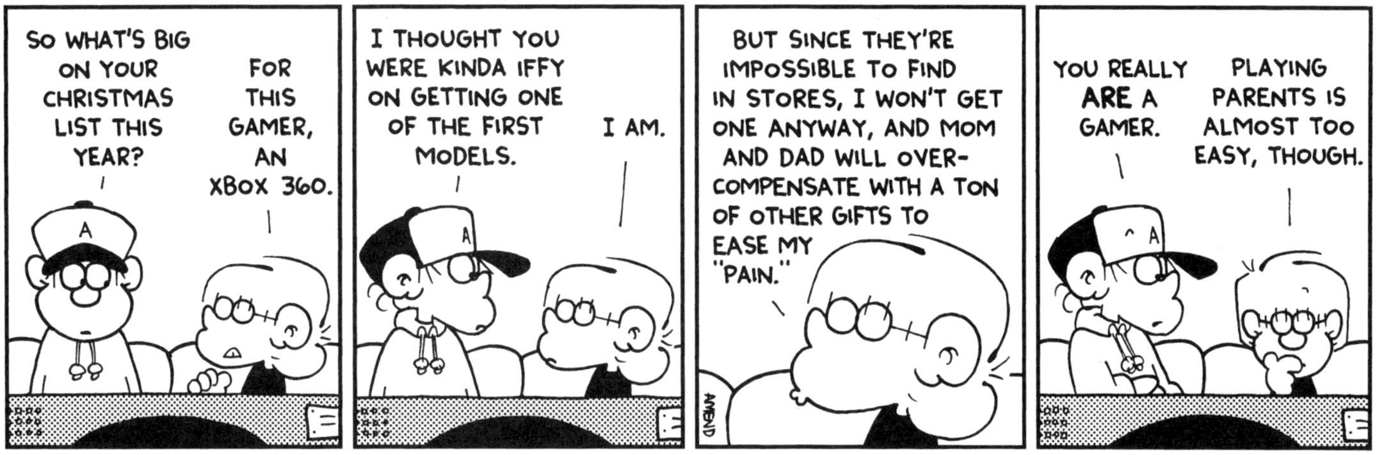
SO WHAT'S BIG ON YOUR CHRISTMAS LIST THIS YEAR?
FOR THIS GAMER, AN XBOX 360.
I THOUGHT YOU WERE KINDA IFFY ON GETTING ONE OF THE FIRST MODELS.
I AM.
BUT SINCE THEY'RE IMPOSSIBLE TO FIND IN STORES, I WON'T GET ONE ANYWAY, AND MOM AND DAD WILL OVER-COMPENSATE WITH A TON OF OTHER GIFTS TO EASE MY "PAIN."
AMEND
YOU REALLY **ARE** A GAMER.
PLAYING PARENTS IS ALMOST TOO EASY, THOUGH.

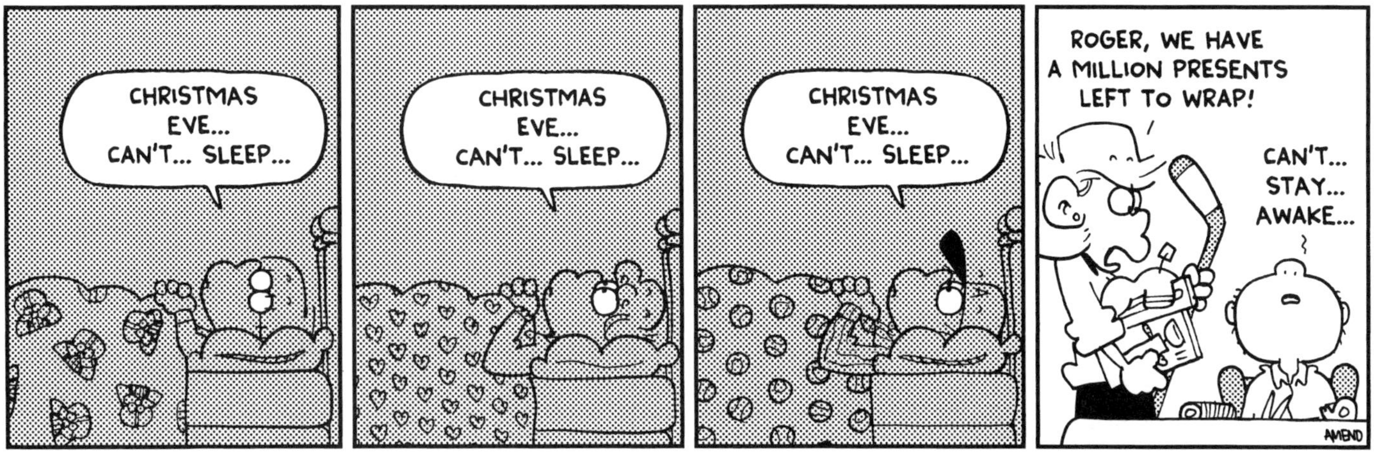
CHRISTMAS EVE... CAN'T... SLEEP...
CHRISTMAS EVE... CAN'T... SLEEP...
CHRISTMAS EVE... CAN'T... SLEEP...
ROGER, WE HAVE A MILLION PRESENTS LEFT TO WRAP!
CAN'T... STAY... AWAKE...
AMEND

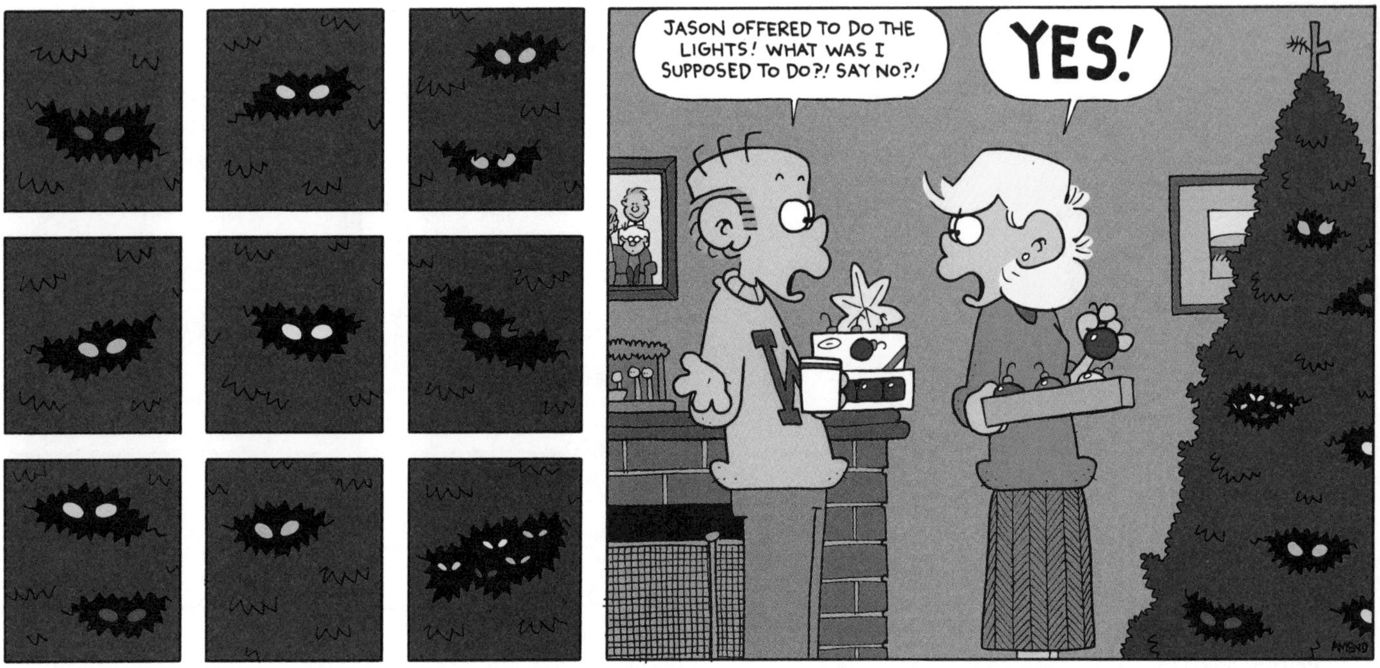
JASON OFFERED TO DO THE LIGHTS! WHAT WAS I SUPPOSED TO DO?! SAY NO?!
YES!
AMEND

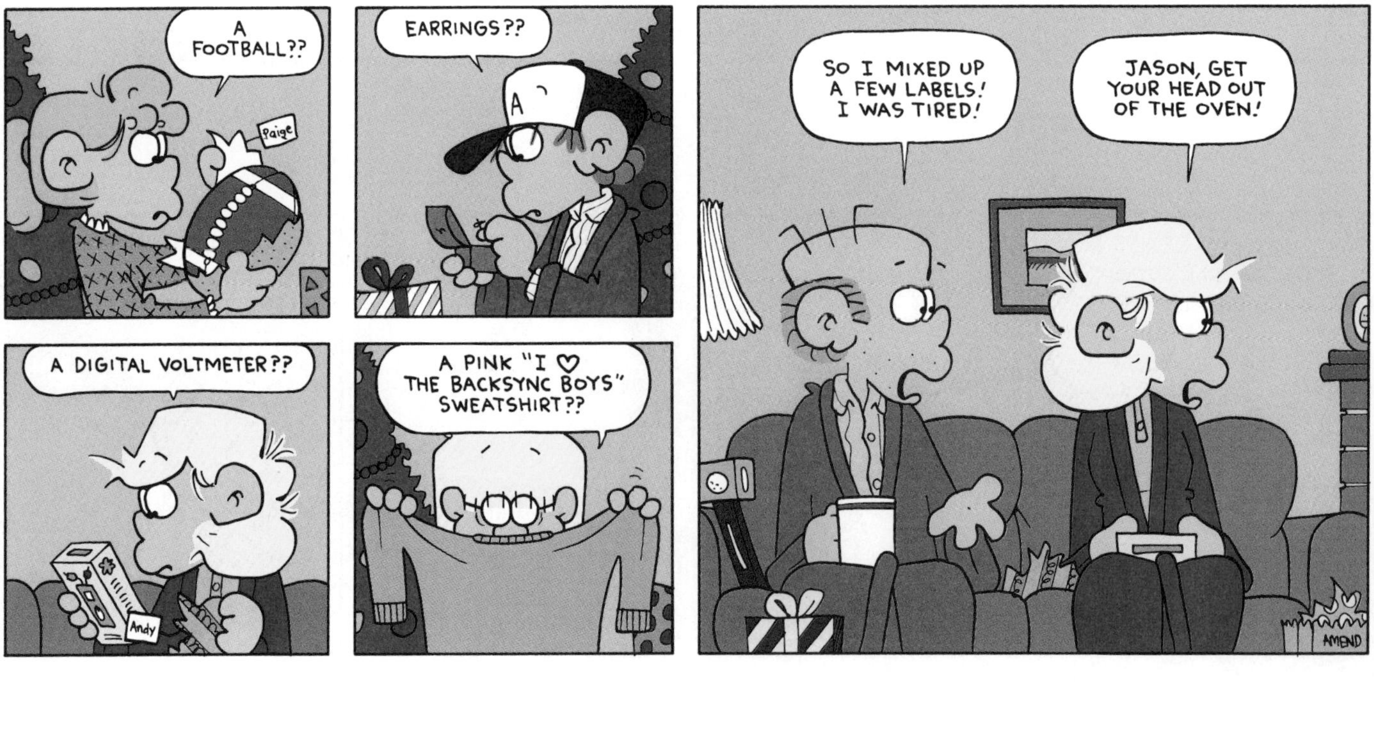
A FOOTBALL??
Paige
EARRINGS??
A DIGITAL VOLTMETER??
Andy
A PINK "I ♡ THE BACKSYNC BOYS" SWEATSHIRT??
SO I MIXED UP A FEW LABELS! I WAS TIRED!
JASON, GET YOUR HEAD OUT OF THE OVEN!
AMEND

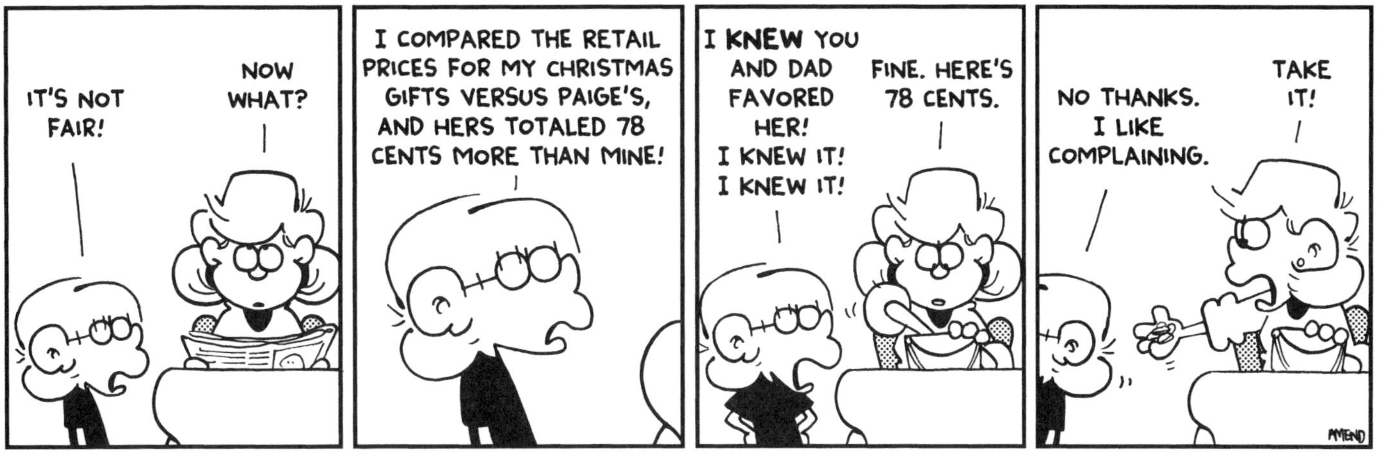
IT'S NOT FAIR!
NOW WHAT?
I COMPARED THE RETAIL PRICES FOR MY CHRISTMAS GIFTS VERSUS PAIGE'S, AND HERS TOTALED 78 CENTS MORE THAN MINE!
I **KNEW** YOU AND DAD FAVORED HER! I KNEW IT! I KNEW IT!
FINE. HERE'S 78 CENTS.
NO THANKS. I LIKE COMPLAINING.
TAKE IT!
AMEND

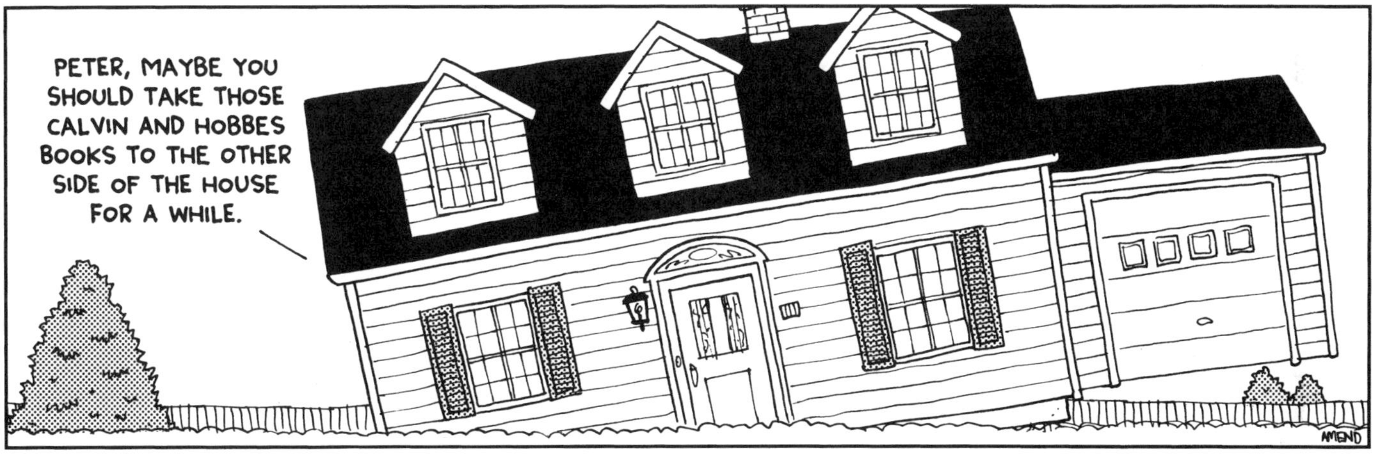
PETER, MAYBE YOU SHOULD TAKE THOSE CALVIN AND HOBBES BOOKS TO THE OTHER SIDE OF THE HOUSE FOR A WHILE.
AMEND

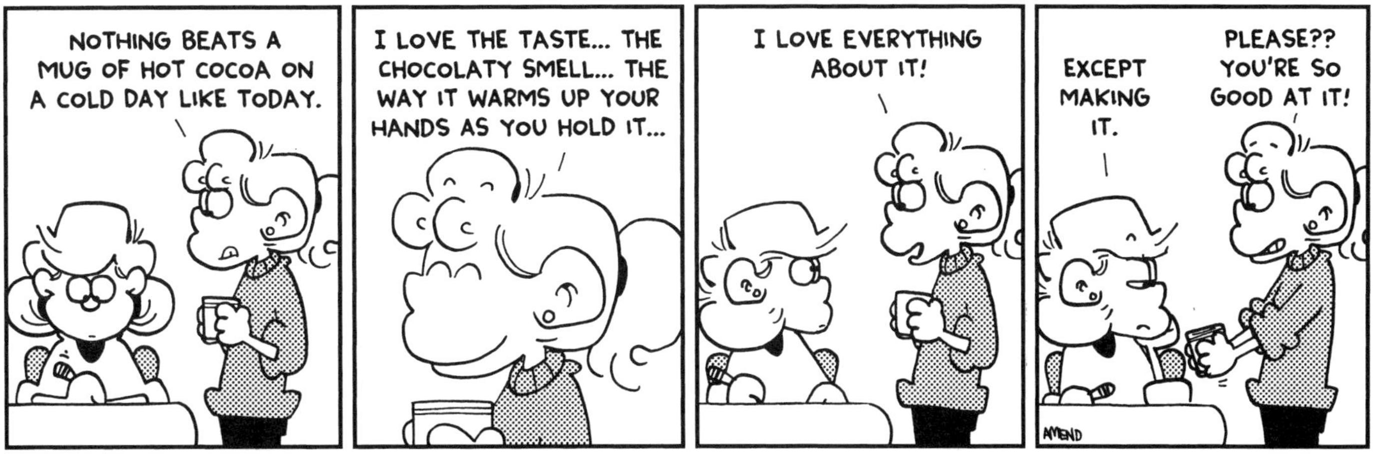
NOTHING BEATS A MUG OF HOT COCOA ON A COLD DAY LIKE TODAY.
I LOVE THE TASTE... THE CHOCOLATY SMELL... THE WAY IT WARMS UP YOUR HANDS AS YOU HOLD IT...
I LOVE EVERYTHING ABOUT IT!
EXCEPT MAKING IT.
PLEASE?? YOU'RE SO GOOD AT IT!
AMEND

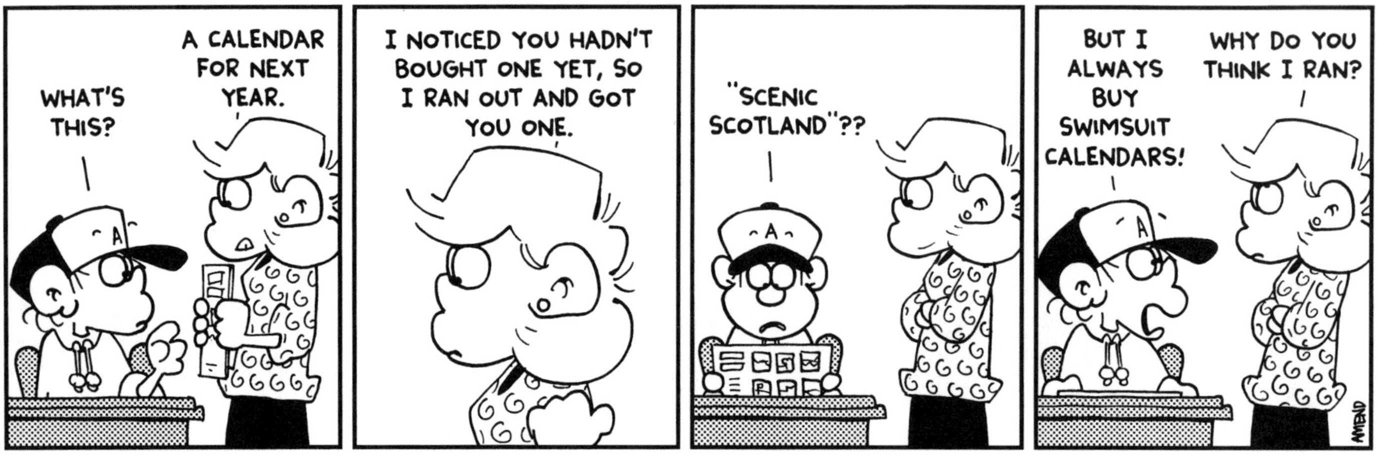
WHAT'S THIS?
A CALENDAR FOR NEXT YEAR.
I NOTICED YOU HADN'T BOUGHT ONE YET, SO I RAN OUT AND GOT YOU ONE.
"SCENIC SCOTLAND"??
BUT I ALWAYS BUY SWIMSUIT CALENDARS!
WHY DO YOU THINK I RAN?

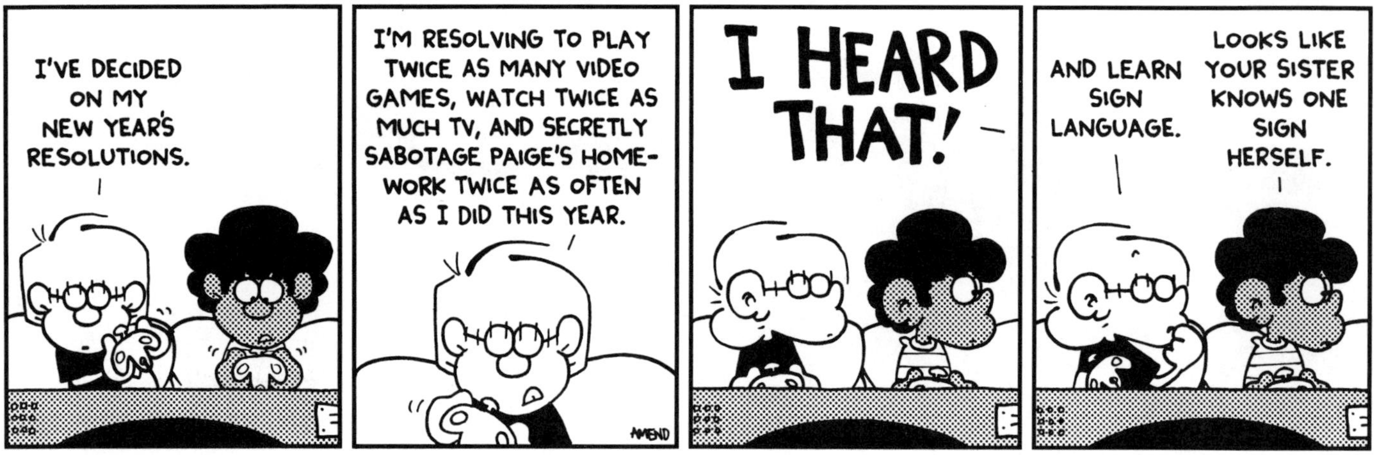
I'VE DECIDED ON MY NEW YEAR'S RESOLUTIONS.
I'M RESOLVING TO PLAY TWICE AS MANY VIDEO GAMES, WATCH TWICE AS MUCH TV, AND SECRETLY SABOTAGE PAIGE'S HOME-WORK TWICE AS OFTEN AS I DID THIS YEAR.
I HEARD THAT!
AND LEARN SIGN LANGUAGE.
LOOKS LIKE YOUR SISTER KNOWS ONE SIGN HERSELF.

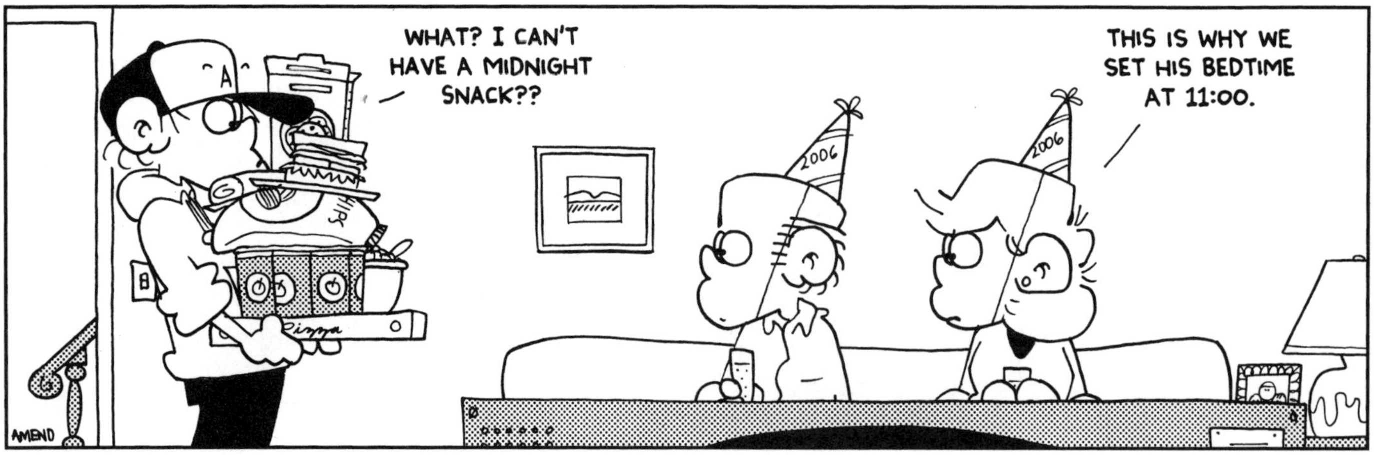
WHAT? I CAN'T HAVE A MIDNIGHT SNACK??
THIS IS WHY WE SET HIS BEDTIME AT 11:00.

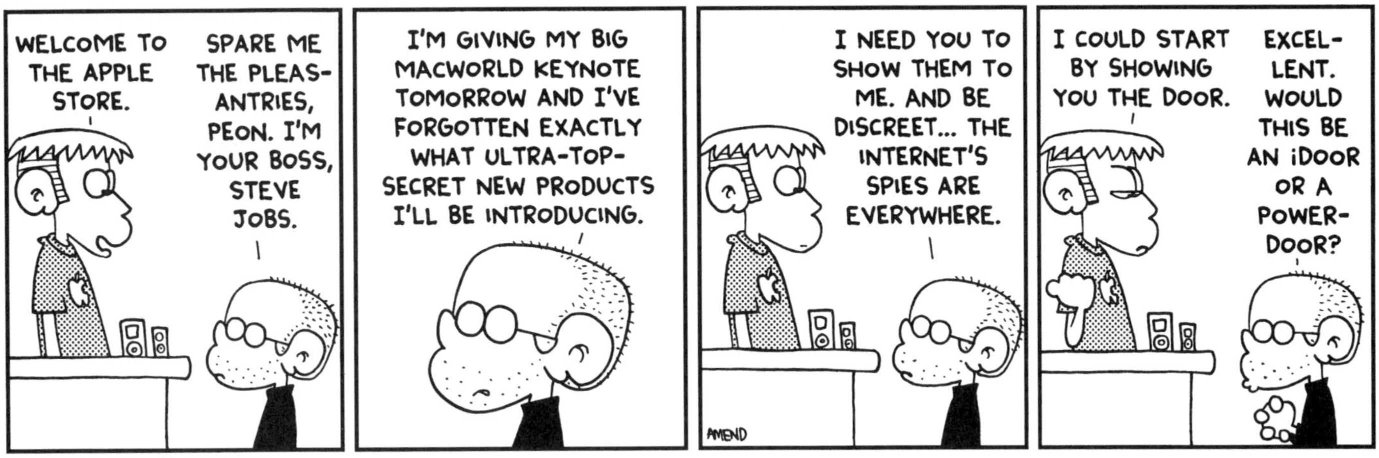
WELCOME TO THE APPLE STORE.
SPARE ME THE PLEASANTRIES, PEON. I'M YOUR BOSS, STEVE JOBS.
I'M GIVING MY BIG MACWORLD KEYNOTE TOMORROW AND I'VE FORGOTTEN EXACTLY WHAT ULTRA-TOP-SECRET NEW PRODUCTS I'LL BE INTRODUCING.
I NEED YOU TO SHOW THEM TO ME. AND BE DISCREET... THE INTERNET'S SPIES ARE EVERYWHERE.
AMEND
I COULD START BY SHOWING YOU THE DOOR.
EXCELLENT. WOULD THIS BE AN iDOOR OR A POWERDOOR?

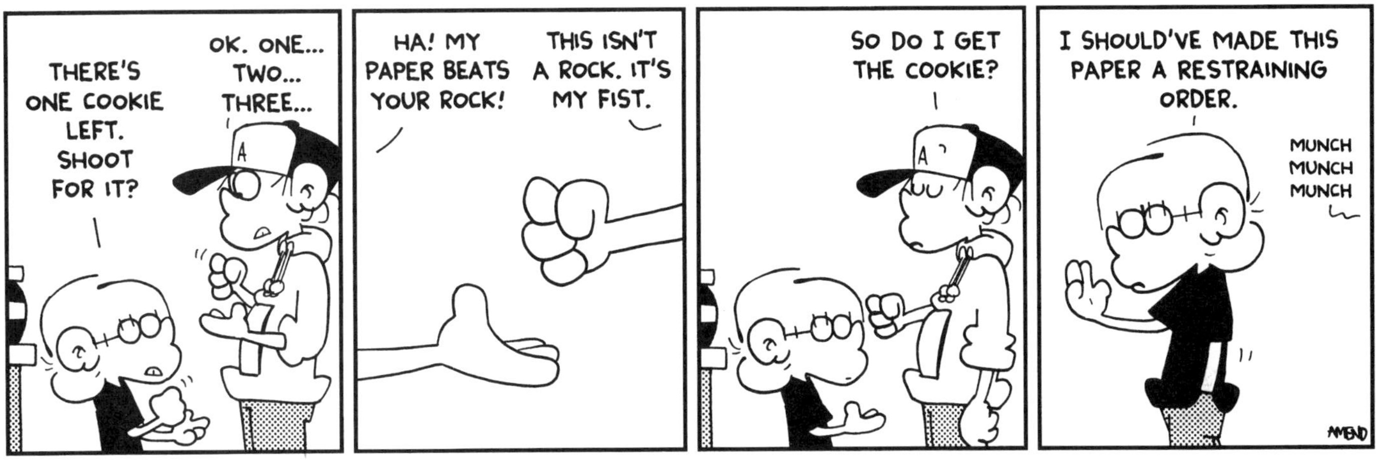
THERE'S ONE COOKIE LEFT. SHOOT FOR IT?
OK. ONE... TWO... THREE...
HA! MY PAPER BEATS YOUR ROCK!
THIS ISN'T A ROCK. IT'S MY FIST.
SO DO I GET THE COOKIE?
I SHOULD'VE MADE THIS PAPER A RESTRAINING ORDER.
MUNCH
MUNCH
MUNCH
AMEND

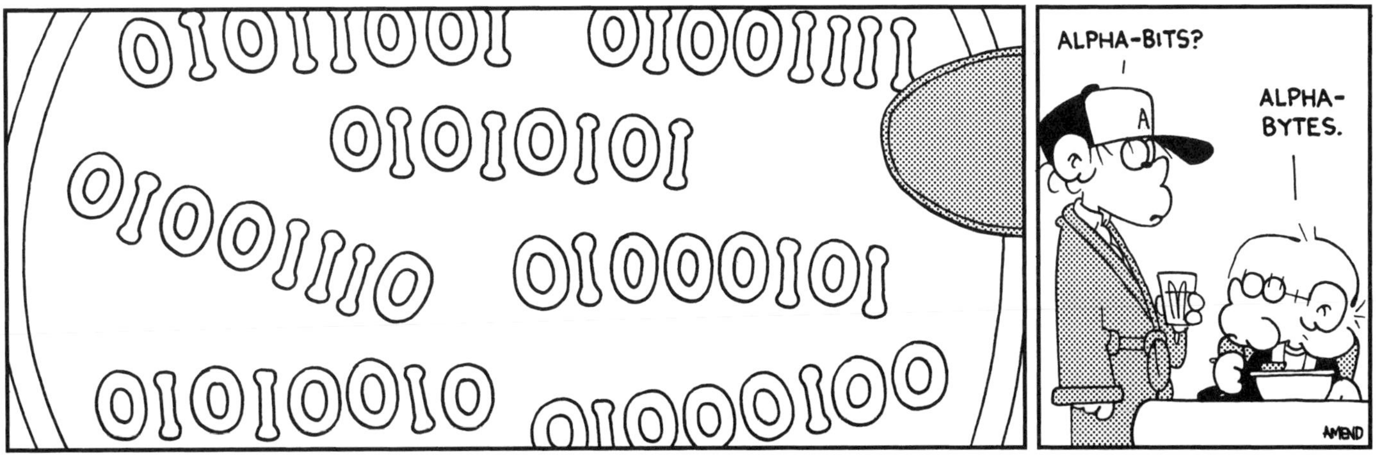
01011001 01001111
01010101
01001110 01000101
01010010 01000100
ALPHA-BITS?
ALPHA-BYTES.
AMEND

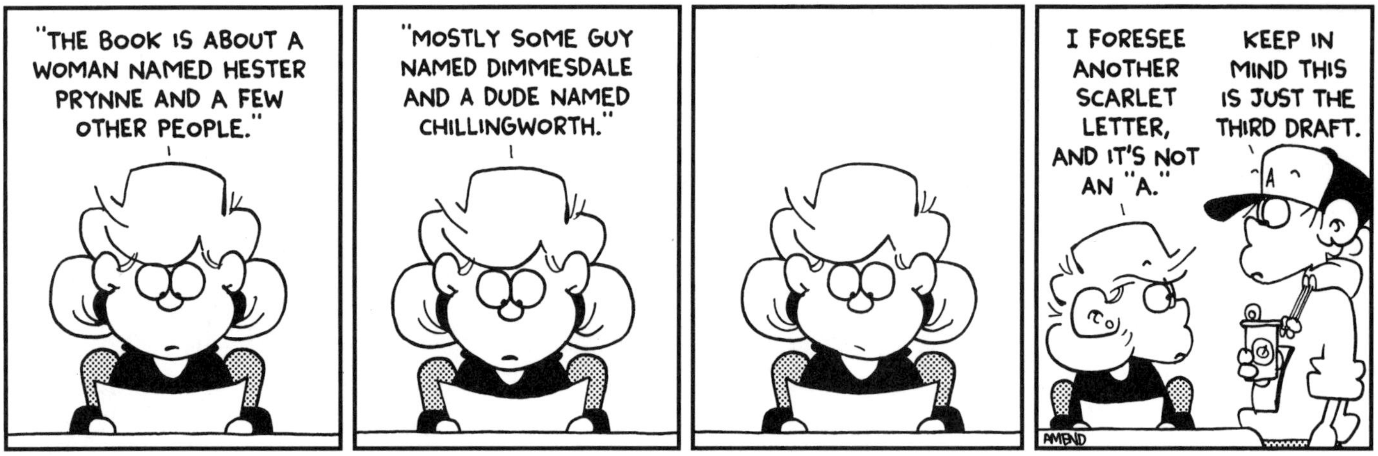
"THE BOOK IS ABOUT A WOMAN NAMED HESTER PRYNNE AND A FEW OTHER PEOPLE."
"MOSTLY SOME GUY NAMED DIMMESDALE AND A DUDE NAMED CHILLINGWORTH."
I FORESEE ANOTHER SCARLET LETTER, AND IT'S NOT AN "A."
KEEP IN MIND THIS IS JUST THE THIRD DRAFT.

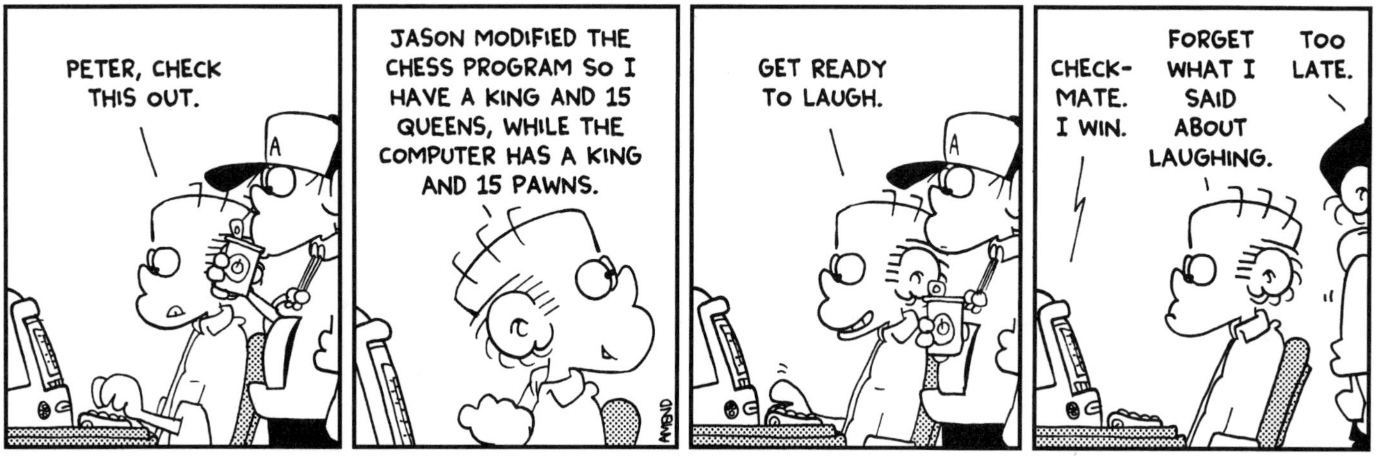
PETER, CHECK THIS OUT.
JASON MODIFIED THE CHESS PROGRAM SO I HAVE A KING AND 15 QUEENS, WHILE THE COMPUTER HAS A KING AND 15 PAWNS.
GET READY TO LAUGH.
CHECK-MATE. I WIN.
FORGET WHAT I SAID ABOUT LAUGHING.
TOO LATE.

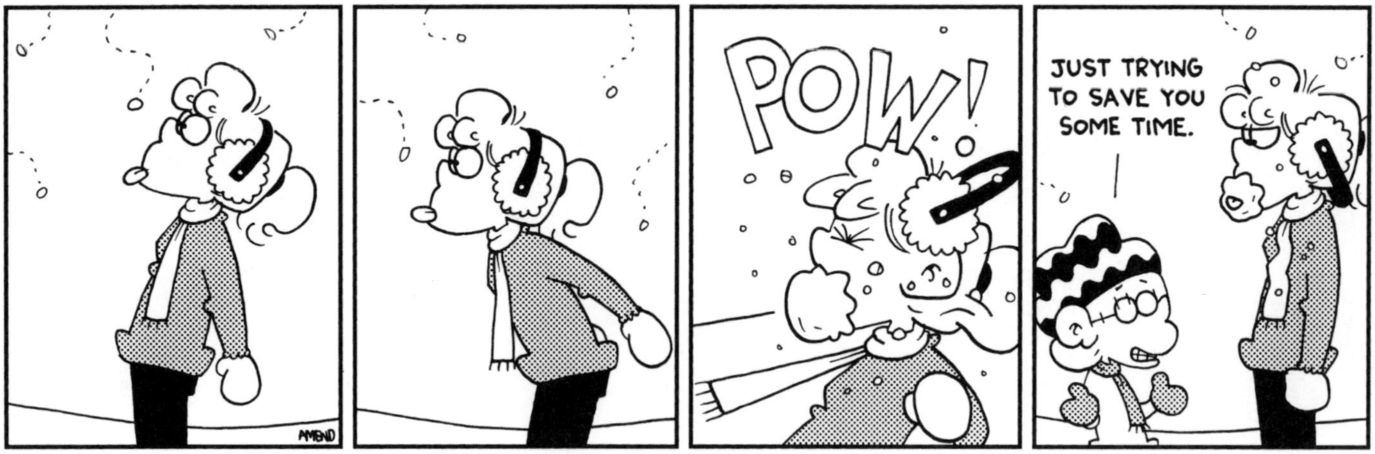
POW!
JUST TRYING TO SAVE YOU SOME TIME.

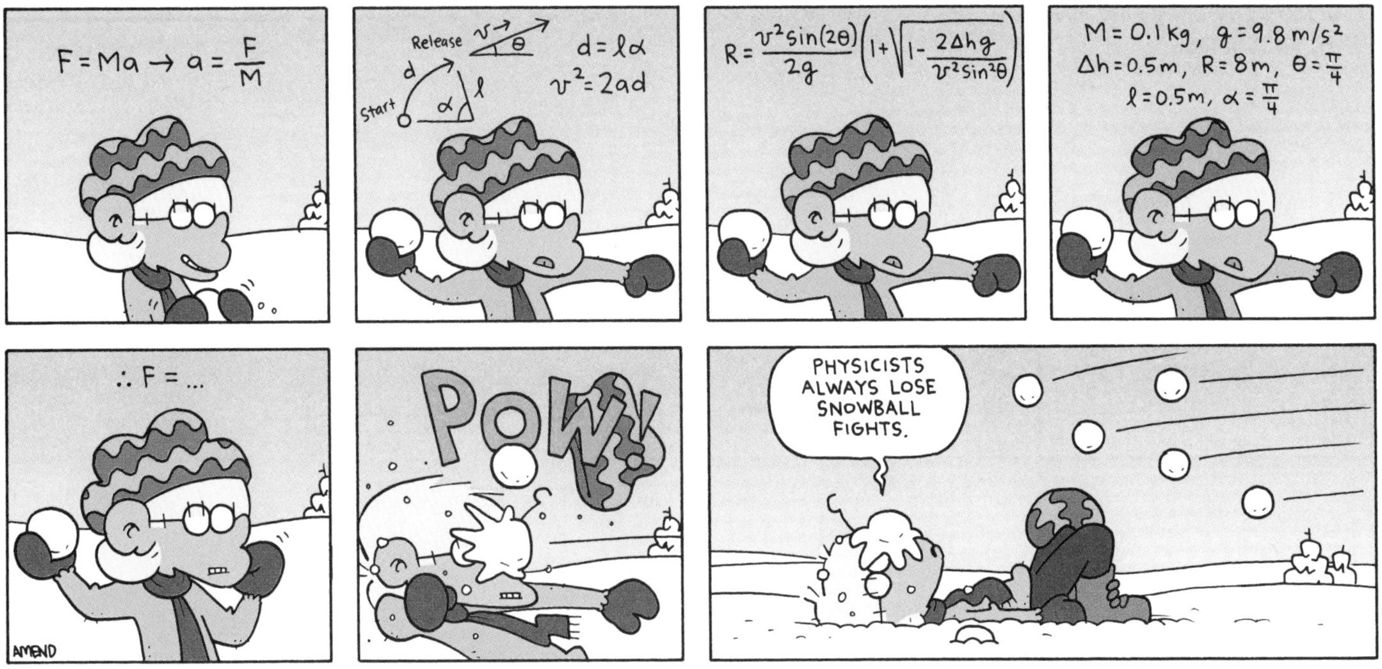
$F = Ma \rightarrow a = \frac{F}{M}$
Release
Start
$d = \ell\alpha$
$v^2 = 2ad$
$R = \frac{v^2 \sin(2\theta)}{2g}\left(1 + \sqrt{1 - \frac{2\Delta h g}{v^2 \sin^2\theta}}\right)$
$M = 0.1\,kg,\ g = 9.8\,m/s^2$
$\Delta h = 0.5\,m,\ R = 8\,m,\ \theta = \frac{\pi}{4}$
$\ell = 0.5\,m,\ \alpha = \frac{\pi}{4}$
$\therefore F = \ldots$
AMEND
POW!
PHYSICISTS ALWAYS LOSE SNOWBALL FIGHTS.

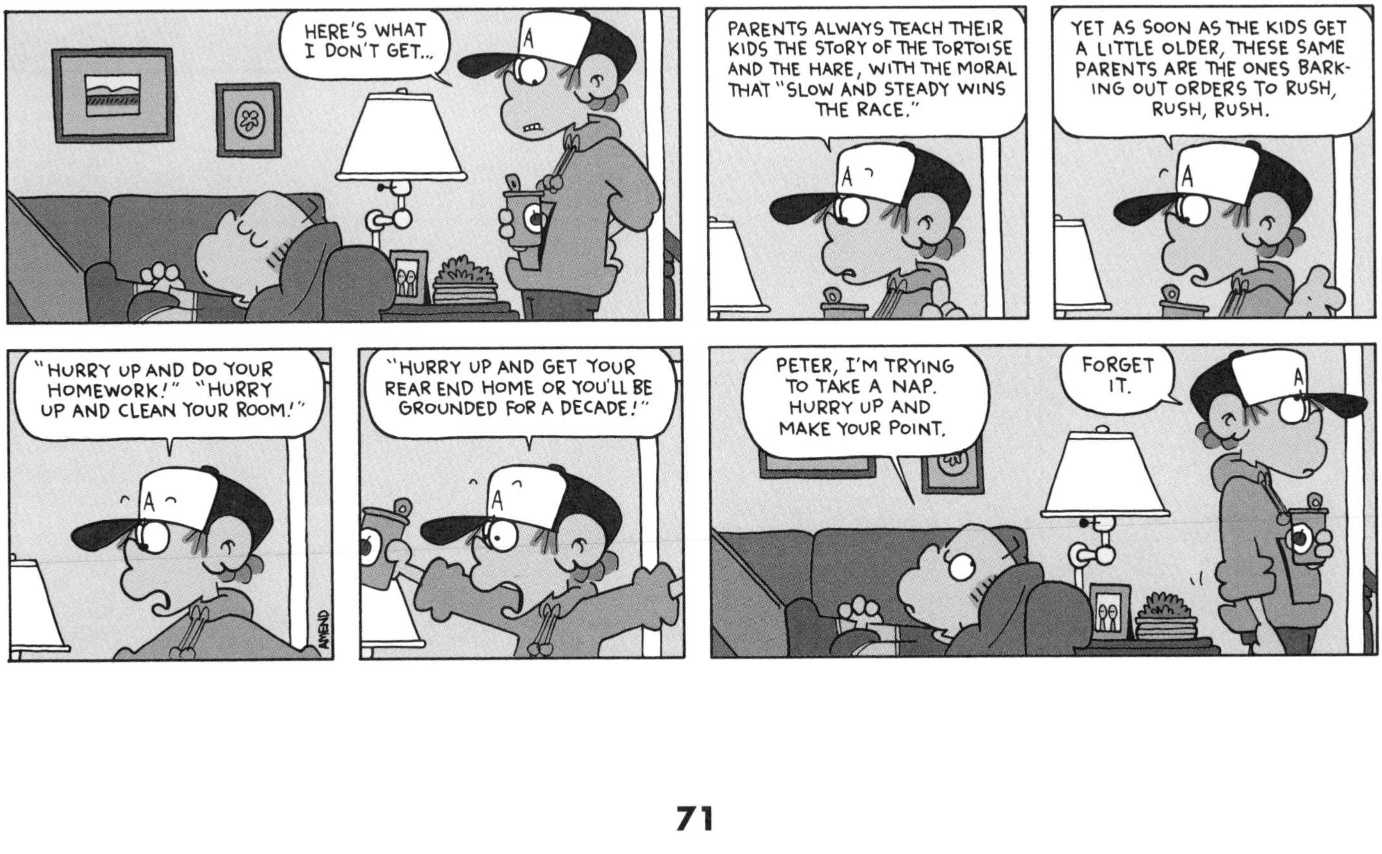
HERE'S WHAT I DON'T GET...
PARENTS ALWAYS TEACH THEIR KIDS THE STORY OF THE TORTOISE AND THE HARE, WITH THE MORAL THAT "SLOW AND STEADY WINS THE RACE."
YET AS SOON AS THE KIDS GET A LITTLE OLDER, THESE SAME PARENTS ARE THE ONES BARK-ING OUT ORDERS TO RUSH, RUSH, RUSH.
"HURRY UP AND DO YOUR HOMEWORK!" "HURRY UP AND CLEAN YOUR ROOM!"
AMEND
"HURRY UP AND GET YOUR REAR END HOME OR YOU'LL BE GROUNDED FOR A DECADE!"
PETER, I'M TRYING TO TAKE A NAP. HURRY UP AND MAKE YOUR POINT.
FORGET IT.

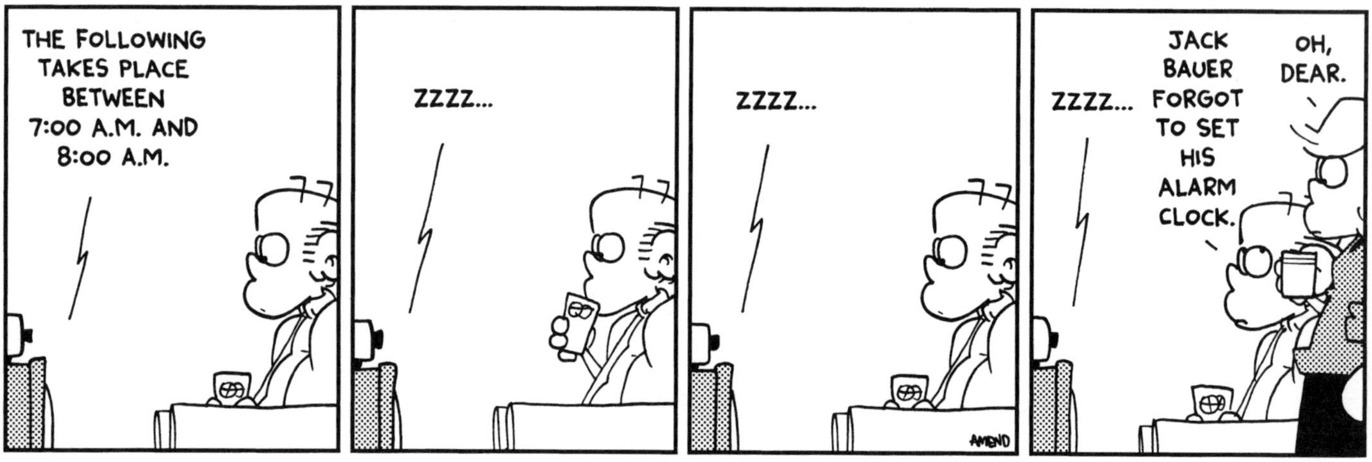
THE FOLLOWING TAKES PLACE BETWEEN 7:00 A.M. AND 8:00 A.M.
ZZZZ...
ZZZZ...
ZZZZ...
JACK BAUER FORGOT TO SET HIS ALARM CLOCK.
OH, DEAR.
AMEND

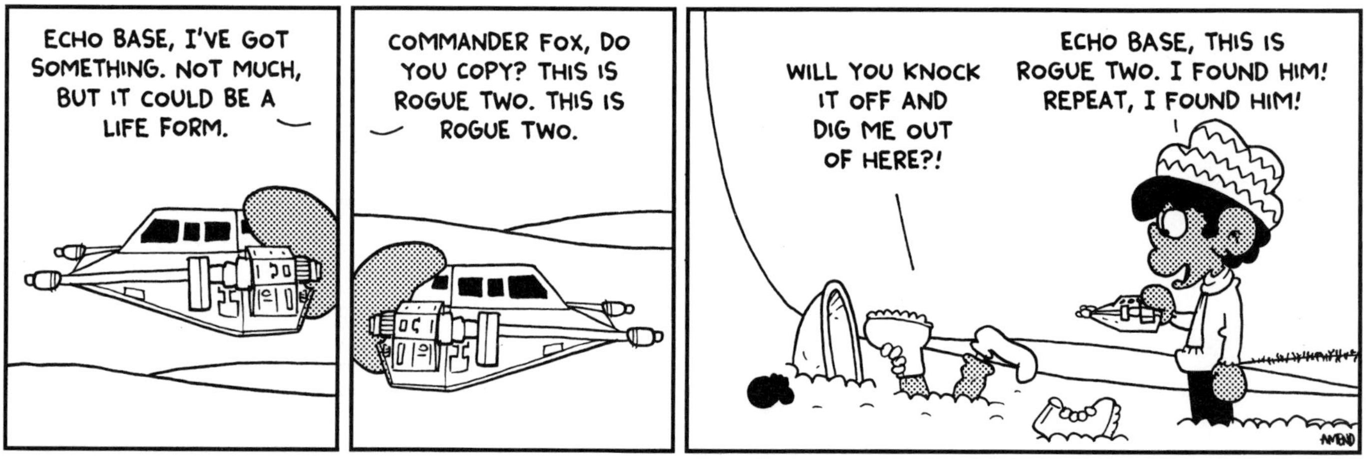
ECHO BASE, I'VE GOT SOMETHING. NOT MUCH, BUT IT COULD BE A LIFE FORM.
COMMANDER FOX, DO YOU COPY? THIS IS ROGUE TWO. THIS IS ROGUE TWO.
ECHO BASE, THIS IS ROGUE TWO. I FOUND HIM! REPEAT, I FOUND HIM!
WILL YOU KNOCK IT OFF AND DIG ME OUT OF HERE?!
AMEND

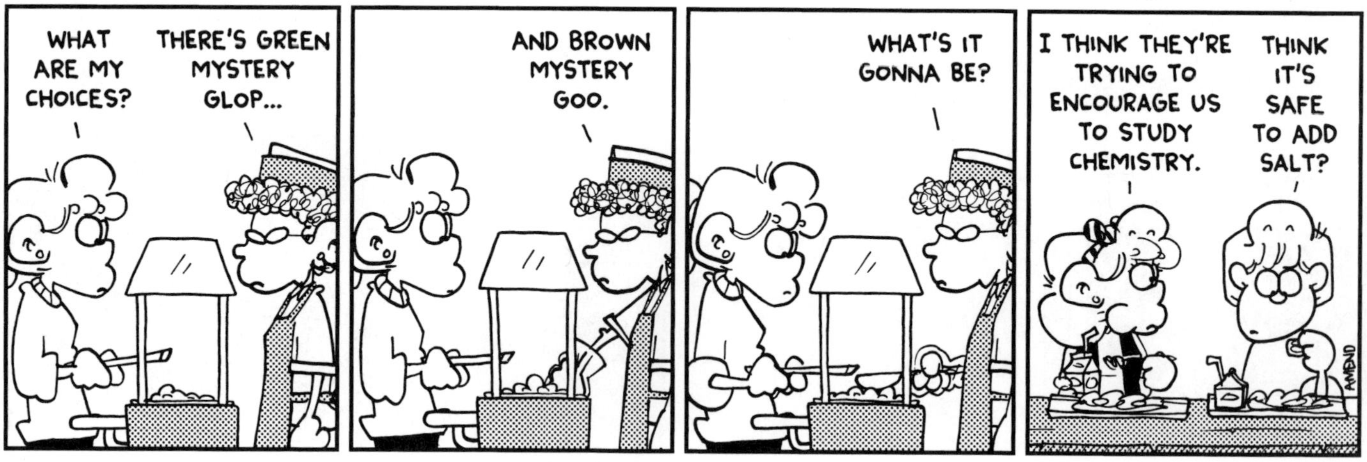
WHAT ARE MY CHOICES?
THERE'S GREEN MYSTERY GLOP...
AND BROWN MYSTERY GOO.
WHAT'S IT GONNA BE?
I THINK THEY'RE TRYING TO ENCOURAGE US TO STUDY CHEMISTRY.
THINK IT'S SAFE TO ADD SALT?
AMEND

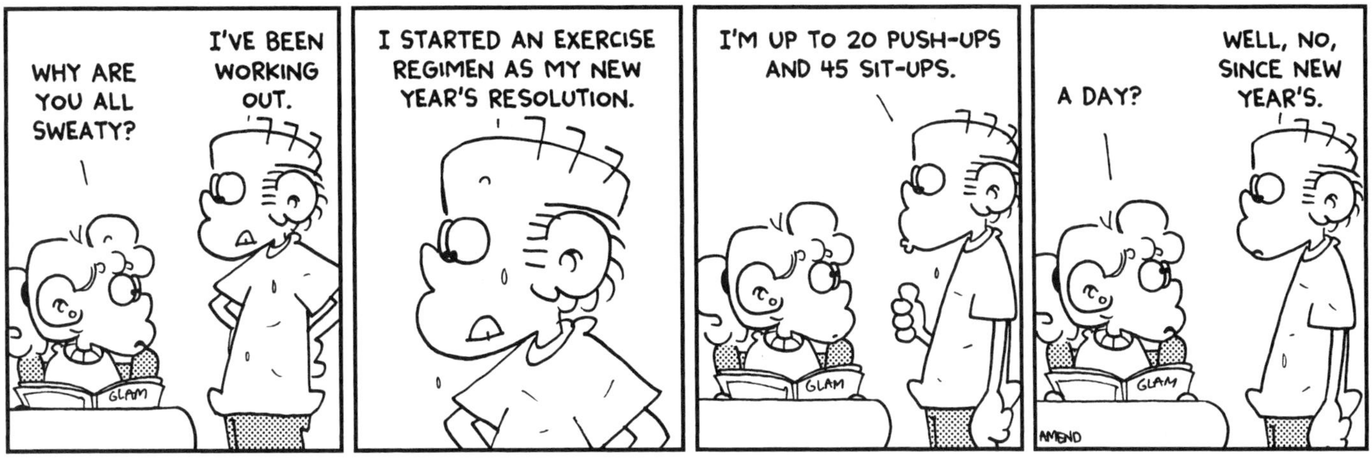
WHY ARE YOU ALL SWEATY?
I'VE BEEN WORKING OUT.
I STARTED AN EXERCISE REGIMEN AS MY NEW YEAR'S RESOLUTION.
I'M UP TO 20 PUSH-UPS AND 45 SIT-UPS.
A DAY?
WELL, NO, SINCE NEW YEAR'S.
GLAM
AMEND

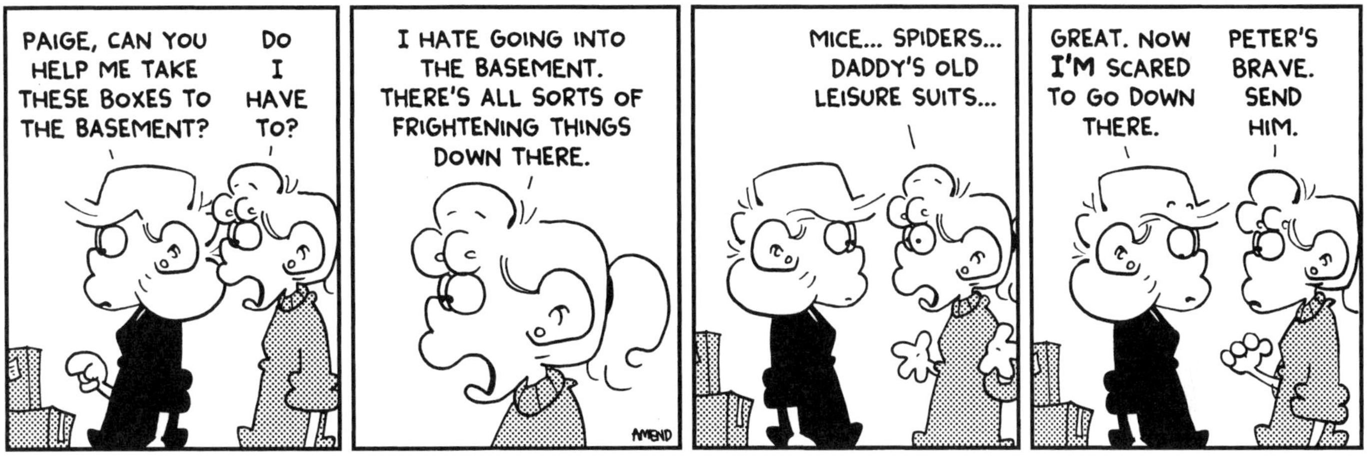
PAIGE, CAN YOU HELP ME TAKE THESE BOXES TO THE BASEMENT?
DO I HAVE TO?
I HATE GOING INTO THE BASEMENT. THERE'S ALL SORTS OF FRIGHTENING THINGS DOWN THERE.
MICE... SPIDERS... DADDY'S OLD LEISURE SUITS...
GREAT. NOW I'M SCARED TO GO DOWN THERE.
PETER'S BRAVE. SEND HIM.
AMEND

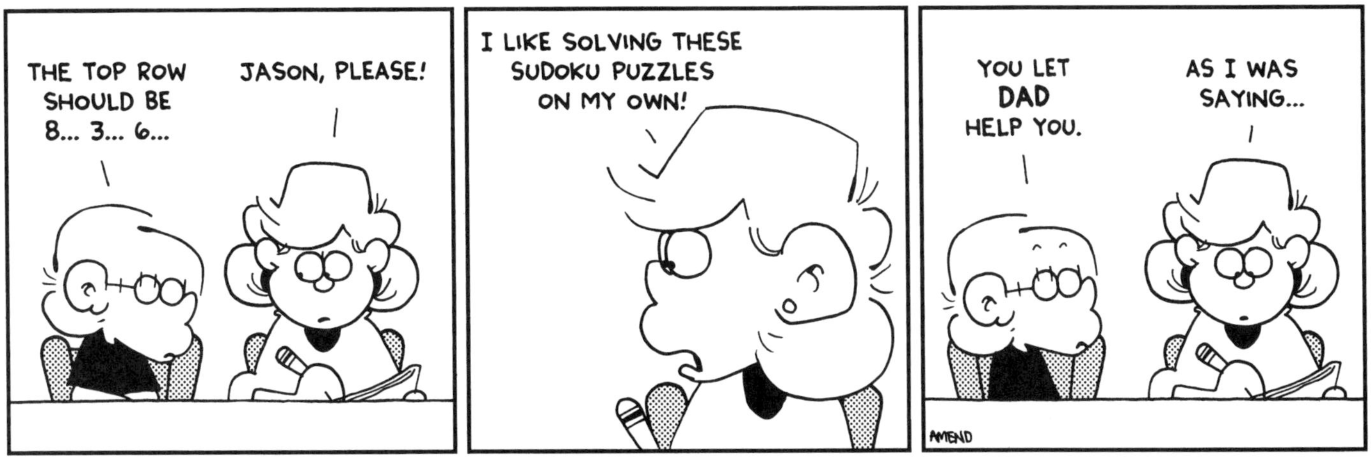
THE TOP ROW SHOULD BE 8... 3... 6...
JASON, PLEASE!
I LIKE SOLVING THESE SUDOKU PUZZLES ON MY OWN!
YOU LET DAD HELP YOU.
AS I WAS SAYING...
AMEND

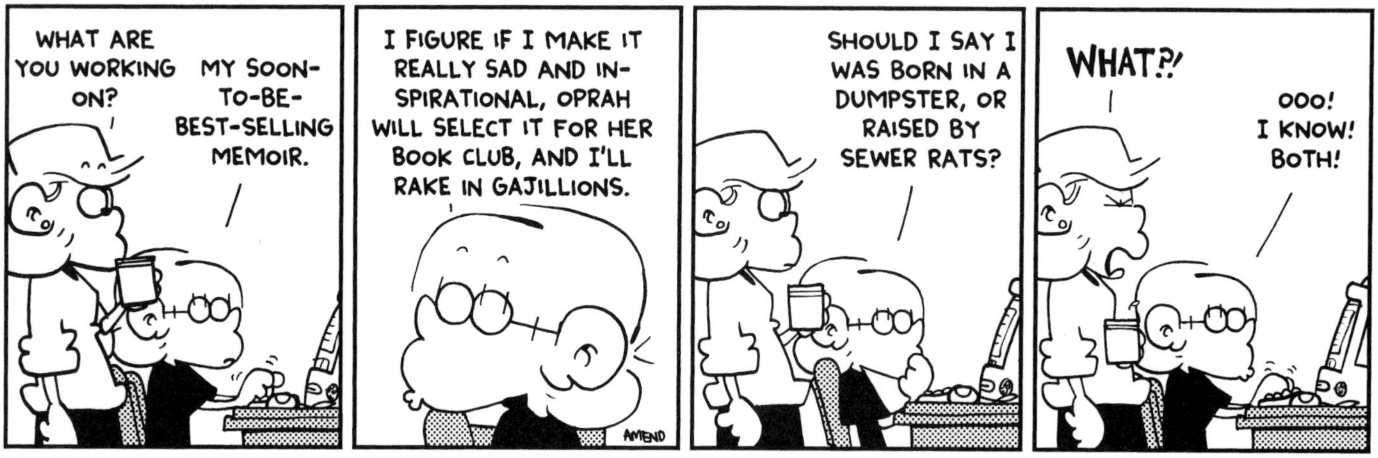
WHAT ARE YOU WORKING ON?
MY SOON-TO-BE-BEST-SELLING MEMOIR.
I FIGURE IF I MAKE IT REALLY SAD AND INSPIRATIONAL, OPRAH WILL SELECT IT FOR HER BOOK CLUB, AND I'LL RAKE IN GAJILLIONS.
AMEND
SHOULD I SAY I WAS BORN IN A DUMPSTER, OR RAISED BY SEWER RATS?
WHAT?!
OOO! I KNOW! BOTH!

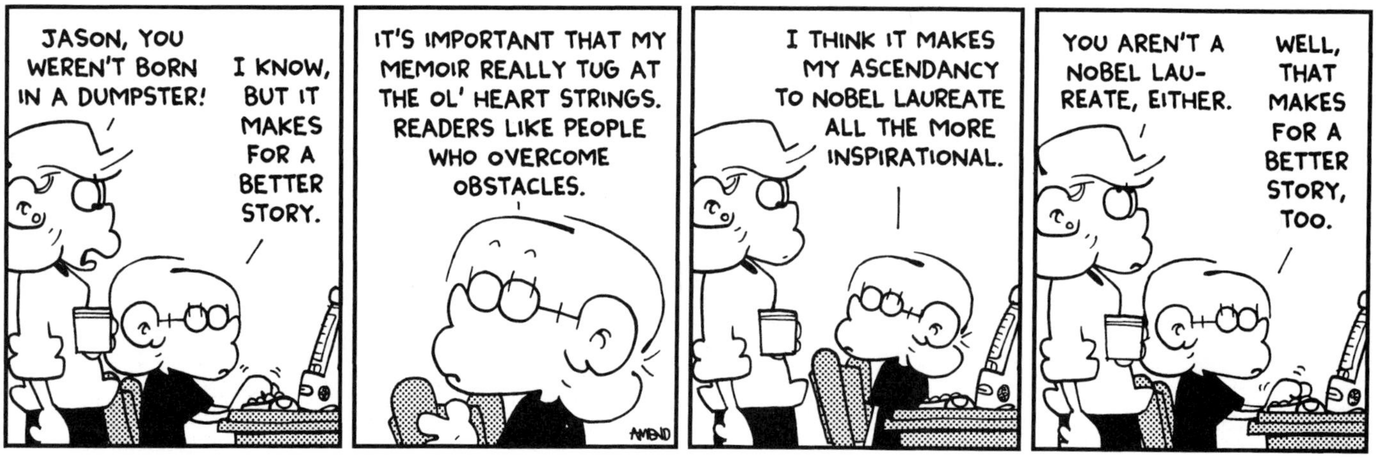
JASON, YOU WEREN'T BORN IN A DUMPSTER!
I KNOW, BUT IT MAKES FOR A BETTER STORY.
IT'S IMPORTANT THAT MY MEMOIR REALLY TUG AT THE OL' HEART STRINGS. READERS LIKE PEOPLE WHO OVERCOME OBSTACLES.
AMEND
I THINK IT MAKES MY ASCENDANCY TO NOBEL LAUREATE ALL THE MORE INSPIRATIONAL.
YOU AREN'T A NOBEL LAUREATE, EITHER.
WELL, THAT MAKES FOR A BETTER STORY, TOO.

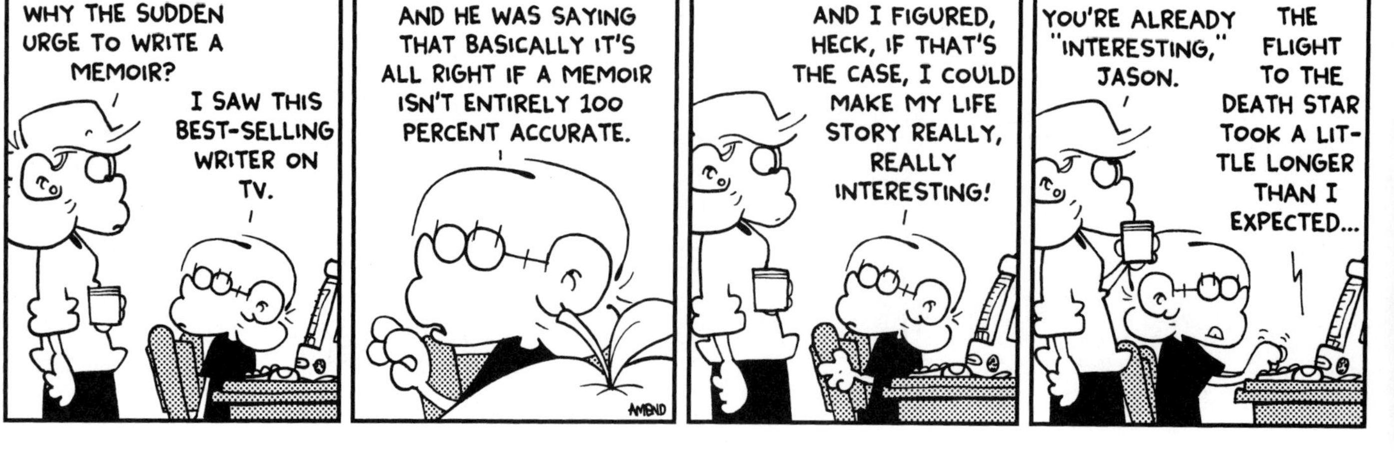
WHY THE SUDDEN URGE TO WRITE A MEMOIR?
I SAW THIS BEST-SELLING WRITER ON TV.
AND HE WAS SAYING THAT BASICALLY IT'S ALL RIGHT IF A MEMOIR ISN'T ENTIRELY 100 PERCENT ACCURATE.
AMEND
AND I FIGURED, HECK, IF THAT'S THE CASE, I COULD MAKE MY LIFE STORY REALLY, REALLY INTERESTING!
YOU'RE ALREADY "INTERESTING," JASON.
THE FLIGHT TO THE DEATH STAR TOOK A LITTLE LONGER THAN I EXPECTED...

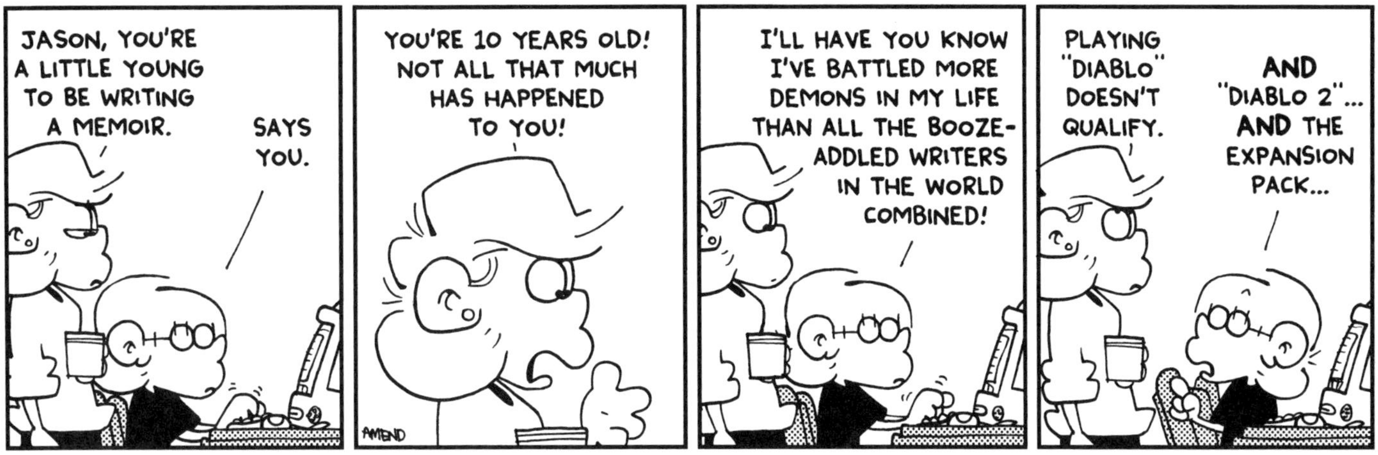
JASON, YOU'RE A LITTLE YOUNG TO BE WRITING A MEMOIR.
SAYS YOU.
YOU'RE 10 YEARS OLD! NOT ALL THAT MUCH HAS HAPPENED TO YOU!
AMEND
I'LL HAVE YOU KNOW I'VE BATTLED MORE DEMONS IN MY LIFE THAN ALL THE BOOZE-ADDLED WRITERS IN THE WORLD COMBINED!
PLAYING "DIABLO" DOESN'T QUALIFY.
AND "DIABLO 2"... AND THE EXPANSION PACK...

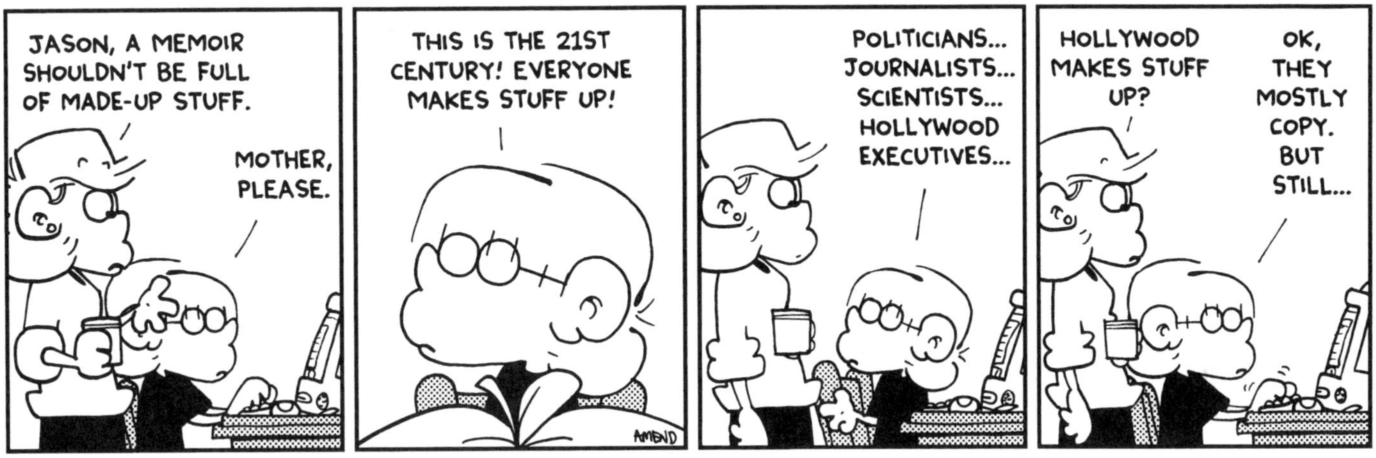
JASON, A MEMOIR SHOULDN'T BE FULL OF MADE-UP STUFF.
MOTHER, PLEASE.
THIS IS THE 21ST CENTURY! EVERYONE MAKES STUFF UP!
AMEND
POLITICIANS... JOURNALISTS... SCIENTISTS... HOLLYWOOD EXECUTIVES...
HOLLYWOOD MAKES STUFF UP?
OK, THEY MOSTLY COPY. BUT STILL...

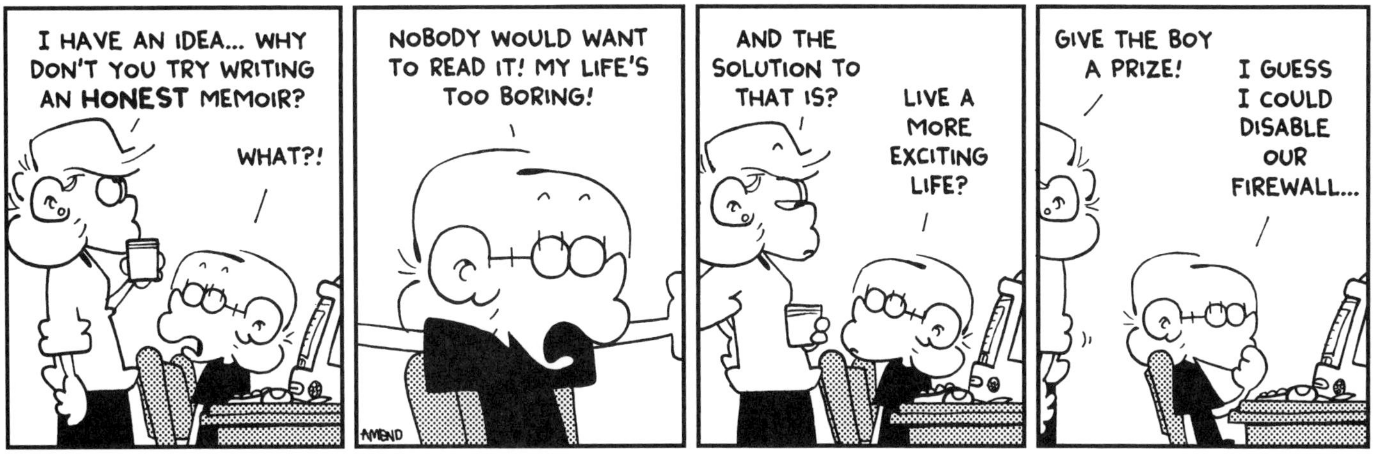
I HAVE AN IDEA... WHY DON'T YOU TRY WRITING AN HONEST MEMOIR?
WHAT?!
NOBODY WOULD WANT TO READ IT! MY LIFE'S TOO BORING!
AMEND
AND THE SOLUTION TO THAT IS?
LIVE A MORE EXCITING LIFE?
GIVE THE BOY A PRIZE!
I GUESS I COULD DISABLE OUR FIREWALL...

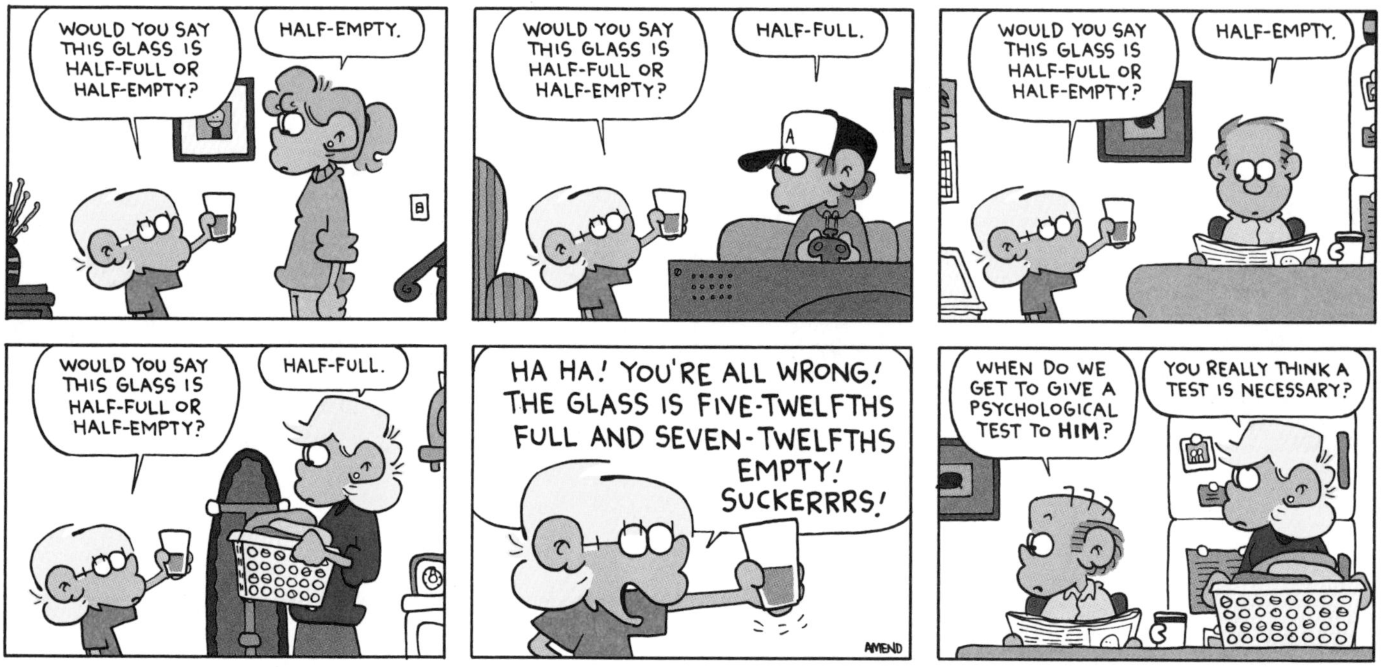
WOULD YOU SAY THIS GLASS IS HALF-FULL OR HALF-EMPTY?
HALF-EMPTY.
WOULD YOU SAY THIS GLASS IS HALF-FULL OR HALF-EMPTY?
HALF-FULL.
WOULD YOU SAY THIS GLASS IS HALF-FULL OR HALF-EMPTY?
HALF-EMPTY.
WOULD YOU SAY THIS GLASS IS HALF-FULL OR HALF-EMPTY?
HALF-FULL.
HA HA! YOU'RE ALL WRONG! THE GLASS IS FIVE-TWELFTHS FULL AND SEVEN-TWELFTHS EMPTY! SUCKERRRS!
AMEND
WHEN DO WE GET TO GIVE A PSYCHOLOGICAL TEST TO HIM?
YOU REALLY THINK A TEST IS NECESSARY?

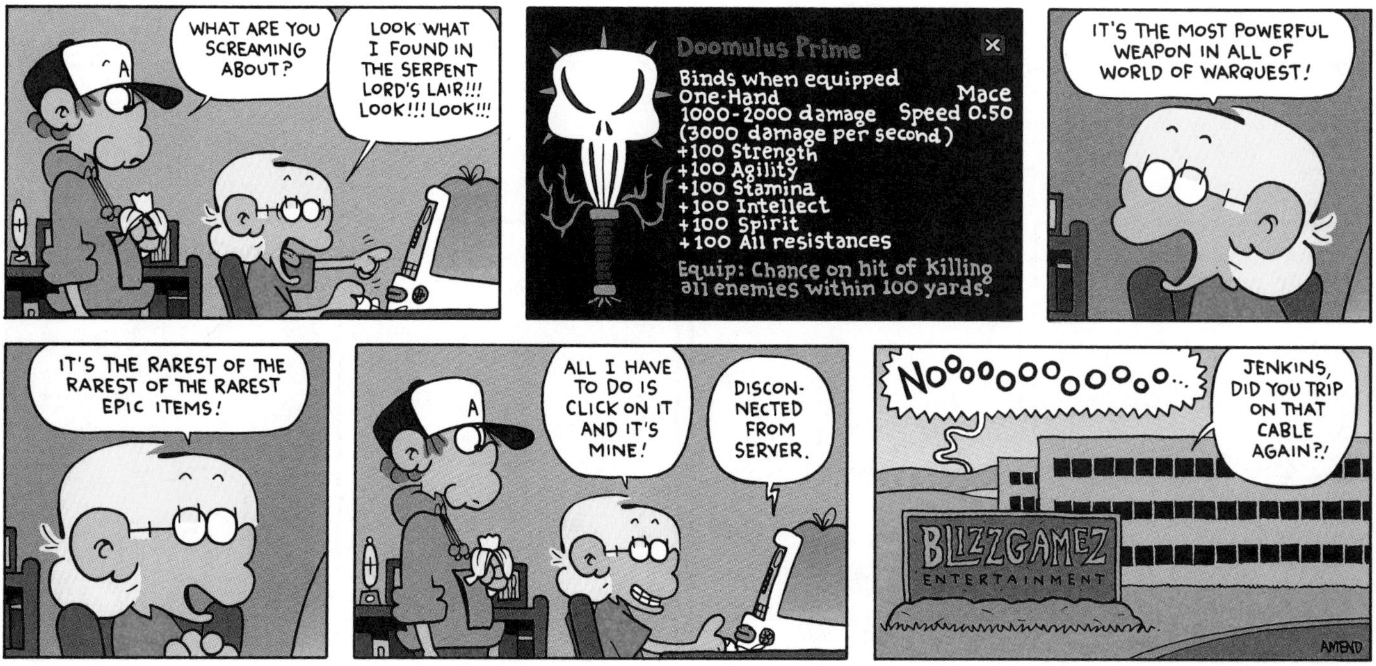
WHAT ARE YOU SCREAMING ABOUT?
LOOK WHAT I FOUND IN THE SERPENT LORD'S LAIR!!! LOOK!!! LOOK!!!
Doomulus Prime
Binds when equipped
One-Hand Mace
1000-2000 damage Speed 0.50
(3000 damage per second)
+100 Strength
+100 Agility
+100 Stamina
+100 Intellect
+100 Spirit
+100 All resistances
Equip: Chance on hit of killing all enemies within 100 yards.
IT'S THE MOST POWERFUL WEAPON IN ALL OF WORLD OF WARQUEST!
IT'S THE RAREST OF THE RAREST OF THE RAREST EPIC ITEMS!
ALL I HAVE TO DO IS CLICK ON IT AND IT'S MINE!
DISCONNECTED FROM SERVER.
NOOOOOOOOOOO...
JENKINS, DID YOU TRIP ON THAT CABLE AGAIN?!
BLIZZGAMEZ ENTERTAINMENT
AMEND

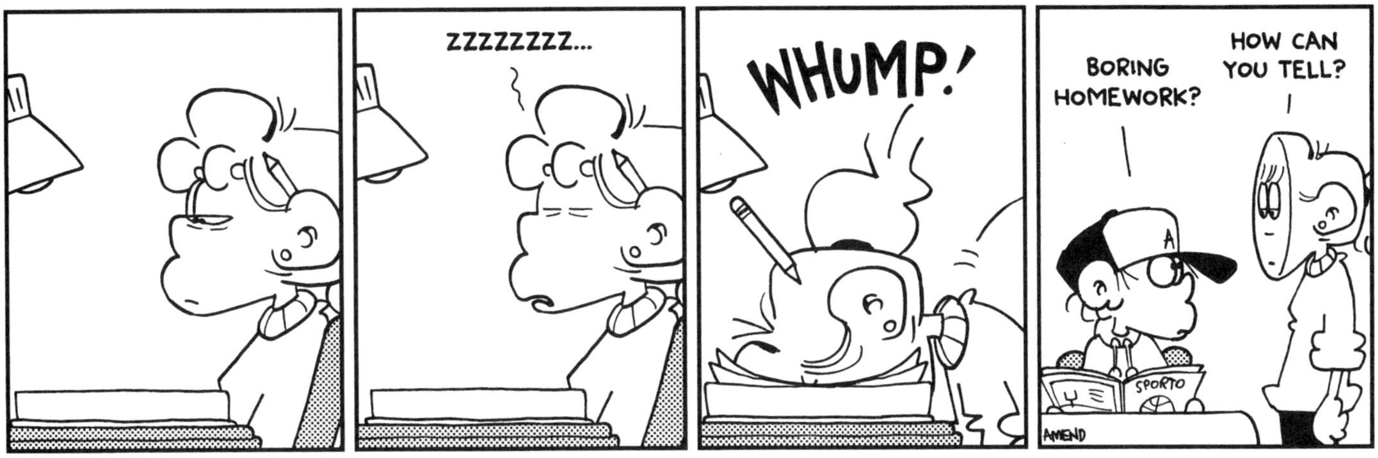
ZZZZZZZZ...
WHUMP!
BORING HOMEWORK?
HOW CAN YOU TELL?
SPORTO
AMEND

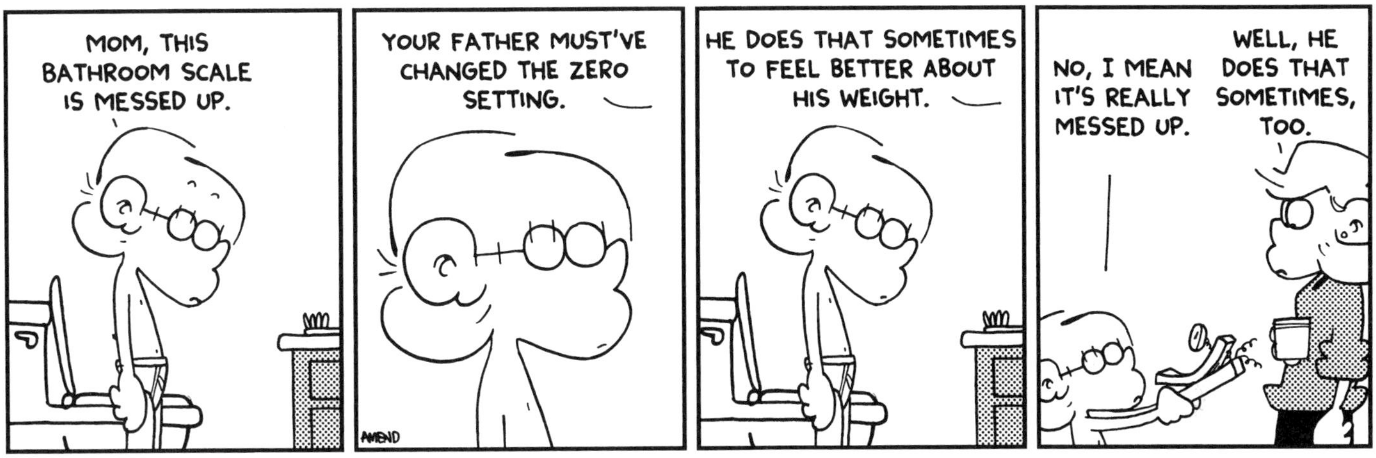
MOM, THIS BATHROOM SCALE IS MESSED UP.
YOUR FATHER MUST'VE CHANGED THE ZERO SETTING.
AMEND
HE DOES THAT SOMETIMES TO FEEL BETTER ABOUT HIS WEIGHT.
NO, I MEAN IT'S REALLY MESSED UP.
WELL, HE DOES THAT SOMETIMES, TOO.

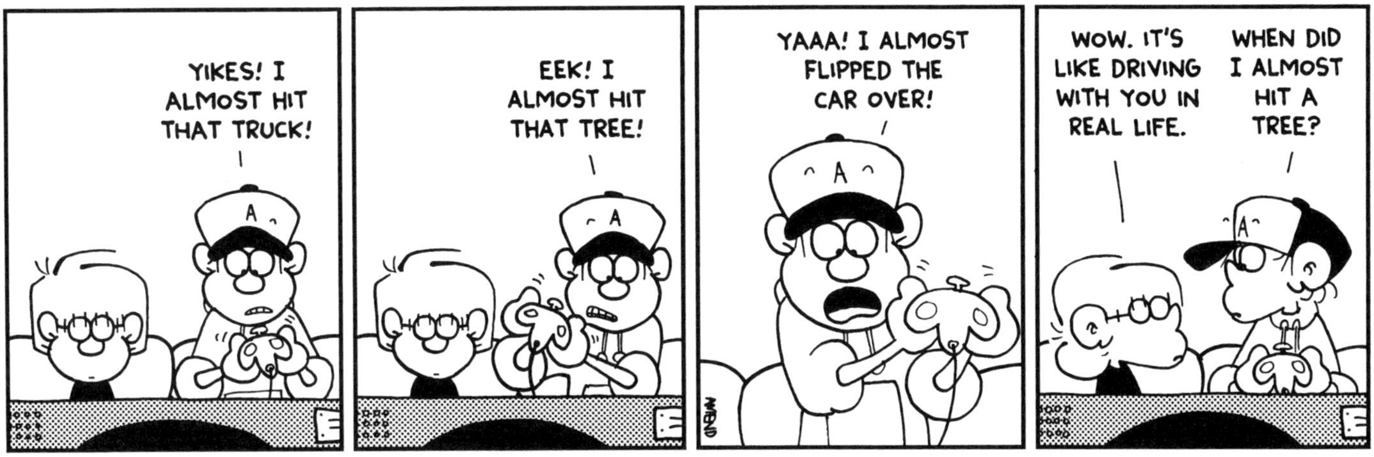
YIKES! I ALMOST HIT THAT TRUCK!
EEK! I ALMOST HIT THAT TREE!
YAAA! I ALMOST FLIPPED THE CAR OVER!
AMEND
WOW. IT'S LIKE DRIVING WITH YOU IN REAL LIFE.
WHEN DID I ALMOST HIT A TREE?

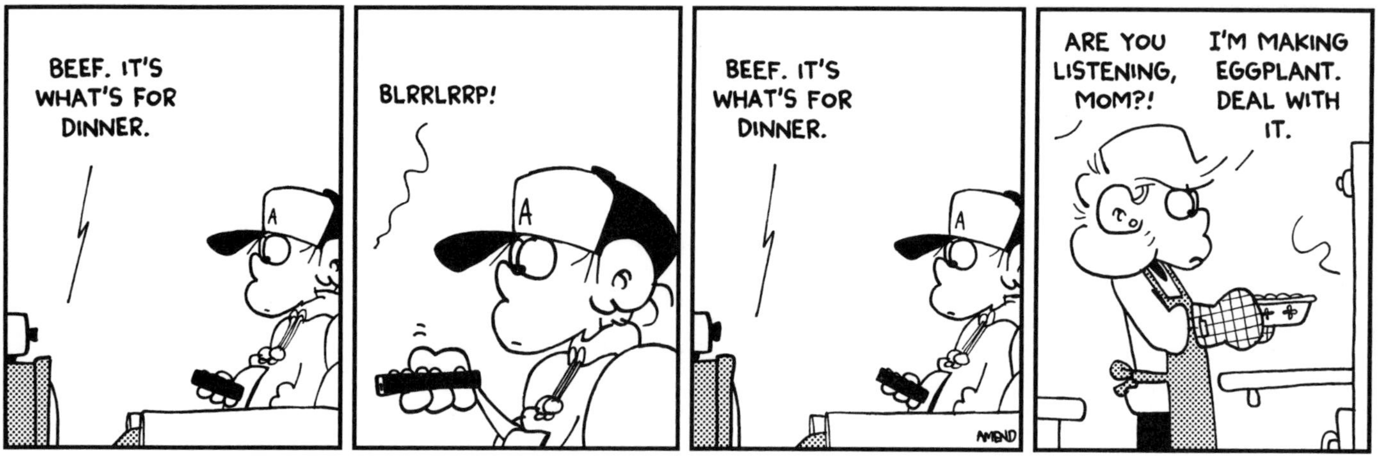
BEEF. IT'S WHAT'S FOR DINNER.
BLRRLRRP!
BEEF. IT'S WHAT'S FOR DINNER.
ARE YOU LISTENING, MOM?!
I'M MAKING EGGPLANT. DEAL WITH IT.

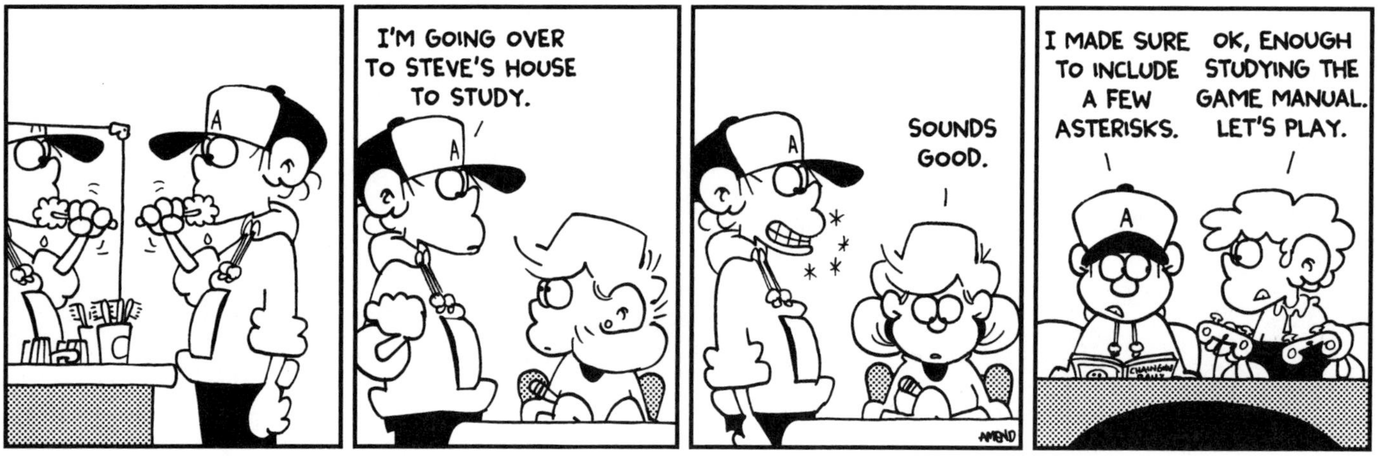
I'M GOING OVER TO STEVE'S HOUSE TO STUDY.
SOUNDS GOOD.
I MADE SURE TO INCLUDE A FEW ASTERISKS.
OK, ENOUGH STUDYING THE GAME MANUAL. LET'S PLAY.

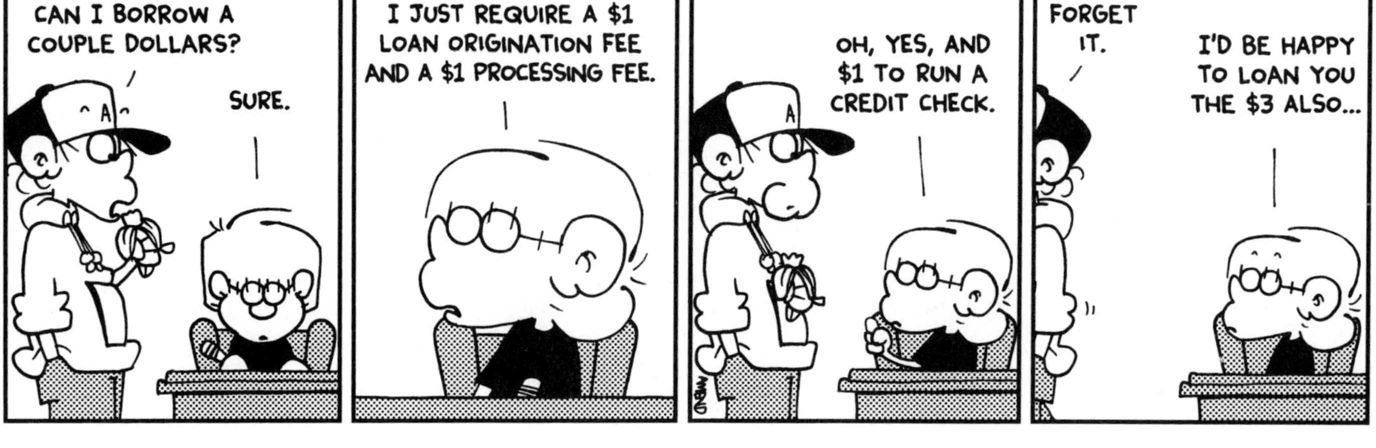
CAN I BORROW A COUPLE DOLLARS?
SURE.
I JUST REQUIRE A $1 LOAN ORIGINATION FEE AND A $1 PROCESSING FEE.
OH, YES, AND $1 TO RUN A CREDIT CHECK.
FORGET IT.
I'D BE HAPPY TO LOAN YOU THE $3 ALSO...

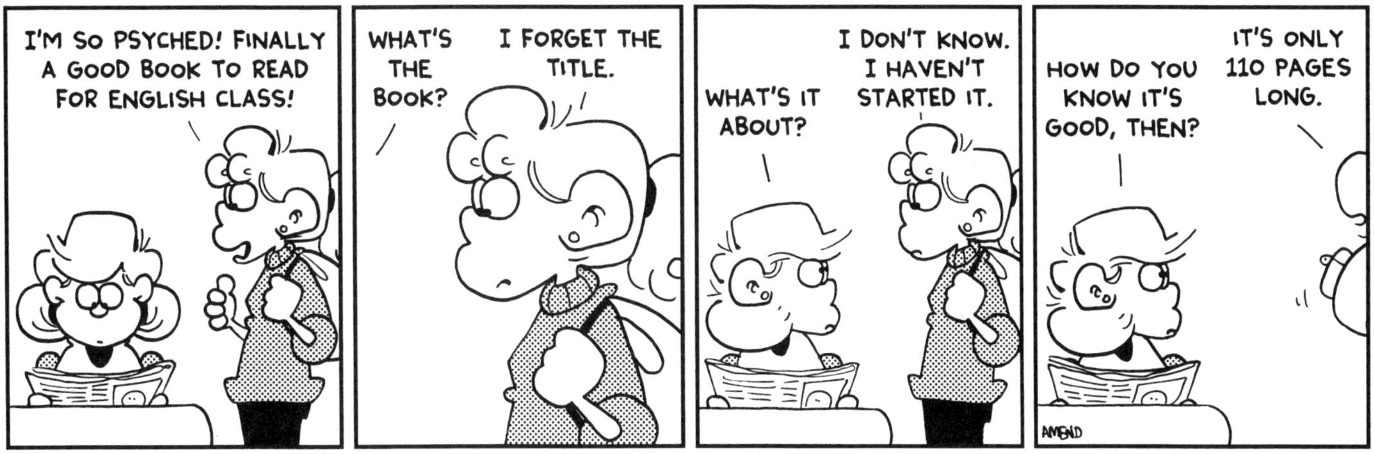
I'M SO PSYCHED! FINALLY A GOOD BOOK TO READ FOR ENGLISH CLASS!
WHAT'S THE BOOK?
I FORGET THE TITLE.
WHAT'S IT ABOUT?
I DON'T KNOW. I HAVEN'T STARTED IT.
HOW DO YOU KNOW IT'S GOOD, THEN?
IT'S ONLY 110 PAGES LONG.
AMEND

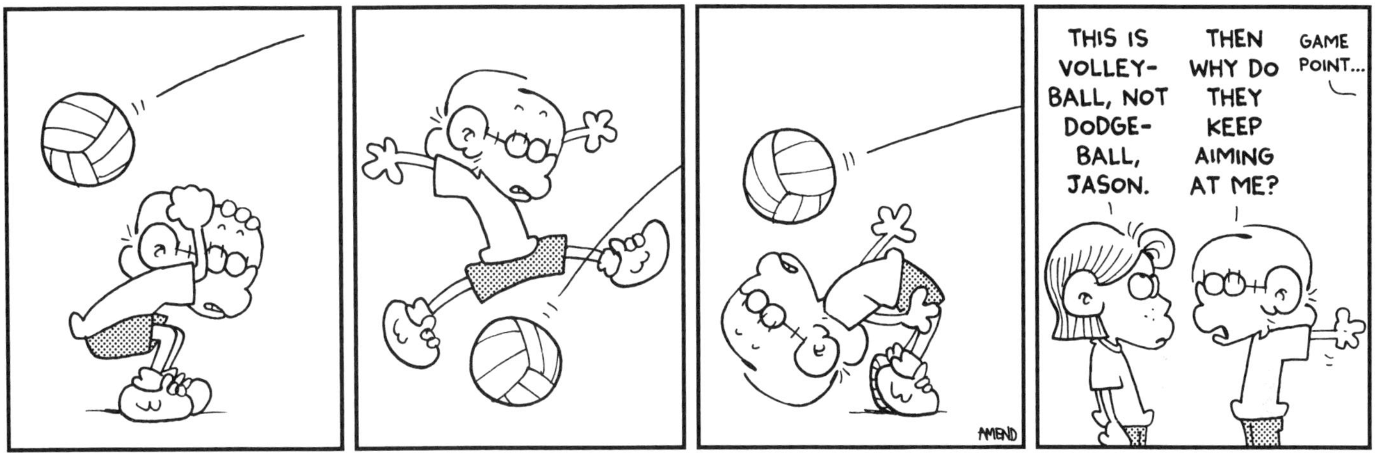
AMEND
THIS IS VOLLEY-BALL, NOT DODGE-BALL, JASON.
THEN WHY DO THEY KEEP AIMING AT ME?
GAME POINT...

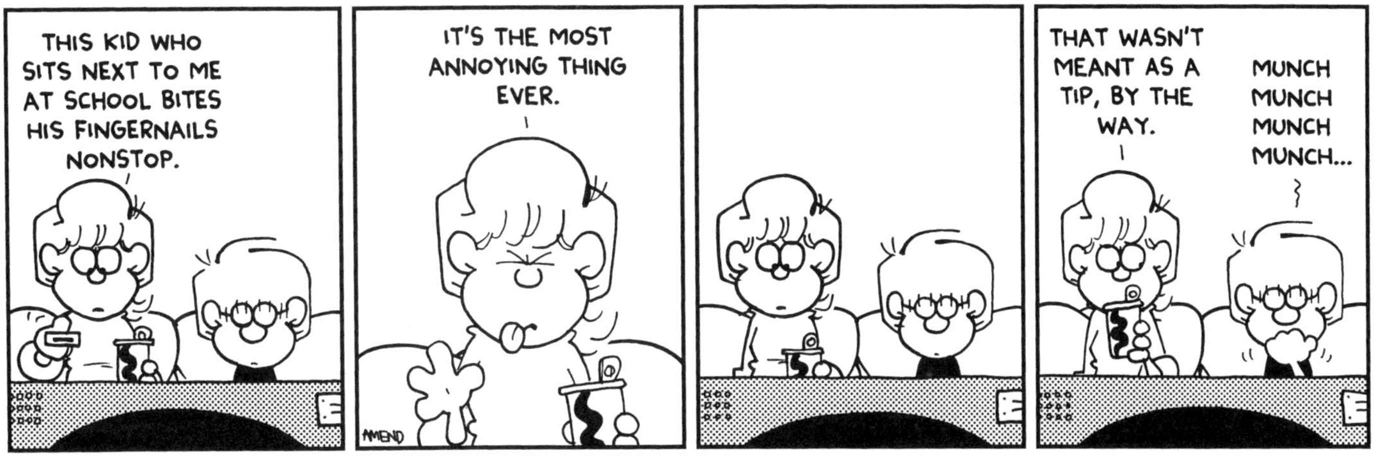
THIS KID WHO SITS NEXT TO ME AT SCHOOL BITES HIS FINGERNAILS NONSTOP.
IT'S THE MOST ANNOYING THING EVER.
AMEND
THAT WASN'T MEANT AS A TIP, BY THE WAY.
MUNCH MUNCH MUNCH MUNCH...

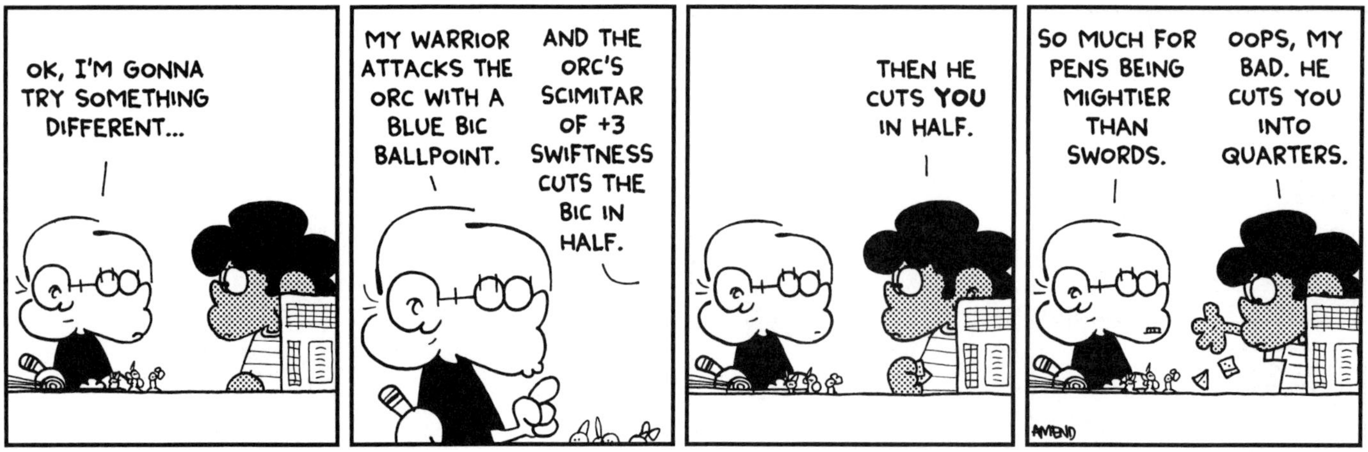
OK, I'M GONNA TRY SOMETHING DIFFERENT...
MY WARRIOR ATTACKS THE ORC WITH A BLUE BIC BALLPOINT.
AND THE ORC'S SCIMITAR OF +3 SWIFTNESS CUTS THE BIC IN HALF.
THEN HE CUTS YOU IN HALF.
SO MUCH FOR PENS BEING MIGHTIER THAN SWORDS.
OOPS, MY BAD. HE CUTS YOU INTO QUARTERS.
AMEND

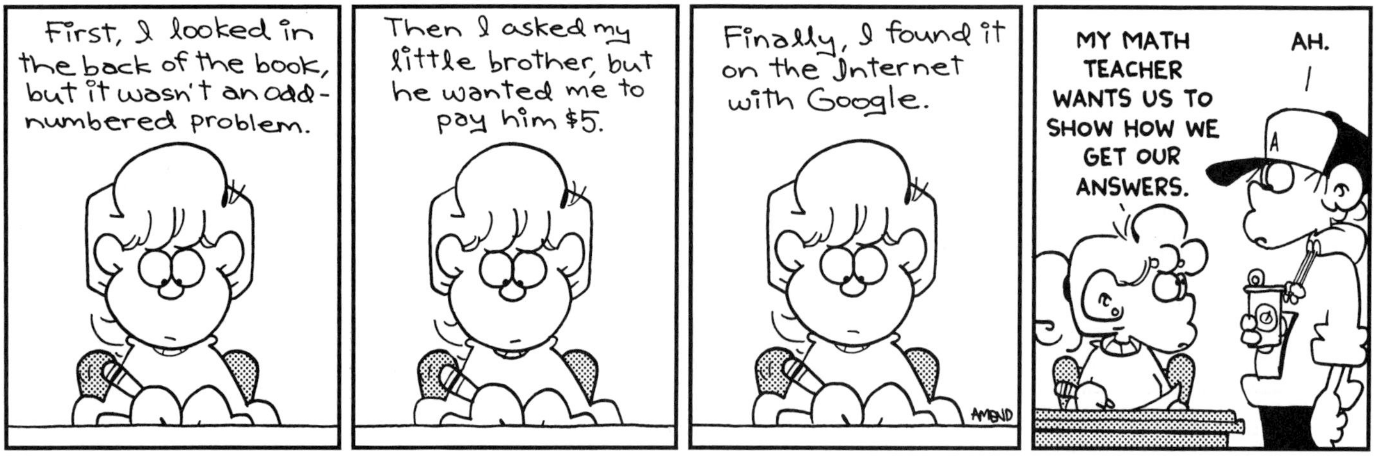
First, I looked in the back of the book, but it wasn't an odd-numbered problem.
Then I asked my little brother, but he wanted me to pay him $5.
Finally, I found it on the Internet with Google.
AMEND
MY MATH TEACHER WANTS US TO SHOW HOW WE GET OUR ANSWERS.
AH.

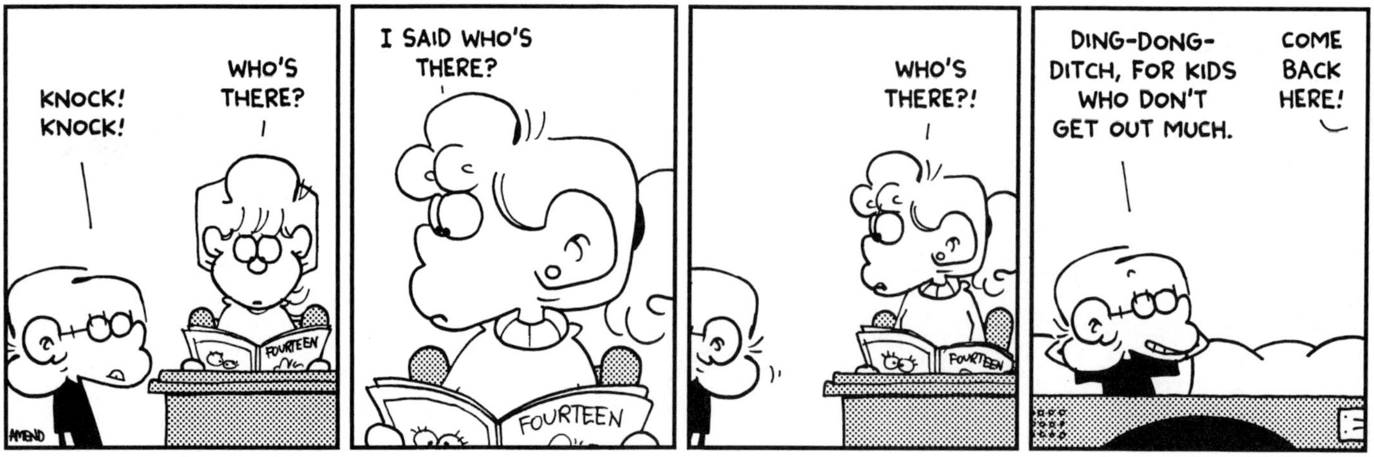
KNOCK! KNOCK!
WHO'S THERE?
AMEND
FOURTEEN
I SAID WHO'S THERE?
FOURTEEN
WHO'S THERE?!
FOURTEEN
DING-DONG-DITCH, FOR KIDS WHO DON'T GET OUT MUCH.
COME BACK HERE!

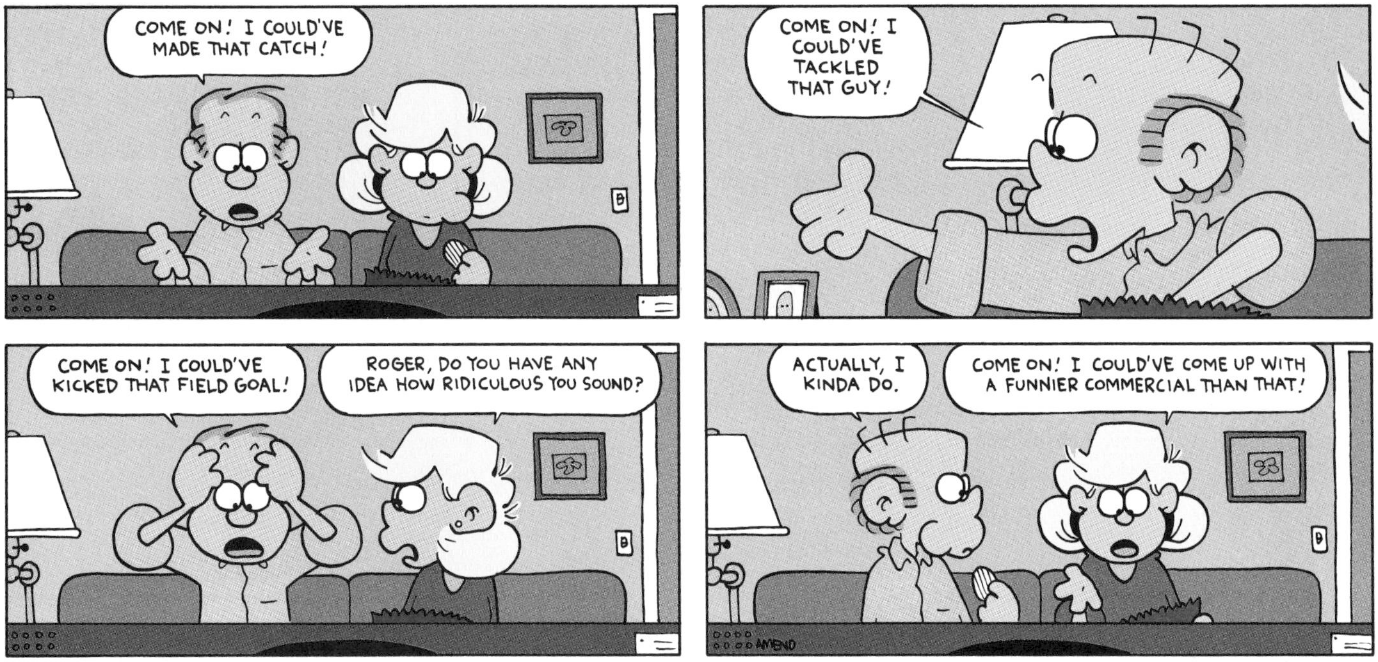
COME ON! I COULD'VE MADE THAT CATCH!
COME ON! I COULD'VE TACKLED THAT GUY!
COME ON! I COULD'VE KICKED THAT FIELD GOAL!
ROGER, DO YOU HAVE ANY IDEA HOW RIDICULOUS YOU SOUND?
ACTUALLY, I KINDA DO.
COME ON! I COULD'VE COME UP WITH A FUNNIER COMMERCIAL THAN THAT!
AMEND

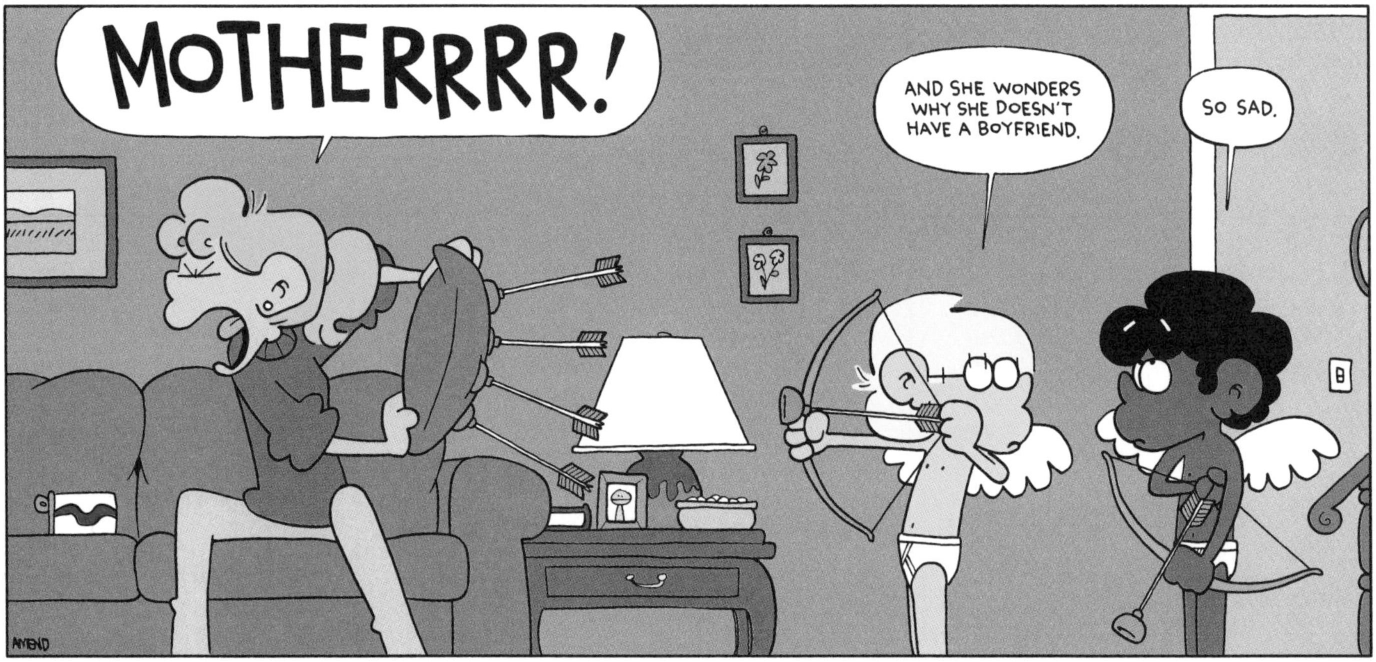
MOTHERRRR!
AND SHE WONDERS WHY SHE DOESN'T HAVE A BOYFRIEND.
SO SAD.
AMEND

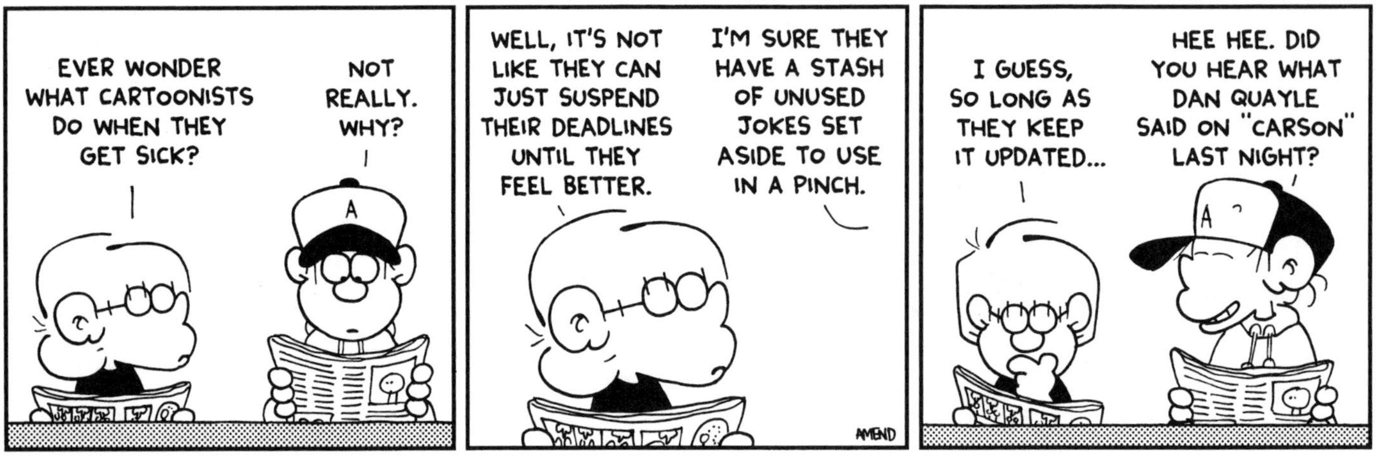
EVER WONDER WHAT CARTOONISTS DO WHEN THEY GET SICK?
NOT REALLY. WHY?
WELL, IT'S NOT LIKE THEY CAN JUST SUSPEND THEIR DEADLINES UNTIL THEY FEEL BETTER.
I'M SURE THEY HAVE A STASH OF UNUSED JOKES SET ASIDE TO USE IN A PINCH.
AMEND
I GUESS, SO LONG AS THEY KEEP IT UPDATED...
HEE HEE. DID YOU HEAR WHAT DAN QUAYLE SAID ON "CARSON" LAST NIGHT?

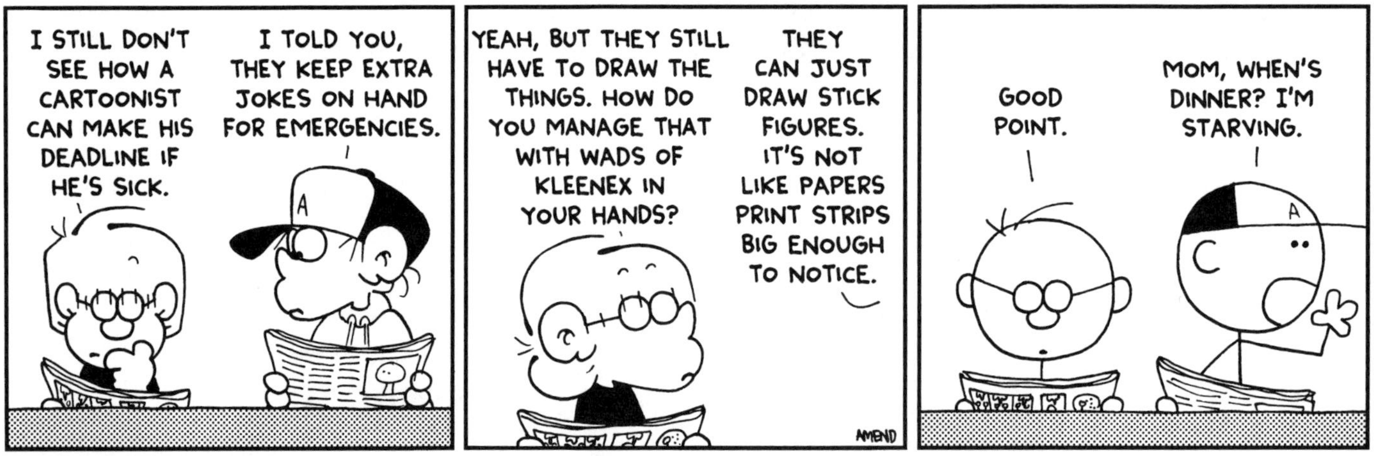
I STILL DON'T SEE HOW A CARTOONIST CAN MAKE HIS DEADLINE IF HE'S SICK.
I TOLD YOU, THEY KEEP EXTRA JOKES ON HAND FOR EMERGENCIES.
YEAH, BUT THEY STILL HAVE TO DRAW THE THINGS. HOW DO YOU MANAGE THAT WITH WADS OF KLEENEX IN YOUR HANDS?
THEY CAN JUST DRAW STICK FIGURES. IT'S NOT LIKE PAPERS PRINT STRIPS BIG ENOUGH TO NOTICE.
AMEND
GOOD POINT.
MOM, WHEN'S DINNER? I'M STARVING.

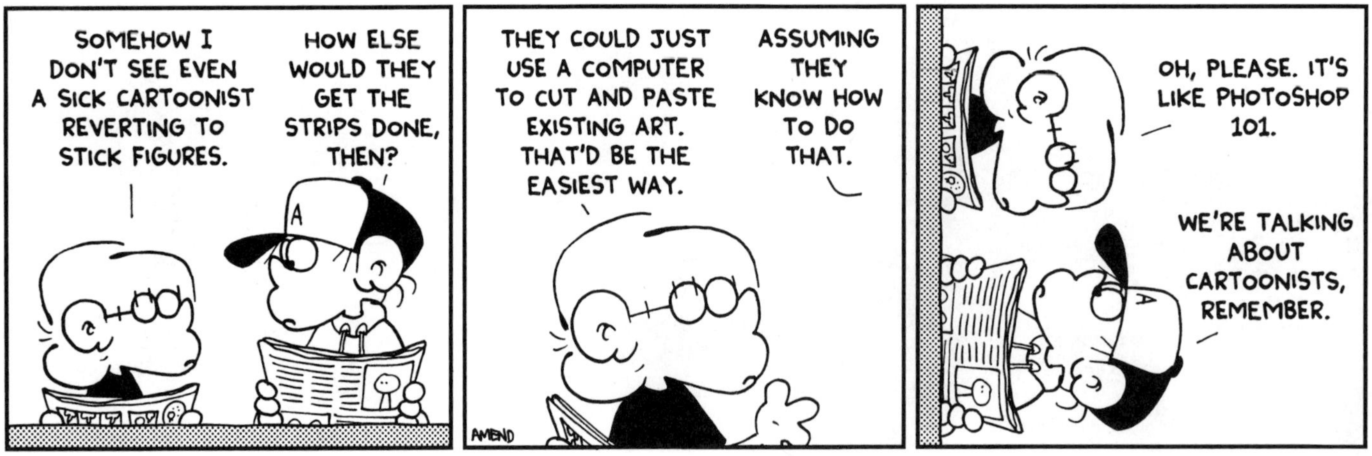
SOMEHOW I DON'T SEE EVEN A SICK CARTOONIST REVERTING TO STICK FIGURES.
HOW ELSE WOULD THEY GET THE STRIPS DONE, THEN?
THEY COULD JUST USE A COMPUTER TO CUT AND PASTE EXISTING ART. THAT'D BE THE EASIEST WAY.
ASSUMING THEY KNOW HOW TO DO THAT.
AMEND
OH, PLEASE. IT'S LIKE PHOTOSHOP 101.
WE'RE TALKING ABOUT CARTOONISTS, REMEMBER.

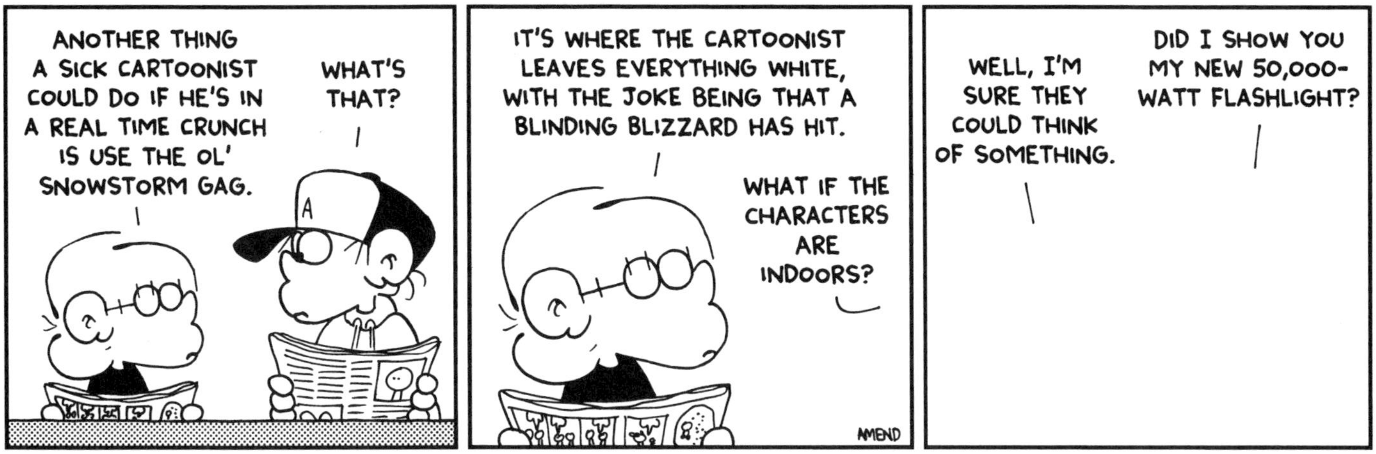
ANOTHER THING A SICK CARTOONIST COULD DO IF HE'S IN A REAL TIME CRUNCH IS USE THE OL' SNOWSTORM GAG.
WHAT'S THAT?
IT'S WHERE THE CARTOONIST LEAVES EVERYTHING WHITE, WITH THE JOKE BEING THAT A BLINDING BLIZZARD HAS HIT.
WHAT IF THE CHARACTERS ARE INDOORS?
WELL, I'M SURE THEY COULD THINK OF SOMETHING.
DID I SHOW YOU MY NEW 50,000-WATT FLASHLIGHT?

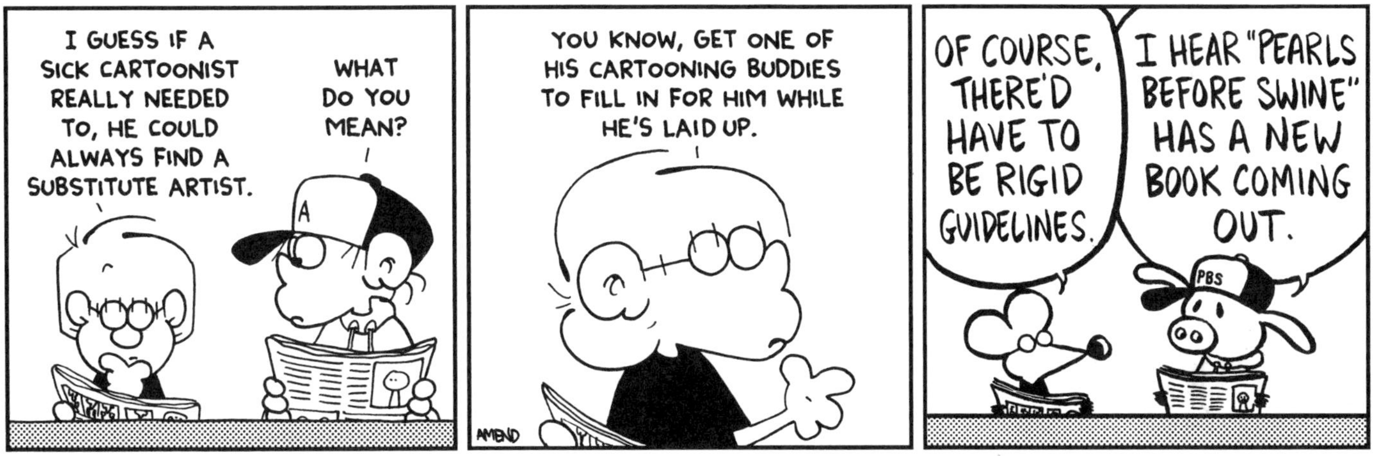
I GUESS IF A SICK CARTOONIST REALLY NEEDED TO, HE COULD ALWAYS FIND A SUBSTITUTE ARTIST.
WHAT DO YOU MEAN?
YOU KNOW, GET ONE OF HIS CARTOONING BUDDIES TO FILL IN FOR HIM WHILE HE'S LAID UP.
OF COURSE, THERE'D HAVE TO BE RIGID GUIDELINES.
I HEAR "PEARLS BEFORE SWINE" HAS A NEW BOOK COMING OUT.
PBS

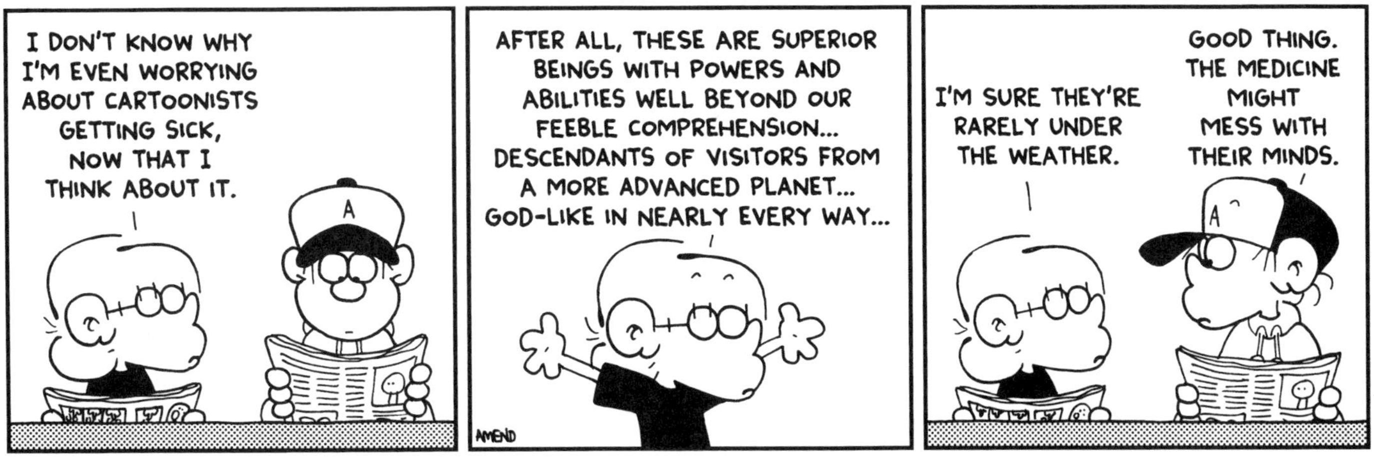
I DON'T KNOW WHY I'M EVEN WORRYING ABOUT CARTOONISTS GETTING SICK, NOW THAT I THINK ABOUT IT.
AFTER ALL, THESE ARE SUPERIOR BEINGS WITH POWERS AND ABILITIES WELL BEYOND OUR FEEBLE COMPREHENSION... DESCENDANTS OF VISITORS FROM A MORE ADVANCED PLANET... GOD-LIKE IN NEARLY EVERY WAY...
I'M SURE THEY'RE RARELY UNDER THE WEATHER.
GOOD THING. THE MEDICINE MIGHT MESS WITH THEIR MINDS.

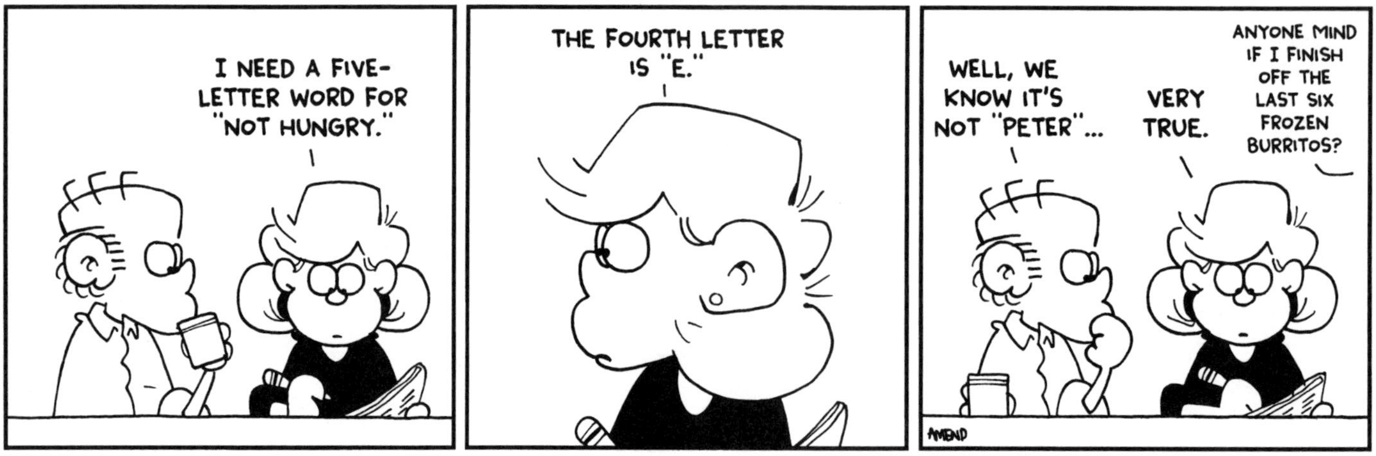
I NEED A FIVE-LETTER WORD FOR "NOT HUNGRY."
THE FOURTH LETTER IS "E."
WELL, WE KNOW IT'S NOT "PETER"...
VERY TRUE.
ANYONE MIND IF I FINISH OFF THE LAST SIX FROZEN BURRITOS?
AMEND

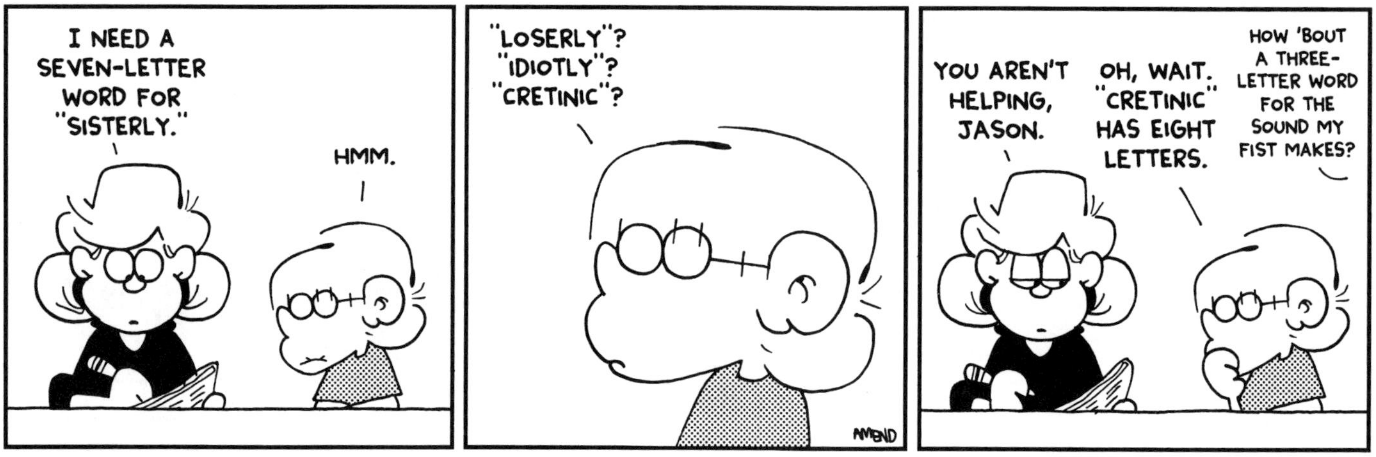
I NEED A SEVEN-LETTER WORD FOR "SISTERLY."
HMM.
"LOSERLY"? "IDIOTLY"? "CRETINIC"?
YOU AREN'T HELPING, JASON.
OH, WAIT. "CRETINIC" HAS EIGHT LETTERS.
HOW 'BOUT A THREE-LETTER WORD FOR THE SOUND MY FIST MAKES?
AMEND

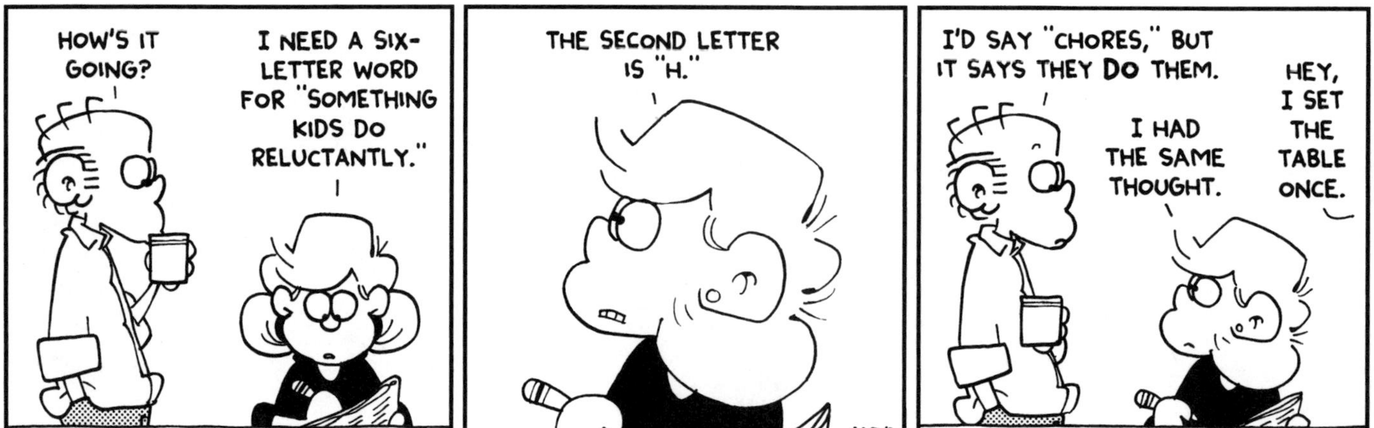
HOW'S IT GOING?
I NEED A SIX-LETTER WORD FOR "SOMETHING KIDS DO RELUCTANTLY."
THE SECOND LETTER IS "H."
I'D SAY "CHORES," BUT IT SAYS THEY DO THEM.
I HAD THE SAME THOUGHT.
HEY, I SET THE TABLE ONCE.
AMEND

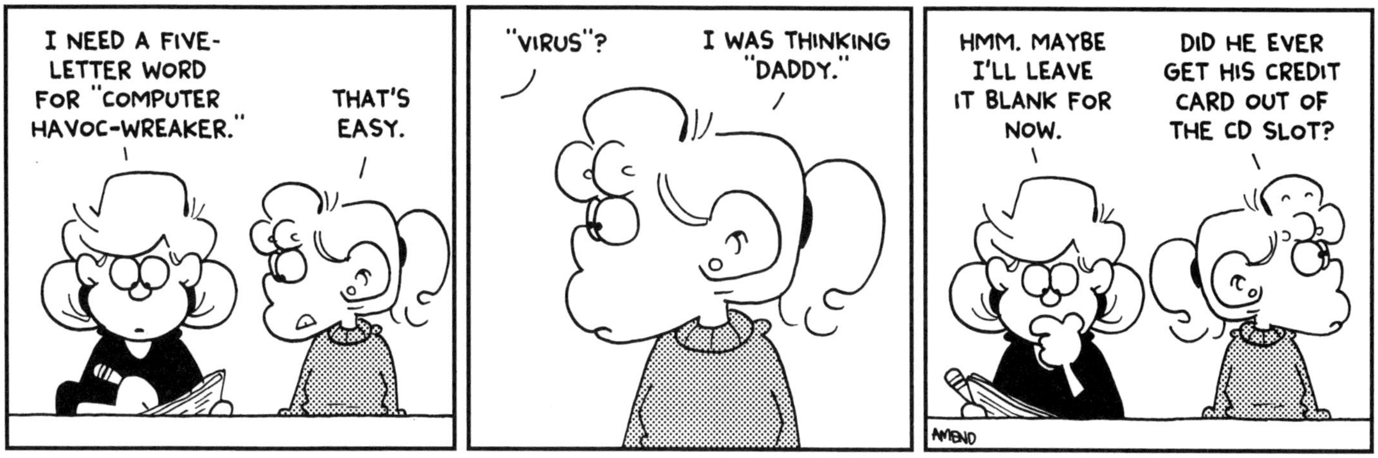
I NEED A FIVE-LETTER WORD FOR "COMPUTER HAVOC-WREAKER."
THAT'S EASY.
"VIRUS"?
I WAS THINKING "DADDY."
HMM. MAYBE I'LL LEAVE IT BLANK FOR NOW.
DID HE EVER GET HIS CREDIT CARD OUT OF THE CD SLOT?
AMEND

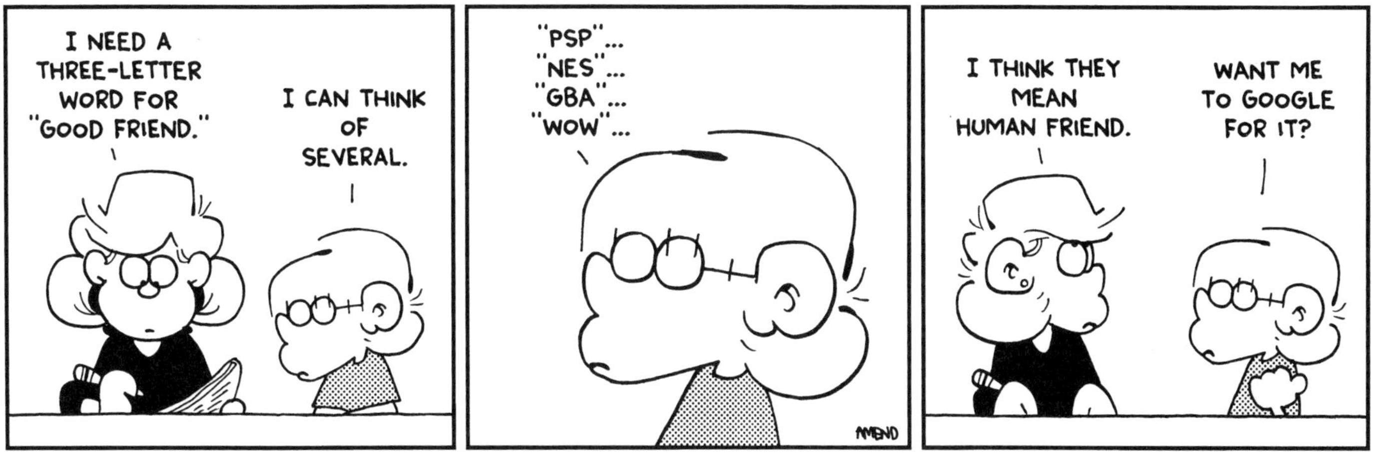
I NEED A THREE-LETTER WORD FOR "GOOD FRIEND."
I CAN THINK OF SEVERAL.
"PSP"... "NES"... "GBA"... "WOW"...
AMEND
I THINK THEY MEAN HUMAN FRIEND.
WANT ME TO GOOGLE FOR IT?

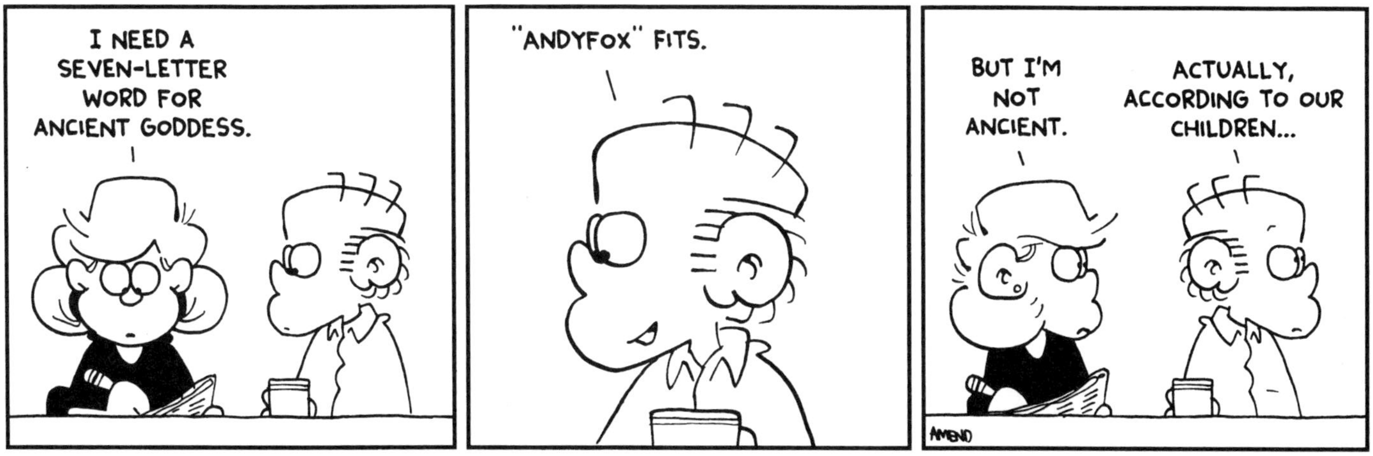
I NEED A SEVEN-LETTER WORD FOR ANCIENT GODDESS.
"ANDYFOX" FITS.
BUT I'M NOT ANCIENT.
ACTUALLY, ACCORDING TO OUR CHILDREN...
AMEND

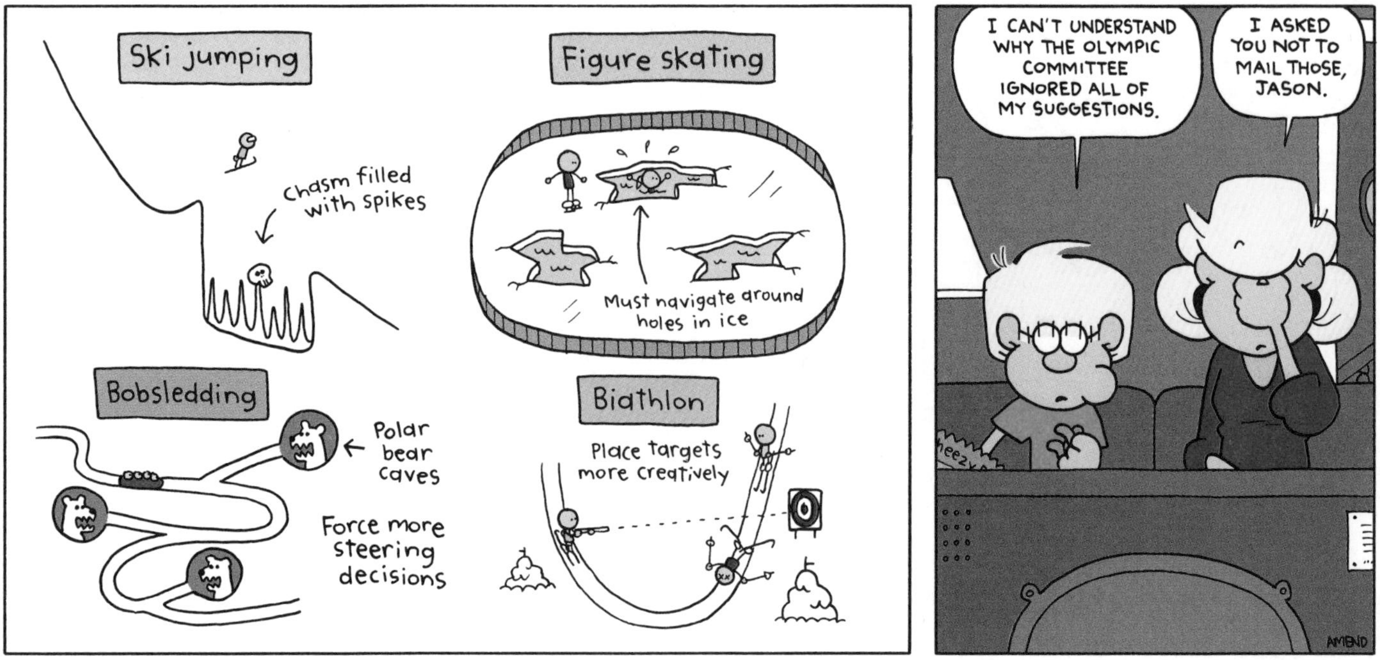
Ski jumping
Chasm filled with spikes
Figure skating
Must navigate around holes in ice
Bobsledding
Polar bear caves
Force more steering decisions
Biathlon
Place targets more creatively
I CAN'T UNDERSTAND WHY THE OLYMPIC COMMITTEE IGNORED ALL OF MY SUGGESTIONS.
I ASKED YOU NOT TO MAIL THOSE, JASON.
AMEND

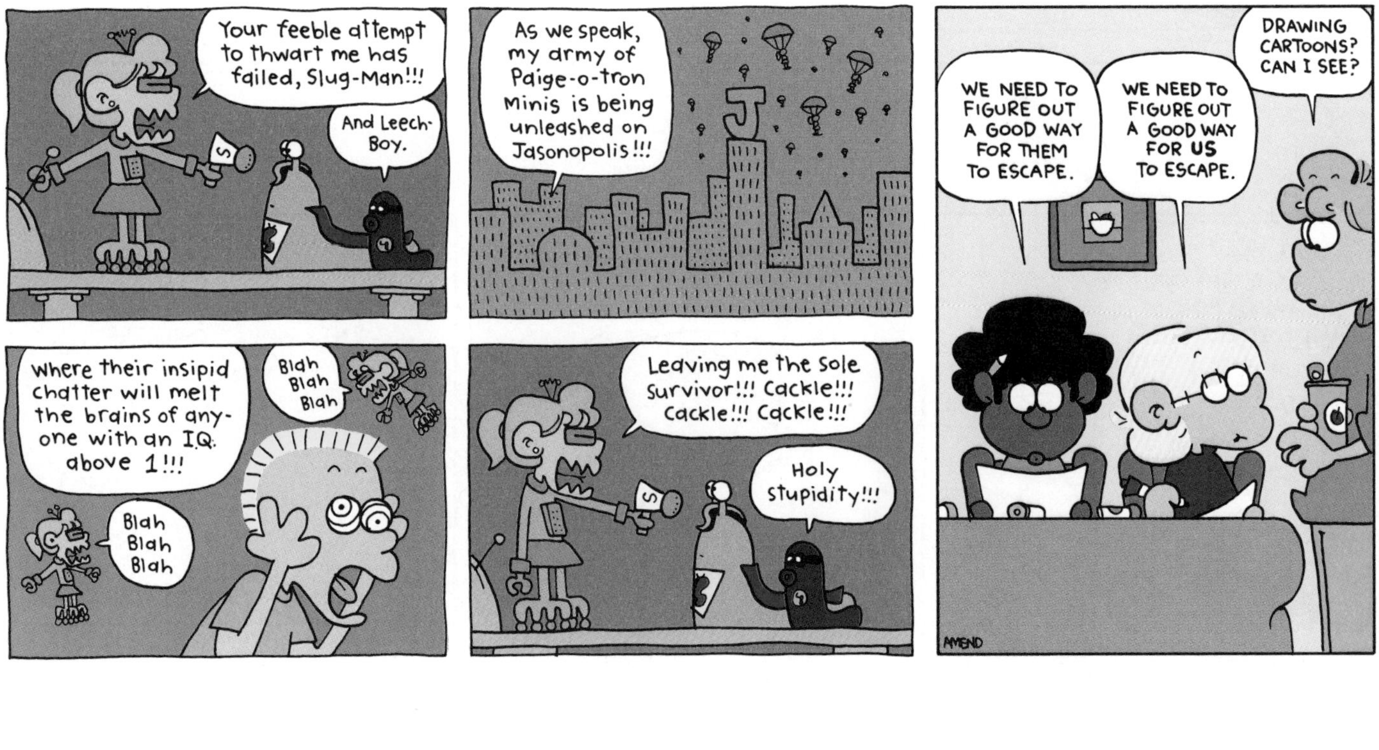
Your feeble attempt to thwart me has failed, Slug-Man!!!
And Leech-Boy.
As we speak, my army of Paige-o-tron Minis is being unleashed on Jasonopolis!!!
Where their insipid chatter will melt the brains of any-one with an I.Q. above 1!!!
Blah Blah Blah
Blah Blah Blah
Leaving me the sole survivor!!! Cackle!!! Cackle!!! Cackle!!!
Holy stupidity!!!
WE NEED TO FIGURE OUT A GOOD WAY FOR THEM TO ESCAPE.
WE NEED TO FIGURE OUT A GOOD WAY FOR **US** TO ESCAPE.
DRAWING CARTOONS? CAN I SEE?
AMEND

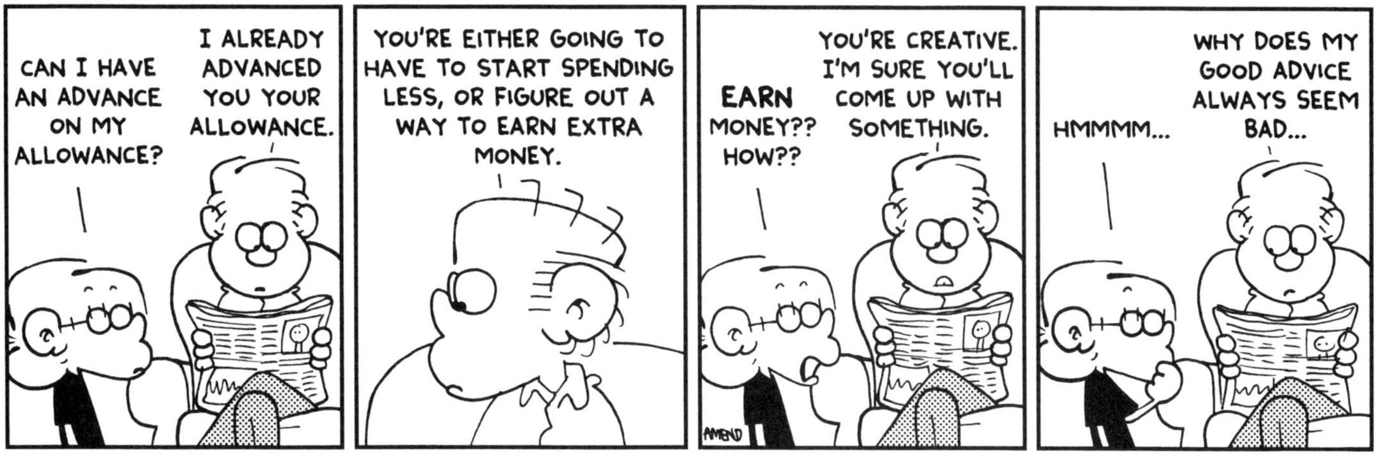
CAN I HAVE AN ADVANCE ON MY ALLOWANCE?
I ALREADY ADVANCED YOU YOUR ALLOWANCE.
YOU'RE EITHER GOING TO HAVE TO START SPENDING LESS, OR FIGURE OUT A WAY TO EARN EXTRA MONEY.
EARN MONEY?? HOW??
YOU'RE CREATIVE. I'M SURE YOU'LL COME UP WITH SOMETHING.
AMEND
HMMMM...
WHY DOES MY GOOD ADVICE ALWAYS SEEM BAD...

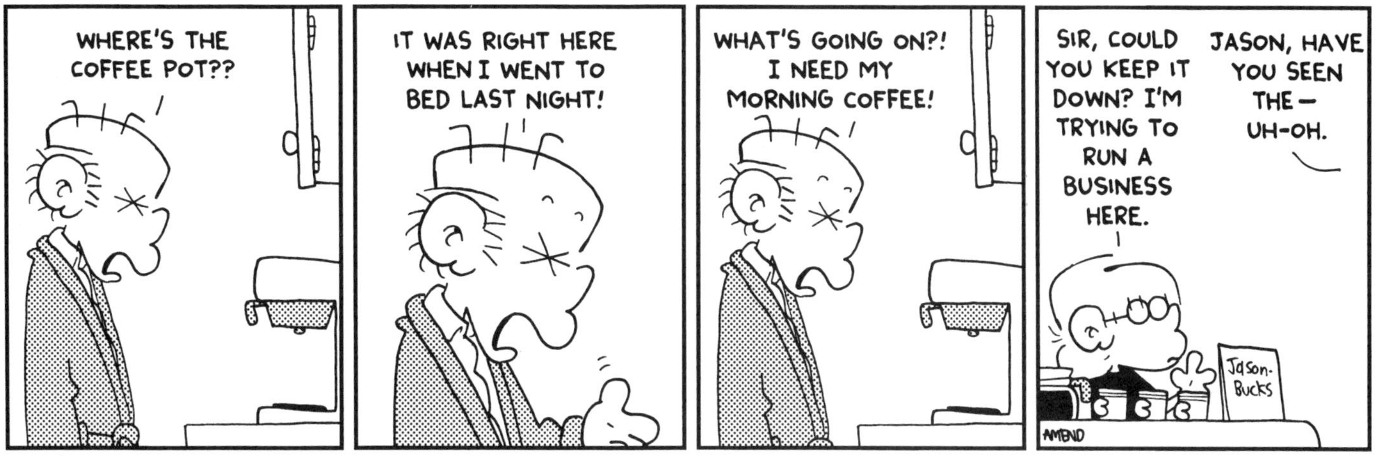
WHERE'S THE COFFEE POT??
IT WAS RIGHT HERE WHEN I WENT TO BED LAST NIGHT!
WHAT'S GOING ON?! I NEED MY MORNING COFFEE!
SIR, COULD YOU KEEP IT DOWN? I'M TRYING TO RUN A BUSINESS HERE.
JASON, HAVE YOU SEEN THE— UH-OH.
Jason-Bucks
AMEND

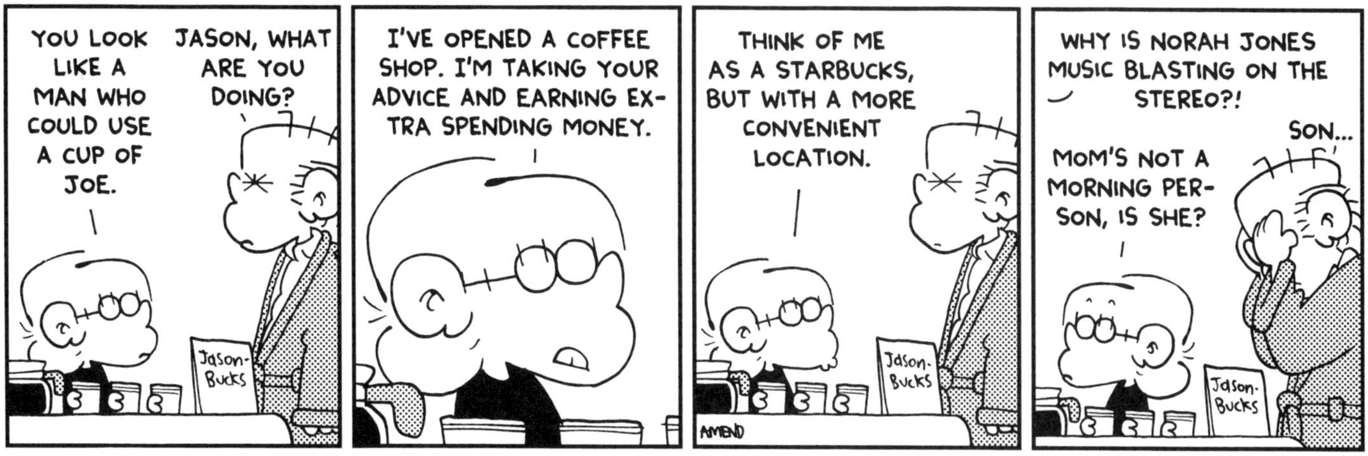
YOU LOOK LIKE A MAN WHO COULD USE A CUP OF JOE.
JASON, WHAT ARE YOU DOING?
Jason-Bucks
I'VE OPENED A COFFEE SHOP. I'M TAKING YOUR ADVICE AND EARNING EXTRA SPENDING MONEY.
THINK OF ME AS A STARBUCKS, BUT WITH A MORE CONVENIENT LOCATION.
Jason-Bucks
AMEND
WHY IS NORAH JONES MUSIC BLASTING ON THE STEREO?!
SON...
MOM'S NOT A MORNING PERSON, IS SHE?
Jason-Bucks

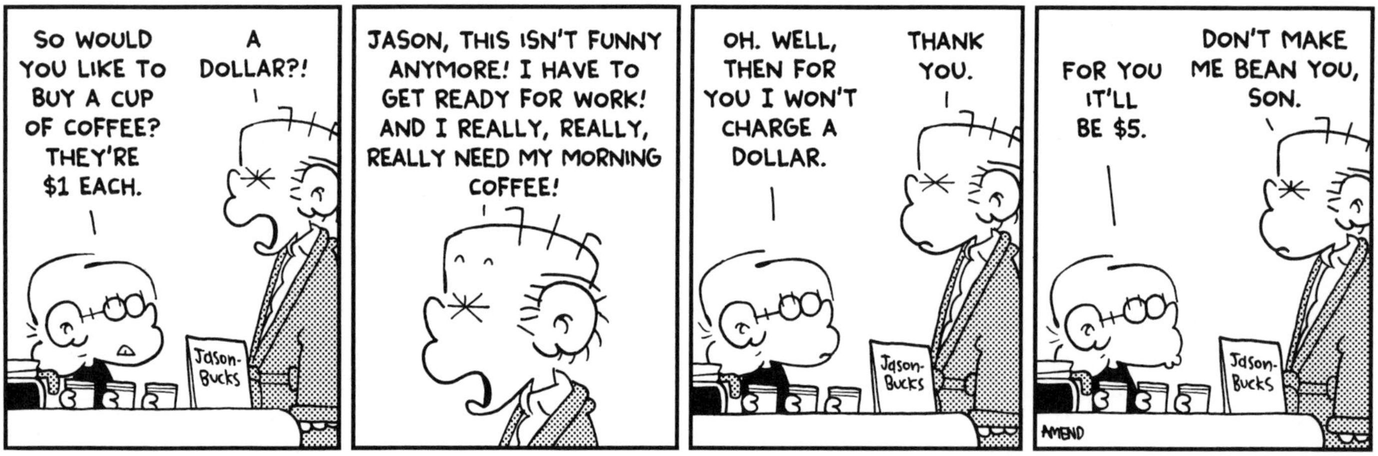
SO WOULD YOU LIKE TO BUY A CUP OF COFFEE? THEY'RE $1 EACH.
A DOLLAR?!
Jason-Bucks
JASON, THIS ISN'T FUNNY ANYMORE! I HAVE TO GET READY FOR WORK! AND I REALLY, REALLY, REALLY NEED MY MORNING COFFEE!
OH. WELL, THEN FOR YOU I WON'T CHARGE A DOLLAR.
THANK YOU.
Jason-Bucks
FOR YOU IT'LL BE $5.
DON'T MAKE ME BEAN YOU, SON.
Jason-Bucks
AMEND

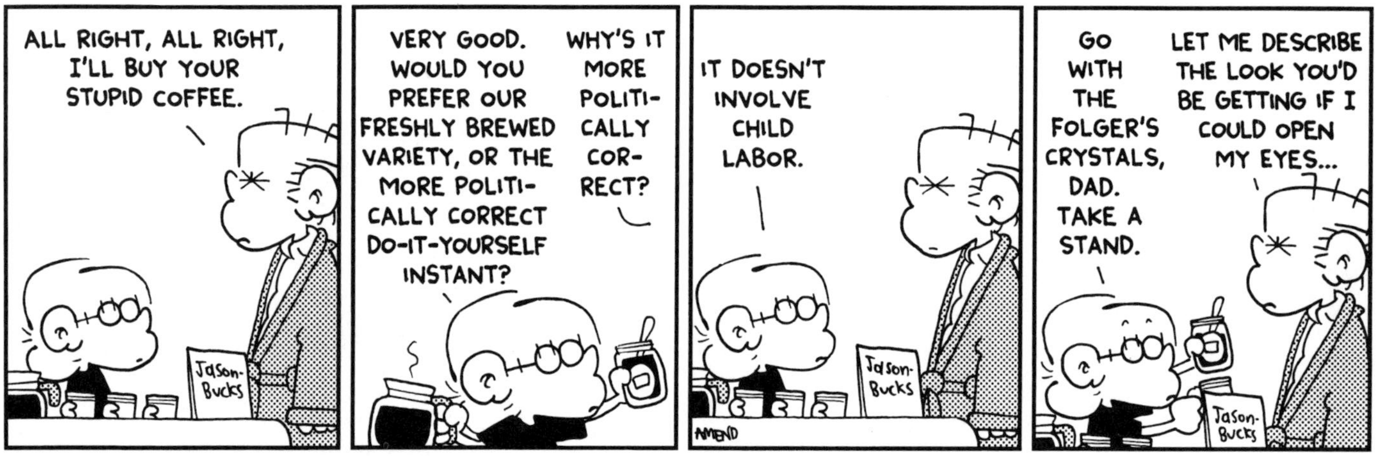
ALL RIGHT, ALL RIGHT, I'LL BUY YOUR STUPID COFFEE.
Jason-Bucks
VERY GOOD. WOULD YOU PREFER OUR FRESHLY BREWED VARIETY, OR THE MORE POLITICALLY CORRECT DO-IT-YOURSELF INSTANT?
WHY'S IT MORE POLITICALLY CORRECT?
IT DOESN'T INVOLVE CHILD LABOR.
Jason-Bucks
AMEND
GO WITH THE FOLGER'S CRYSTALS, DAD. TAKE A STAND.
LET ME DESCRIBE THE LOOK YOU'D BE GETTING IF I COULD OPEN MY EYES...
Jason-Bucks

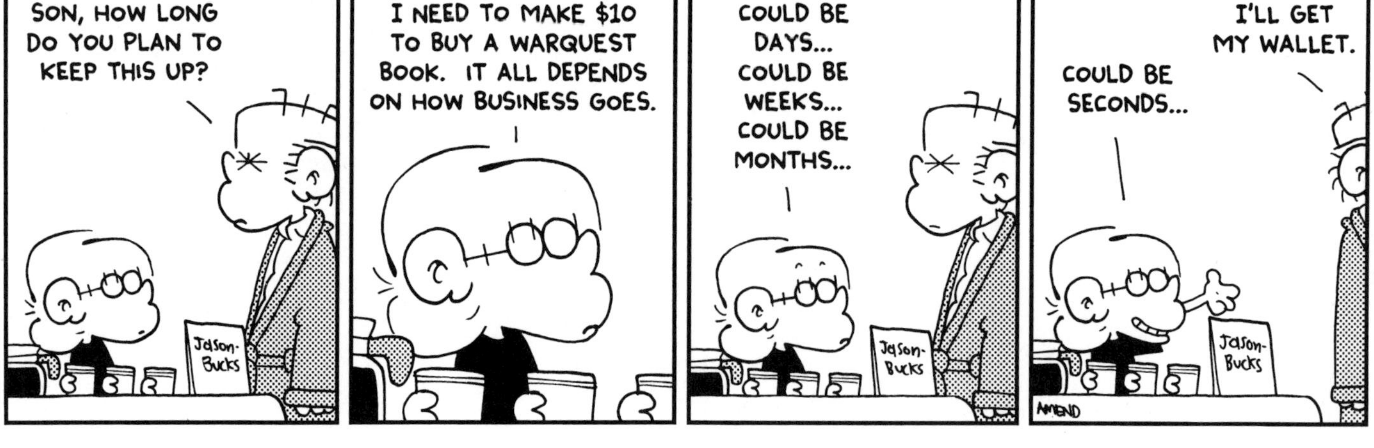
SON, HOW LONG DO YOU PLAN TO KEEP THIS UP?
Jason-Bucks
I NEED TO MAKE $10 TO BUY A WARQUEST BOOK. IT ALL DEPENDS ON HOW BUSINESS GOES.
COULD BE DAYS... COULD BE WEEKS... COULD BE MONTHS...
Jason-Bucks
COULD BE SECONDS...
I'LL GET MY WALLET.
Jason-Bucks
AMEND

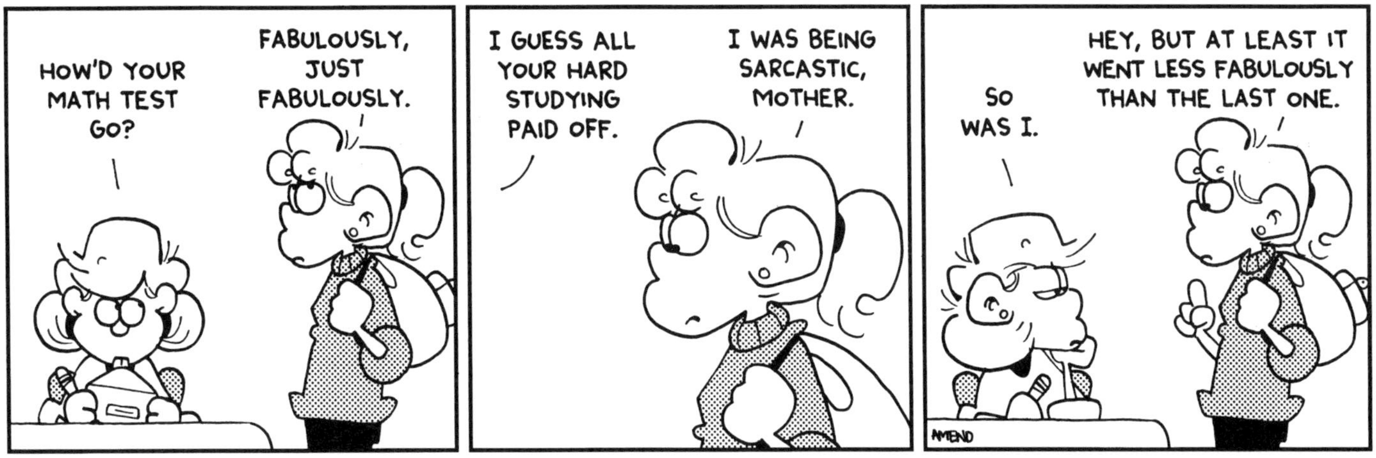
HOW'D YOUR MATH TEST GO?
FABULOUSLY, JUST FABULOUSLY.
I GUESS ALL YOUR HARD STUDYING PAID OFF.
I WAS BEING SARCASTIC, MOTHER.
SO WAS I.
HEY, BUT AT LEAST IT WENT LESS FABULOUSLY THAN THE LAST ONE.
AMEND

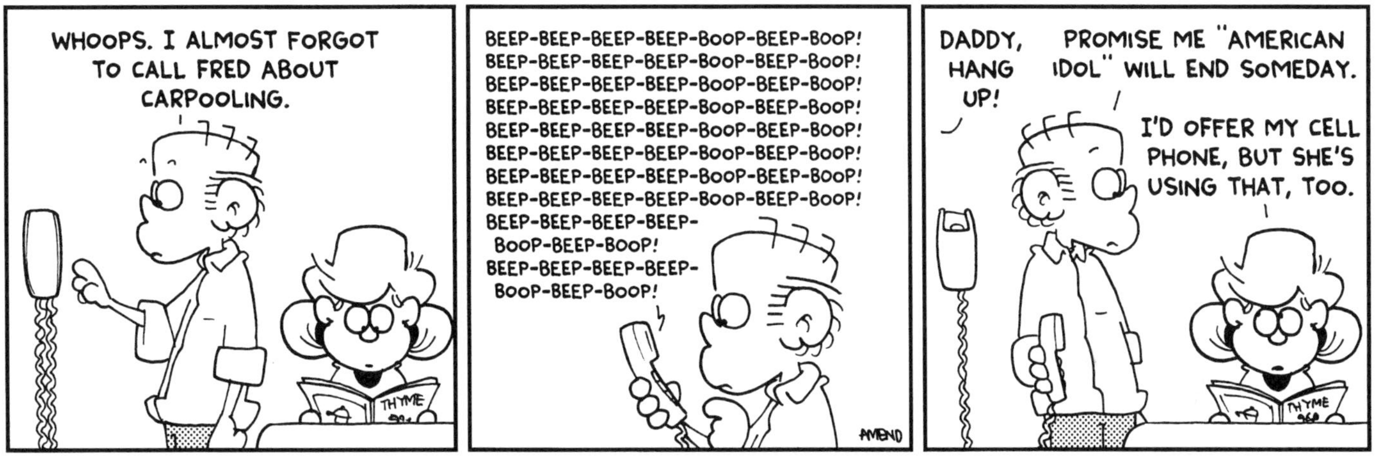
WHOOPS. I ALMOST FORGOT TO CALL FRED ABOUT CARPOOLING.
BEEP-BEEP-BEEP-BEEP-BOOP-BEEP-BOOP! BEEP-BEEP-BEEP-BEEP-BOOP-BEEP-BOOP! BEEP-BEEP-BEEP-BEEP-BOOP-BEEP-BOOP! BEEP-BEEP-BEEP-BEEP-BOOP-BEEP-BOOP! BEEP-BEEP-BEEP-BEEP-BOOP-BEEP-BOOP! BEEP-BEEP-BEEP-BEEP-BOOP-BEEP-BOOP! BEEP-BEEP-BEEP-BEEP-BOOP-BEEP-BOOP! BEEP-BEEP-BEEP-BEEP-BOOP-BEEP-BOOP! BEEP-BEEP-BEEP-BEEP-BOOP-BEEP-BOOP! BEEP-BEEP-BEEP-BEEP-BOOP-BEEP-BOOP!
AMEND
DADDY, HANG UP!
PROMISE ME "AMERICAN IDOL" WILL END SOMEDAY.
I'D OFFER MY CELL PHONE, BUT SHE'S USING THAT, TOO.

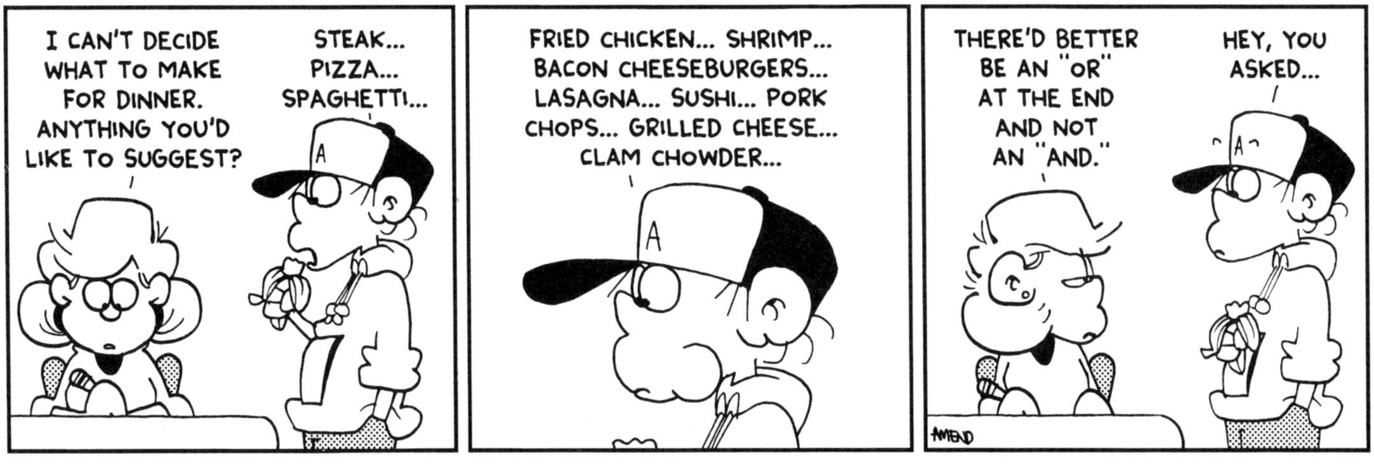
I CAN'T DECIDE WHAT TO MAKE FOR DINNER. ANYTHING YOU'D LIKE TO SUGGEST?
STEAK... PIZZA... SPAGHETTI...
FRIED CHICKEN... SHRIMP... BACON CHEESEBURGERS... LASAGNA... SUSHI... PORK CHOPS... GRILLED CHEESE... CLAM CHOWDER...
THERE'D BETTER BE AN "OR" AT THE END AND NOT AN "AND."
HEY, YOU ASKED...
AMEND

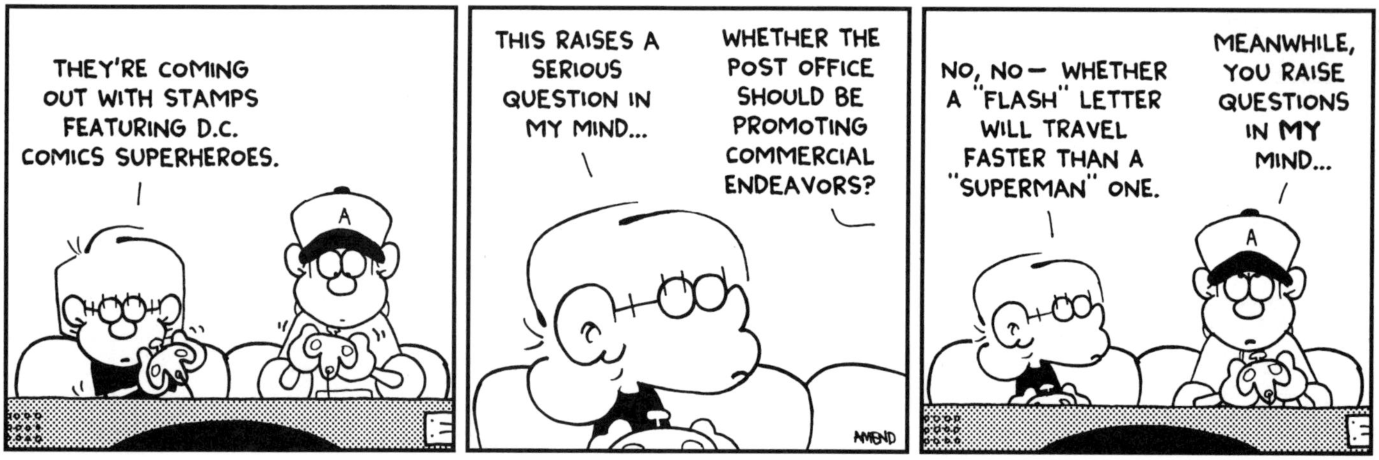
THEY'RE COMING OUT WITH STAMPS FEATURING D.C. COMICS SUPERHEROES.
THIS RAISES A SERIOUS QUESTION IN MY MIND...
WHETHER THE POST OFFICE SHOULD BE PROMOTING COMMERCIAL ENDEAVORS?
NO, NO— WHETHER A "FLASH" LETTER WILL TRAVEL FASTER THAN A "SUPERMAN" ONE.
MEANWHILE, YOU RAISE QUESTIONS IN MY MIND...
AMEND

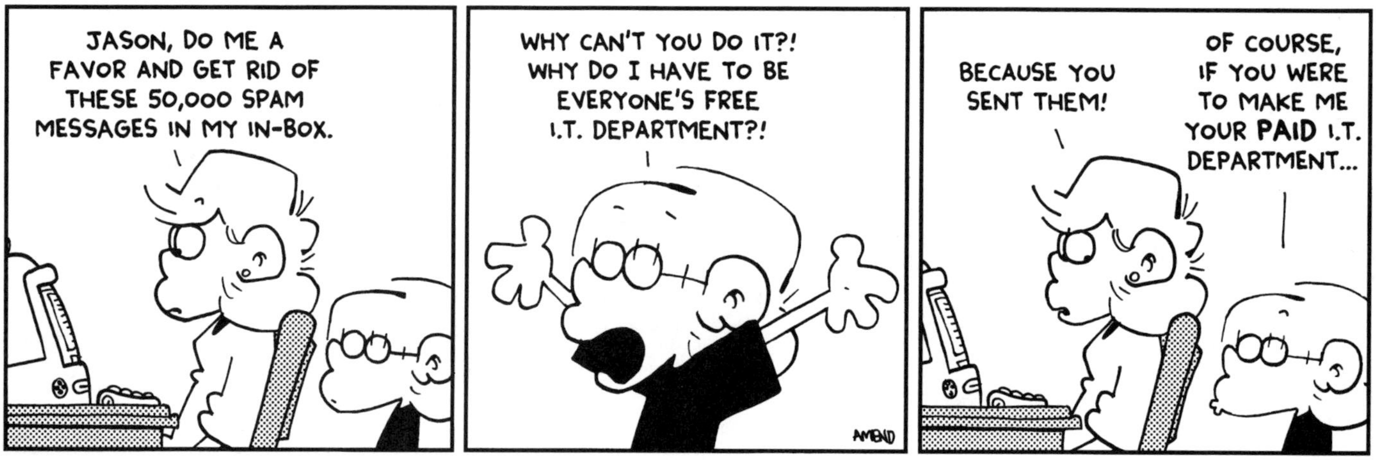
JASON, DO ME A FAVOR AND GET RID OF THESE 50,000 SPAM MESSAGES IN MY IN-BOX.
WHY CAN'T YOU DO IT?! WHY DO I HAVE TO BE EVERYONE'S FREE I.T. DEPARTMENT?!
BECAUSE YOU SENT THEM!
OF COURSE, IF YOU WERE TO MAKE ME YOUR PAID I.T. DEPARTMENT...
AMEND

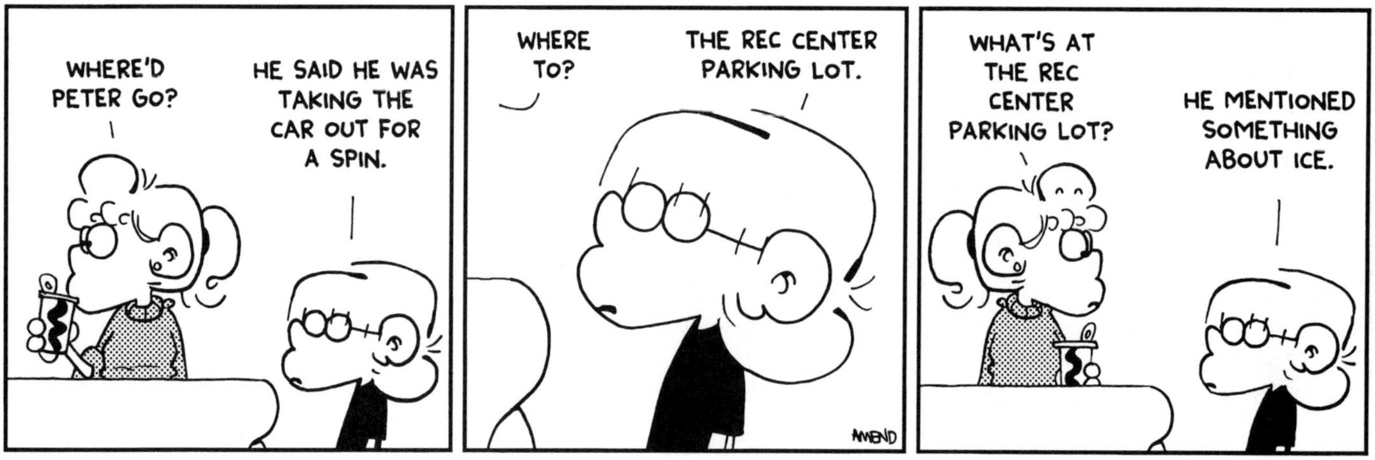
WHERE'D PETER GO?
HE SAID HE WAS TAKING THE CAR OUT FOR A SPIN.
WHERE TO?
THE REC CENTER PARKING LOT.
WHAT'S AT THE REC CENTER PARKING LOT?
HE MENTIONED SOMETHING ABOUT ICE.
AMEND

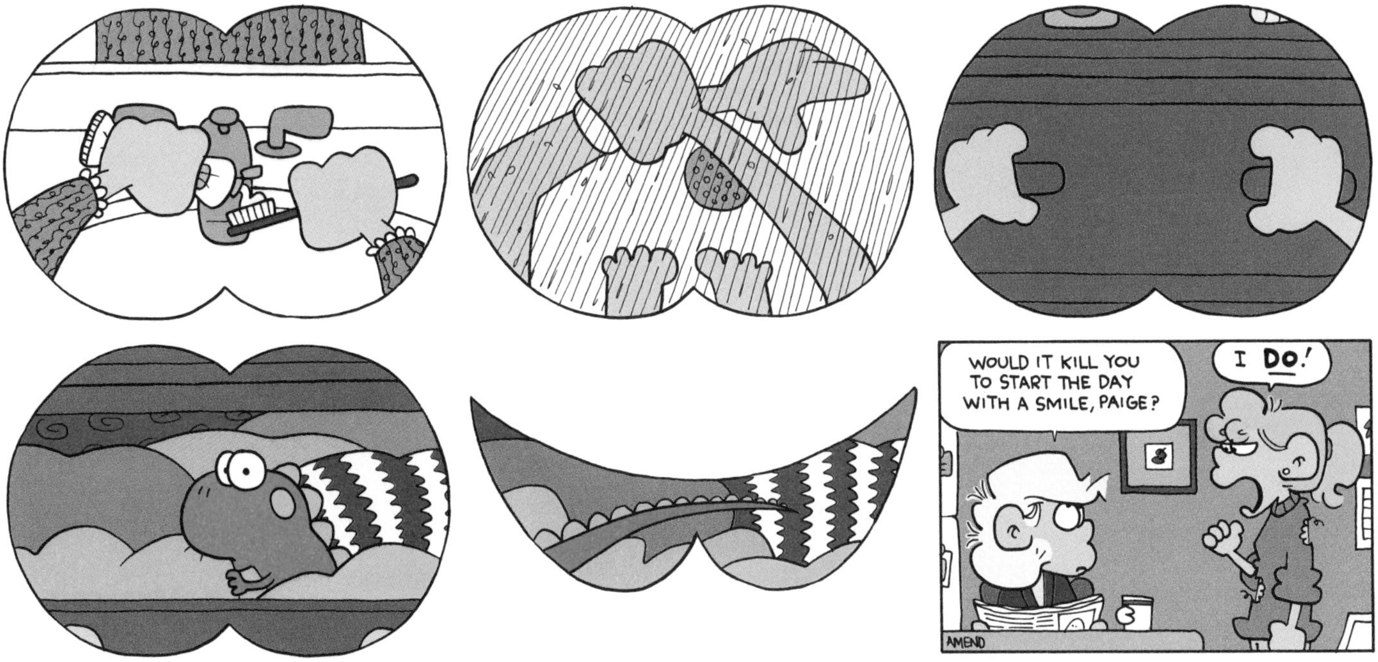
WOULD IT KILL YOU TO START THE DAY WITH A SMILE, PAIGE?
I DO!
AMEND

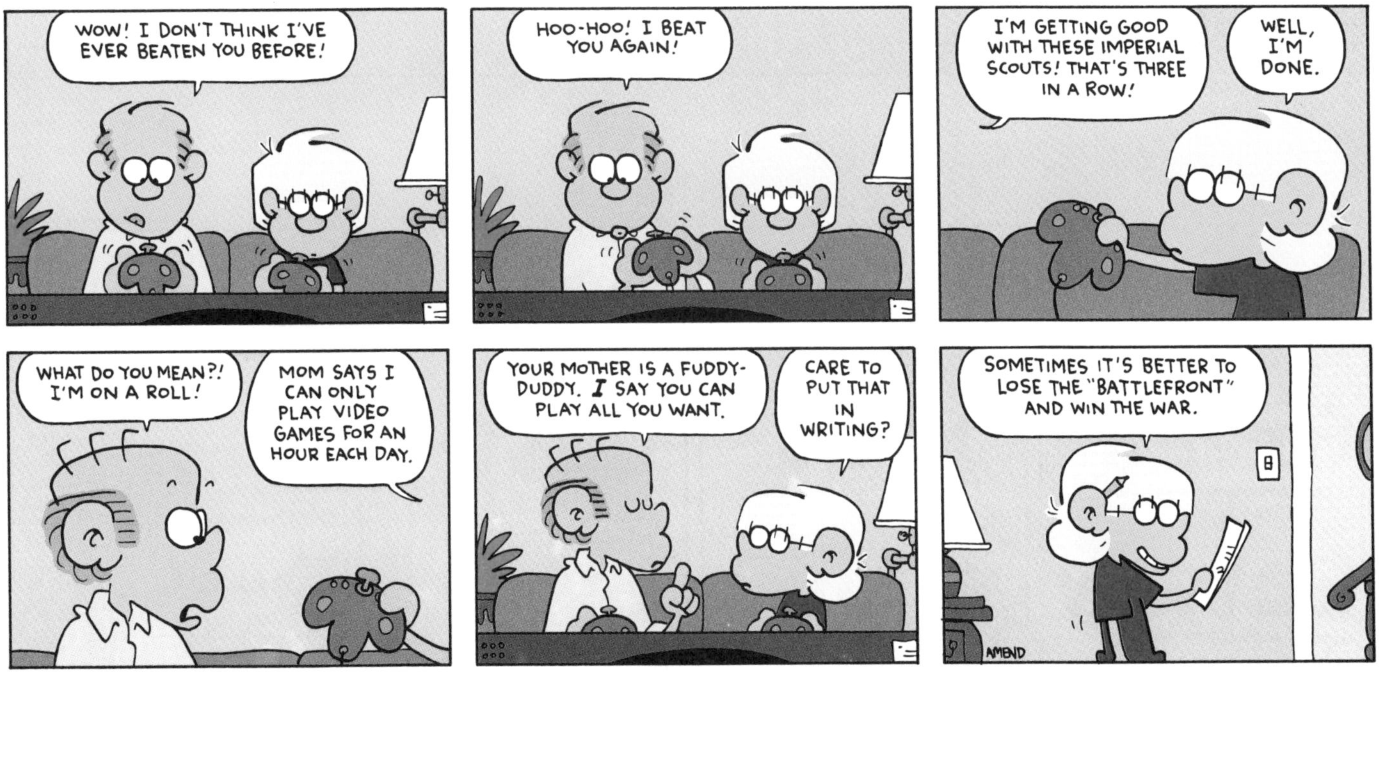
WOW! I DON'T THINK I'VE EVER BEATEN YOU BEFORE!
HOO-HOO! I BEAT YOU AGAIN!
I'M GETTING GOOD WITH THESE IMPERIAL SCOUTS! THAT'S THREE IN A ROW!
WELL, I'M DONE.
WHAT DO YOU MEAN?! I'M ON A ROLL!
MOM SAYS I CAN ONLY PLAY VIDEO GAMES FOR AN HOUR EACH DAY.
YOUR MOTHER IS A FUDDY-DUDDY. I SAY YOU CAN PLAY ALL YOU WANT.
CARE TO PUT THAT IN WRITING?
SOMETIMES IT'S BETTER TO LOSE THE "BATTLEFRONT" AND WIN THE WAR.
AMEND

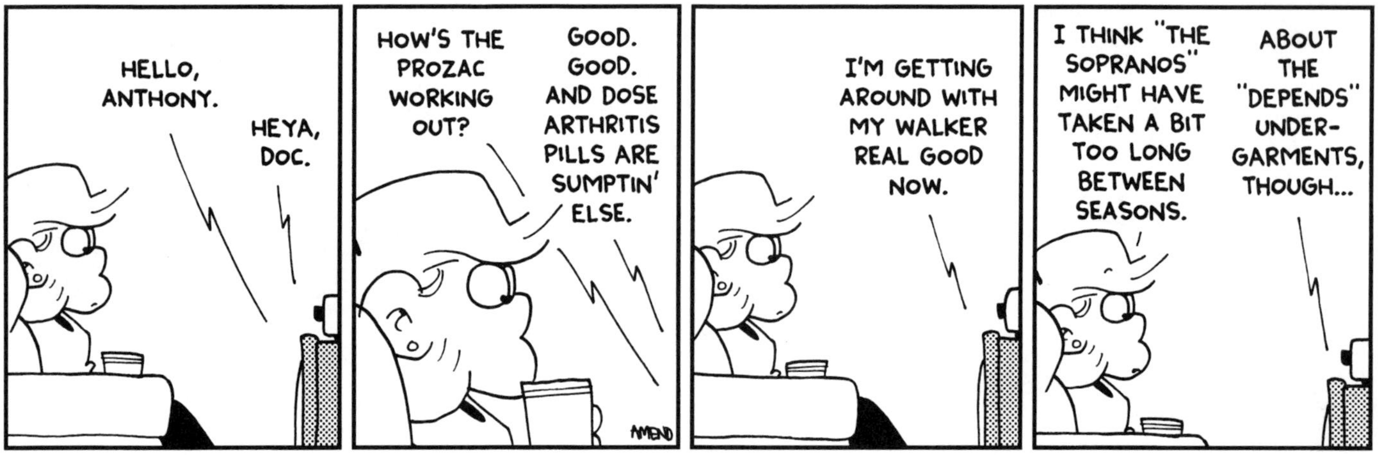
HELLO, ANTHONY.
HEYA, DOC.
HOW'S THE PROZAC WORKING OUT?
GOOD. GOOD. AND DOSE ARTHRITIS PILLS ARE SUMPTIN' ELSE.
I'M GETTING AROUND WITH MY WALKER REAL GOOD NOW.
I THINK "THE SOPRANOS" MIGHT HAVE TAKEN A BIT TOO LONG BETWEEN SEASONS.
ABOUT THE "DEPENDS" UNDER-GARMENTS, THOUGH...
AMEND

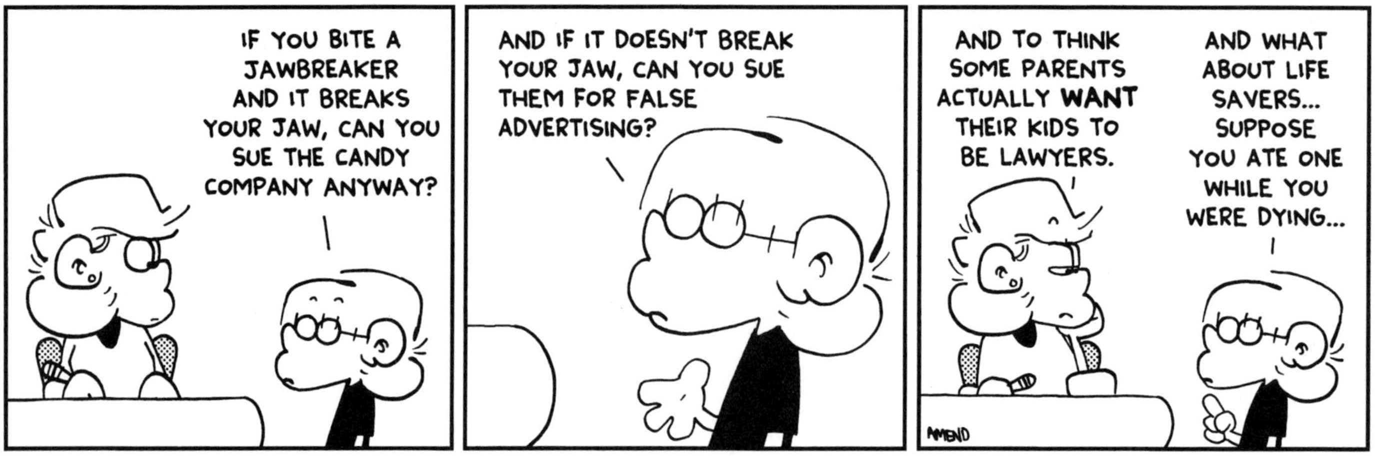
IF YOU BITE A JAWBREAKER AND IT BREAKS YOUR JAW, CAN YOU SUE THE CANDY COMPANY ANYWAY?
AND IF IT DOESN'T BREAK YOUR JAW, CAN YOU SUE THEM FOR FALSE ADVERTISING?
AND TO THINK SOME PARENTS ACTUALLY **WANT** THEIR KIDS TO BE LAWYERS.
AND WHAT ABOUT LIFE SAVERS... SUPPOSE YOU ATE ONE WHILE YOU WERE DYING...
AMEND

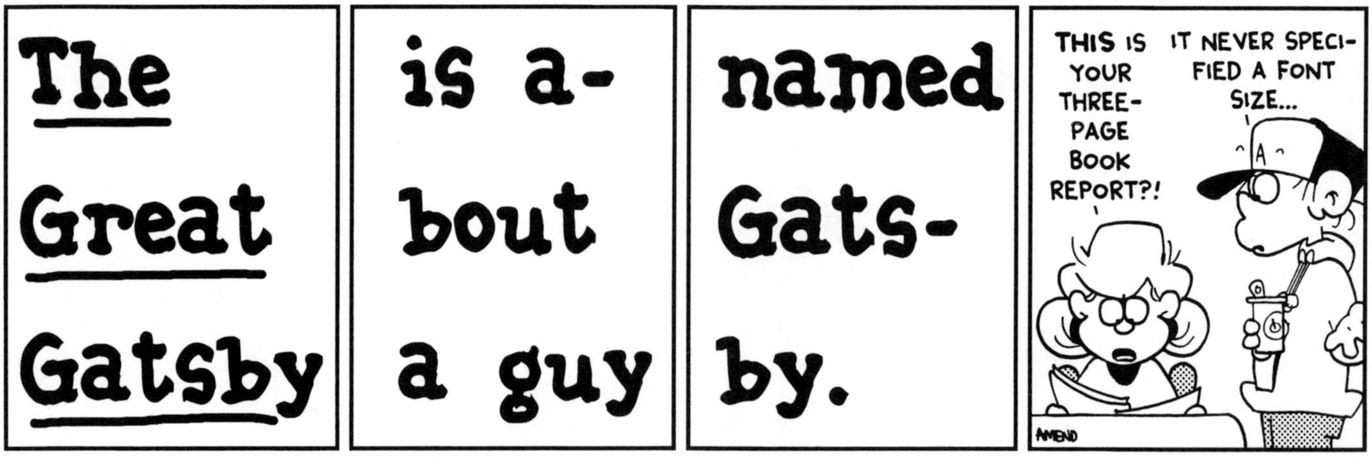
The Great Gatsby
is a- bout a guy
named Gats- by.
THIS IS YOUR THREE-PAGE BOOK REPORT?!
IT NEVER SPECI-FIED A FONT SIZE...
A
AMEND

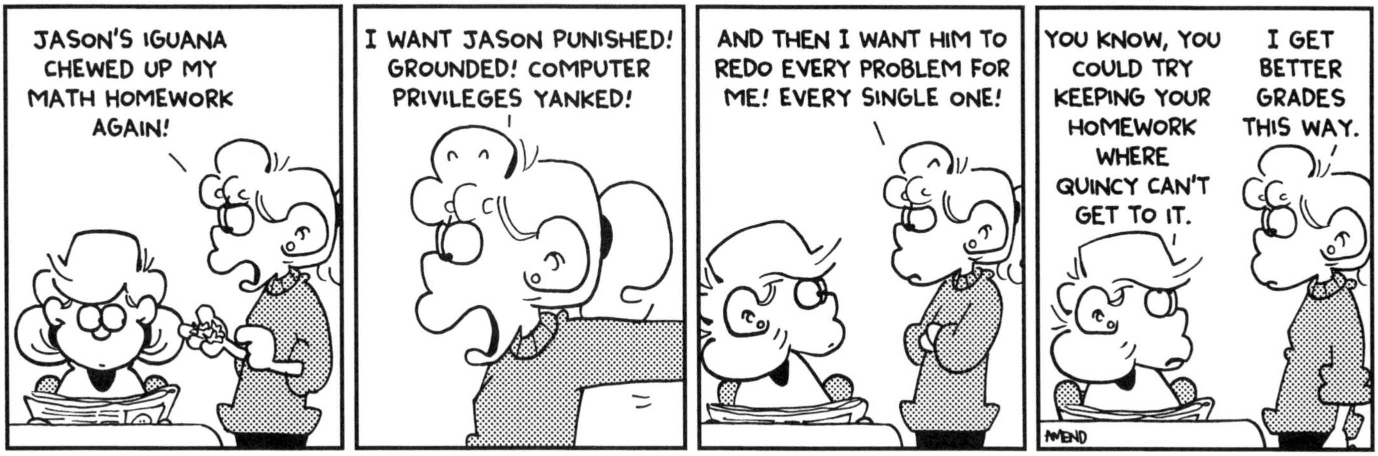
JASON'S IGUANA CHEWED UP MY MATH HOMEWORK AGAIN!
I WANT JASON PUNISHED! GROUNDED! COMPUTER PRIVILEGES YANKED!
AND THEN I WANT HIM TO REDO EVERY PROBLEM FOR ME! EVERY SINGLE ONE!
YOU KNOW, YOU COULD TRY KEEPING YOUR HOMEWORK WHERE QUINCY CAN'T GET TO IT.
I GET BETTER GRADES THIS WAY.
AMEND

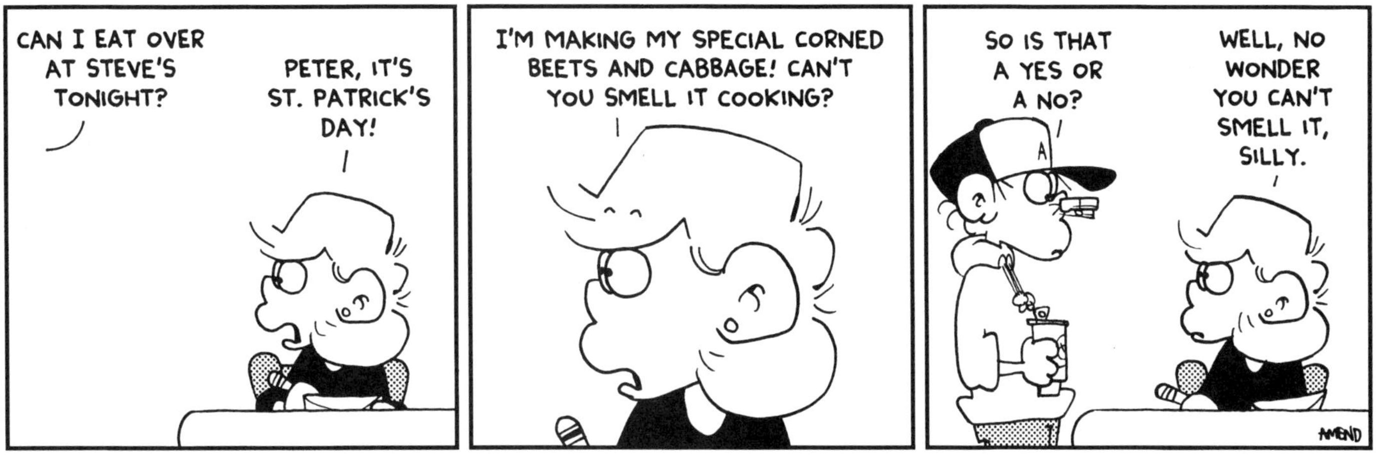
CAN I EAT OVER AT STEVE'S TONIGHT?
PETER, IT'S ST. PATRICK'S DAY!
I'M MAKING MY SPECIAL CORNED BEETS AND CABBAGE! CAN'T YOU SMELL IT COOKING?
SO IS THAT A YES OR A NO?
WELL, NO WONDER YOU CAN'T SMELL IT, SILLY.
AMEND

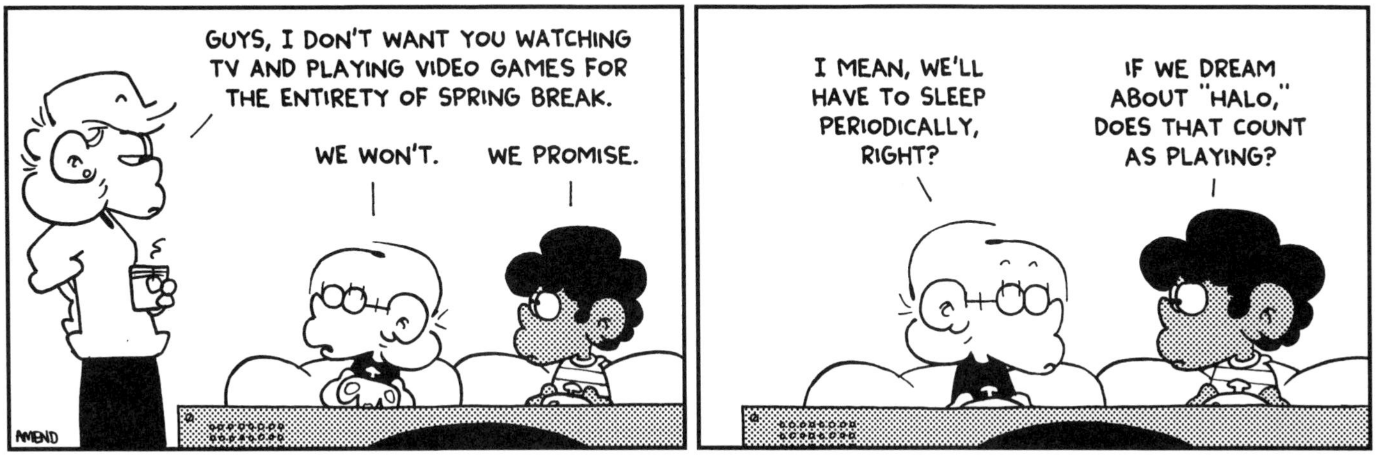
GUYS, I DON'T WANT YOU WATCHING TV AND PLAYING VIDEO GAMES FOR THE ENTIRETY OF SPRING BREAK.
WE WON'T.
WE PROMISE.
AMEND
I MEAN, WE'LL HAVE TO SLEEP PERIODICALLY, RIGHT?
IF WE DREAM ABOUT "HALO," DOES THAT COUNT AS PLAYING?

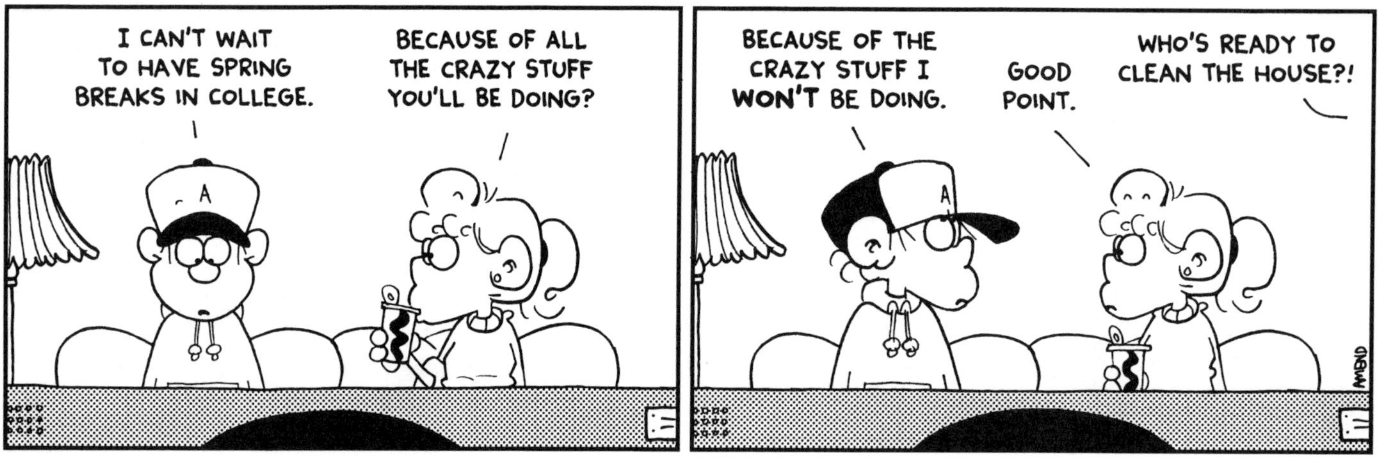
I CAN'T WAIT TO HAVE SPRING BREAKS IN COLLEGE.
BECAUSE OF ALL THE CRAZY STUFF YOU'LL BE DOING?
BECAUSE OF THE CRAZY STUFF I WON'T BE DOING.
GOOD POINT.
WHO'S READY TO CLEAN THE HOUSE?!
AMEND

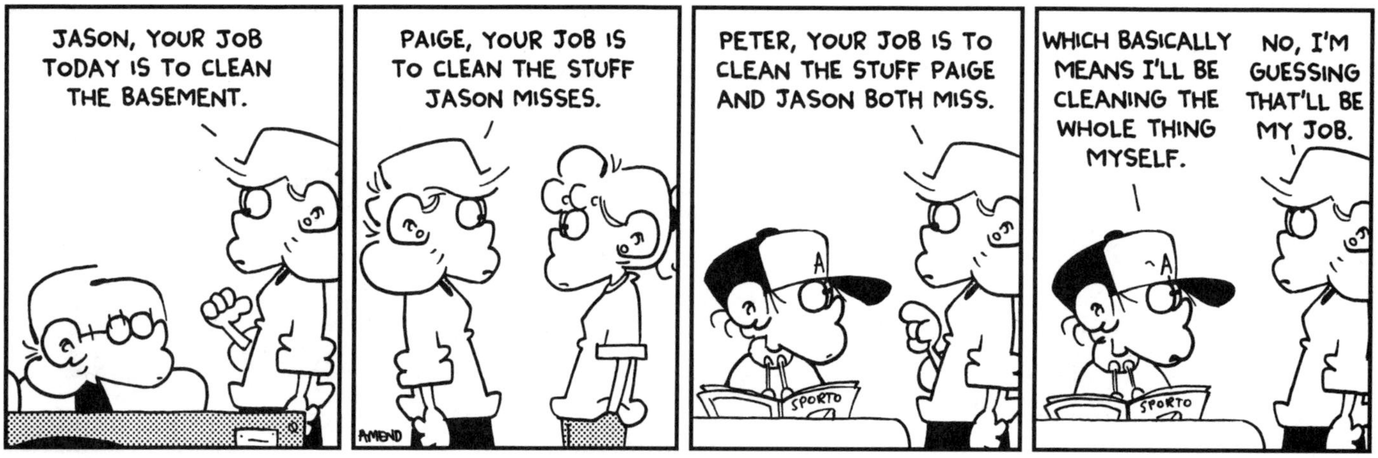
JASON, YOUR JOB TODAY IS TO CLEAN THE BASEMENT.
PAIGE, YOUR JOB IS TO CLEAN THE STUFF JASON MISSES.
AMEND
PETER, YOUR JOB IS TO CLEAN THE STUFF PAIGE AND JASON BOTH MISS.
SPORTO
WHICH BASICALLY MEANS I'LL BE CLEANING THE WHOLE THING MYSELF.
NO, I'M GUESSING THAT'LL BE MY JOB.
SPORTO

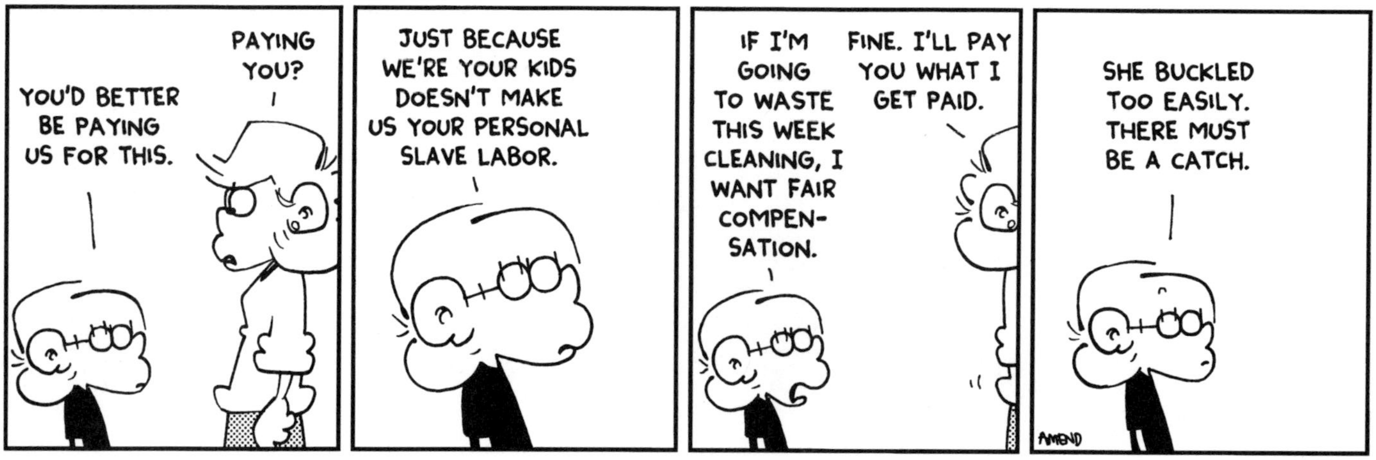
YOU'D BETTER BE PAYING US FOR THIS.
PAYING YOU?
JUST BECAUSE WE'RE YOUR KIDS DOESN'T MAKE US YOUR PERSONAL SLAVE LABOR.
IF I'M GOING TO WASTE THIS WEEK CLEANING, I WANT FAIR COMPEN-SATION.
FINE. I'LL PAY YOU WHAT I GET PAID.
SHE BUCKLED TOO EASILY. THERE MUST BE A CATCH.
AMEND

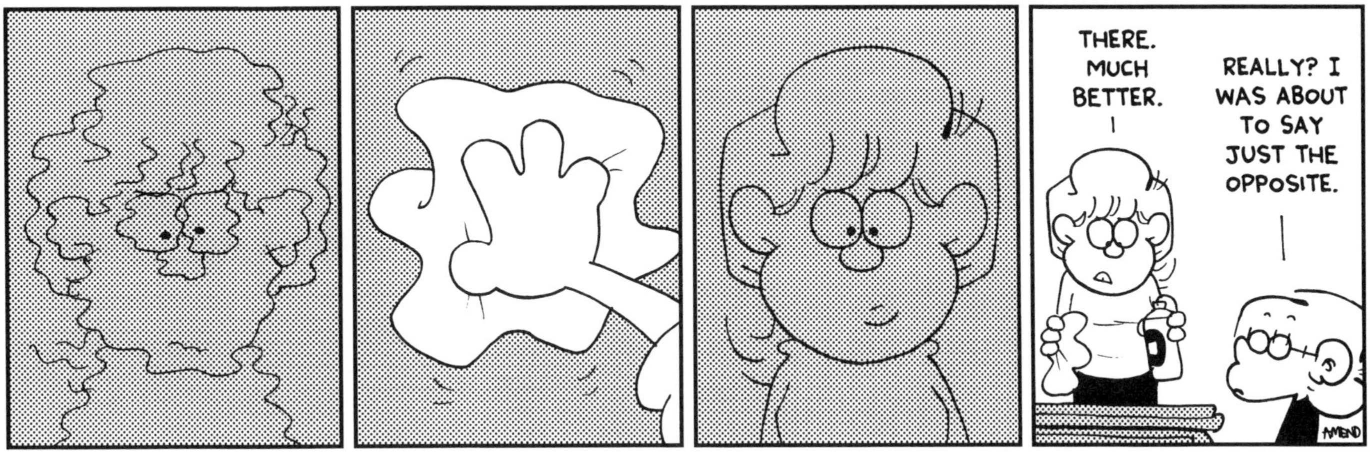
THERE. MUCH BETTER.
REALLY? I WAS ABOUT TO SAY JUST THE OPPOSITE.
AMEND

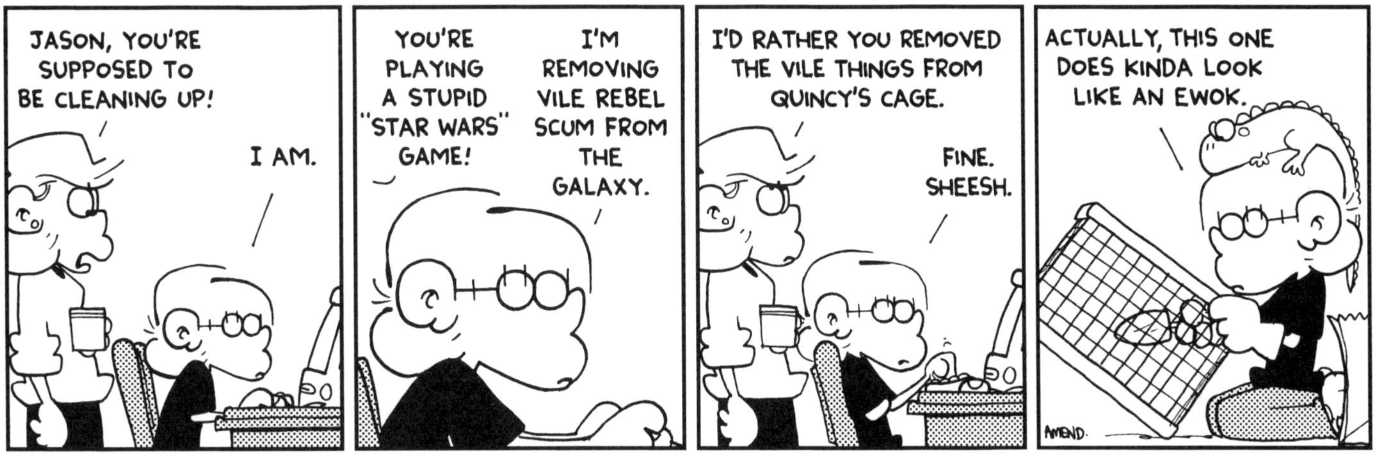
JASON, YOU'RE SUPPOSED TO BE CLEANING UP!
I AM.
YOU'RE PLAYING A STUPID "STAR WARS" GAME!
I'M REMOVING VILE REBEL SCUM FROM THE GALAXY.
I'D RATHER YOU REMOVED THE VILE THINGS FROM QUINCY'S CAGE.
FINE. SHEESH.
ACTUALLY, THIS ONE DOES KINDA LOOK LIKE AN EWOK.
AMEND

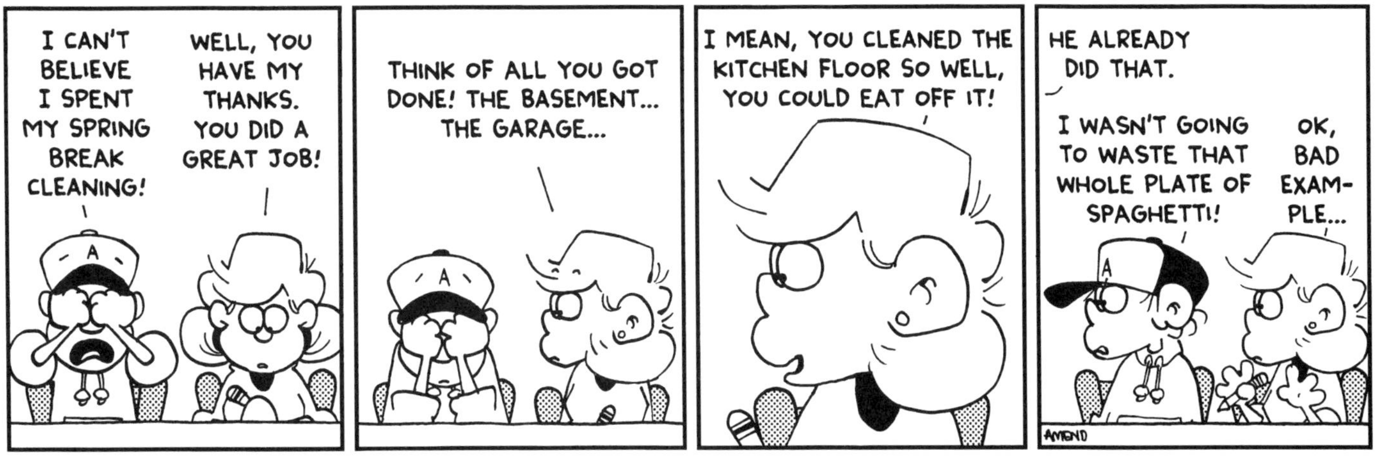
I CAN'T BELIEVE I SPENT MY SPRING BREAK CLEANING!
WELL, YOU HAVE MY THANKS. YOU DID A GREAT JOB!
THINK OF ALL YOU GOT DONE! THE BASEMENT... THE GARAGE...
I MEAN, YOU CLEANED THE KITCHEN FLOOR SO WELL, YOU COULD EAT OFF IT!
HE ALREADY DID THAT.
I WASN'T GOING TO WASTE THAT WHOLE PLATE OF SPAGHETTI!
OK, BAD EXAM-PLE...
AMEND

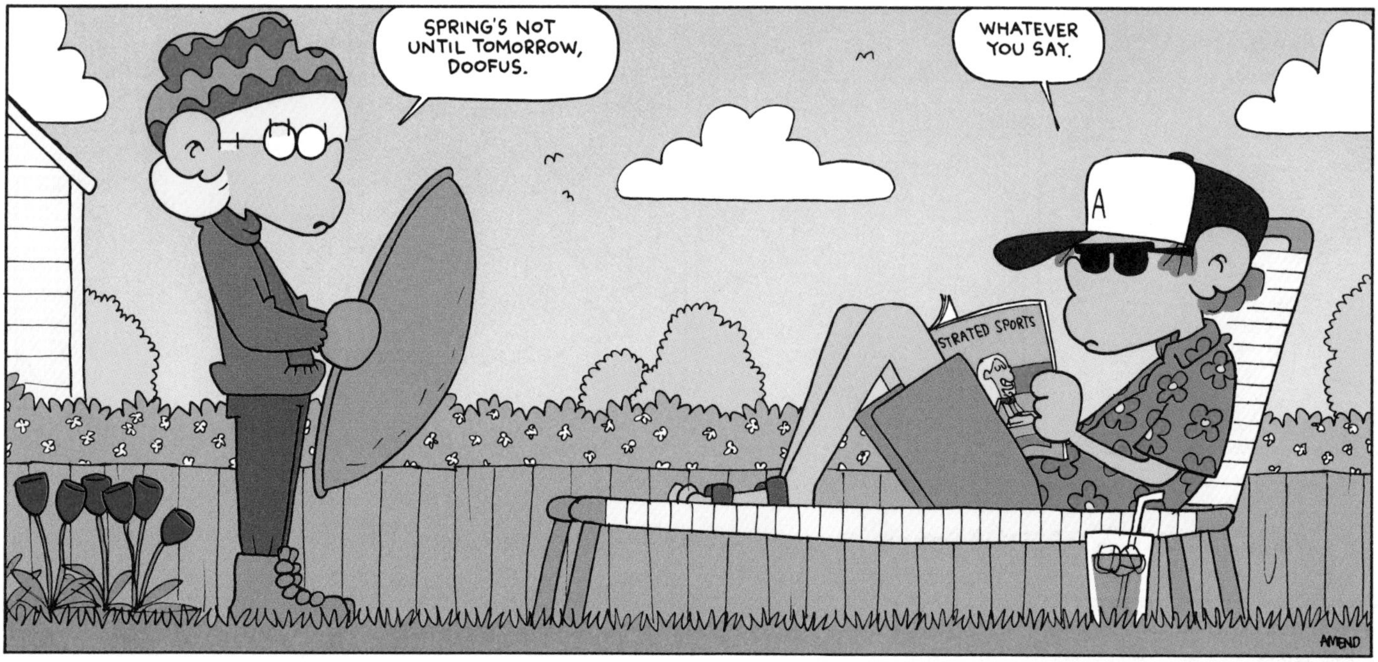
SPRING'S NOT UNTIL TOMORROW, DOOFUS.
WHATEVER YOU SAY.
STRATED SPORTS
AMEND

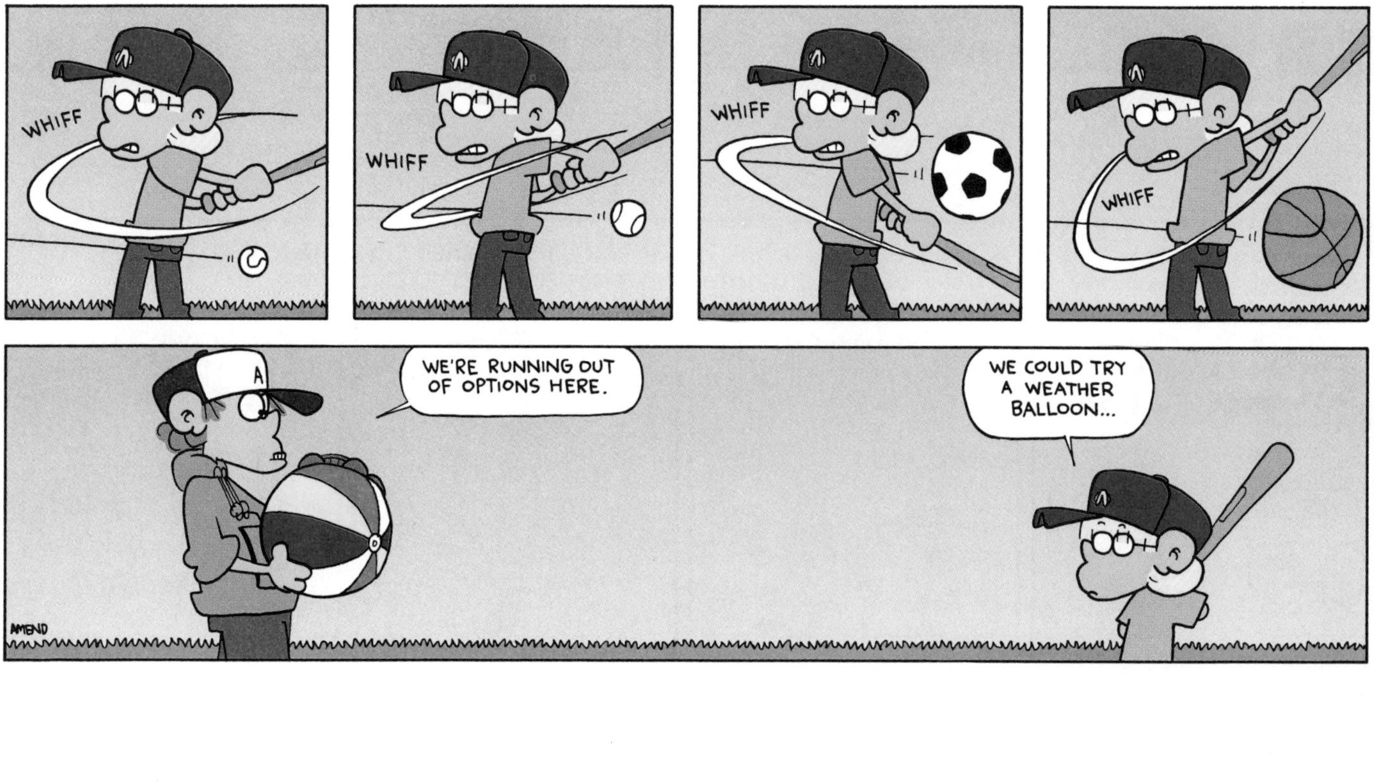
WHIFF
WHIFF
WHIFF
WHIFF
WE'RE RUNNING OUT OF OPTIONS HERE.
WE COULD TRY A WEATHER BALLOON...
AMEND

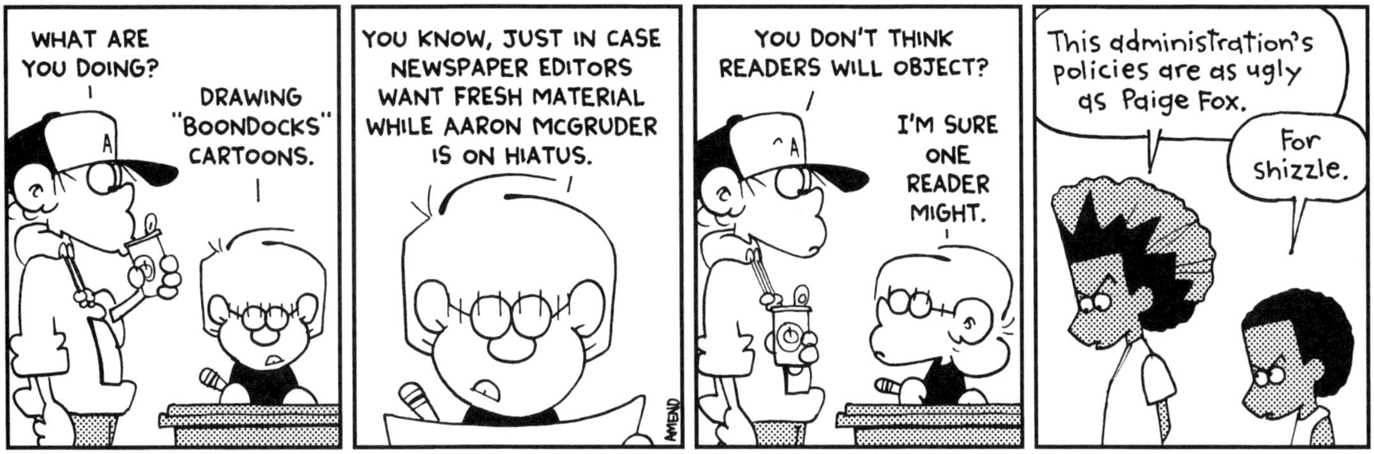
WHAT ARE YOU DOING?
DRAWING "BOONDOCKS" CARTOONS.
YOU KNOW, JUST IN CASE NEWSPAPER EDITORS WANT FRESH MATERIAL WHILE AARON MCGRUDER IS ON HIATUS.
AMEND
YOU DON'T THINK READERS WILL OBJECT?
I'M SURE ONE READER MIGHT.
This administration's policies are as ugly as Paige Fox.
For shizzle.

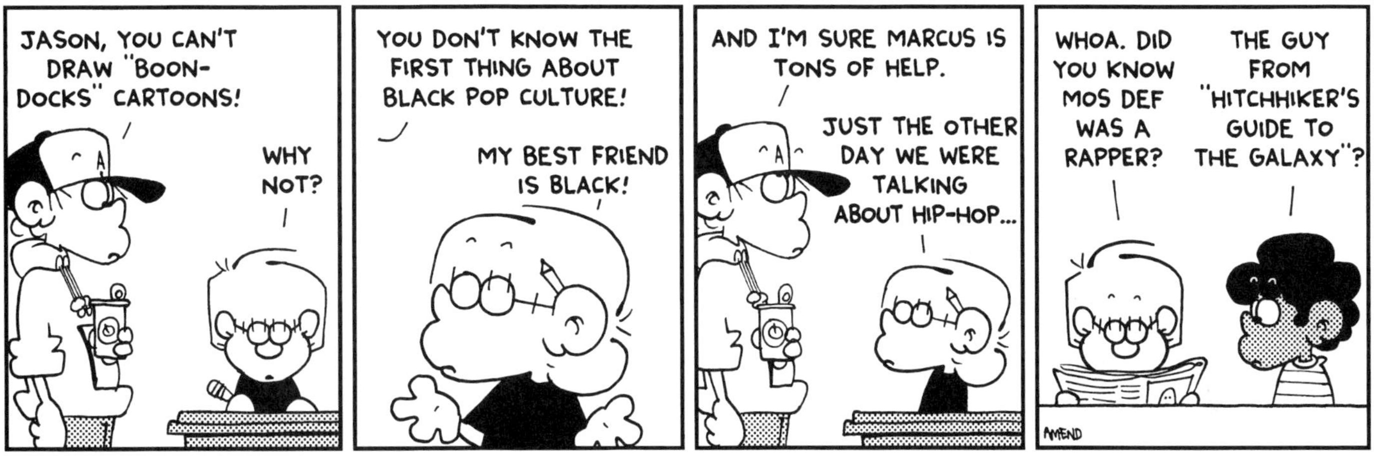
JASON, YOU CAN'T DRAW "BOON-DOCKS" CARTOONS!
WHY NOT?
YOU DON'T KNOW THE FIRST THING ABOUT BLACK POP CULTURE!
MY BEST FRIEND IS BLACK!
AND I'M SURE MARCUS IS TONS OF HELP.
JUST THE OTHER DAY WE WERE TALKING ABOUT HIP-HOP...
WHOA. DID YOU KNOW MOS DEF WAS A RAPPER?
THE GUY FROM "HITCHHIKER'S GUIDE TO THE GALAXY"?
AMEND

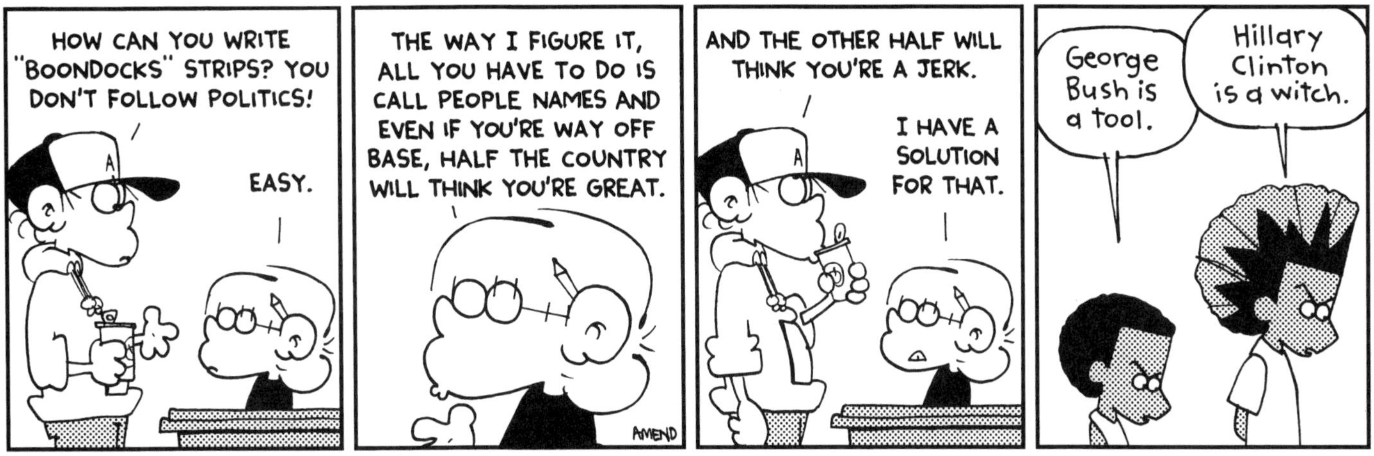
HOW CAN YOU WRITE "BOONDOCKS" STRIPS? YOU DON'T FOLLOW POLITICS!
EASY.
THE WAY I FIGURE IT, ALL YOU HAVE TO DO IS CALL PEOPLE NAMES AND EVEN IF YOU'RE WAY OFF BASE, HALF THE COUNTRY WILL THINK YOU'RE GREAT.
AMEND
AND THE OTHER HALF WILL THINK YOU'RE A JERK.
I HAVE A SOLUTION FOR THAT.
George Bush is a tool.
Hillary Clinton is a witch.

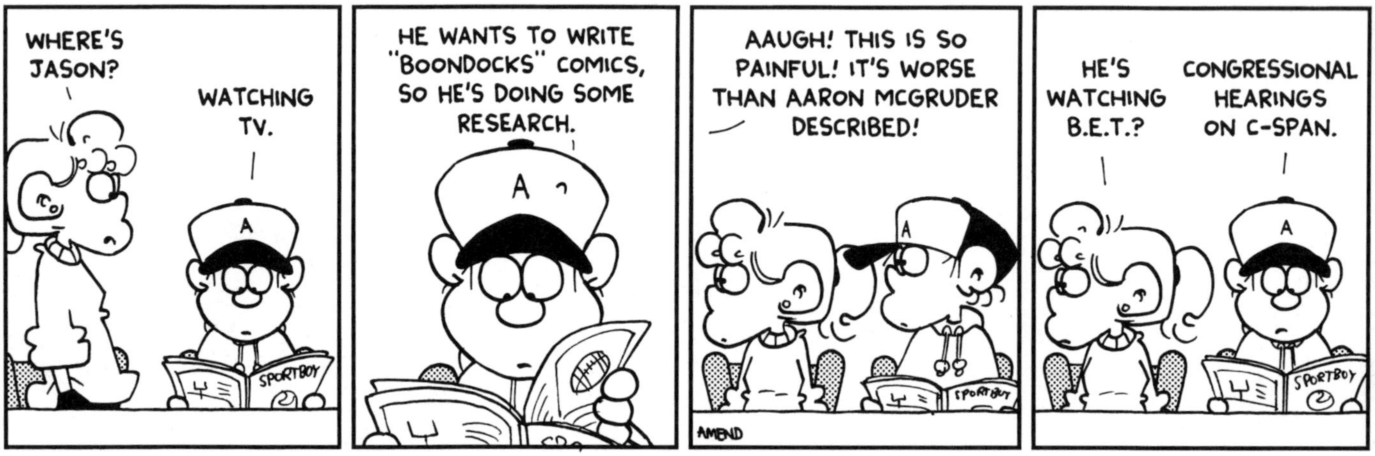
WHERE'S JASON?
WATCHING TV.
HE WANTS TO WRITE "BOONDOCKS" COMICS, SO HE'S DOING SOME RESEARCH.
AAUGH! THIS IS SO PAINFUL! IT'S WORSE THAN AARON MCGRUDER DESCRIBED!
HE'S WATCHING B.E.T.?
CONGRESSIONAL HEARINGS ON C-SPAN.

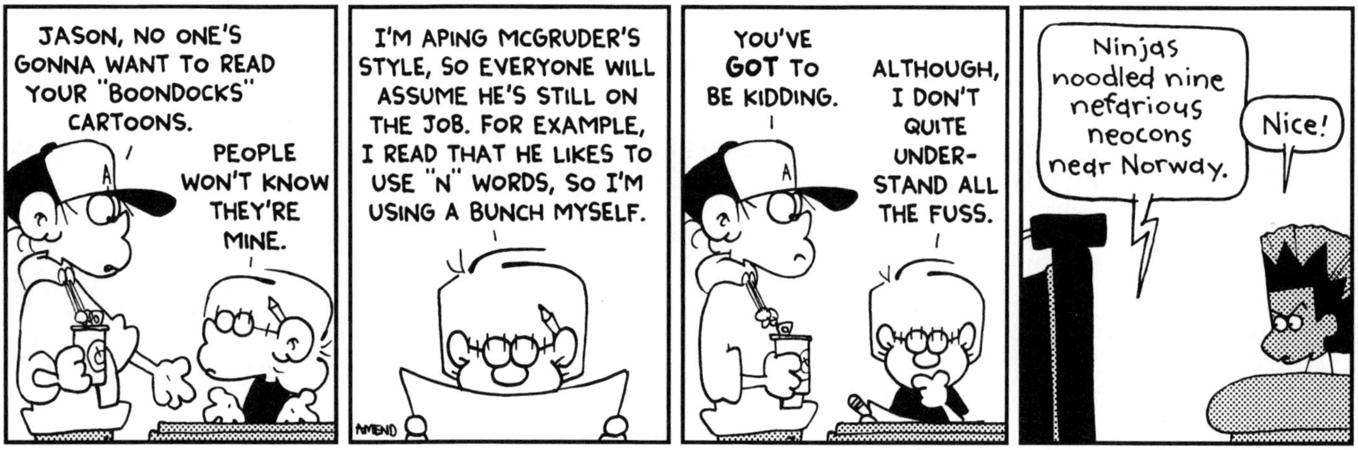
JASON, NO ONE'S GONNA WANT TO READ YOUR "BOONDOCKS" CARTOONS.
PEOPLE WON'T KNOW THEY'RE MINE.
I'M APING MCGRUDER'S STYLE, SO EVERYONE WILL ASSUME HE'S STILL ON THE JOB. FOR EXAMPLE, I READ THAT HE LIKES TO USE "N" WORDS, SO I'M USING A BUNCH MYSELF.
YOU'VE **GOT** TO BE KIDDING.
ALTHOUGH, I DON'T QUITE UNDERSTAND ALL THE FUSS.
Ninjas noodled nine nefarious neocons near Norway.
Nice!

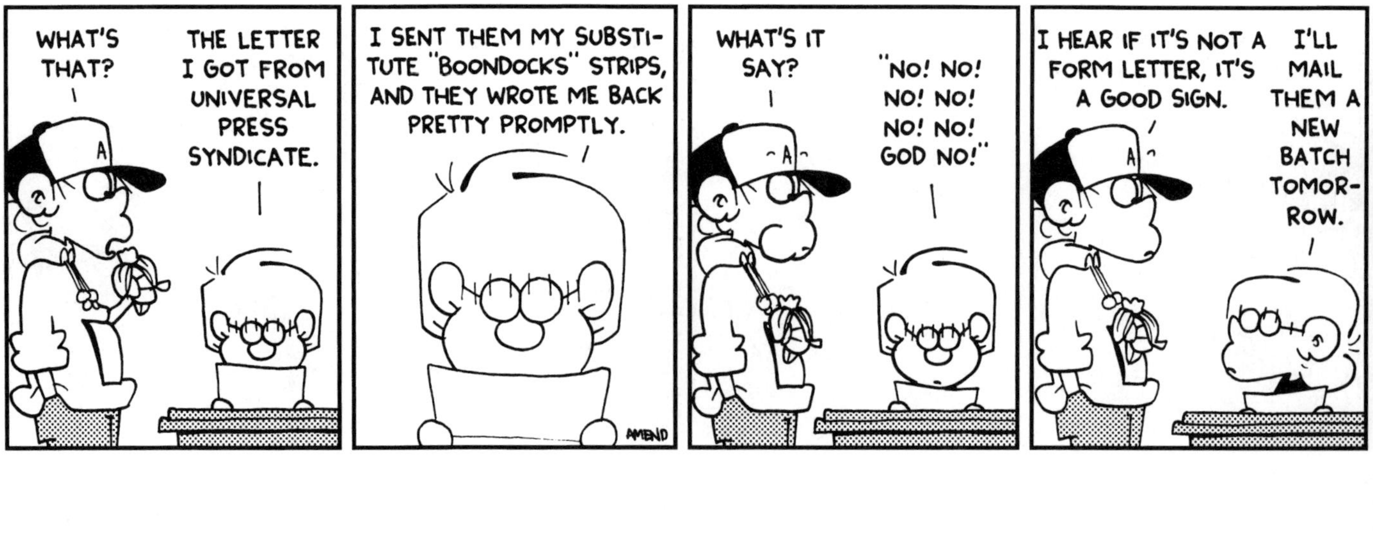
WHAT'S THAT?
THE LETTER I GOT FROM UNIVERSAL PRESS SYNDICATE.
I SENT THEM MY SUBSTITUTE "BOONDOCKS" STRIPS, AND THEY WROTE ME BACK PRETTY PROMPTLY.
WHAT'S IT SAY?
"NO! NO! NO! NO! NO! NO! GOD NO!"
I HEAR IF IT'S NOT A FORM LETTER, IT'S A GOOD SIGN.
I'LL MAIL THEM A NEW BATCH TOMORROW.

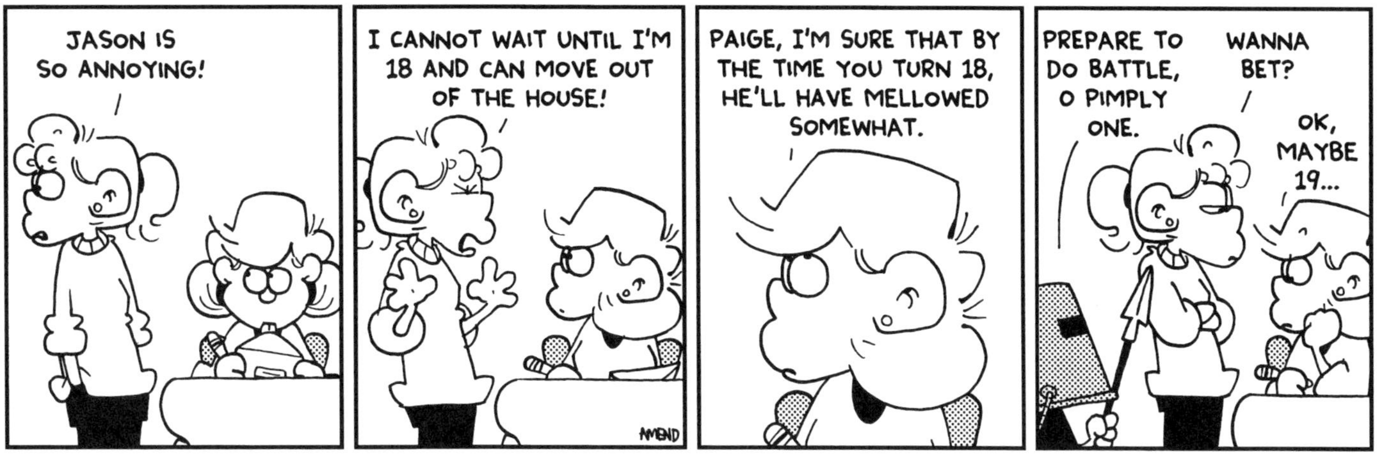
JASON IS SO ANNOYING!
I CANNOT WAIT UNTIL I'M 18 AND CAN MOVE OUT OF THE HOUSE!
AMEND
PAIGE, I'M SURE THAT BY THE TIME YOU TURN 18, HE'LL HAVE MELLOWED SOMEWHAT.
PREPARE TO DO BATTLE, O PIMPLY ONE.
WANNA BET?
OK, MAYBE 19...

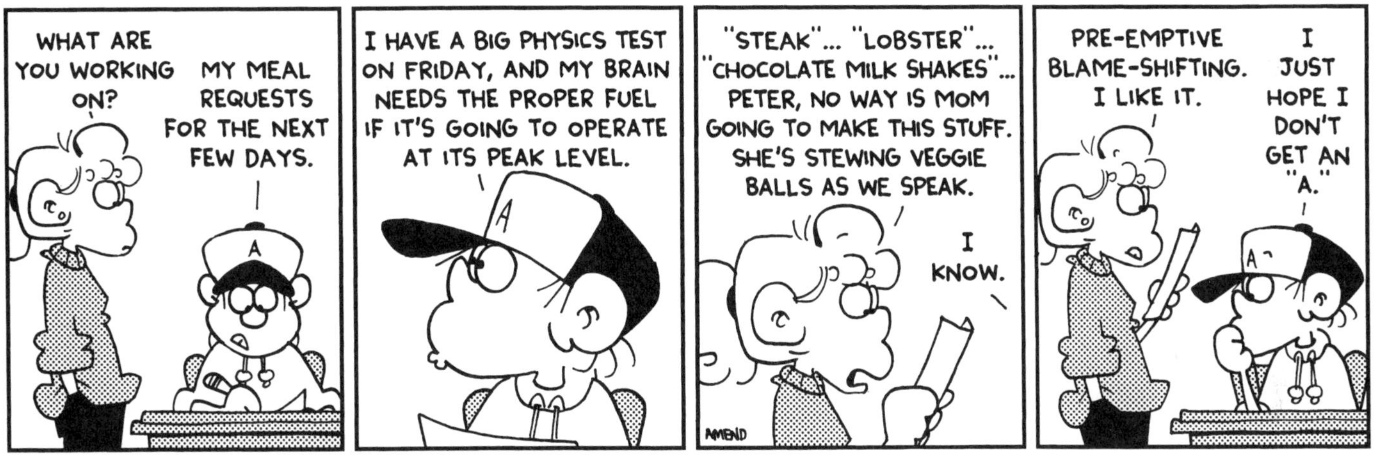
WHAT ARE YOU WORKING ON?
MY MEAL REQUESTS FOR THE NEXT FEW DAYS.
I HAVE A BIG PHYSICS TEST ON FRIDAY, AND MY BRAIN NEEDS THE PROPER FUEL IF IT'S GOING TO OPERATE AT ITS PEAK LEVEL.
"STEAK"... "LOBSTER"... "CHOCOLATE MILK SHAKES"... PETER, NO WAY IS MOM GOING TO MAKE THIS STUFF. SHE'S STEWING VEGGIE BALLS AS WE SPEAK.
I KNOW.
AMEND
PRE-EMPTIVE BLAME-SHIFTING. I LIKE IT.
I JUST HOPE I DON'T GET AN "A."

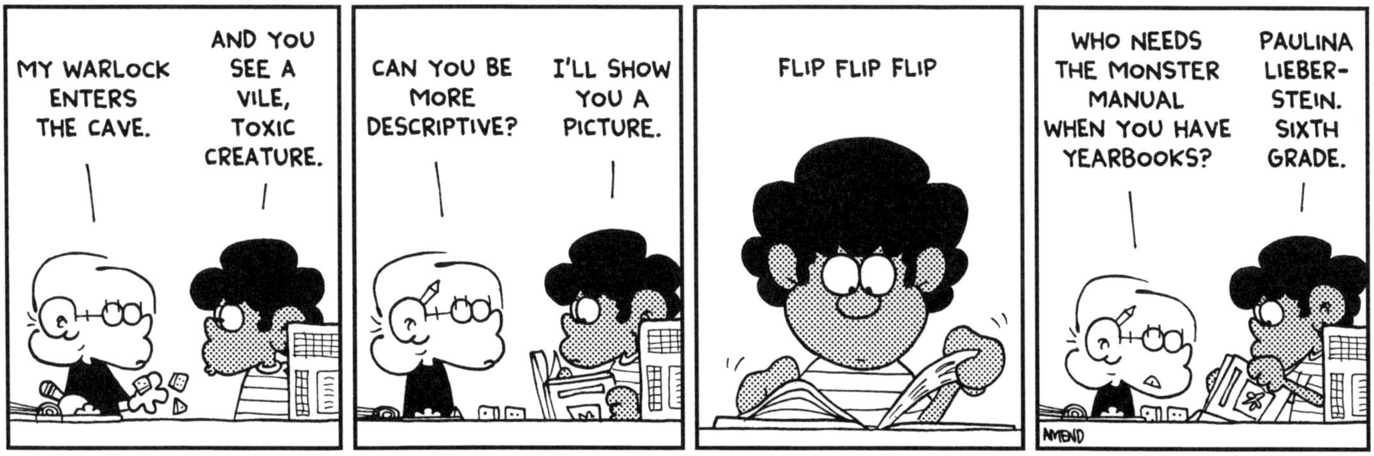
MY WARLOCK ENTERS THE CAVE.
AND YOU SEE A VILE, TOXIC CREATURE.
CAN YOU BE MORE DESCRIPTIVE?
I'LL SHOW YOU A PICTURE.
FLIP FLIP FLIP
WHO NEEDS THE MONSTER MANUAL WHEN YOU HAVE YEARBOOKS?
PAULINA LIEBER-STEIN. SIXTH GRADE.
AMEND

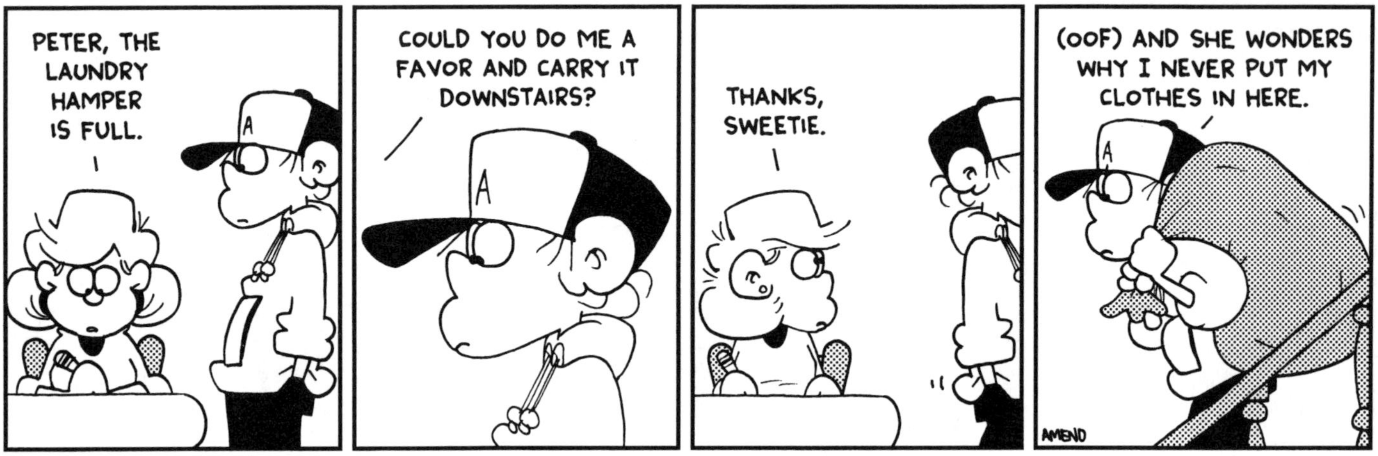
PETER, THE LAUNDRY HAMPER IS FULL.
COULD YOU DO ME A FAVOR AND CARRY IT DOWNSTAIRS?
THANKS, SWEETIE.
(OOF) AND SHE WONDERS WHY I NEVER PUT MY CLOTHES IN HERE.
AMEND

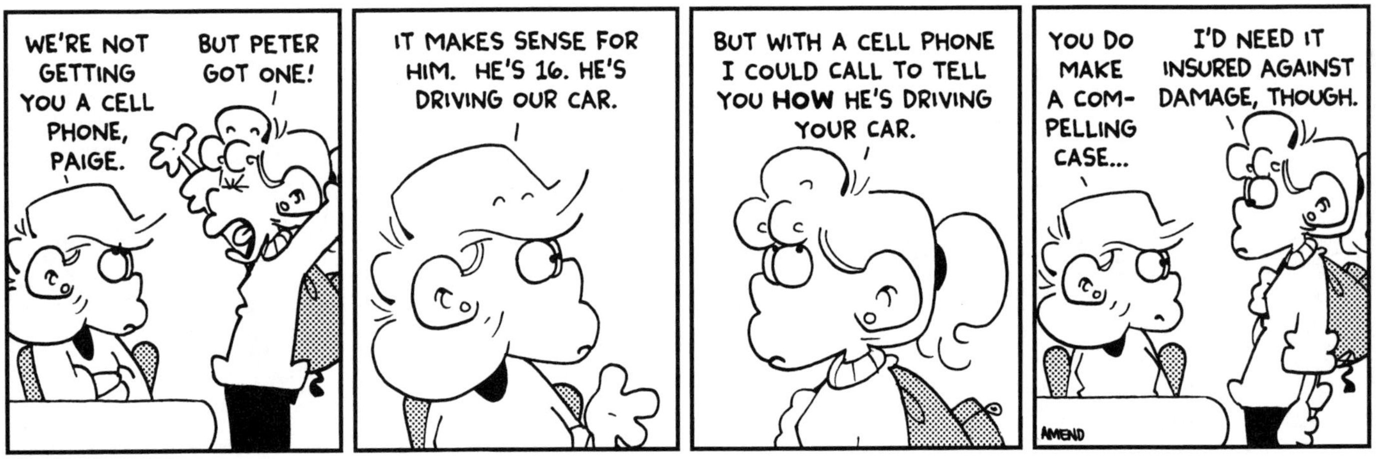
WE'RE NOT GETTING YOU A CELL PHONE, PAIGE.
BUT PETER GOT ONE!
IT MAKES SENSE FOR HIM. HE'S 16. HE'S DRIVING OUR CAR.
BUT WITH A CELL PHONE I COULD CALL TO TELL YOU **HOW** HE'S DRIVING YOUR CAR.
YOU DO MAKE A COM-PELLING CASE...
I'D NEED IT INSURED AGAINST DAMAGE, THOUGH.
AMEND

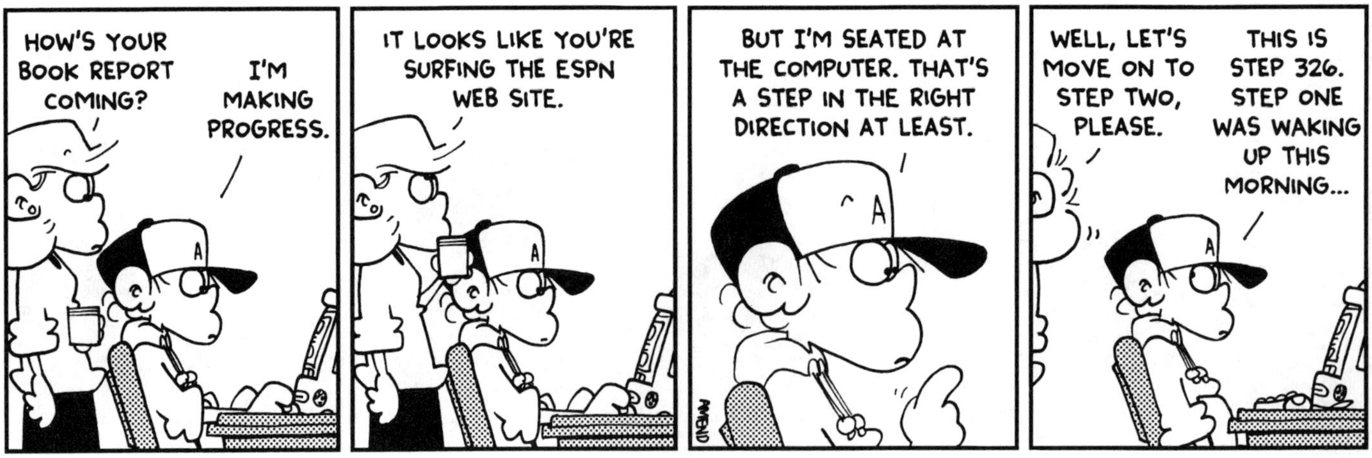
HOW'S YOUR BOOK REPORT COMING?
I'M MAKING PROGRESS.
IT LOOKS LIKE YOU'RE SURFING THE ESPN WEB SITE.
BUT I'M SEATED AT THE COMPUTER. THAT'S A STEP IN THE RIGHT DIRECTION AT LEAST.
AMEND
WELL, LET'S MOVE ON TO STEP TWO, PLEASE.
THIS IS STEP 326. STEP ONE WAS WAKING UP THIS MORNING...

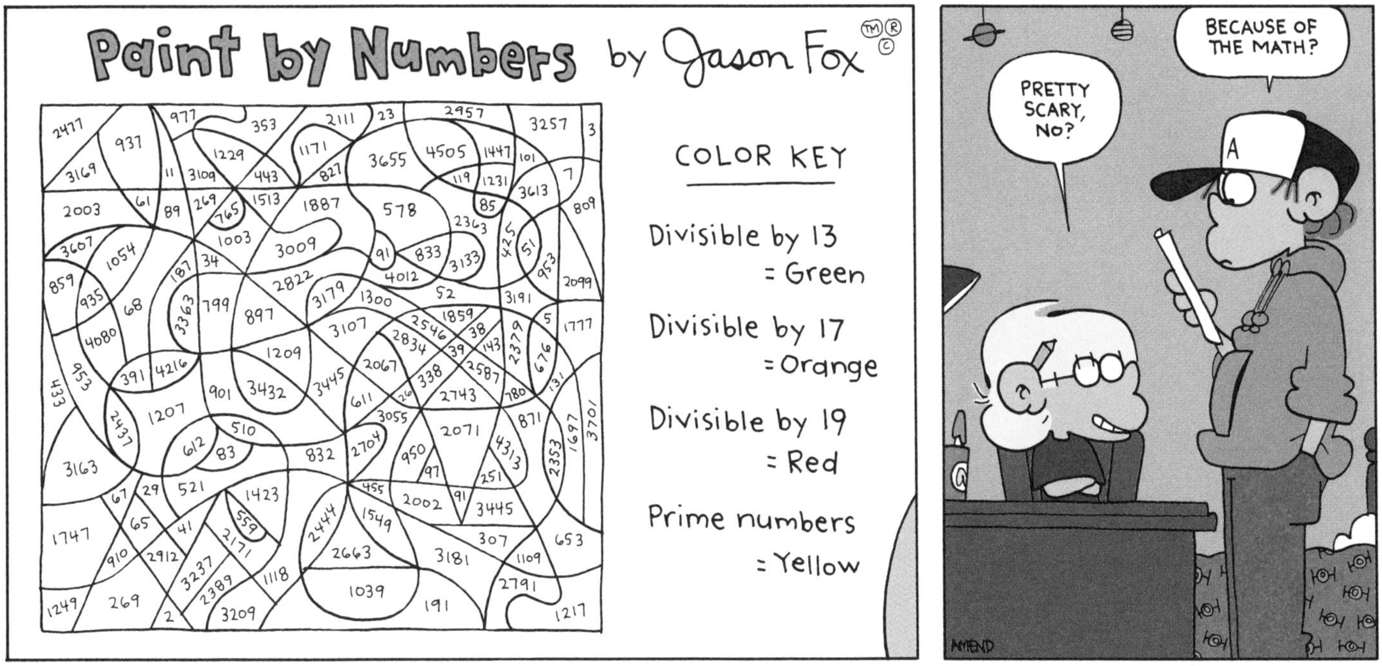
Paint by Numbers by Jason Fox
COLOR KEY
Divisible by 13 = Green
Divisible by 17 = Orange
Divisible by 19 = Red
Prime numbers = Yellow
PRETTY SCARY, NO?
BECAUSE OF THE MATH?
AMEND

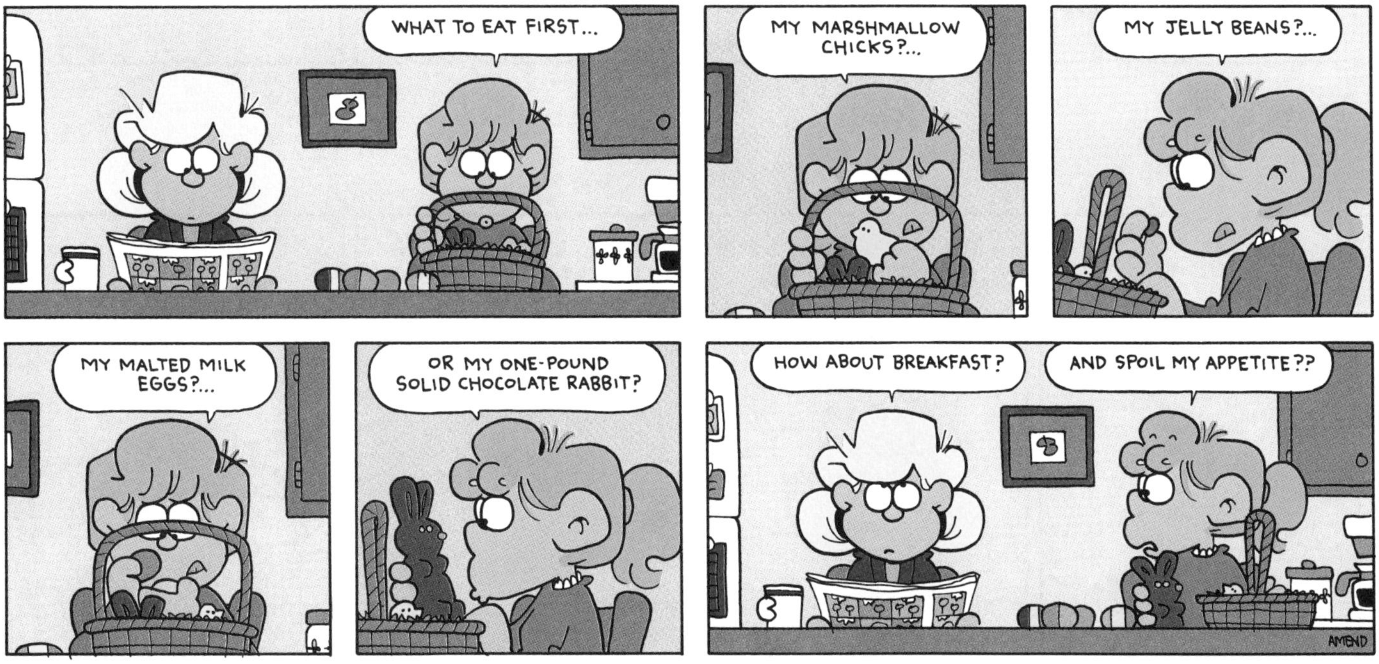
WHAT TO EAT FIRST...
MY MARSHMALLOW CHICKS?...
MY JELLY BEANS?...
MY MALTED MILK EGGS?...
OR MY ONE-POUND SOLID CHOCOLATE RABBIT?
HOW ABOUT BREAKFAST?
AND SPOIL MY APPETITE??
AMEND

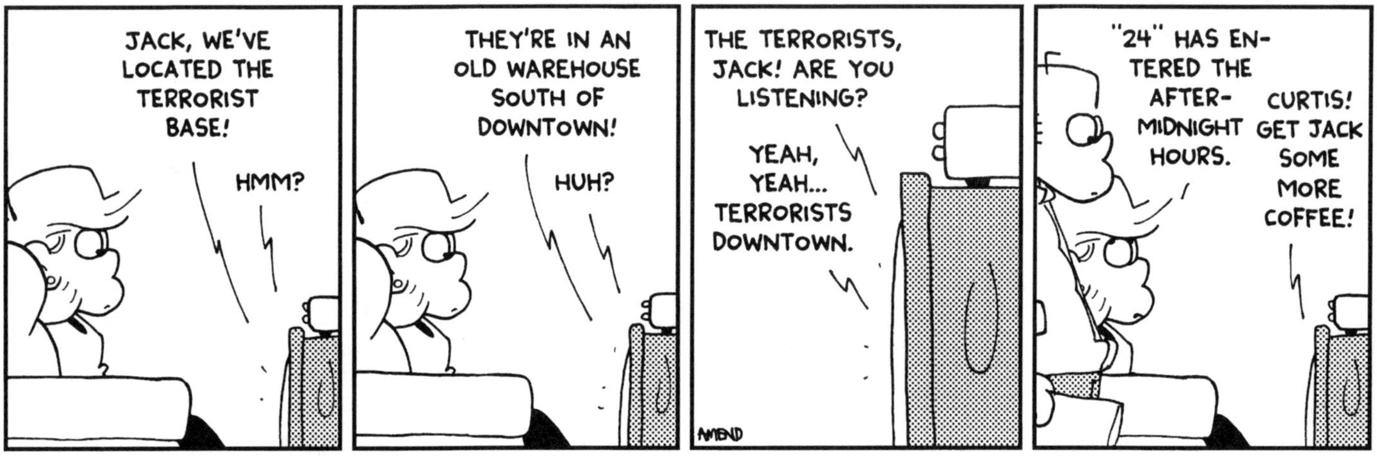
JACK, WE'VE LOCATED THE TERRORIST BASE!
HMM?
THEY'RE IN AN OLD WAREHOUSE SOUTH OF DOWNTOWN!
HUH?
THE TERRORISTS, JACK! ARE YOU LISTENING?
YEAH, YEAH... TERRORISTS DOWNTOWN.
AMEND
"24" HAS ENTERED THE AFTER-MIDNIGHT HOURS.
CURTIS! GET JACK SOME MORE COFFEE!

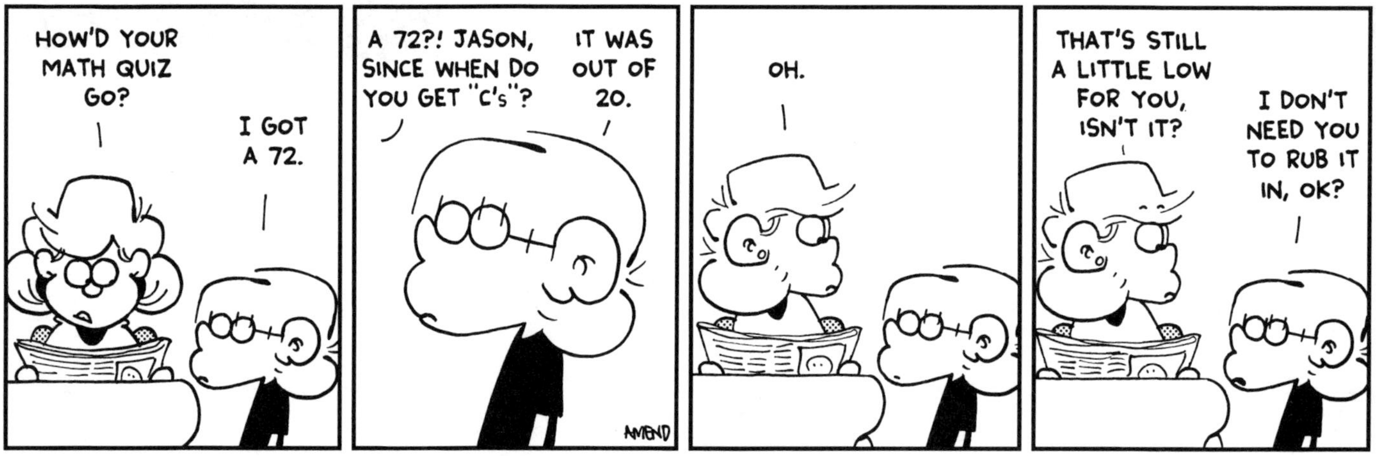
HOW'D YOUR MATH QUIZ GO?
I GOT A 72.
A 72?! JASON, SINCE WHEN DO YOU GET "C's"?
IT WAS OUT OF 20.
AMEND
OH.
THAT'S STILL A LITTLE LOW FOR YOU, ISN'T IT?
I DON'T NEED YOU TO RUB IT IN, OK?

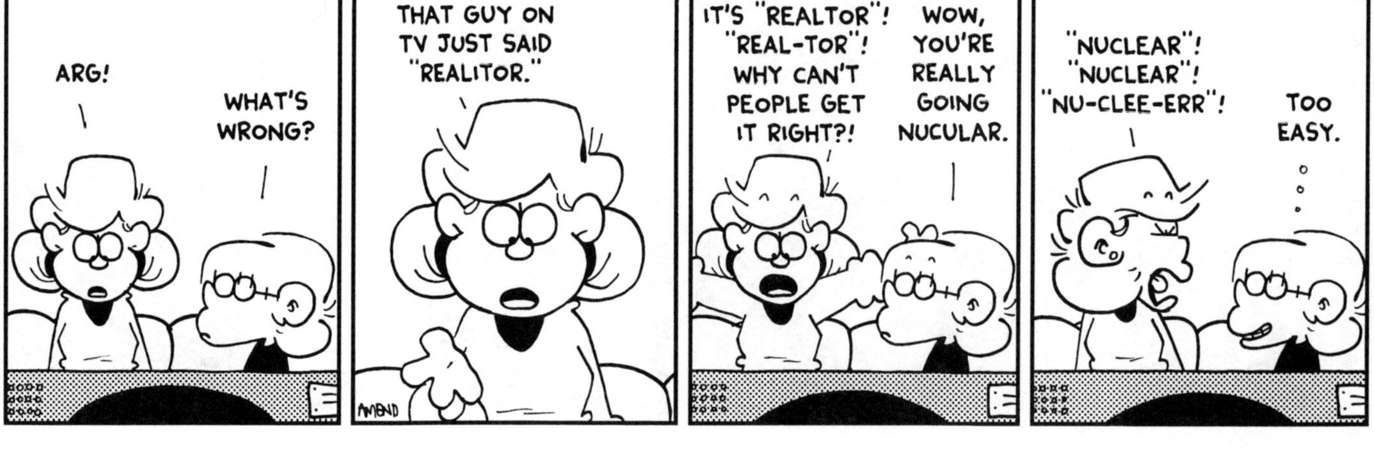
ARG!
WHAT'S WRONG?
THAT GUY ON TV JUST SAID "REALITOR."
AMEND
IT'S "REALTOR"! "REAL-TOR"! WHY CAN'T PEOPLE GET IT RIGHT?!
WOW, YOU'RE REALLY GOING NUCULAR.
"NUCLEAR"! "NUCLEAR"! "NU-CLEE-ERR"!
TOO EASY.

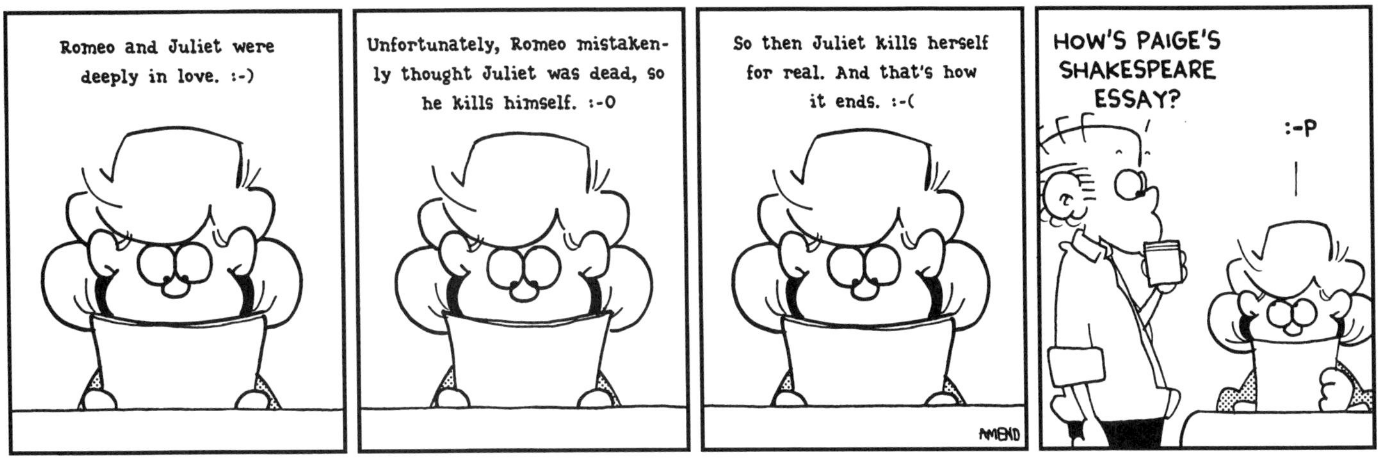
Romeo and Juliet were deeply in love. :-)
Unfortunately, Romeo mistakenly thought Juliet was dead, so he kills himself. :-O
So then Juliet kills herself for real. And that's how it ends. :-(
HOW'S PAIGE'S SHAKESPEARE ESSAY?
:-P
AMEND

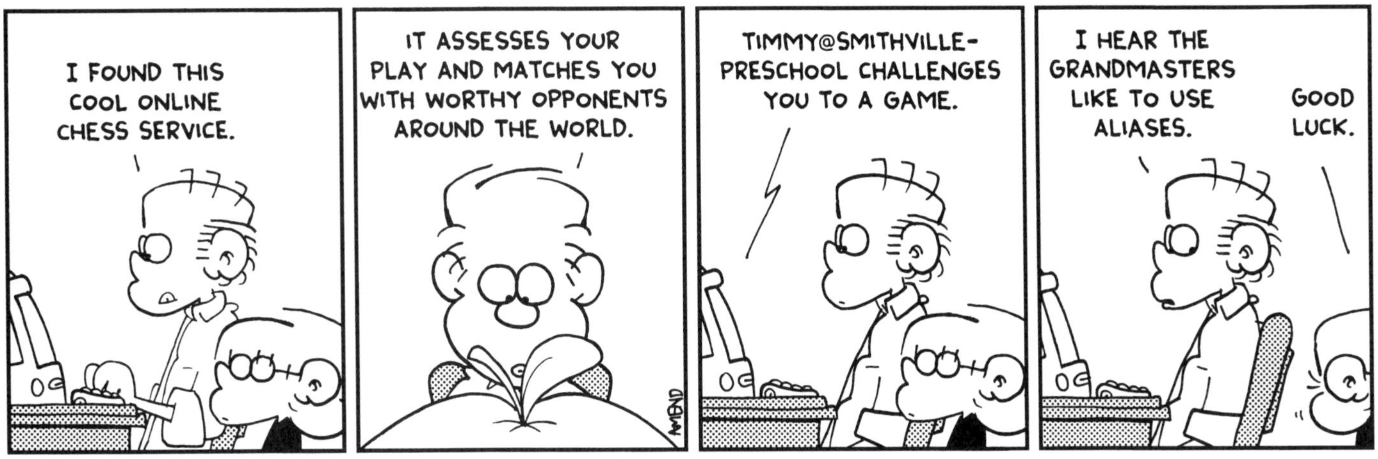
I FOUND THIS COOL ONLINE CHESS SERVICE.
IT ASSESSES YOUR PLAY AND MATCHES YOU WITH WORTHY OPPONENTS AROUND THE WORLD.
AMEND
TIMMY@SMITHVILLE-PRESCHOOL CHALLENGES YOU TO A GAME.
I HEAR THE GRANDMASTERS LIKE TO USE ALIASES.
GOOD LUCK.

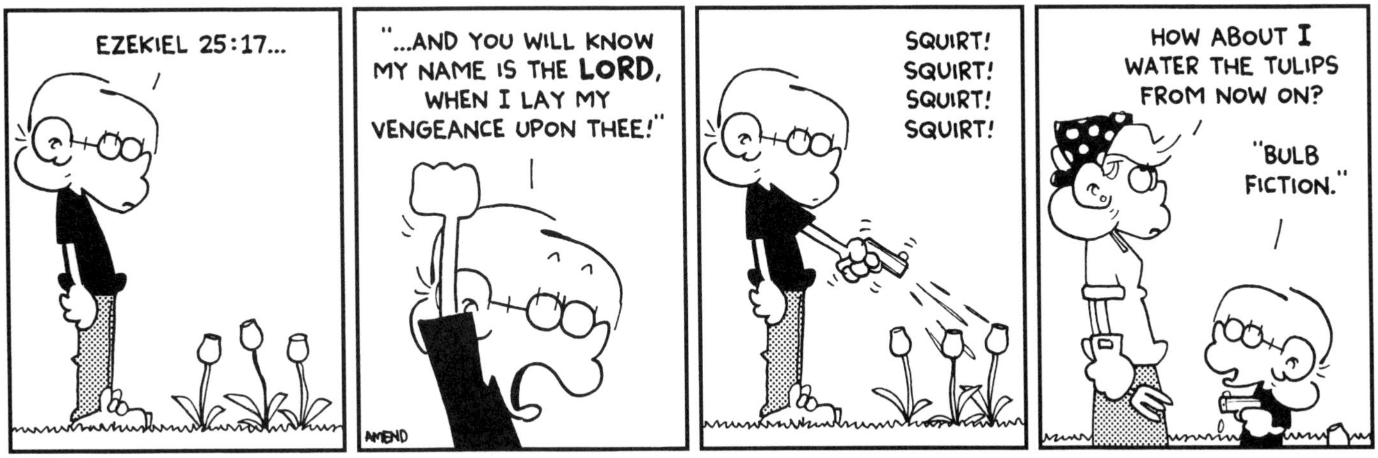
EZEKIEL 25:17...
"...AND YOU WILL KNOW MY NAME IS THE LORD, WHEN I LAY MY VENGEANCE UPON THEE!"
AMEND
SQUIRT! SQUIRT! SQUIRT! SQUIRT!
HOW ABOUT I WATER THE TULIPS FROM NOW ON?
"BULB FICTION."

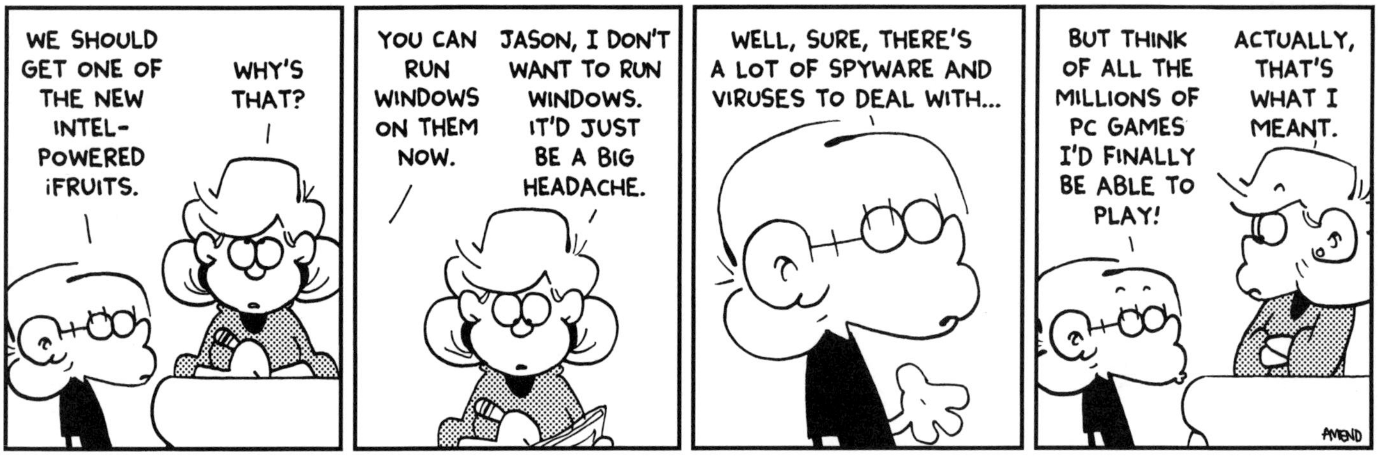
WE SHOULD GET ONE OF THE NEW INTEL-POWERED iFRUITS.
WHY'S THAT?
YOU CAN RUN WINDOWS ON THEM NOW.
JASON, I DON'T WANT TO RUN WINDOWS. IT'D JUST BE A BIG HEADACHE.
WELL, SURE, THERE'S A LOT OF SPYWARE AND VIRUSES TO DEAL WITH...
BUT THINK OF ALL THE MILLIONS OF PC GAMES I'D FINALLY BE ABLE TO PLAY!
ACTUALLY, THAT'S WHAT I MEANT.

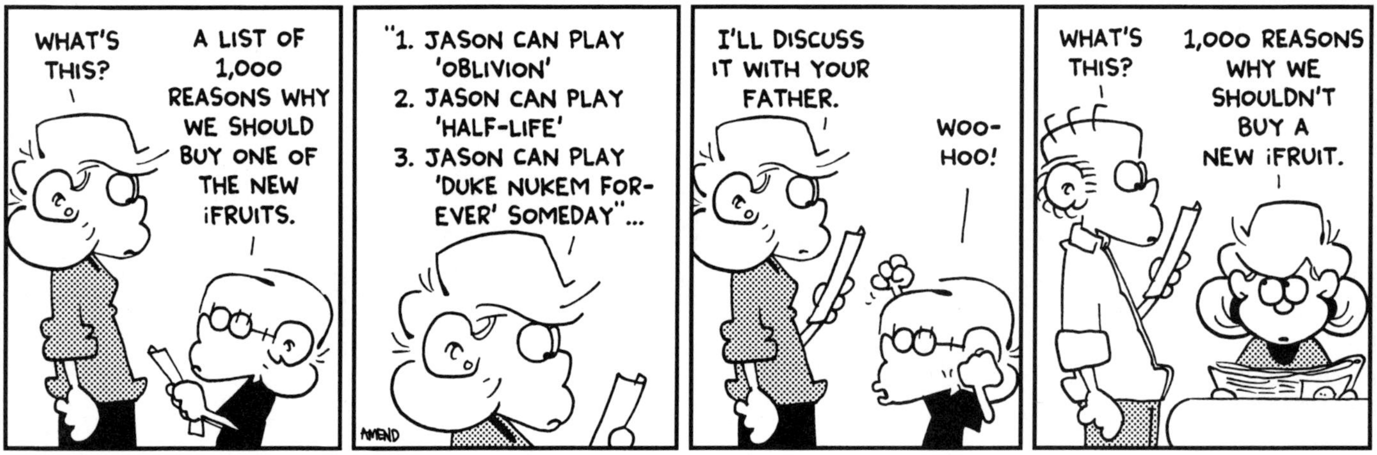
WHAT'S THIS?
A LIST OF 1,000 REASONS WHY WE SHOULD BUY ONE OF THE NEW iFRUITS.
"1. JASON CAN PLAY 'OBLIVION' 2. JASON CAN PLAY 'HALF-LIFE' 3. JASON CAN PLAY 'DUKE NUKEM FOREVER' SOMEDAY"...
I'LL DISCUSS IT WITH YOUR FATHER.
WOO-HOO!
WHAT'S THIS?
1,000 REASONS WHY WE SHOULDN'T BUY A NEW iFRUIT.

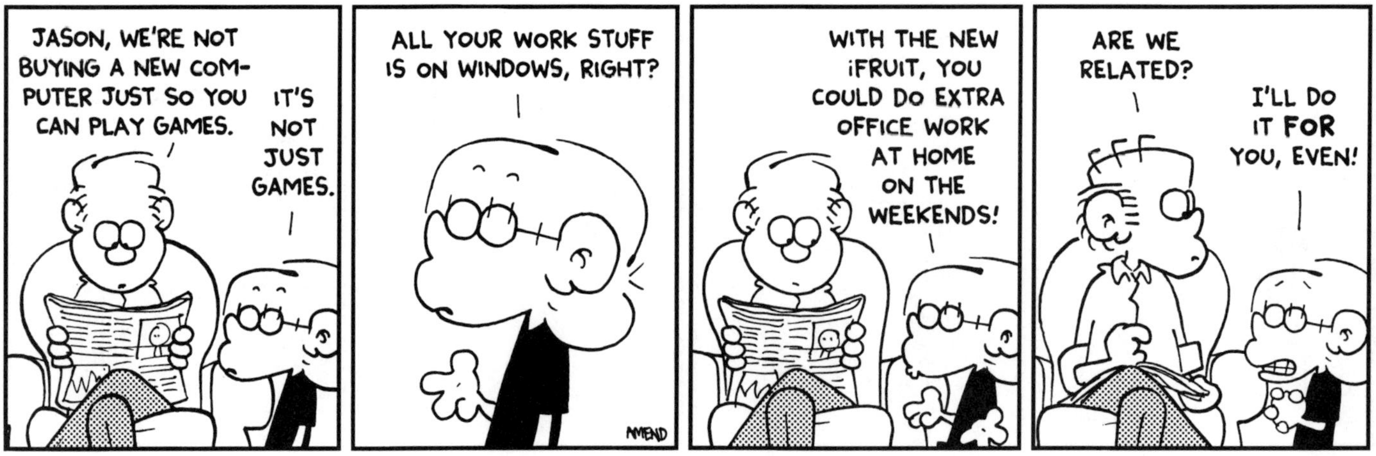
JASON, WE'RE NOT BUYING A NEW COMPUTER JUST SO YOU CAN PLAY GAMES.
IT'S NOT JUST GAMES.
ALL YOUR WORK STUFF IS ON WINDOWS, RIGHT?
WITH THE NEW iFRUIT, YOU COULD DO EXTRA OFFICE WORK AT HOME ON THE WEEKENDS!
ARE WE RELATED?
I'LL DO IT FOR YOU, EVEN!

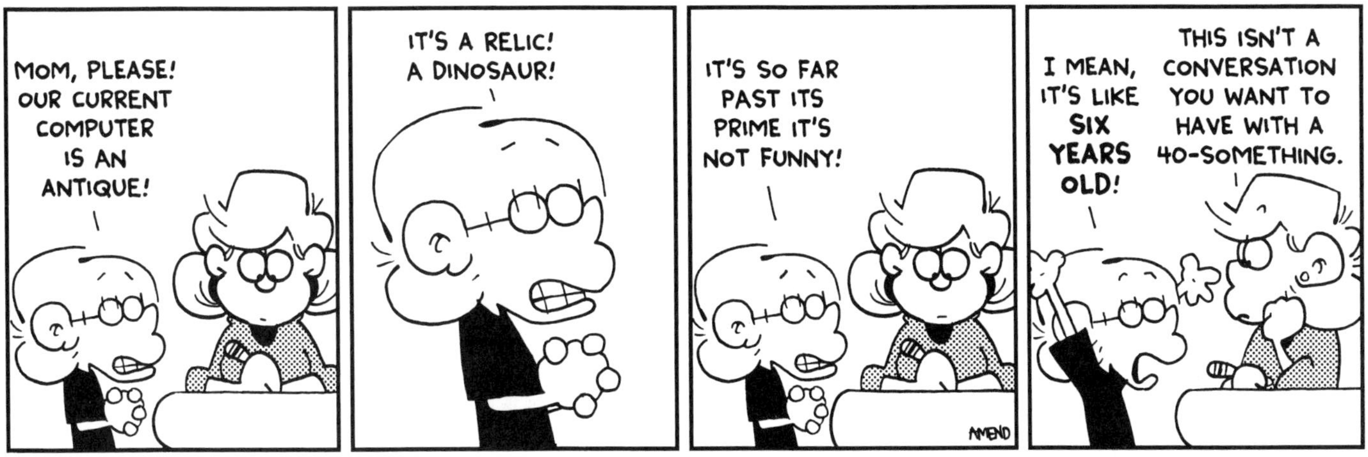
MOM, PLEASE! OUR CURRENT COMPUTER IS AN ANTIQUE!
IT'S A RELIC! A DINOSAUR!
IT'S SO FAR PAST ITS PRIME IT'S NOT FUNNY!
I MEAN, IT'S LIKE **SIX YEARS OLD**!
THIS ISN'T A CONVERSATION YOU WANT TO HAVE WITH A 40-SOMETHING.
AMEND

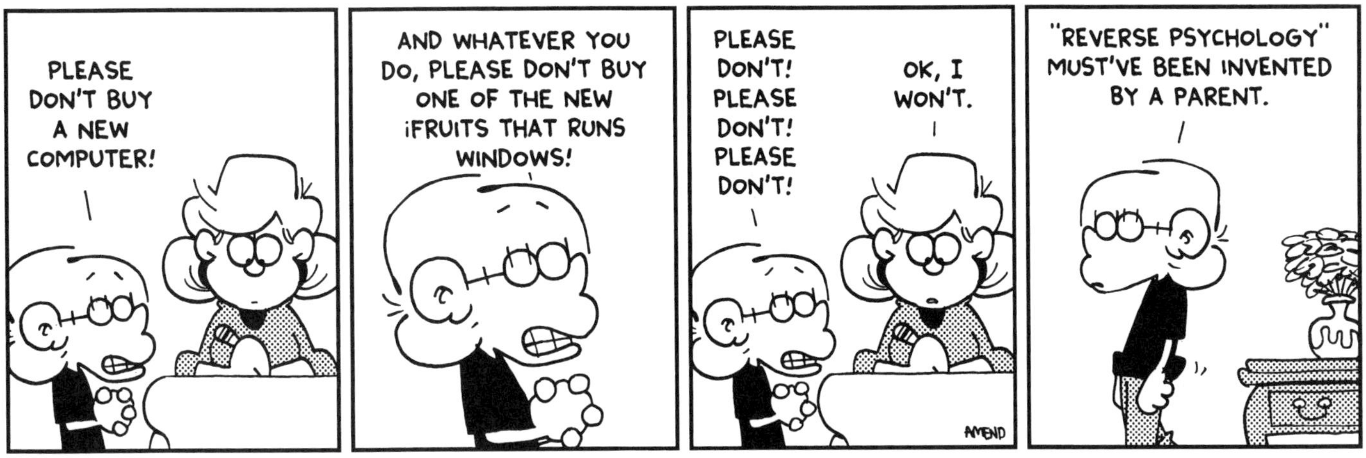
PLEASE DON'T BUY A NEW COMPUTER!
AND WHATEVER YOU DO, PLEASE DON'T BUY ONE OF THE NEW iFRUITS THAT RUNS WINDOWS!
PLEASE DON'T! PLEASE DON'T! PLEASE DON'T!
OK, I WON'T.
AMEND
"REVERSE PSYCHOLOGY" MUST'VE BEEN INVENTED BY A PARENT.

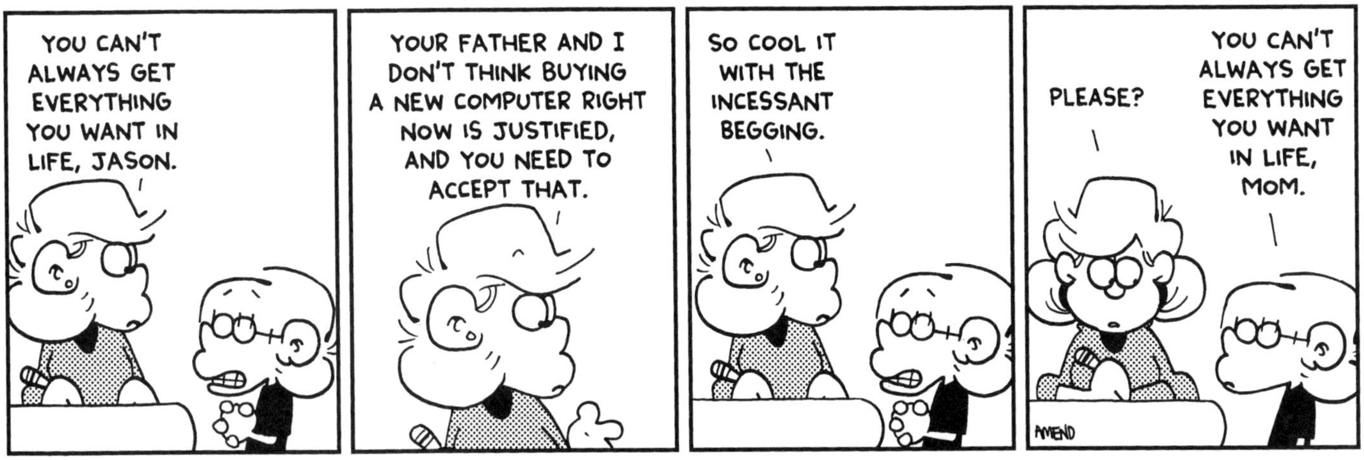
YOU CAN'T ALWAYS GET EVERYTHING YOU WANT IN LIFE, JASON.
YOUR FATHER AND I DON'T THINK BUYING A NEW COMPUTER RIGHT NOW IS JUSTIFIED, AND YOU NEED TO ACCEPT THAT.
SO COOL IT WITH THE INCESSANT BEGGING.
PLEASE?
YOU CAN'T ALWAYS GET EVERYTHING YOU WANT IN LIFE, MOM.
AMEND

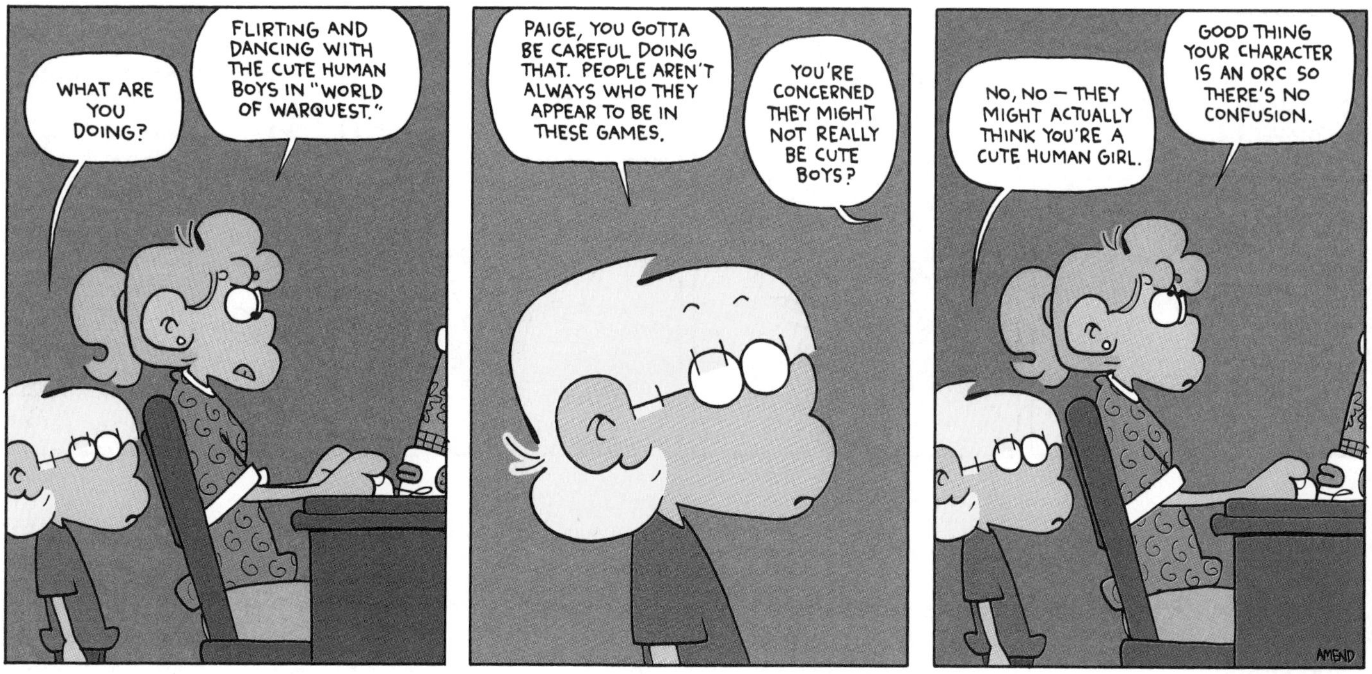
WHAT ARE YOU DOING?
FLIRTING AND DANCING WITH THE CUTE HUMAN BOYS IN "WORLD OF WARQUEST."
PAIGE, YOU GOTTA BE CAREFUL DOING THAT. PEOPLE AREN'T ALWAYS WHO THEY APPEAR TO BE IN THESE GAMES.
YOU'RE CONCERNED THEY MIGHT NOT REALLY BE CUTE BOYS?
NO, NO — THEY MIGHT ACTUALLY THINK YOU'RE A CUTE HUMAN GIRL.
GOOD THING YOUR CHARACTER IS AN ORC SO THERE'S NO CONFUSION.
AMEND

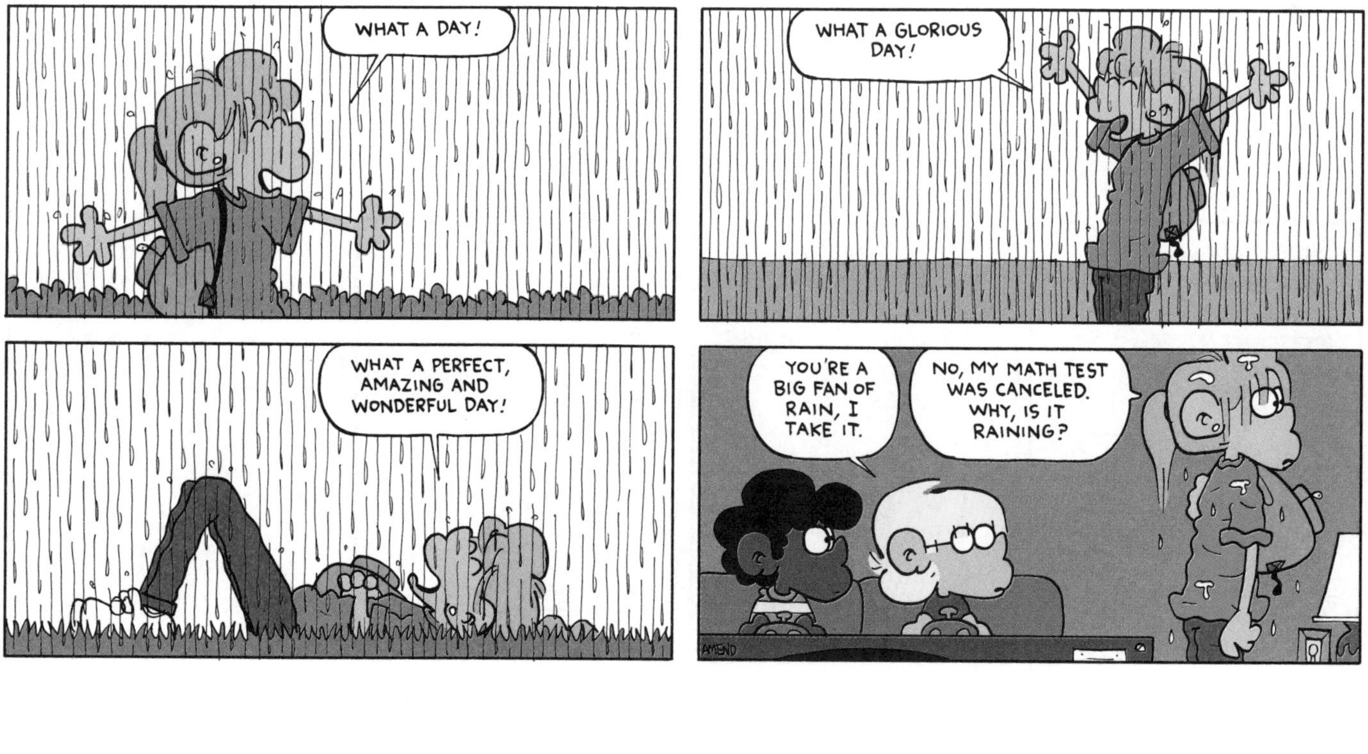
WHAT A DAY!
WHAT A GLORIOUS DAY!
WHAT A PERFECT, AMAZING AND WONDERFUL DAY!
YOU'RE A BIG FAN OF RAIN, I TAKE IT.
NO, MY MATH TEST WAS CANCELED. WHY, IS IT RAINING?
AMEND

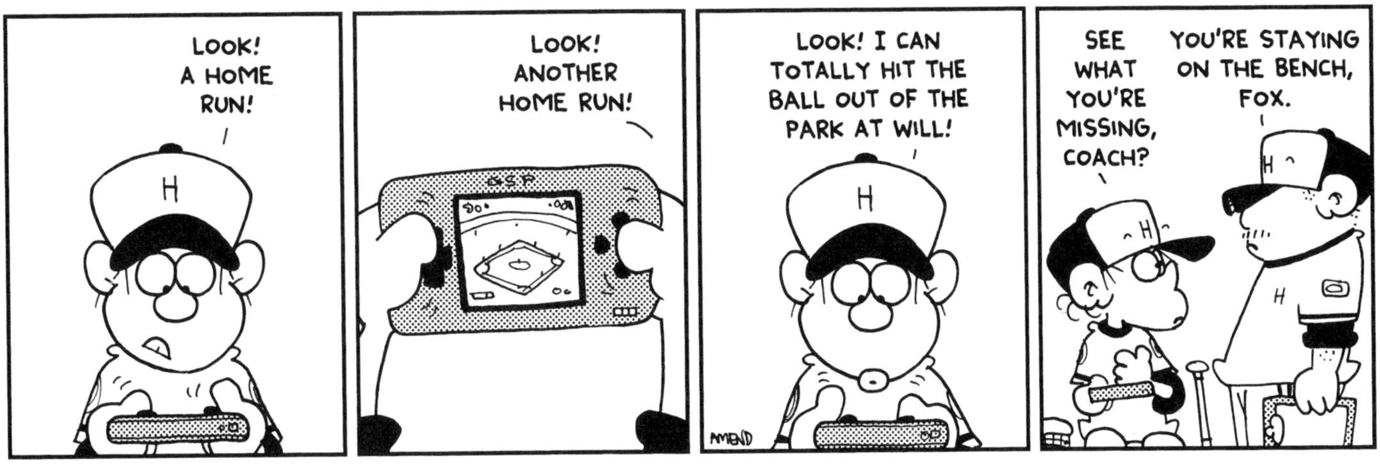
LOOK! A HOME RUN!
LOOK! ANOTHER HOME RUN!
LOOK! I CAN TOTALLY HIT THE BALL OUT OF THE PARK AT WILL!
AMEND
SEE WHAT YOU'RE MISSING, COACH?
YOU'RE STAYING ON THE BENCH, FOX.

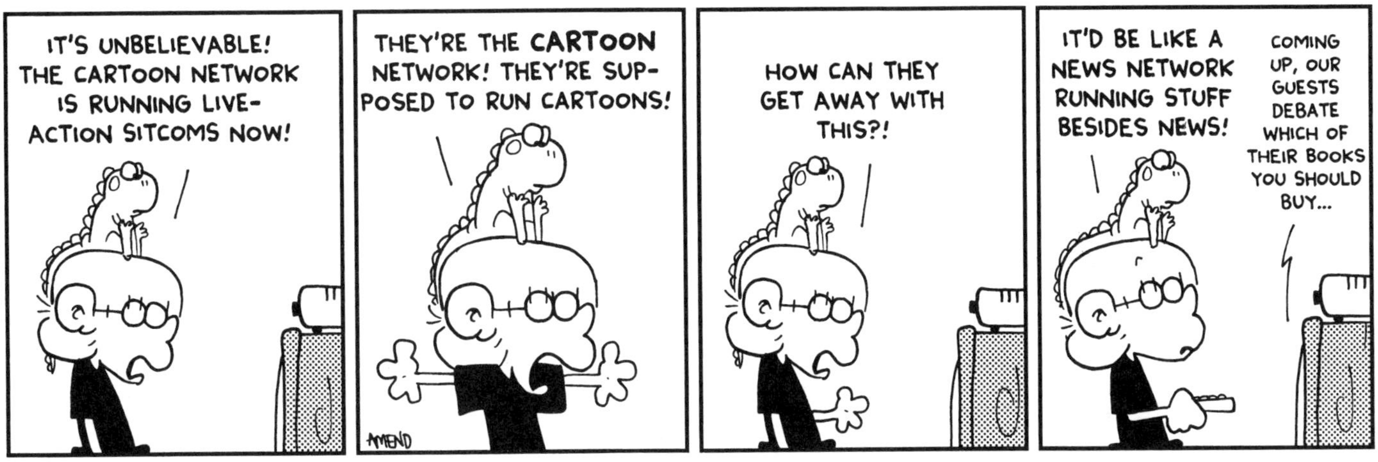
IT'S UNBELIEVABLE! THE CARTOON NETWORK IS RUNNING LIVE-ACTION SITCOMS NOW!
THEY'RE THE CARTOON NETWORK! THEY'RE SUP-POSED TO RUN CARTOONS!
AMEND
HOW CAN THEY GET AWAY WITH THIS?!
IT'D BE LIKE A NEWS NETWORK RUNNING STUFF BESIDES NEWS!
COMING UP, OUR GUESTS DEBATE WHICH OF THEIR BOOKS YOU SHOULD BUY...

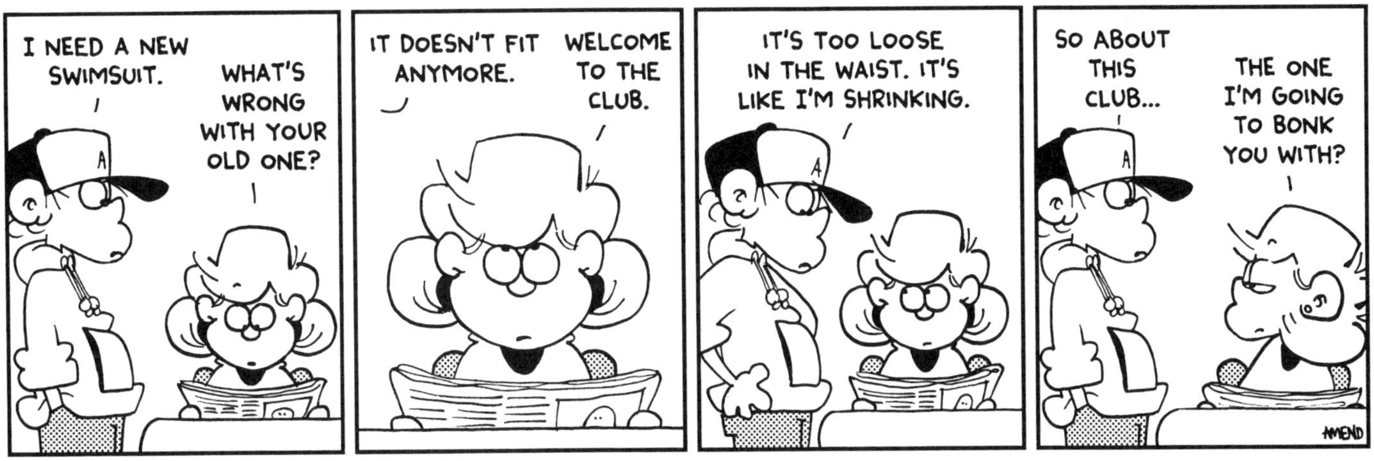
I NEED A NEW SWIMSUIT.
WHAT'S WRONG WITH YOUR OLD ONE?
IT DOESN'T FIT ANYMORE.
WELCOME TO THE CLUB.
IT'S TOO LOOSE IN THE WAIST. IT'S LIKE I'M SHRINKING.
SO ABOUT THIS CLUB...
THE ONE I'M GOING TO BONK YOU WITH?
AMEND

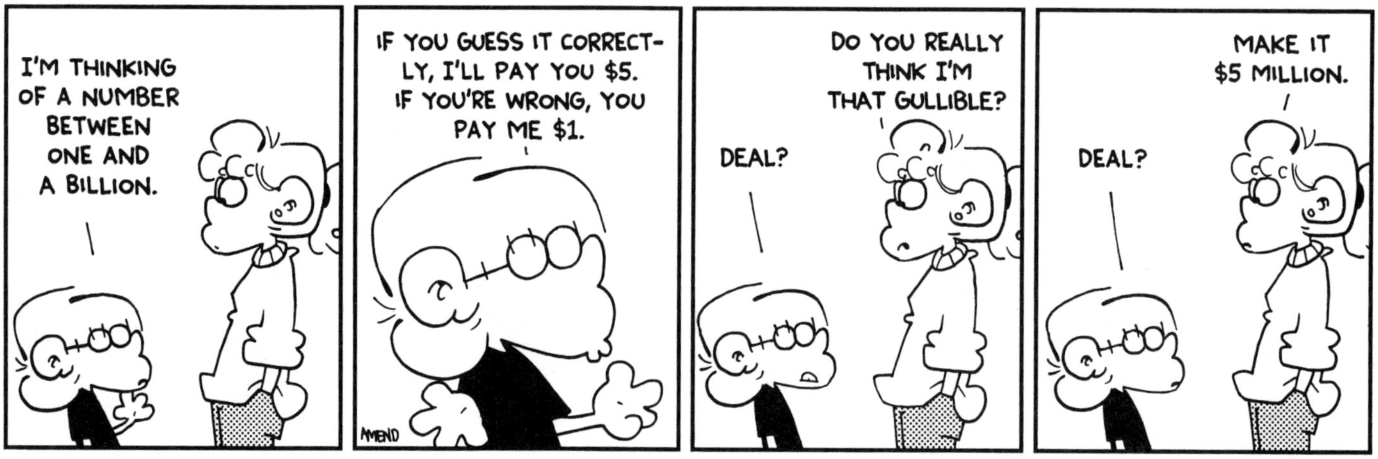
I'M THINKING OF A NUMBER BETWEEN ONE AND A BILLION.
IF YOU GUESS IT CORRECTLY, I'LL PAY YOU $5. IF YOU'RE WRONG, YOU PAY ME $1.
AMEND
DEAL?
DO YOU REALLY THINK I'M THAT GULLIBLE?
DEAL?
MAKE IT $5 MILLION.

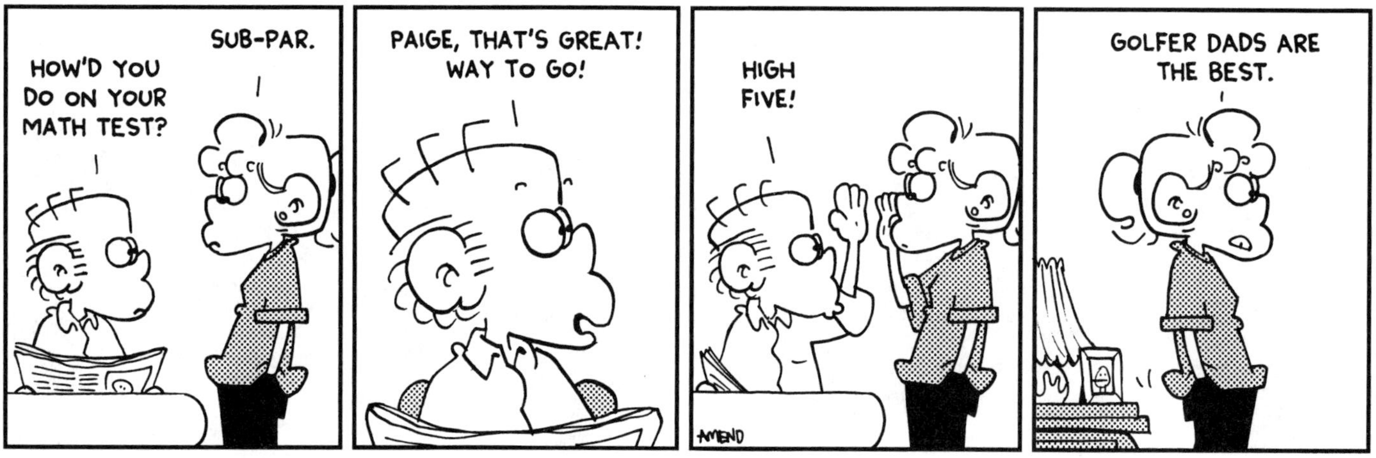
HOW'D YOU DO ON YOUR MATH TEST?
SUB-PAR.
PAIGE, THAT'S GREAT! WAY TO GO!
HIGH FIVE!
AMEND
GOLFER DADS ARE THE BEST.

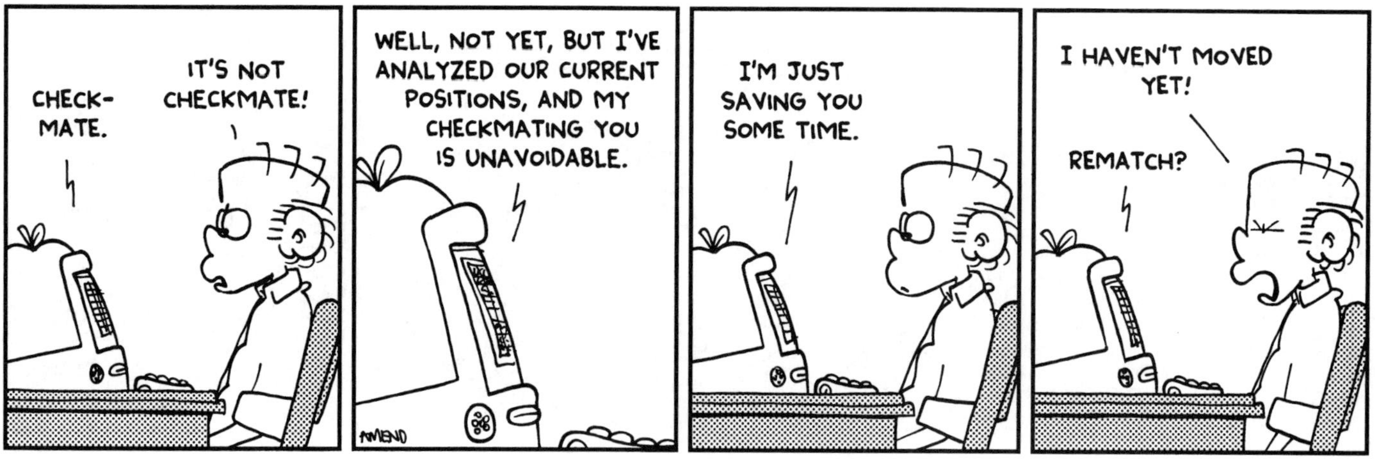
CHECK-MATE.
IT'S NOT CHECKMATE!
WELL, NOT YET, BUT I'VE ANALYZED OUR CURRENT POSITIONS, AND MY CHECKMATING YOU IS UNAVOIDABLE.
AMEND
I'M JUST SAVING YOU SOME TIME.
I HAVEN'T MOVED YET!
REMATCH?

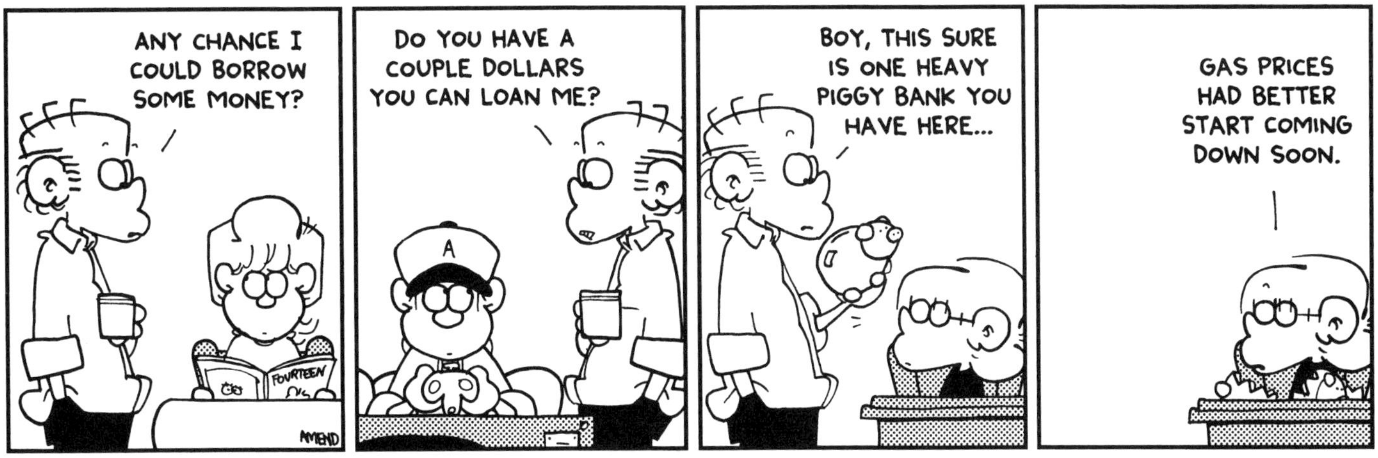
ANY CHANCE I COULD BORROW SOME MONEY?
DO YOU HAVE A COUPLE DOLLARS YOU CAN LOAN ME?
BOY, THIS SURE IS ONE HEAVY PIGGY BANK YOU HAVE HERE...
GAS PRICES HAD BETTER START COMING DOWN SOON.

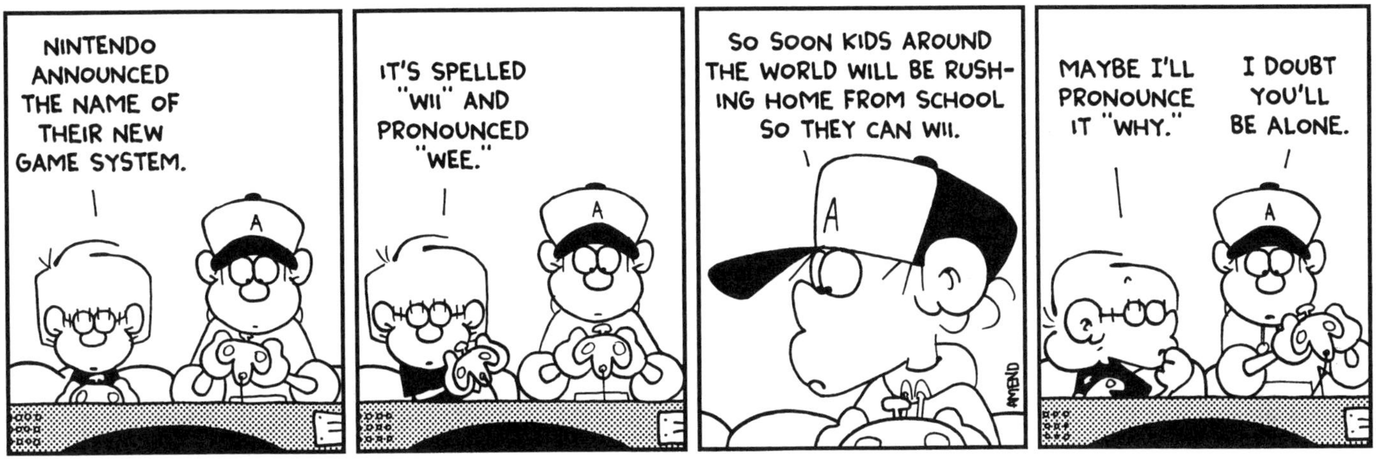
NINTENDO ANNOUNCED THE NAME OF THEIR NEW GAME SYSTEM.
IT'S SPELLED "WII" AND PRONOUNCED "WEE."
SO SOON KIDS AROUND THE WORLD WILL BE RUSH-ING HOME FROM SCHOOL SO THEY CAN WII.
MAYBE I'LL PRONOUNCE IT "WHY."
I DOUBT YOU'LL BE ALONE.

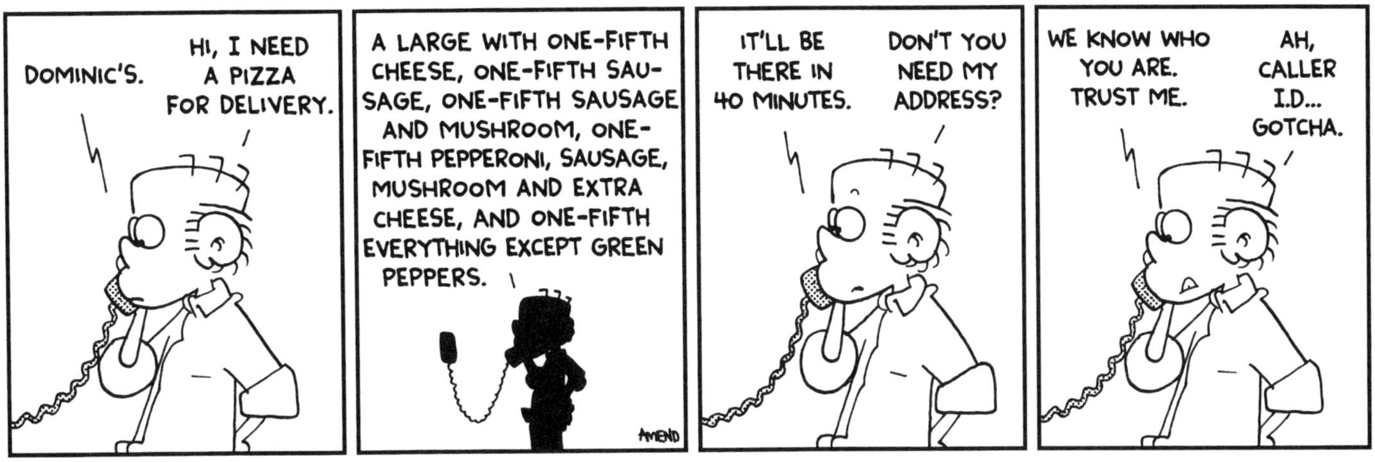
DOMINIC'S.
HI, I NEED A PIZZA FOR DELIVERY.
A LARGE WITH ONE-FIFTH CHEESE, ONE-FIFTH SAU-SAGE, ONE-FIFTH SAUSAGE AND MUSHROOM, ONE-FIFTH PEPPERONI, SAUSAGE, MUSHROOM AND EXTRA CHEESE, AND ONE-FIFTH EVERYTHING EXCEPT GREEN PEPPERS.
IT'LL BE THERE IN 40 MINUTES.
DON'T YOU NEED MY ADDRESS?
WE KNOW WHO YOU ARE. TRUST ME.
AH, CALLER I.D... GOTCHA.

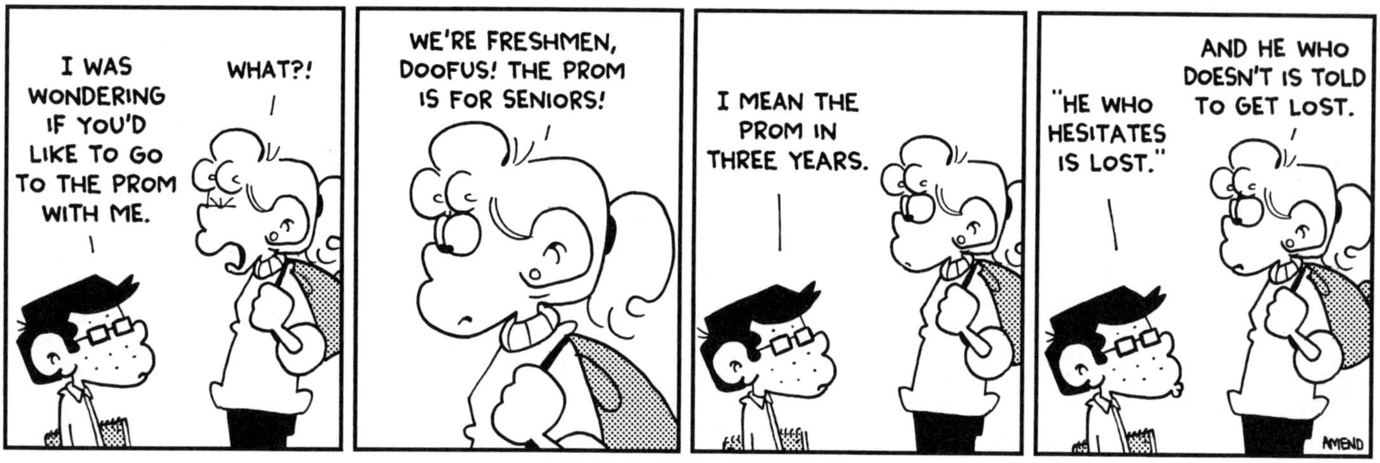
I WAS WONDERING IF YOU'D LIKE TO GO TO THE PROM WITH ME.
WHAT?!
WE'RE FRESHMEN, DOOFUS! THE PROM IS FOR SENIORS!
I MEAN THE PROM IN THREE YEARS.
"HE WHO HESITATES IS LOST."
AND HE WHO DOESN'T IS TOLD TO GET LOST.
AMEND

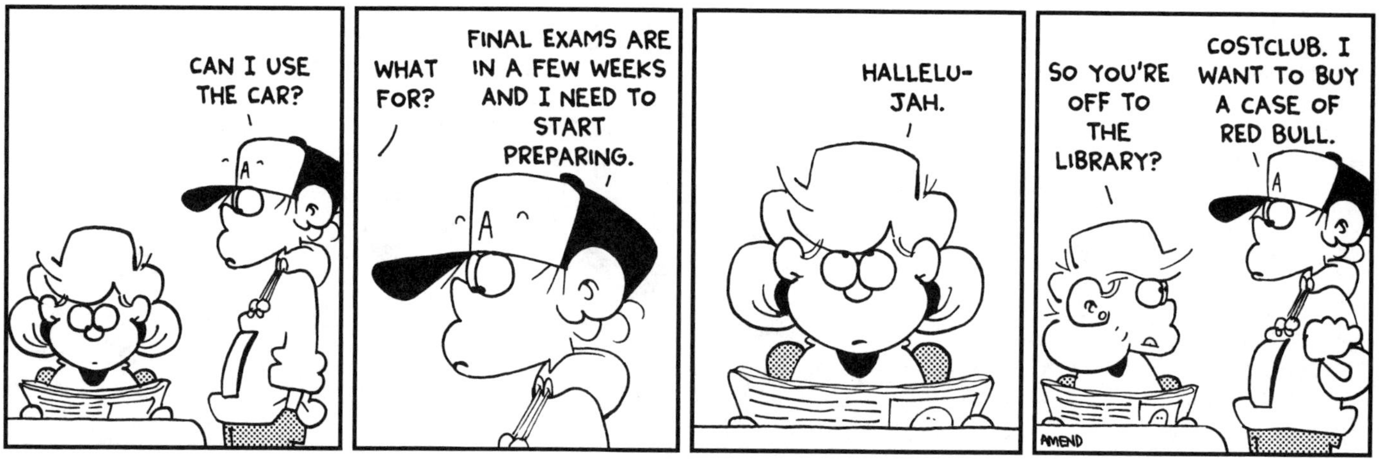
CAN I USE THE CAR?
WHAT FOR?
FINAL EXAMS ARE IN A FEW WEEKS AND I NEED TO START PREPARING.
HALLELU-JAH.
SO YOU'RE OFF TO THE LIBRARY?
COSTCLUB. I WANT TO BUY A CASE OF RED BULL.
AMEND

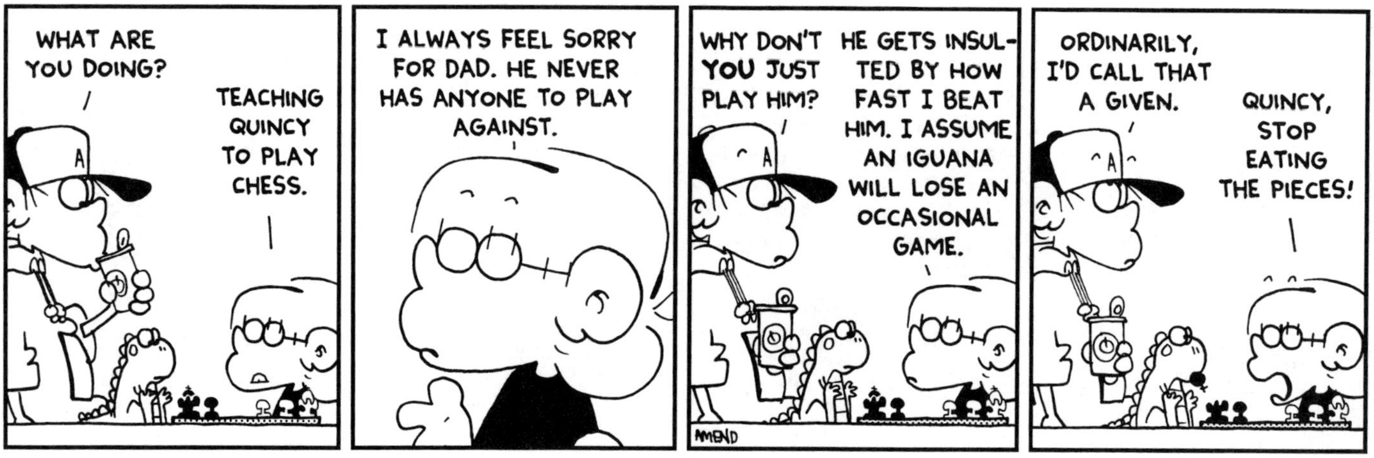
WHAT ARE YOU DOING?
TEACHING QUINCY TO PLAY CHESS.
I ALWAYS FEEL SORRY FOR DAD. HE NEVER HAS ANYONE TO PLAY AGAINST.
WHY DON'T YOU JUST PLAY HIM?
HE GETS INSUL-TED BY HOW FAST I BEAT HIM. I ASSUME AN IGUANA WILL LOSE AN OCCASIONAL GAME.
AMEND
ORDINARILY, I'D CALL THAT A GIVEN.
QUINCY, STOP EATING THE PIECES!

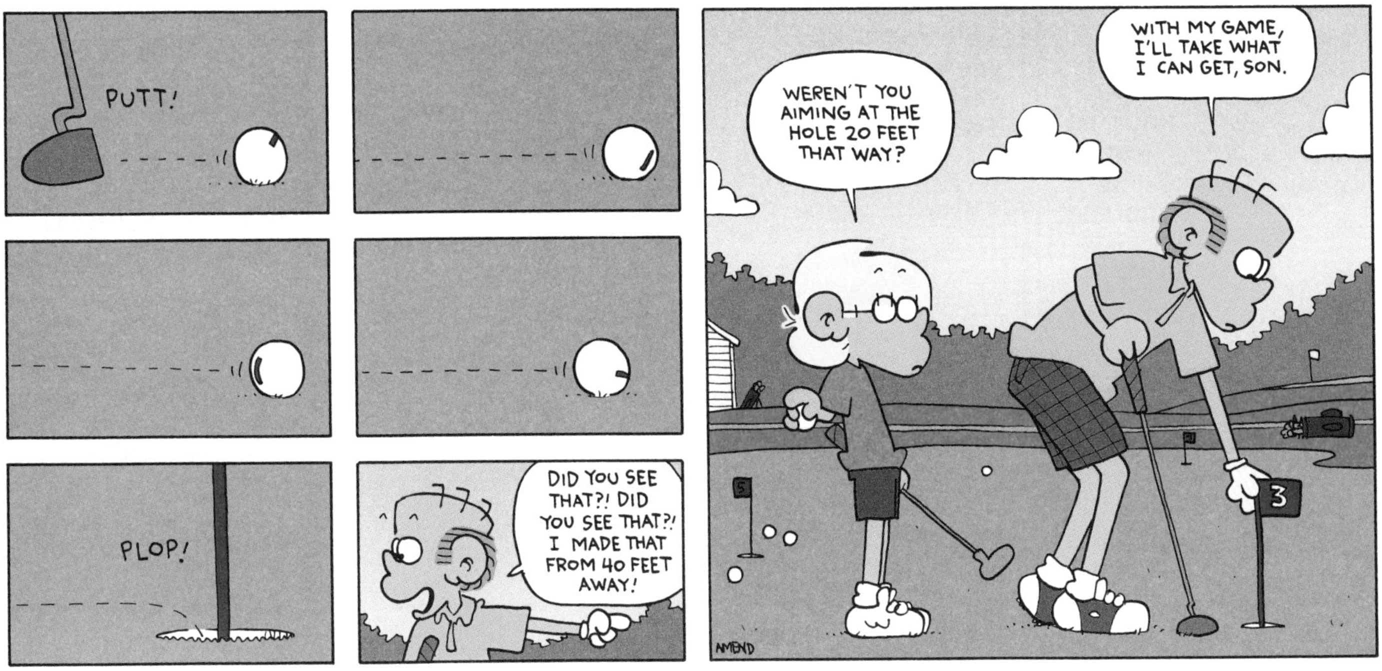
PUTT!
PLOP!
DID YOU SEE THAT?! DID YOU SEE THAT?! I MADE THAT FROM 40 FEET AWAY!
WEREN'T YOU AIMING AT THE HOLE 20 FEET THAT WAY?
WITH MY GAME, I'LL TAKE WHAT I CAN GET, SON.
AMEND

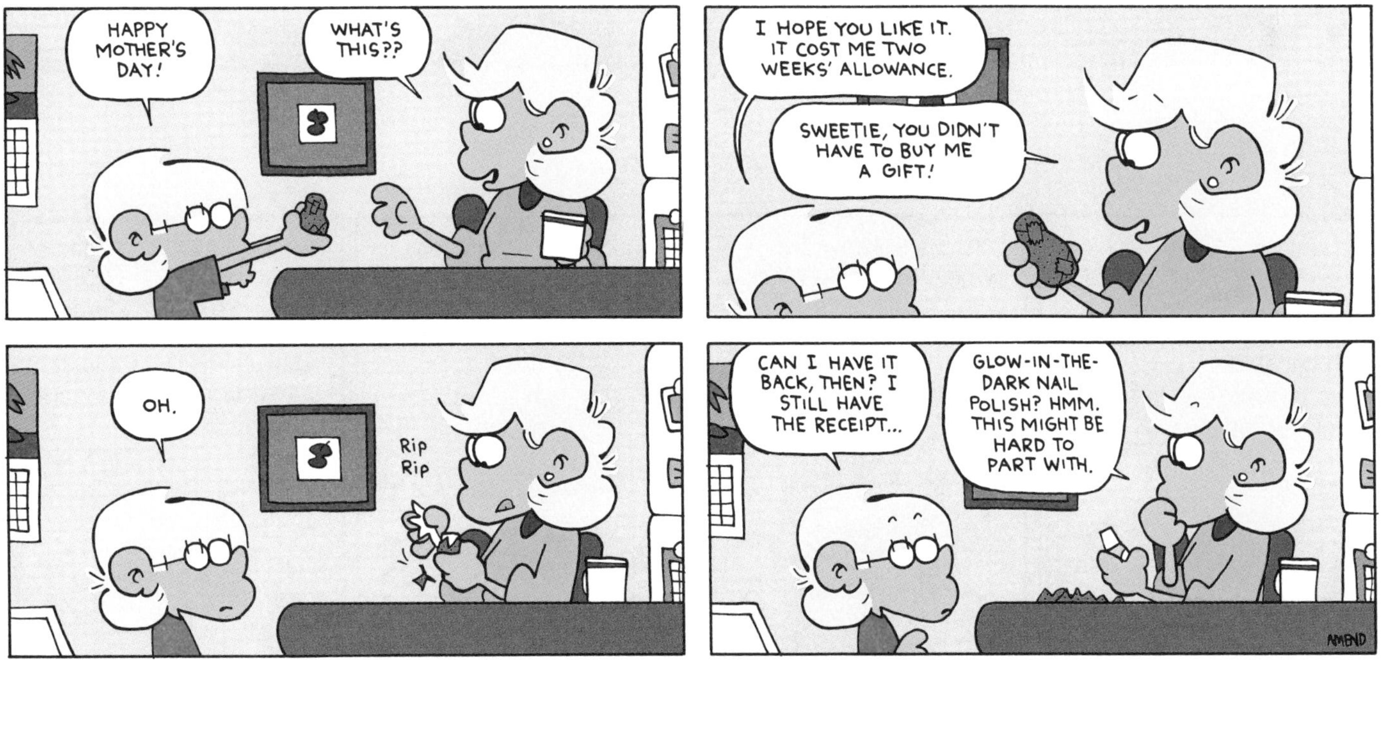
HAPPY MOTHER'S DAY!
WHAT'S THIS??
I HOPE YOU LIKE IT. IT COST ME TWO WEEKS' ALLOWANCE.
SWEETIE, YOU DIDN'T HAVE TO BUY ME A GIFT!
OH.
Rip Rip
CAN I HAVE IT BACK, THEN? I STILL HAVE THE RECEIPT...
GLOW-IN-THE-DARK NAIL POLISH? HMM. THIS MIGHT BE HARD TO PART WITH.
AMEND

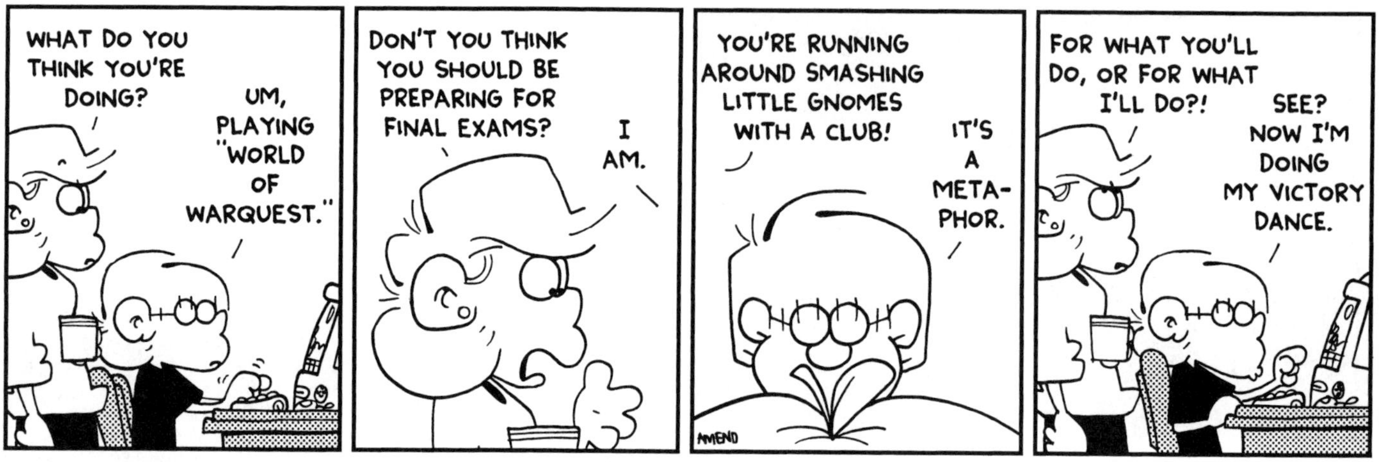
WHAT DO YOU THINK YOU'RE DOING?
UM, PLAYING "WORLD OF WARQUEST."
DON'T YOU THINK YOU SHOULD BE PREPARING FOR FINAL EXAMS?
I AM.
YOU'RE RUNNING AROUND SMASHING LITTLE GNOMES WITH A CLUB!
IT'S A META-PHOR.
AMEND
FOR WHAT YOU'LL DO, OR FOR WHAT I'LL DO?!
SEE? NOW I'M DOING MY VICTORY DANCE.

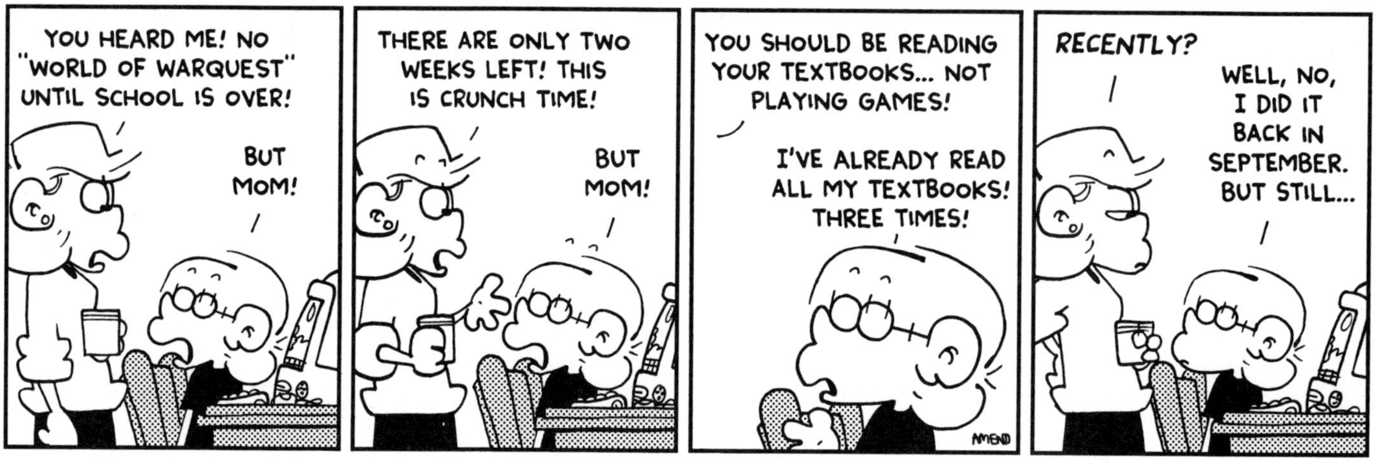
YOU HEARD ME! NO "WORLD OF WARQUEST" UNTIL SCHOOL IS OVER!
BUT MOM!
THERE ARE ONLY TWO WEEKS LEFT! THIS IS CRUNCH TIME!
BUT MOM!
YOU SHOULD BE READING YOUR TEXTBOOKS... NOT PLAYING GAMES!
I'VE ALREADY READ ALL MY TEXTBOOKS! THREE TIMES!
AMEND
RECENTLY?
WELL, NO, I DID IT BACK IN SEPTEMBER. BUT STILL...

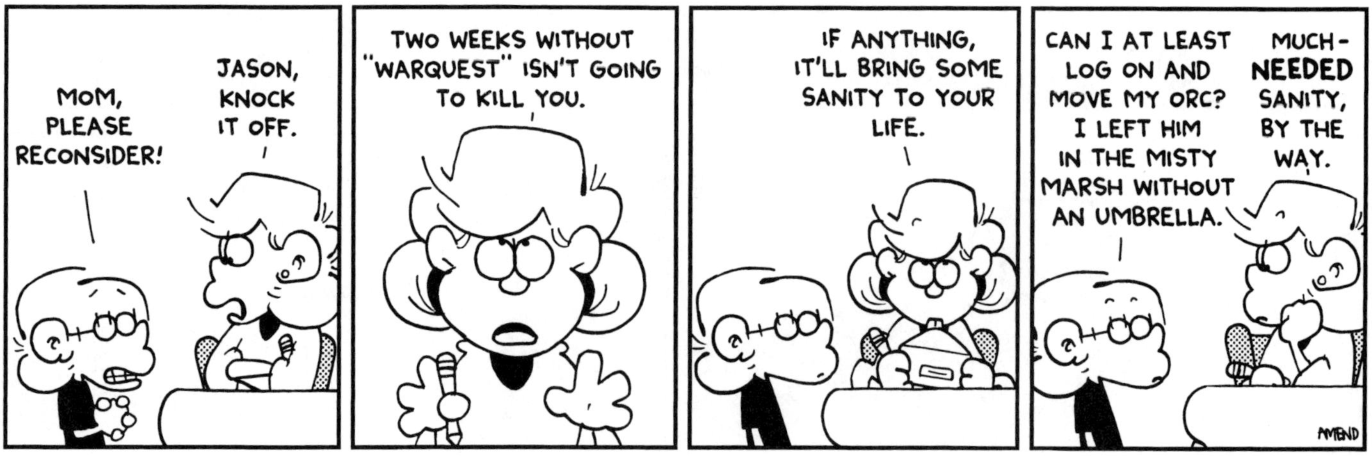
MOM, PLEASE RECONSIDER!
JASON, KNOCK IT OFF.
TWO WEEKS WITHOUT "WARQUEST" ISN'T GOING TO KILL YOU.
IF ANYTHING, IT'LL BRING SOME SANITY TO YOUR LIFE.
CAN I AT LEAST LOG ON AND MOVE MY ORC? I LEFT HIM IN THE MISTY MARSH WITHOUT AN UMBRELLA.
MUCH-**NEEDED** SANITY, BY THE WAY.
AMEND

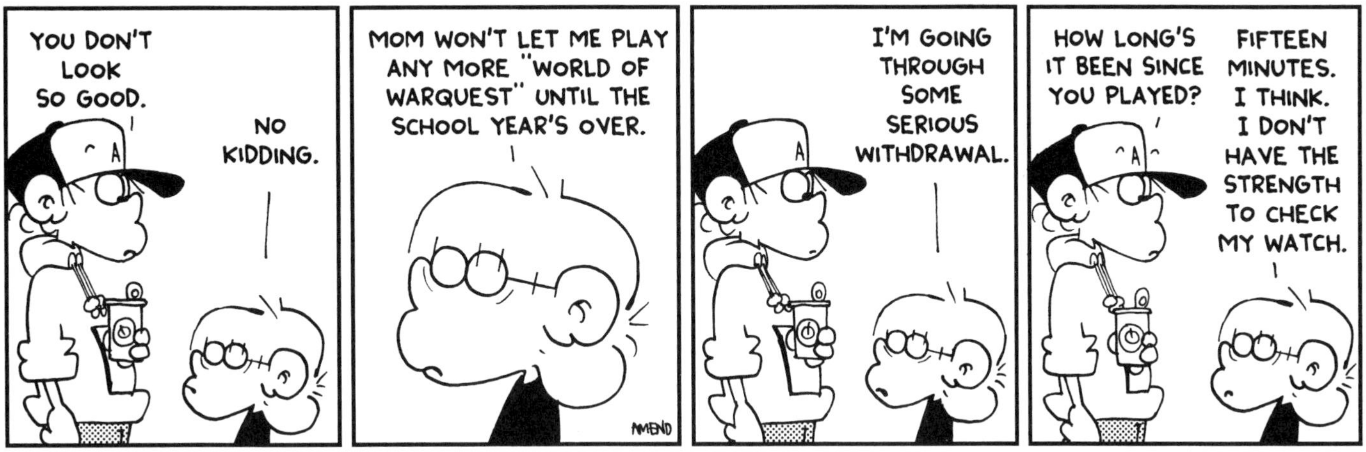
YOU DON'T LOOK SO GOOD.
NO KIDDING.
MOM WON'T LET ME PLAY ANY MORE "WORLD OF WARQUEST" UNTIL THE SCHOOL YEAR'S OVER.
I'M GOING THROUGH SOME SERIOUS WITHDRAWAL.
HOW LONG'S IT BEEN SINCE YOU PLAYED?
FIFTEEN MINUTES. I THINK. I DON'T HAVE THE STRENGTH TO CHECK MY WATCH.

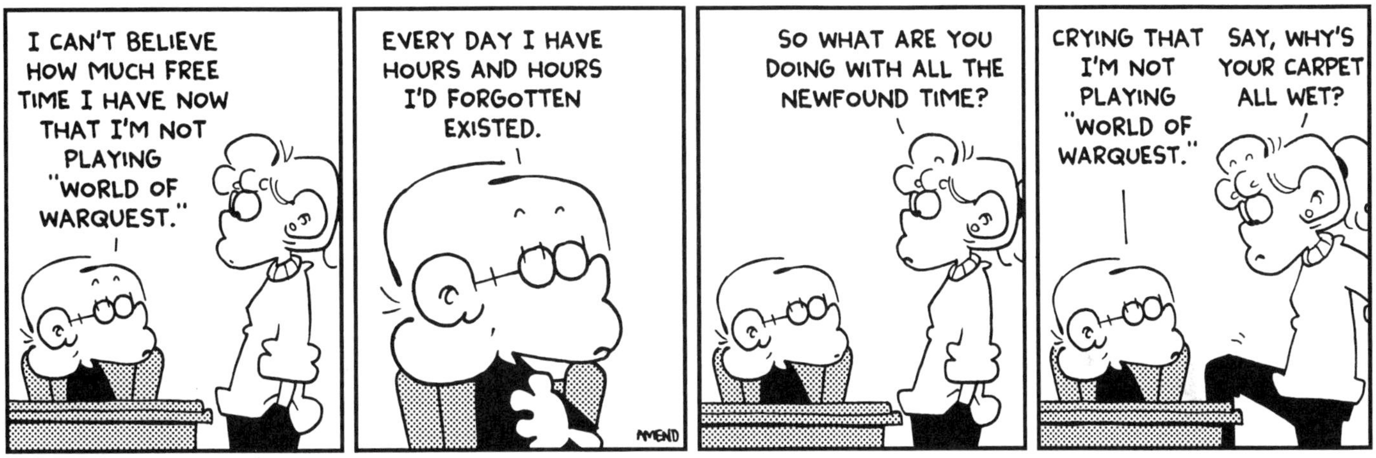
I CAN'T BELIEVE HOW MUCH FREE TIME I HAVE NOW THAT I'M NOT PLAYING "WORLD OF WARQUEST."
EVERY DAY I HAVE HOURS AND HOURS I'D FORGOTTEN EXISTED.
SO WHAT ARE YOU DOING WITH ALL THE NEWFOUND TIME?
CRYING THAT I'M NOT PLAYING "WORLD OF WARQUEST."
SAY, WHY'S YOUR CARPET ALL WET?

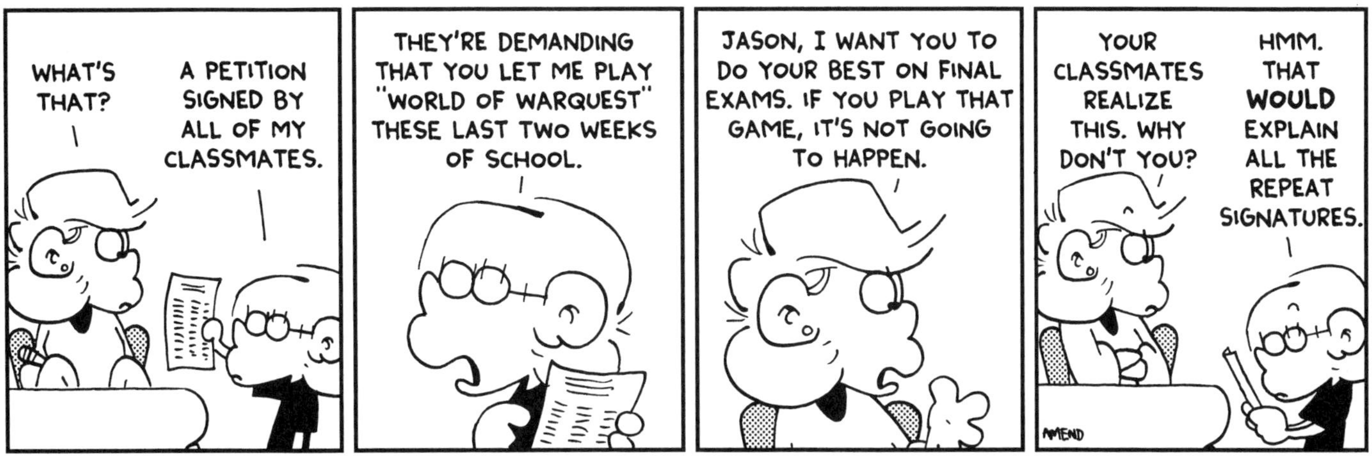
WHAT'S THAT?
A PETITION SIGNED BY ALL OF MY CLASSMATES.
THEY'RE DEMANDING THAT YOU LET ME PLAY "WORLD OF WARQUEST" THESE LAST TWO WEEKS OF SCHOOL.
JASON, I WANT YOU TO DO YOUR BEST ON FINAL EXAMS. IF YOU PLAY THAT GAME, IT'S NOT GOING TO HAPPEN.
YOUR CLASSMATES REALIZE THIS. WHY DON'T YOU?
HMM. THAT **WOULD** EXPLAIN ALL THE REPEAT SIGNATURES.

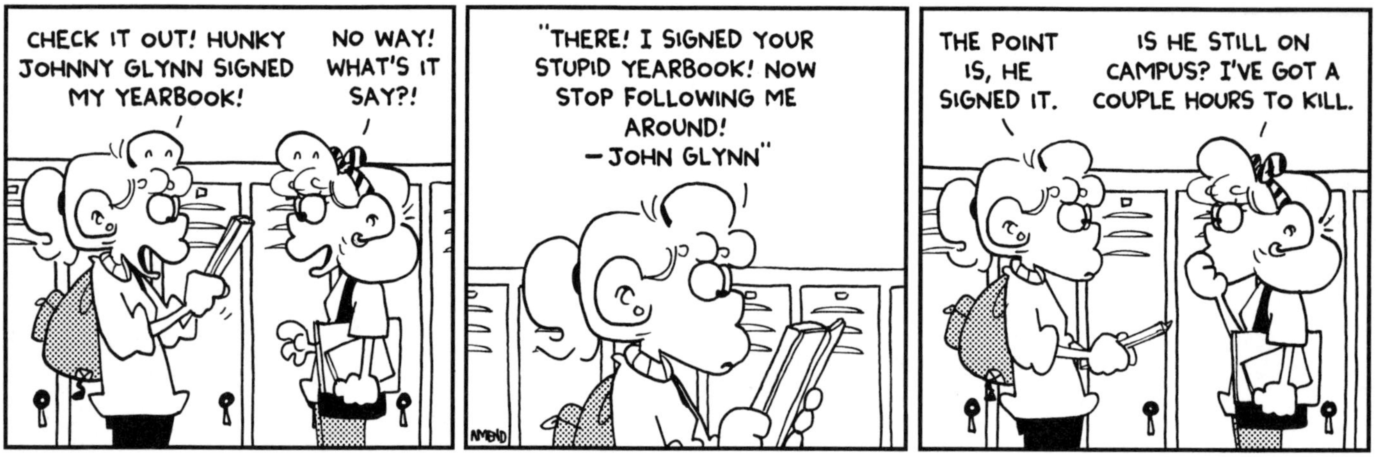
CHECK IT OUT! HUNKY JOHNNY GLYNN SIGNED MY YEARBOOK!
NO WAY! WHAT'S IT SAY?!
"THERE! I SIGNED YOUR STUPID YEARBOOK! NOW STOP FOLLOWING ME AROUND! —JOHN GLYNN"
THE POINT IS, HE SIGNED IT.
IS HE STILL ON CAMPUS? I'VE GOT A COUPLE HOURS TO KILL.
AMEND

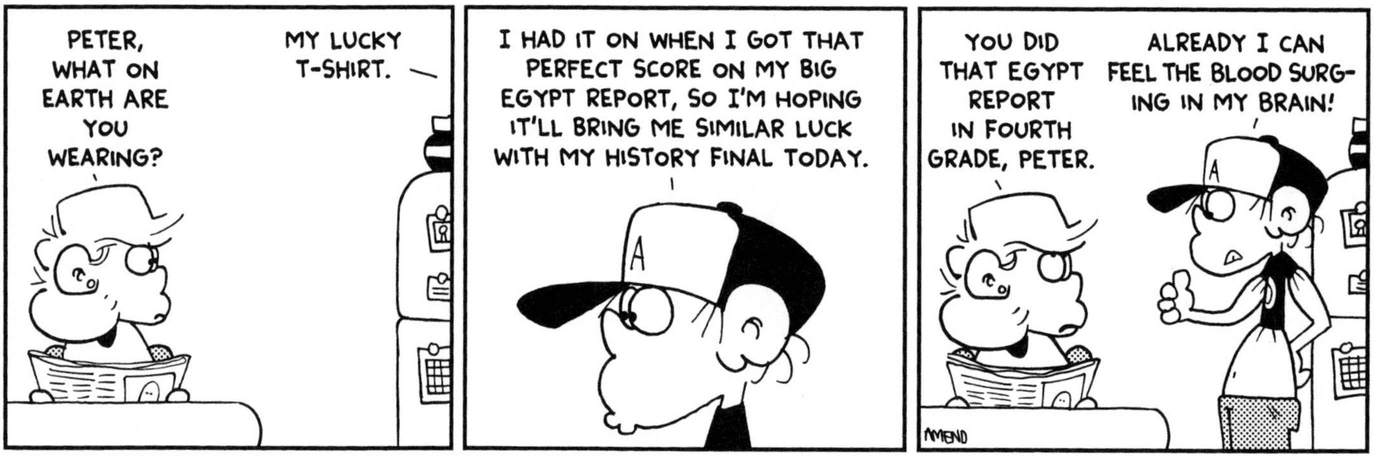
PETER, WHAT ON EARTH ARE YOU WEARING?
MY LUCKY T-SHIRT.
I HAD IT ON WHEN I GOT THAT PERFECT SCORE ON MY BIG EGYPT REPORT, SO I'M HOPING IT'LL BRING ME SIMILAR LUCK WITH MY HISTORY FINAL TODAY.
YOU DID THAT EGYPT REPORT IN FOURTH GRADE, PETER.
ALREADY I CAN FEEL THE BLOOD SURGING IN MY BRAIN!
AMEND

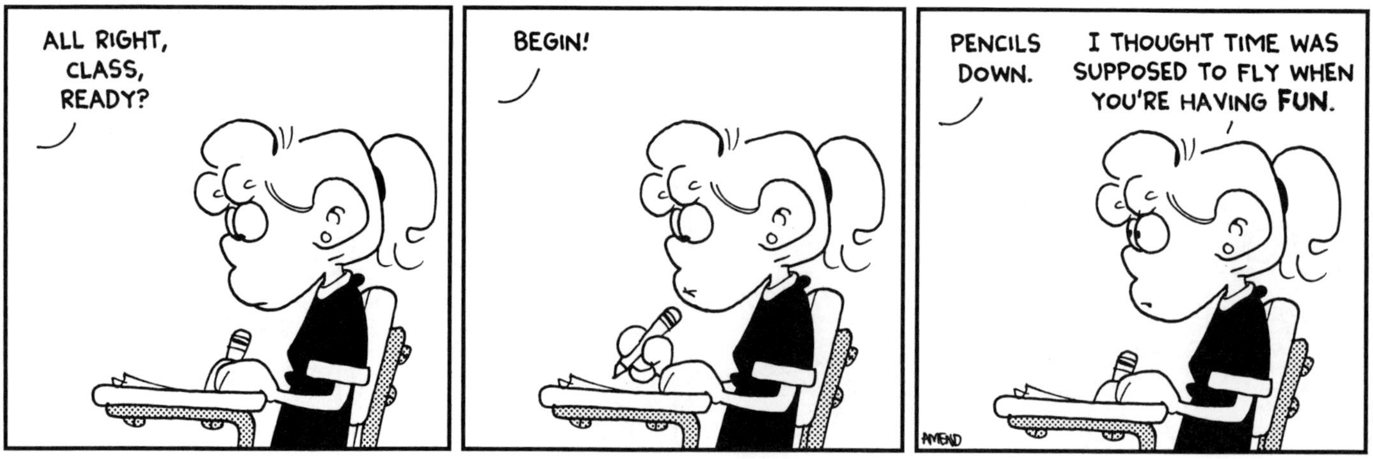
ALL RIGHT, CLASS, READY?
BEGIN!
PENCILS DOWN.
I THOUGHT TIME WAS SUPPOSED TO FLY WHEN YOU'RE HAVING FUN.
AMEND

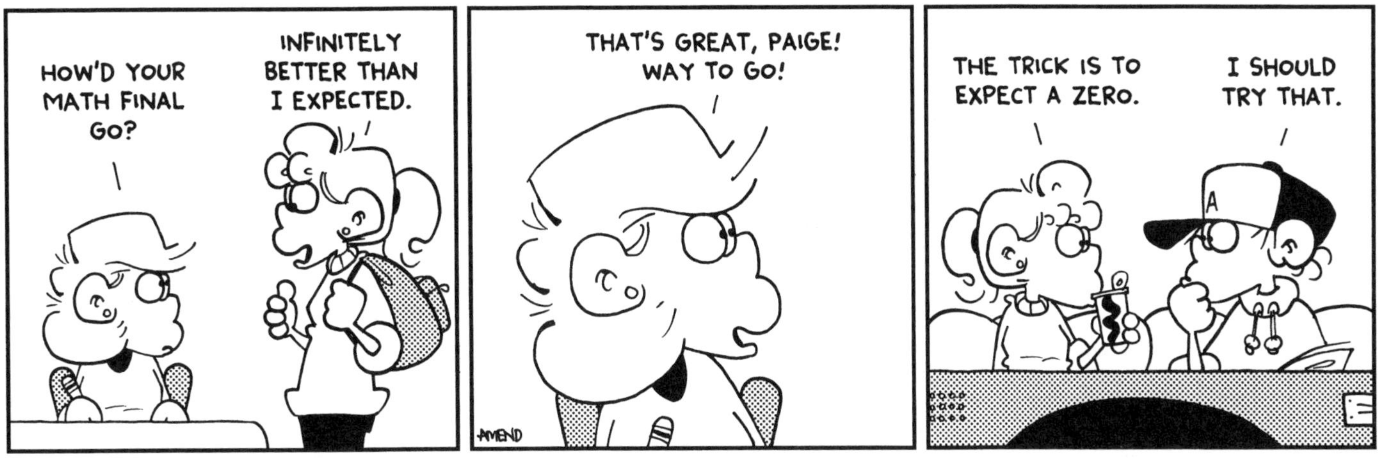
HOW'D YOUR MATH FINAL GO?
INFINITELY BETTER THAN I EXPECTED.
THAT'S GREAT, PAIGE! WAY TO GO!
THE TRICK IS TO EXPECT A ZERO.
I SHOULD TRY THAT.

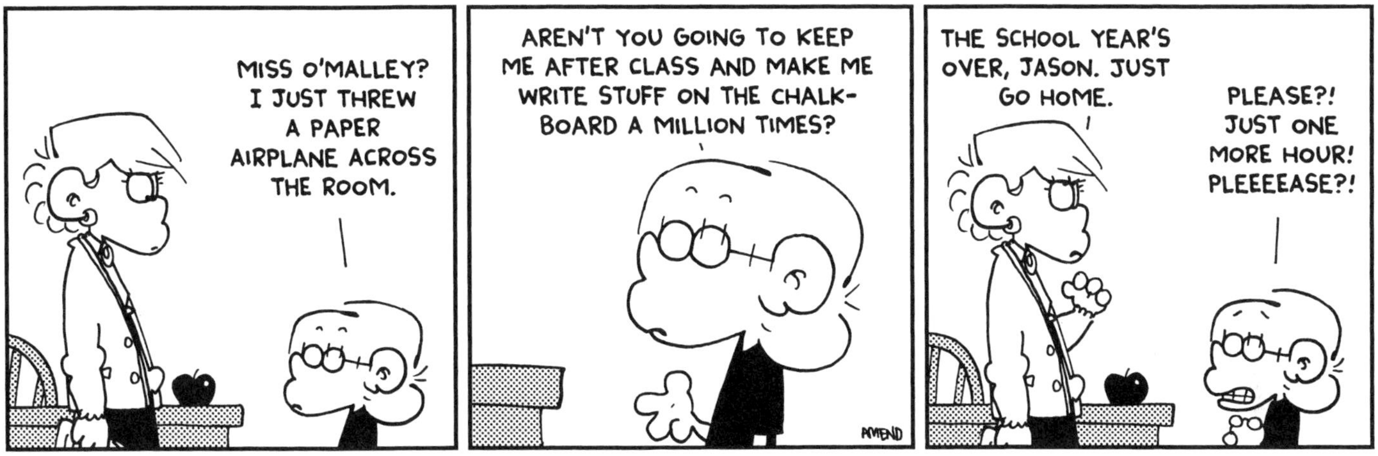
MISS O'MALLEY? I JUST THREW A PAPER AIRPLANE ACROSS THE ROOM.
AREN'T YOU GOING TO KEEP ME AFTER CLASS AND MAKE ME WRITE STUFF ON THE CHALK-BOARD A MILLION TIMES?
THE SCHOOL YEAR'S OVER, JASON. JUST GO HOME.
PLEASE?! JUST ONE MORE HOUR! PLEEEEASE?!

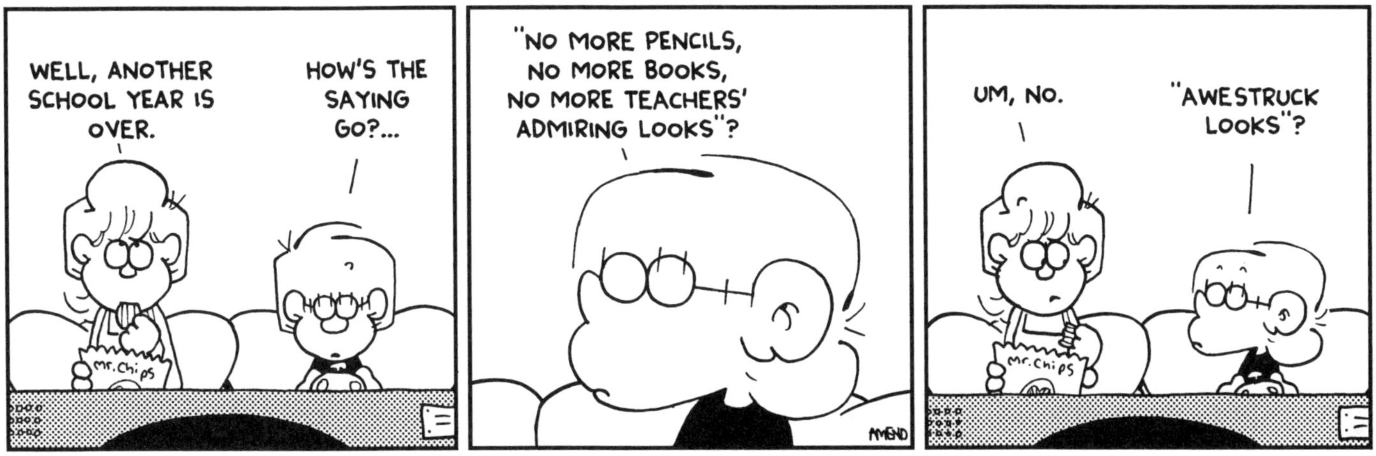
WELL, ANOTHER SCHOOL YEAR IS OVER.
HOW'S THE SAYING GO?...
"NO MORE PENCILS, NO MORE BOOKS, NO MORE TEACHERS' ADMIRING LOOKS"?
UM, NO.
"AWESTRUCK LOOKS"?

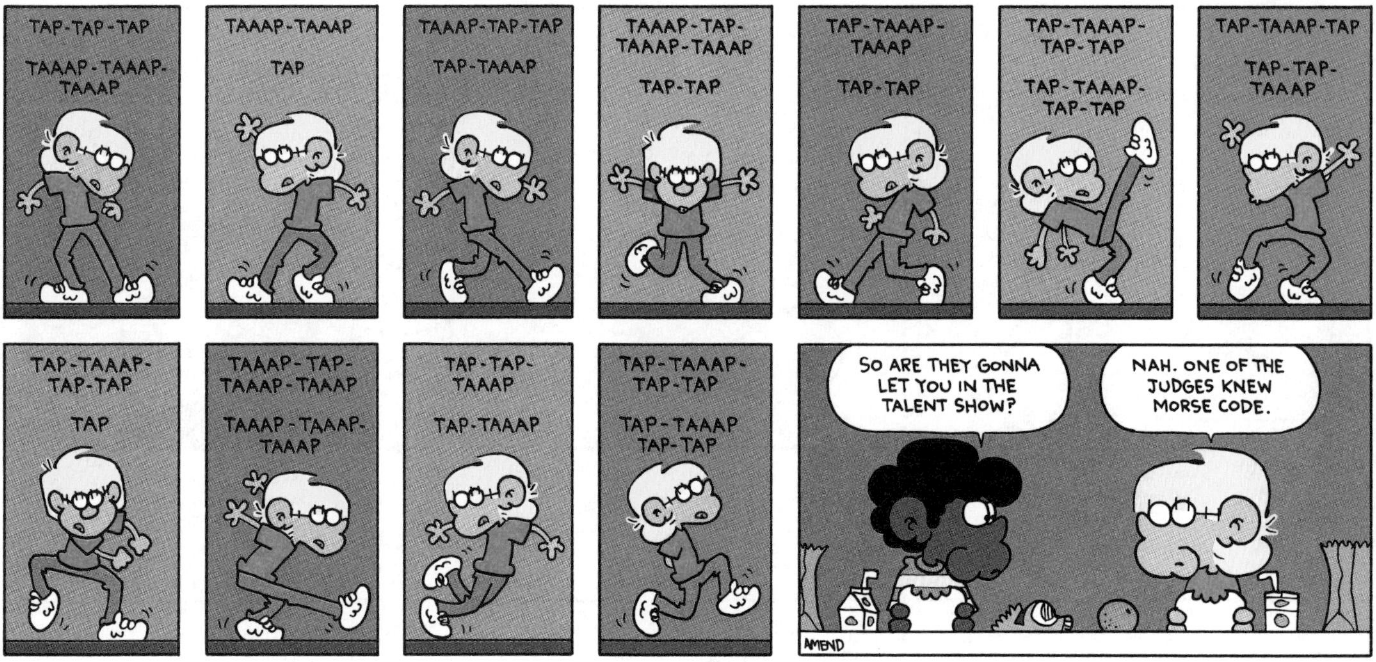
TAP-TAP-TAP
TAAAP-TAAAP-TAAAP
TAAAP-TAAAP
TAP
TAAAP-TAP-TAP
TAP-TAAAP
TAAAP-TAP-TAAAP-TAAAP
TAP-TAP
TAP-TAAAP-TAAAP
TAP-TAP
TAP-TAAAP-TAP-TAP
TAP-TAAAP-TAP-TAP
TAP-TAAAP-TAP
TAP-TAP-TAAAP
TAP-TAAAP-TAP-TAP
TAP
TAAAP-TAP-TAAAP-TAAAP
TAAAP-TAAAP-TAAAP
TAP-TAP-TAAAP
TAP-TAAAP
TAP-TAAAP-TAP-TAP
TAP-TAAAP TAP-TAP
SO ARE THEY GONNA LET YOU IN THE TALENT SHOW?
NAH. ONE OF THE JUDGES KNEW MORSE CODE.
AMEND

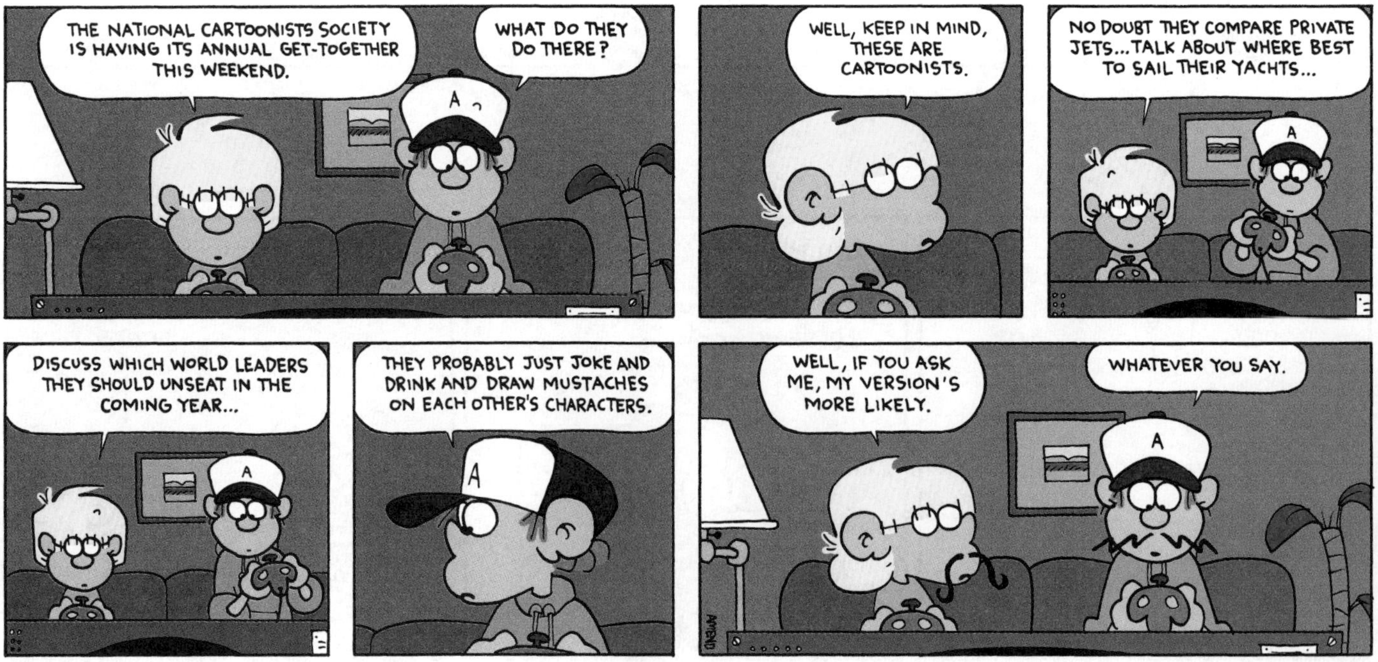
THE NATIONAL CARTOONISTS SOCIETY IS HAVING ITS ANNUAL GET-TOGETHER THIS WEEKEND.
WHAT DO THEY DO THERE?
WELL, KEEP IN MIND, THESE ARE CARTOONISTS.
NO DOUBT THEY COMPARE PRIVATE JETS... TALK ABOUT WHERE BEST TO SAIL THEIR YACHTS...
DISCUSS WHICH WORLD LEADERS THEY SHOULD UNSEAT IN THE COMING YEAR...
THEY PROBABLY JUST JOKE AND DRINK AND DRAW MUSTACHES ON EACH OTHER'S CHARACTERS.
WELL, IF YOU ASK ME, MY VERSION'S MORE LIKELY.
WHATEVER YOU SAY.
AMEND

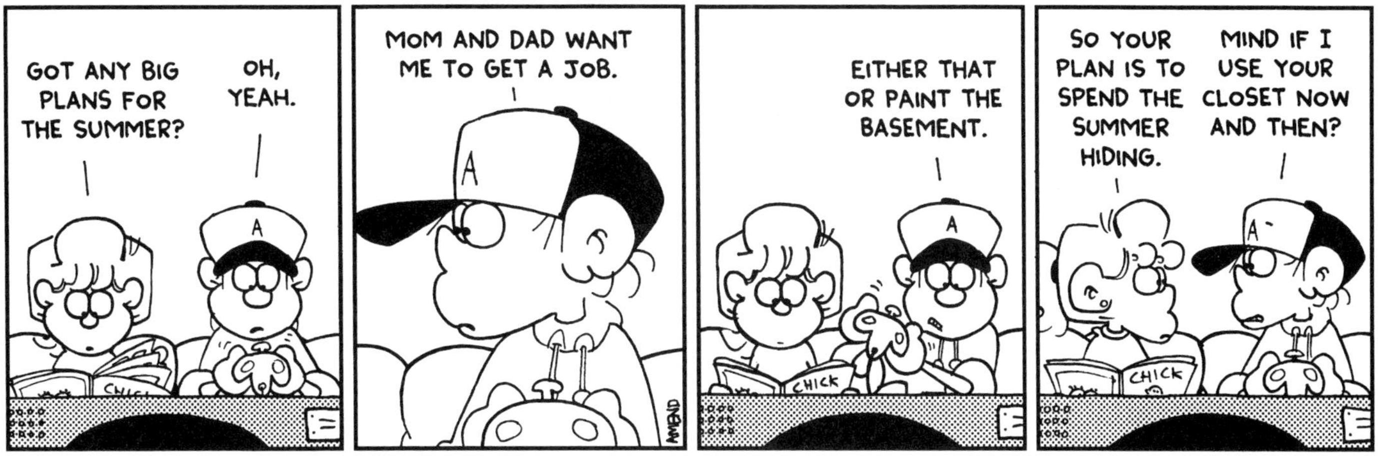
GOT ANY BIG PLANS FOR THE SUMMER?
OH, YEAH.
MOM AND DAD WANT ME TO GET A JOB.
EITHER THAT OR PAINT THE BASEMENT.
SO YOUR PLAN IS TO SPEND THE SUMMER HIDING.
MIND IF I USE YOUR CLOSET NOW AND THEN?
CHICK
AMEND

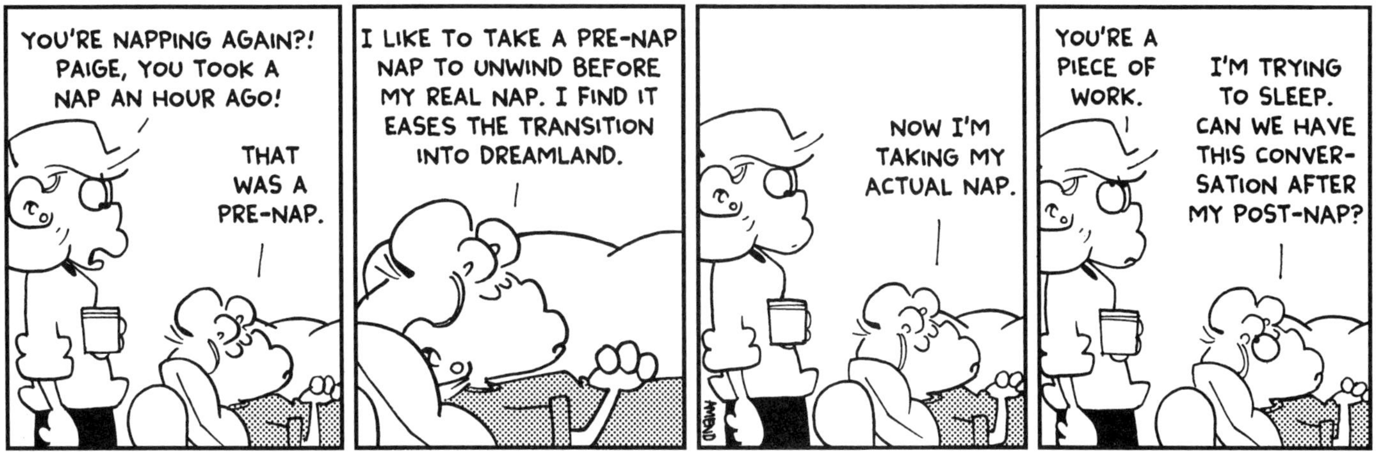
YOU'RE NAPPING AGAIN?! PAIGE, YOU TOOK A NAP AN HOUR AGO!
THAT WAS A PRE-NAP.
I LIKE TO TAKE A PRE-NAP NAP TO UNWIND BEFORE MY REAL NAP. I FIND IT EASES THE TRANSITION INTO DREAMLAND.
NOW I'M TAKING MY ACTUAL NAP.
YOU'RE A PIECE OF WORK.
I'M TRYING TO SLEEP. CAN WE HAVE THIS CONVERSATION AFTER MY POST-NAP?
AMEND

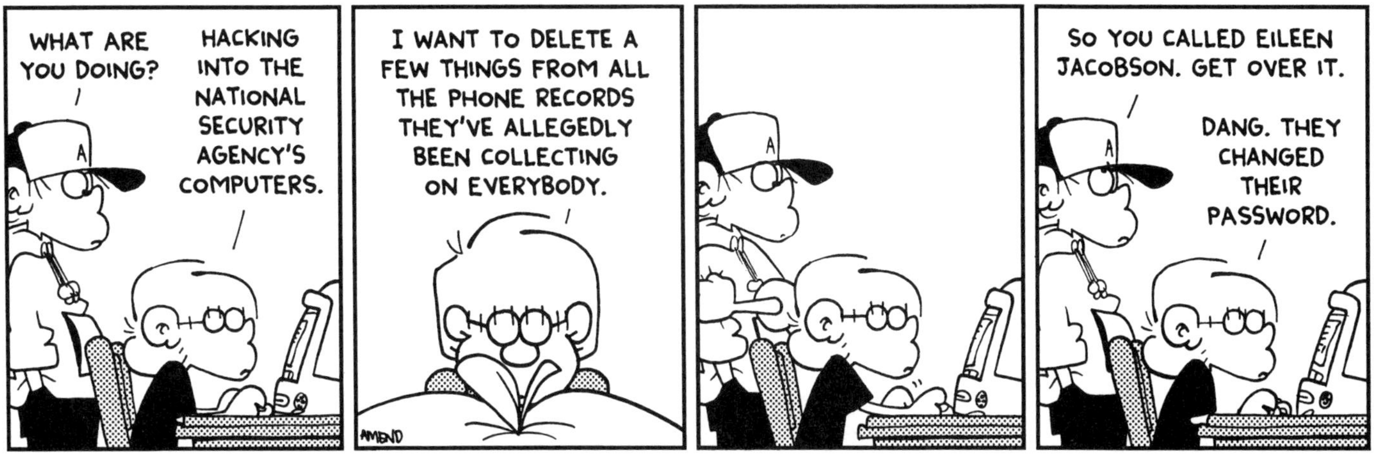
WHAT ARE YOU DOING?
HACKING INTO THE NATIONAL SECURITY AGENCY'S COMPUTERS.
I WANT TO DELETE A FEW THINGS FROM ALL THE PHONE RECORDS THEY'VE ALLEGEDLY BEEN COLLECTING ON EVERYBODY.
SO YOU CALLED EILEEN JACOBSON. GET OVER IT.
DANG. THEY CHANGED THEIR PASSWORD.
AMEND

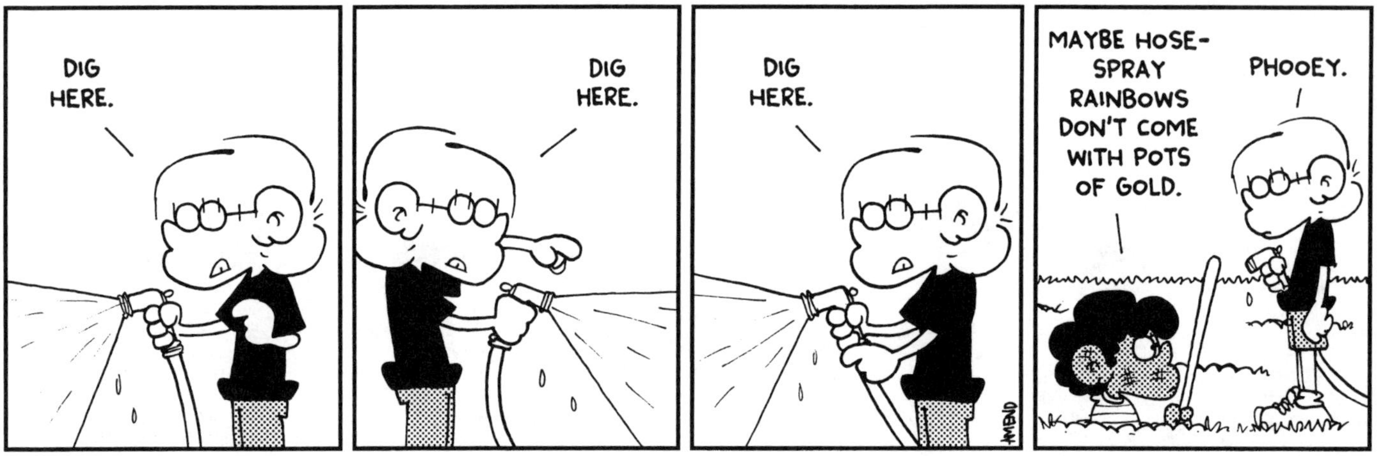
DIG HERE.
DIG HERE.
DIG HERE.
MAYBE HOSE-SPRAY RAINBOWS DON'T COME WITH POTS OF GOLD.
PHOOEY.

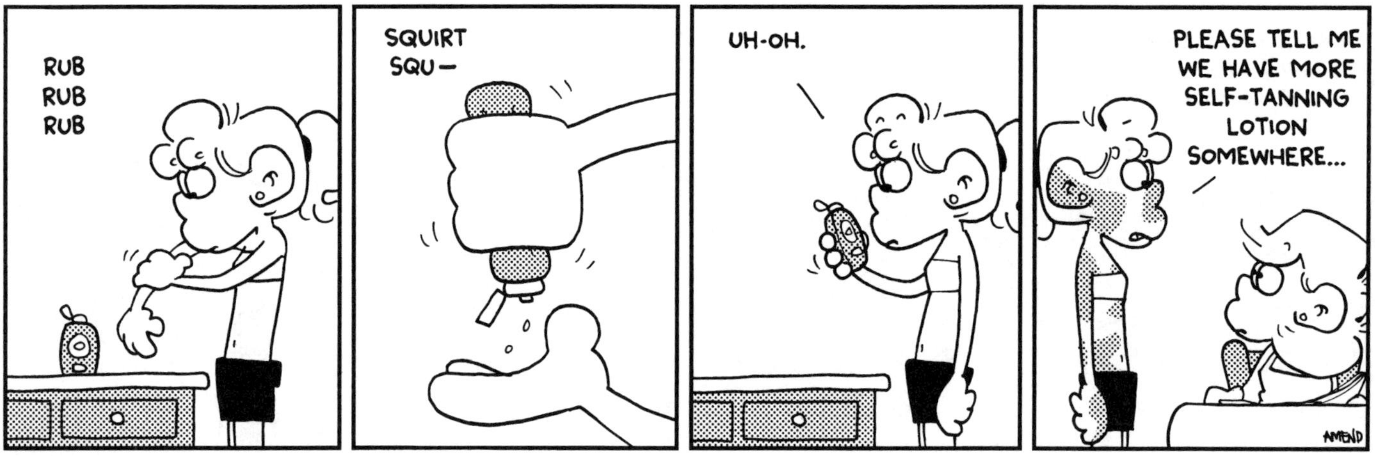
RUB RUB RUB
SQUIRT SQU—
UH-OH.
PLEASE TELL ME WE HAVE MORE SELF-TANNING LOTION SOMEWHERE...

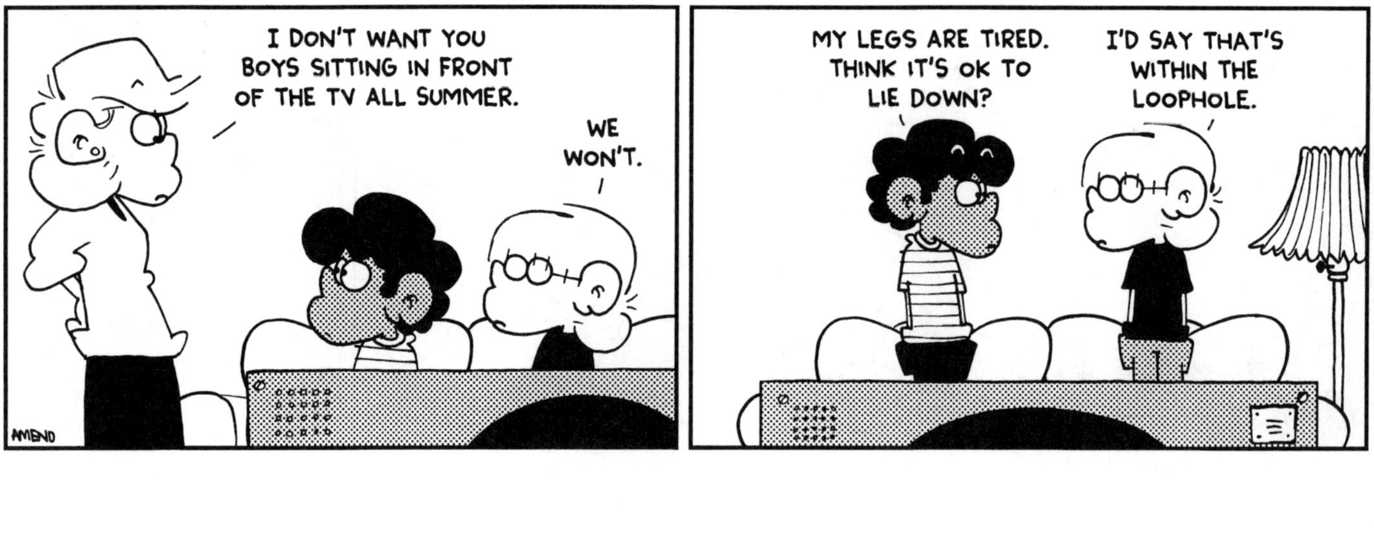
I DON'T WANT YOU BOYS SITTING IN FRONT OF THE TV ALL SUMMER.
WE WON'T.
MY LEGS ARE TIRED. THINK IT'S OK TO LIE DOWN?
I'D SAY THAT'S WITHIN THE LOOPHOLE.

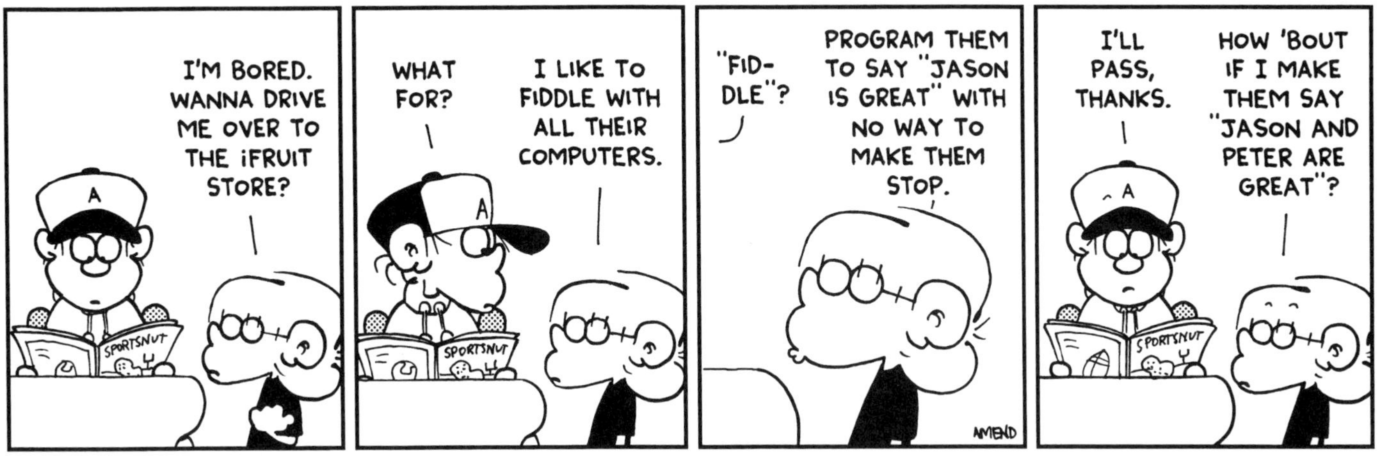
I'M BORED. WANNA DRIVE ME OVER TO THE iFRUIT STORE?
WHAT FOR?
I LIKE TO FIDDLE WITH ALL THEIR COMPUTERS.
"FID-DLE"?
PROGRAM THEM TO SAY "JASON IS GREAT" WITH NO WAY TO MAKE THEM STOP.
AMEND
I'LL PASS, THANKS.
HOW 'BOUT IF I MAKE THEM SAY "JASON AND PETER ARE GREAT"?
SPORTSNUT

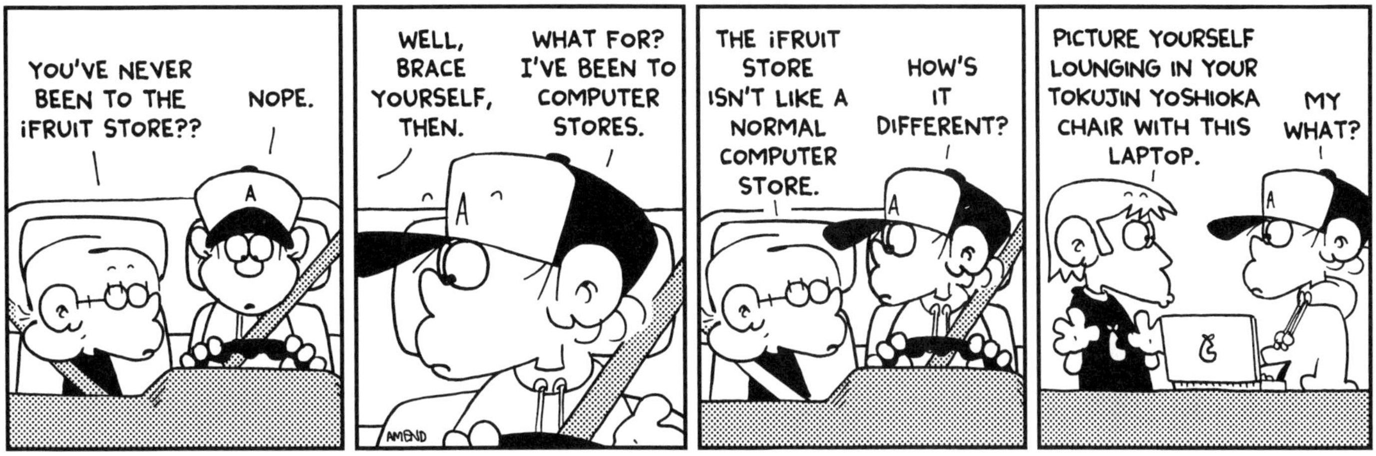
YOU'VE NEVER BEEN TO THE iFRUIT STORE??
NOPE.
WELL, BRACE YOURSELF, THEN.
WHAT FOR? I'VE BEEN TO COMPUTER STORES.
AMEND
THE iFRUIT STORE ISN'T LIKE A NORMAL COMPUTER STORE.
HOW'S IT DIFFERENT?
PICTURE YOURSELF LOUNGING IN YOUR TOKUJIN YOSHIOKA CHAIR WITH THIS LAPTOP.
MY WHAT?

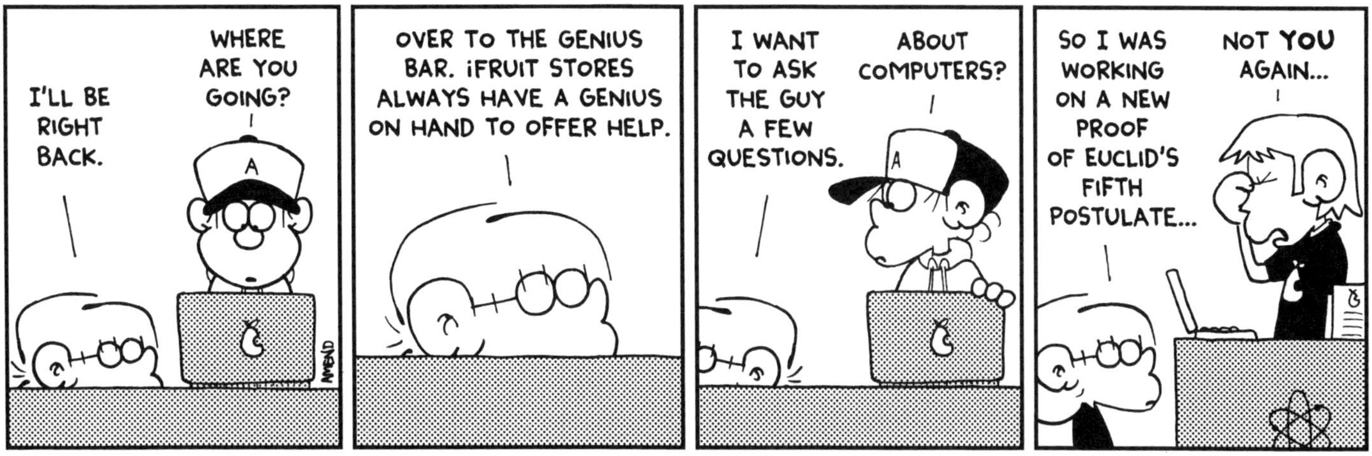
I'LL BE RIGHT BACK.
WHERE ARE YOU GOING?
AMEND
OVER TO THE GENIUS BAR. iFRUIT STORES ALWAYS HAVE A GENIUS ON HAND TO OFFER HELP.
I WANT TO ASK THE GUY A FEW QUESTIONS.
ABOUT COMPUTERS?
SO I WAS WORKING ON A NEW PROOF OF EUCLID'S FIFTH POSTULATE...
NOT **YOU** AGAIN...

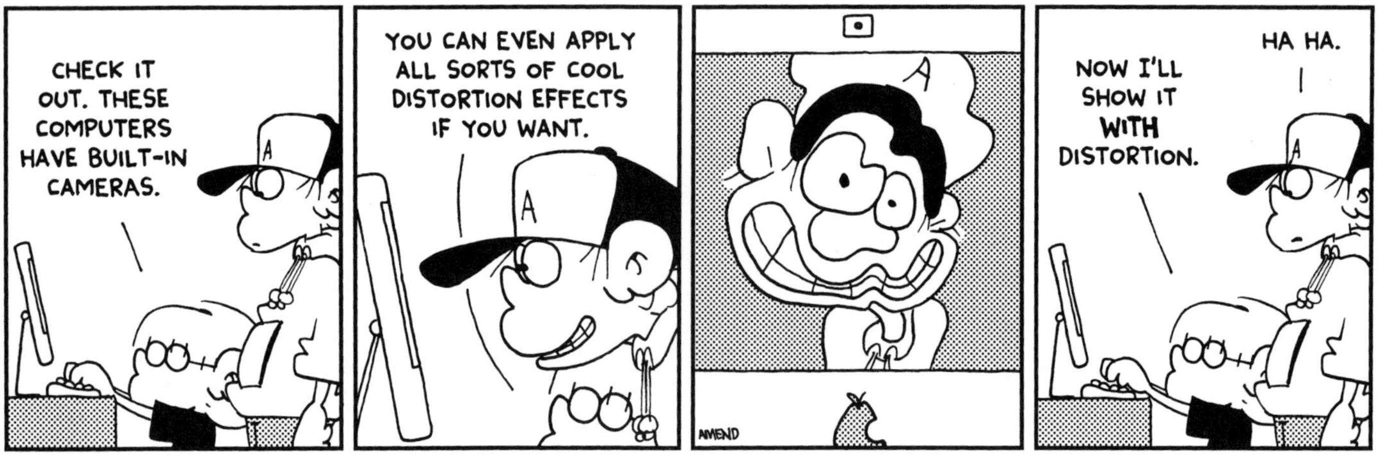
CHECK IT OUT. THESE COMPUTERS HAVE BUILT-IN CAMERAS.
YOU CAN EVEN APPLY ALL SORTS OF COOL DISTORTION EFFECTS IF YOU WANT.
AMEND
NOW I'LL SHOW IT **WITH** DISTORTION.
HA HA.

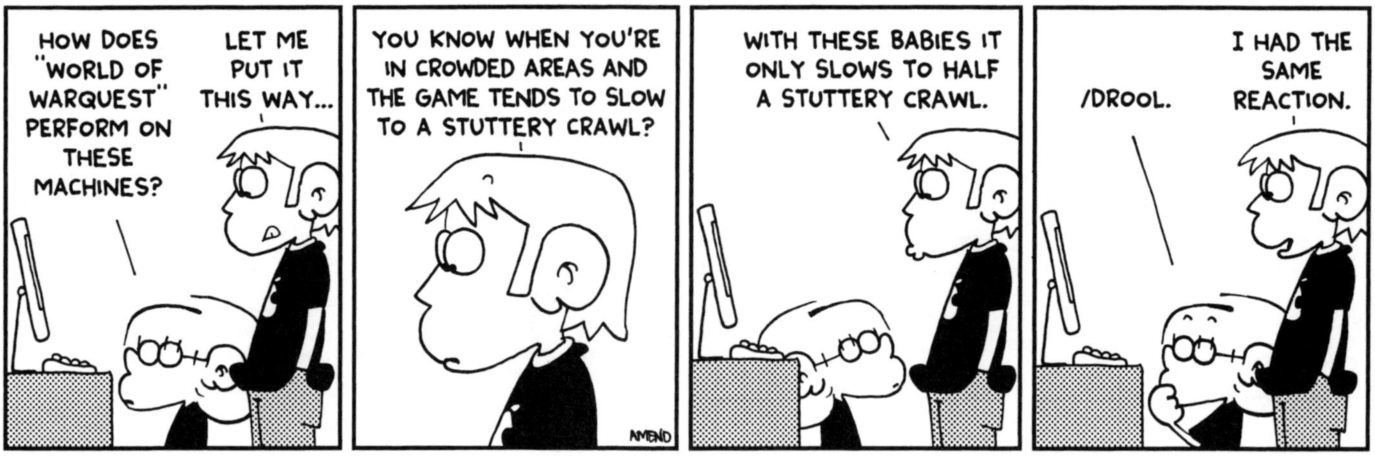
HOW DOES "WORLD OF WARQUEST" PERFORM ON THESE MACHINES?
LET ME PUT IT THIS WAY...
YOU KNOW WHEN YOU'RE IN CROWDED AREAS AND THE GAME TENDS TO SLOW TO A STUTTERY CRAWL?
AMEND
WITH THESE BABIES IT ONLY SLOWS TO HALF A STUTTERY CRAWL.
/DROOL.
I HAD THE SAME REACTION.

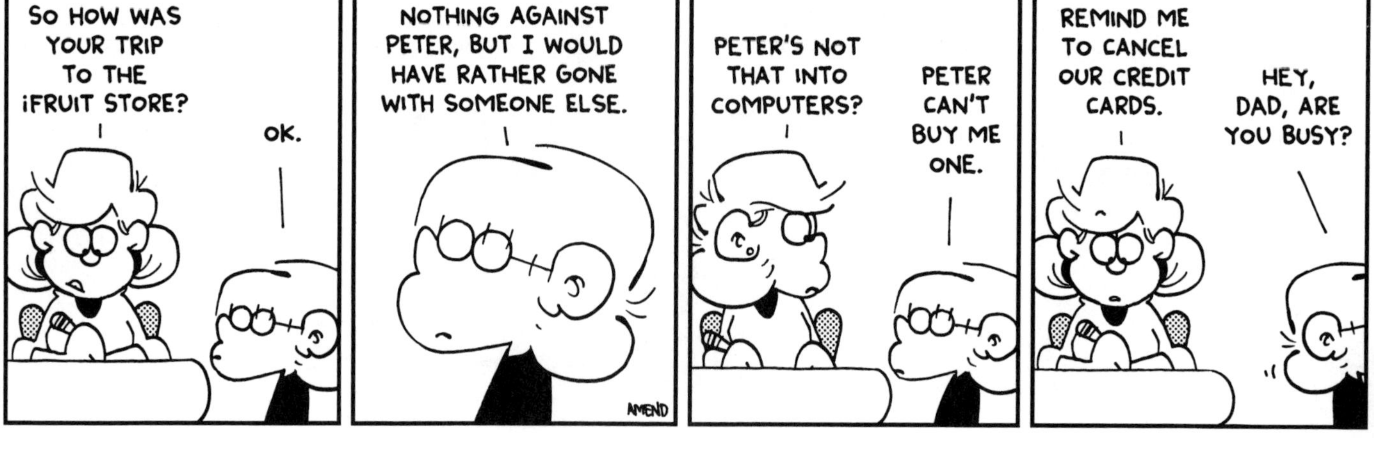
SO HOW WAS YOUR TRIP TO THE iFRUIT STORE?
OK.
NOTHING AGAINST PETER, BUT I WOULD HAVE RATHER GONE WITH SOMEONE ELSE.
AMEND
PETER'S NOT THAT INTO COMPUTERS?
PETER CAN'T BUY ME ONE.
REMIND ME TO CANCEL OUR CREDIT CARDS.
HEY, DAD, ARE YOU BUSY?

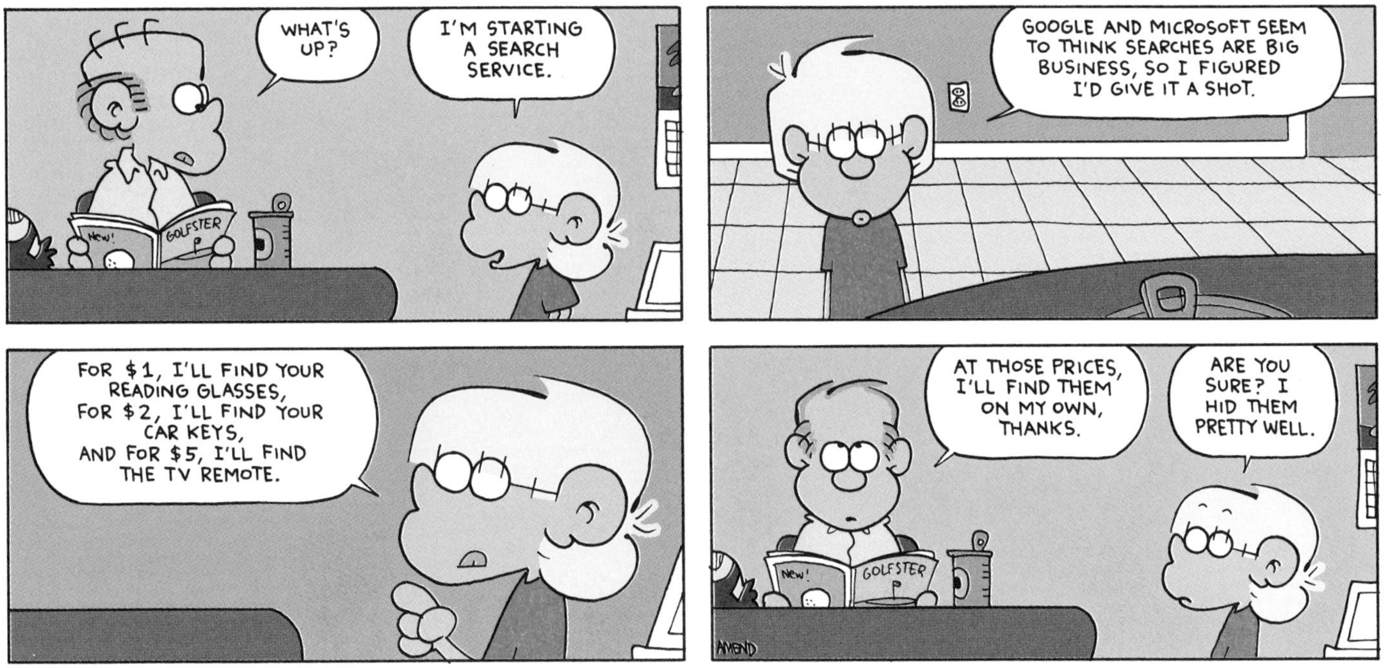
WHAT'S UP?
I'M STARTING A SEARCH SERVICE.
GOOGLE AND MICROSOFT SEEM TO THINK SEARCHES ARE BIG BUSINESS, SO I FIGURED I'D GIVE IT A SHOT.
FOR $1, I'LL FIND YOUR READING GLASSES, FOR $2, I'LL FIND YOUR CAR KEYS, AND FOR $5, I'LL FIND THE TV REMOTE.
AT THOSE PRICES, I'LL FIND THEM ON MY OWN, THANKS.
ARE YOU SURE? I HID THEM PRETTY WELL.
GOLFSTER
New!
AMEND

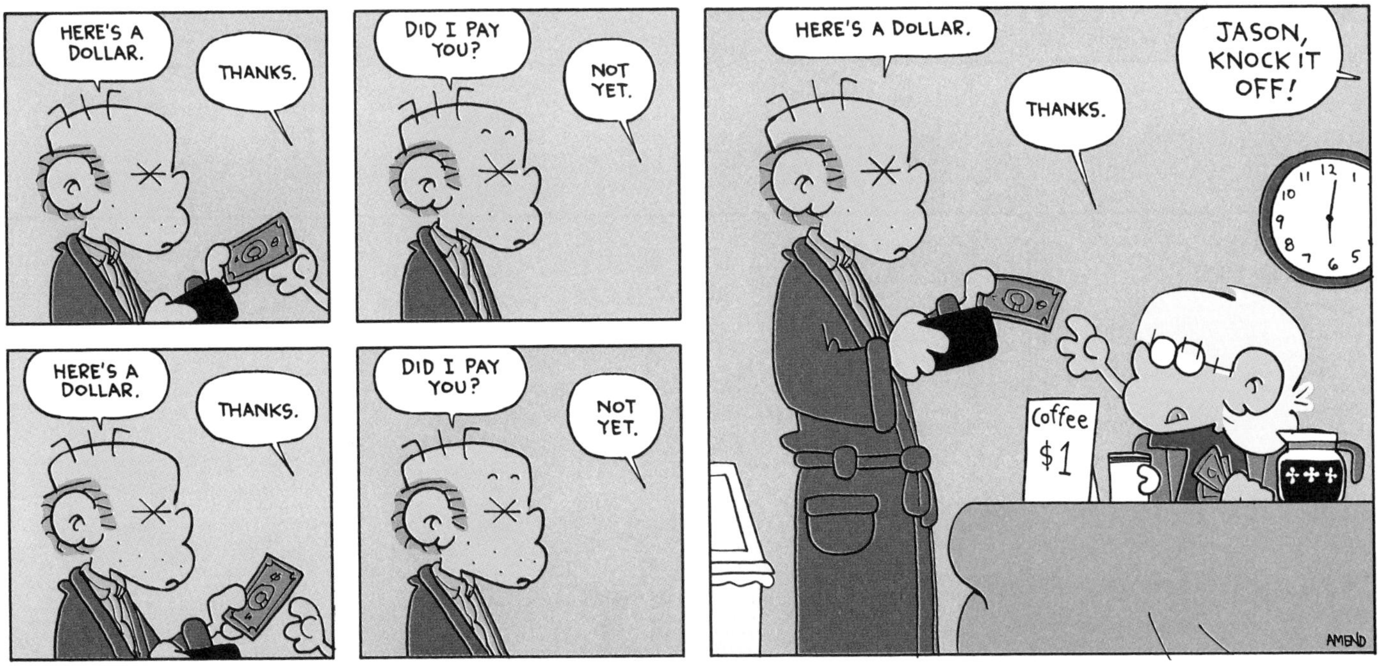
HERE'S A DOLLAR.
THANKS.
DID I PAY YOU?
NOT YET.
HERE'S A DOLLAR.
THANKS.
DID I PAY YOU?
NOT YET.
HERE'S A DOLLAR.
THANKS.
JASON, KNOCK IT OFF!
Coffee $1
AMEND

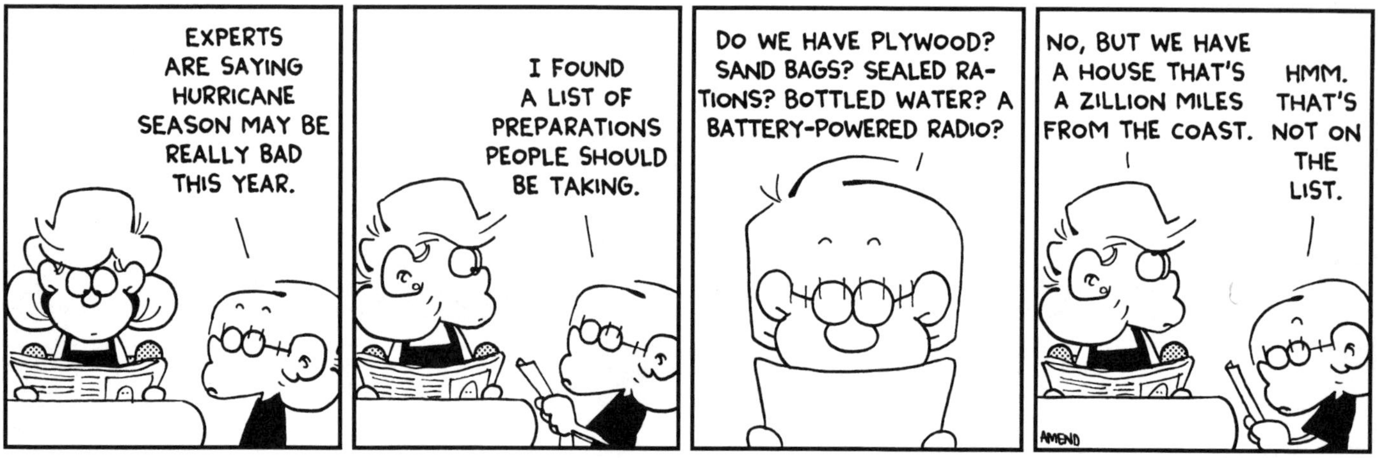
EXPERTS ARE SAYING HURRICANE SEASON MAY BE REALLY BAD THIS YEAR.
I FOUND A LIST OF PREPARATIONS PEOPLE SHOULD BE TAKING.
DO WE HAVE PLYWOOD? SAND BAGS? SEALED RATIONS? BOTTLED WATER? A BATTERY-POWERED RADIO?
NO, BUT WE HAVE A HOUSE THAT'S A ZILLION MILES FROM THE COAST.
HMM. THAT'S NOT ON THE LIST.
AMEND

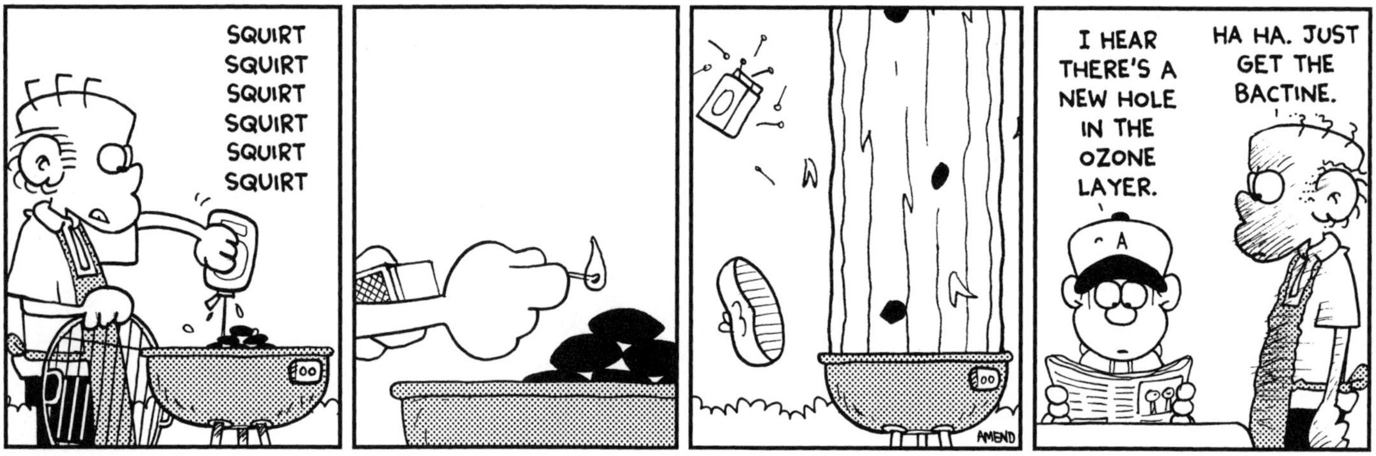
SQUIRT SQUIRT SQUIRT SQUIRT SQUIRT SQUIRT
AMEND
I HEAR THERE'S A NEW HOLE IN THE OZONE LAYER.
HA HA. JUST GET THE BACTINE.

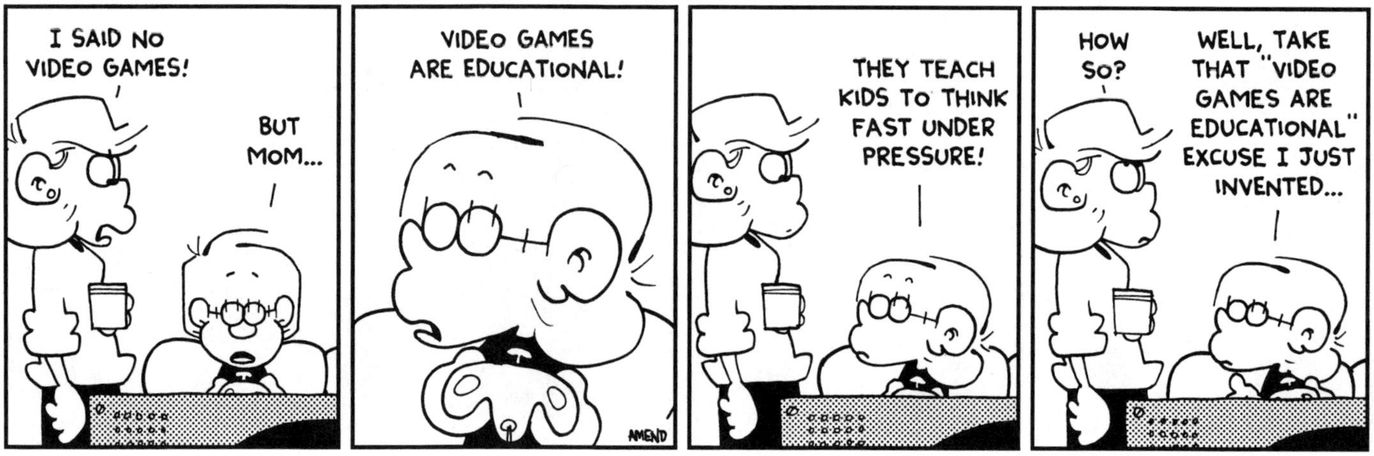
I SAID NO VIDEO GAMES!
BUT MOM...
VIDEO GAMES ARE EDUCATIONAL!
AMEND
THEY TEACH KIDS TO THINK FAST UNDER PRESSURE!
HOW SO?
WELL, TAKE THAT "VIDEO GAMES ARE EDUCATIONAL" EXCUSE I JUST INVENTED...

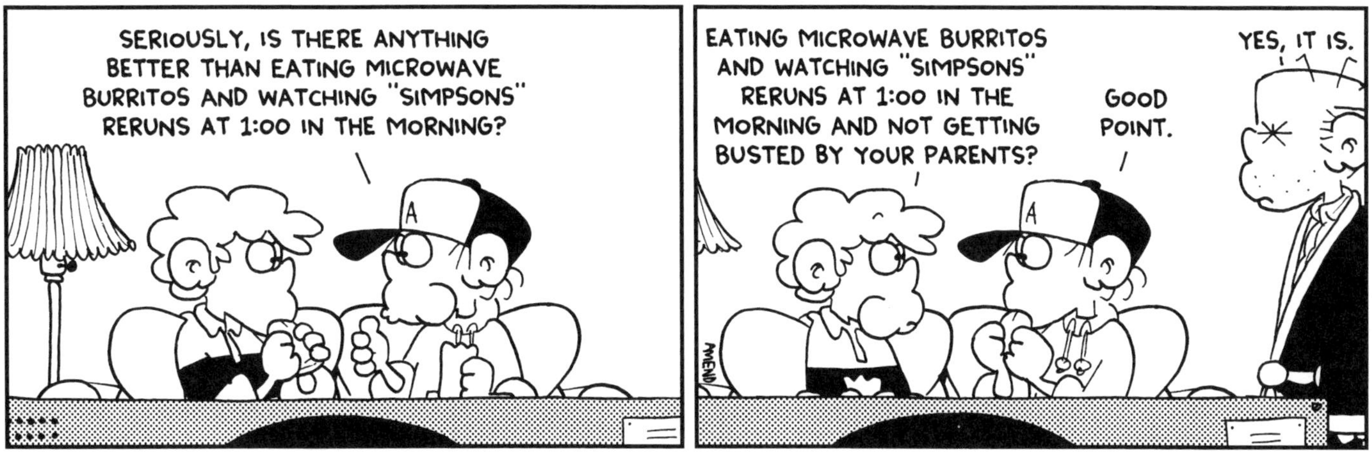
SERIOUSLY, IS THERE ANYTHING BETTER THAN EATING MICROWAVE BURRITOS AND WATCHING "SIMPSONS" RERUNS AT 1:00 IN THE MORNING?
EATING MICROWAVE BURRITOS AND WATCHING "SIMPSONS" RERUNS AT 1:00 IN THE MORNING AND NOT GETTING BUSTED BY YOUR PARENTS?
GOOD POINT.
YES, IT IS.
AMEND

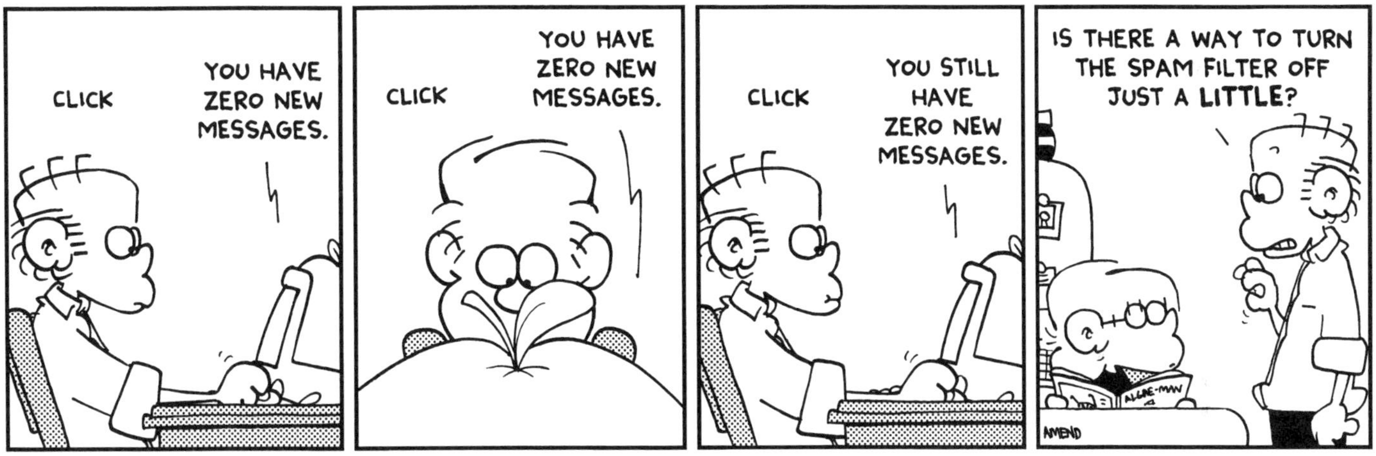
CLICK
YOU HAVE ZERO NEW MESSAGES.
CLICK
YOU HAVE ZERO NEW MESSAGES.
CLICK
YOU STILL HAVE ZERO NEW MESSAGES.
IS THERE A WAY TO TURN THE SPAM FILTER OFF JUST A **LITTLE**?
ALGAE-MAN
AMEND

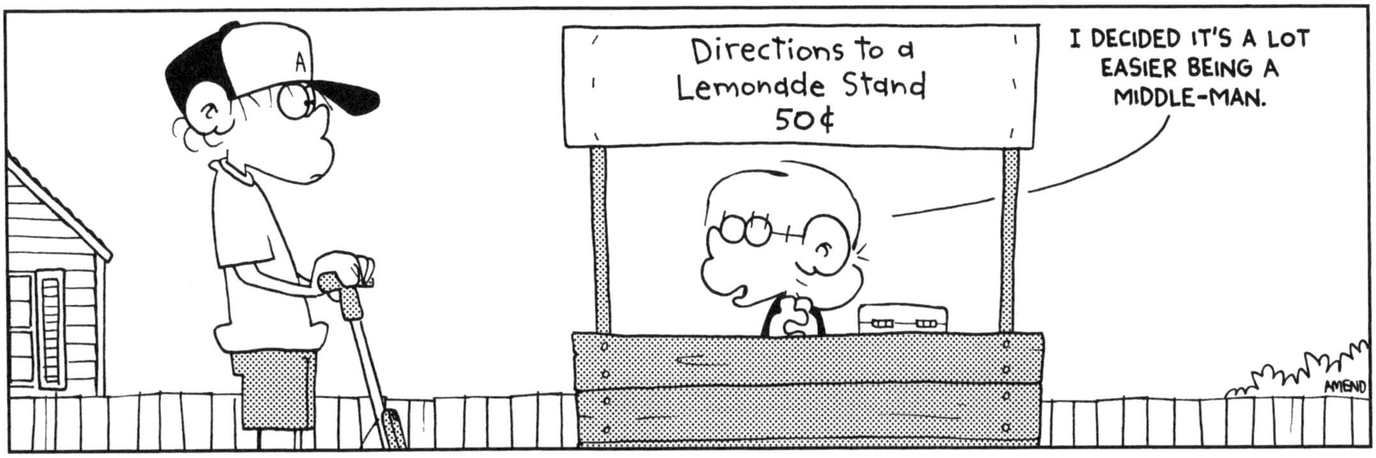
Directions to a Lemondde Stand 50¢
I DECIDED IT'S A LOT EASIER BEING A MIDDLE-MAN.
AMEND

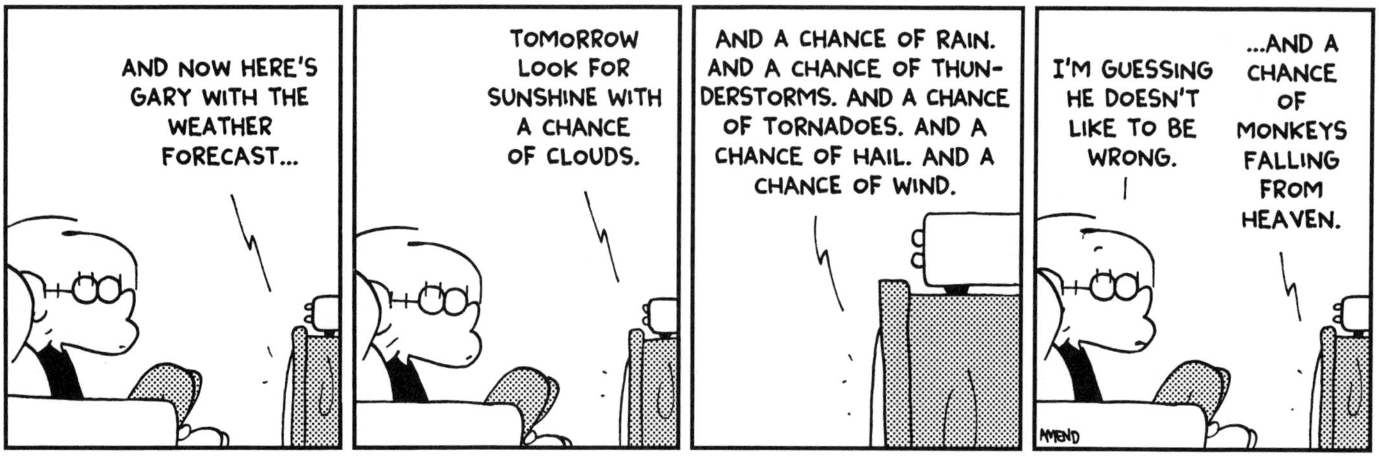
AND NOW HERE'S GARY WITH THE WEATHER FORECAST...
TOMORROW LOOK FOR SUNSHINE WITH A CHANCE OF CLOUDS.
AND A CHANCE OF RAIN. AND A CHANCE OF THUNDERSTORMS. AND A CHANCE OF TORNADOES. AND A CHANCE OF HAIL. AND A CHANCE OF WIND.
I'M GUESSING HE DOESN'T LIKE TO BE WRONG.
...AND A CHANCE OF MONKEYS FALLING FROM HEAVEN.
AMEND

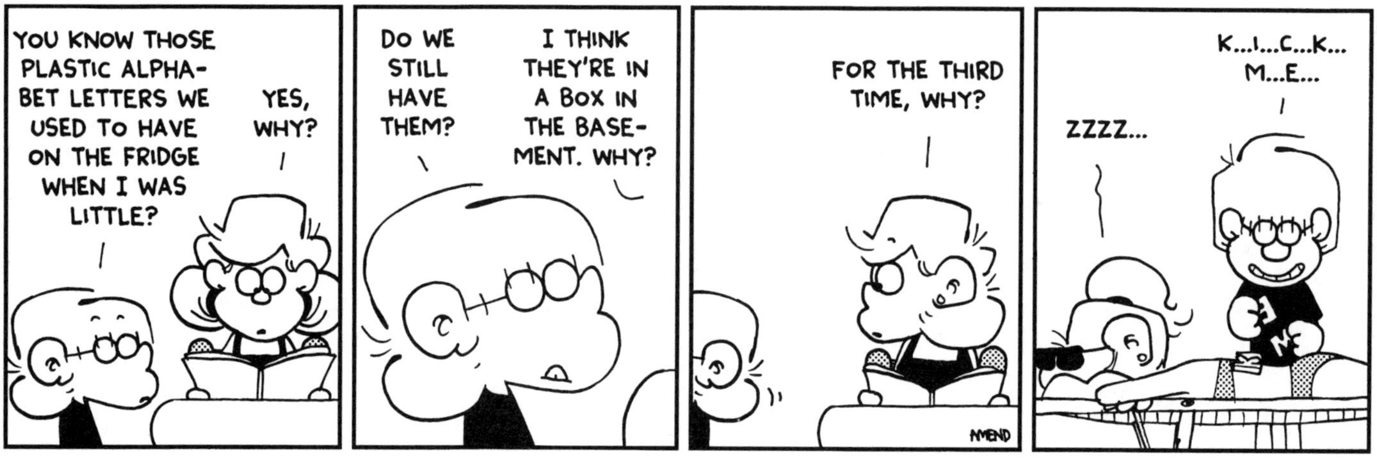
YOU KNOW THOSE PLASTIC ALPHABET LETTERS WE USED TO HAVE ON THE FRIDGE WHEN I WAS LITTLE?
YES, WHY?
DO WE STILL HAVE THEM?
I THINK THEY'RE IN A BOX IN THE BASEMENT. WHY?
FOR THE THIRD TIME, WHY?
AMEND
ZZZZ...
K...I...C...K... M...E...

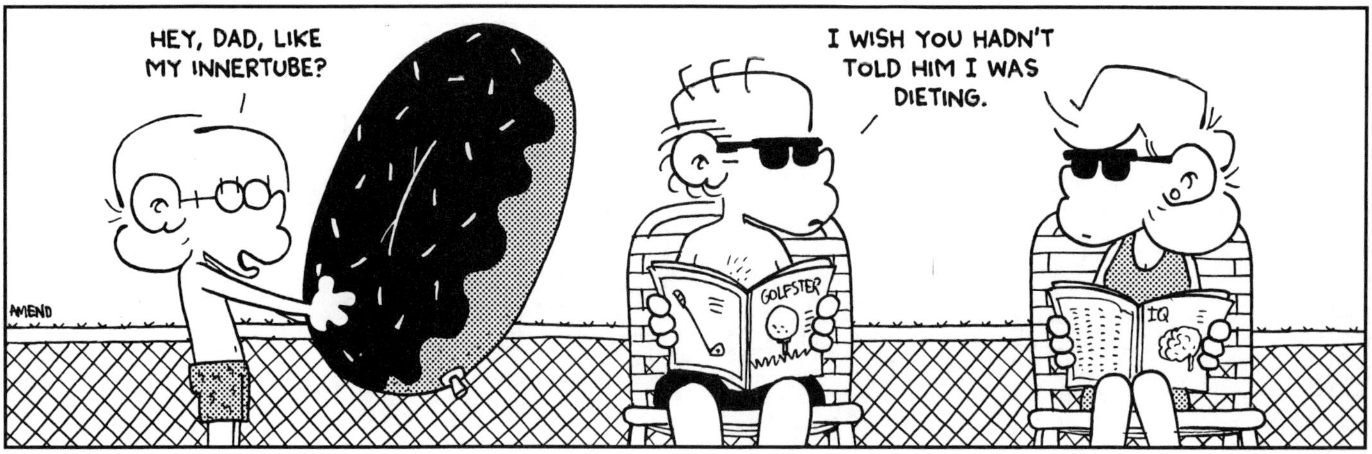
HEY, DAD, LIKE MY INNERTUBE?
I WISH YOU HADN'T TOLD HIM I WAS DIETING.
AMEND
GOLFSTER
IQ

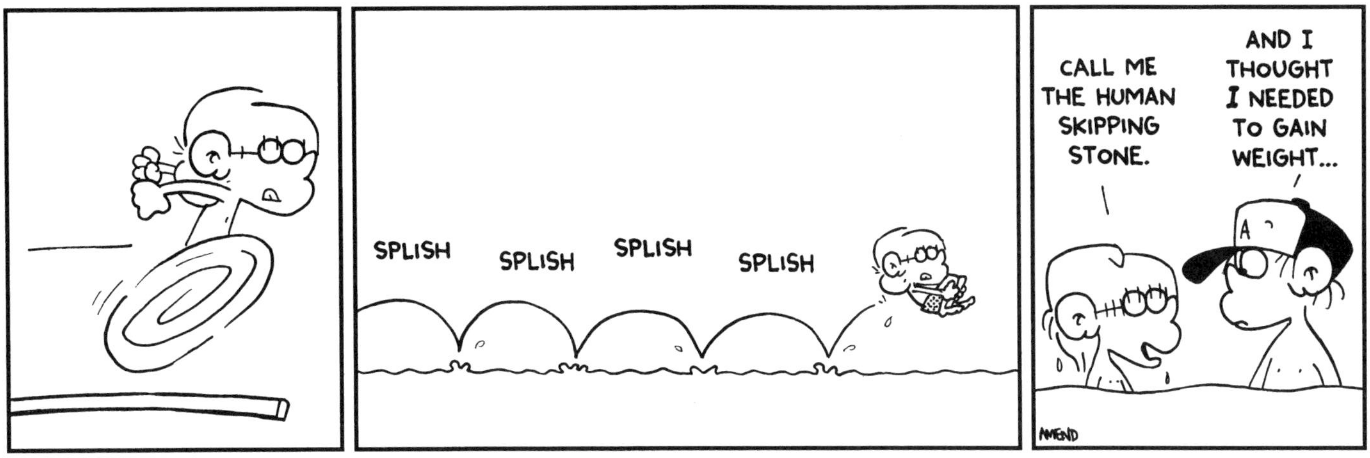
SPLISH
SPLISH
SPLISH
SPLISH
CALL ME THE HUMAN SKIPPING STONE.
AND I THOUGHT I NEEDED TO GAIN WEIGHT...
AMEND

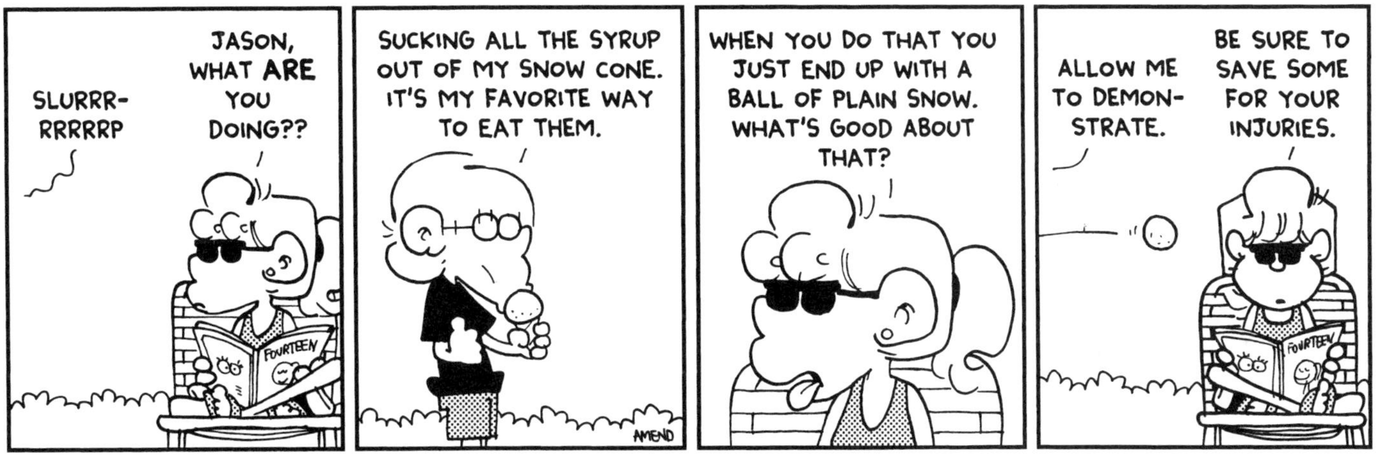
SLURRR-RRRRRP
JASON, WHAT ARE YOU DOING??
FOURTEEN
SUCKING ALL THE SYRUP OUT OF MY SNOW CONE. IT'S MY FAVORITE WAY TO EAT THEM.
AMEND
WHEN YOU DO THAT YOU JUST END UP WITH A BALL OF PLAIN SNOW. WHAT'S GOOD ABOUT THAT?
ALLOW ME TO DEMON-STRATE.
BE SURE TO SAVE SOME FOR YOUR INJURIES.
FOURTEEN

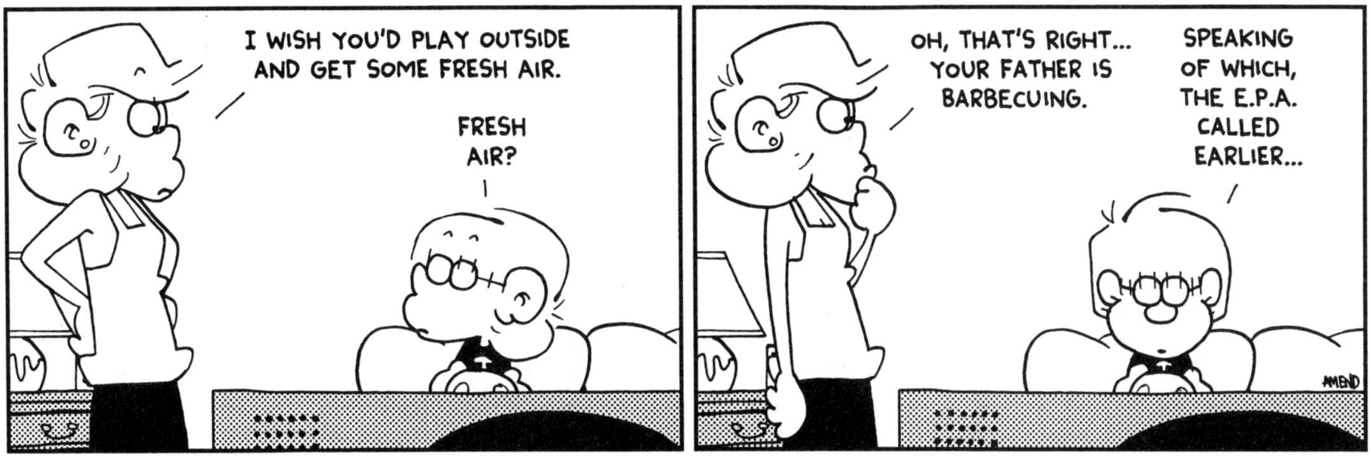
I WISH YOU'D PLAY OUTSIDE AND GET SOME FRESH AIR.
FRESH AIR?
OH, THAT'S RIGHT... YOUR FATHER IS BARBECUING.
SPEAKING OF WHICH, THE E.P.A. CALLED EARLIER...
AMEND

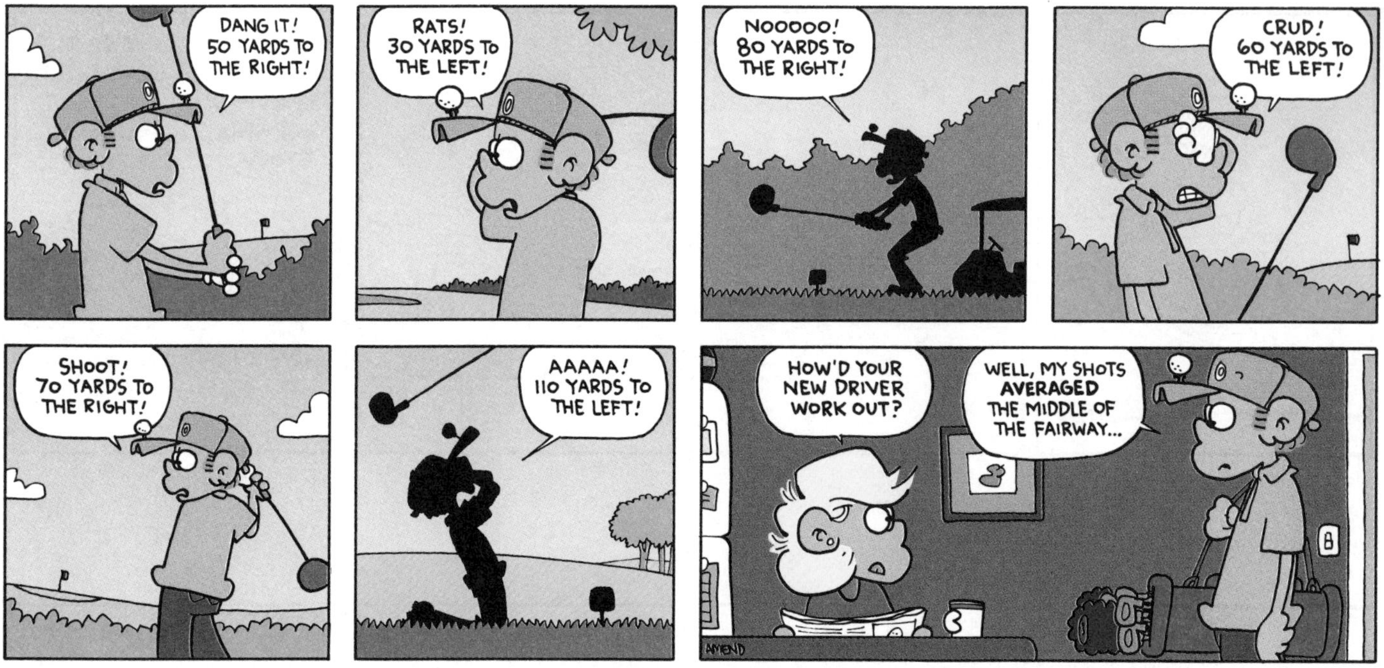
DANG IT! 50 YARDS TO THE RIGHT!
RATS! 30 YARDS TO THE LEFT!
NOOOOO! 80 YARDS TO THE RIGHT!
CRUD! 60 YARDS TO THE LEFT!
SHOOT! 70 YARDS TO THE RIGHT!
AAAAA! 110 YARDS TO THE LEFT!
HOW'D YOUR NEW DRIVER WORK OUT?
WELL, MY SHOTS **AVERAGED** THE MIDDLE OF THE FAIRWAY...
AMEND

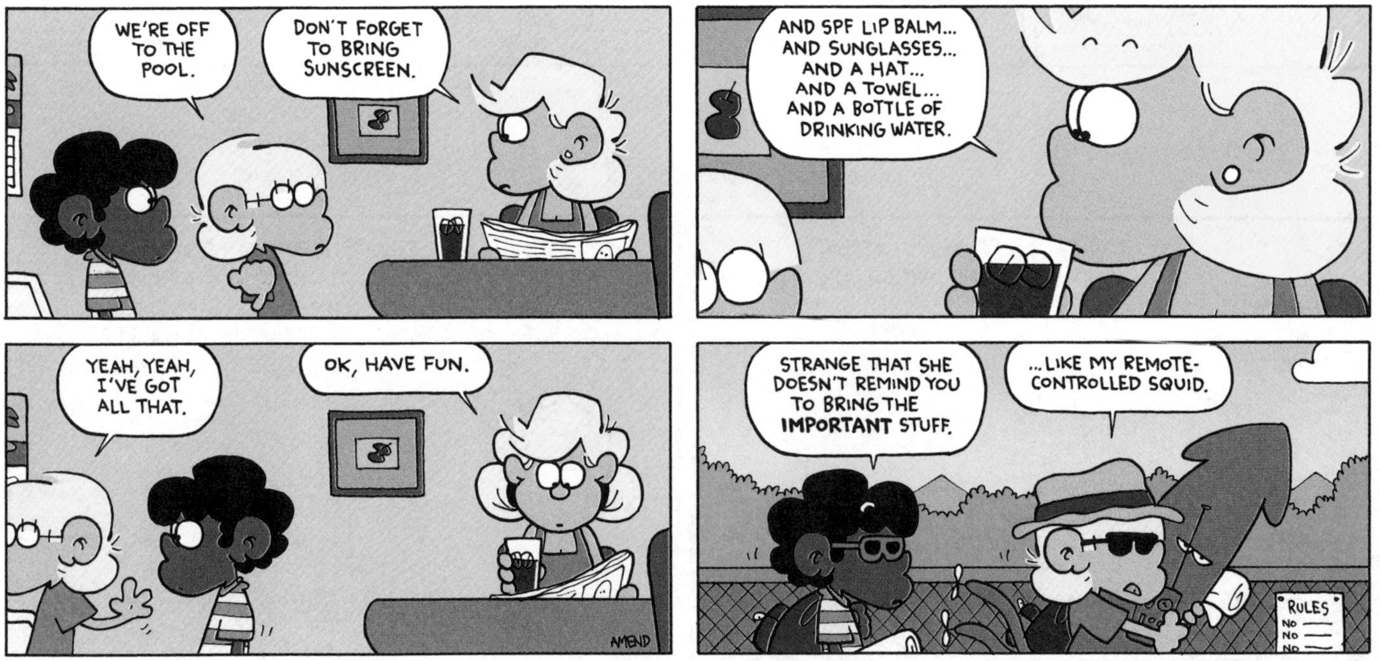
WE'RE OFF TO THE POOL.
DON'T FORGET TO BRING SUNSCREEN.
AND SPF LIP BALM... AND SUNGLASSES... AND A HAT... AND A TOWEL... AND A BOTTLE OF DRINKING WATER.
YEAH, YEAH, I'VE GOT ALL THAT.
OK, HAVE FUN.
AMEND
STRANGE THAT SHE DOESN'T REMIND YOU TO BRING THE **IMPORTANT** STUFF.
...LIKE MY REMOTE-CONTROLLED SQUID.
RULES
NO
NO
NO

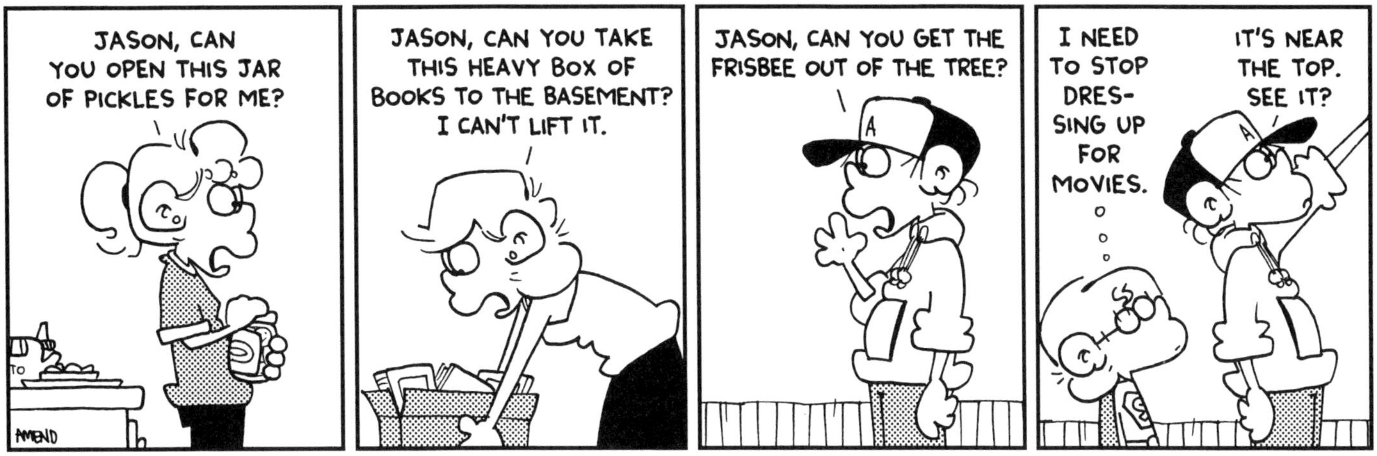
JASON, CAN YOU OPEN THIS JAR OF PICKLES FOR ME?
AMEND
JASON, CAN YOU TAKE THIS HEAVY BOX OF BOOKS TO THE BASEMENT? I CAN'T LIFT IT.
JASON, CAN YOU GET THE FRISBEE OUT OF THE TREE?
I NEED TO STOP DRES-SING UP FOR MOVIES.
IT'S NEAR THE TOP. SEE IT?

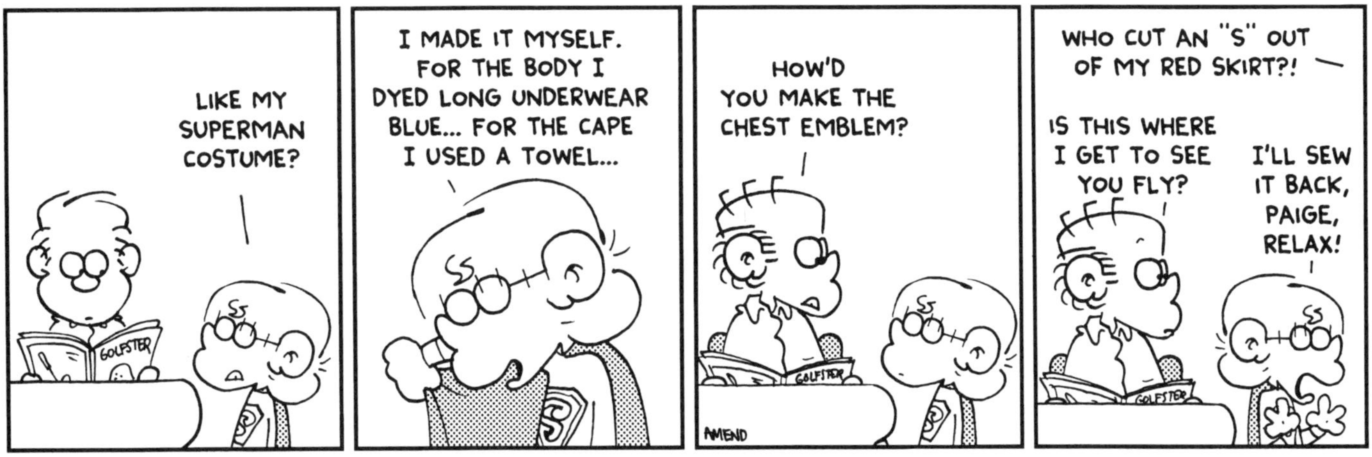
LIKE MY SUPERMAN COSTUME?
GOLFSTER
I MADE IT MYSELF. FOR THE BODY I DYED LONG UNDERWEAR BLUE... FOR THE CAPE I USED A TOWEL...
HOW'D YOU MAKE THE CHEST EMBLEM?
AMEND
WHO CUT AN "S" OUT OF MY RED SKIRT?!
IS THIS WHERE I GET TO SEE YOU FLY?
I'LL SEW IT BACK, PAIGE, RELAX!

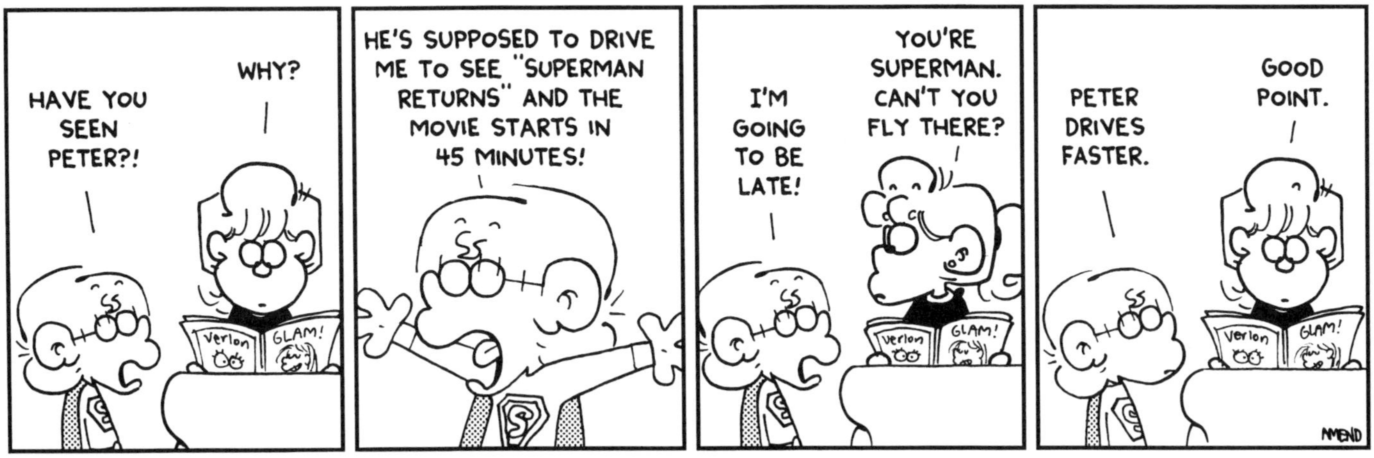
HAVE YOU SEEN PETER?!
WHY?
Verlon
GLAM!
HE'S SUPPOSED TO DRIVE ME TO SEE "SUPERMAN RETURNS" AND THE MOVIE STARTS IN 45 MINUTES!
I'M GOING TO BE LATE!
YOU'RE SUPERMAN. CAN'T YOU FLY THERE?
PETER DRIVES FASTER.
GOOD POINT.
AMEND

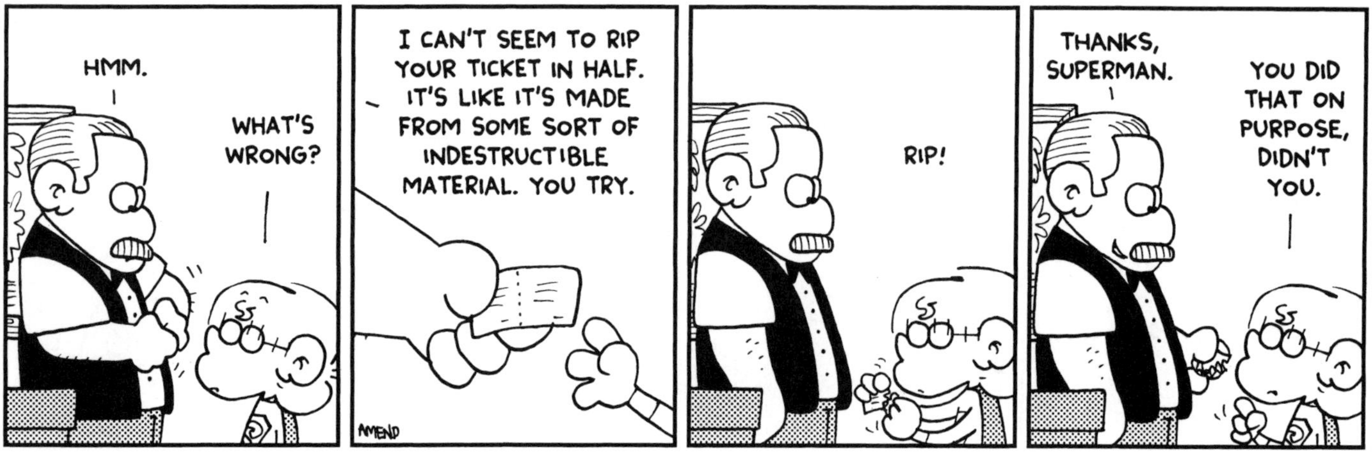
HMM.
WHAT'S WRONG?
I CAN'T SEEM TO RIP YOUR TICKET IN HALF. IT'S LIKE IT'S MADE FROM SOME SORT OF INDESTRUCTIBLE MATERIAL. YOU TRY.
AMEND
RIP!
THANKS, SUPERMAN.
YOU DID THAT ON PURPOSE, DIDN'T YOU.

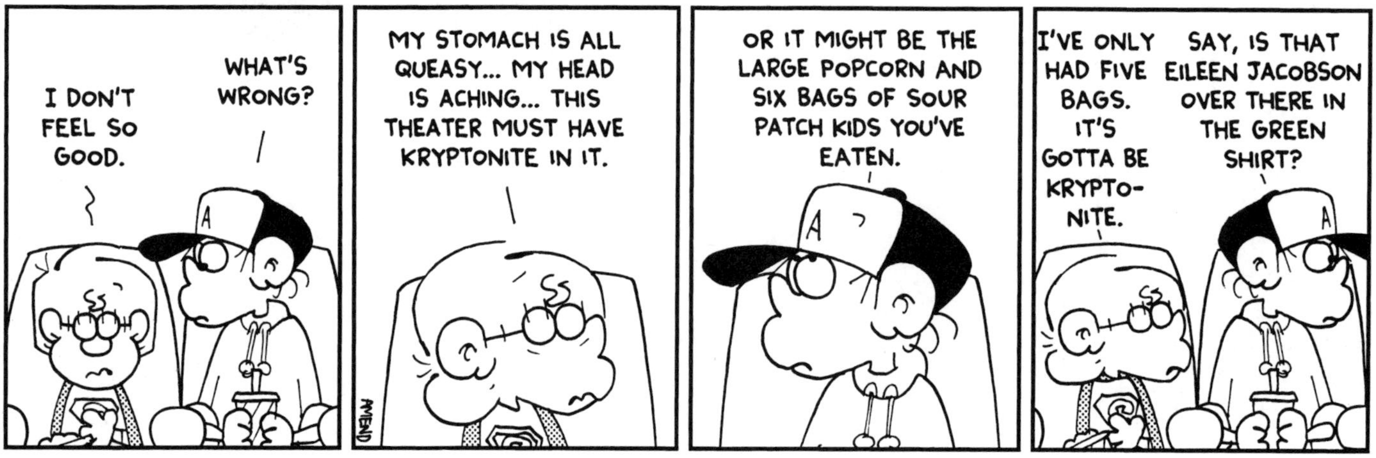
I DON'T FEEL SO GOOD.
WHAT'S WRONG?
MY STOMACH IS ALL QUEASY... MY HEAD IS ACHING... THIS THEATER MUST HAVE KRYPTONITE IN IT.
AMEND
OR IT MIGHT BE THE LARGE POPCORN AND SIX BAGS OF SOUR PATCH KIDS YOU'VE EATEN.
I'VE ONLY HAD FIVE BAGS. IT'S GOTTA BE KRYPTO-NITE.
SAY, IS THAT EILEEN JACOBSON OVER THERE IN THE GREEN SHIRT?

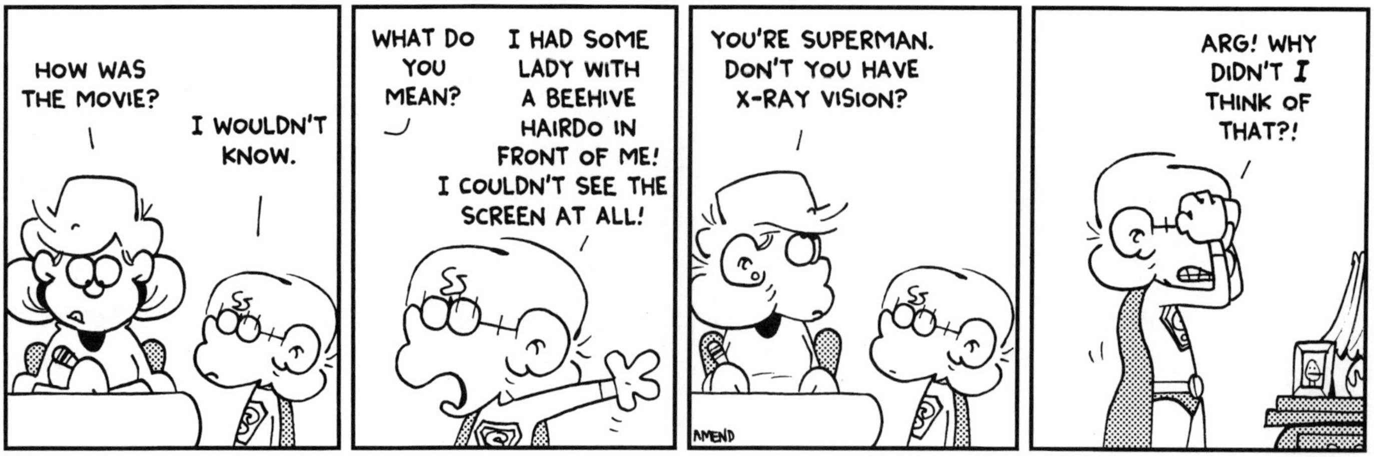
HOW WAS THE MOVIE?
I WOULDN'T KNOW.
WHAT DO YOU MEAN?
I HAD SOME LADY WITH A BEEHIVE HAIRDO IN FRONT OF ME! I COULDN'T SEE THE SCREEN AT ALL!
YOU'RE SUPERMAN. DON'T YOU HAVE X-RAY VISION?
AMEND
ARG! WHY DIDN'T *I* THINK OF THAT?!

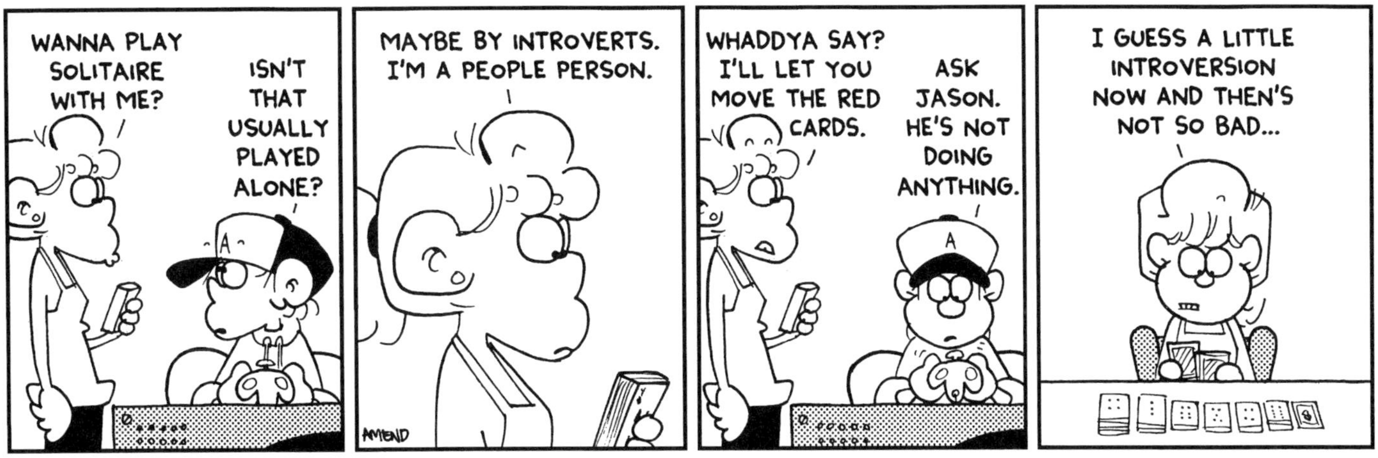
WANNA PLAY SOLITAIRE WITH ME?
ISN'T THAT USUALLY PLAYED ALONE?
MAYBE BY INTROVERTS. I'M A PEOPLE PERSON.
AMEND
WHADDYA SAY? I'LL LET YOU MOVE THE RED CARDS.
ASK JASON. HE'S NOT DOING ANYTHING.
I GUESS A LITTLE INTROVERSION NOW AND THEN'S NOT SO BAD...

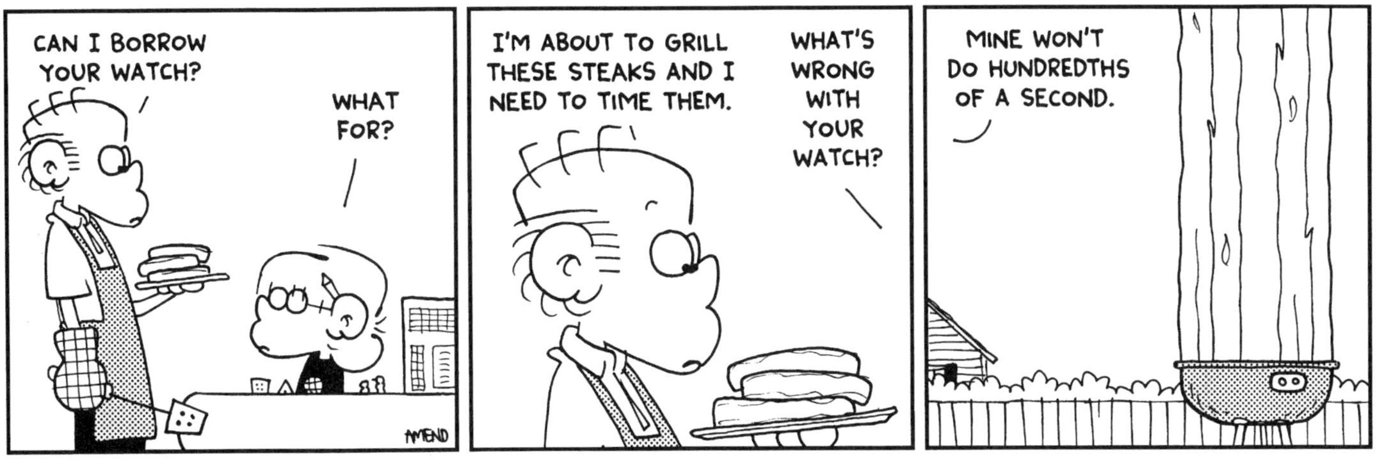
CAN I BORROW YOUR WATCH?
WHAT FOR?
AMEND
I'M ABOUT TO GRILL THESE STEAKS AND I NEED TO TIME THEM.
WHAT'S WRONG WITH YOUR WATCH?
MINE WON'T DO HUNDREDTHS OF A SECOND.

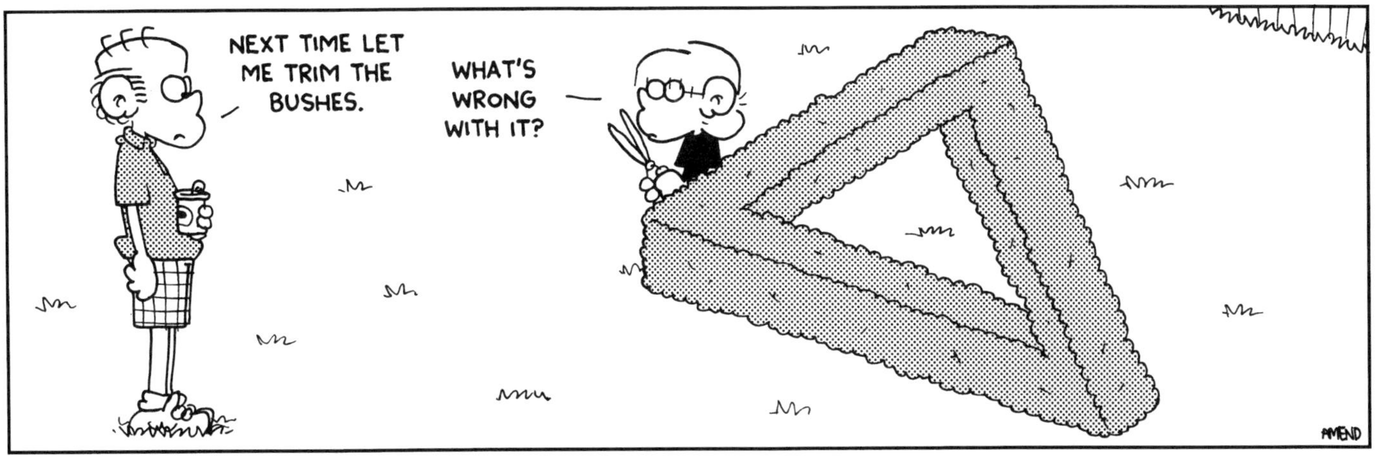
NEXT TIME LET ME TRIM THE BUSHES.
WHAT'S WRONG WITH IT?
AMEND

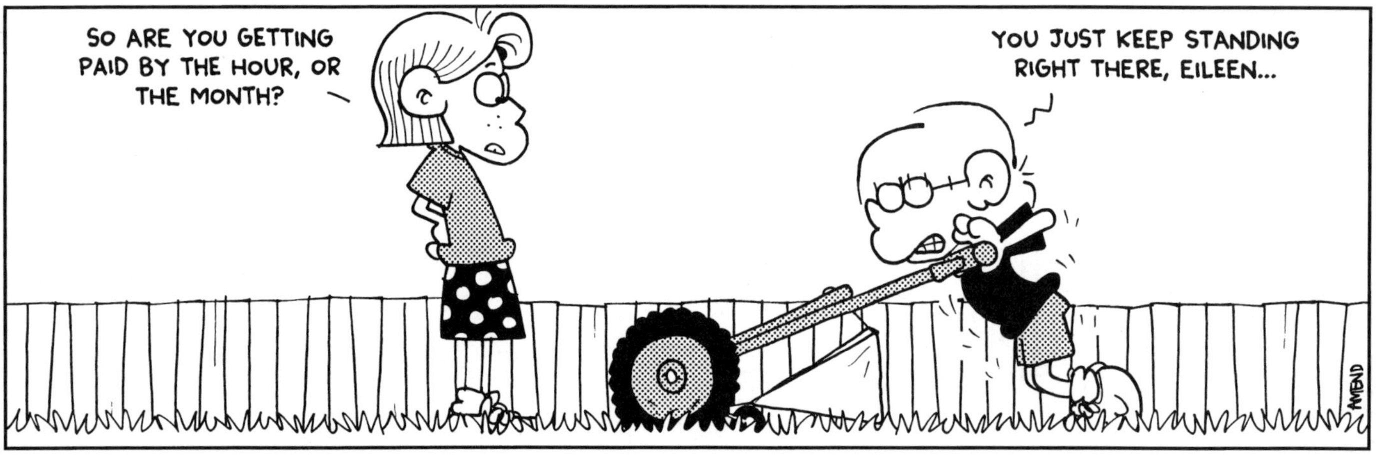
SO ARE YOU GETTING PAID BY THE HOUR, OR THE MONTH?
YOU JUST KEEP STANDING RIGHT THERE, EILEEN...
AMEND

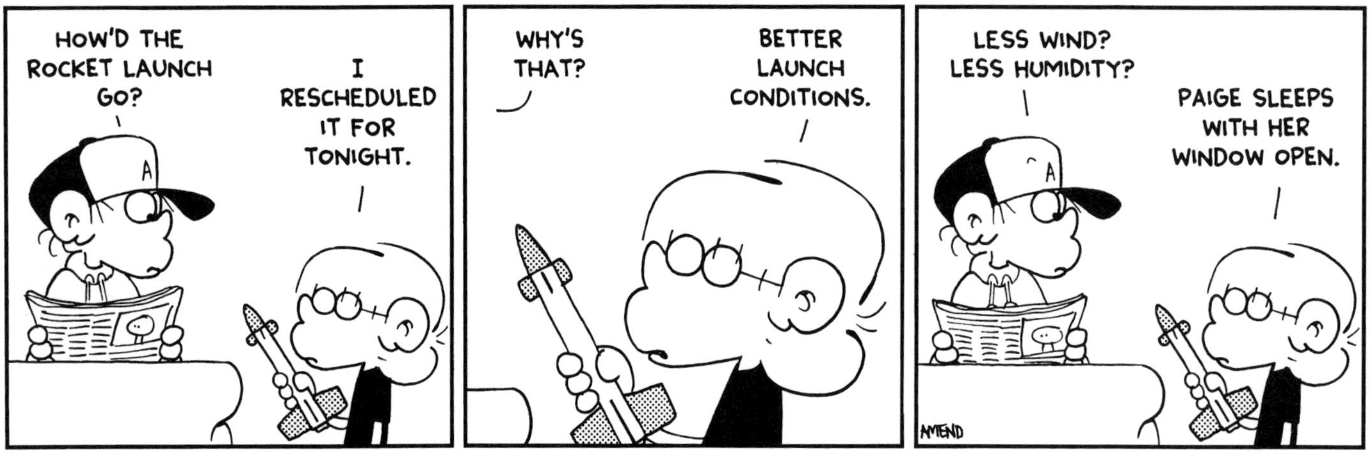
HOW'D THE ROCKET LAUNCH GO?
I RESCHEDULED IT FOR TONIGHT.
WHY'S THAT?
BETTER LAUNCH CONDITIONS.
LESS WIND? LESS HUMIDITY?
PAIGE SLEEPS WITH HER WINDOW OPEN.
AMEND

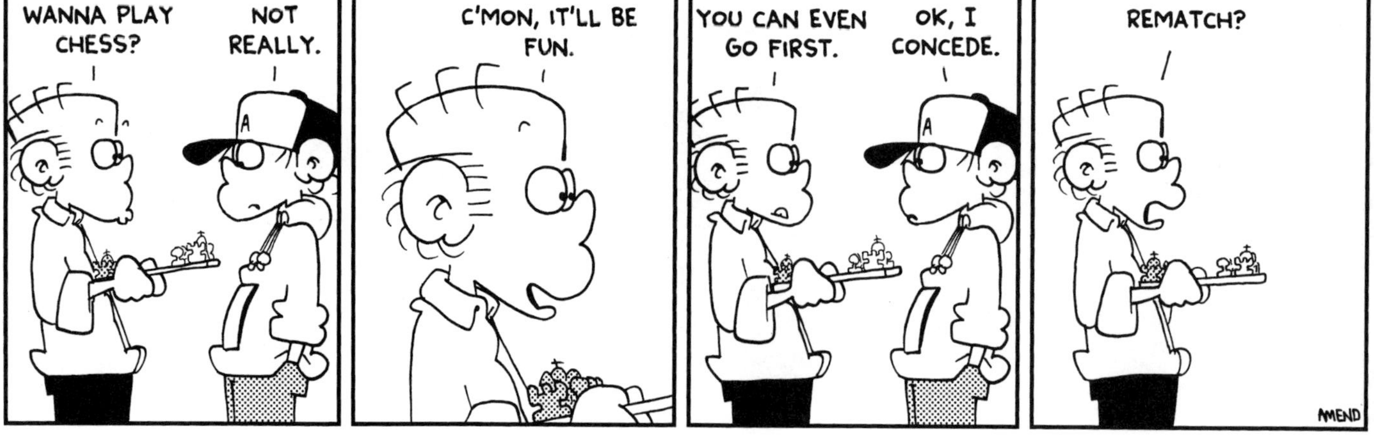
WANNA PLAY CHESS?
NOT REALLY.
C'MON, IT'LL BE FUN.
YOU CAN EVEN GO FIRST.
OK, I CONCEDE.
REMATCH?
AMEND

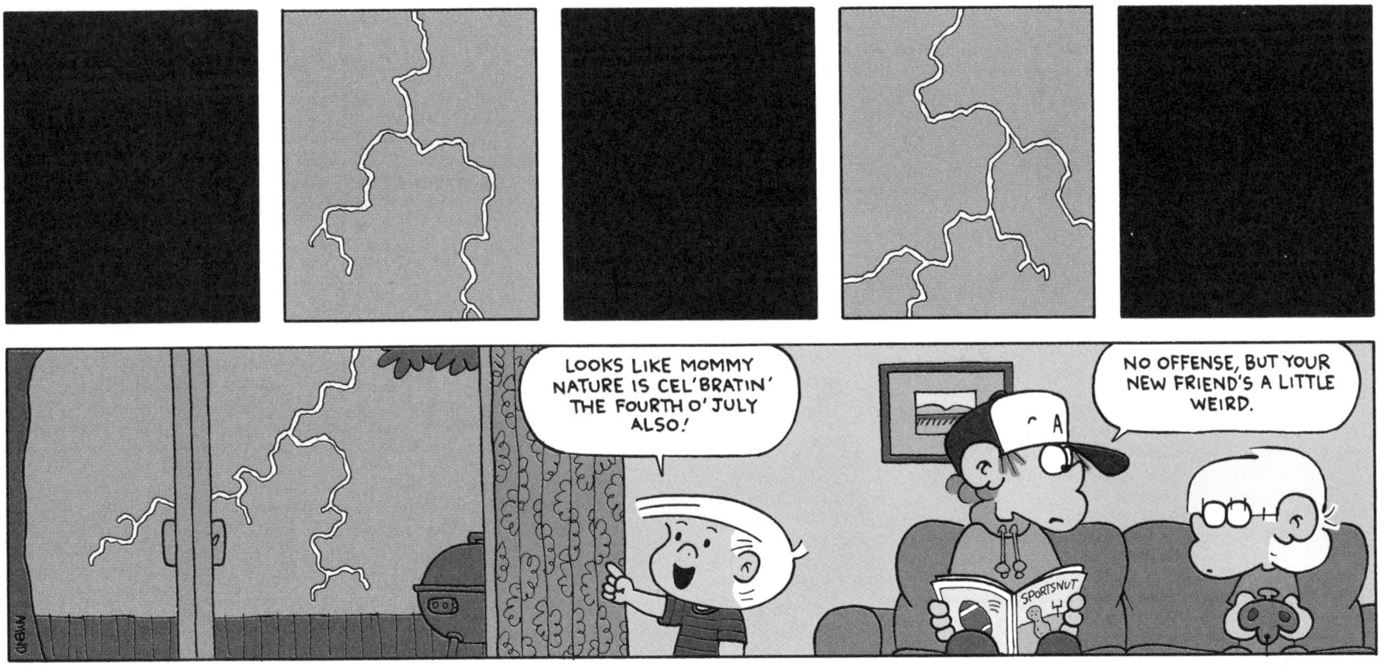
LOOKS LIKE MOMMY NATURE IS CEL'BRATIN' THE FOURTH O' JULY ALSO!
NO OFFENSE, BUT YOUR NEW FRIEND'S A LITTLE WEIRD.
SPORTSNUT
AMEND

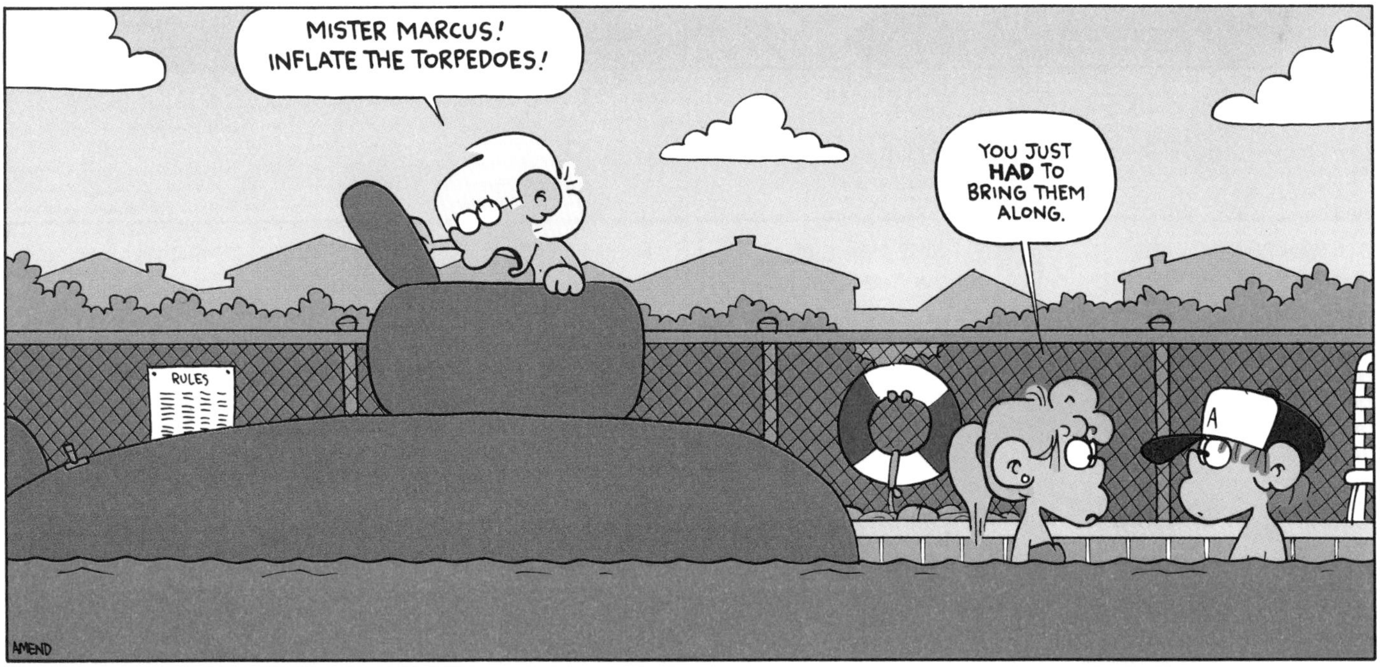
MISTER MARCUS! INFLATE THE TORPEDOES!
YOU JUST **HAD** TO BRING THEM ALONG.
RULES
AMEND

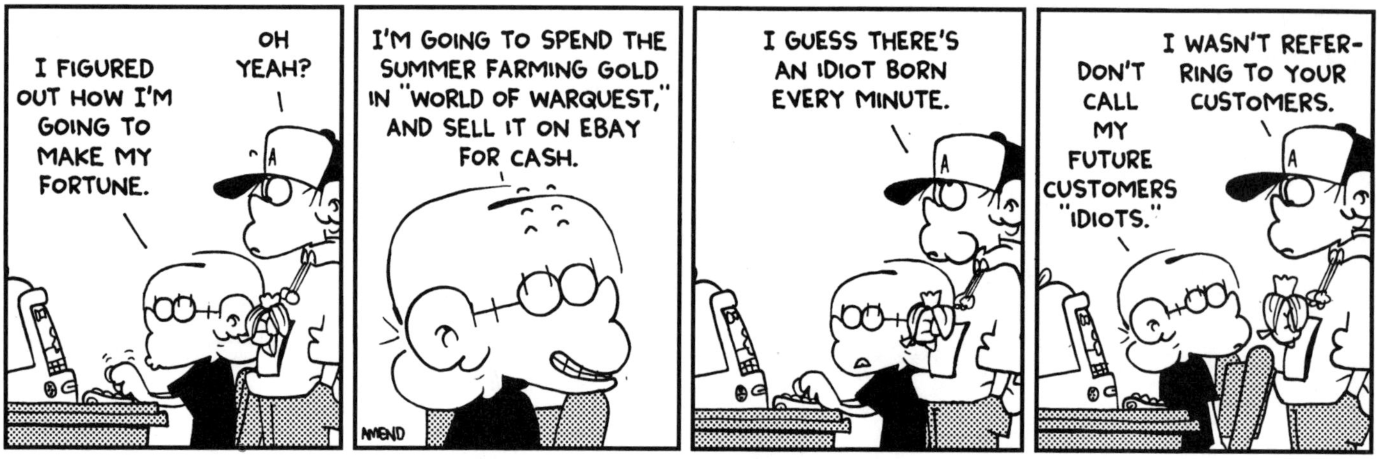
I FIGURED OUT HOW I'M GOING TO MAKE MY FORTUNE.
OH YEAH?
I'M GOING TO SPEND THE SUMMER FARMING GOLD IN "WORLD OF WARQUEST," AND SELL IT ON EBAY FOR CASH.
AMEND
I GUESS THERE'S AN IDIOT BORN EVERY MINUTE.
DON'T CALL MY FUTURE CUSTOMERS "IDIOTS."
I WASN'T REFER-RING TO YOUR CUSTOMERS.

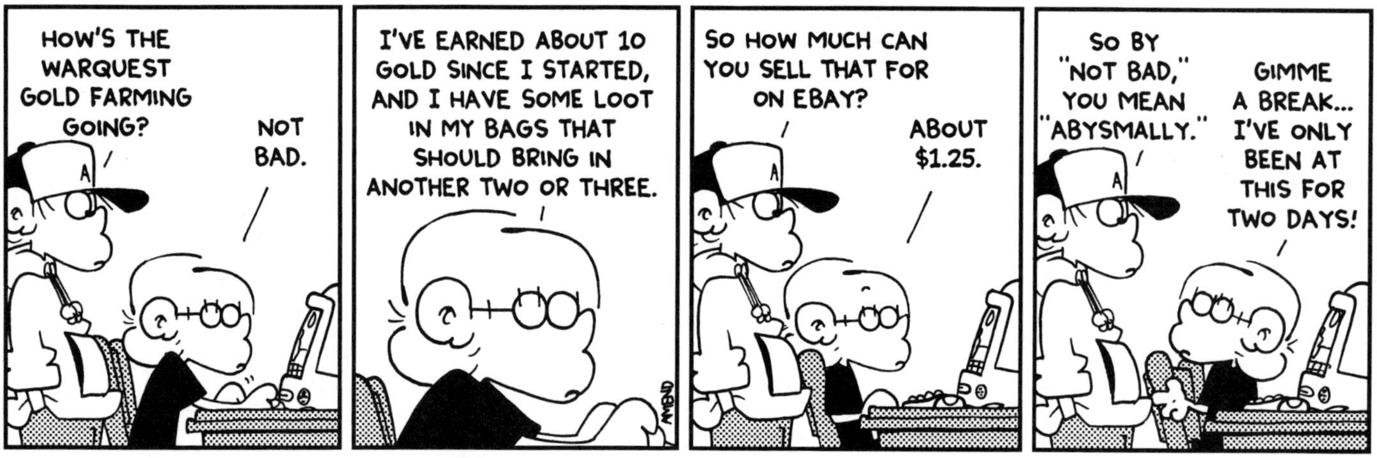
HOW'S THE WARQUEST GOLD FARMING GOING?
NOT BAD.
I'VE EARNED ABOUT 10 GOLD SINCE I STARTED, AND I HAVE SOME LOOT IN MY BAGS THAT SHOULD BRING IN ANOTHER TWO OR THREE.
AMEND
SO HOW MUCH CAN YOU SELL THAT FOR ON EBAY?
ABOUT $1.25.
SO BY "NOT BAD," YOU MEAN "ABYSMALLY."
GIMME A BREAK... I'VE ONLY BEEN AT THIS FOR TWO DAYS!

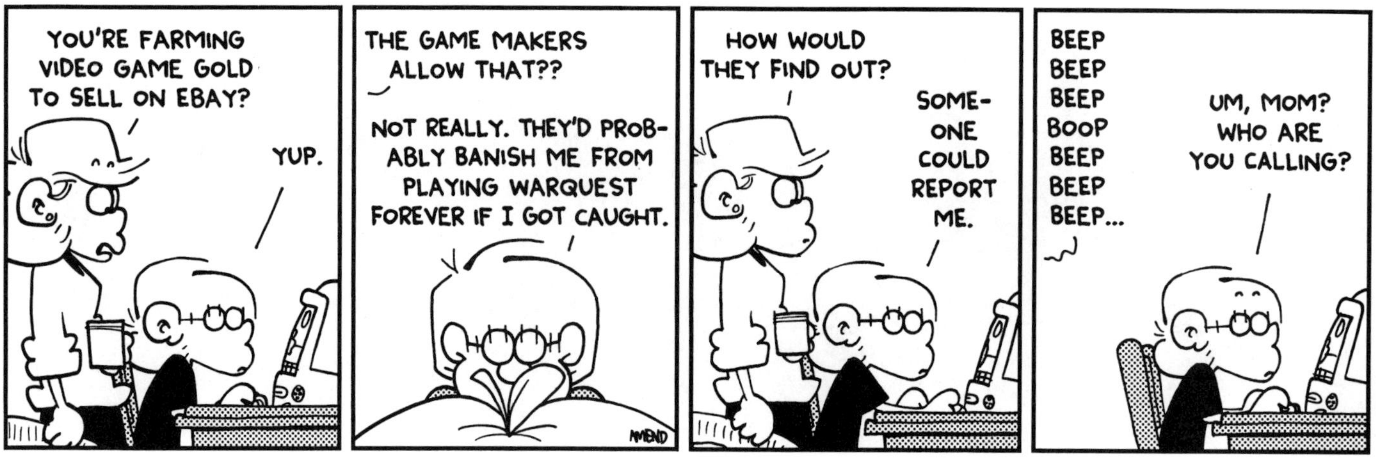
YOU'RE FARMING VIDEO GAME GOLD TO SELL ON EBAY?
YUP.
THE GAME MAKERS ALLOW THAT??
NOT REALLY. THEY'D PROB-ABLY BANISH ME FROM PLAYING WARQUEST FOREVER IF I GOT CAUGHT.
AMEND
HOW WOULD THEY FIND OUT?
SOME-ONE COULD REPORT ME.
BEEP BEEP BEEP BOOP BEEP BEEP BEEP...
UM, MOM? WHO ARE YOU CALLING?

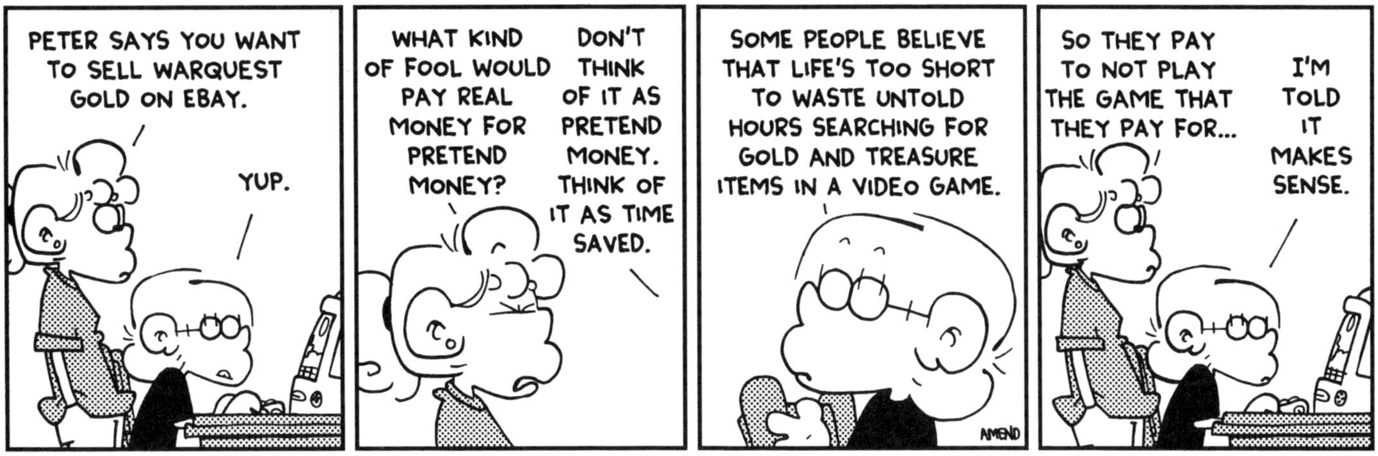
PETER SAYS YOU WANT TO SELL WARQUEST GOLD ON EBAY.
YUP.
WHAT KIND OF FOOL WOULD PAY REAL MONEY FOR PRETEND MONEY?
DON'T THINK OF IT AS PRETEND MONEY. THINK OF IT AS TIME SAVED.
SOME PEOPLE BELIEVE THAT LIFE'S TOO SHORT TO WASTE UNTOLD HOURS SEARCHING FOR GOLD AND TREASURE ITEMS IN A VIDEO GAME.
AMEND
SO THEY PAY TO NOT PLAY THE GAME THAT THEY PAY FOR...
I'M TOLD IT MAKES SENSE.

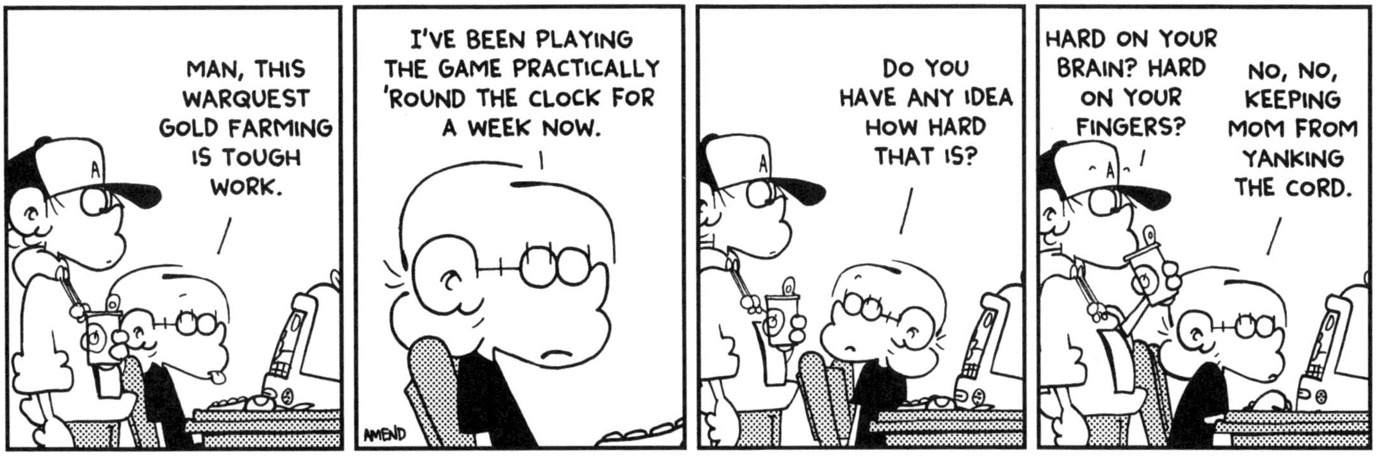
MAN, THIS WARQUEST GOLD FARMING IS TOUGH WORK.
I'VE BEEN PLAYING THE GAME PRACTICALLY 'ROUND THE CLOCK FOR A WEEK NOW.
AMEND
DO YOU HAVE ANY IDEA HOW HARD THAT IS?
HARD ON YOUR BRAIN? HARD ON YOUR FINGERS?
NO, NO, KEEPING MOM FROM YANKING THE CORD.

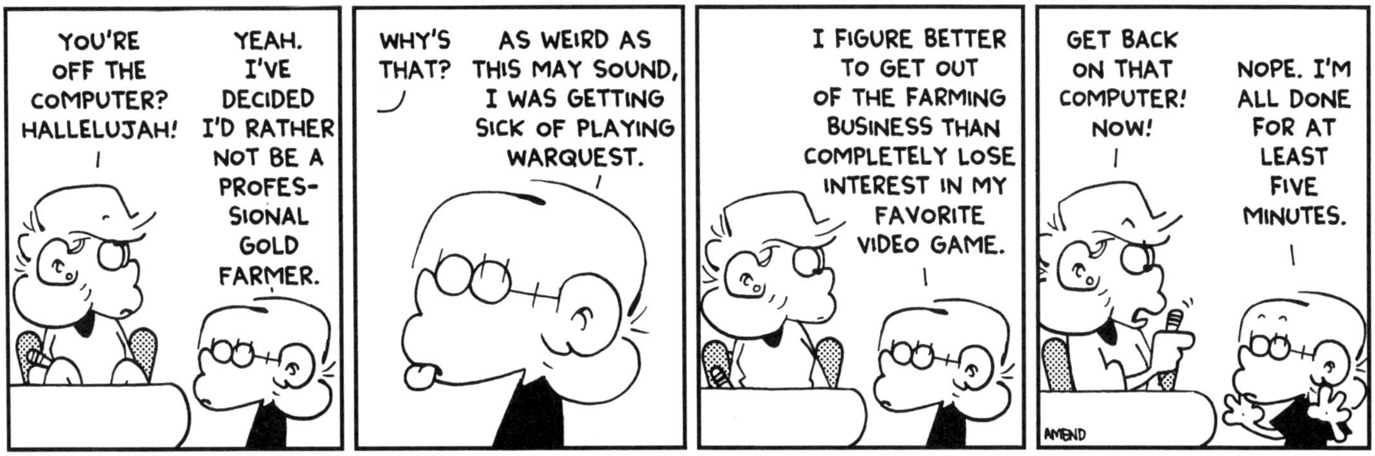
YOU'RE OFF THE COMPUTER? HALLELUJAH!
YEAH. I'VE DECIDED I'D RATHER NOT BE A PROFES-SIONAL GOLD FARMER.
WHY'S THAT?
AS WEIRD AS THIS MAY SOUND, I WAS GETTING SICK OF PLAYING WARQUEST.
I FIGURE BETTER TO GET OUT OF THE FARMING BUSINESS THAN COMPLETELY LOSE INTEREST IN MY FAVORITE VIDEO GAME.
GET BACK ON THAT COMPUTER! NOW!
NOPE. I'M ALL DONE FOR AT LEAST FIVE MINUTES.
AMEND

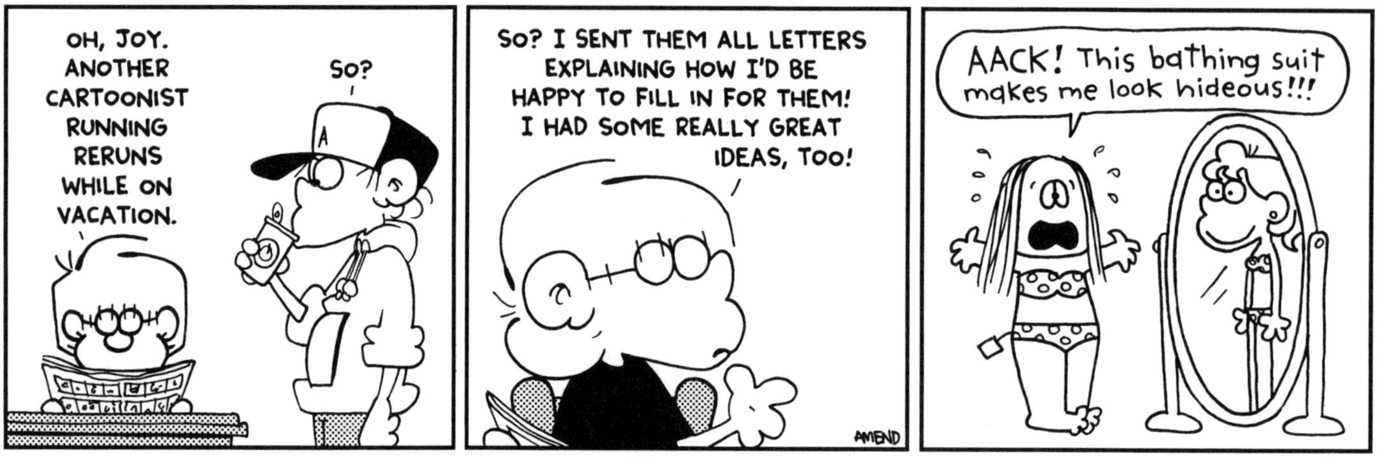
OH, JOY. ANOTHER CARTOONIST RUNNING RERUNS WHILE ON VACATION.
SO?
SO? I SENT THEM ALL LETTERS EXPLAINING HOW I'D BE HAPPY TO FILL IN FOR THEM! I HAD SOME REALLY GREAT IDEAS, TOO!
AMEND
AACK! This bathing suit makes me look hideous!!!

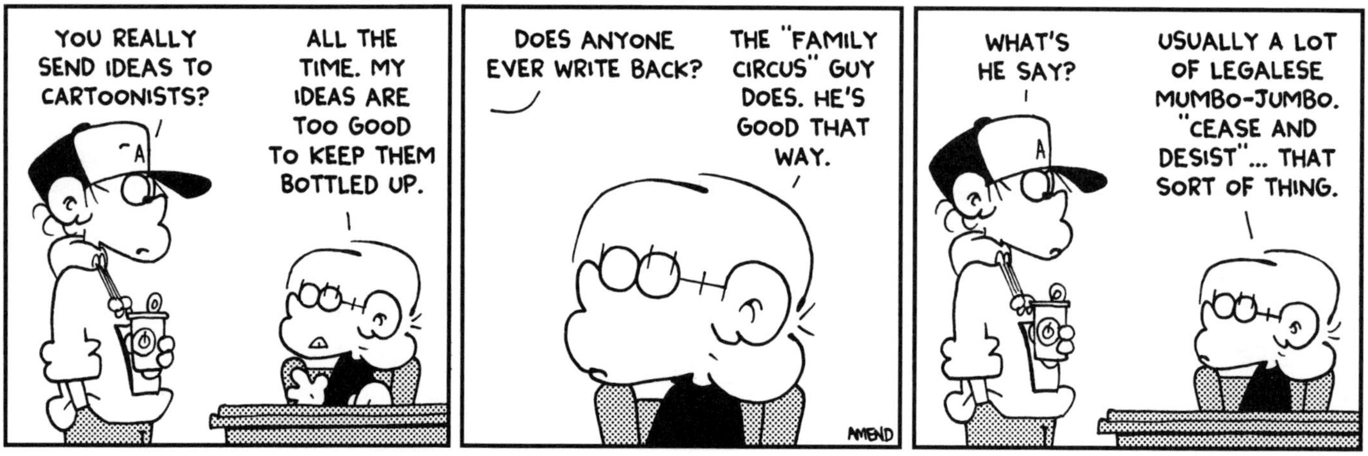
YOU REALLY SEND IDEAS TO CARTOONISTS?
ALL THE TIME. MY IDEAS ARE TOO GOOD TO KEEP THEM BOTTLED UP.
DOES ANYONE EVER WRITE BACK?
THE "FAMILY CIRCUS" GUY DOES. HE'S GOOD THAT WAY.
AMEND
WHAT'S HE SAY?
USUALLY A LOT OF LEGALESE MUMBO-JUMBO. "CEASE AND DESIST"... THAT SORT OF THING.

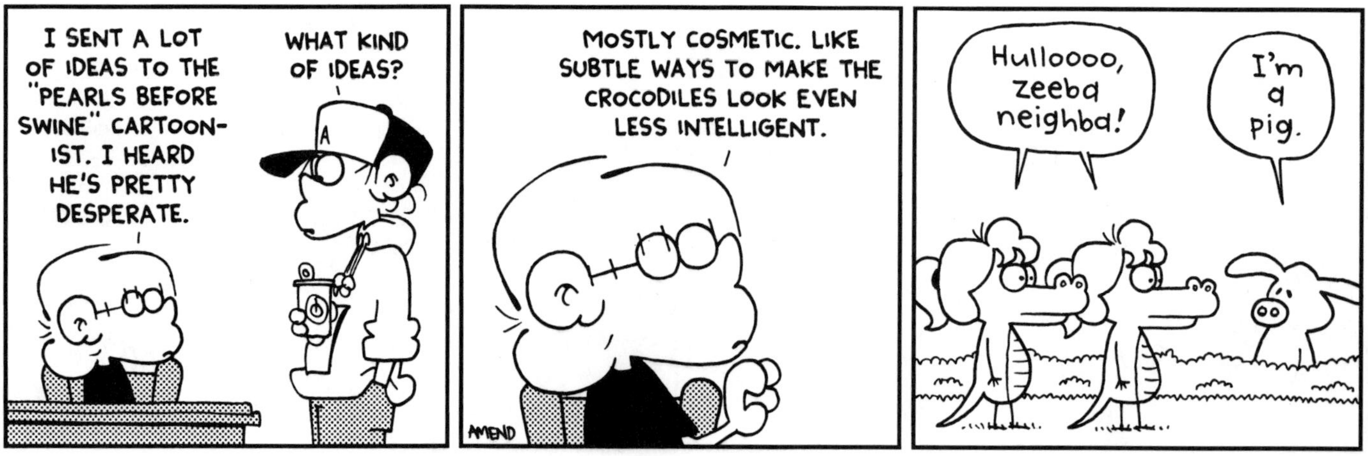
I SENT A LOT OF IDEAS TO THE "PEARLS BEFORE SWINE" CARTOON-IST. I HEARD HE'S PRETTY DESPERATE.
WHAT KIND OF IDEAS?
MOSTLY COSMETIC. LIKE SUBTLE WAYS TO MAKE THE CROCODILES LOOK EVEN LESS INTELLIGENT.
AMEND
Hulloooo, zeeba neighba!
I'm a pig.

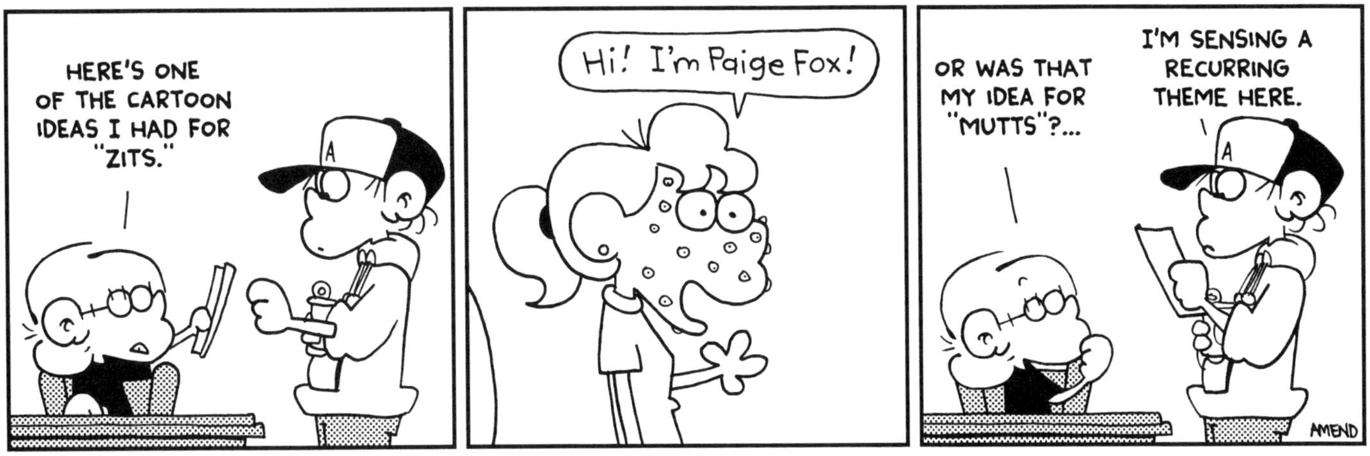
HERE'S ONE OF THE CARTOON IDEAS I HAD FOR "ZITS."
Hi! I'm Paige Fox!
OR WAS THAT MY IDEA FOR "MUTTS"?...
I'M SENSING A RECURRING THEME HERE.
AMEND

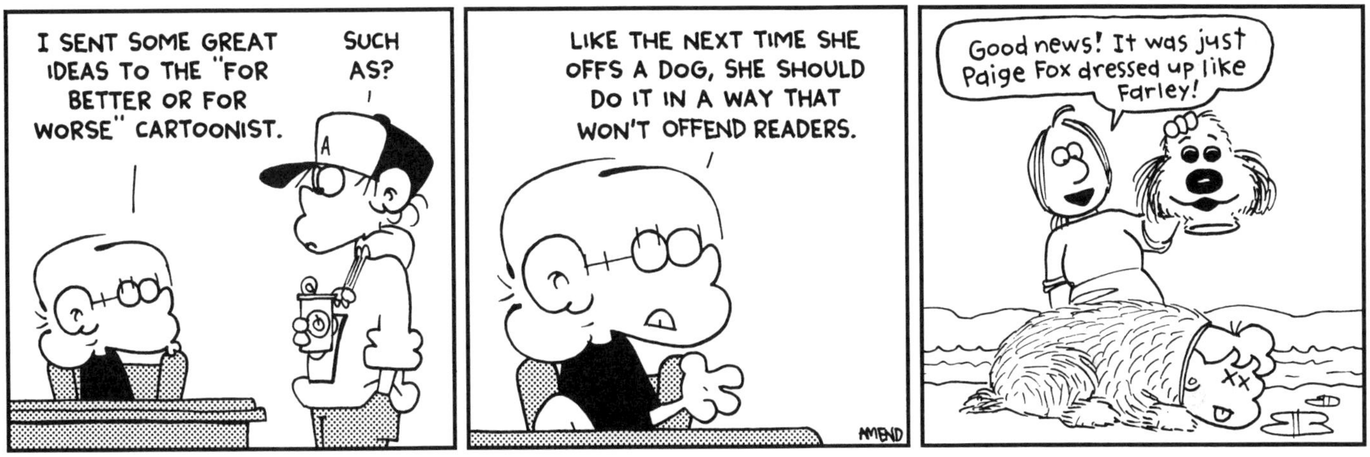
I SENT SOME GREAT IDEAS TO THE "FOR BETTER OR FOR WORSE" CARTOONIST.
SUCH AS?
LIKE THE NEXT TIME SHE OFFS A DOG, SHE SHOULD DO IT IN A WAY THAT WON'T OFFEND READERS.
AMEND
Good news! It was just Paige Fox dressed up like Farley!

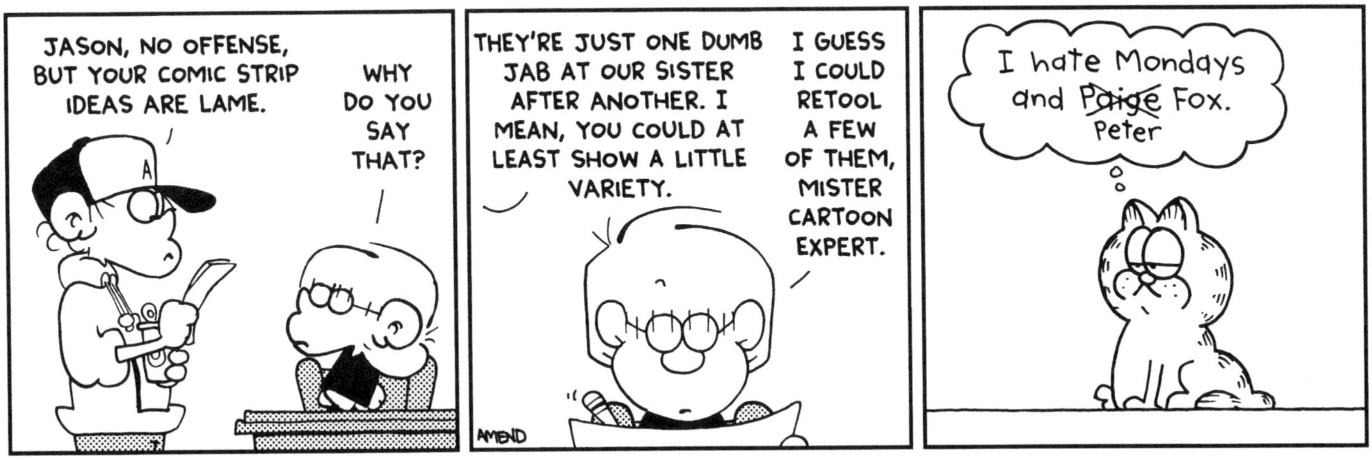
JASON, NO OFFENSE, BUT YOUR COMIC STRIP IDEAS ARE LAME.
WHY DO YOU SAY THAT?
THEY'RE JUST ONE DUMB JAB AT OUR SISTER AFTER ANOTHER. I MEAN, YOU COULD AT LEAST SHOW A LITTLE VARIETY.
I GUESS I COULD RETOOL A FEW OF THEM, MISTER CARTOON EXPERT.
AMEND
I hate Mondays and ~~Paige~~ Fox.
Peter

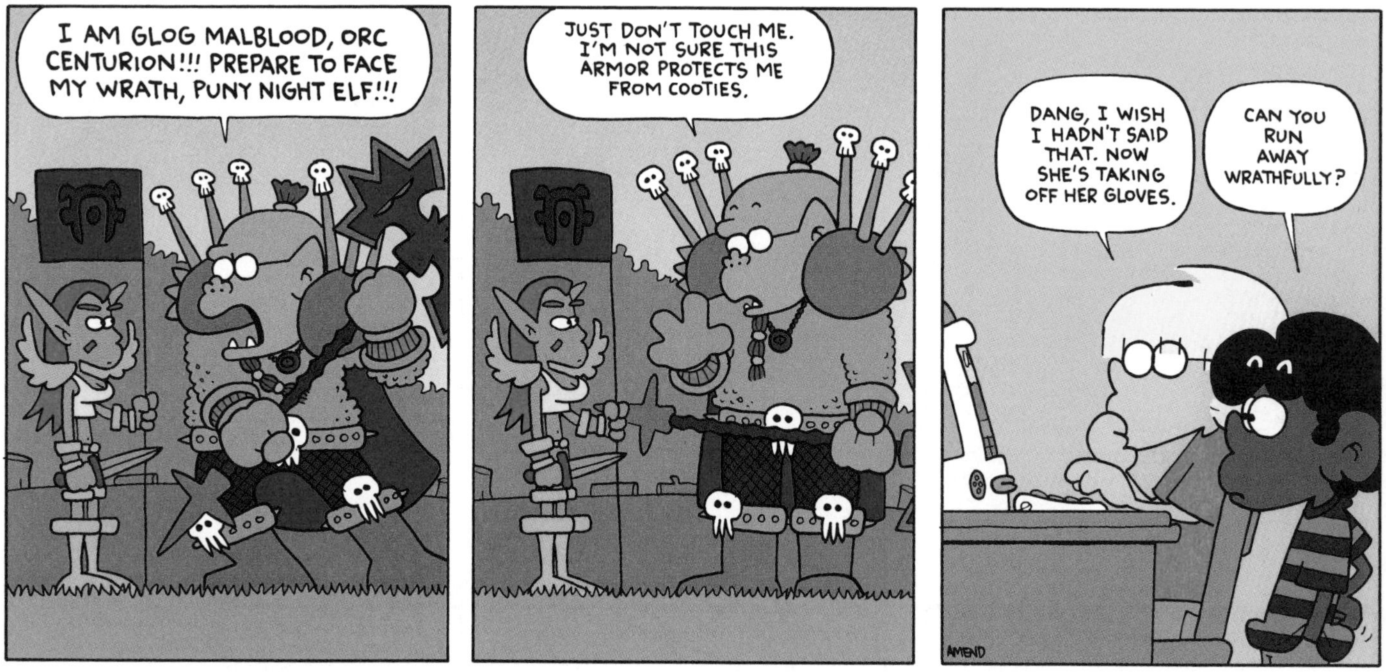
I AM GLOG MALBLOOD, ORC CENTURION!!! PREPARE TO FACE MY WRATH, PUNY NIGHT ELF!!!
JUST DON'T TOUCH ME. I'M NOT SURE THIS ARMOR PROTECTS ME FROM COOTIES.
DANG, I WISH I HADN'T SAID THAT. NOW SHE'S TAKING OFF HER GLOVES.
CAN YOU RUN AWAY WRATHFULLY?
AMEND

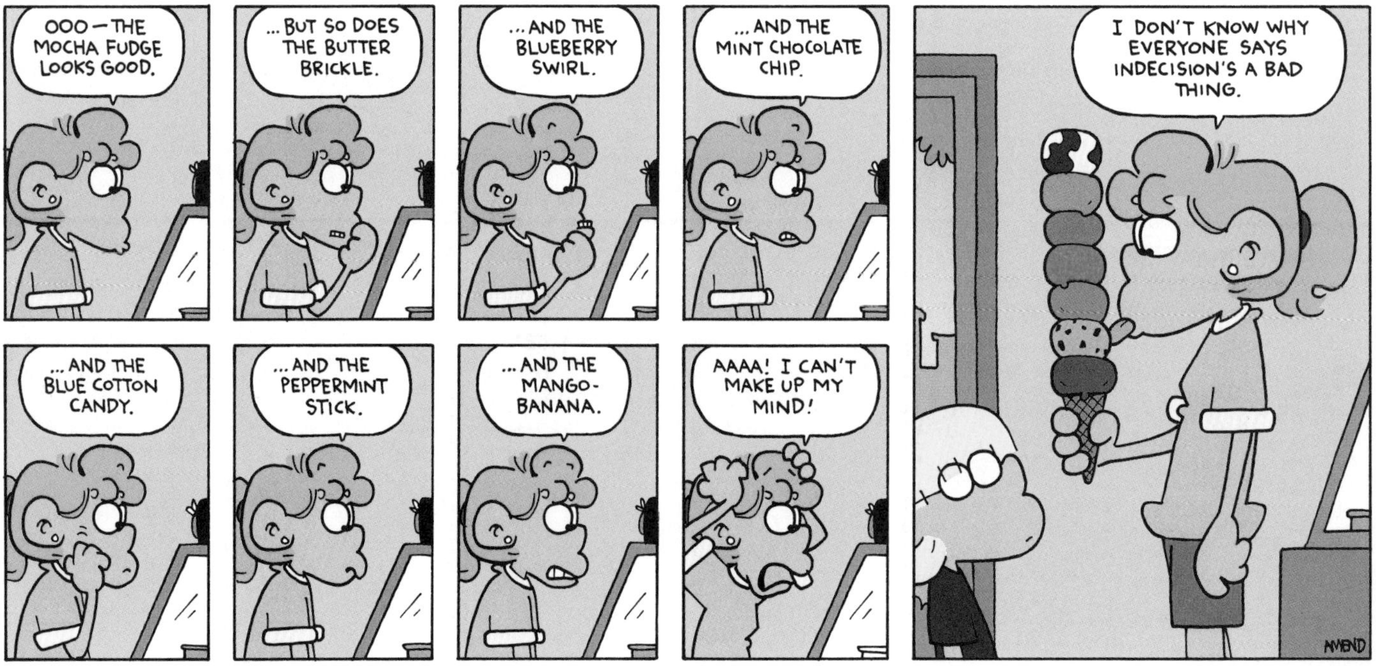
OOO—THE MOCHA FUDGE LOOKS GOOD.
...BUT SO DOES THE BUTTER BRICKLE.
...AND THE BLUEBERRY SWIRL.
...AND THE MINT CHOCOLATE CHIP.
...AND THE BLUE COTTON CANDY.
...AND THE PEPPERMINT STICK.
...AND THE MANGO-BANANA.
AAAA! I CAN'T MAKE UP MY MIND!
I DON'T KNOW WHY EVERYONE SAYS INDECISION'S A BAD THING.
AMEND

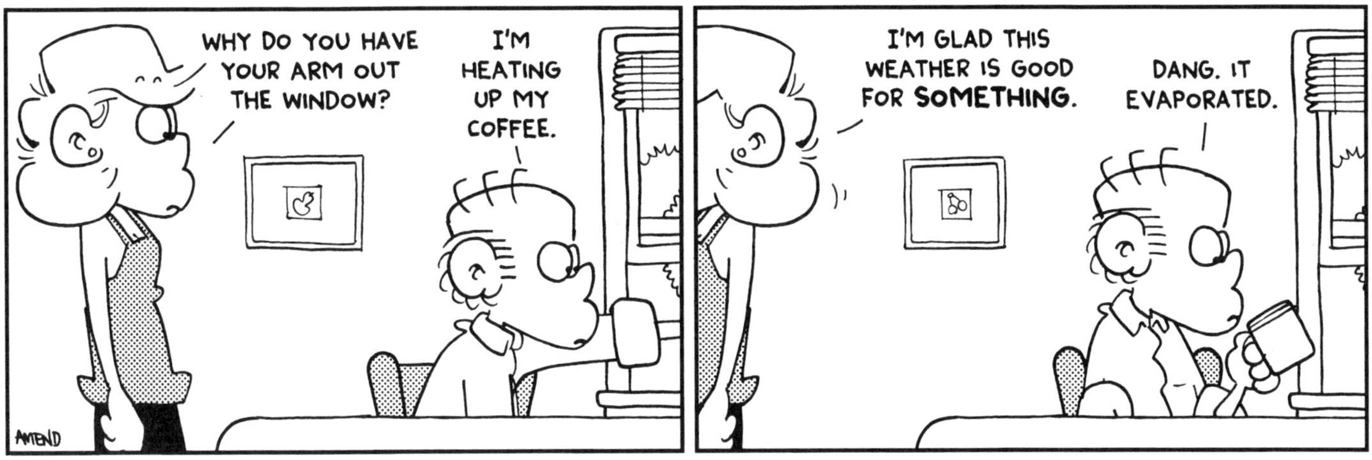
WHY DO YOU HAVE YOUR ARM OUT THE WINDOW?
I'M HEATING UP MY COFFEE.
AMEND
I'M GLAD THIS WEATHER IS GOOD FOR **SOMETHING**.
DANG. IT EVAPORATED.

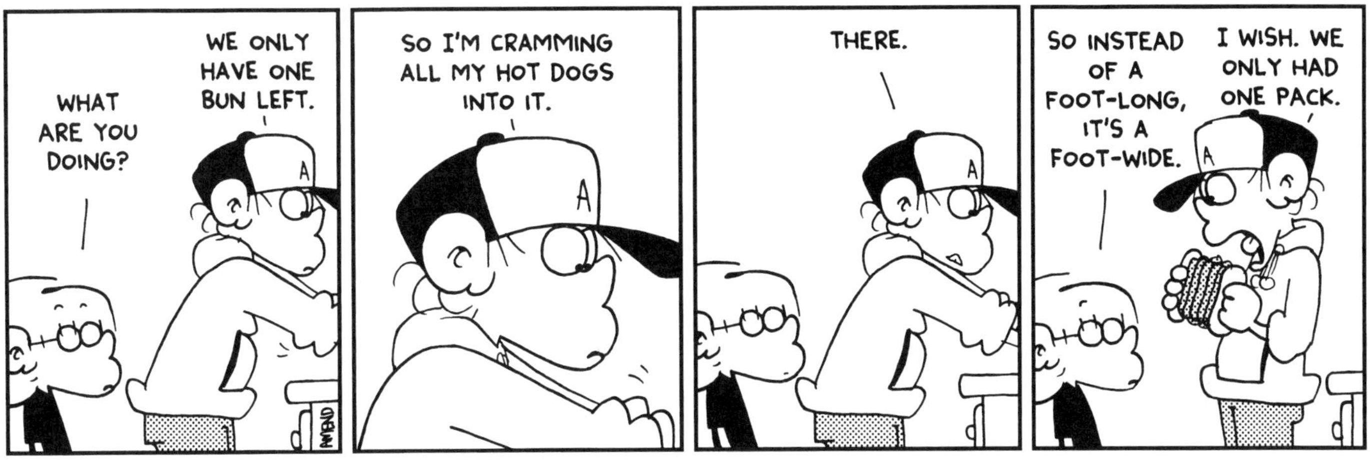
WHAT ARE YOU DOING?
WE ONLY HAVE ONE BUN LEFT.
AMEND
SO I'M CRAMMING ALL MY HOT DOGS INTO IT.
THERE.
SO INSTEAD OF A FOOT-LONG, IT'S A FOOT-WIDE.
I WISH. WE ONLY HAD ONE PACK.

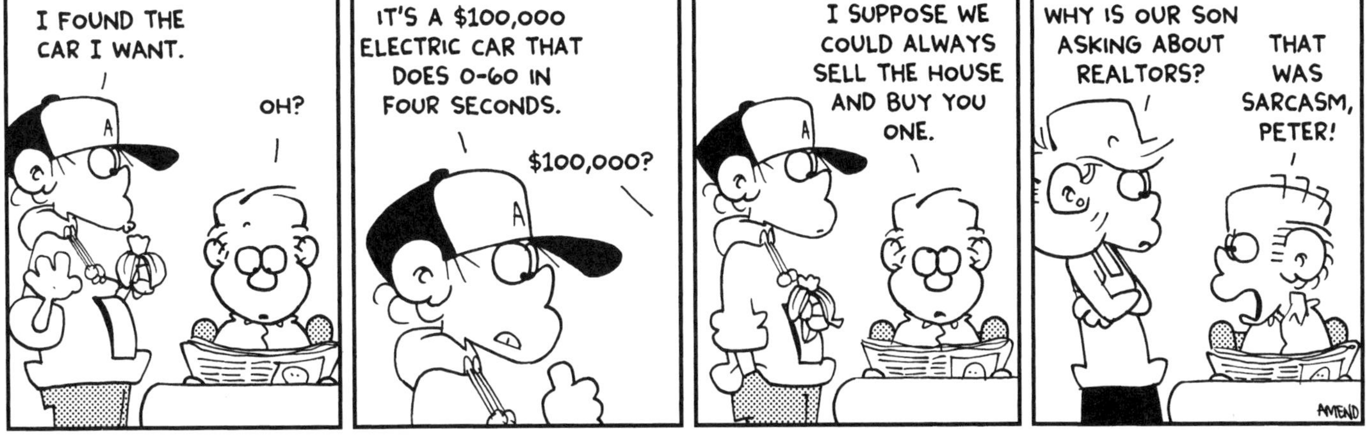
I FOUND THE CAR I WANT.
OH?
IT'S A $100,000 ELECTRIC CAR THAT DOES 0-60 IN FOUR SECONDS.
$100,000?
I SUPPOSE WE COULD ALWAYS SELL THE HOUSE AND BUY YOU ONE.
WHY IS OUR SON ASKING ABOUT REALTORS?
THAT WAS SARCASM, PETER!
AMEND

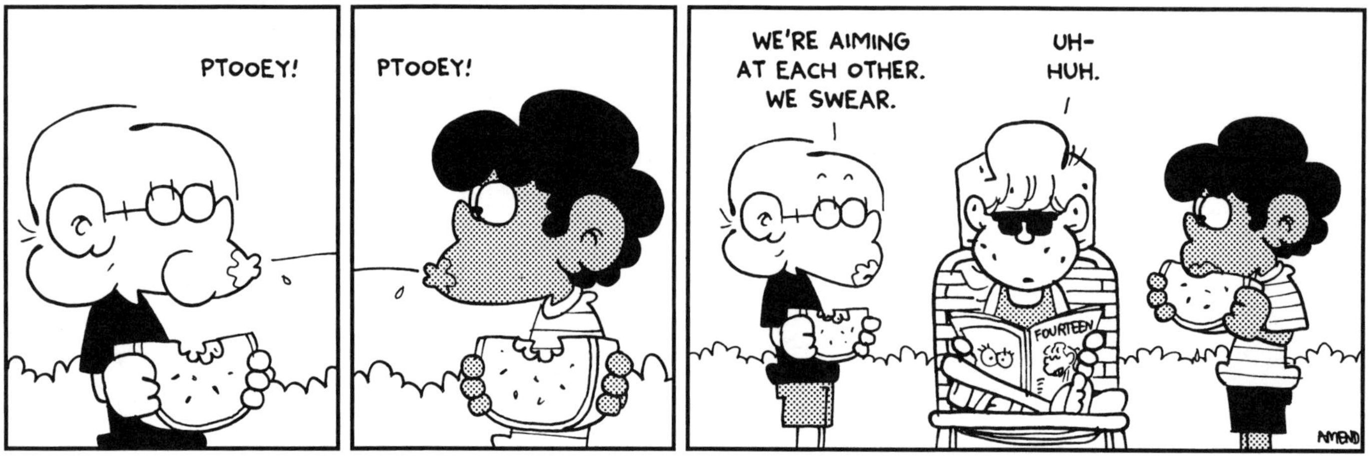
PTOOEY!
PTOOEY!
WE'RE AIMING AT EACH OTHER. WE SWEAR.
UH-HUH.
FOURTEEN
AMEND

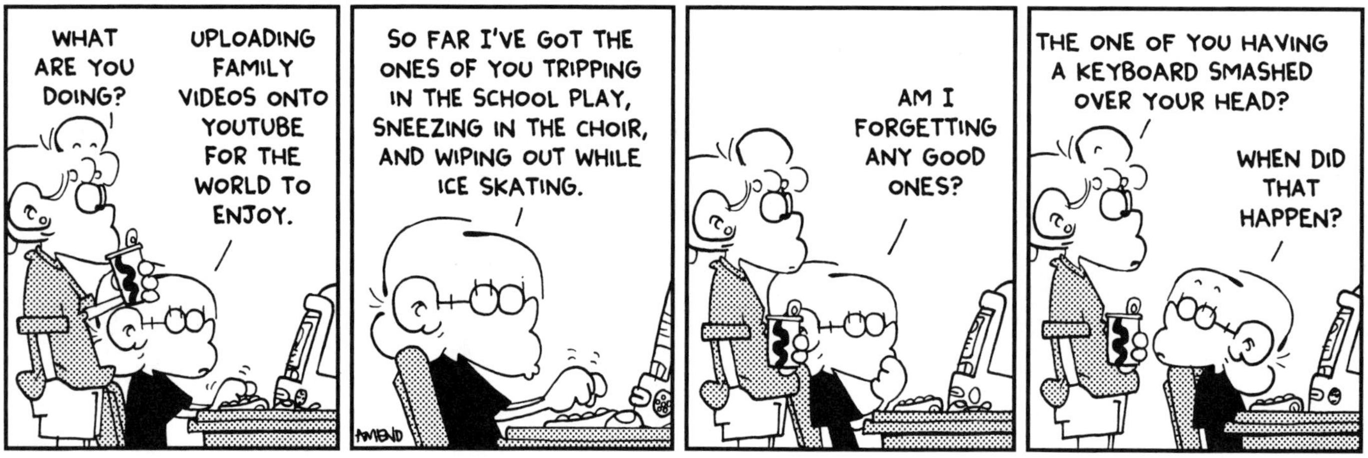
WHAT ARE YOU DOING?
UPLOADING FAMILY VIDEOS ONTO YOUTUBE FOR THE WORLD TO ENJOY.
SO FAR I'VE GOT THE ONES OF YOU TRIPPING IN THE SCHOOL PLAY, SNEEZING IN THE CHOIR, AND WIPING OUT WHILE ICE SKATING.
AMEND
AM I FORGETTING ANY GOOD ONES?
THE ONE OF YOU HAVING A KEYBOARD SMASHED OVER YOUR HEAD?
WHEN DID THAT HAPPEN?

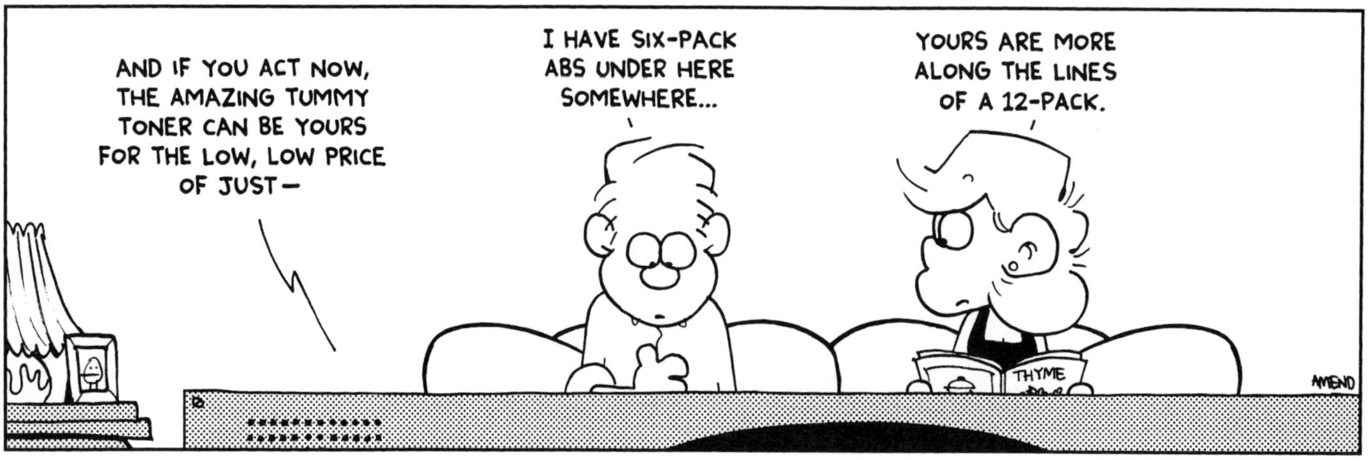
AND IF YOU ACT NOW, THE AMAZING TUMMY TONER CAN BE YOURS FOR THE LOW, LOW PRICE OF JUST—
I HAVE SIX-PACK ABS UNDER HERE SOMEWHERE...
YOURS ARE MORE ALONG THE LINES OF A 12-PACK.
THYME
AMEND

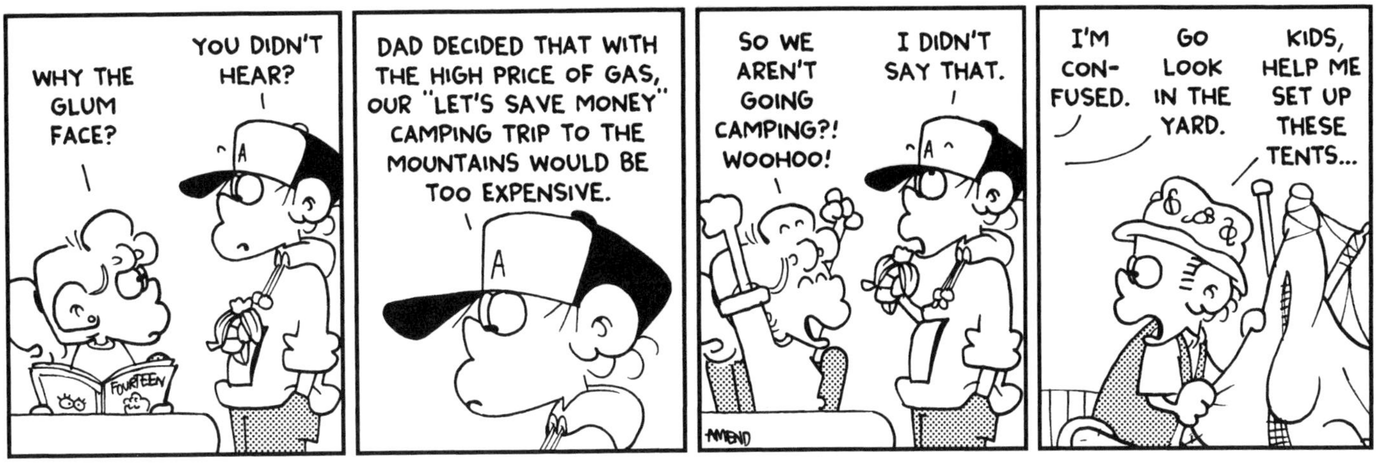
WHY THE GLUM FACE?
YOU DIDN'T HEAR?
FOURTEEN
DAD DECIDED THAT WITH THE HIGH PRICE OF GAS, OUR "LET'S SAVE MONEY" CAMPING TRIP TO THE MOUNTAINS WOULD BE TOO EXPENSIVE.
SO WE AREN'T GOING CAMPING?! WOOHOO!
I DIDN'T SAY THAT.
AMEND
I'M CON-FUSED.
GO LOOK IN THE YARD.
KIDS, HELP ME SET UP THESE TENTS...

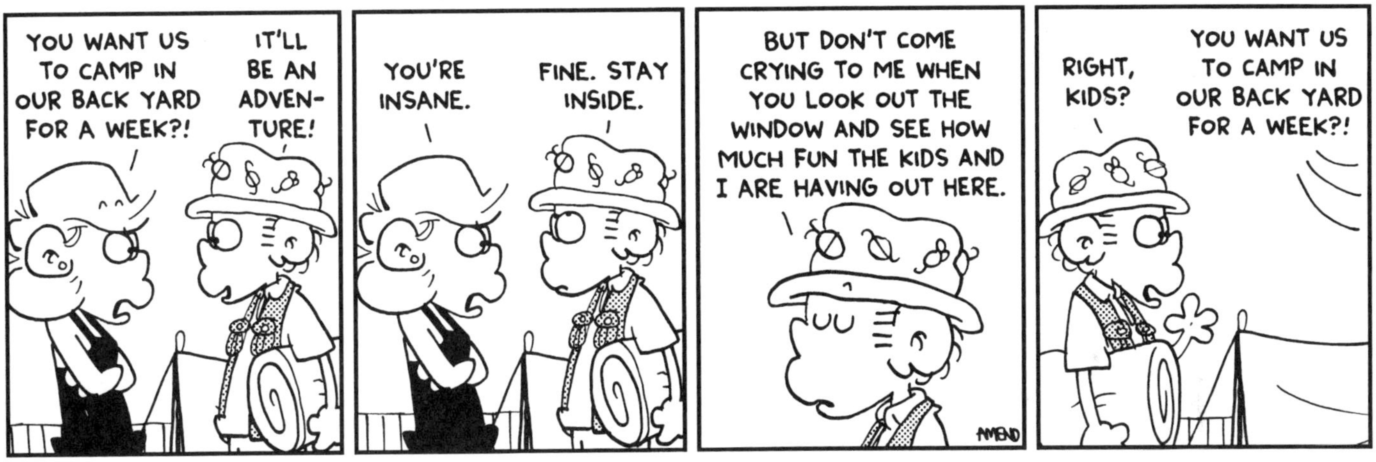
YOU WANT US TO CAMP IN OUR BACK YARD FOR A WEEK?!
IT'LL BE AN ADVEN-TURE!
YOU'RE INSANE.
FINE. STAY INSIDE.
BUT DON'T COME CRYING TO ME WHEN YOU LOOK OUT THE WINDOW AND SEE HOW MUCH FUN THE KIDS AND I ARE HAVING OUT HERE.
AMEND
RIGHT, KIDS?
YOU WANT US TO CAMP IN OUR BACK YARD FOR A WEEK?!

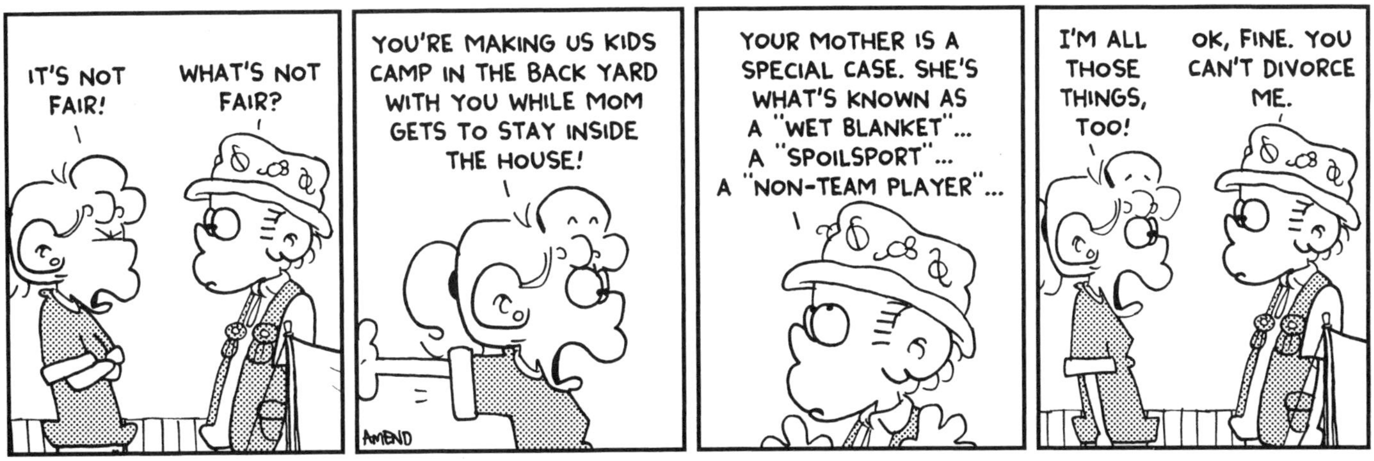
IT'S NOT FAIR!
WHAT'S NOT FAIR?
YOU'RE MAKING US KIDS CAMP IN THE BACK YARD WITH YOU WHILE MOM GETS TO STAY INSIDE THE HOUSE!
AMEND
YOUR MOTHER IS A SPECIAL CASE. SHE'S WHAT'S KNOWN AS A "WET BLANKET"... A "SPOILSPORT"... A "NON-TEAM PLAYER"...
I'M ALL THOSE THINGS, TOO!
OK, FINE. YOU CAN'T DIVORCE ME.

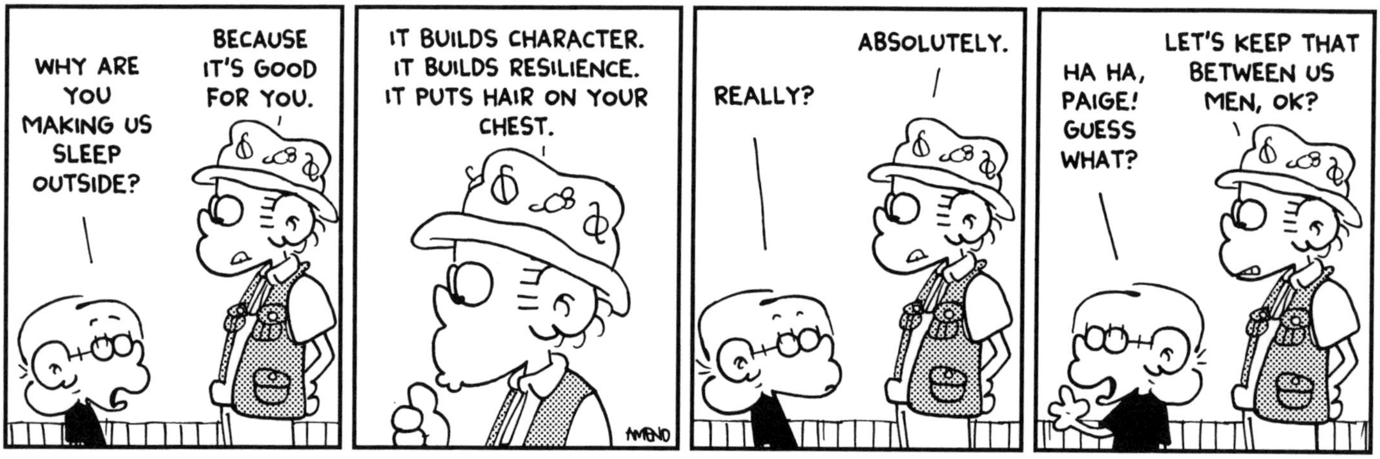
WHY ARE YOU MAKING US SLEEP OUTSIDE?
BECAUSE IT'S GOOD FOR YOU.
IT BUILDS CHARACTER. IT BUILDS RESILIENCE. IT PUTS HAIR ON YOUR CHEST.
REALLY?
ABSOLUTELY.
HA HA, PAIGE! GUESS WHAT?
LET'S KEEP THAT BETWEEN US MEN, OK?

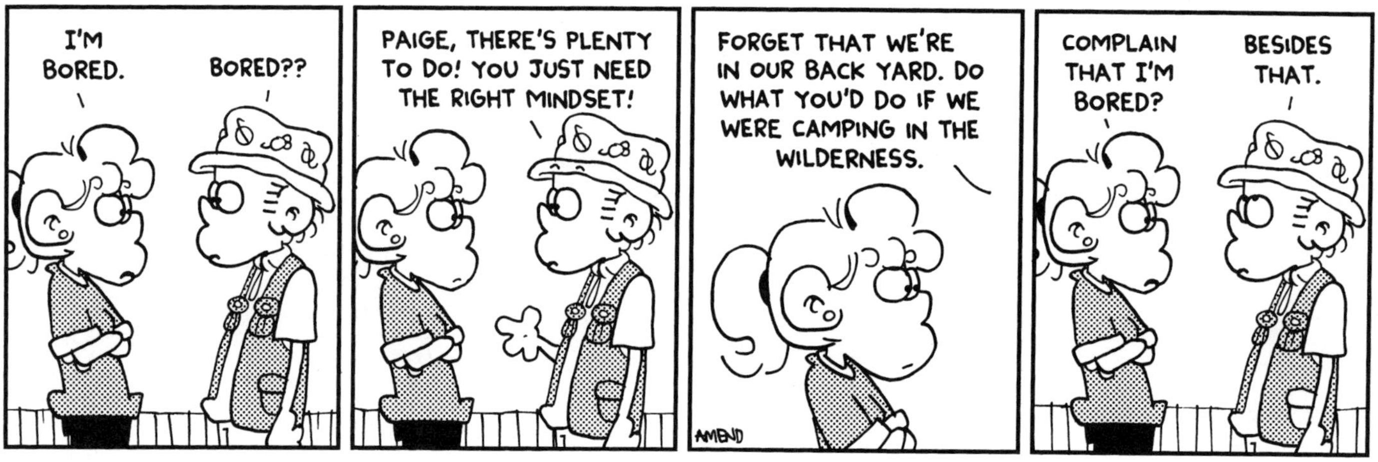
I'M BORED.
BORED??
PAIGE, THERE'S PLENTY TO DO! YOU JUST NEED THE RIGHT MINDSET!
FORGET THAT WE'RE IN OUR BACK YARD. DO WHAT YOU'D DO IF WE WERE CAMPING IN THE WILDERNESS.
COMPLAIN THAT I'M BORED?
BESIDES THAT.

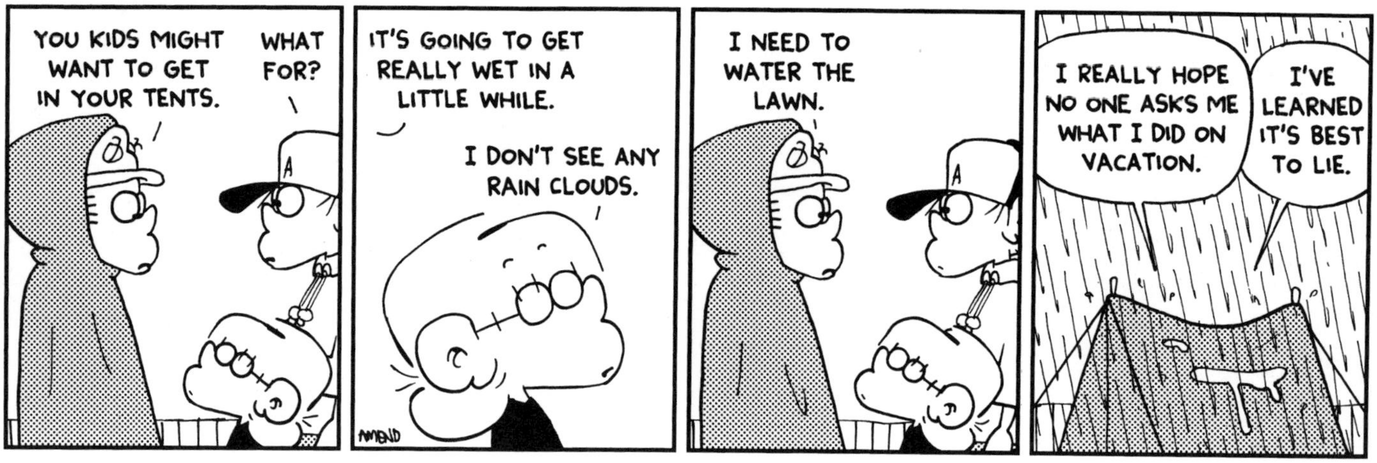
YOU KIDS MIGHT WANT TO GET IN YOUR TENTS.
WHAT FOR?
IT'S GOING TO GET REALLY WET IN A LITTLE WHILE.
I DON'T SEE ANY RAIN CLOUDS.
I NEED TO WATER THE LAWN.
I REALLY HOPE NO ONE ASKS ME WHAT I DID ON VACATION.
I'VE LEARNED IT'S BEST TO LIE.

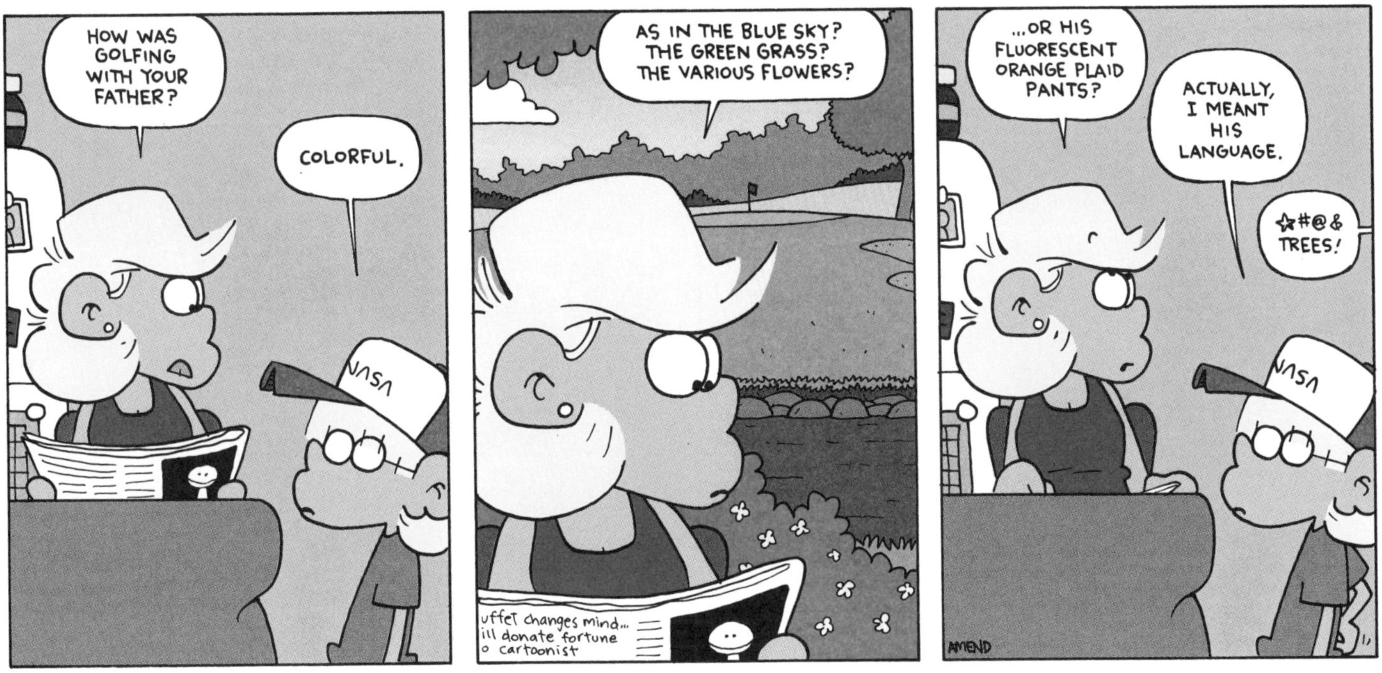
HOW WAS GOLFING WITH YOUR FATHER?
COLORFUL.
AS IN THE BLUE SKY? THE GREEN GRASS? THE VARIOUS FLOWERS?
uffet changes mind... ill donate fortune o cartoonist
...OR HIS FLUORESCENT ORANGE PLAID PANTS?
ACTUALLY, I MEANT HIS LANGUAGE.
☆#@& TREES!
AMEND

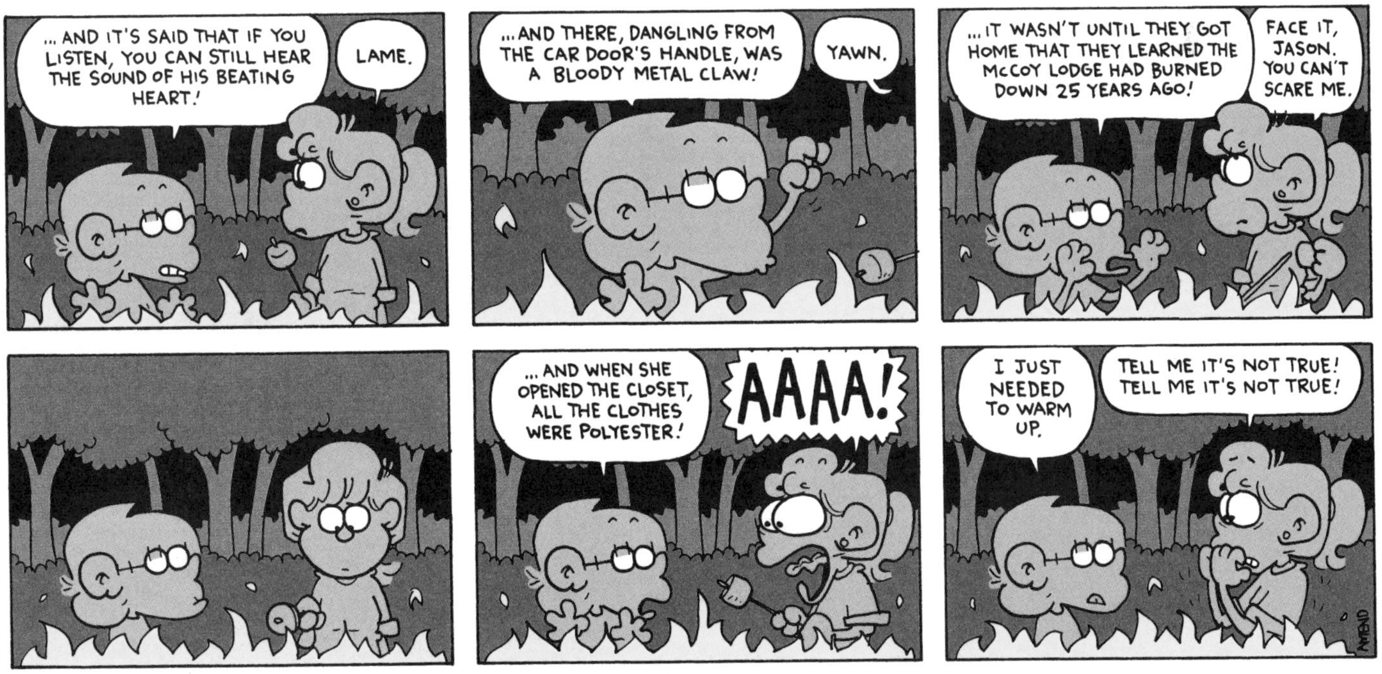
... AND IT'S SAID THAT IF YOU LISTEN, YOU CAN STILL HEAR THE SOUND OF HIS BEATING HEART!
LAME.
... AND THERE, DANGLING FROM THE CAR DOOR'S HANDLE, WAS A BLOODY METAL CLAW!
YAWN.
... IT WASN'T UNTIL THEY GOT HOME THAT THEY LEARNED THE McCOY LODGE HAD BURNED DOWN 25 YEARS AGO!
FACE IT, JASON. YOU CAN'T SCARE ME.
... AND WHEN SHE OPENED THE CLOSET, ALL THE CLOTHES WERE POLYESTER!
AAAA!
I JUST NEEDED TO WARM UP.
TELL ME IT'S NOT TRUE! TELL ME IT'S NOT TRUE!
AMEND

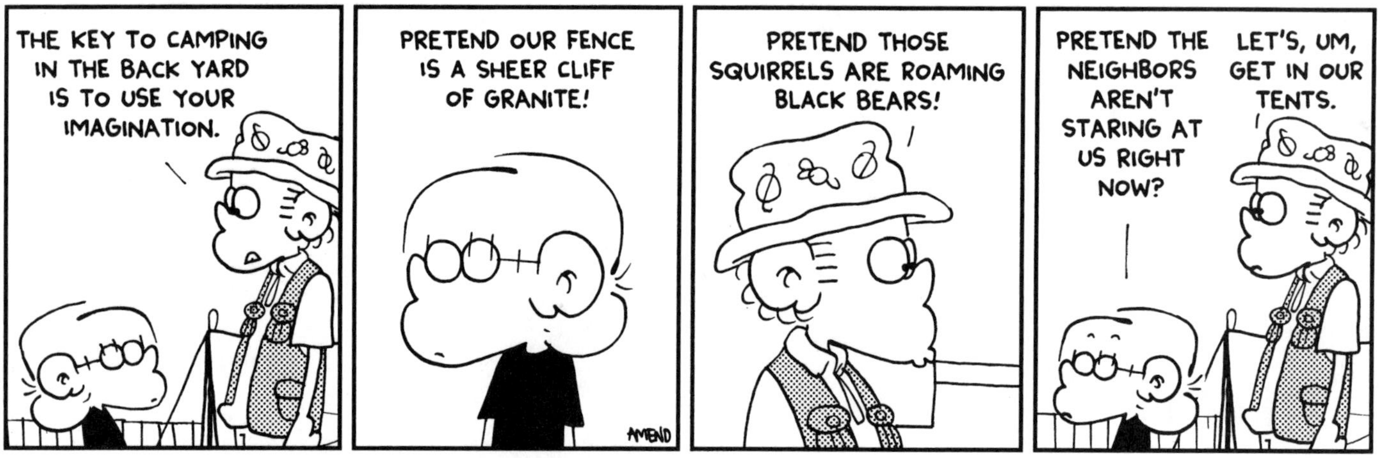
THE KEY TO CAMPING IN THE BACK YARD IS TO USE YOUR IMAGINATION.
PRETEND OUR FENCE IS A SHEER CLIFF OF GRANITE!
AMEND
PRETEND THOSE SQUIRRELS ARE ROAMING BLACK BEARS!
PRETEND THE NEIGHBORS AREN'T STARING AT US RIGHT NOW?
LET'S, UM, GET IN OUR TENTS.

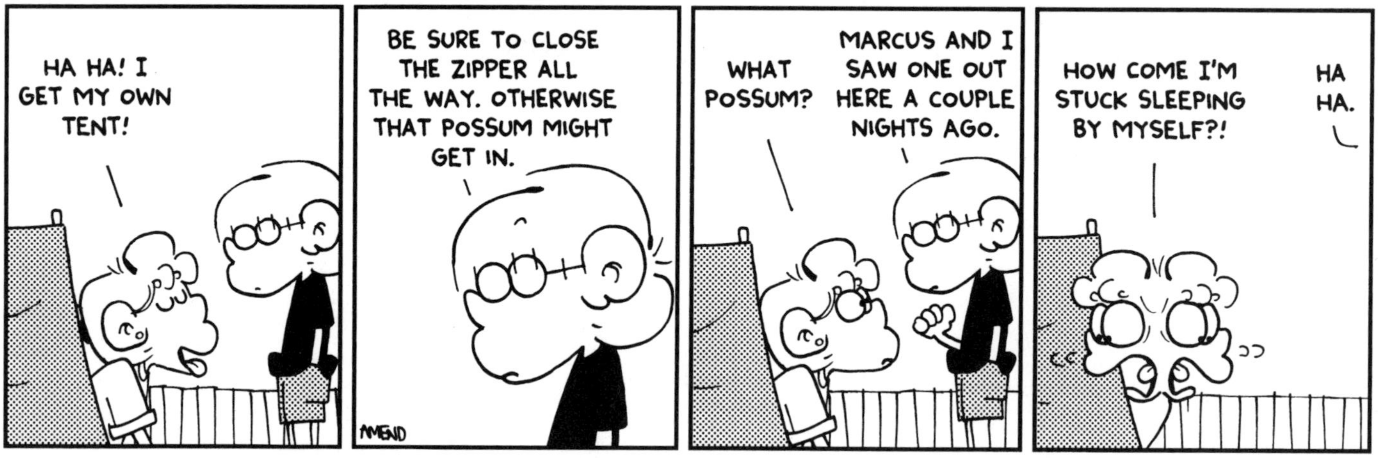
HA HA! I GET MY OWN TENT!
BE SURE TO CLOSE THE ZIPPER ALL THE WAY. OTHERWISE THAT POSSUM MIGHT GET IN.
AMEND
WHAT POSSUM?
MARCUS AND I SAW ONE OUT HERE A COUPLE NIGHTS AGO.
HOW COME I'M STUCK SLEEPING BY MYSELF?!
HA HA.

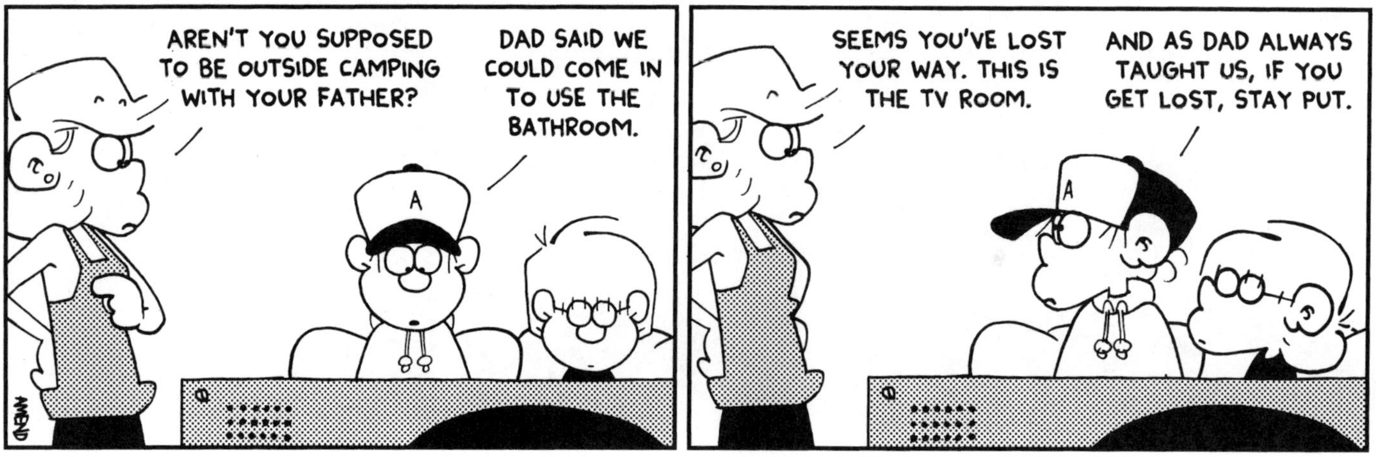
AREN'T YOU SUPPOSED TO BE OUTSIDE CAMPING WITH YOUR FATHER?
DAD SAID WE COULD COME IN TO USE THE BATHROOM.
AMEND
SEEMS YOU'VE LOST YOUR WAY. THIS IS THE TV ROOM.
AND AS DAD ALWAYS TAUGHT US, IF YOU GET LOST, STAY PUT.

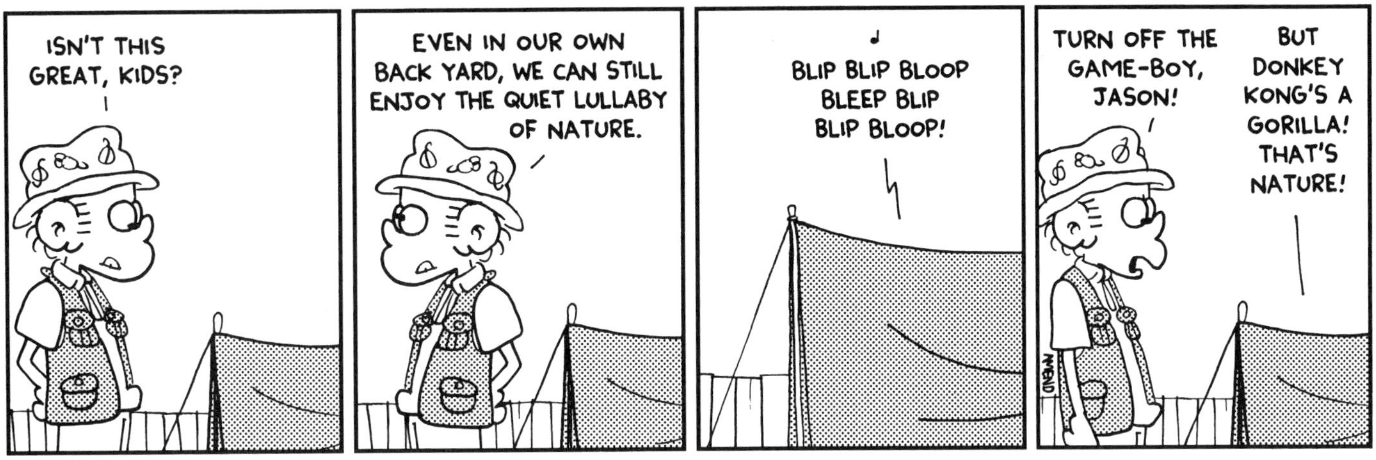
ISN'T THIS GREAT, KIDS?
EVEN IN OUR OWN BACK YARD, WE CAN STILL ENJOY THE QUIET LULLABY OF NATURE.
BLIP BLIP BLOOP BLEEP BLIP BLIP BLOOP!
TURN OFF THE GAME-BOY, JASON!
BUT DONKEY KONG'S A GORILLA! THAT'S NATURE!
AMEND

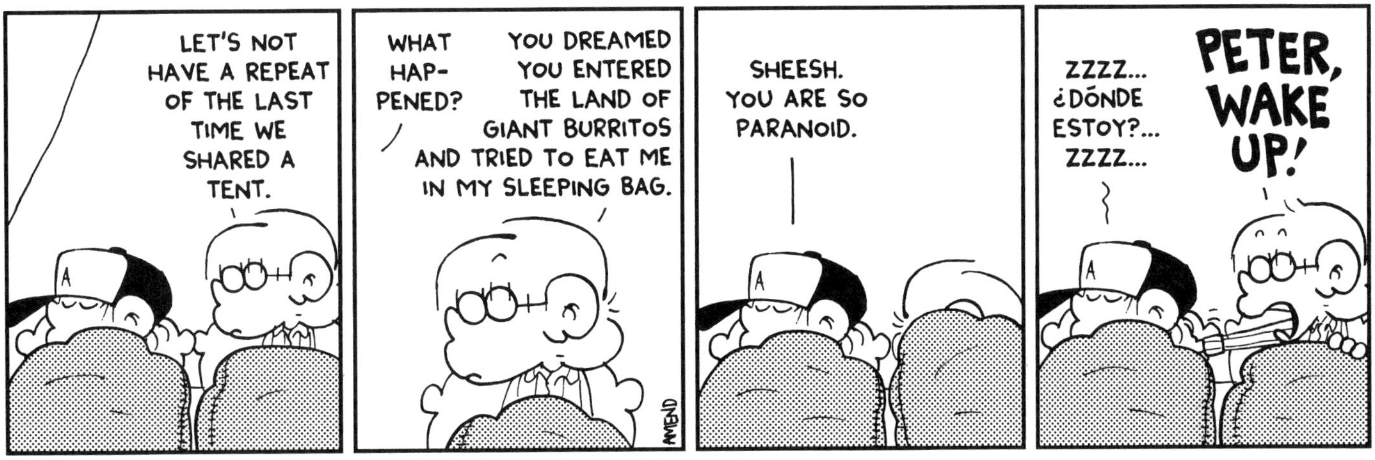
LET'S NOT HAVE A REPEAT OF THE LAST TIME WE SHARED A TENT.
WHAT HAPPENED?
YOU DREAMED YOU ENTERED THE LAND OF GIANT BURRITOS AND TRIED TO EAT ME IN MY SLEEPING BAG.
AMEND
SHEESH. YOU ARE SO PARANOID.
ZZZZ... ¿DÓNDE ESTOY?... ZZZZ...
PETER, WAKE UP!

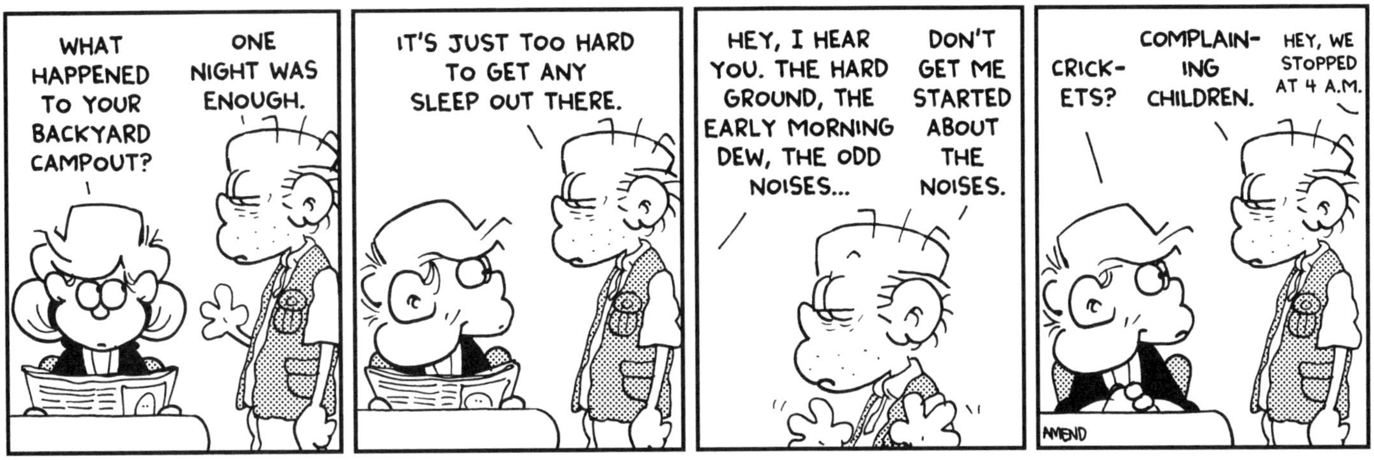
WHAT HAPPENED TO YOUR BACKYARD CAMPOUT?
ONE NIGHT WAS ENOUGH.
IT'S JUST TOO HARD TO GET ANY SLEEP OUT THERE.
HEY, I HEAR YOU. THE HARD GROUND, THE EARLY MORNING DEW, THE ODD NOISES...
DON'T GET ME STARTED ABOUT THE NOISES.
CRICKETS?
COMPLAINING CHILDREN.
HEY, WE STOPPED AT 4 A.M.
AMEND

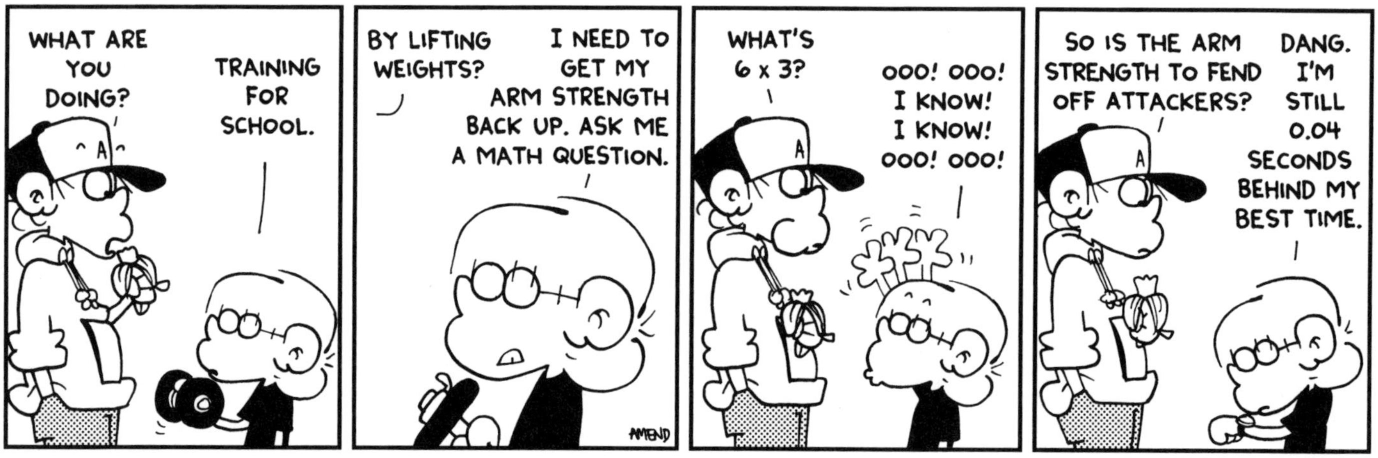
WHAT ARE YOU DOING?
TRAINING FOR SCHOOL.
BY LIFTING WEIGHTS?
I NEED TO GET MY ARM STRENGTH BACK UP. ASK ME A MATH QUESTION.
WHAT'S 6 x 3?
OOO! OOO! I KNOW! I KNOW! OOO! OOO!
SO IS THE ARM STRENGTH TO FEND OFF ATTACKERS?
DANG. I'M STILL 0.04 SECONDS BEHIND MY BEST TIME.

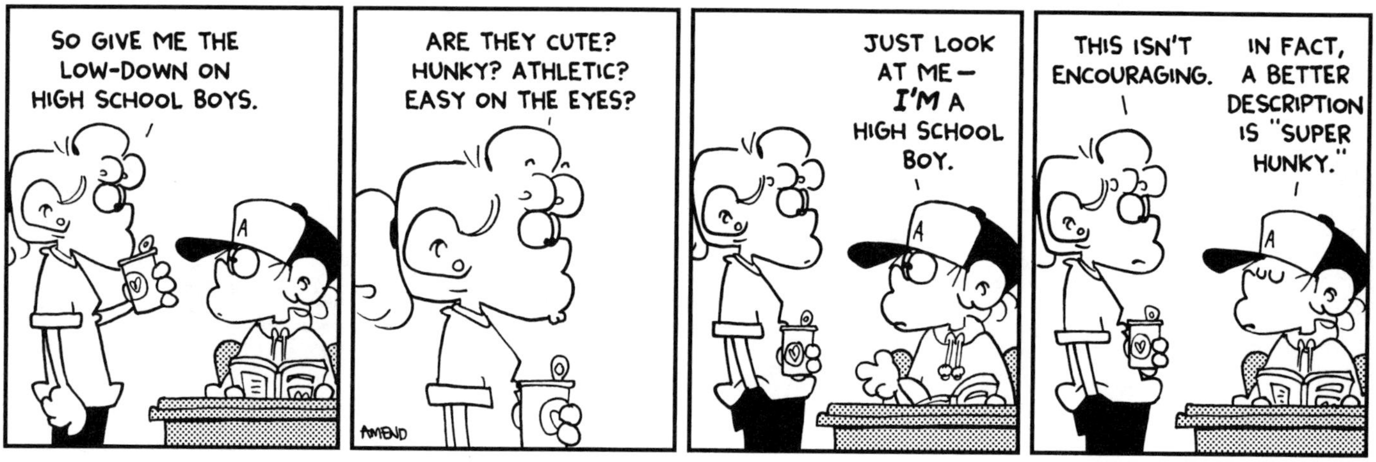
SO GIVE ME THE LOW-DOWN ON HIGH SCHOOL BOYS.
ARE THEY CUTE? HUNKY? ATHLETIC? EASY ON THE EYES?
JUST LOOK AT ME— I'M A HIGH SCHOOL BOY.
THIS ISN'T ENCOURAGING.
IN FACT, A BETTER DESCRIPTION IS "SUPER HUNKY."

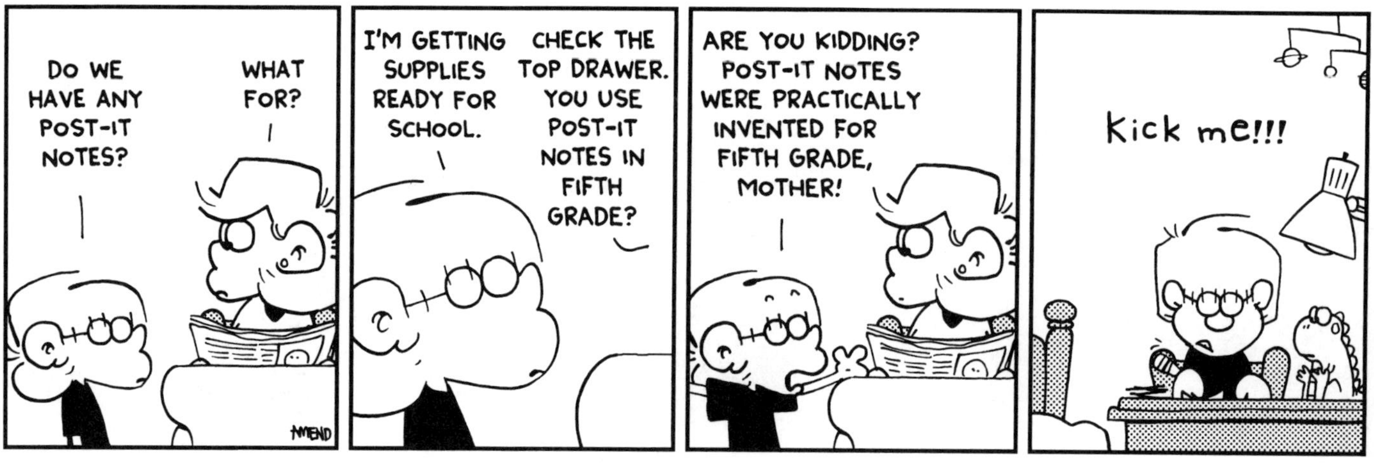
DO WE HAVE ANY POST-IT NOTES?
WHAT FOR?
I'M GETTING SUPPLIES READY FOR SCHOOL.
CHECK THE TOP DRAWER. YOU USE POST-IT NOTES IN FIFTH GRADE?
ARE YOU KIDDING? POST-IT NOTES WERE PRACTICALLY INVENTED FOR FIFTH GRADE, MOTHER!
Kick me!!!

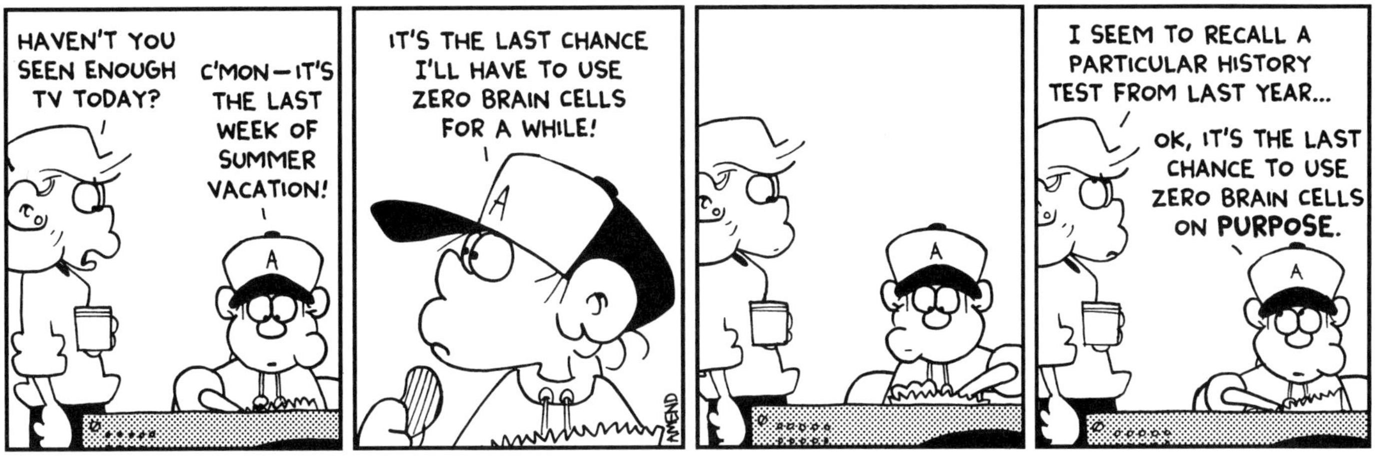
HAVEN'T YOU SEEN ENOUGH TV TODAY?
C'MON—IT'S THE LAST WEEK OF SUMMER VACATION!
IT'S THE LAST CHANCE I'LL HAVE TO USE ZERO BRAIN CELLS FOR A WHILE!
AMEND
I SEEM TO RECALL A PARTICULAR HISTORY TEST FROM LAST YEAR...
OK, IT'S THE LAST CHANCE TO USE ZERO BRAIN CELLS ON **PURPOSE**.

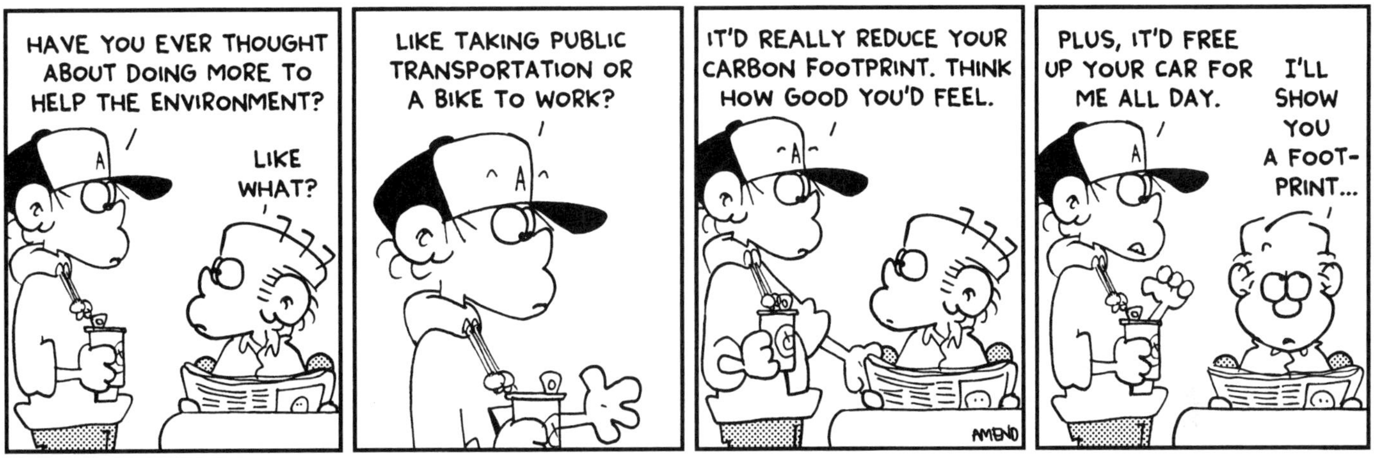
HAVE YOU EVER THOUGHT ABOUT DOING MORE TO HELP THE ENVIRONMENT?
LIKE WHAT?
LIKE TAKING PUBLIC TRANSPORTATION OR A BIKE TO WORK?
IT'D REALLY REDUCE YOUR CARBON FOOTPRINT. THINK HOW GOOD YOU'D FEEL.
AMEND
PLUS, IT'D FREE UP YOUR CAR FOR ME ALL DAY.
I'LL SHOW YOU A FOOT-PRINT...

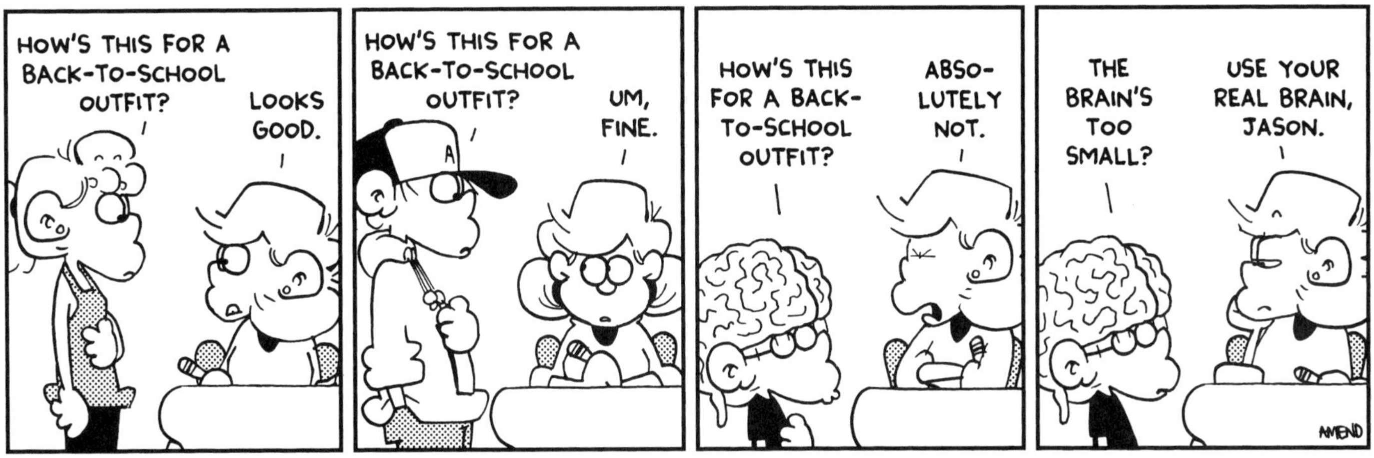
HOW'S THIS FOR A BACK-TO-SCHOOL OUTFIT?
LOOKS GOOD.
HOW'S THIS FOR A BACK-TO-SCHOOL OUTFIT?
UM, FINE.
HOW'S THIS FOR A BACK-TO-SCHOOL OUTFIT?
ABSO-LUTELY NOT.
THE BRAIN'S TOO SMALL?
USE YOUR REAL BRAIN, JASON.
AMEND

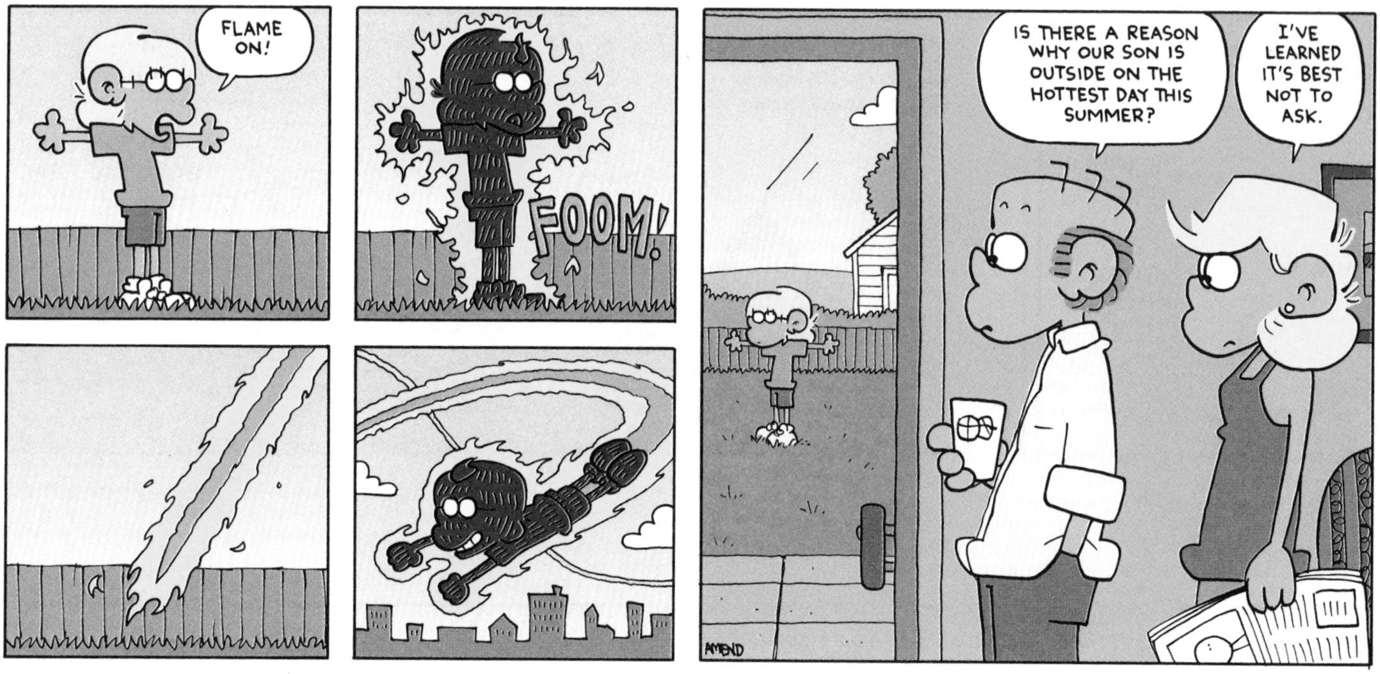
FLAME ON!
FOOM!
IS THERE A REASON WHY OUR SON IS OUTSIDE ON THE HOTTEST DAY THIS SUMMER?
I'VE LEARNED IT'S BEST NOT TO ASK.
AMEND

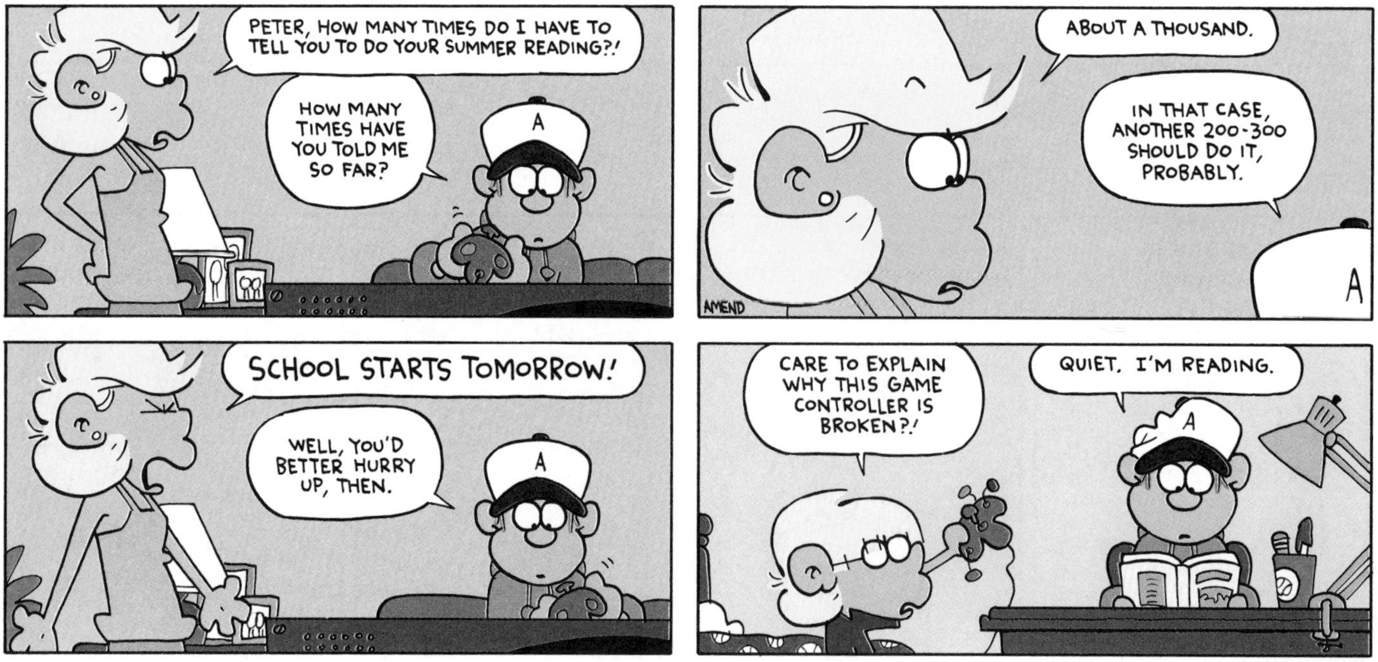
PETER, HOW MANY TIMES DO I HAVE TO TELL YOU TO DO YOUR SUMMER READING?!
HOW MANY TIMES HAVE YOU TOLD ME SO FAR?
ABOUT A THOUSAND.
IN THAT CASE, ANOTHER 200-300 SHOULD DO IT, PROBABLY.
AMEND
SCHOOL STARTS TOMORROW!
WELL, YOU'D BETTER HURRY UP, THEN.
CARE TO EXPLAIN WHY THIS GAME CONTROLLER IS BROKEN?!
QUIET, I'M READING.

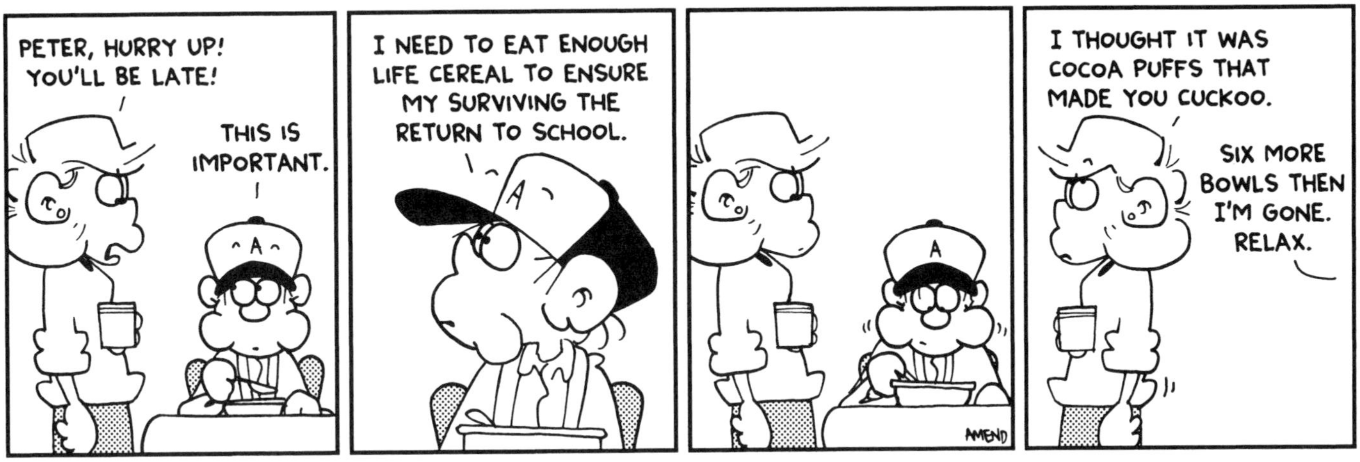
PETER, HURRY UP! YOU'LL BE LATE!
THIS IS IMPORTANT.
I NEED TO EAT ENOUGH LIFE CEREAL TO ENSURE MY SURVIVING THE RETURN TO SCHOOL.
I THOUGHT IT WAS COCOA PUFFS THAT MADE YOU CUCKOO.
SIX MORE BOWLS THEN I'M GONE. RELAX.
AMEND

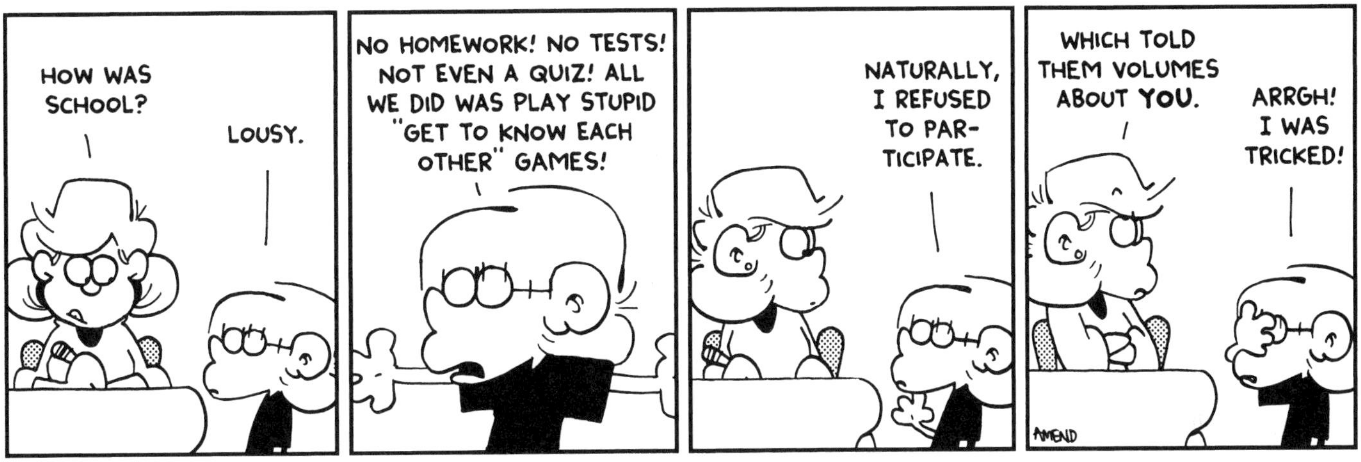
HOW WAS SCHOOL?
LOUSY.
NO HOMEWORK! NO TESTS! NOT EVEN A QUIZ! ALL WE DID WAS PLAY STUPID "GET TO KNOW EACH OTHER" GAMES!
NATURALLY, I REFUSED TO PAR-TICIPATE.
WHICH TOLD THEM VOLUMES ABOUT **YOU**.
ARRGH! I WAS TRICKED!
AMEND

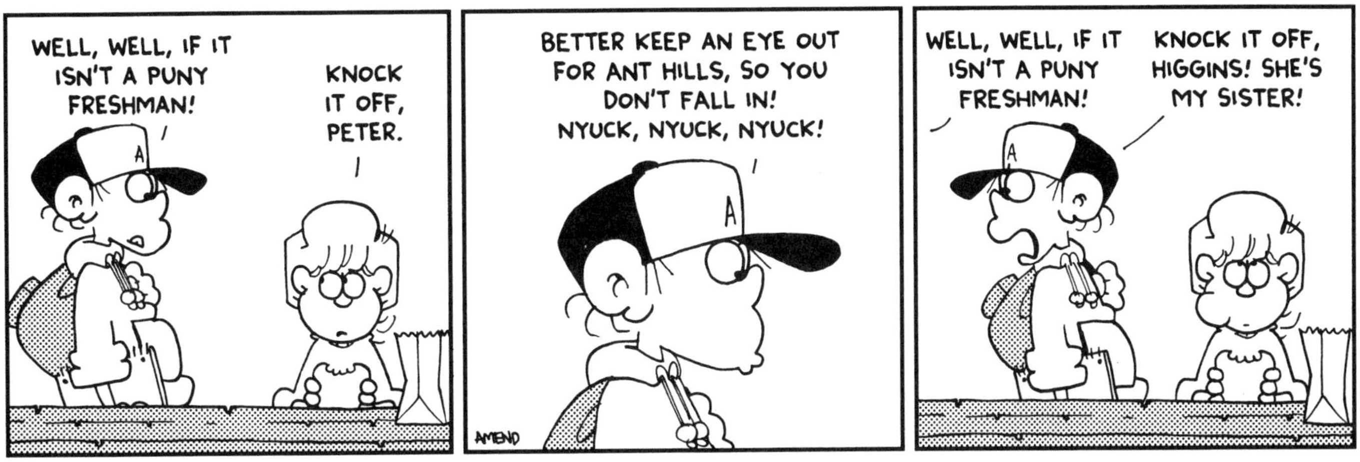
WELL, WELL, IF IT ISN'T A PUNY FRESHMAN!
KNOCK IT OFF, PETER.
BETTER KEEP AN EYE OUT FOR ANT HILLS, SO YOU DON'T FALL IN! NYUCK, NYUCK, NYUCK!
AMEND
WELL, WELL, IF IT ISN'T A PUNY FRESHMAN!
KNOCK IT OFF, HIGGINS! SHE'S MY SISTER!

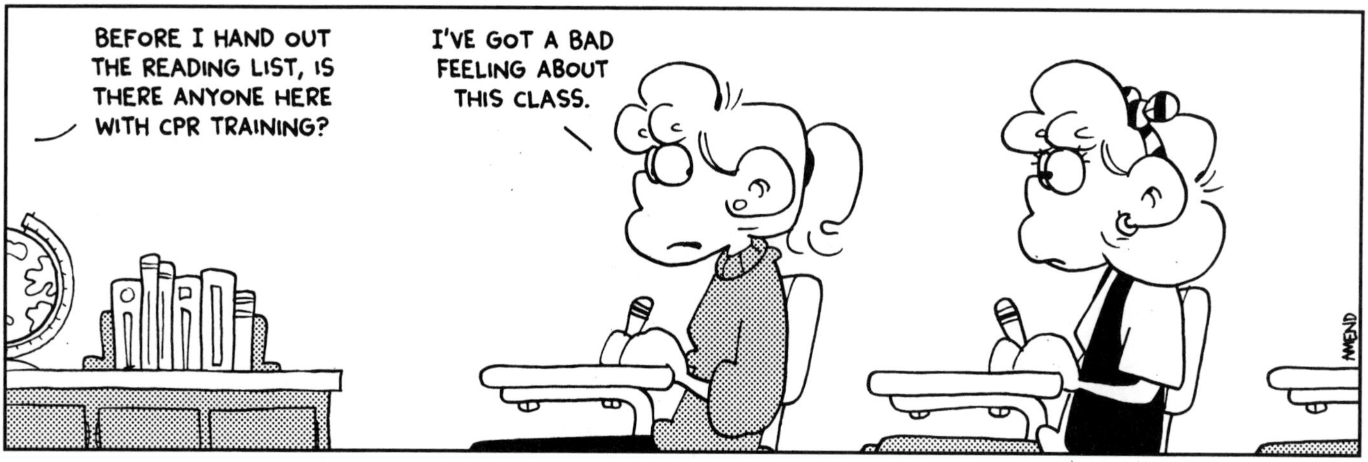
BEFORE I HAND OUT THE READING LIST, IS THERE ANYONE HERE WITH CPR TRAINING?
I'VE GOT A BAD FEELING ABOUT THIS CLASS.
AMEND

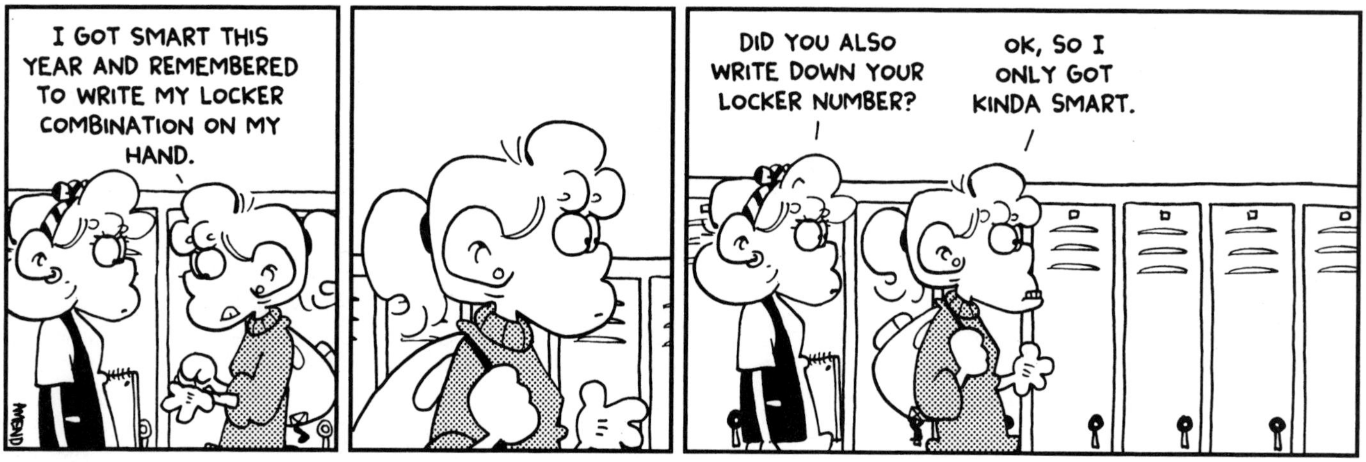
I GOT SMART THIS YEAR AND REMEMBERED TO WRITE MY LOCKER COMBINATION ON MY HAND.
AMEND
DID YOU ALSO WRITE DOWN YOUR LOCKER NUMBER?
OK, SO I ONLY GOT KINDA SMART.

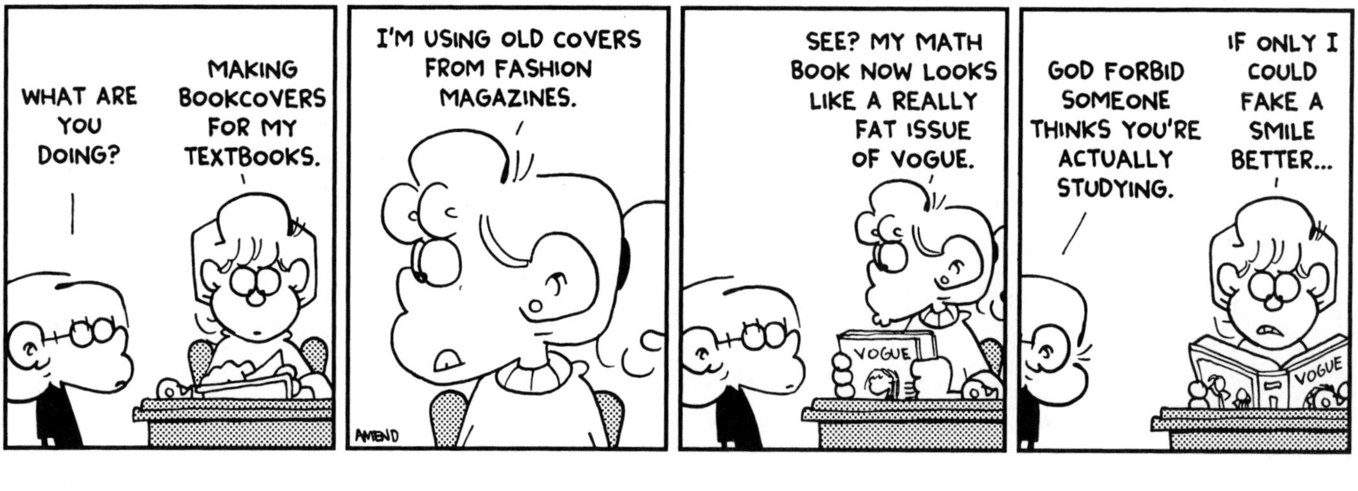
WHAT ARE YOU DOING?
MAKING BOOKCOVERS FOR MY TEXTBOOKS.
I'M USING OLD COVERS FROM FASHION MAGAZINES.
AMEND
SEE? MY MATH BOOK NOW LOOKS LIKE A REALLY FAT ISSUE OF VOGUE.
VOGUE
GOD FORBID SOMEONE THINKS YOU'RE ACTUALLY STUDYING.
IF ONLY I COULD FAKE A SMILE BETTER...
VOGUE

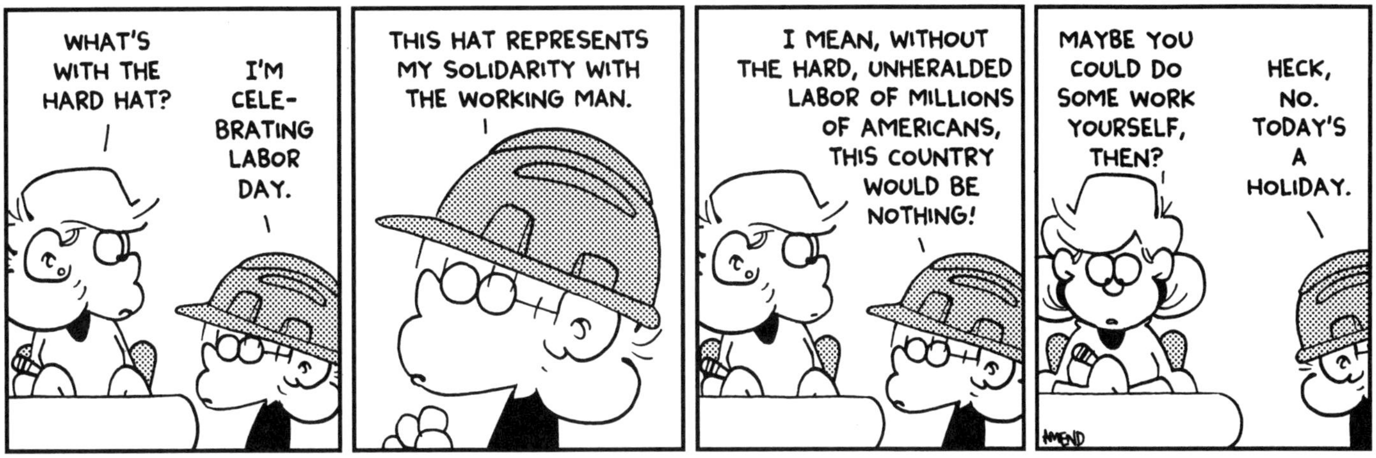
WHAT'S WITH THE HARD HAT?
I'M CELE-BRATING LABOR DAY.
THIS HAT REPRESENTS MY SOLIDARITY WITH THE WORKING MAN.
I MEAN, WITHOUT THE HARD, UNHERALDED LABOR OF MILLIONS OF AMERICANS, THIS COUNTRY WOULD BE NOTHING!
MAYBE YOU COULD DO SOME WORK YOURSELF, THEN?
HECK, NO. TODAY'S A HOLIDAY.

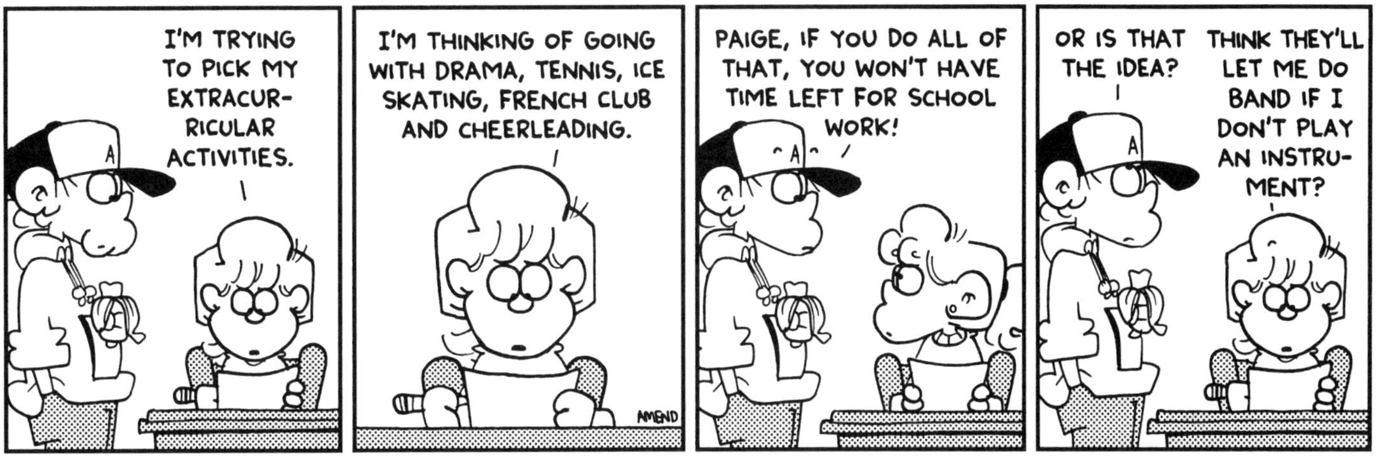
I'M TRYING TO PICK MY EXTRACUR-RICULAR ACTIVITIES.
I'M THINKING OF GOING WITH DRAMA, TENNIS, ICE SKATING, FRENCH CLUB AND CHEERLEADING.
PAIGE, IF YOU DO ALL OF THAT, YOU WON'T HAVE TIME LEFT FOR SCHOOL WORK!
OR IS THAT THE IDEA?
THINK THEY'LL LET ME DO BAND IF I DON'T PLAY AN INSTRU-MENT?

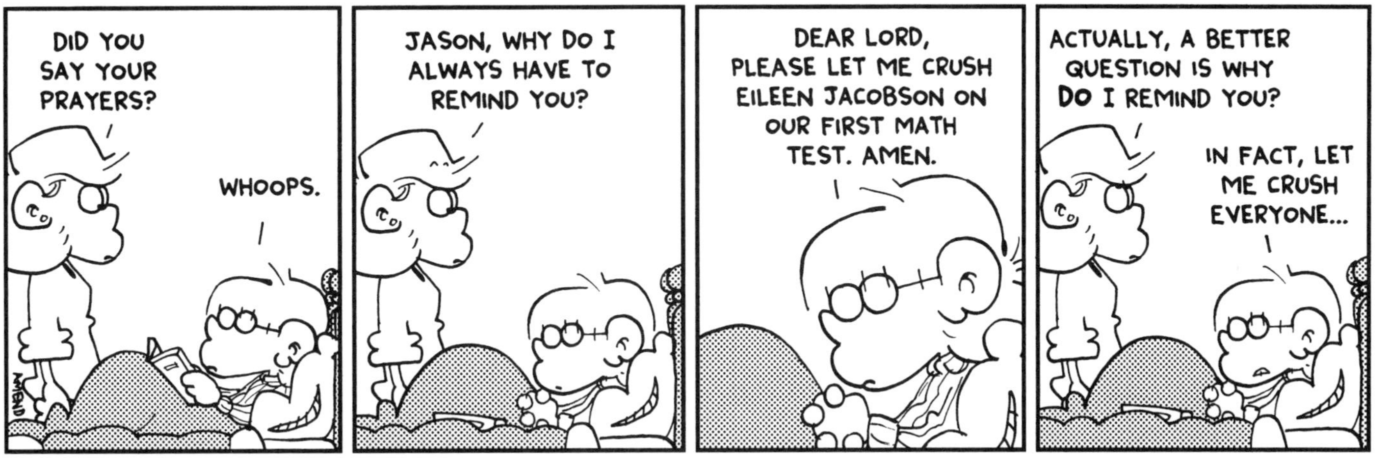
DID YOU SAY YOUR PRAYERS?
WHOOPS.
JASON, WHY DO I ALWAYS HAVE TO REMIND YOU?
DEAR LORD, PLEASE LET ME CRUSH EILEEN JACOBSON ON OUR FIRST MATH TEST. AMEN.
ACTUALLY, A BETTER QUESTION IS WHY DO I REMIND YOU?
IN FACT, LET ME CRUSH EVERYONE...

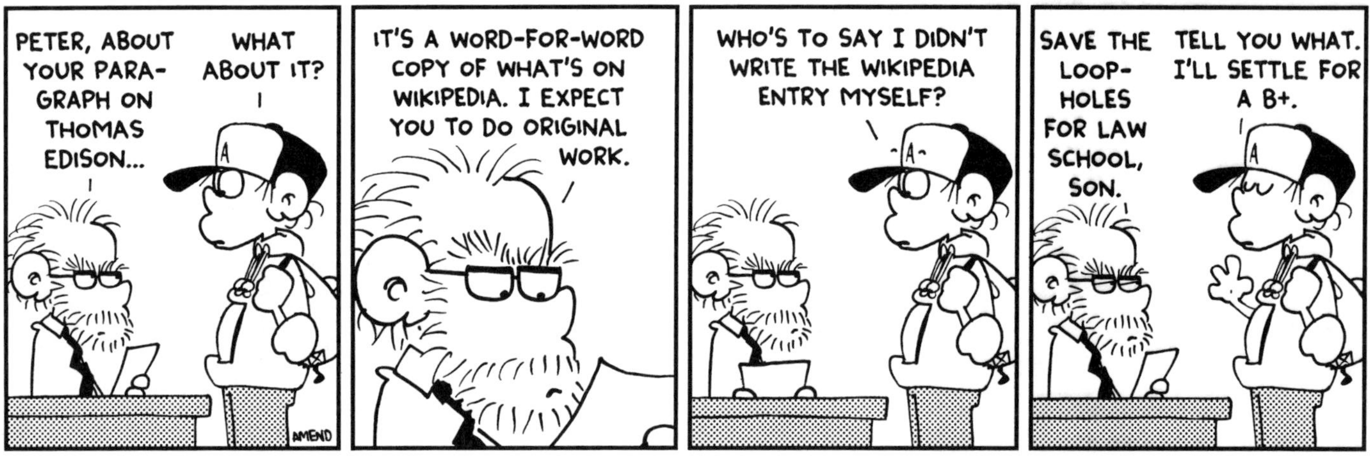
PETER, ABOUT YOUR PARA-GRAPH ON THOMAS EDISON...
WHAT ABOUT IT?
IT'S A WORD-FOR-WORD COPY OF WHAT'S ON WIKIPEDIA. I EXPECT YOU TO DO ORIGINAL WORK.
WHO'S TO SAY I DIDN'T WRITE THE WIKIPEDIA ENTRY MYSELF?
SAVE THE LOOP-HOLES FOR LAW SCHOOL, SON.
TELL YOU WHAT. I'LL SETTLE FOR A B+.

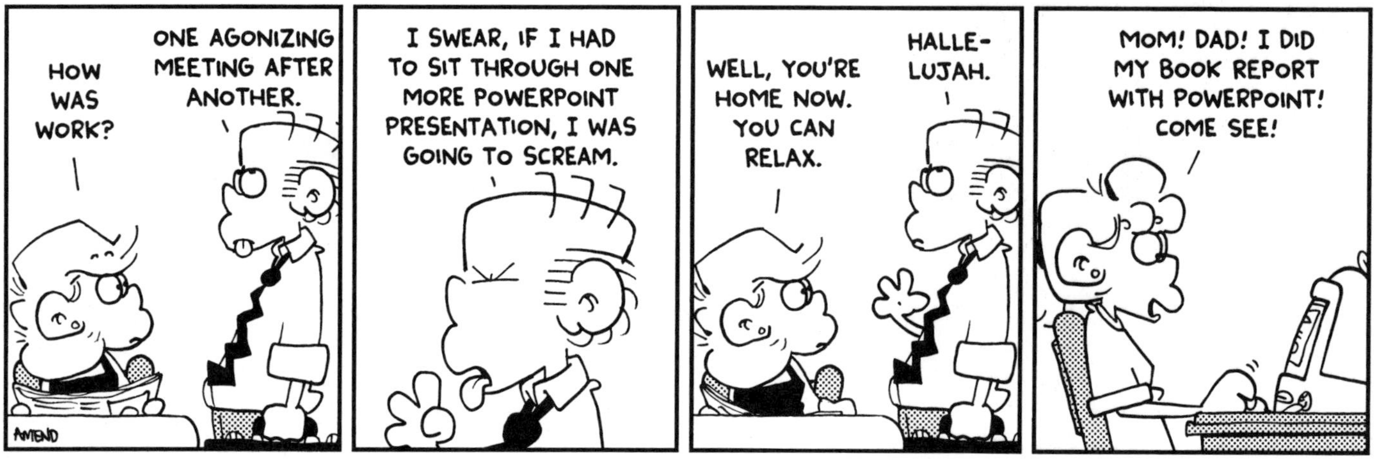
HOW WAS WORK?
ONE AGONIZING MEETING AFTER ANOTHER.
I SWEAR, IF I HAD TO SIT THROUGH ONE MORE POWERPOINT PRESENTATION, I WAS GOING TO SCREAM.
WELL, YOU'RE HOME NOW. YOU CAN RELAX.
HALLE-LUJAH.
MOM! DAD! I DID MY BOOK REPORT WITH POWERPOINT! COME SEE!

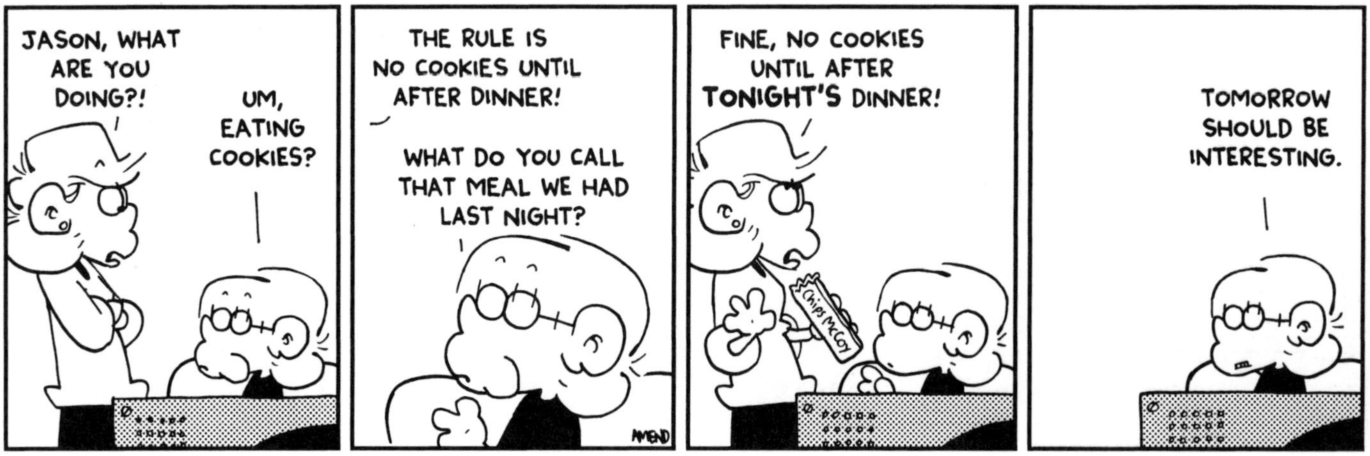
JASON, WHAT ARE YOU DOING?!
UM, EATING COOKIES?
THE RULE IS NO COOKIES UNTIL AFTER DINNER!
WHAT DO YOU CALL THAT MEAL WE HAD LAST NIGHT?
FINE, NO COOKIES UNTIL AFTER **TONIGHT'S** DINNER!
TOMORROW SHOULD BE INTERESTING.

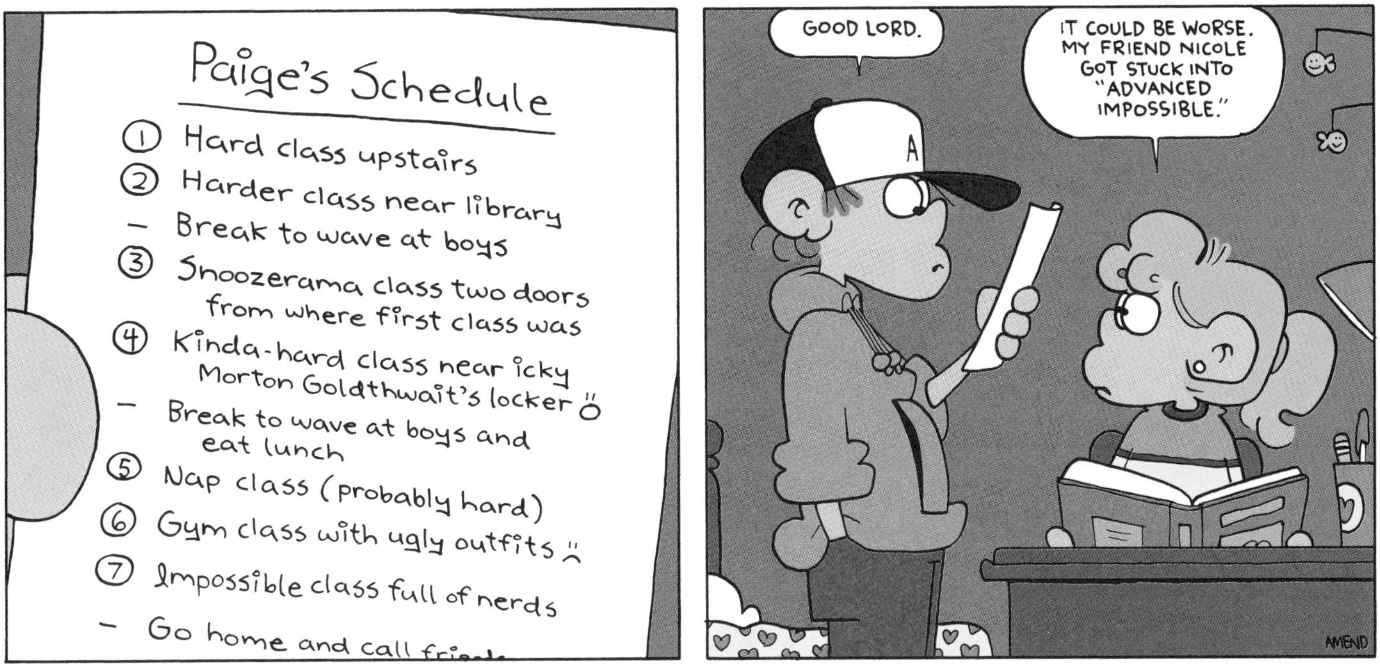
Paige's Schedule
① Hard class upstairs
② Harder class near library
– Break to wave at boys
③ Snoozerama class two doors from where first class was
④ Kinda-hard class near icky Morton Goldthwait's locker
– Break to wave at boys and eat lunch
⑤ Nap class (probably hard)
⑥ Gym class with ugly outfits
⑦ Impossible class full of nerds
– Go home and call
GOOD LORD.
IT COULD BE WORSE. MY FRIEND NICOLE GOT STUCK INTO "ADVANCED IMPOSSIBLE."
AMEND

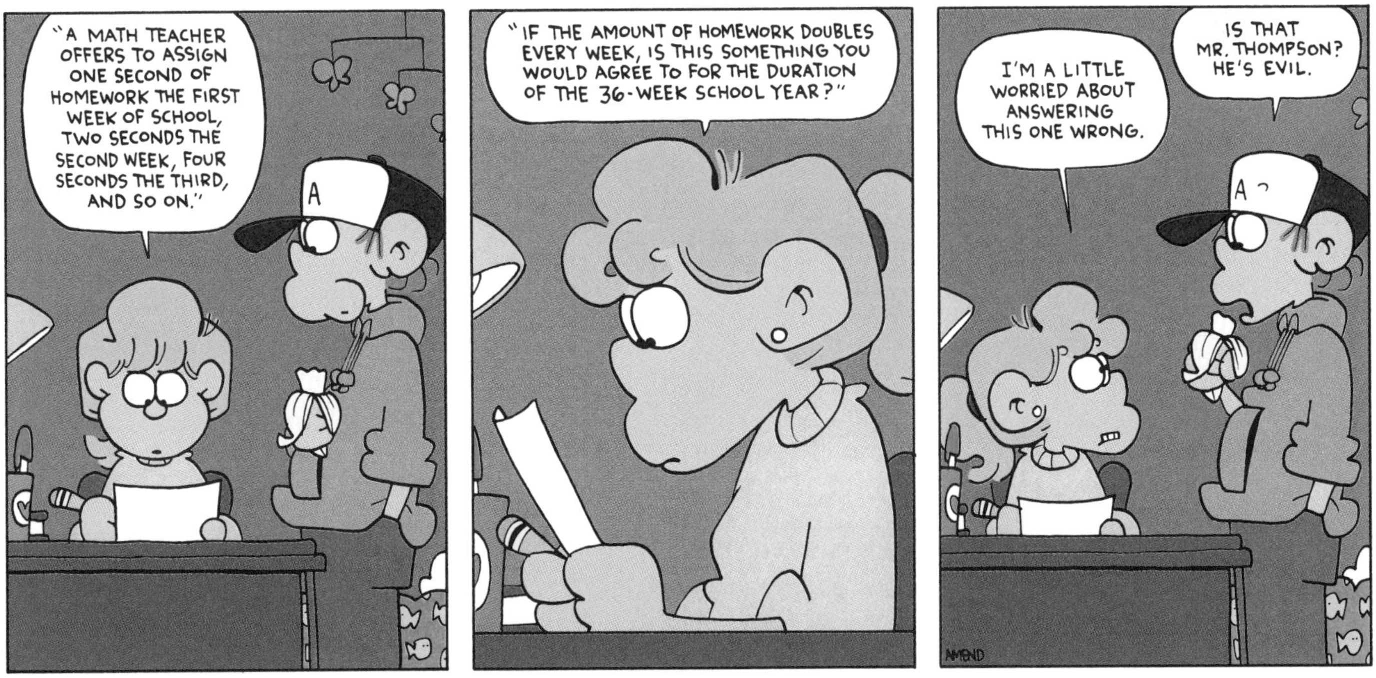
"A MATH TEACHER OFFERS TO ASSIGN ONE SECOND OF HOMEWORK THE FIRST WEEK OF SCHOOL, TWO SECONDS THE SECOND WEEK, FOUR SECONDS THE THIRD, AND SO ON."
"IF THE AMOUNT OF HOMEWORK DOUBLES EVERY WEEK, IS THIS SOMETHING YOU WOULD AGREE TO FOR THE DURATION OF THE 36-WEEK SCHOOL YEAR?"
I'M A LITTLE WORRIED ABOUT ANSWERING THIS ONE WRONG.
IS THAT MR. THOMPSON? HE'S EVIL.
AMEND

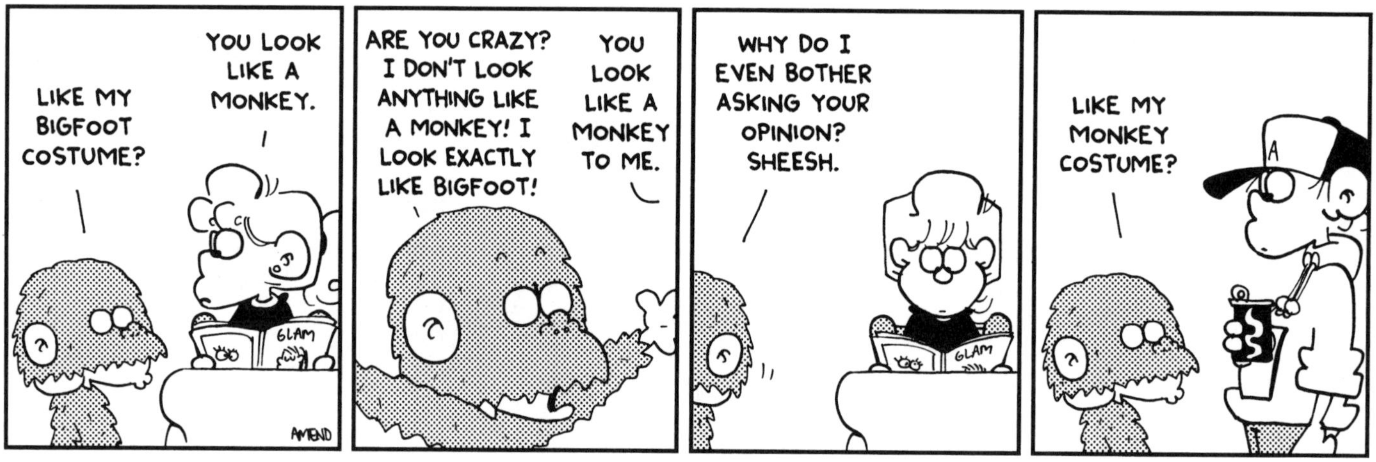
LIKE MY BIGFOOT COSTUME?
YOU LOOK LIKE A MONKEY.
ARE YOU CRAZY? I DON'T LOOK ANYTHING LIKE A MONKEY! I LOOK EXACTLY LIKE BIGFOOT!
YOU LOOK LIKE A MONKEY TO ME.
WHY DO I EVEN BOTHER ASKING YOUR OPINION? SHEESH.
LIKE MY MONKEY COSTUME?

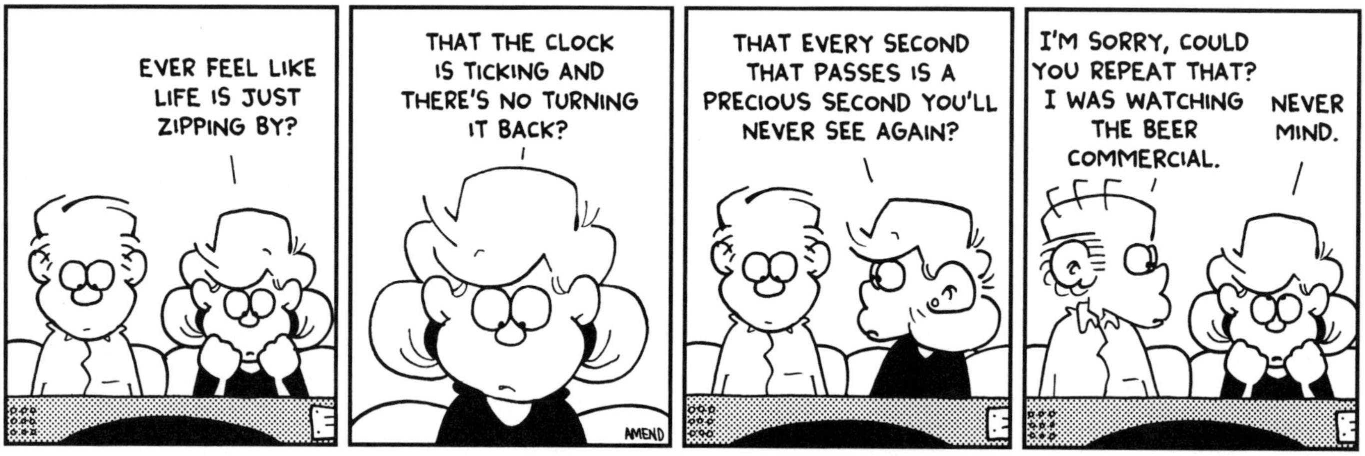
EVER FEEL LIKE LIFE IS JUST ZIPPING BY?
THAT THE CLOCK IS TICKING AND THERE'S NO TURNING IT BACK?
THAT EVERY SECOND THAT PASSES IS A PRECIOUS SECOND YOU'LL NEVER SEE AGAIN?
I'M SORRY, COULD YOU REPEAT THAT? I WAS WATCHING THE BEER COMMERCIAL.
NEVER MIND.

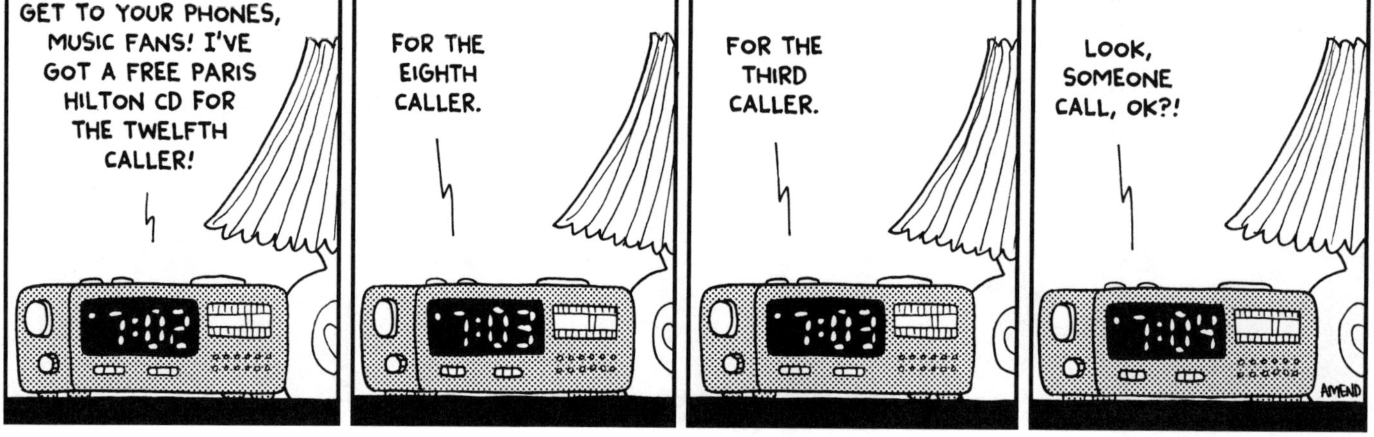
GET TO YOUR PHONES, MUSIC FANS! I'VE GOT A FREE PARIS HILTON CD FOR THE TWELFTH CALLER!
FOR THE EIGHTH CALLER.
FOR THE THIRD CALLER.
LOOK, SOMEONE CALL, OK?!

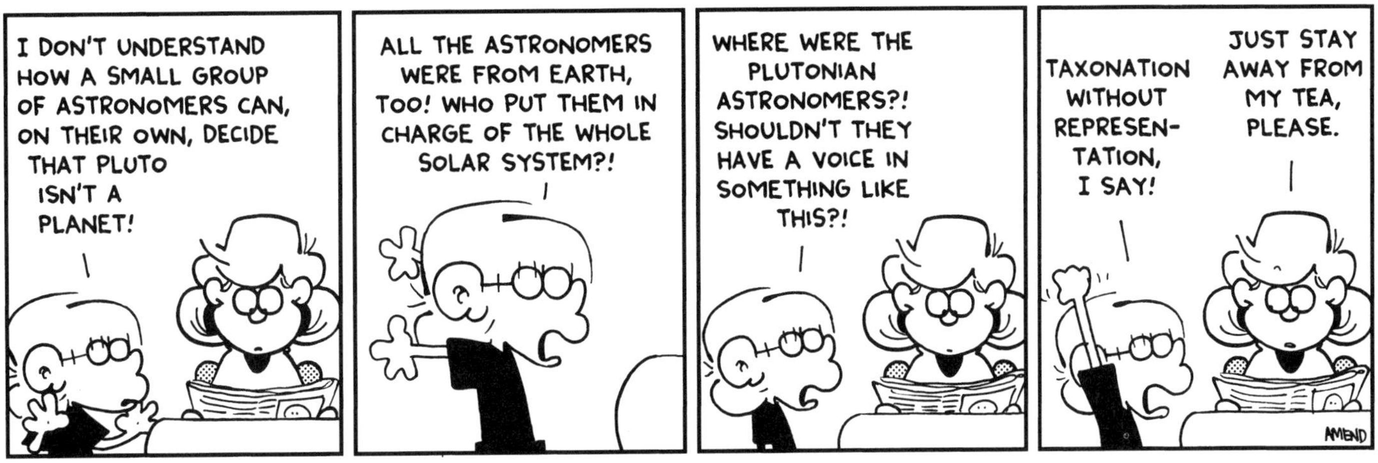
I DON'T UNDERSTAND HOW A SMALL GROUP OF ASTRONOMERS CAN, ON THEIR OWN, DECIDE THAT PLUTO ISN'T A PLANET!
ALL THE ASTRONOMERS WERE FROM EARTH, TOO! WHO PUT THEM IN CHARGE OF THE WHOLE SOLAR SYSTEM?!
WHERE WERE THE PLUTONIAN ASTRONOMERS?! SHOULDN'T THEY HAVE A VOICE IN SOMETHING LIKE THIS?!
TAXONATION WITHOUT REPRESEN-TATION, I SAY!
JUST STAY AWAY FROM MY TEA, PLEASE.
AMEND

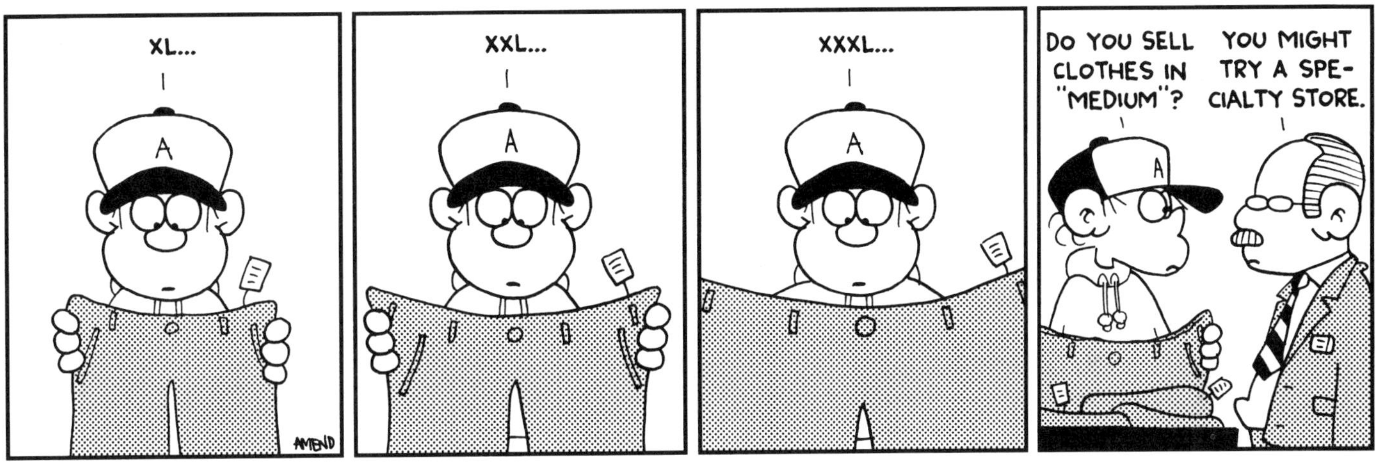
XL...
XXL...
XXXL...
DO YOU SELL CLOTHES IN "MEDIUM"?
YOU MIGHT TRY A SPE-CIALTY STORE.
AMEND

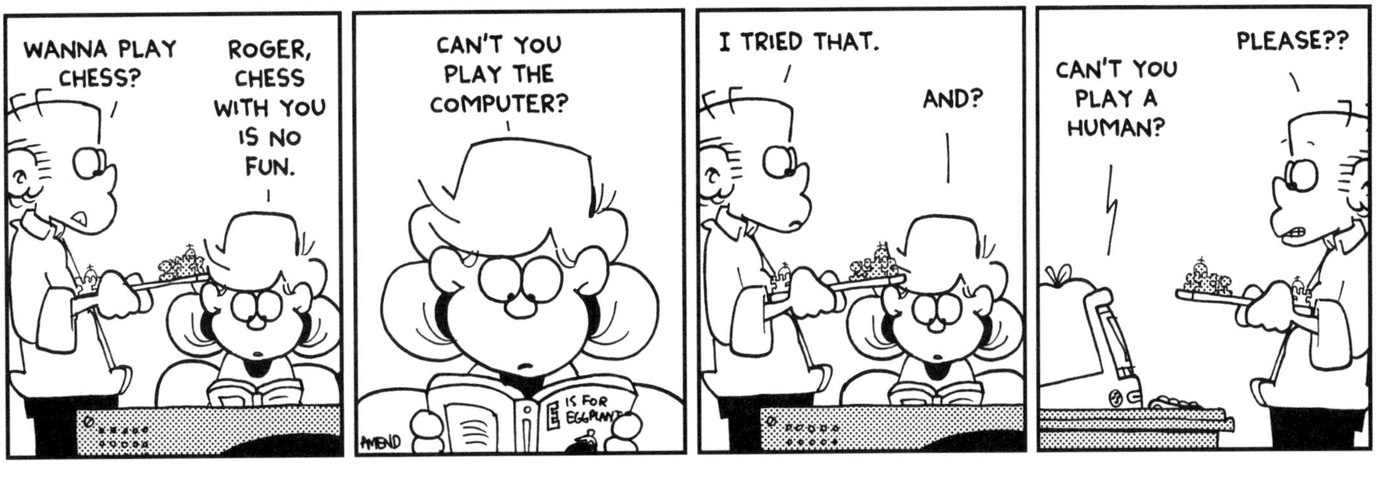
WANNA PLAY CHESS?
ROGER, CHESS WITH YOU IS NO FUN.
CAN'T YOU PLAY THE COMPUTER?
I TRIED THAT.
AND?
CAN'T YOU PLAY A HUMAN?
PLEASE??
AMEND

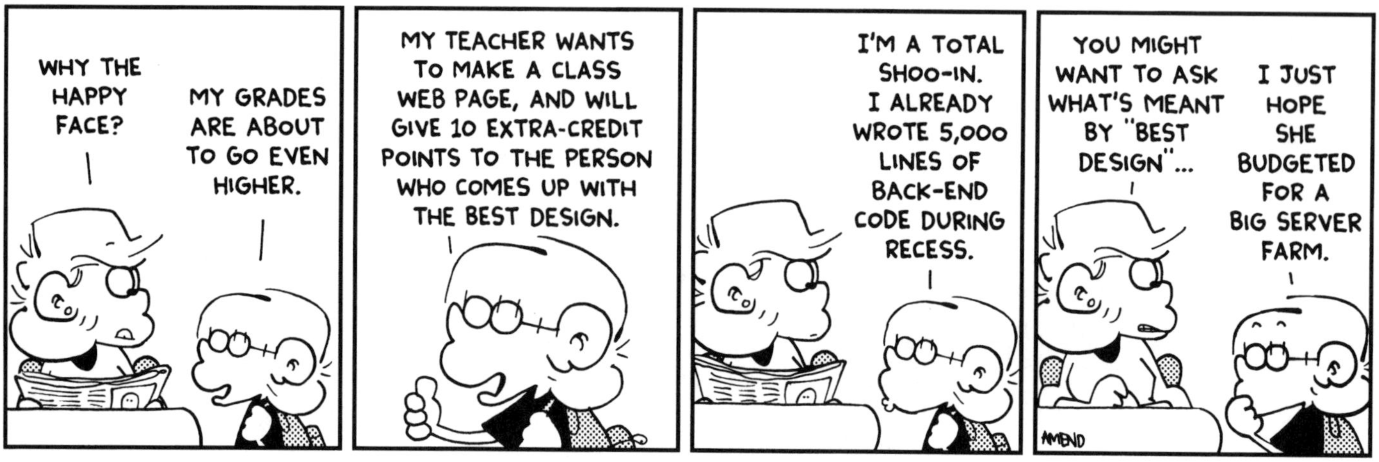
WHY THE HAPPY FACE?
MY GRADES ARE ABOUT TO GO EVEN HIGHER.
MY TEACHER WANTS TO MAKE A CLASS WEB PAGE, AND WILL GIVE 10 EXTRA-CREDIT POINTS TO THE PERSON WHO COMES UP WITH THE BEST DESIGN.
I'M A TOTAL SHOO-IN. I ALREADY WROTE 5,000 LINES OF BACK-END CODE DURING RECESS.
YOU MIGHT WANT TO ASK WHAT'S MEANT BY "BEST DESIGN"...
I JUST HOPE SHE BUDGETED FOR A BIG SERVER FARM.
AMEND

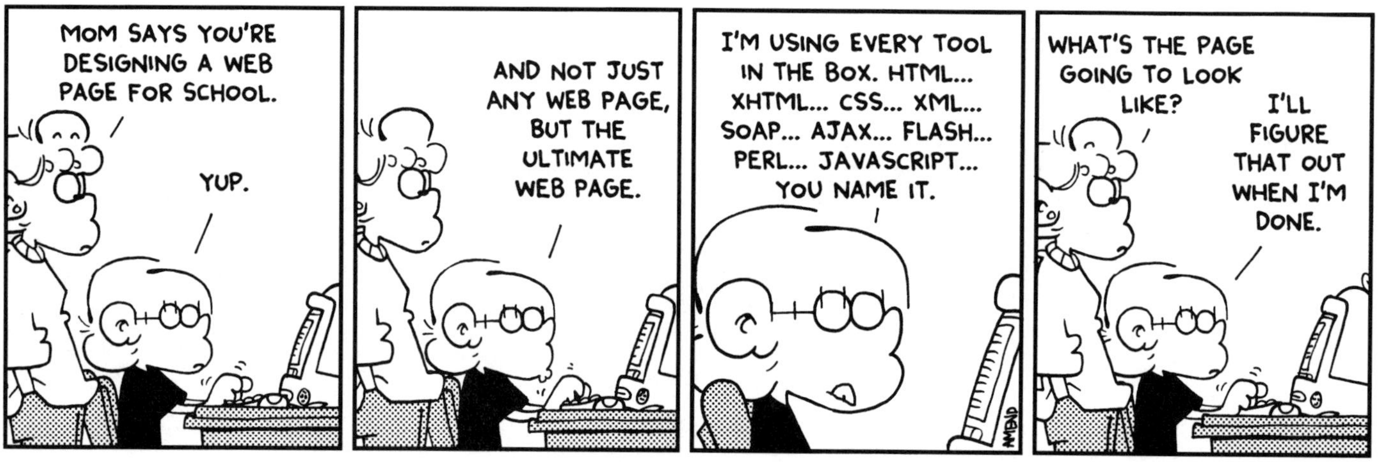
MOM SAYS YOU'RE DESIGNING A WEB PAGE FOR SCHOOL.
YUP.
AND NOT JUST ANY WEB PAGE, BUT THE ULTIMATE WEB PAGE.
I'M USING EVERY TOOL IN THE BOX. HTML... XHTML... CSS... XML... SOAP... AJAX... FLASH... PERL... JAVASCRIPT... YOU NAME IT.
AMEND
WHAT'S THE PAGE GOING TO LOOK LIKE?
I'LL FIGURE THAT OUT WHEN I'M DONE.

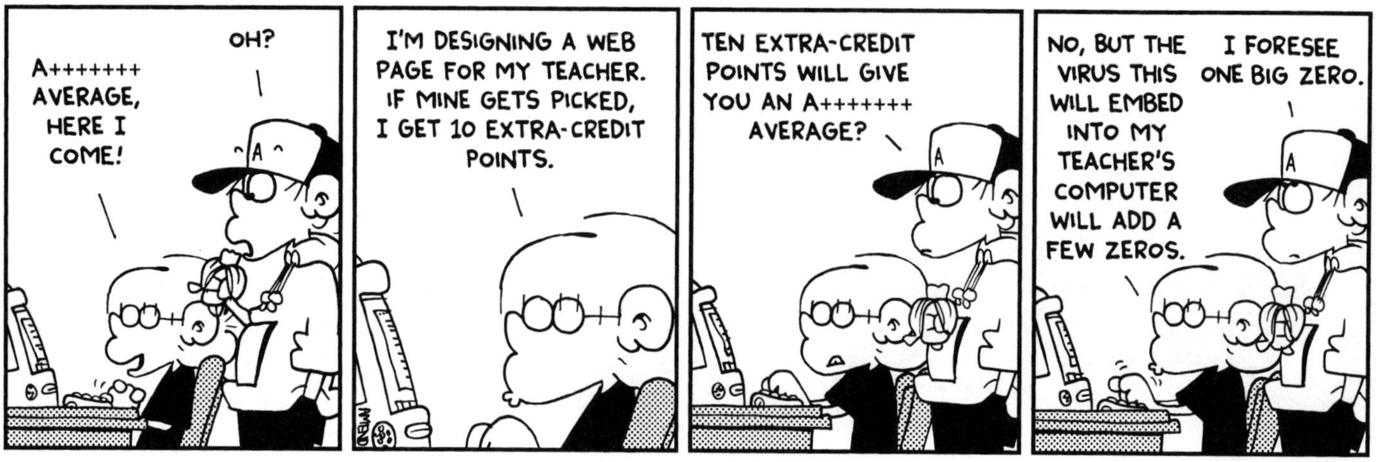
A+++++++ AVERAGE, HERE I COME!
OH?
I'M DESIGNING A WEB PAGE FOR MY TEACHER. IF MINE GETS PICKED, I GET 10 EXTRA-CREDIT POINTS.
TEN EXTRA-CREDIT POINTS WILL GIVE YOU AN A+++++++ AVERAGE?
NO, BUT THE VIRUS THIS WILL EMBED INTO MY TEACHER'S COMPUTER WILL ADD A FEW ZEROS.
I FORESEE ONE BIG ZERO.

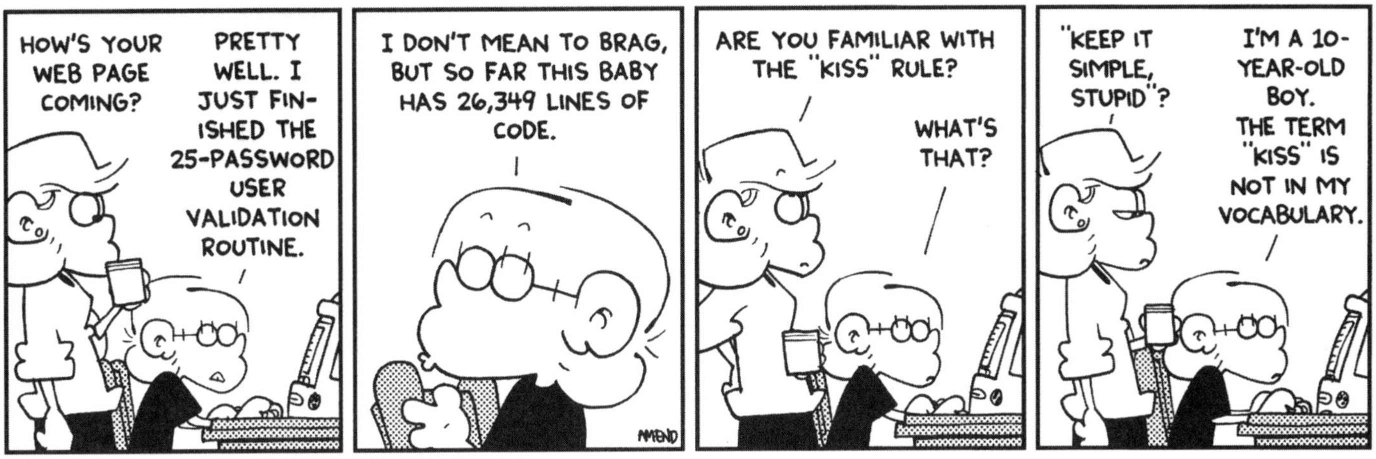
HOW'S YOUR WEB PAGE COMING?
PRETTY WELL. I JUST FIN-ISHED THE 25-PASSWORD USER VALIDATION ROUTINE.
I DON'T MEAN TO BRAG, BUT SO FAR THIS BABY HAS 26,349 LINES OF CODE.
ARE YOU FAMILIAR WITH THE "KISS" RULE?
WHAT'S THAT?
"KEEP IT SIMPLE, STUPID"?
I'M A 10-YEAR-OLD BOY. THE TERM "KISS" IS NOT IN MY VOCABULARY.
AMEND

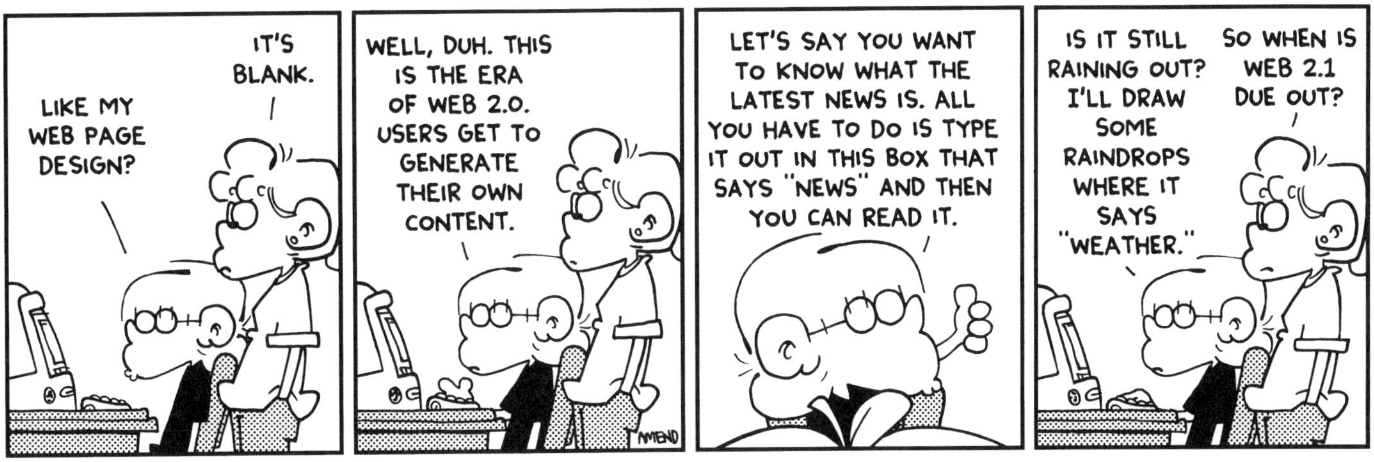
LIKE MY WEB PAGE DESIGN?
IT'S BLANK.
WELL, DUH. THIS IS THE ERA OF WEB 2.0. USERS GET TO GENERATE THEIR OWN CONTENT.
AMEND
LET'S SAY YOU WANT TO KNOW WHAT THE LATEST NEWS IS. ALL YOU HAVE TO DO IS TYPE IT OUT IN THIS BOX THAT SAYS "NEWS" AND THEN YOU CAN READ IT.
IS IT STILL RAINING OUT? I'LL DRAW SOME RAINDROPS WHERE IT SAYS "WEATHER."
SO WHEN IS WEB 2.1 DUE OUT?

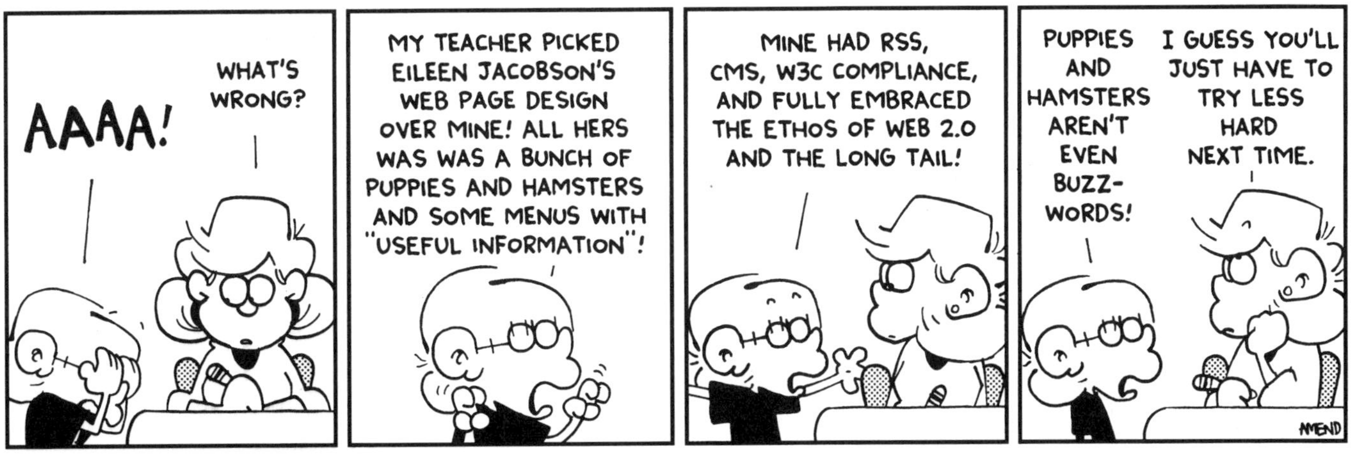
AAAA!
WHAT'S WRONG?
MY TEACHER PICKED EILEEN JACOBSON'S WEB PAGE DESIGN OVER MINE! ALL HERS WAS WAS A BUNCH OF PUPPIES AND HAMSTERS AND SOME MENUS WITH "USEFUL INFORMATION"!
MINE HAD RSS, CMS, W3C COMPLIANCE, AND FULLY EMBRACED THE ETHOS OF WEB 2.0 AND THE LONG TAIL!
PUPPIES AND HAMSTERS AREN'T EVEN BUZZ-WORDS!
I GUESS YOU'LL JUST HAVE TO TRY LESS HARD NEXT TIME.
AMEND

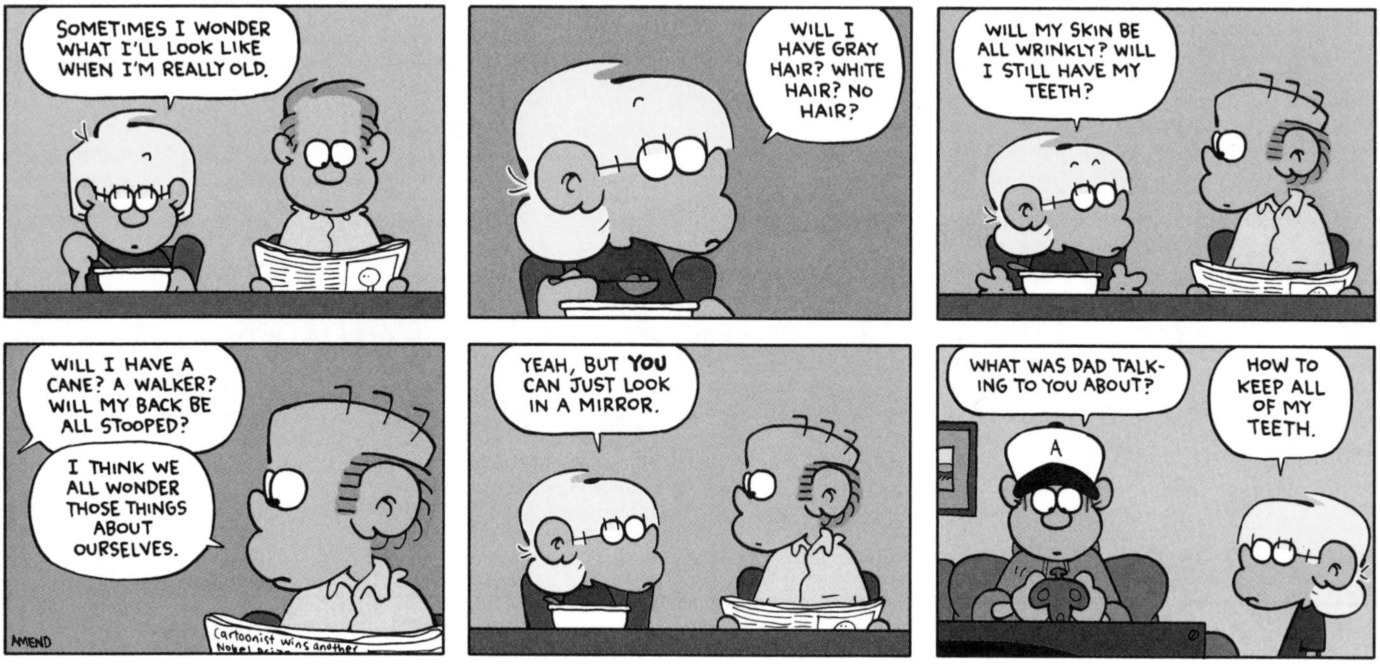
SOMETIMES I WONDER WHAT I'LL LOOK LIKE WHEN I'M REALLY OLD.
WILL I HAVE GRAY HAIR? WHITE HAIR? NO HAIR?
WILL MY SKIN BE ALL WRINKLY? WILL I STILL HAVE MY TEETH?
WILL I HAVE A CANE? A WALKER? WILL MY BACK BE ALL STOOPED?
I THINK WE ALL WONDER THOSE THINGS ABOUT OURSELVES.
Cartoonist wins another
AMEND
YEAH, BUT **YOU** CAN JUST LOOK IN A MIRROR.
WHAT WAS DAD TALKING TO YOU ABOUT?
HOW TO KEEP ALL OF MY TEETH.

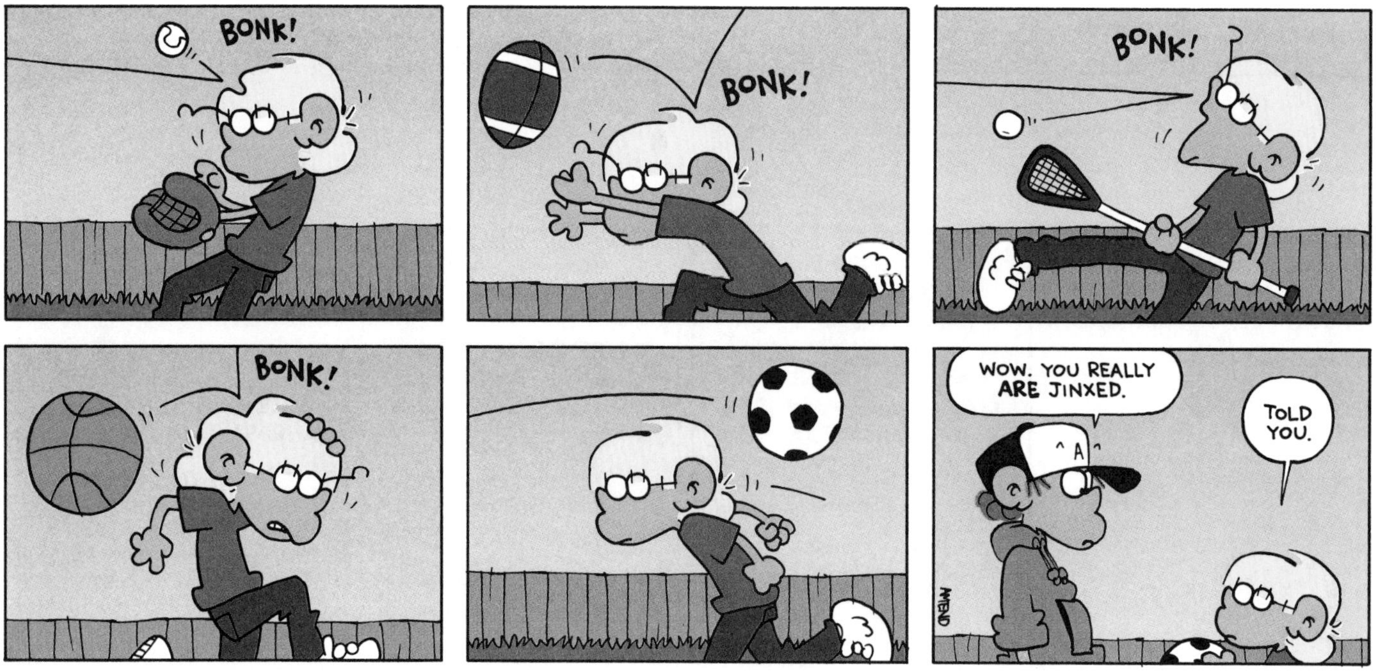
BONK!
BONK!
BONK!
BONK!
WOW. YOU REALLY **ARE** JINXED.
TOLD YOU.
AMEND

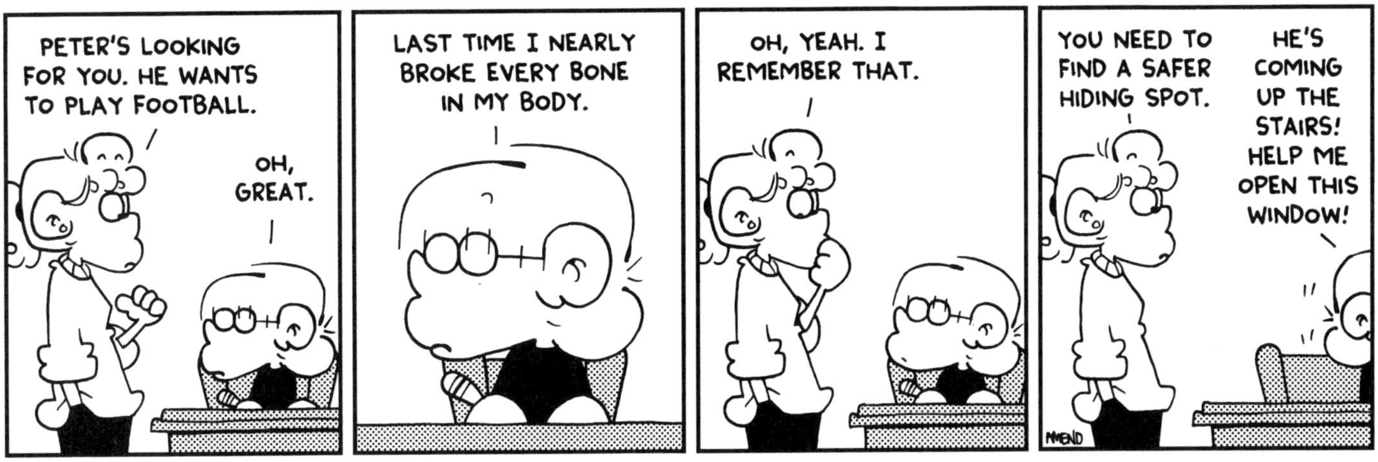
PETER'S LOOKING FOR YOU. HE WANTS TO PLAY FOOTBALL.
OH, GREAT.
LAST TIME I NEARLY BROKE EVERY BONE IN MY BODY.
OH, YEAH. I REMEMBER THAT.
YOU NEED TO FIND A SAFER HIDING SPOT.
HE'S COMING UP THE STAIRS! HELP ME OPEN THIS WINDOW!
AMEND

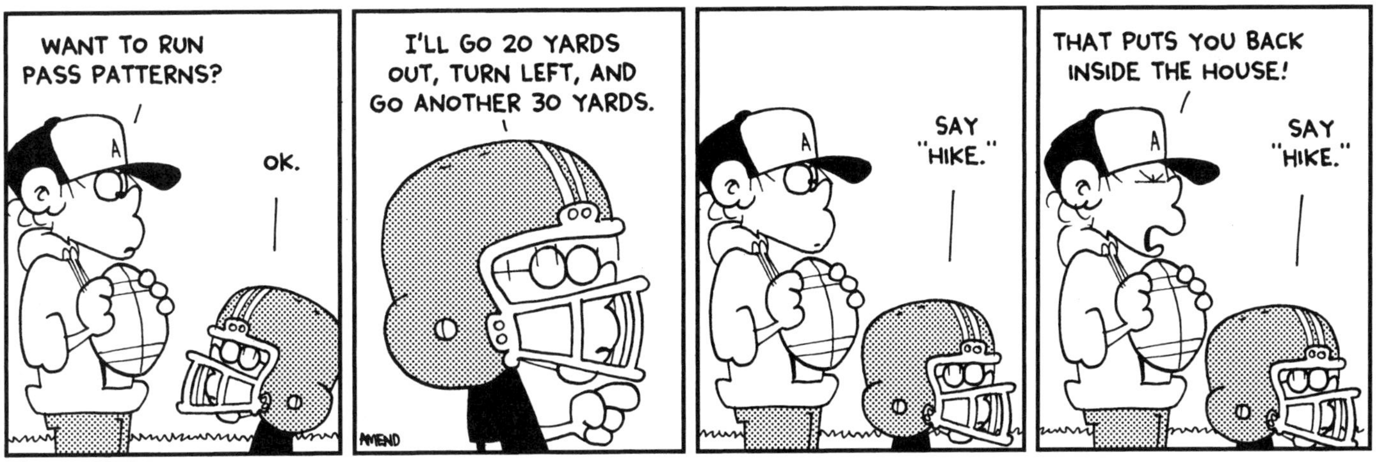
WANT TO RUN PASS PATTERNS?
OK.
I'LL GO 20 YARDS OUT, TURN LEFT, AND GO ANOTHER 30 YARDS.
AMEND
SAY "HIKE."
THAT PUTS YOU BACK INSIDE THE HOUSE!
SAY "HIKE."

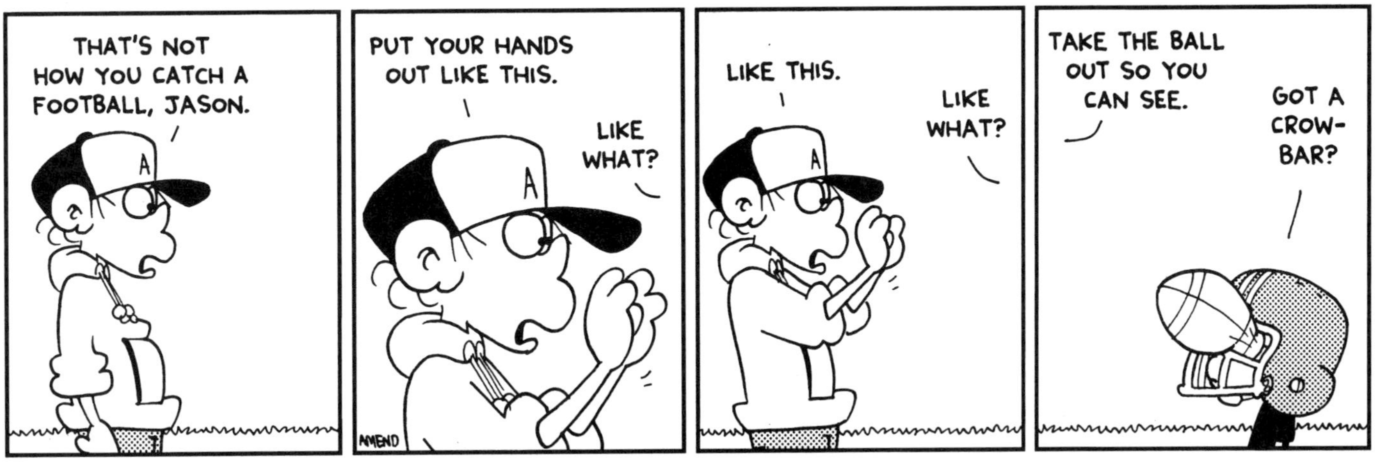
THAT'S NOT HOW YOU CATCH A FOOTBALL, JASON.
PUT YOUR HANDS OUT LIKE THIS.
LIKE WHAT?
AMEND
LIKE THIS.
LIKE WHAT?
TAKE THE BALL OUT SO YOU CAN SEE.
GOT A CROW-BAR?

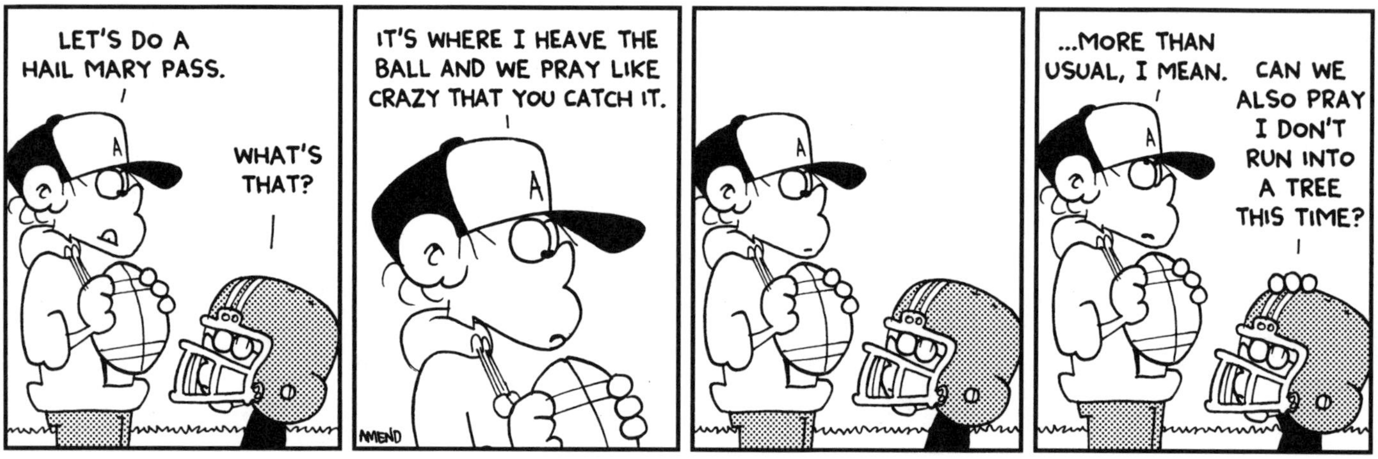
LET'S DO A HAIL MARY PASS.
WHAT'S THAT?
IT'S WHERE I HEAVE THE BALL AND WE PRAY LIKE CRAZY THAT YOU CATCH IT.
AMEND
...MORE THAN USUAL, I MEAN.
CAN WE ALSO PRAY I DON'T RUN INTO A TREE THIS TIME?

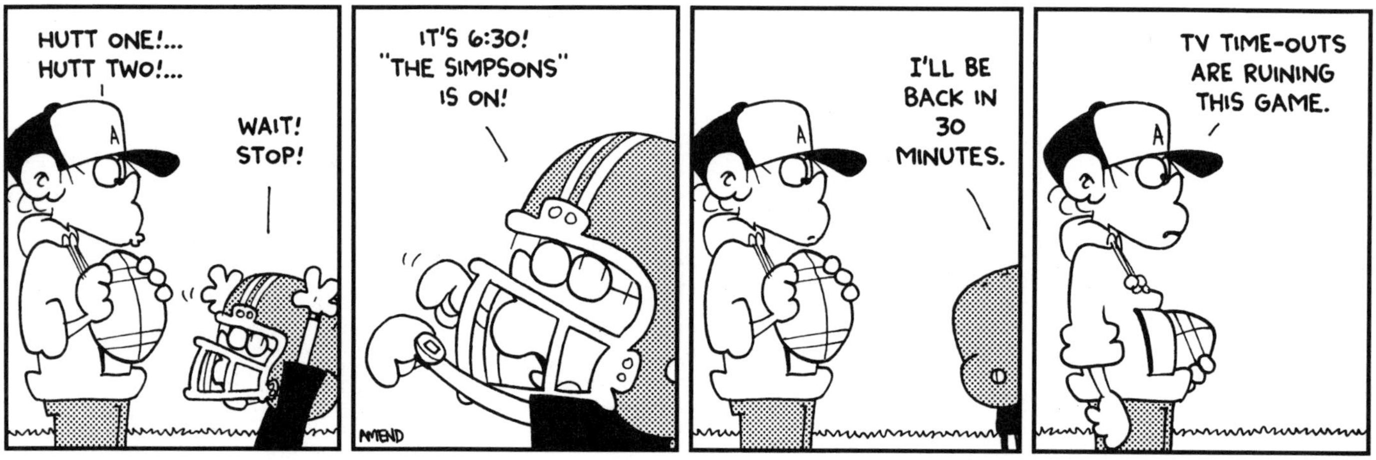
HUTT ONE!... HUTT TWO!...
WAIT! STOP!
IT'S 6:30! "THE SIMPSONS" IS ON!
AMEND
I'LL BE BACK IN 30 MINUTES.
TV TIME-OUTS ARE RUINING THIS GAME.

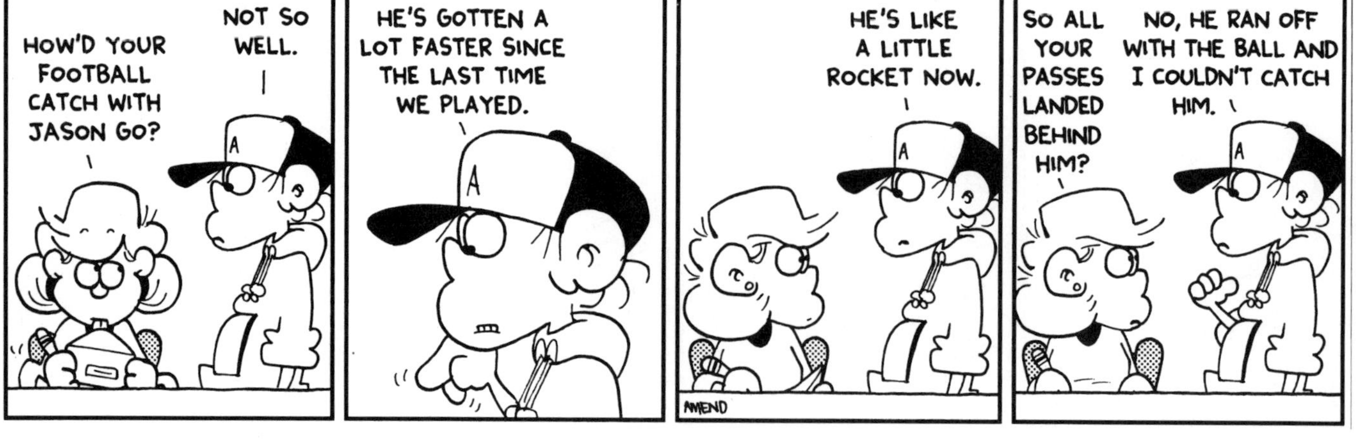
HOW'D YOUR FOOTBALL CATCH WITH JASON GO?
NOT SO WELL.
HE'S GOTTEN A LOT FASTER SINCE THE LAST TIME WE PLAYED.
HE'S LIKE A LITTLE ROCKET NOW.
AMEND
SO ALL YOUR PASSES LANDED BEHIND HIM?
NO, HE RAN OFF WITH THE BALL AND I COULDN'T CATCH HIM.

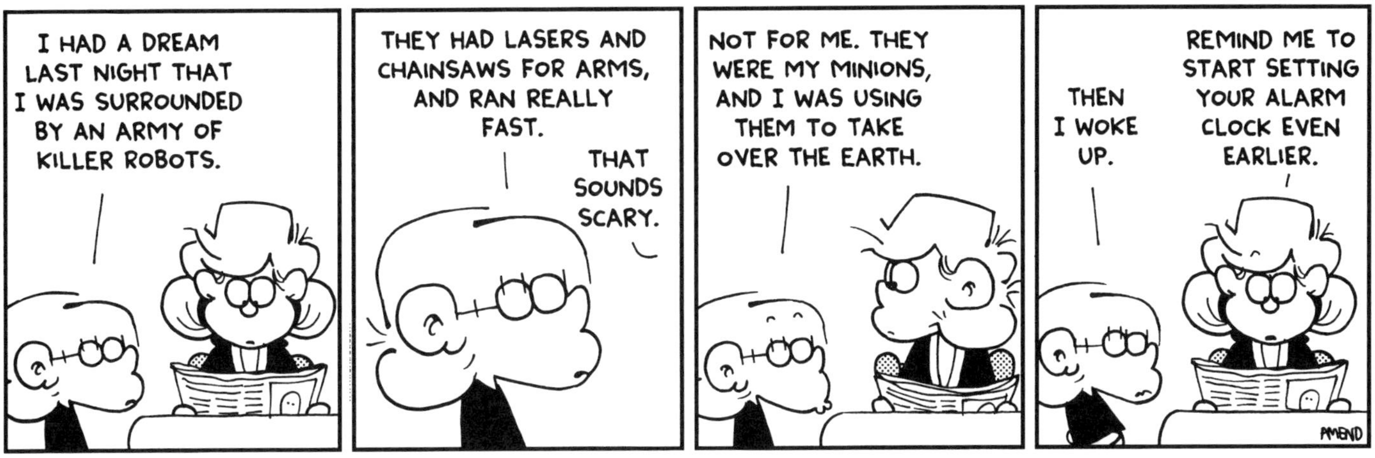
I HAD A DREAM LAST NIGHT THAT I WAS SURROUNDED BY AN ARMY OF KILLER ROBOTS.
THEY HAD LASERS AND CHAINSAWS FOR ARMS, AND RAN REALLY FAST.
THAT SOUNDS SCARY.
NOT FOR ME. THEY WERE MY MINIONS, AND I WAS USING THEM TO TAKE OVER THE EARTH.
THEN I WOKE UP.
REMIND ME TO START SETTING YOUR ALARM CLOCK EVEN EARLIER.
AMEND

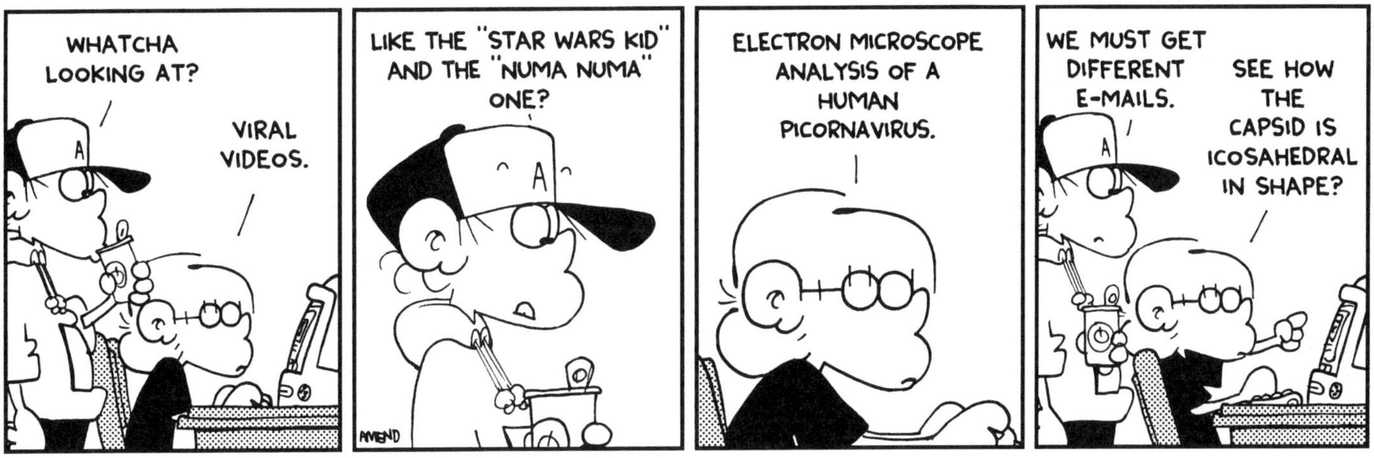
WHATCHA LOOKING AT?
VIRAL VIDEOS.
LIKE THE "STAR WARS KID" AND THE "NUMA NUMA" ONE?
AMEND
ELECTRON MICROSCOPE ANALYSIS OF A HUMAN PICORNAVIRUS.
WE MUST GET DIFFERENT E-MAILS.
SEE HOW THE CAPSID IS ICOSAHEDRAL IN SHAPE?

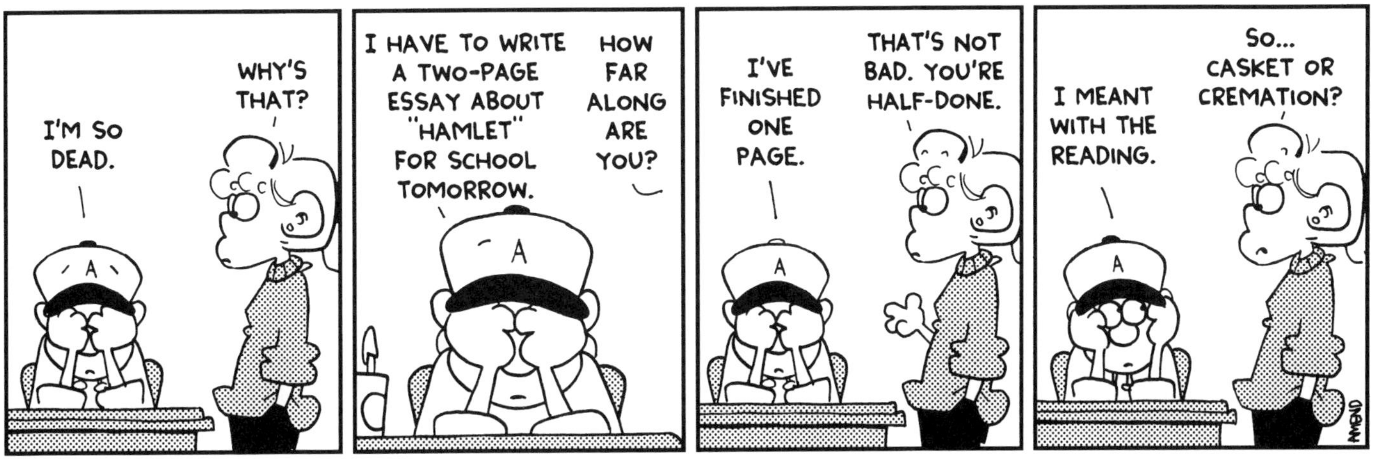
I'M SO DEAD.
WHY'S THAT?
I HAVE TO WRITE A TWO-PAGE ESSAY ABOUT "HAMLET" FOR SCHOOL TOMORROW.
HOW FAR ALONG ARE YOU?
I'VE FINISHED ONE PAGE.
THAT'S NOT BAD. YOU'RE HALF-DONE.
I MEANT WITH THE READING.
SO... CASKET OR CREMATION?
AMEND

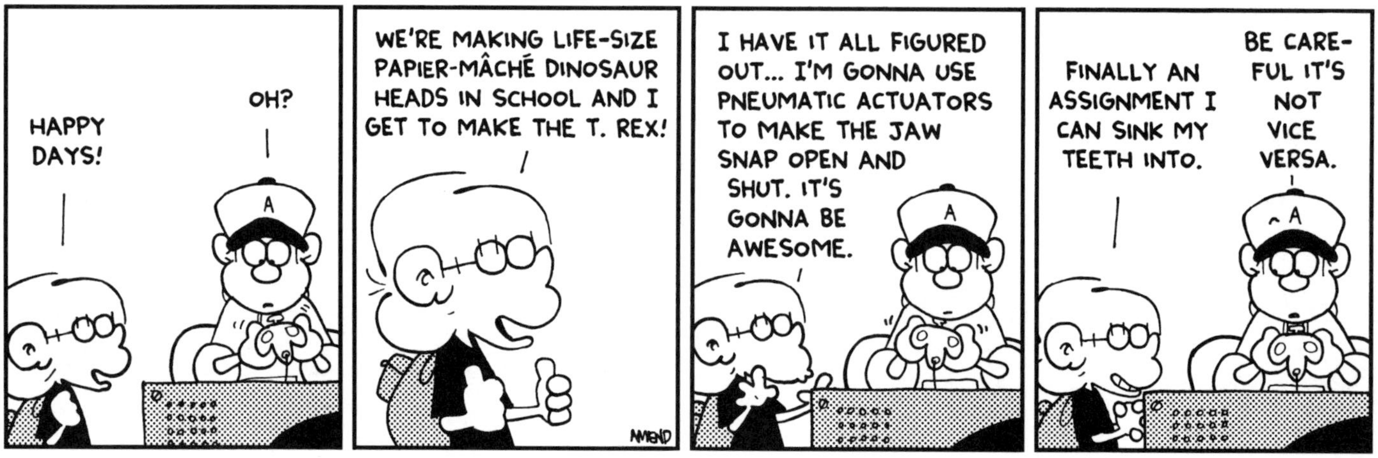
HAPPY DAYS!
OH?
WE'RE MAKING LIFE-SIZE PAPIER-MÂCHÉ DINOSAUR HEADS IN SCHOOL AND I GET TO MAKE THE T. REX!
I HAVE IT ALL FIGURED OUT... I'M GONNA USE PNEUMATIC ACTUATORS TO MAKE THE JAW SNAP OPEN AND SHUT. IT'S GONNA BE AWESOME.
FINALLY AN ASSIGNMENT I CAN SINK MY TEETH INTO.
BE CARE-FUL IT'S NOT VICE VERSA.
AMEND

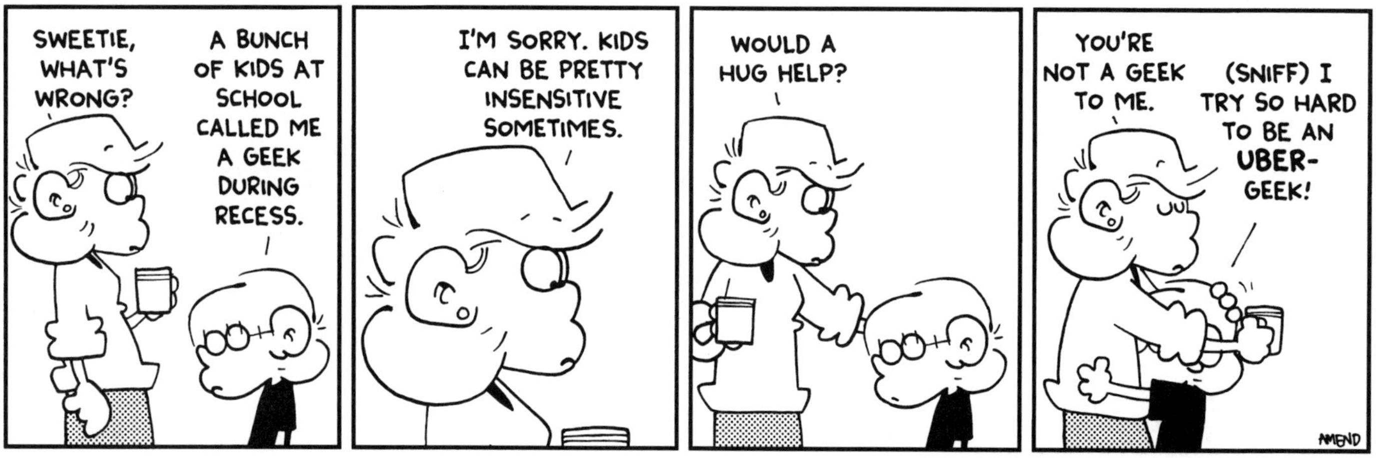
SWEETIE, WHAT'S WRONG?
A BUNCH OF KIDS AT SCHOOL CALLED ME A GEEK DURING RECESS.
I'M SORRY. KIDS CAN BE PRETTY INSENSITIVE SOMETIMES.
WOULD A HUG HELP?
YOU'RE NOT A GEEK TO ME.
(SNIFF) I TRY SO HARD TO BE AN UBER-GEEK!
AMEND

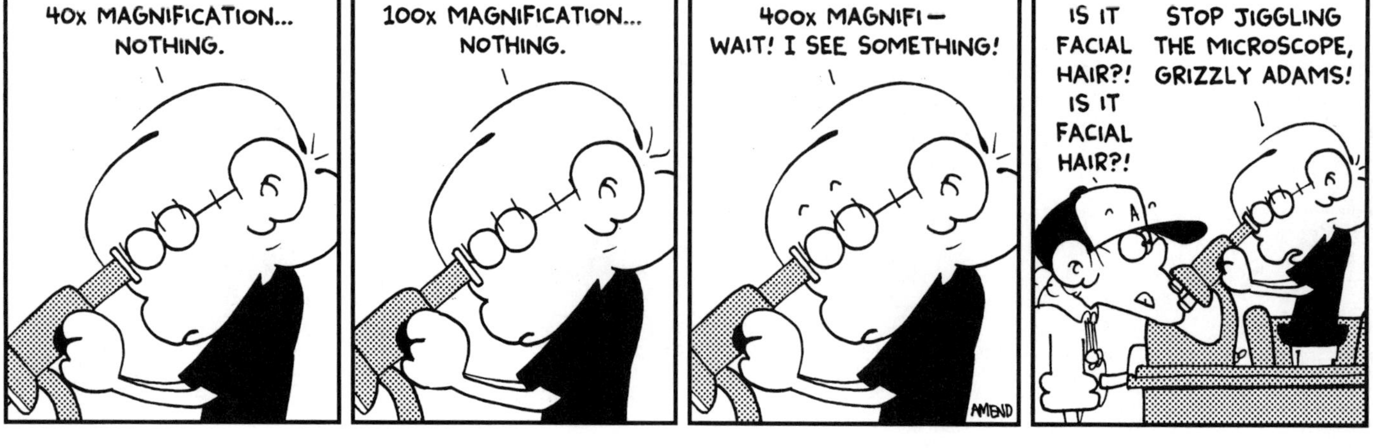
40x MAGNIFICATION... NOTHING.
100x MAGNIFICATION... NOTHING.
400x MAGNIFI— WAIT! I SEE SOMETHING!
IS IT FACIAL HAIR?! IS IT FACIAL HAIR?!
STOP JIGGLING THE MICROSCOPE, GRIZZLY ADAMS!
AMEND

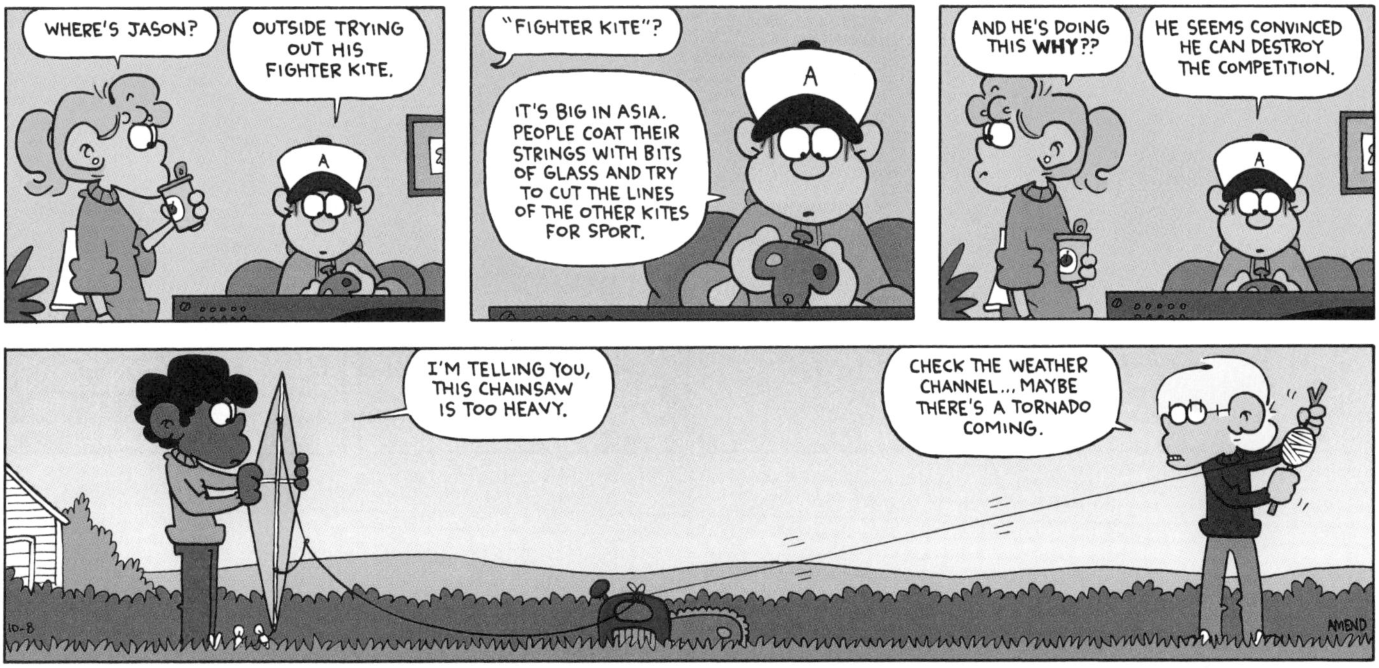
WHERE'S JASON?
OUTSIDE TRYING OUT HIS FIGHTER KITE.
"FIGHTER KITE"?
IT'S BIG IN ASIA. PEOPLE COAT THEIR STRINGS WITH BITS OF GLASS AND TRY TO CUT THE LINES OF THE OTHER KITES FOR SPORT.
AND HE'S DOING THIS **WHY**??
HE SEEMS CONVINCED HE CAN DESTROY THE COMPETITION.
I'M TELLING YOU, THIS CHAINSAW IS TOO HEAVY.
CHECK THE WEATHER CHANNEL... MAYBE THERE'S A TORNADO COMING.
10-8
AMEND

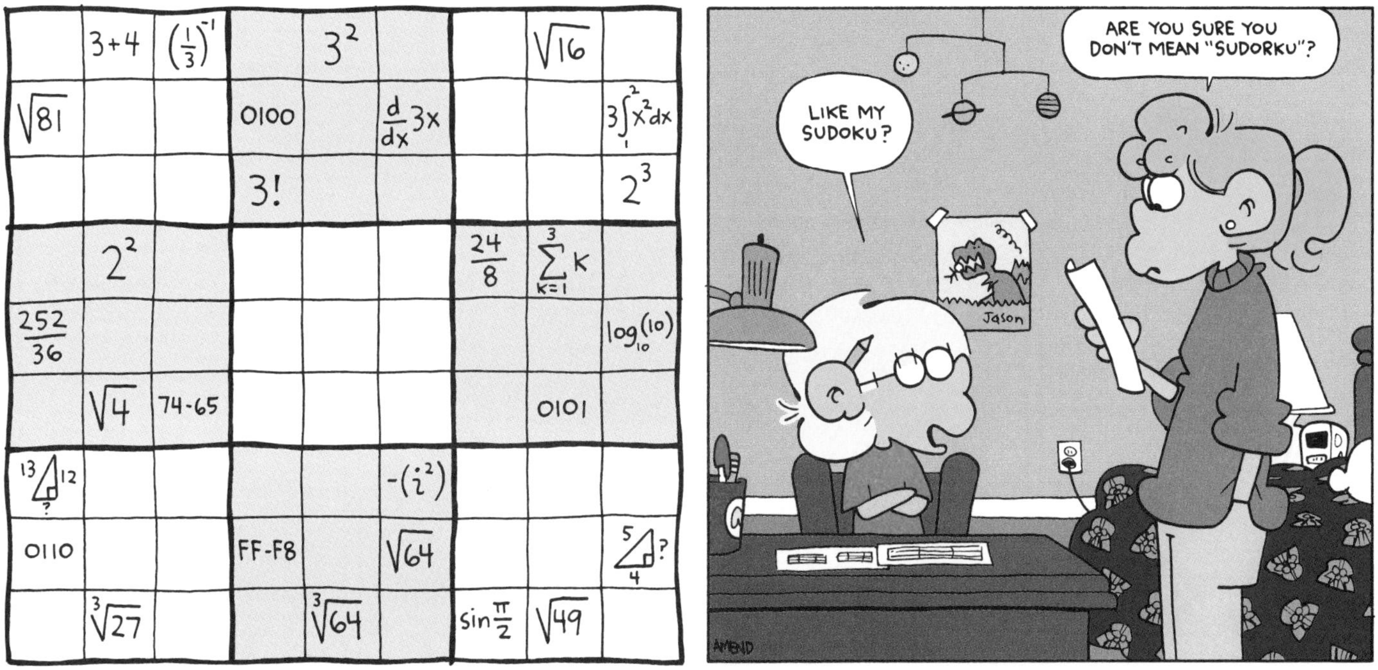
$3+4$ $\left(\frac{1}{3}\right)^{-1}$ 3^2 $\sqrt{16}$
$\sqrt{81}$ 0100 $\frac{d}{dx}3x$ $3\int_1^2 x^2 dx$
$3!$ 2^3
2^2 $\frac{24}{8}$ $\sum_{k=1}^{3} k$
$\frac{252}{36}$ $\log_{10}(10)$
$\sqrt{4}$ 74-65 0101
13 12 ? $-(i^2)$
0110 FF-F8 $\sqrt{64}$ 5 4 ?
$\sqrt[3]{27}$ $\sqrt[3]{64}$ $\sin\frac{\pi}{2}$ $\sqrt{49}$
LIKE MY SUDOKU?
ARE YOU SURE YOU DON'T MEAN "SUDORKU"?
Jason
AMEND

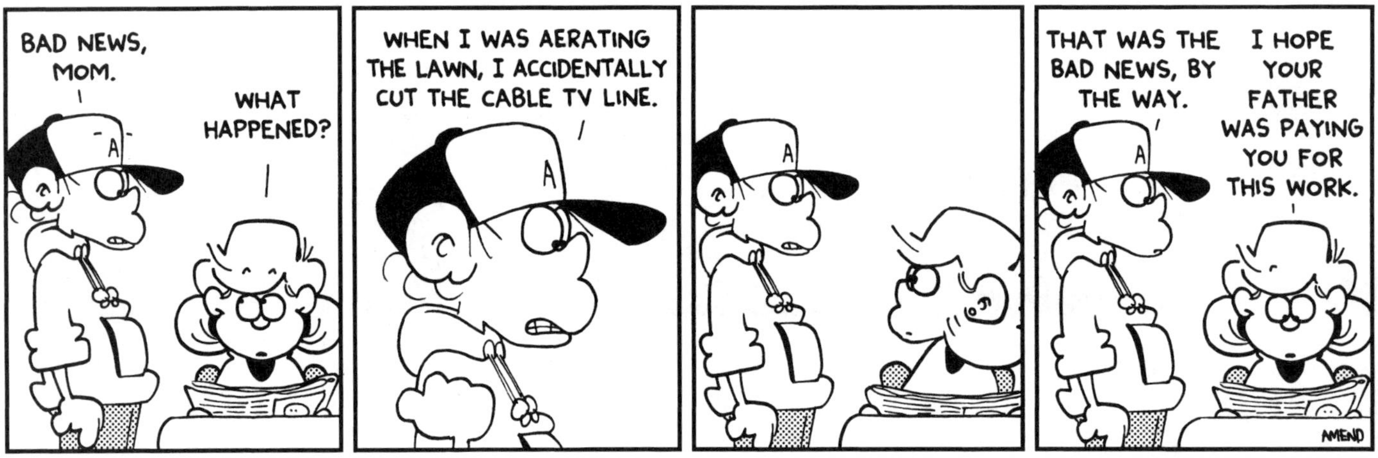
BAD NEWS, MOM.
WHAT HAPPENED?
WHEN I WAS AERATING THE LAWN, I ACCIDENTALLY CUT THE CABLE TV LINE.
THAT WAS THE BAD NEWS, BY THE WAY.
I HOPE YOUR FATHER WAS PAYING YOU FOR THIS WORK.
AMEND

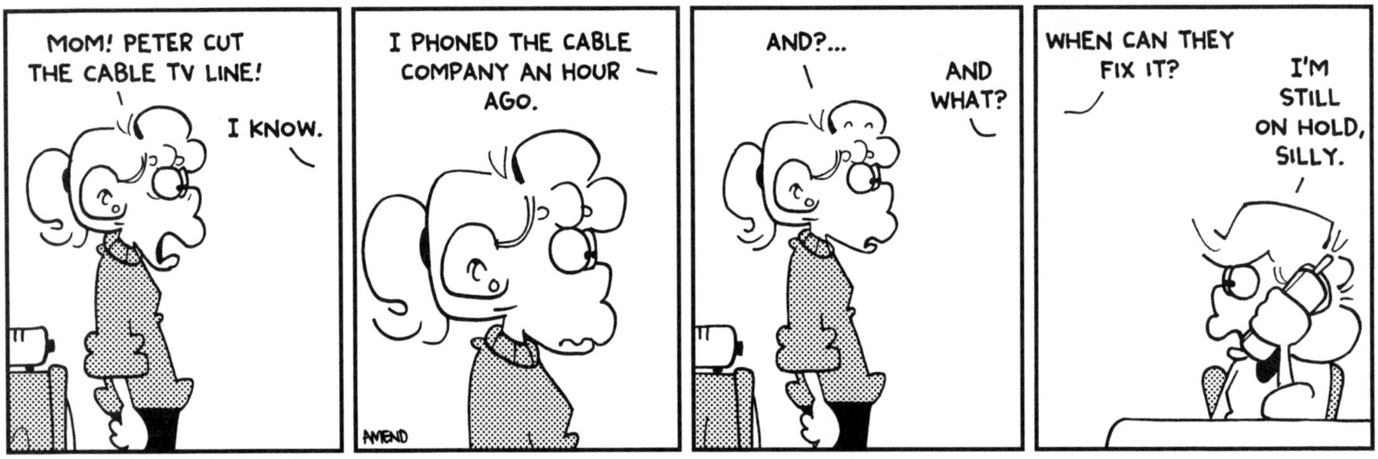
MOM! PETER CUT THE CABLE TV LINE!
I KNOW.
I PHONED THE CABLE COMPANY AN HOUR AGO.
AMEND
AND?...
AND WHAT?
WHEN CAN THEY FIX IT?
I'M STILL ON HOLD, SILLY.

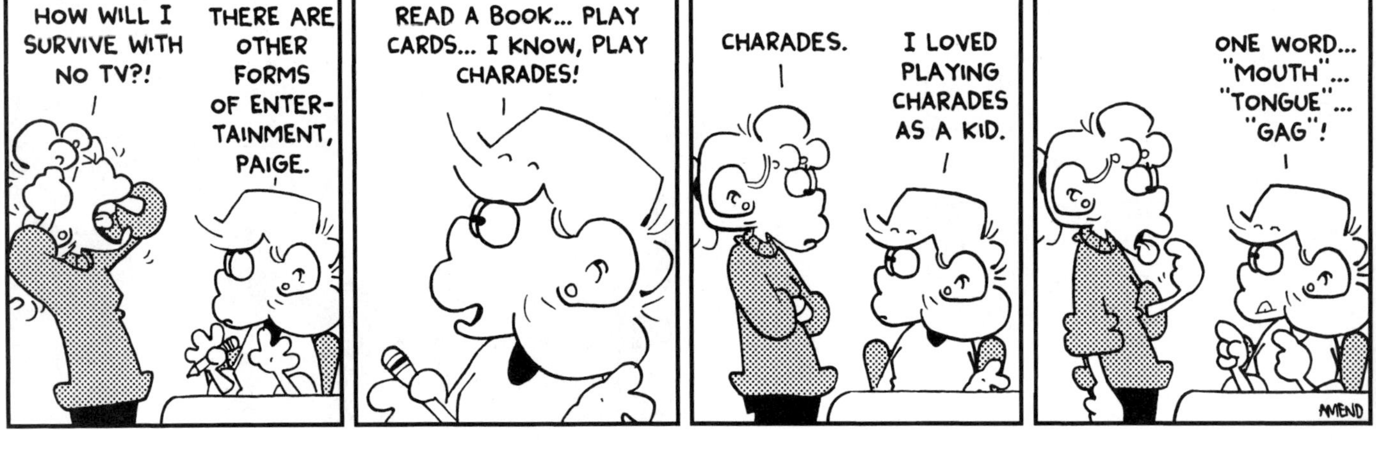
HOW WILL I SURVIVE WITH NO TV?!
THERE ARE OTHER FORMS OF ENTER-TAINMENT, PAIGE.
READ A BOOK... PLAY CARDS... I KNOW, PLAY CHARADES!
CHARADES.
I LOVED PLAYING CHARADES AS A KID.
ONE WORD... "MOUTH"... "TONGUE"... "GAG"!
AMEND

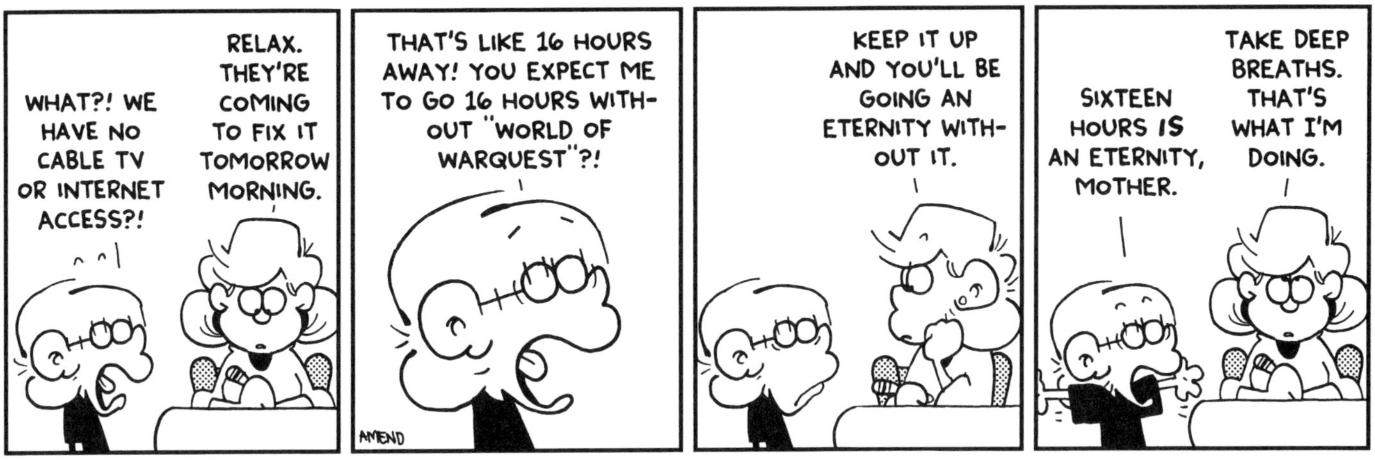
WHAT?! WE HAVE NO CABLE TV OR INTERNET ACCESS?!
RELAX. THEY'RE COMING TO FIX IT TOMORROW MORNING.
THAT'S LIKE 16 HOURS AWAY! YOU EXPECT ME TO GO 16 HOURS WITH-OUT "WORLD OF WARQUEST"?!
AMEND
KEEP IT UP AND YOU'LL BE GOING AN ETERNITY WITH-OUT IT.
SIXTEEN HOURS **IS** AN ETERNITY, MOTHER.
TAKE DEEP BREATHS. THAT'S WHAT I'M DOING.

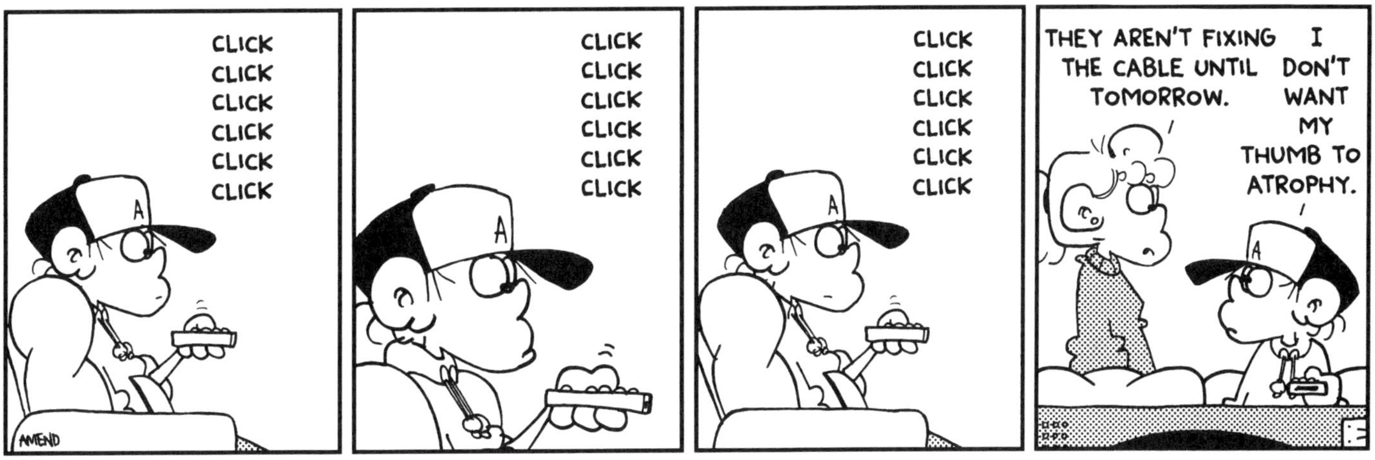
CLICK CLICK CLICK CLICK CLICK CLICK
AMEND
CLICK CLICK CLICK CLICK CLICK CLICK
CLICK CLICK CLICK CLICK CLICK CLICK
THEY AREN'T FIXING THE CABLE UNTIL TOMORROW.
I DON'T WANT MY THUMB TO ATROPHY.

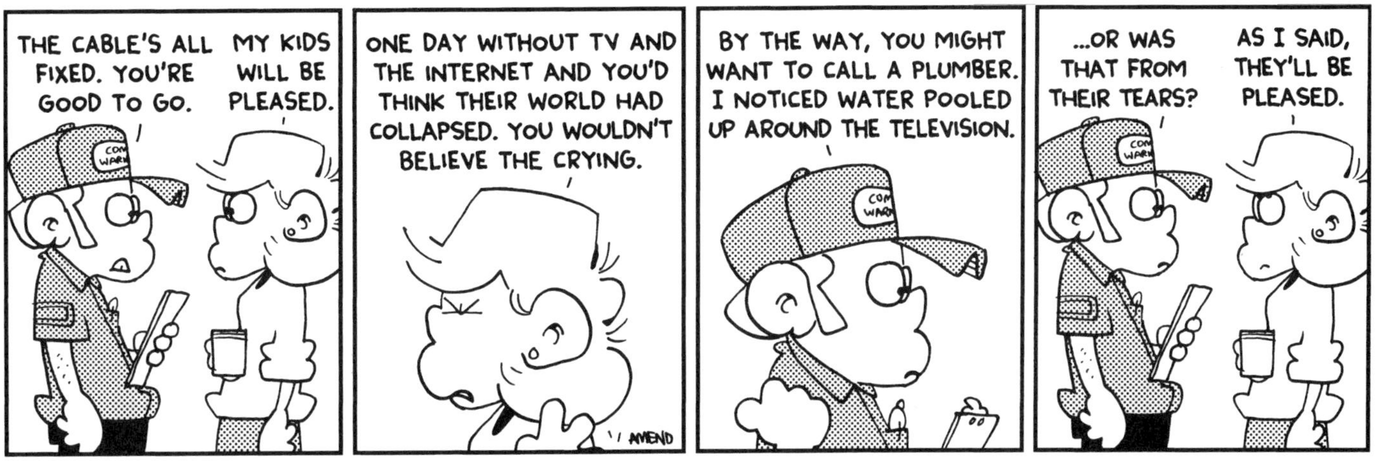
THE CABLE'S ALL FIXED. YOU'RE GOOD TO GO.
MY KIDS WILL BE PLEASED.
ONE DAY WITHOUT TV AND THE INTERNET AND YOU'D THINK THEIR WORLD HAD COLLAPSED. YOU WOULDN'T BELIEVE THE CRYING.
AMEND
BY THE WAY, YOU MIGHT WANT TO CALL A PLUMBER. I NOTICED WATER POOLED UP AROUND THE TELEVISION.
...OR WAS THAT FROM THEIR TEARS?
AS I SAID, THEY'LL BE PLEASED.

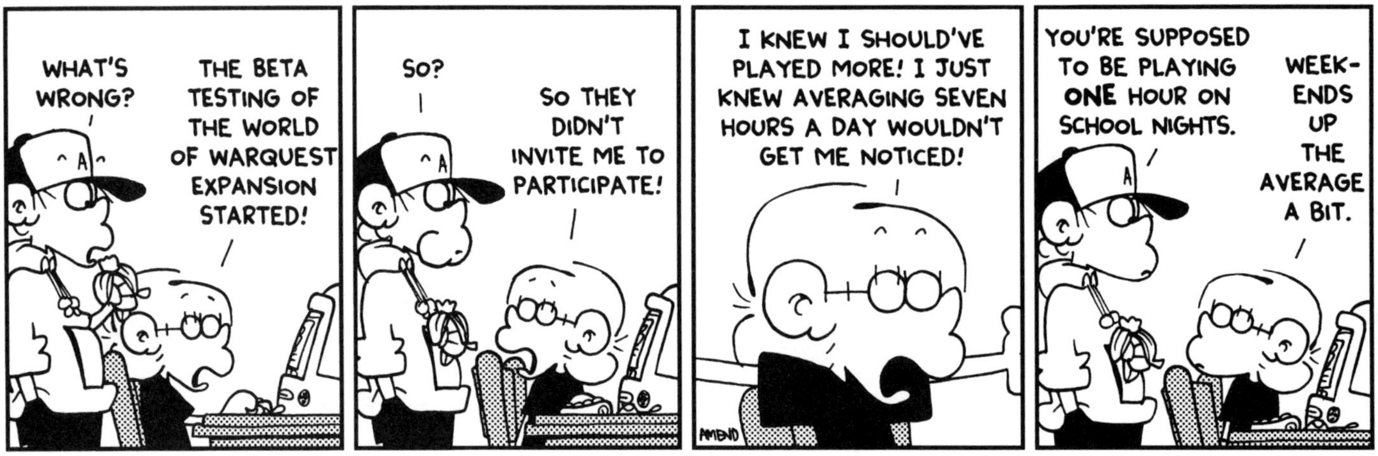
WHAT'S WRONG?
THE BETA TESTING OF THE WORLD OF WARQUEST EXPANSION STARTED!
SO?
SO THEY DIDN'T INVITE ME TO PARTICIPATE!
I KNEW I SHOULD'VE PLAYED MORE! I JUST KNEW AVERAGING SEVEN HOURS A DAY WOULDN'T GET ME NOTICED!
AMEND
YOU'RE SUPPOSED TO BE PLAYING ONE HOUR ON SCHOOL NIGHTS.
WEEK-ENDS UP THE AVERAGE A BIT.

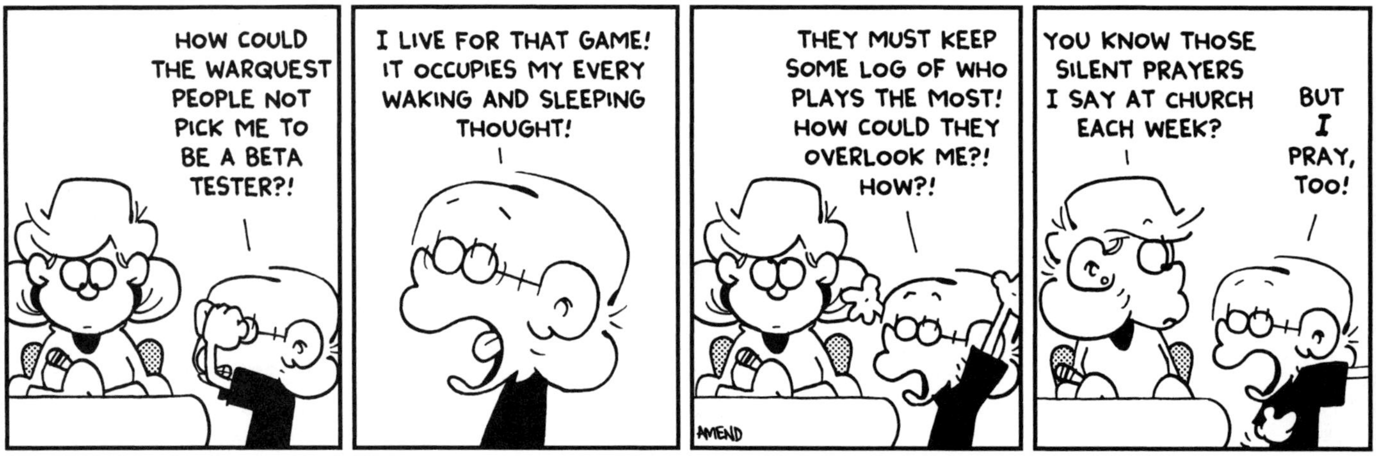
HOW COULD THE WARQUEST PEOPLE NOT PICK ME TO BE A BETA TESTER?!
I LIVE FOR THAT GAME! IT OCCUPIES MY EVERY WAKING AND SLEEPING THOUGHT!
THEY MUST KEEP SOME LOG OF WHO PLAYS THE MOST! HOW COULD THEY OVERLOOK ME?! HOW?!
AMEND
YOU KNOW THOSE SILENT PRAYERS I SAY AT CHURCH EACH WEEK?
BUT I PRAY, TOO!

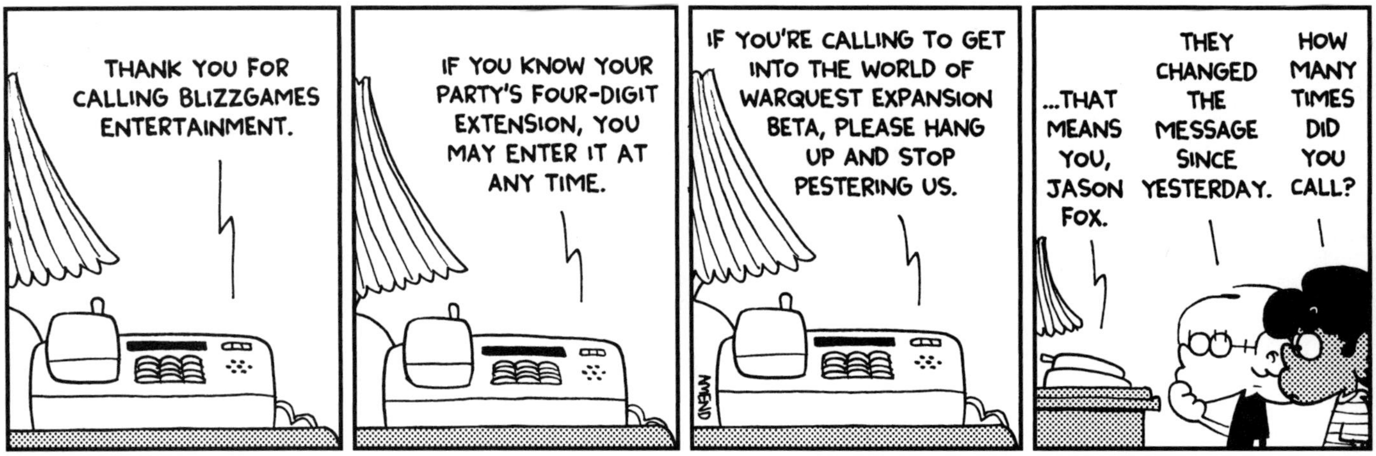
THANK YOU FOR CALLING BLIZZGAMES ENTERTAINMENT.
IF YOU KNOW YOUR PARTY'S FOUR-DIGIT EXTENSION, YOU MAY ENTER IT AT ANY TIME.
IF YOU'RE CALLING TO GET INTO THE WORLD OF WARQUEST EXPANSION BETA, PLEASE HANG UP AND STOP PESTERING US.
AMEND
...THAT MEANS YOU, JASON FOX.
THEY CHANGED THE MESSAGE SINCE YESTERDAY.
HOW MANY TIMES DID YOU CALL?

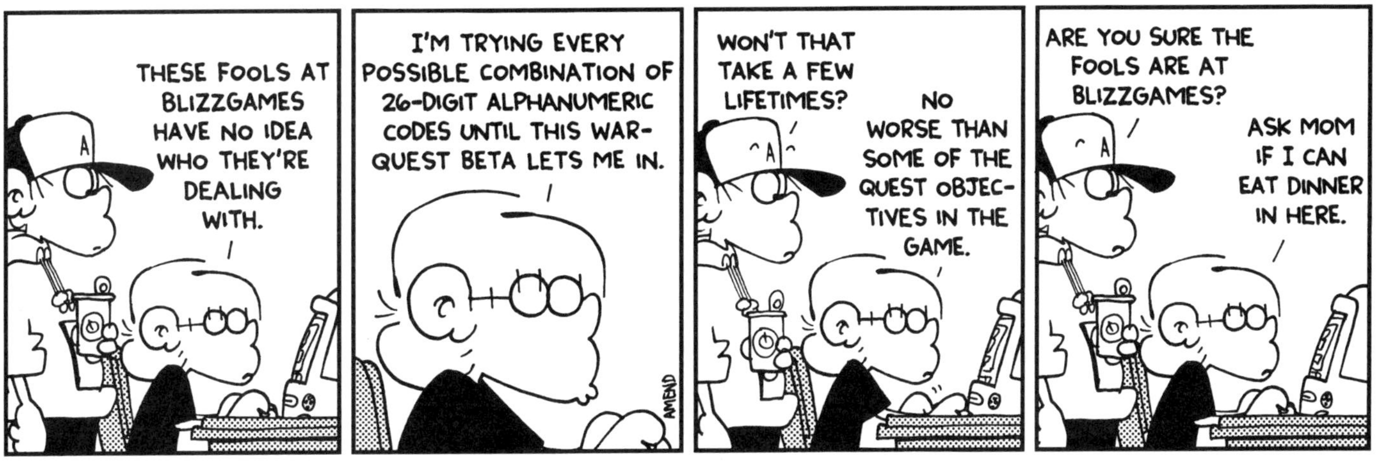
THESE FOOLS AT BLIZZGAMES HAVE NO IDEA WHO THEY'RE DEALING WITH.
I'M TRYING EVERY POSSIBLE COMBINATION OF 26-DIGIT ALPHANUMERIC CODES UNTIL THIS WARQUEST BETA LETS ME IN.
AMEND
WON'T THAT TAKE A FEW LIFETIMES?
NO WORSE THAN SOME OF THE QUEST OBJECTIVES IN THE GAME.
ARE YOU SURE THE FOOLS ARE AT BLIZZGAMES?
ASK MOM IF I CAN EAT DINNER IN HERE.

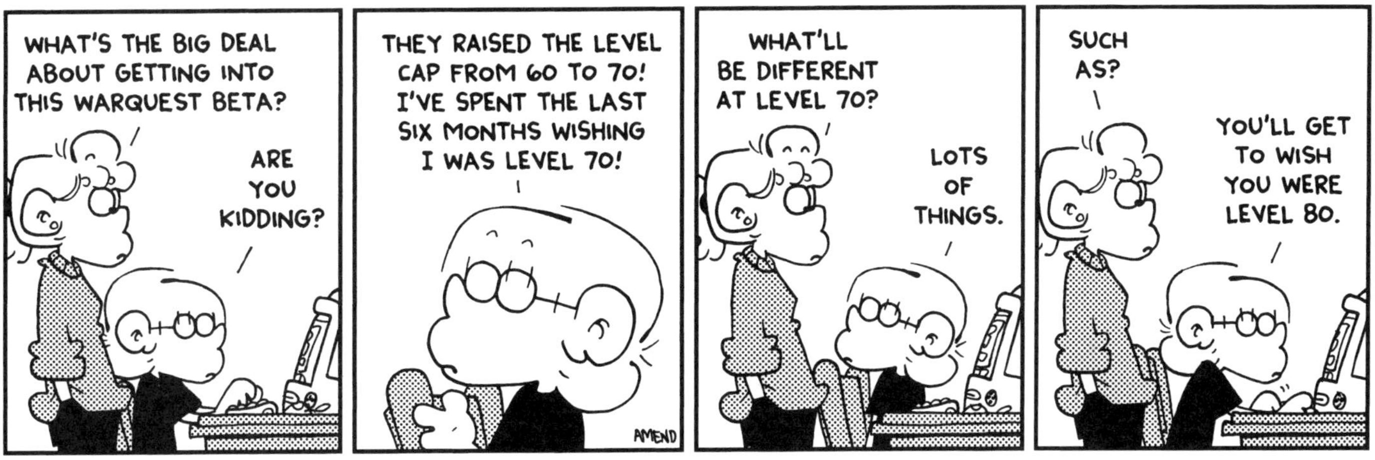
WHAT'S THE BIG DEAL ABOUT GETTING INTO THIS WARQUEST BETA?
ARE YOU KIDDING?
THEY RAISED THE LEVEL CAP FROM 60 TO 70! I'VE SPENT THE LAST SIX MONTHS WISHING I WAS LEVEL 70!
AMEND
WHAT'LL BE DIFFERENT AT LEVEL 70?
LOTS OF THINGS.
SUCH AS?
YOU'LL GET TO WISH YOU WERE LEVEL 80.

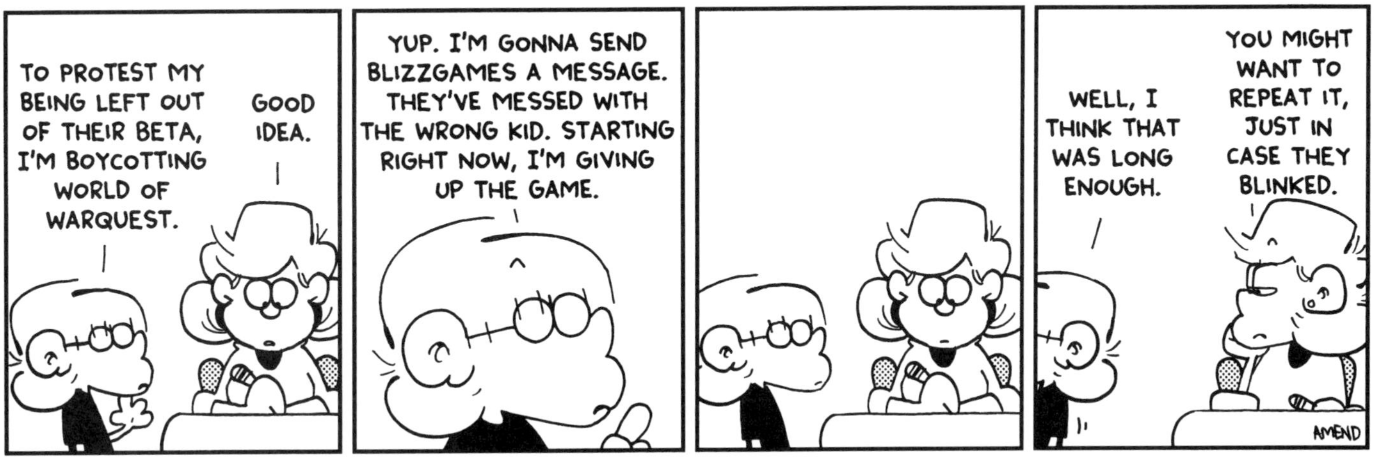
TO PROTEST MY BEING LEFT OUT OF THEIR BETA, I'M BOYCOTTING WORLD OF WARQUEST.
GOOD IDEA.
YUP. I'M GONNA SEND BLIZZGAMES A MESSAGE. THEY'VE MESSED WITH THE WRONG KID. STARTING RIGHT NOW, I'M GIVING UP THE GAME.
WELL, I THINK THAT WAS LONG ENOUGH.
YOU MIGHT WANT TO REPEAT IT, JUST IN CASE THEY BLINKED.
AMEND

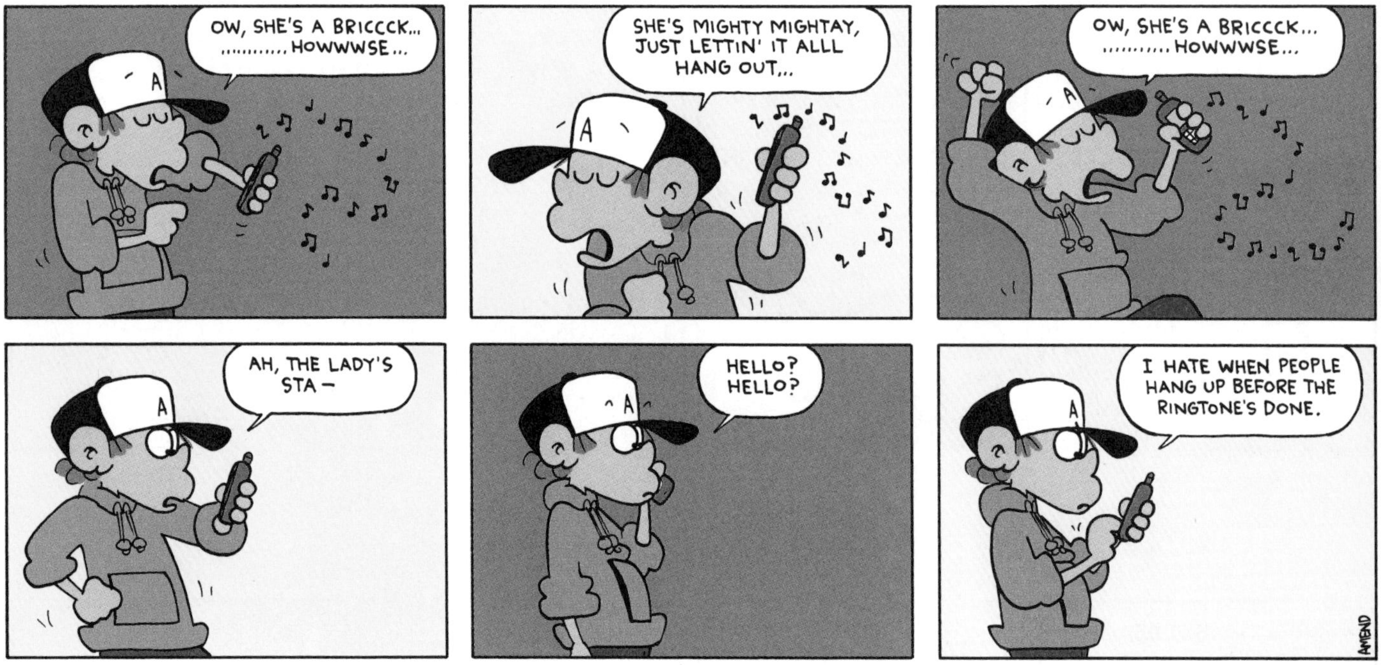
OW, SHE'S A BRICCCK...
...........HOWWWSE...
SHE'S MIGHTY MIGHTAY, JUST LETTIN' IT ALLL HANG OUT...
OW, SHE'S A BRICCCK...
...........HOWWWSE...
AH, THE LADY'S STA —
HELLO? HELLO?
I HATE WHEN PEOPLE HANG UP BEFORE THE RINGTONE'S DONE.
AMEND

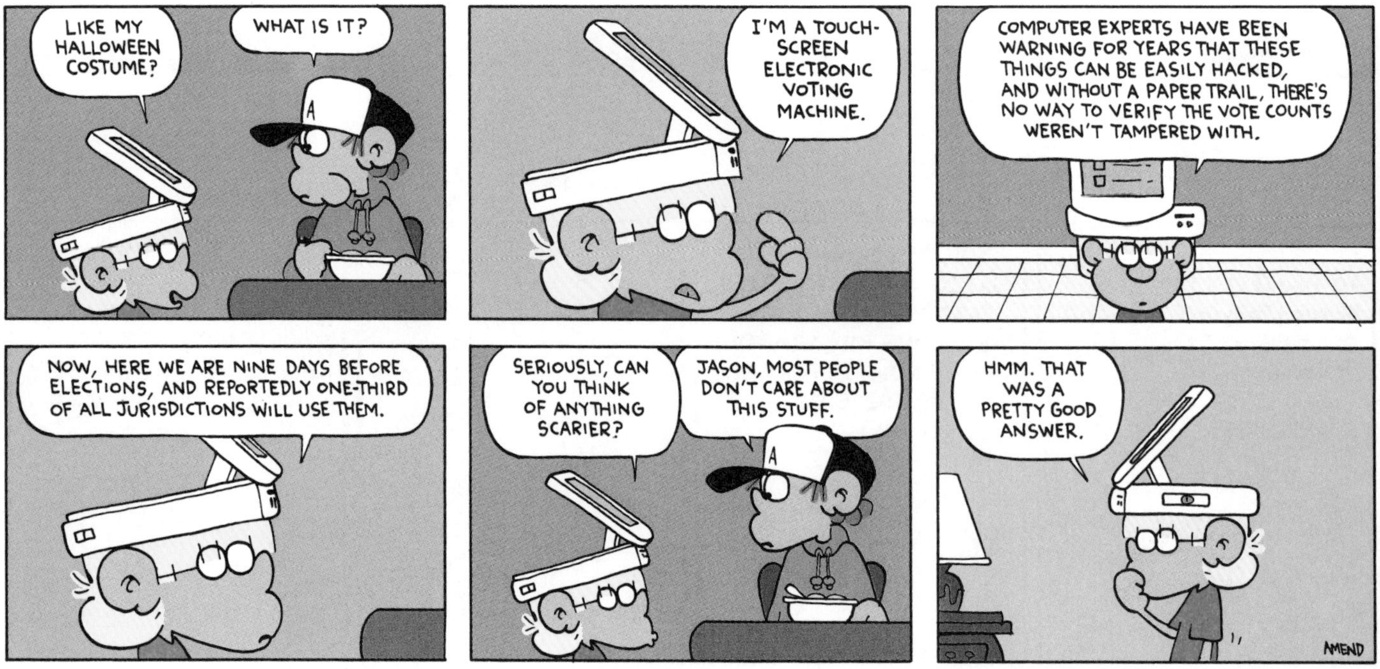
LIKE MY HALLOWEEN COSTUME?
WHAT IS IT?
I'M A TOUCH-SCREEN ELECTRONIC VOTING MACHINE.
COMPUTER EXPERTS HAVE BEEN WARNING FOR YEARS THAT THESE THINGS CAN BE EASILY HACKED, AND WITHOUT A PAPER TRAIL, THERE'S NO WAY TO VERIFY THE VOTE COUNTS WEREN'T TAMPERED WITH.
NOW, HERE WE ARE NINE DAYS BEFORE ELECTIONS, AND REPORTEDLY ONE-THIRD OF ALL JURISDICTIONS WILL USE THEM.
SERIOUSLY, CAN YOU THINK OF ANYTHING SCARIER?
JASON, MOST PEOPLE DON'T CARE ABOUT THIS STUFF.
HMM. THAT WAS A PRETTY GOOD ANSWER.
AMEND

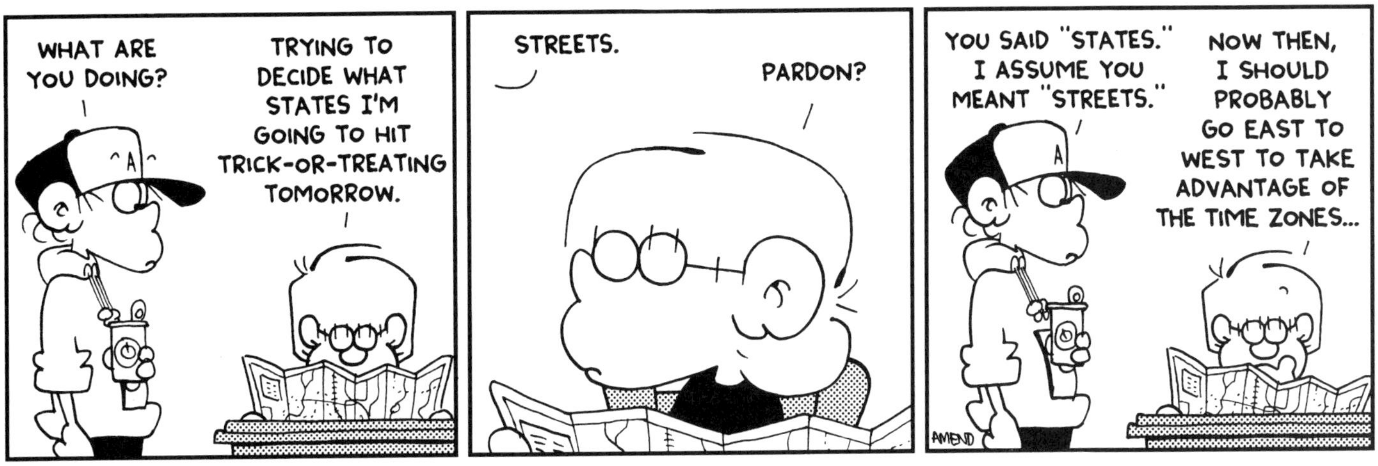
WHAT ARE YOU DOING?
TRYING TO DECIDE WHAT STATES I'M GOING TO HIT TRICK-OR-TREATING TOMORROW.
STREETS.
PARDON?
YOU SAID "STATES." I ASSUME YOU MEANT "STREETS."
NOW THEN, I SHOULD PROBABLY GO EAST TO WEST TO TAKE ADVANTAGE OF THE TIME ZONES...
AMEND

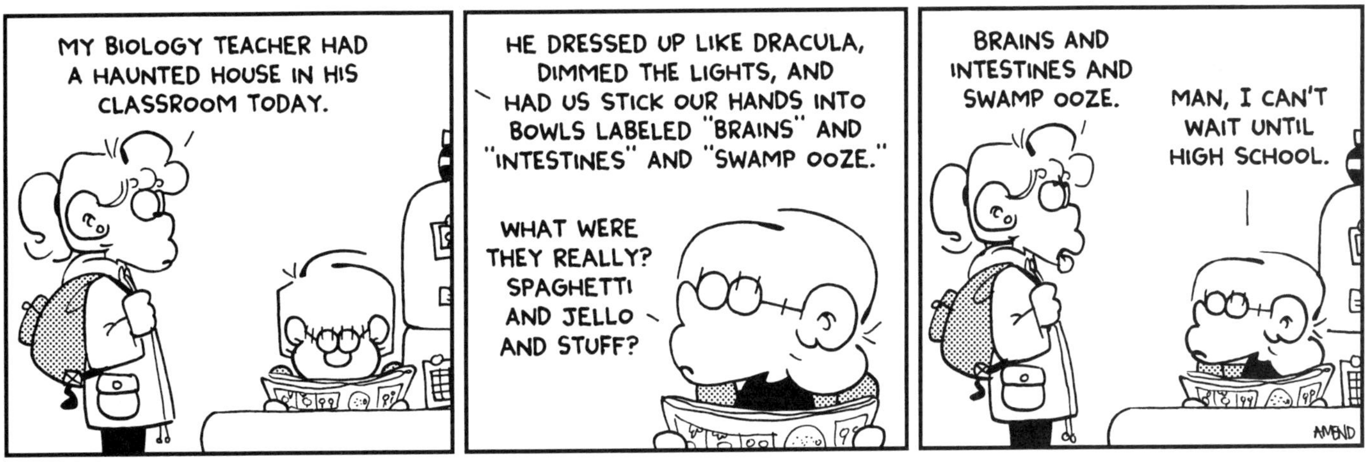
MY BIOLOGY TEACHER HAD A HAUNTED HOUSE IN HIS CLASSROOM TODAY.
HE DRESSED UP LIKE DRACULA, DIMMED THE LIGHTS, AND HAD US STICK OUR HANDS INTO BOWLS LABELED "BRAINS" AND "INTESTINES" AND "SWAMP OOZE."
WHAT WERE THEY REALLY? SPAGHETTI AND JELLO AND STUFF?
BRAINS AND INTESTINES AND SWAMP OOZE.
MAN, I CAN'T WAIT UNTIL HIGH SCHOOL.
AMEND

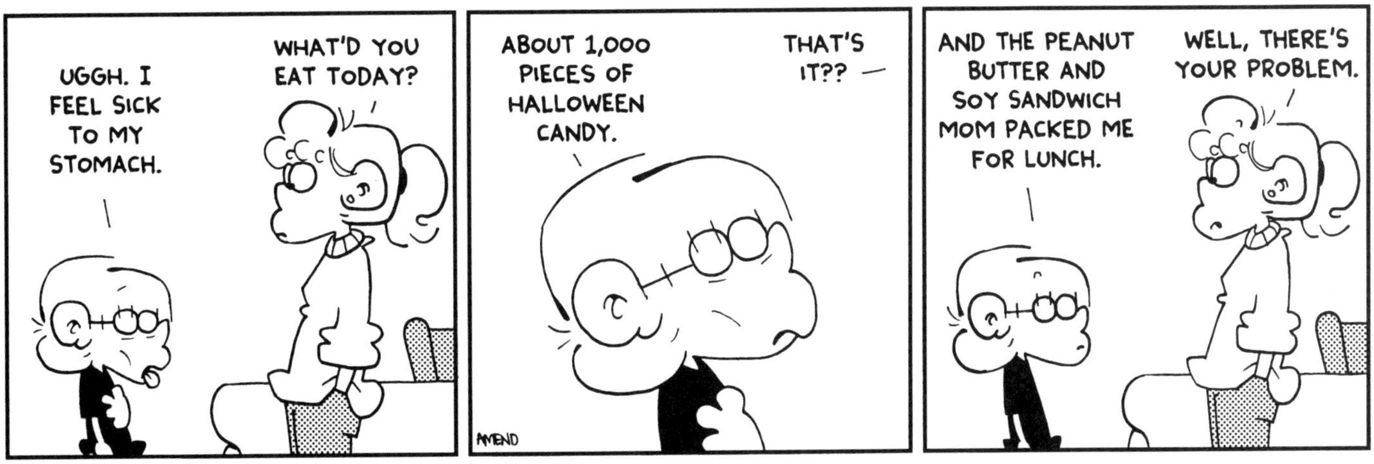
UGGH. I FEEL SICK TO MY STOMACH.
WHAT'D YOU EAT TODAY?
ABOUT 1,000 PIECES OF HALLOWEEN CANDY.
THAT'S IT??
AMEND
AND THE PEANUT BUTTER AND SOY SANDWICH MOM PACKED ME FOR LUNCH.
WELL, THERE'S YOUR PROBLEM.

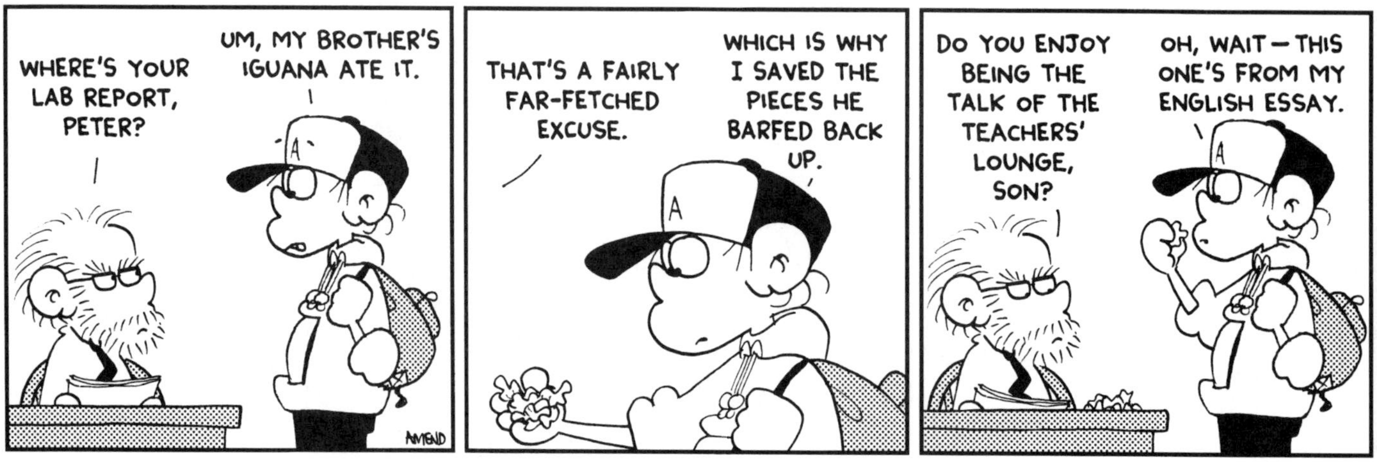
WHERE'S YOUR LAB REPORT, PETER?
UM, MY BROTHER'S IGUANA ATE IT.
THAT'S A FAIRLY FAR-FETCHED EXCUSE.
WHICH IS WHY I SAVED THE PIECES HE BARFED BACK UP.
DO YOU ENJOY BEING THE TALK OF THE TEACHERS' LOUNGE, SON?
OH, WAIT—THIS ONE'S FROM MY ENGLISH ESSAY.
AMEND

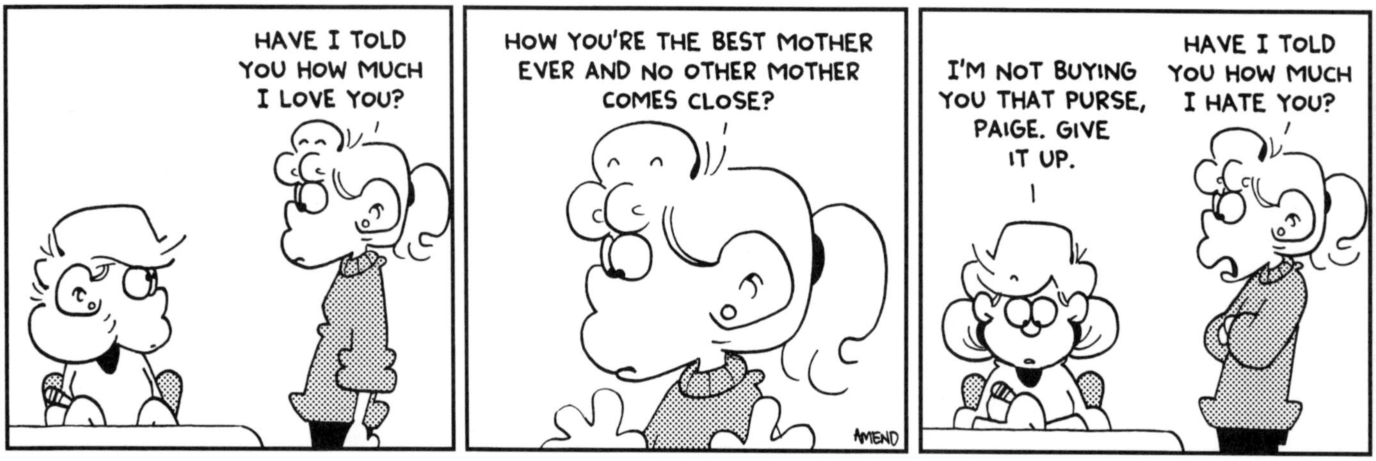
HAVE I TOLD YOU HOW MUCH I LOVE YOU?
HOW YOU'RE THE BEST MOTHER EVER AND NO OTHER MOTHER COMES CLOSE?
I'M NOT BUYING YOU THAT PURSE, PAIGE. GIVE IT UP.
HAVE I TOLD YOU HOW MUCH I HATE YOU?
AMEND

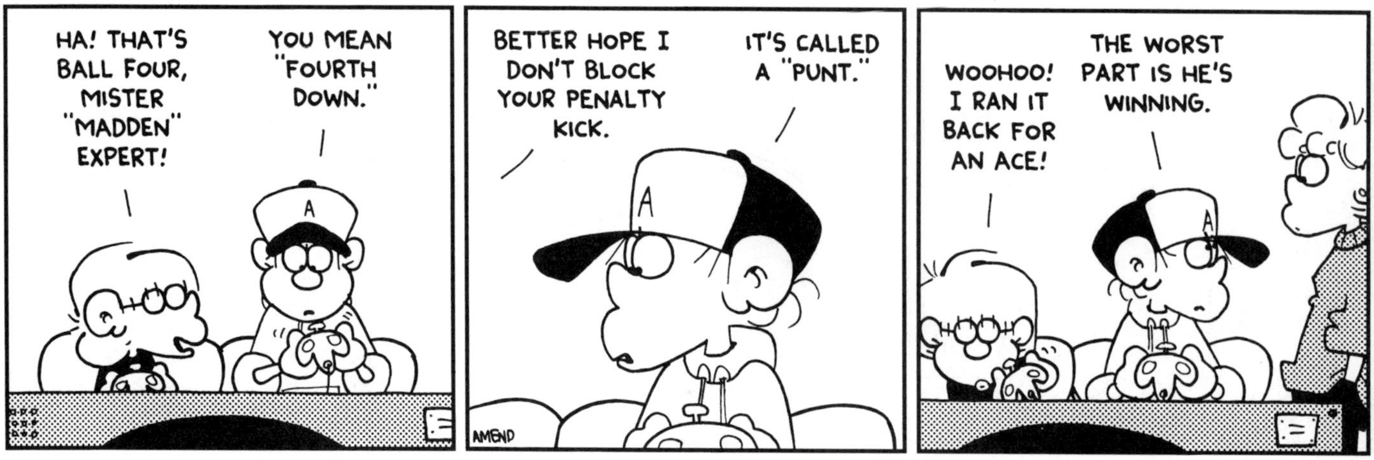
HA! THAT'S BALL FOUR, MISTER "MADDEN" EXPERT!
YOU MEAN "FOURTH DOWN."
BETTER HOPE I DON'T BLOCK YOUR PENALTY KICK.
IT'S CALLED A "PUNT."
WOOHOO! I RAN IT BACK FOR AN ACE!
THE WORST PART IS HE'S WINNING.
AMEND

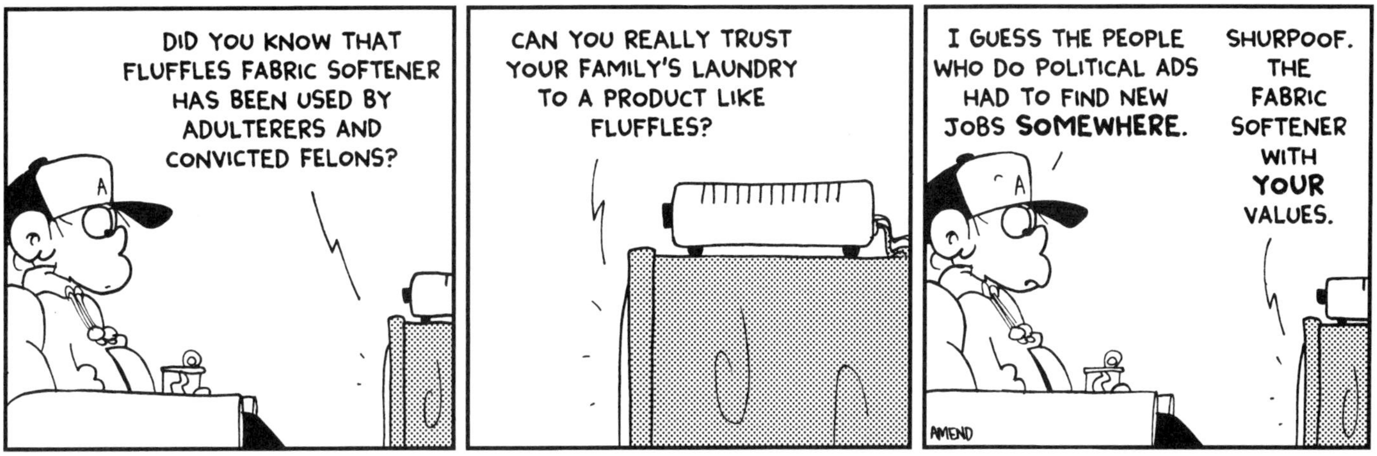
DID YOU KNOW THAT FLUFFLES FABRIC SOFTENER HAS BEEN USED BY ADULTERERS AND CONVICTED FELONS?
CAN YOU REALLY TRUST YOUR FAMILY'S LAUNDRY TO A PRODUCT LIKE FLUFFLES?
I GUESS THE PEOPLE WHO DO POLITICAL ADS HAD TO FIND NEW JOBS **SOMEWHERE**.
SHURPOOF. THE FABRIC SOFTENER WITH **YOUR** VALUES.
AMEND

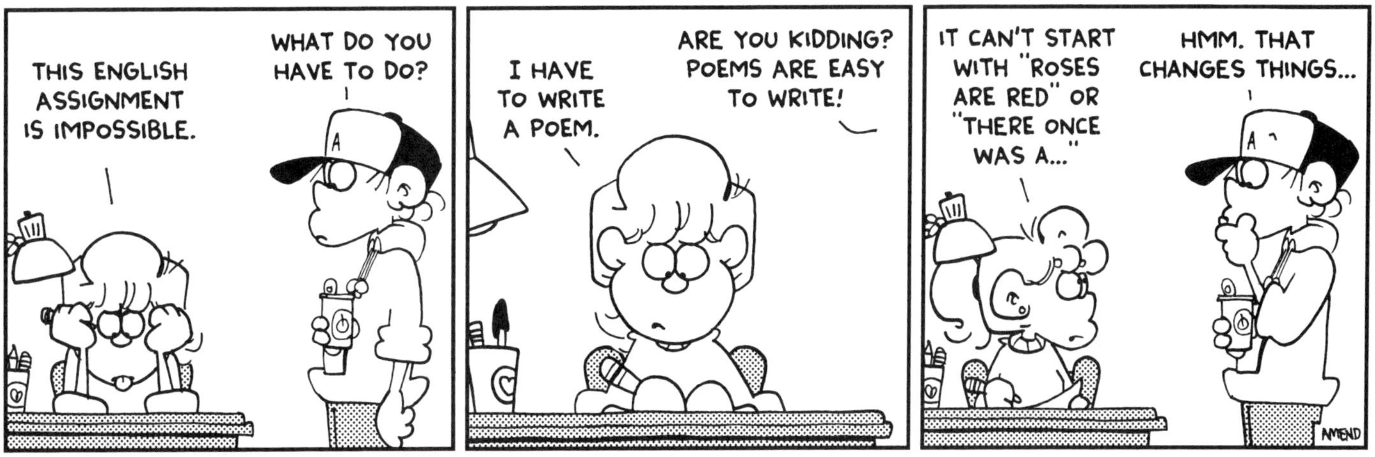
THIS ENGLISH ASSIGNMENT IS IMPOSSIBLE.
WHAT DO YOU HAVE TO DO?
I HAVE TO WRITE A POEM.
ARE YOU KIDDING? POEMS ARE EASY TO WRITE!
IT CAN'T START WITH "ROSES ARE RED" OR "THERE ONCE WAS A..."
HMM. THAT CHANGES THINGS...
AMEND

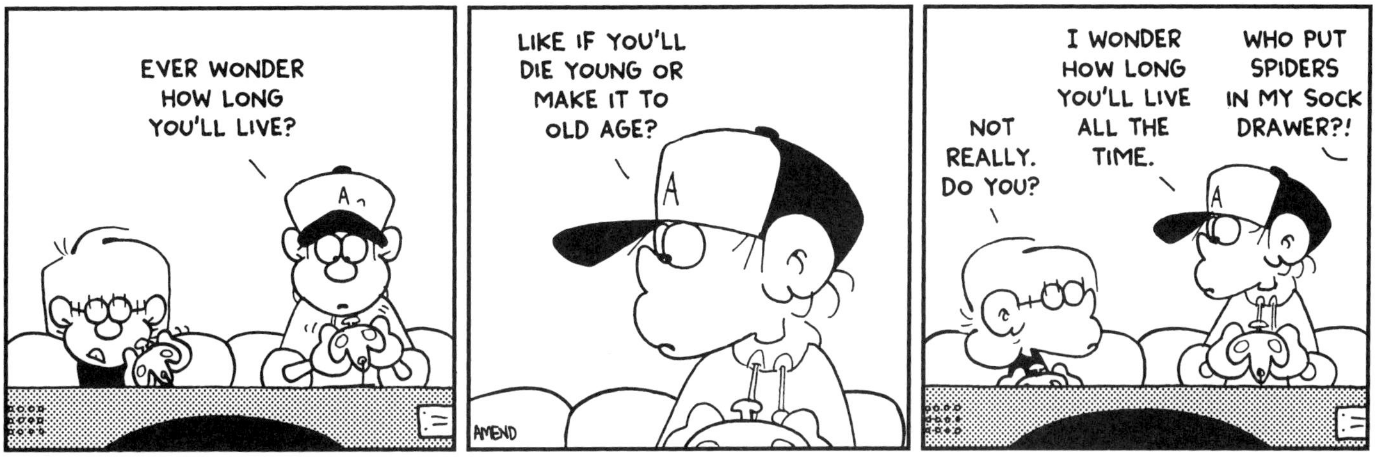
EVER WONDER HOW LONG YOU'LL LIVE?
LIKE IF YOU'LL DIE YOUNG OR MAKE IT TO OLD AGE?
AMEND
NOT REALLY. DO YOU?
I WONDER HOW LONG YOU'LL LIVE ALL THE TIME.
WHO PUT SPIDERS IN MY SOCK DRAWER?!

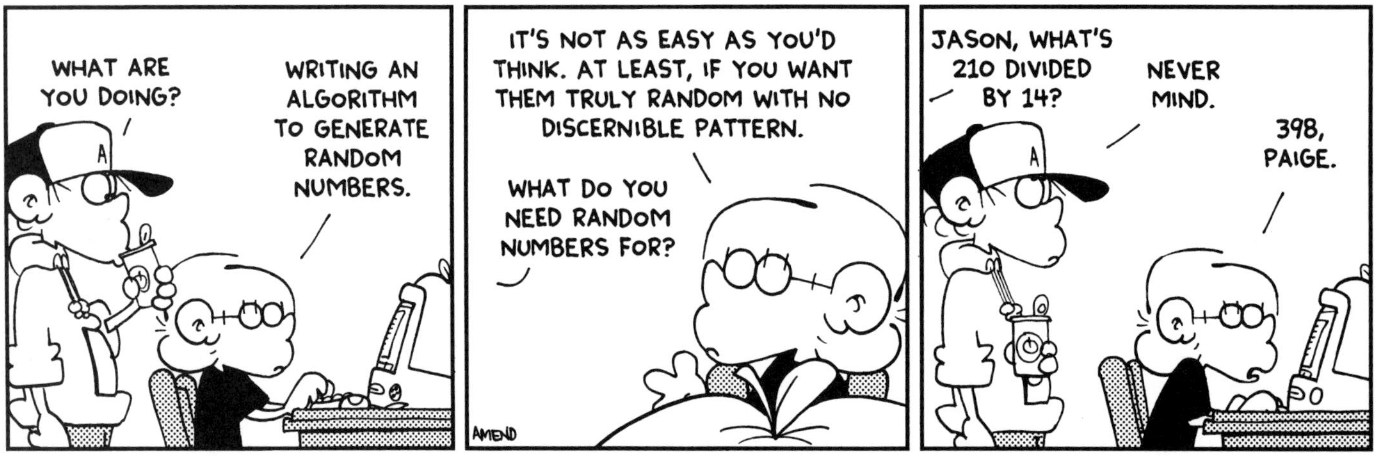
WHAT ARE YOU DOING?
WRITING AN ALGORITHM TO GENERATE RANDOM NUMBERS.
IT'S NOT AS EASY AS YOU'D THINK. AT LEAST, IF YOU WANT THEM TRULY RANDOM WITH NO DISCERNIBLE PATTERN.
WHAT DO YOU NEED RANDOM NUMBERS FOR?
JASON, WHAT'S 210 DIVIDED BY 14?
NEVER MIND.
398, PAIGE.
AMEND

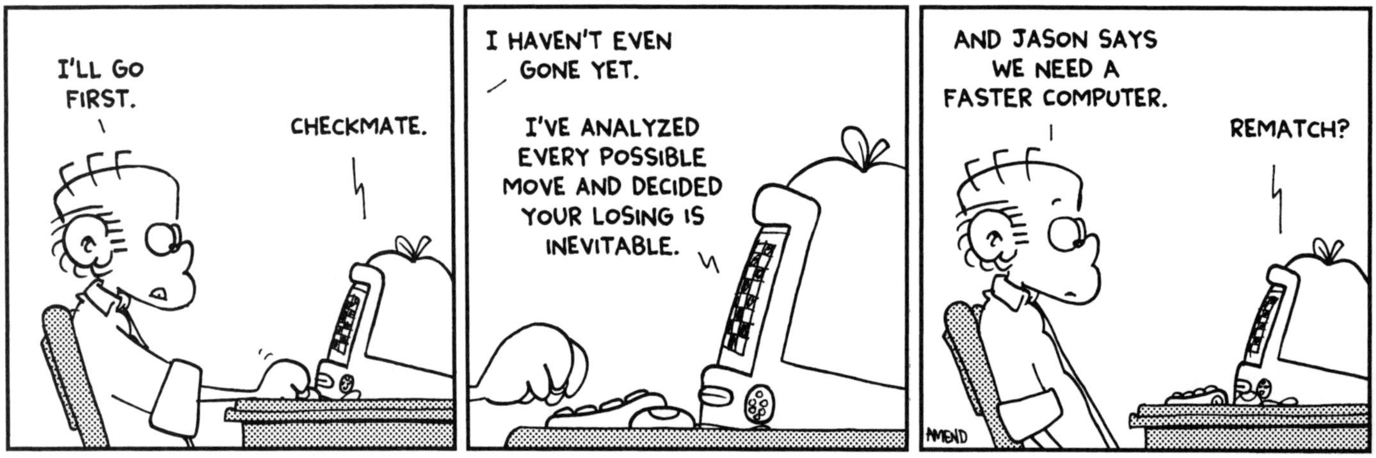
I'LL GO FIRST.
CHECKMATE.
I HAVEN'T EVEN GONE YET.
I'VE ANALYZED EVERY POSSIBLE MOVE AND DECIDED YOUR LOSING IS INEVITABLE.
AND JASON SAYS WE NEED A FASTER COMPUTER.
REMATCH?
AMEND

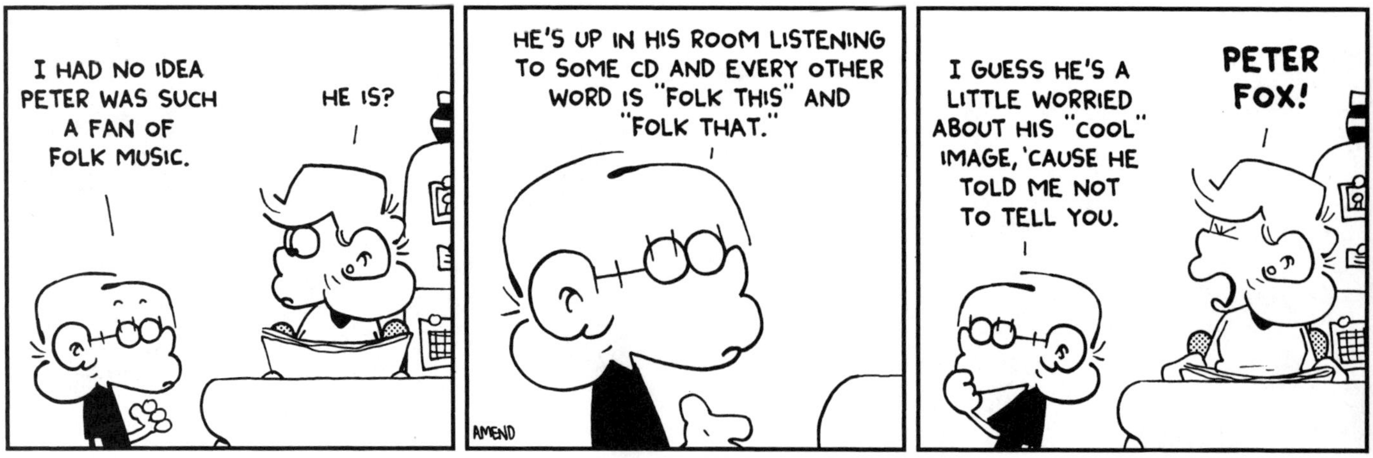
I HAD NO IDEA PETER WAS SUCH A FAN OF FOLK MUSIC.
HE IS?
HE'S UP IN HIS ROOM LISTENING TO SOME CD AND EVERY OTHER WORD IS "FOLK THIS" AND "FOLK THAT."
I GUESS HE'S A LITTLE WORRIED ABOUT HIS "COOL" IMAGE, 'CAUSE HE TOLD ME NOT TO TELL YOU.
PETER FOX!
AMEND

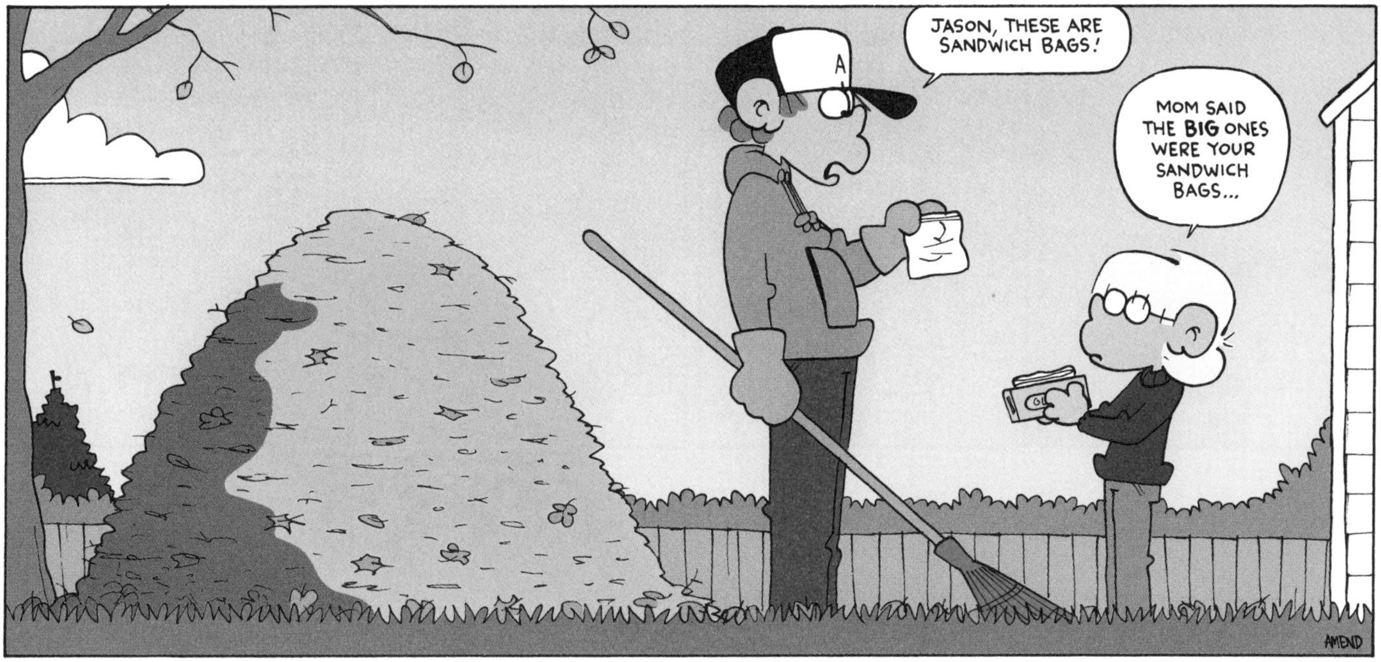
JASON, THESE ARE SANDWICH BAGS!
MOM SAID THE **BIG** ONES WERE YOUR SANDWICH BAGS...
AMEND

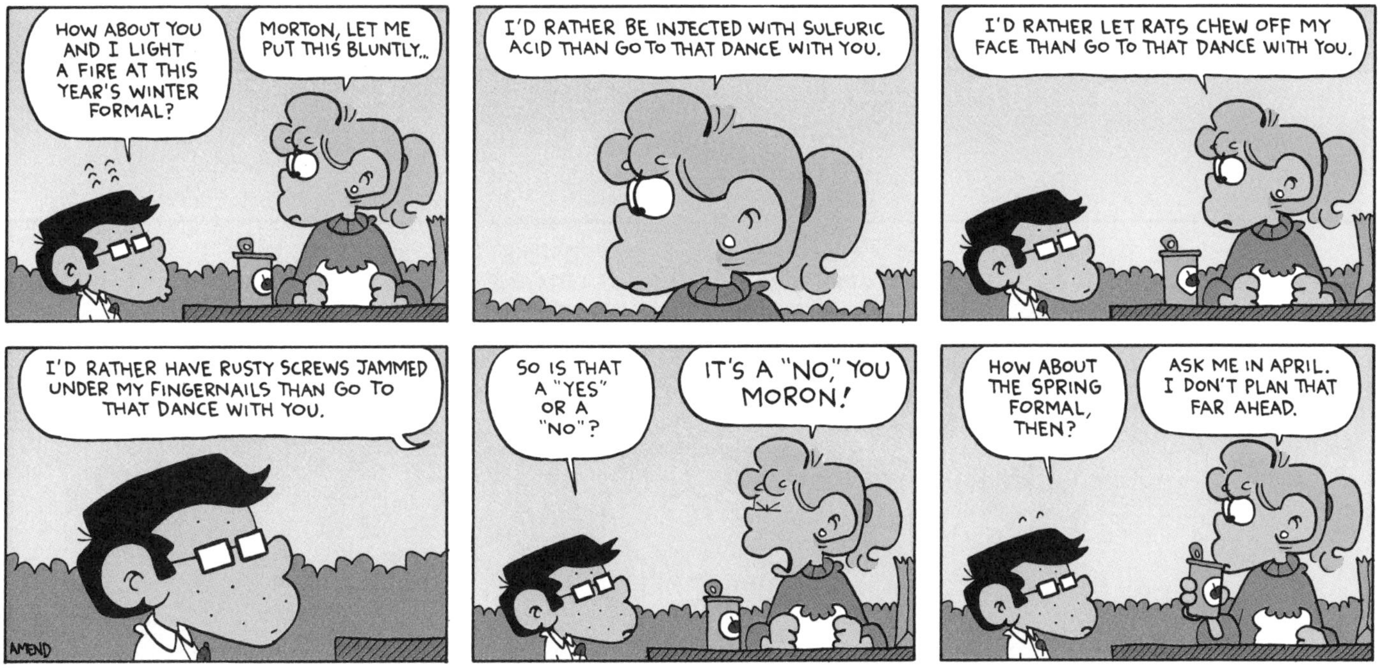
HOW ABOUT YOU AND I LIGHT A FIRE AT THIS YEAR'S WINTER FORMAL?
MORTON, LET ME PUT THIS BLUNTLY...
I'D RATHER BE INJECTED WITH SULFURIC ACID THAN GO TO THAT DANCE WITH YOU.
I'D RATHER LET RATS CHEW OFF MY FACE THAN GO TO THAT DANCE WITH YOU.
I'D RATHER HAVE RUSTY SCREWS JAMMED UNDER MY FINGERNAILS THAN GO TO THAT DANCE WITH YOU.
AMEND
SO IS THAT A "YES" OR A "NO"?
IT'S A "NO," YOU MORON!
HOW ABOUT THE SPRING FORMAL, THEN?
ASK ME IN APRIL. I DON'T PLAN THAT FAR AHEAD.

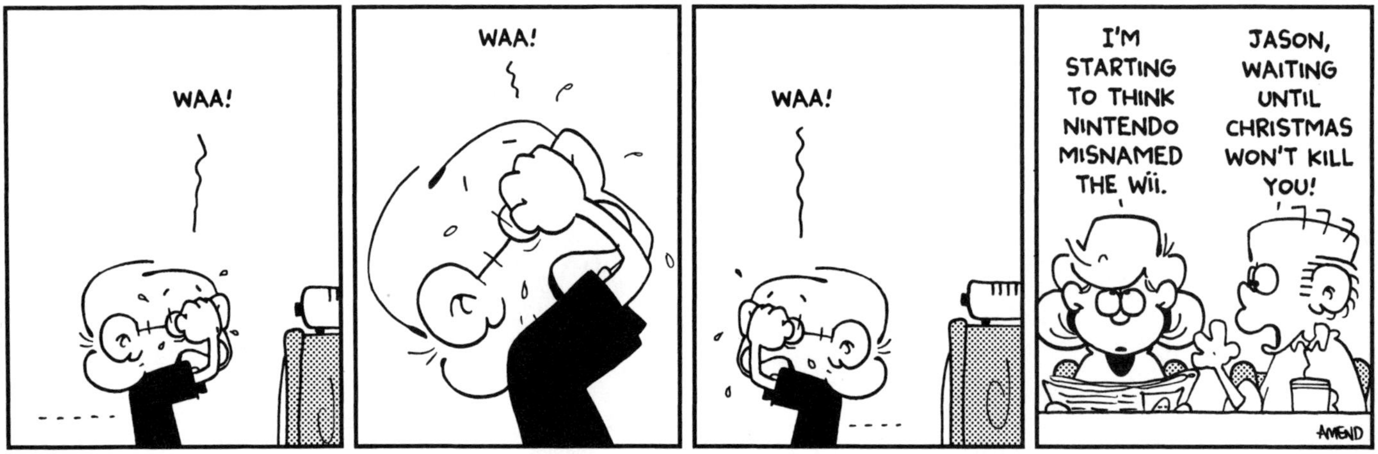
WAA!
WAA!
WAA!
I'M STARTING TO THINK NINTENDO MISNAMED THE Wii.
JASON, WAITING UNTIL CHRISTMAS WON'T KILL YOU!
AMEND

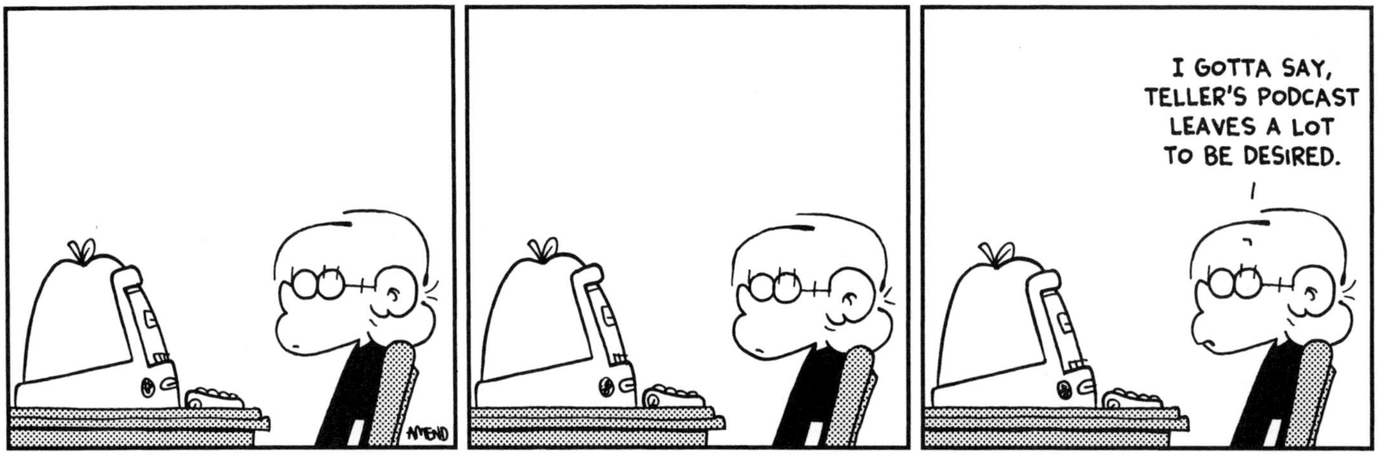
AMEND
I GOTTA SAY, TELLER'S PODCAST LEAVES A LOT TO BE DESIRED.

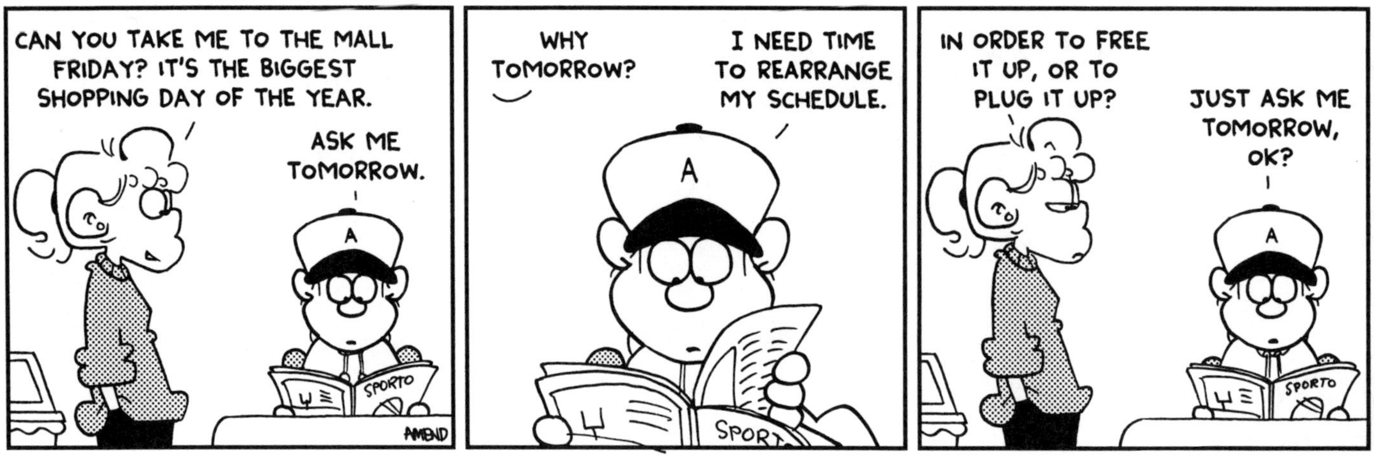
CAN YOU TAKE ME TO THE MALL FRIDAY? IT'S THE BIGGEST SHOPPING DAY OF THE YEAR.
ASK ME TOMORROW.
SPORTO
AMEND
WHY TOMORROW?
I NEED TIME TO REARRANGE MY SCHEDULE.
IN ORDER TO FREE IT UP, OR TO PLUG IT UP?
JUST ASK ME TOMORROW, OK?
SPORTO

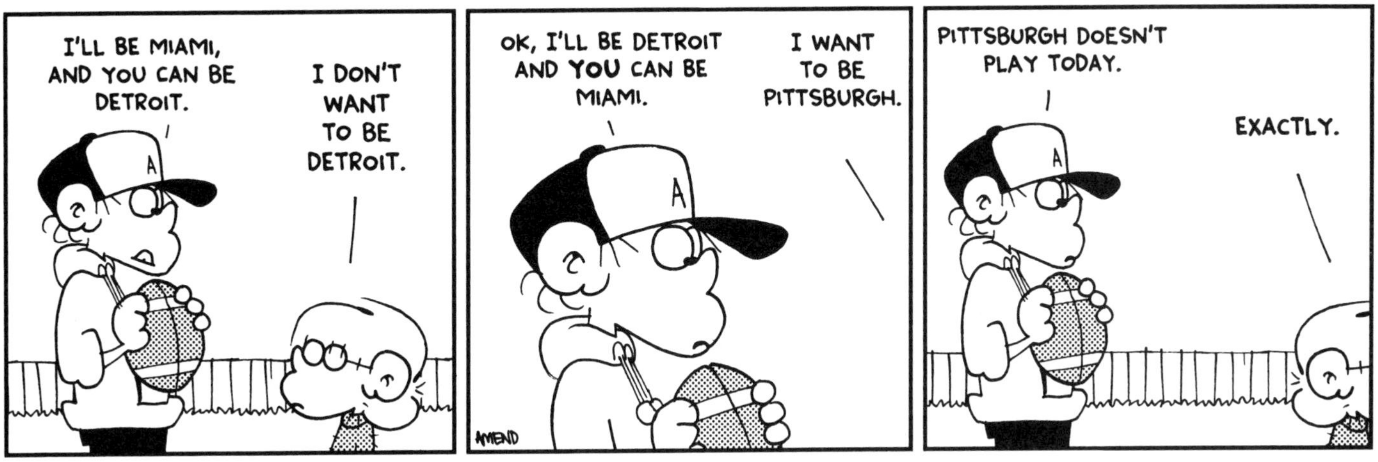
I'LL BE MIAMI, AND YOU CAN BE DETROIT.
I DON'T WANT TO BE DETROIT.
OK, I'LL BE DETROIT AND YOU CAN BE MIAMI.
I WANT TO BE PITTSBURGH.
PITTSBURGH DOESN'T PLAY TODAY.
EXACTLY.
AMEND

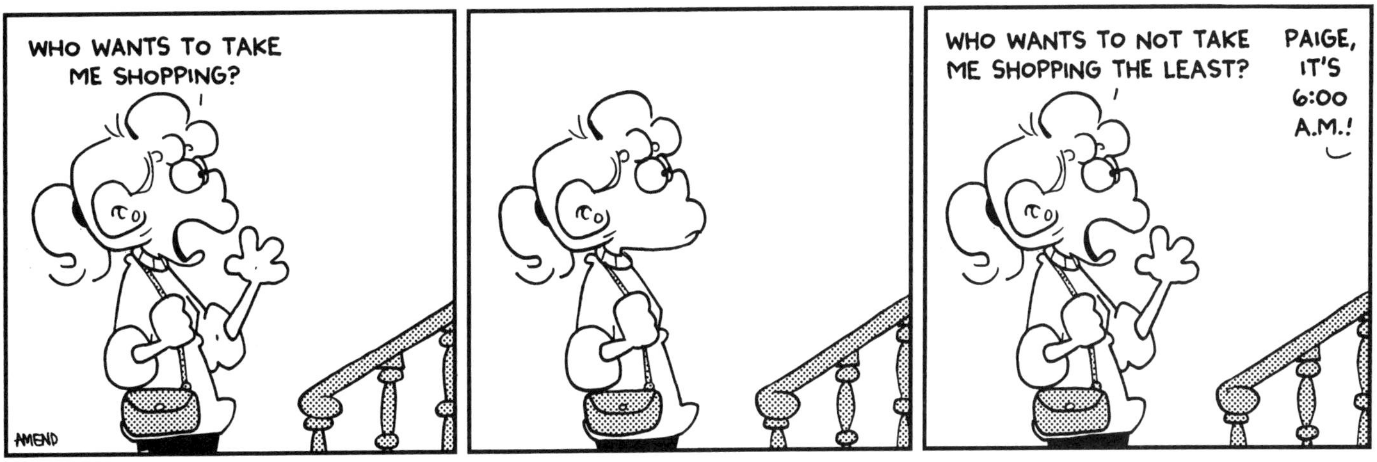
WHO WANTS TO TAKE ME SHOPPING?
AMEND
WHO WANTS TO NOT TAKE ME SHOPPING THE LEAST?
PAIGE, IT'S 6:00 A.M.!

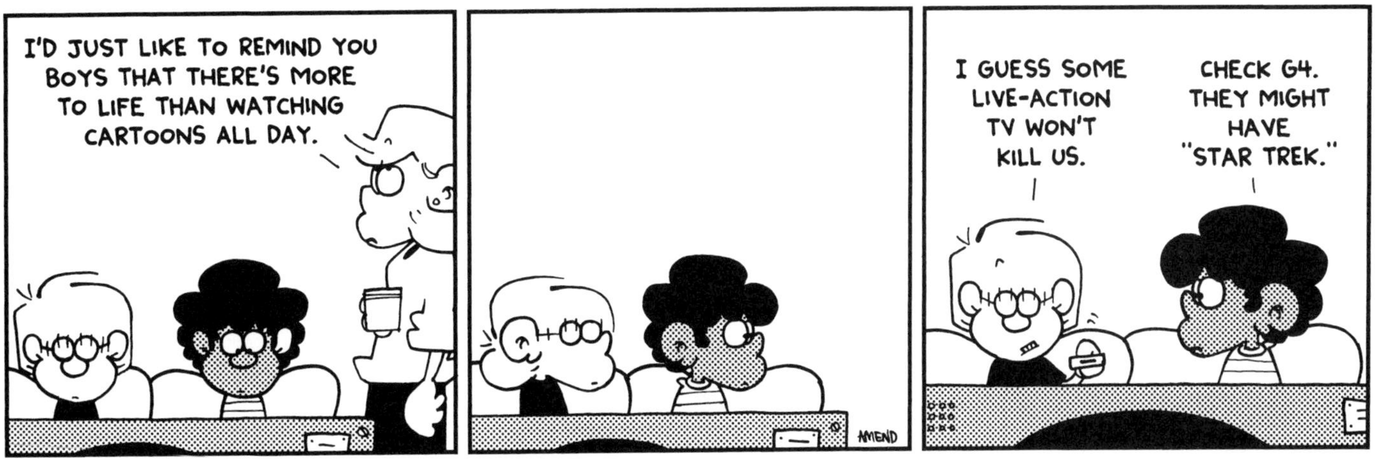
I'D JUST LIKE TO REMIND YOU BOYS THAT THERE'S MORE TO LIFE THAN WATCHING CARTOONS ALL DAY.
AMEND
I GUESS SOME LIVE-ACTION TV WON'T KILL US.
CHECK G4. THEY MIGHT HAVE "STAR TREK."

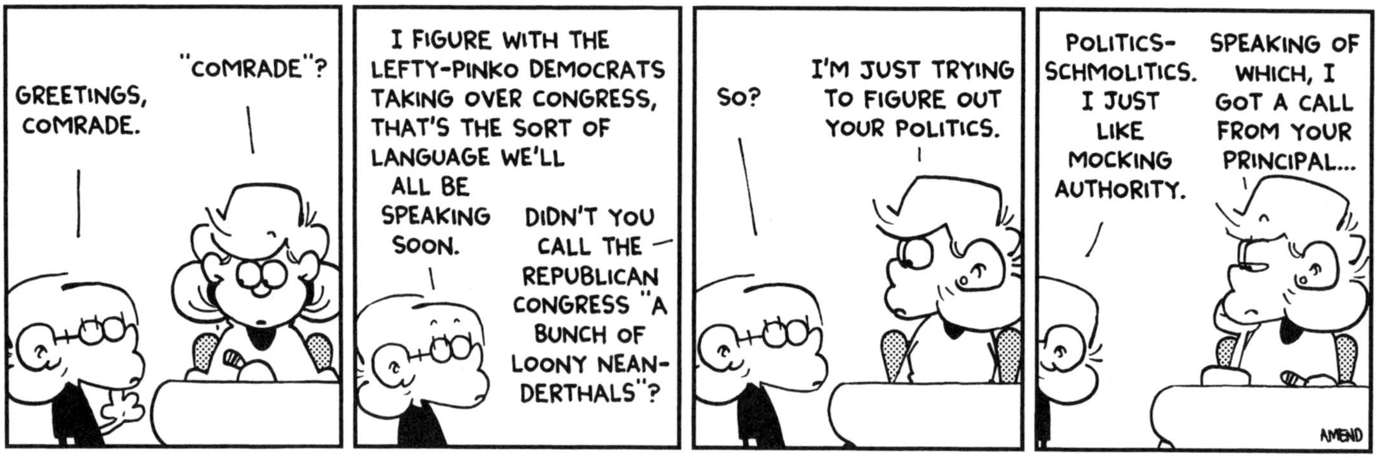
GREETINGS, COMRADE.
"COMRADE"?
I FIGURE WITH THE LEFTY-PINKO DEMOCRATS TAKING OVER CONGRESS, THAT'S THE SORT OF LANGUAGE WE'LL ALL BE SPEAKING SOON.
DIDN'T YOU CALL THE REPUBLICAN CONGRESS "A BUNCH OF LOONY NEANDERTHALS"?
SO?
I'M JUST TRYING TO FIGURE OUT YOUR POLITICS.
POLITICS-SCHMOLITICS. I JUST LIKE MOCKING AUTHORITY.
SPEAKING OF WHICH, I GOT A CALL FROM YOUR PRINCIPAL...
AMEND

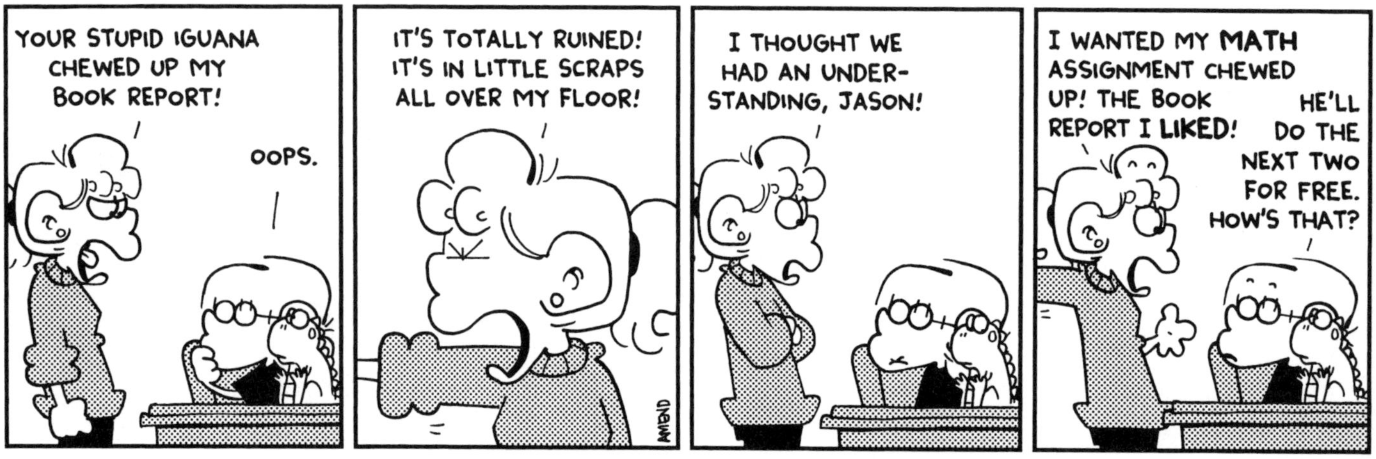
YOUR STUPID IGUANA CHEWED UP MY BOOK REPORT!
OOPS.
IT'S TOTALLY RUINED! IT'S IN LITTLE SCRAPS ALL OVER MY FLOOR!
AMEND
I THOUGHT WE HAD AN UNDER-STANDING, JASON!
I WANTED MY **MATH** ASSIGNMENT CHEWED UP! THE BOOK REPORT I **LIKED**!
HE'LL DO THE NEXT TWO FOR FREE. HOW'S THAT?

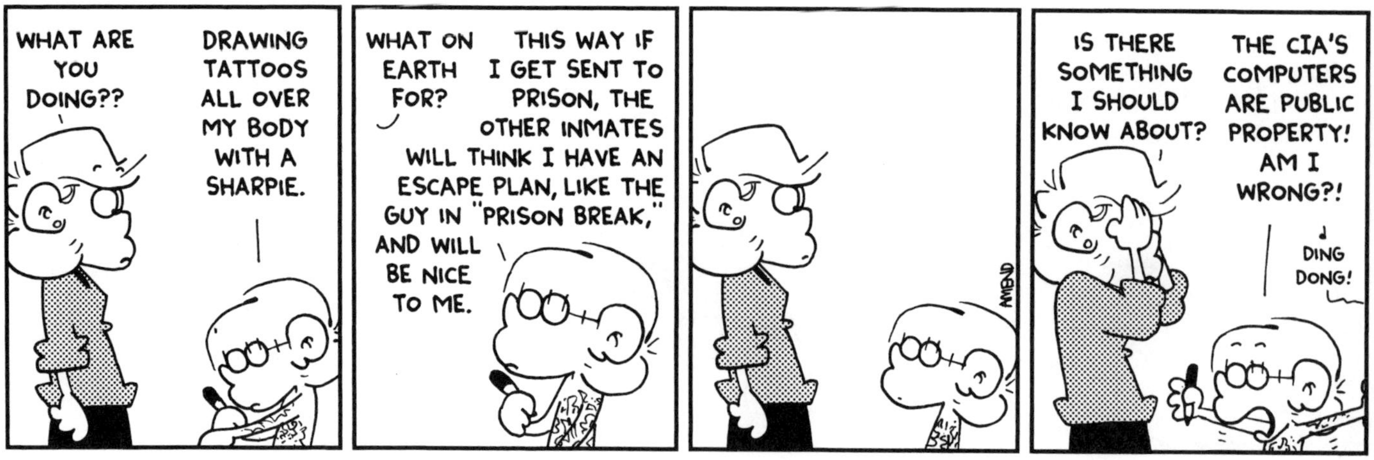
WHAT ARE YOU DOING??
DRAWING TATTOOS ALL OVER MY BODY WITH A SHARPIE.
WHAT ON EARTH FOR?
THIS WAY IF I GET SENT TO PRISON, THE OTHER INMATES WILL THINK I HAVE AN ESCAPE PLAN, LIKE THE GUY IN "PRISON BREAK," AND WILL BE NICE TO ME.
AMEND
IS THERE SOMETHING I SHOULD KNOW ABOUT?
THE CIA'S COMPUTERS ARE PUBLIC PROPERTY! AM I WRONG?!
DING DONG!

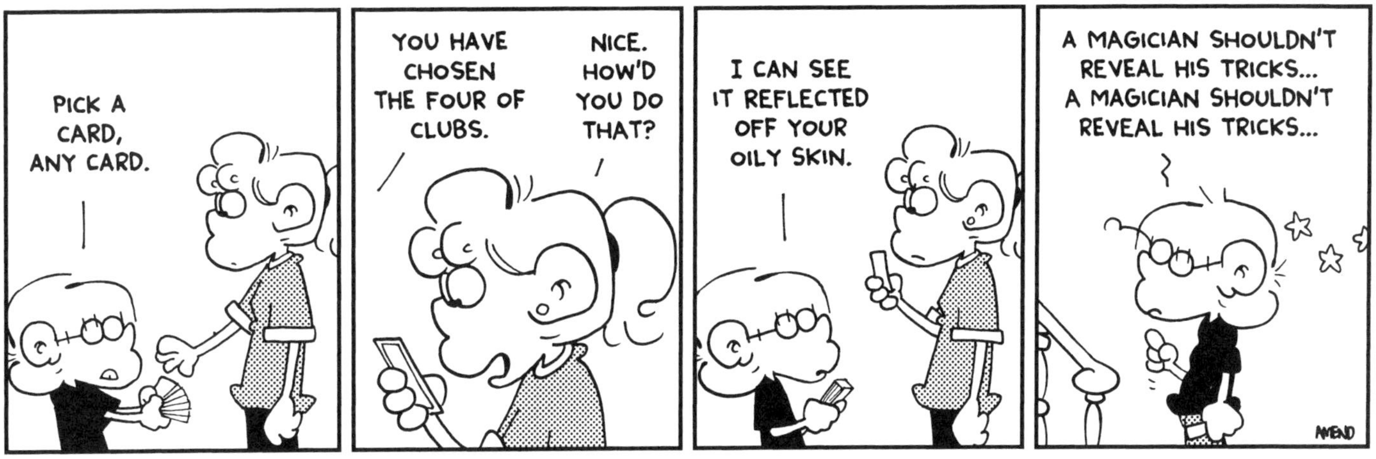
PICK A CARD, ANY CARD.
YOU HAVE CHOSEN THE FOUR OF CLUBS.
NICE. HOW'D YOU DO THAT?
I CAN SEE IT REFLECTED OFF YOUR OILY SKIN.
A MAGICIAN SHOULDN'T REVEAL HIS TRICKS... A MAGICIAN SHOULDN'T REVEAL HIS TRICKS...
AMEND

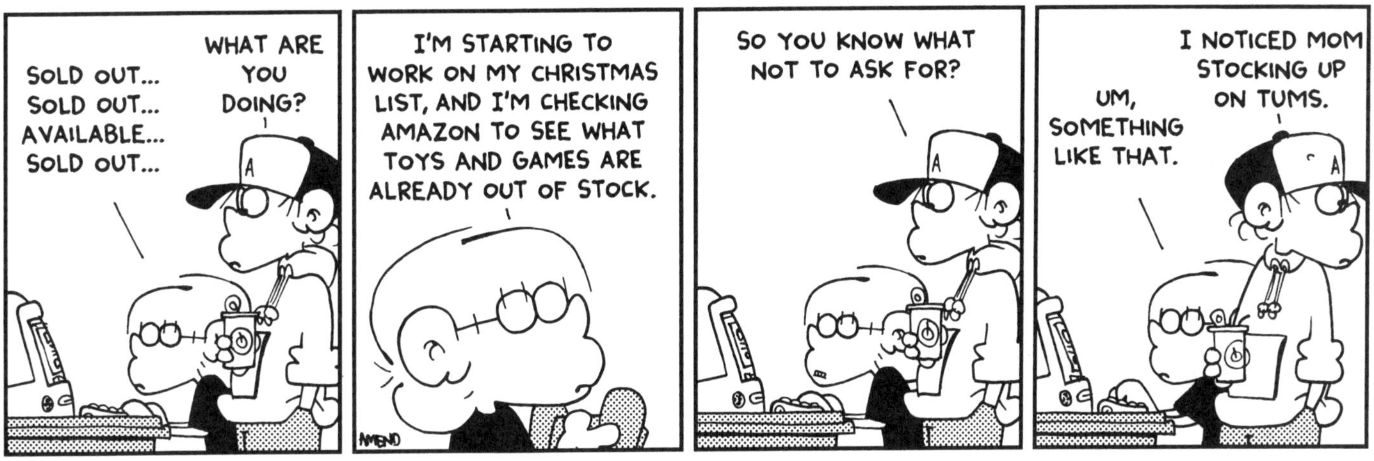
SOLD OUT... SOLD OUT... AVAILABLE... SOLD OUT...
WHAT ARE YOU DOING?
I'M STARTING TO WORK ON MY CHRISTMAS LIST, AND I'M CHECKING AMAZON TO SEE WHAT TOYS AND GAMES ARE ALREADY OUT OF STOCK.
AMEND
SO YOU KNOW WHAT NOT TO ASK FOR?
UM, SOMETHING LIKE THAT.
I NOTICED MOM STOCKING UP ON TUMS.

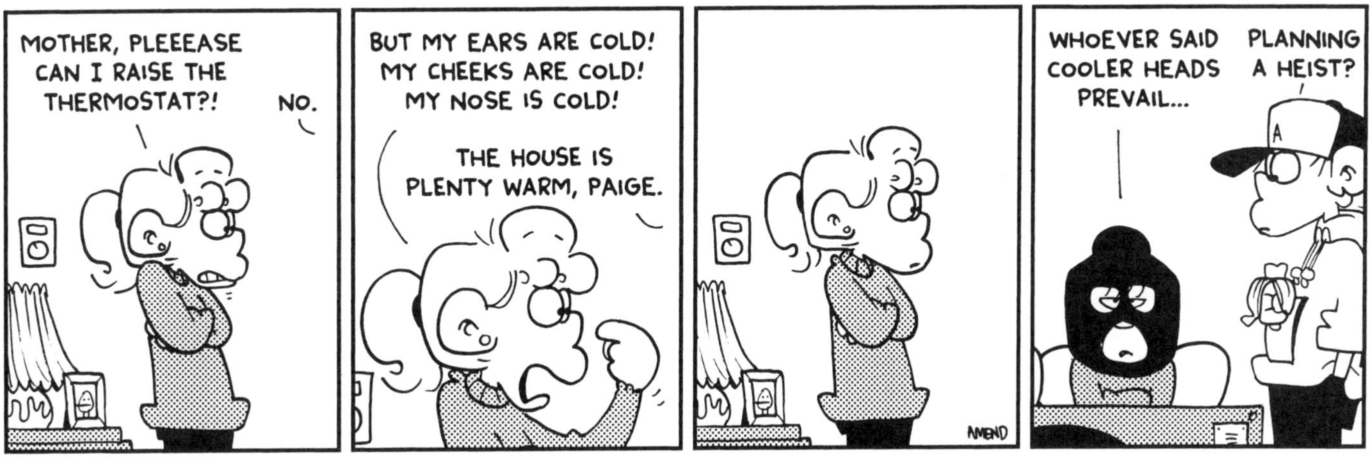
MOTHER, PLEEEASE CAN I RAISE THE THERMOSTAT?!
NO.
BUT MY EARS ARE COLD! MY CHEEKS ARE COLD! MY NOSE IS COLD!
THE HOUSE IS PLENTY WARM, PAIGE.
AMEND
WHOEVER SAID COOLER HEADS PREVAIL...
PLANNING A HEIST?

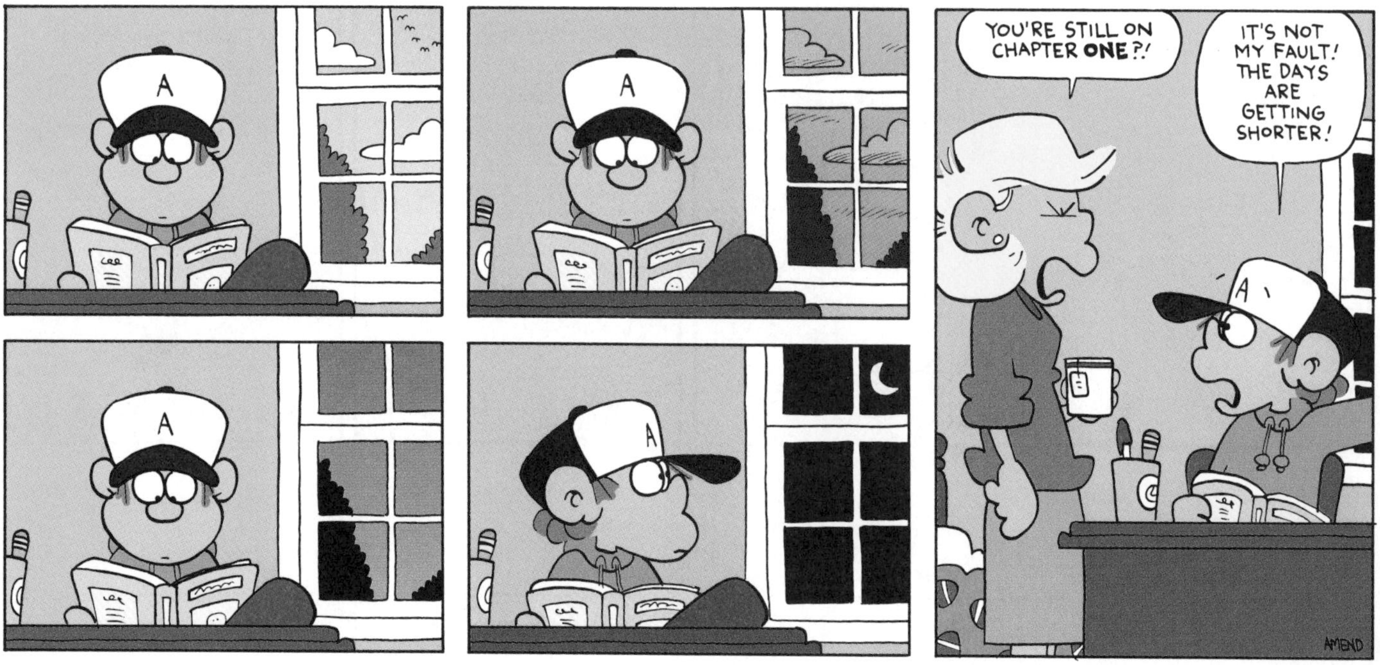
YOU'RE STILL ON CHAPTER ONE?!
IT'S NOT MY FAULT! THE DAYS ARE GETTING SHORTER!
AMEND

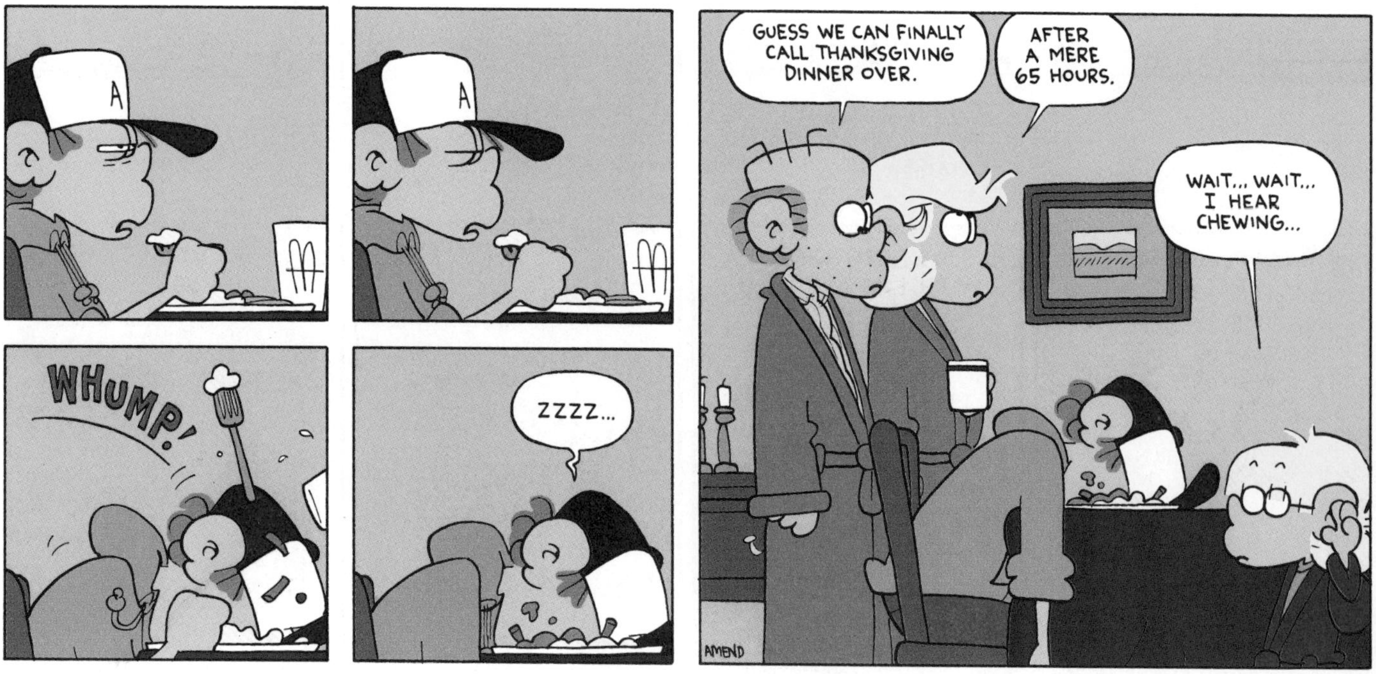
WHUMP!
ZZZZ...
GUESS WE CAN FINALLY CALL THANKSGIVING DINNER OVER.
AFTER A MERE 65 HOURS.
WAIT... WAIT... I HEAR CHEWING...
AMEND

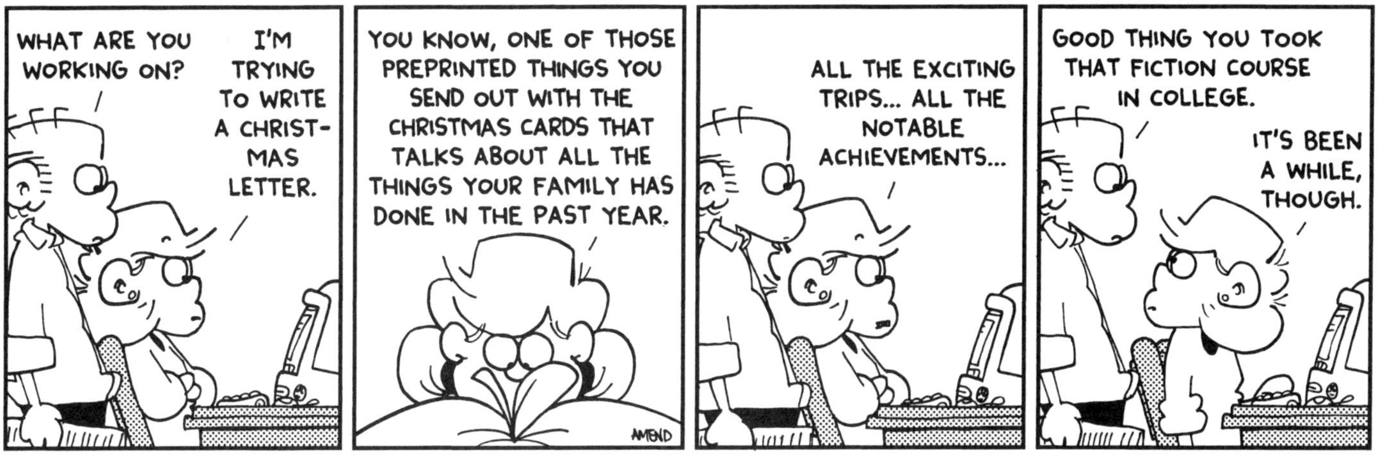
WHAT ARE YOU WORKING ON?
I'M TRYING TO WRITE A CHRIST-MAS LETTER.
YOU KNOW, ONE OF THOSE PREPRINTED THINGS YOU SEND OUT WITH THE CHRISTMAS CARDS THAT TALKS ABOUT ALL THE THINGS YOUR FAMILY HAS DONE IN THE PAST YEAR.
AMEND
ALL THE EXCITING TRIPS... ALL THE NOTABLE ACHIEVEMENTS...
GOOD THING YOU TOOK THAT FICTION COURSE IN COLLEGE.
IT'S BEEN A WHILE, THOUGH.

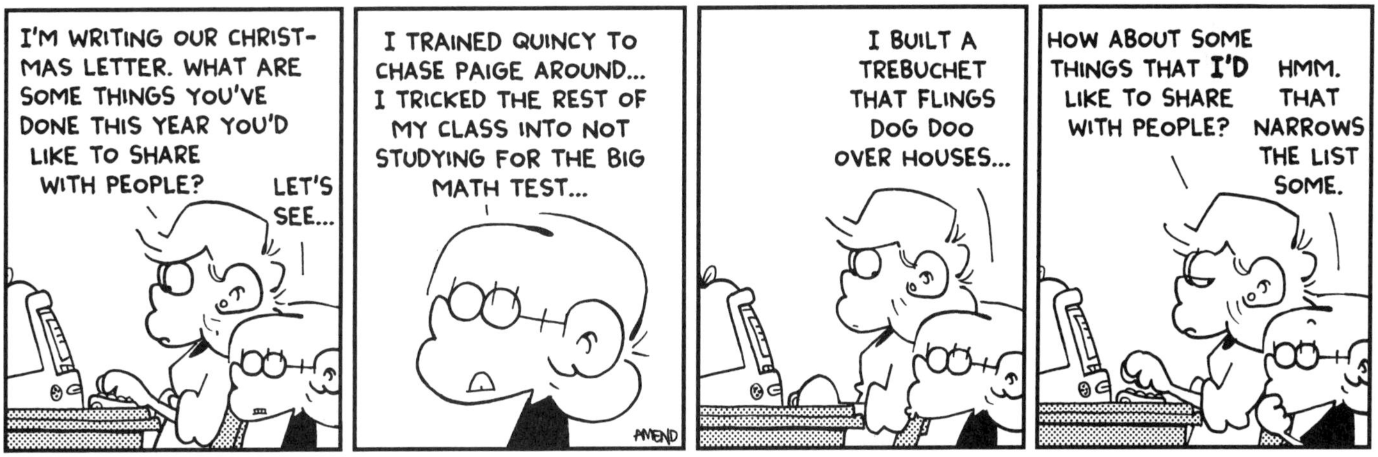
I'M WRITING OUR CHRIST-MAS LETTER. WHAT ARE SOME THINGS YOU'VE DONE THIS YEAR YOU'D LIKE TO SHARE WITH PEOPLE?
LET'S SEE...
I TRAINED QUINCY TO CHASE PAIGE AROUND... I TRICKED THE REST OF MY CLASS INTO NOT STUDYING FOR THE BIG MATH TEST...
AMEND
I BUILT A TREBUCHET THAT FLINGS DOG DOO OVER HOUSES...
HOW ABOUT SOME THINGS THAT **I'D** LIKE TO SHARE WITH PEOPLE?
HMM. THAT NARROWS THE LIST SOME.

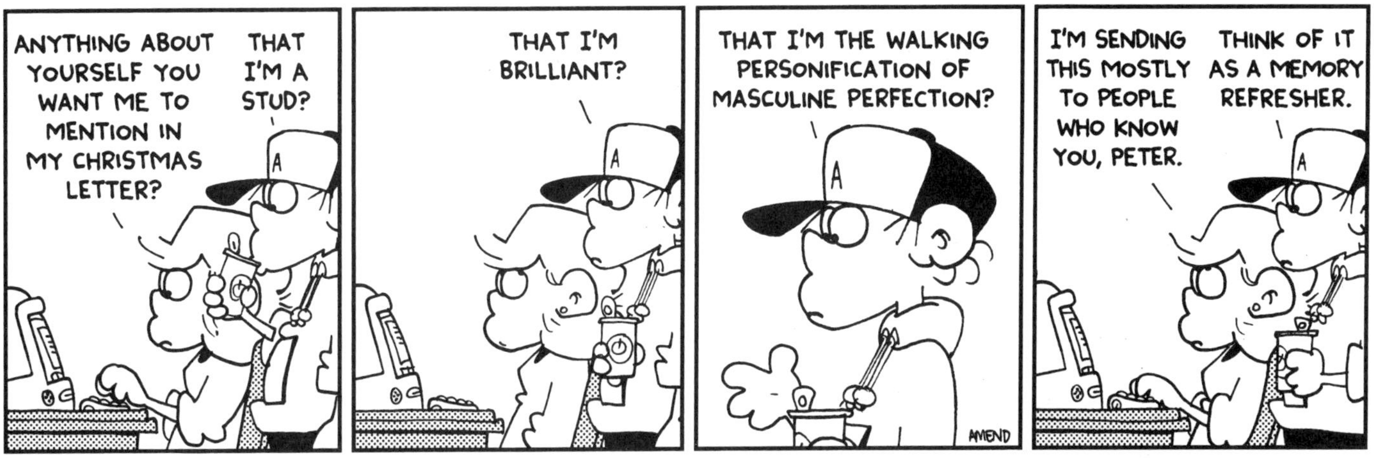
ANYTHING ABOUT YOURSELF YOU WANT ME TO MENTION IN MY CHRISTMAS LETTER?
THAT I'M A STUD?
THAT I'M BRILLIANT?
THAT I'M THE WALKING PERSONIFICATION OF MASCULINE PERFECTION?
AMEND
I'M SENDING THIS MOSTLY TO PEOPLE WHO KNOW YOU, PETER.
THINK OF IT AS A MEMORY REFRESHER.

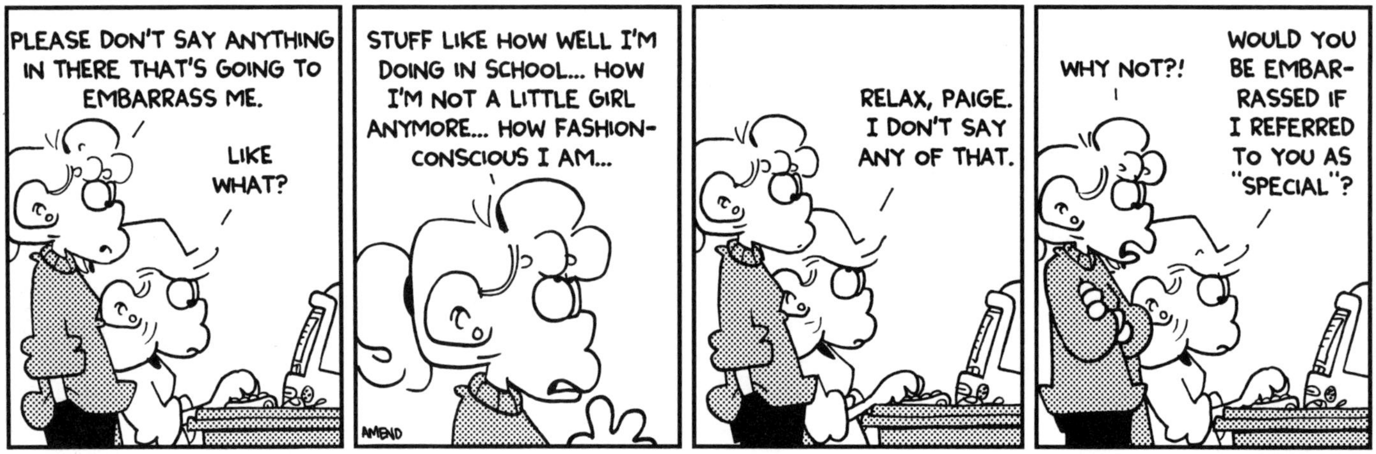
PLEASE DON'T SAY ANYTHING IN THERE THAT'S GOING TO EMBARRASS ME.
LIKE WHAT?
STUFF LIKE HOW WELL I'M DOING IN SCHOOL... HOW I'M NOT A LITTLE GIRL ANYMORE... HOW FASHION-CONSCIOUS I AM...
AMEND
RELAX, PAIGE. I DON'T SAY ANY OF THAT.
WHY NOT?!
WOULD YOU BE EMBARRASSED IF I REFERRED TO YOU AS "SPECIAL"?

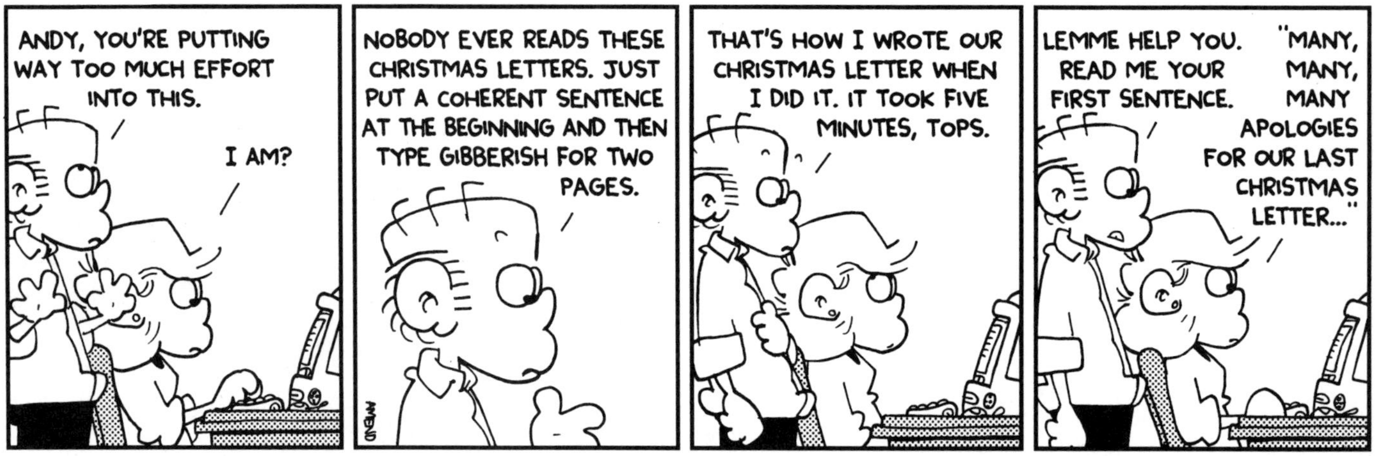
ANDY, YOU'RE PUTTING WAY TOO MUCH EFFORT INTO THIS.
I AM?
NOBODY EVER READS THESE CHRISTMAS LETTERS. JUST PUT A COHERENT SENTENCE AT THE BEGINNING AND THEN TYPE GIBBERISH FOR TWO PAGES.
AMEND
THAT'S HOW I WROTE OUR CHRISTMAS LETTER WHEN I DID IT. IT TOOK FIVE MINUTES, TOPS.
LEMME HELP YOU. READ ME YOUR FIRST SENTENCE.
"MANY, MANY, MANY APOLOGIES FOR OUR LAST CHRISTMAS LETTER..."

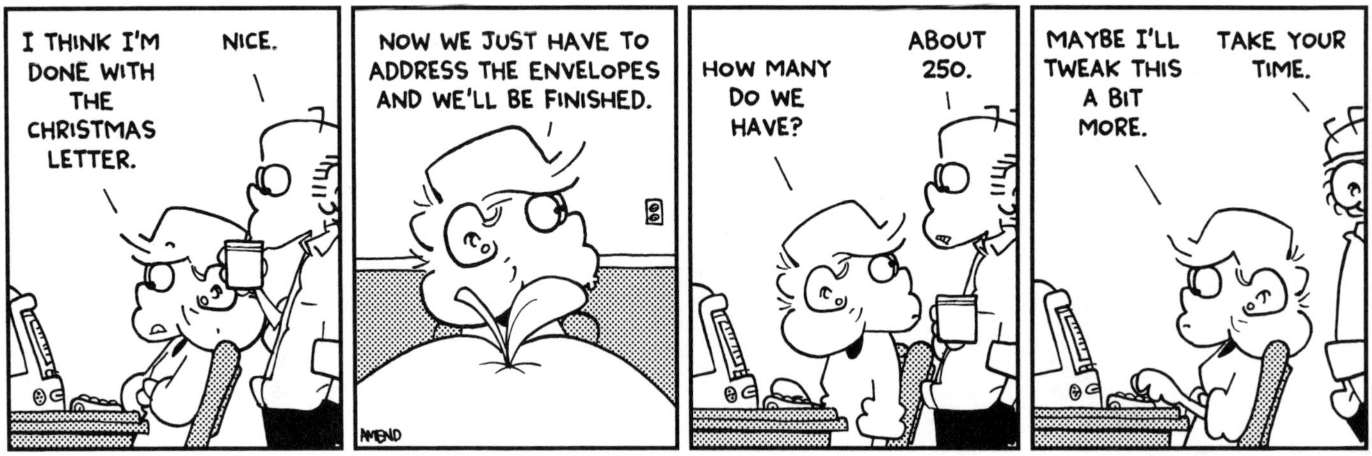
I THINK I'M DONE WITH THE CHRISTMAS LETTER.
NICE.
NOW WE JUST HAVE TO ADDRESS THE ENVELOPES AND WE'LL BE FINISHED.
AMEND
HOW MANY DO WE HAVE?
ABOUT 250.
MAYBE I'LL TWEAK THIS A BIT MORE.
TAKE YOUR TIME.

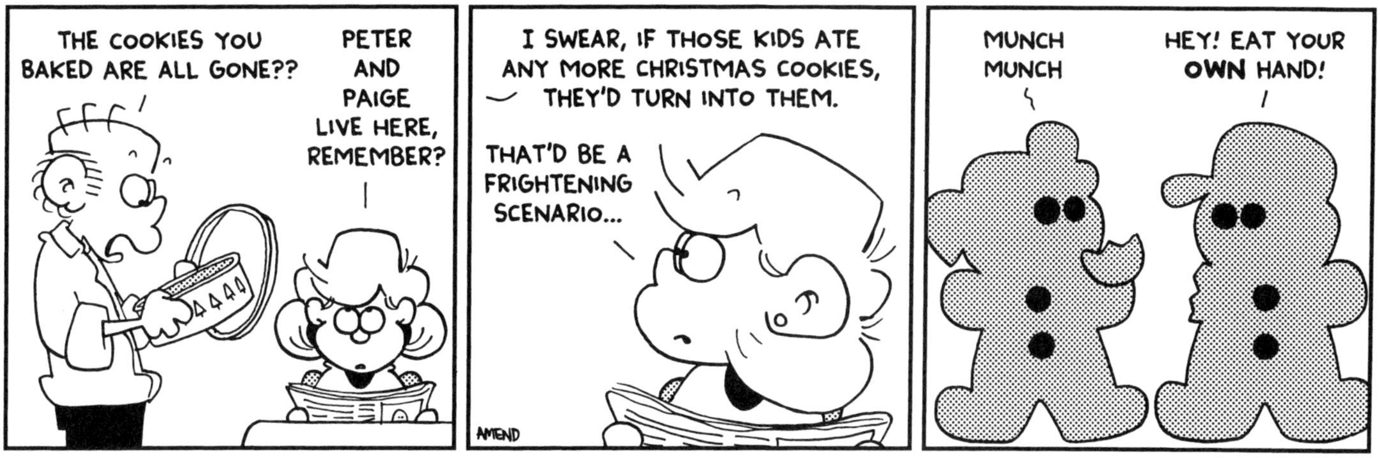
THE COOKIES YOU BAKED ARE ALL GONE??
PETER AND PAIGE LIVE HERE, REMEMBER?
I SWEAR, IF THOSE KIDS ATE ANY MORE CHRISTMAS COOKIES, THEY'D TURN INTO THEM.
THAT'D BE A FRIGHTENING SCENARIO...
AMEND
MUNCH MUNCH
HEY! EAT YOUR **OWN** HAND!

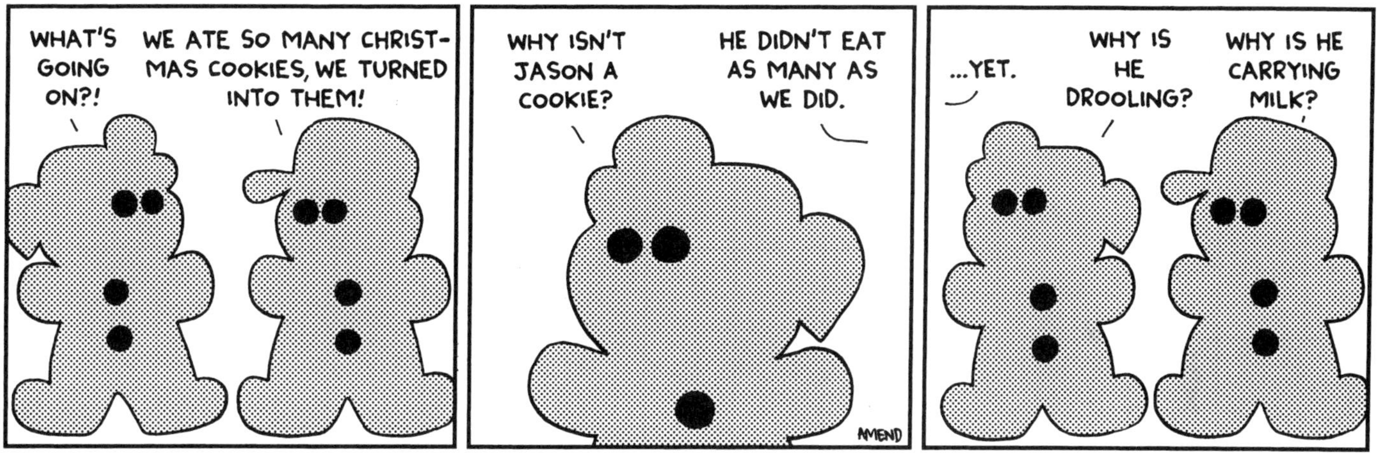
WHAT'S GOING ON?!
WE ATE SO MANY CHRIST-MAS COOKIES, WE TURNED INTO THEM!
WHY ISN'T JASON A COOKIE?
HE DIDN'T EAT AS MANY AS WE DID.
AMEND
...YET.
WHY IS HE DROOLING?
WHY IS HE CARRYING MILK?

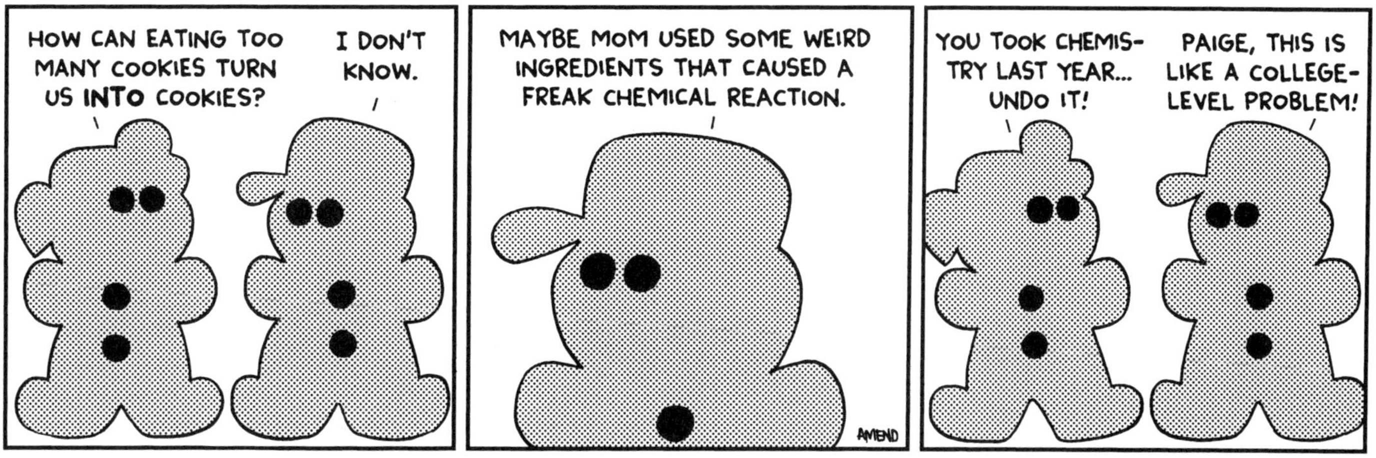
HOW CAN EATING TOO MANY COOKIES TURN US **INTO** COOKIES?
I DON'T KNOW.
MAYBE MOM USED SOME WEIRD INGREDIENTS THAT CAUSED A FREAK CHEMICAL REACTION.
AMEND
YOU TOOK CHEMIS-TRY LAST YEAR... UNDO IT!
PAIGE, THIS IS LIKE A COLLEGE-LEVEL PROBLEM!

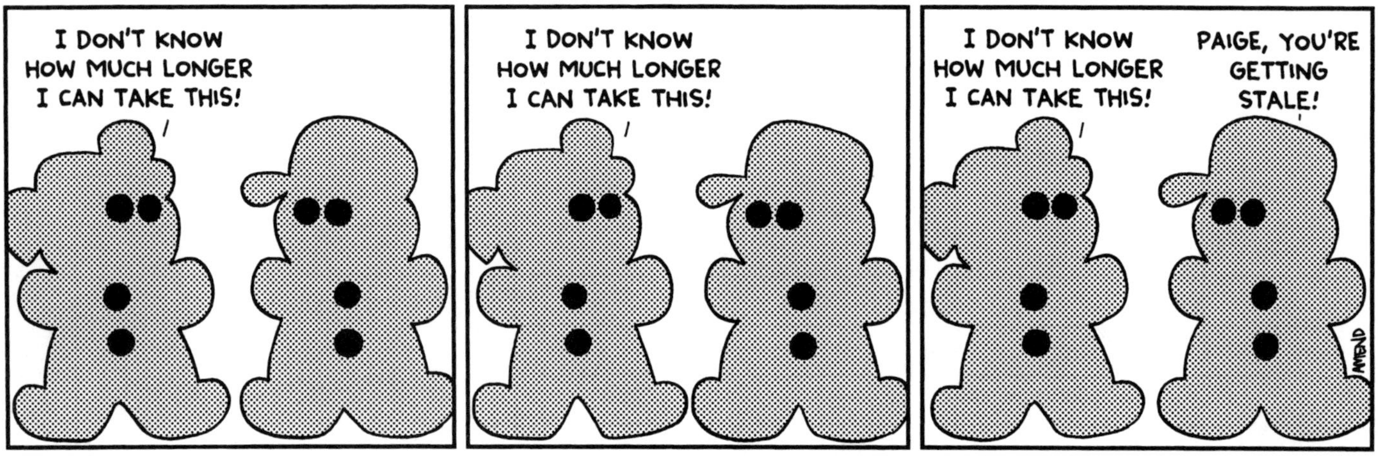
I DON'T KNOW HOW MUCH LONGER I CAN TAKE THIS!
I DON'T KNOW HOW MUCH LONGER I CAN TAKE THIS!
I DON'T KNOW HOW MUCH LONGER I CAN TAKE THIS!
PAIGE, YOU'RE GETTING STALE!
AMEND

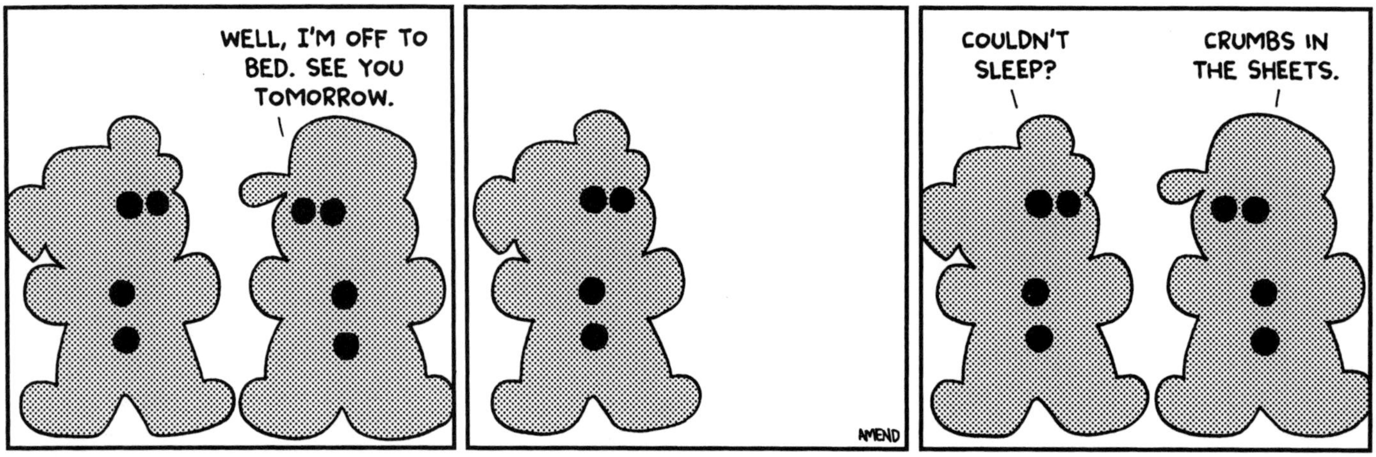
WELL, I'M OFF TO BED. SEE YOU TOMORROW.
AMEND
COULDN'T SLEEP?
CRUMBS IN THE SHEETS.

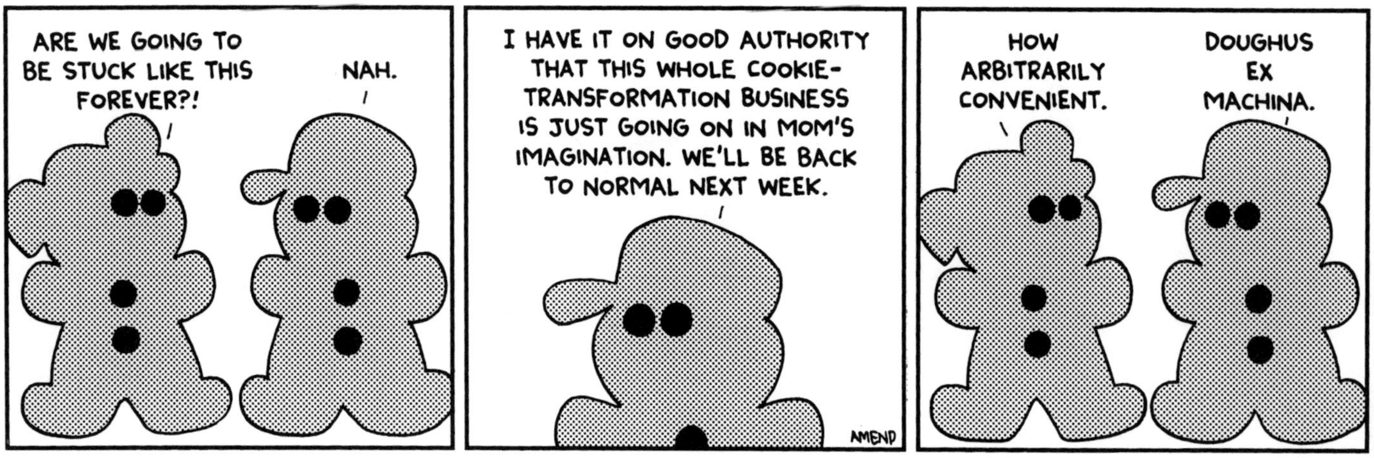
ARE WE GOING TO BE STUCK LIKE THIS FOREVER?!
NAH.
I HAVE IT ON GOOD AUTHORITY THAT THIS WHOLE COOKIE-TRANSFORMATION BUSINESS IS JUST GOING ON IN MOM'S IMAGINATION. WE'LL BE BACK TO NORMAL NEXT WEEK.
AMEND
HOW ARBITRARILY CONVENIENT.
DOUGHUS EX MACHINA.

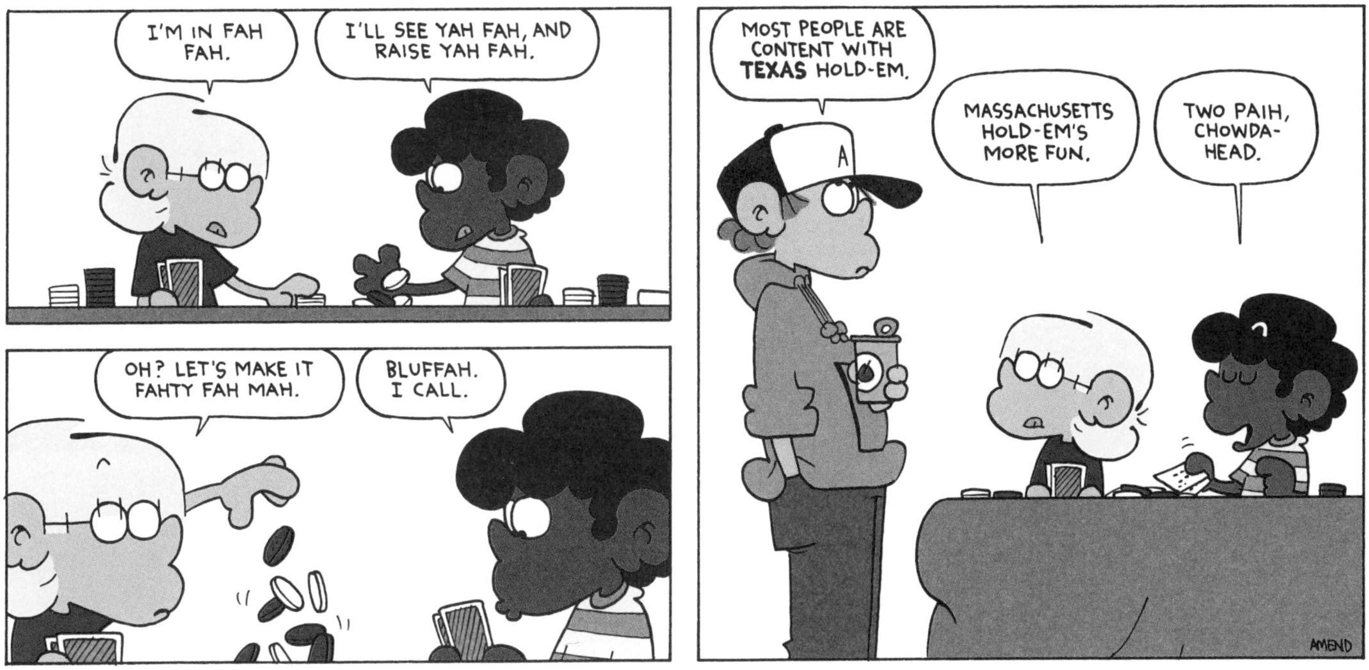
I'M IN FAH FAH.
I'LL SEE YAH FAH, AND RAISE YAH FAH.
OH? LET'S MAKE IT FAHTY FAH MAH.
BLUFFAH. I CALL.
MOST PEOPLE ARE CONTENT WITH **TEXAS** HOLD-EM.
MASSACHUSETTS HOLD-EM'S MORE FUN.
TWO PAIH, CHOWDA-HEAD.
AMEND

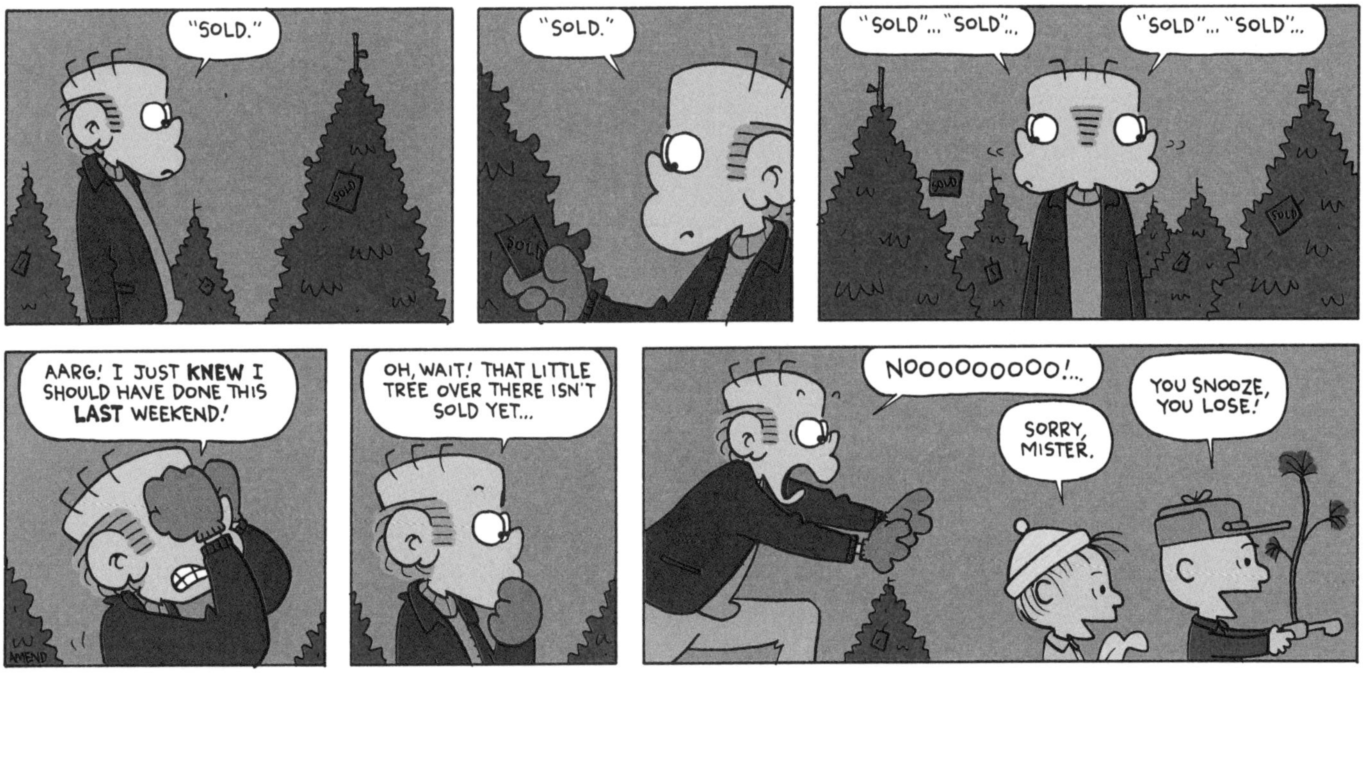
"SOLD."
"SOLD."
"SOLD"..."SOLD"...
"SOLD"..."SOLD"...
AARG! I JUST **KNEW** I SHOULD HAVE DONE THIS **LAST** WEEKEND!
AMEND
OH, WAIT! THAT LITTLE TREE OVER THERE ISN'T SOLD YET...
NOOOOOOOOO!...
SORRY, MISTER.
YOU SNOOZE, YOU LOSE!

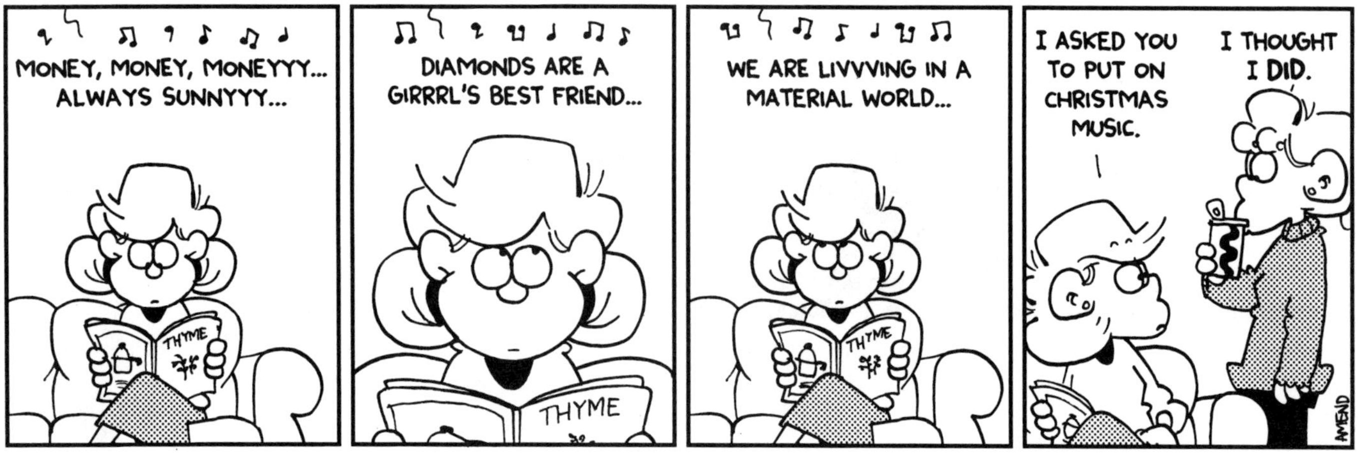
MONEY, MONEY, MONEYYY... ALWAYS SUNNYYY...
DIAMONDS ARE A GIRRRL'S BEST FRIEND...
WE ARE LIVVVING IN A MATERIAL WORLD...
I ASKED YOU TO PUT ON CHRISTMAS MUSIC.
I THOUGHT I DID.
THYME
AMEND

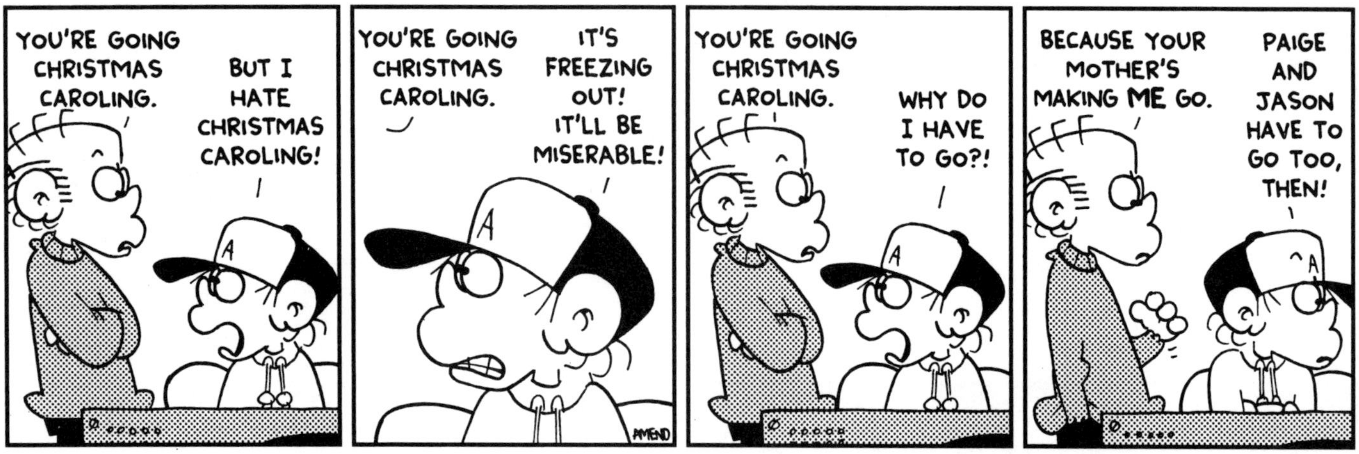
YOU'RE GOING CHRISTMAS CAROLING.
BUT I HATE CHRISTMAS CAROLING!
YOU'RE GOING CHRISTMAS CAROLING.
IT'S FREEZING OUT! IT'LL BE MISERABLE!
YOU'RE GOING CHRISTMAS CAROLING.
WHY DO I HAVE TO GO?!
BECAUSE YOUR MOTHER'S MAKING ME GO.
PAIGE AND JASON HAVE TO GO TOO, THEN!
AMEND

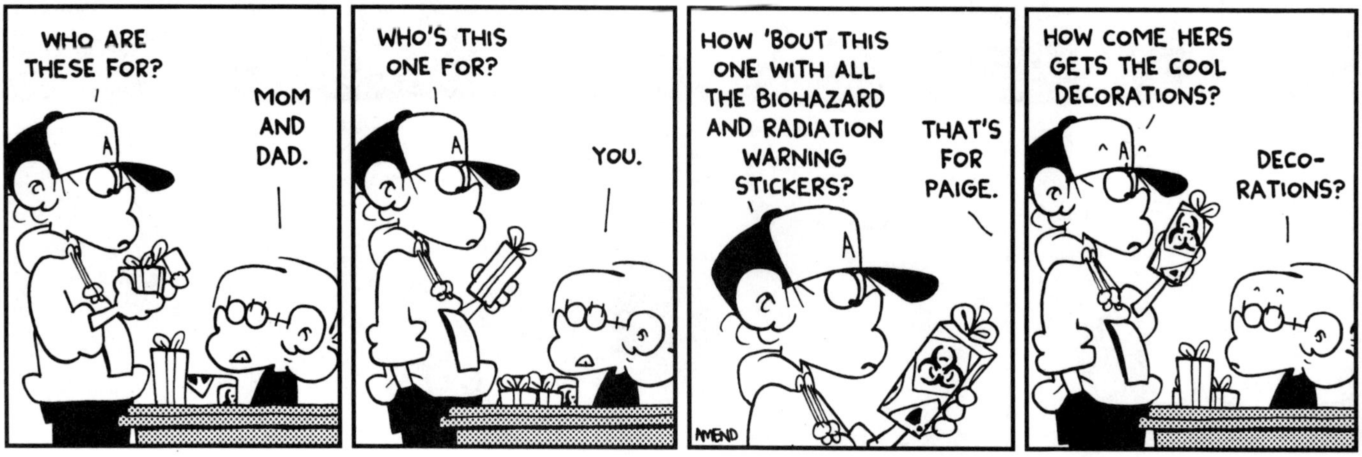
WHO ARE THESE FOR?
MOM AND DAD.
WHO'S THIS ONE FOR?
YOU.
HOW 'BOUT THIS ONE WITH ALL THE BIOHAZARD AND RADIATION WARNING STICKERS?
THAT'S FOR PAIGE.
HOW COME HERS GETS THE COOL DECORATIONS?
DECO-RATIONS?
AMEND

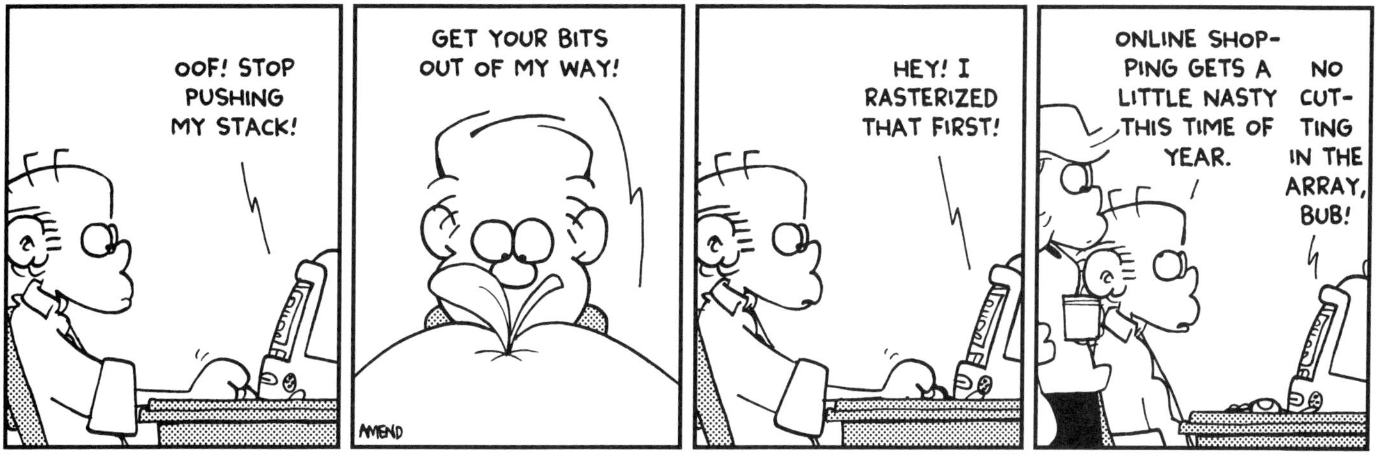
OOF! STOP PUSHING MY STACK!
GET YOUR BITS OUT OF MY WAY!
HEY! I RASTERIZED THAT FIRST!
ONLINE SHOPPING GETS A LITTLE NASTY THIS TIME OF YEAR.
NO CUTTING IN THE ARRAY, BUB!
AMEND

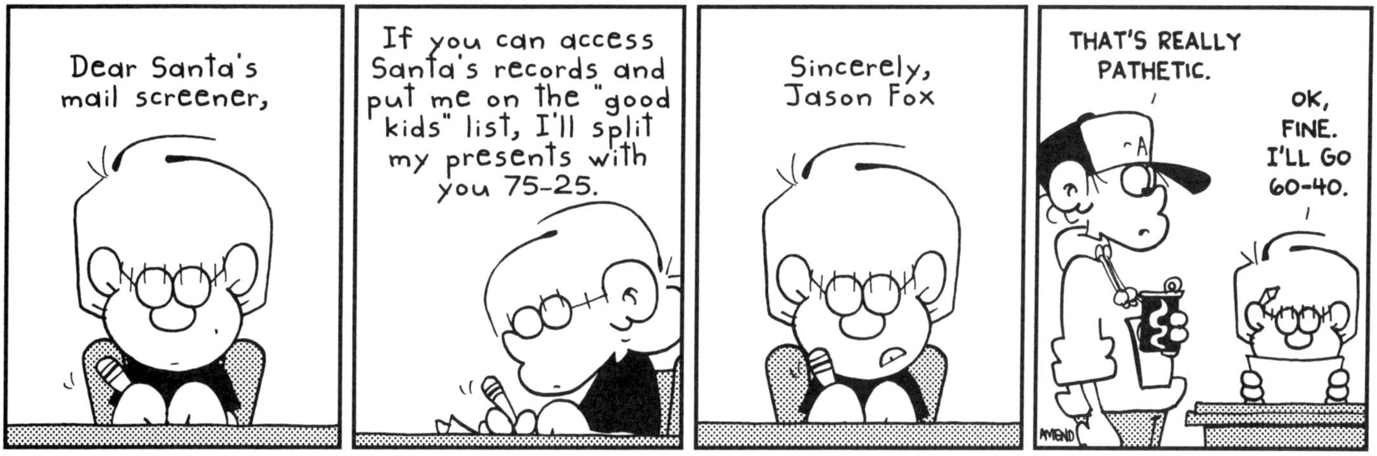
Dear Santa's mail screener,
If you can access Santa's records and put me on the "good kids" list, I'll split my presents with you 75-25.
Sincerely, Jason Fox
THAT'S REALLY PATHETIC.
OK, FINE. I'LL GO 60-40.
AMEND

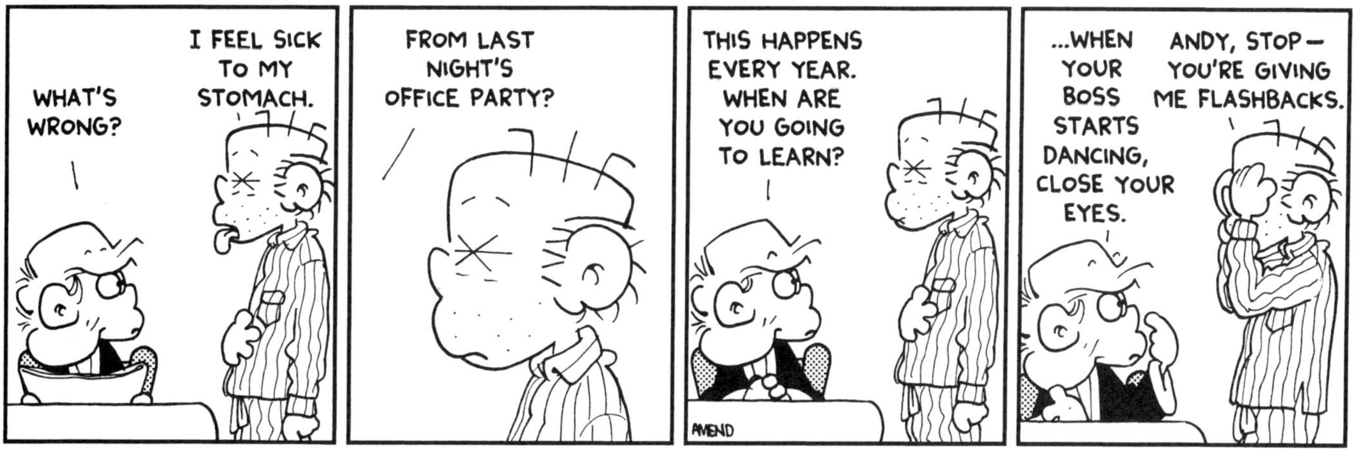
WHAT'S WRONG?
I FEEL SICK TO MY STOMACH.
FROM LAST NIGHT'S OFFICE PARTY?
THIS HAPPENS EVERY YEAR. WHEN ARE YOU GOING TO LEARN?
...WHEN YOUR BOSS STARTS DANCING, CLOSE YOUR EYES.
ANDY, STOP— YOU'RE GIVING ME FLASHBACKS.
AMEND

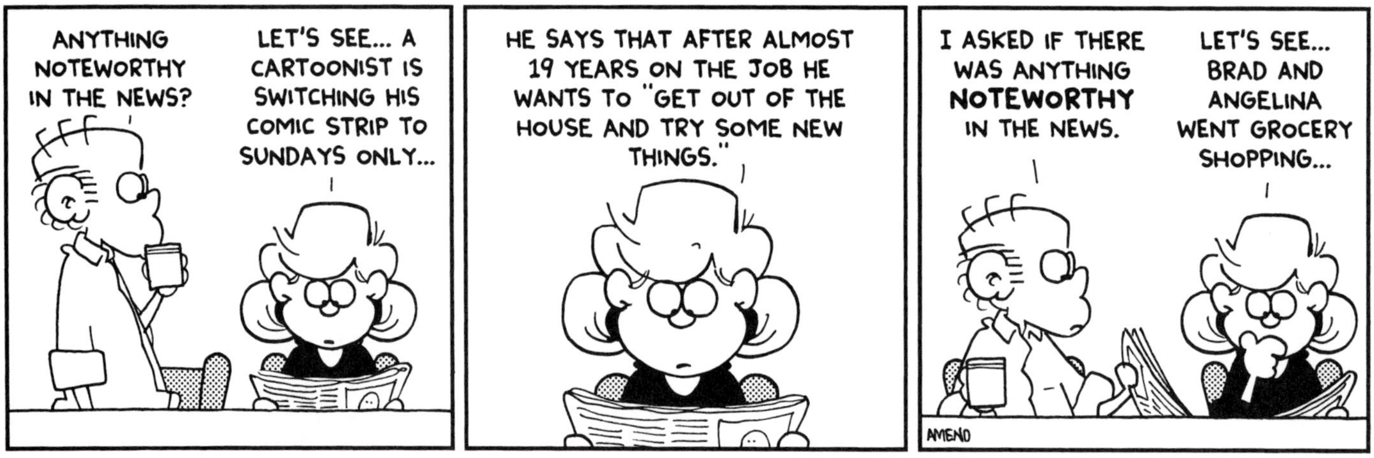
ANYTHING NOTEWORTHY IN THE NEWS?
LET'S SEE... A CARTOONIST IS SWITCHING HIS COMIC STRIP TO SUNDAYS ONLY...
HE SAYS THAT AFTER ALMOST 19 YEARS ON THE JOB HE WANTS TO "GET OUT OF THE HOUSE AND TRY SOME NEW THINGS."
I ASKED IF THERE WAS ANYTHING NOTEWORTHY IN THE NEWS.
LET'S SEE... BRAD AND ANGELINA WENT GROCERY SHOPPING...
AMEND

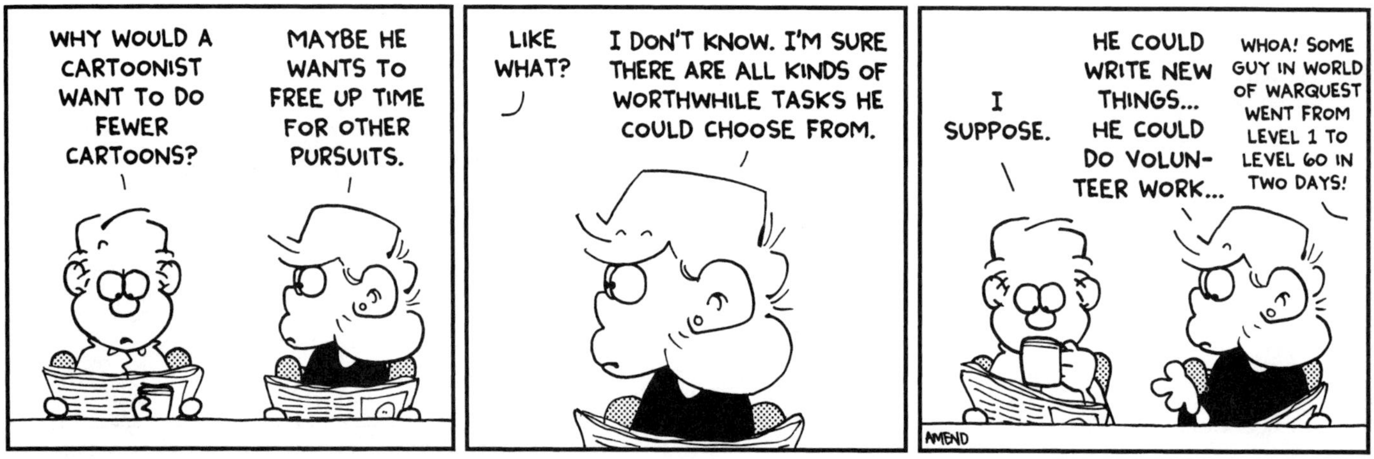
WHY WOULD A CARTOONIST WANT TO DO FEWER CARTOONS?
MAYBE HE WANTS TO FREE UP TIME FOR OTHER PURSUITS.
LIKE WHAT?
I DON'T KNOW. I'M SURE THERE ARE ALL KINDS OF WORTHWHILE TASKS HE COULD CHOOSE FROM.
I SUPPOSE.
HE COULD WRITE NEW THINGS... HE COULD DO VOLUNTEER WORK...
WHOA! SOME GUY IN WORLD OF WARQUEST WENT FROM LEVEL 1 TO LEVEL 60 IN TWO DAYS!
AMEND

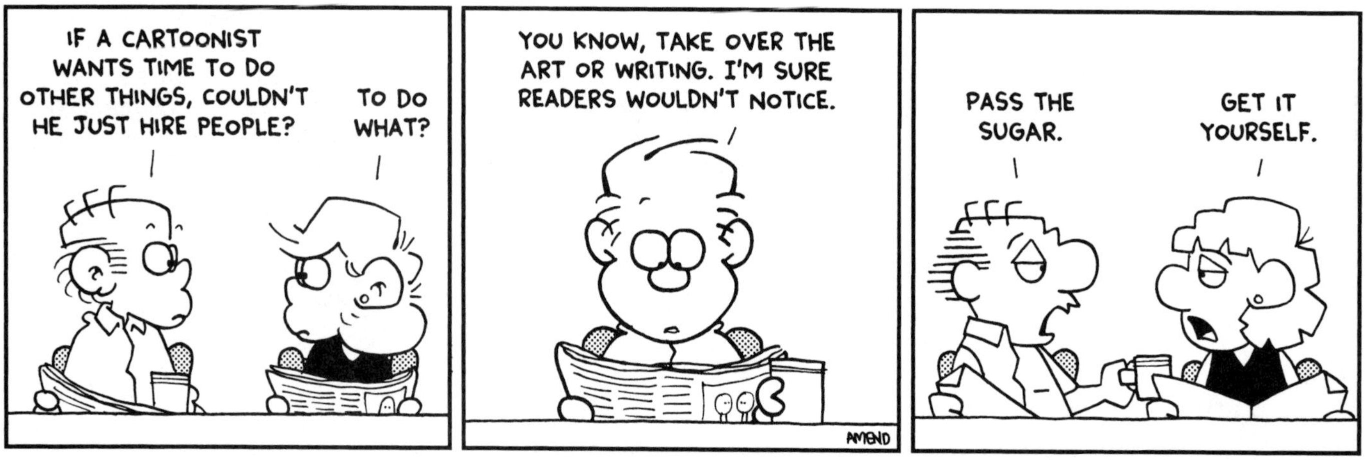
IF A CARTOONIST WANTS TIME TO DO OTHER THINGS, COULDN'T HE JUST HIRE PEOPLE?
TO DO WHAT?
YOU KNOW, TAKE OVER THE ART OR WRITING. I'M SURE READERS WOULDN'T NOTICE.
AMEND
PASS THE SUGAR.
GET IT YOURSELF.

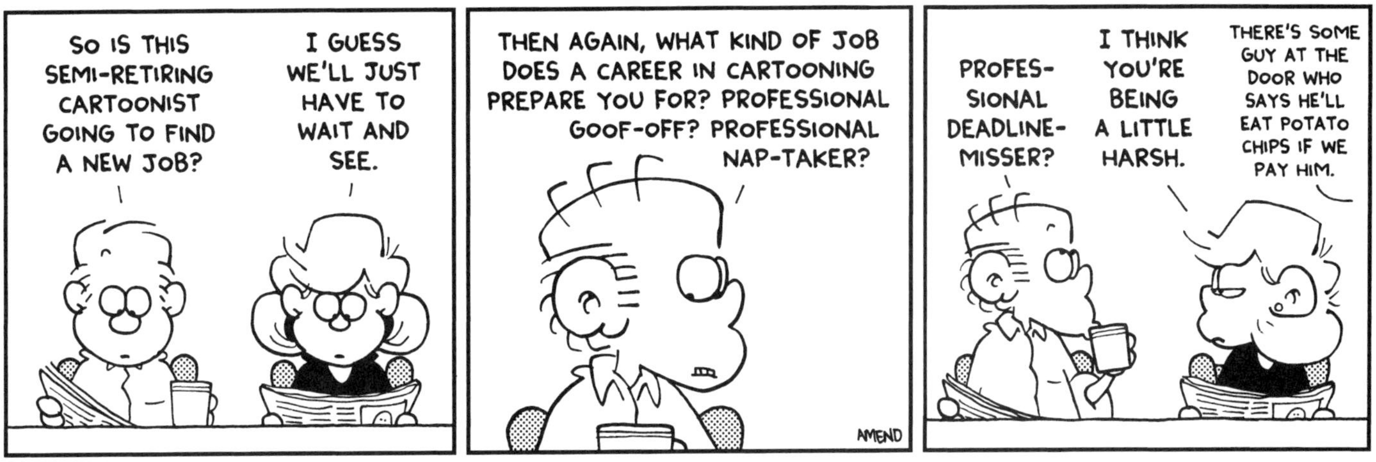
SO IS THIS SEMI-RETIRING CARTOONIST GOING TO FIND A NEW JOB?
I GUESS WE'LL JUST HAVE TO WAIT AND SEE.
THEN AGAIN, WHAT KIND OF JOB DOES A CAREER IN CARTOONING PREPARE YOU FOR? PROFESSIONAL GOOF-OFF? PROFESSIONAL NAP-TAKER?
PROFES-SIONAL DEADLINE-MISSER?
I THINK YOU'RE BEING A LITTLE HARSH.
THERE'S SOME GUY AT THE DOOR WHO SAYS HE'LL EAT POTATO CHIPS IF WE PAY HIM.
AMEND

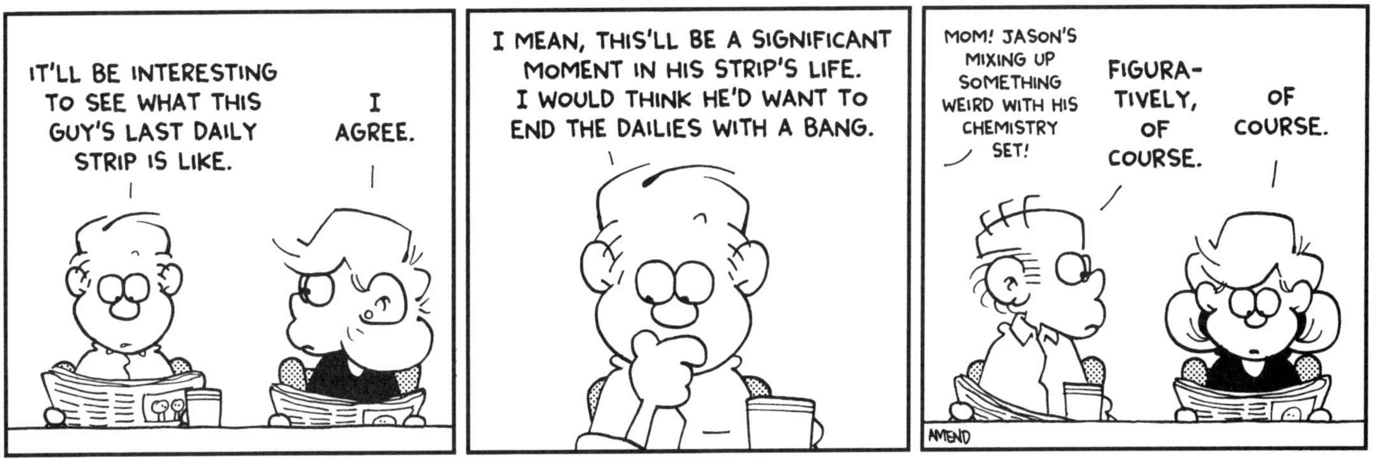
IT'LL BE INTERESTING TO SEE WHAT THIS GUY'S LAST DAILY STRIP IS LIKE.
I AGREE.
I MEAN, THIS'LL BE A SIGNIFICANT MOMENT IN HIS STRIP'S LIFE. I WOULD THINK HE'D WANT TO END THE DAILIES WITH A BANG.
MOM! JASON'S MIXING UP SOMETHING WEIRD WITH HIS CHEMISTRY SET!
FIGURA-TIVELY, OF COURSE.
OF COURSE.
AMEND

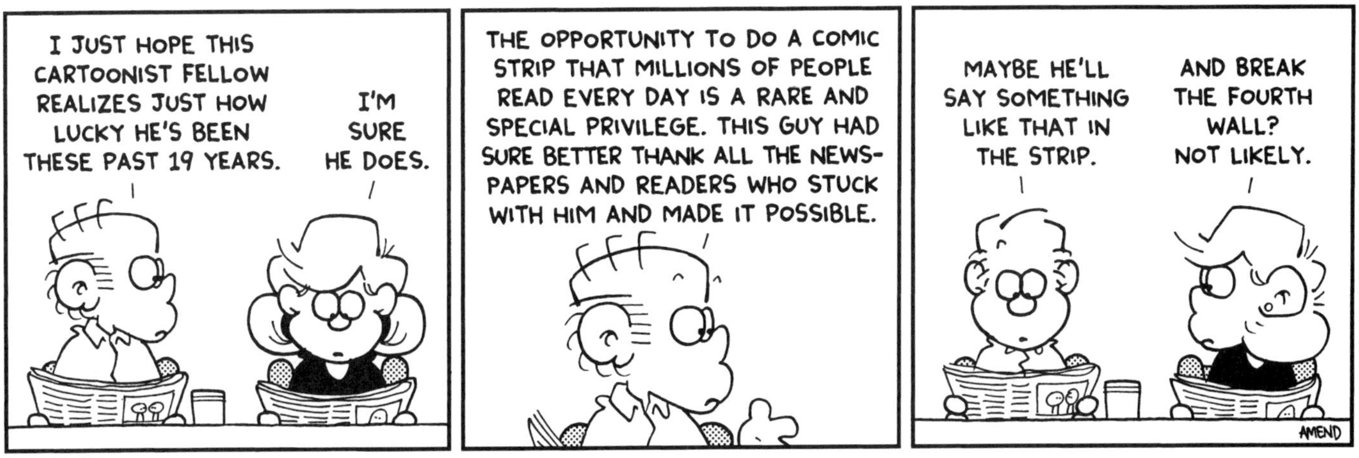
I JUST HOPE THIS CARTOONIST FELLOW REALIZES JUST HOW LUCKY HE'S BEEN THESE PAST 19 YEARS.
I'M SURE HE DOES.
THE OPPORTUNITY TO DO A COMIC STRIP THAT MILLIONS OF PEOPLE READ EVERY DAY IS A RARE AND SPECIAL PRIVILEGE. THIS GUY HAD SURE BETTER THANK ALL THE NEWS-PAPERS AND READERS WHO STUCK WITH HIM AND MADE IT POSSIBLE.
MAYBE HE'LL SAY SOMETHING LIKE THAT IN THE STRIP.
AND BREAK THE FOURTH WALL? NOT LIKELY.
AMEND

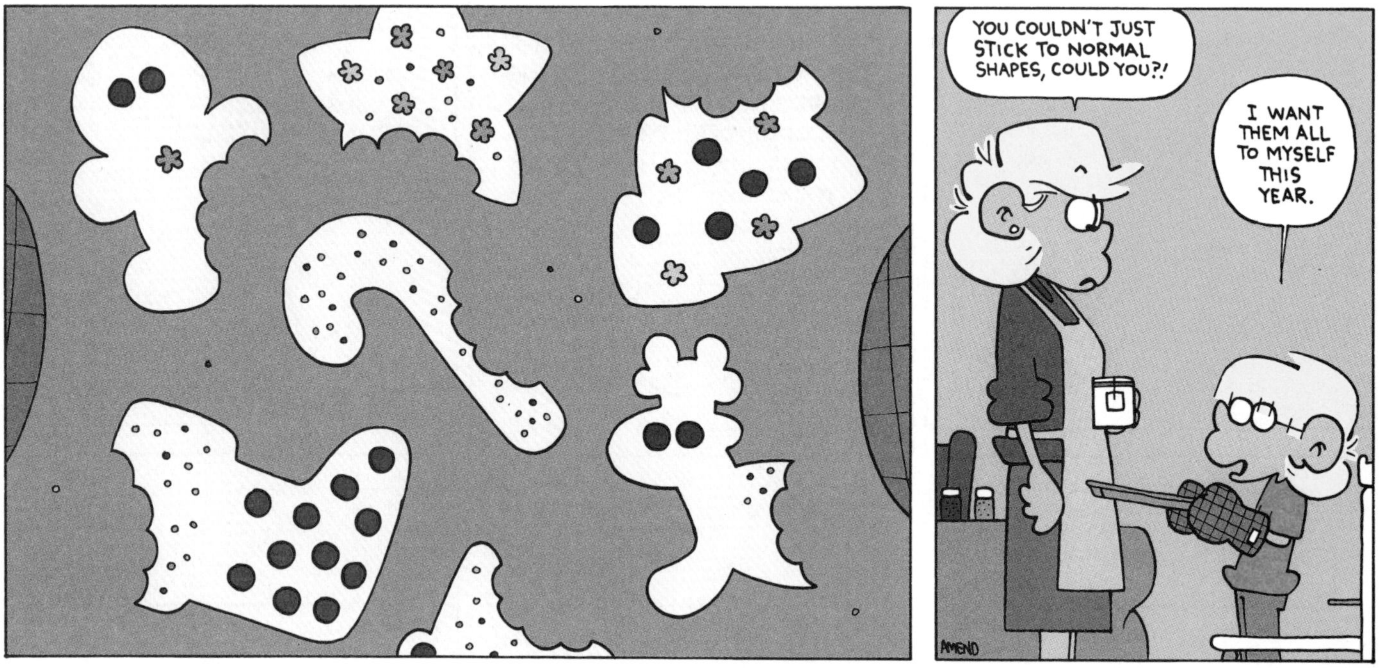
YOU COULDN'T JUST STICK TO NORMAL SHAPES, COULD YOU?!
I WANT THEM ALL TO MYSELF THIS YEAR.
AMEND

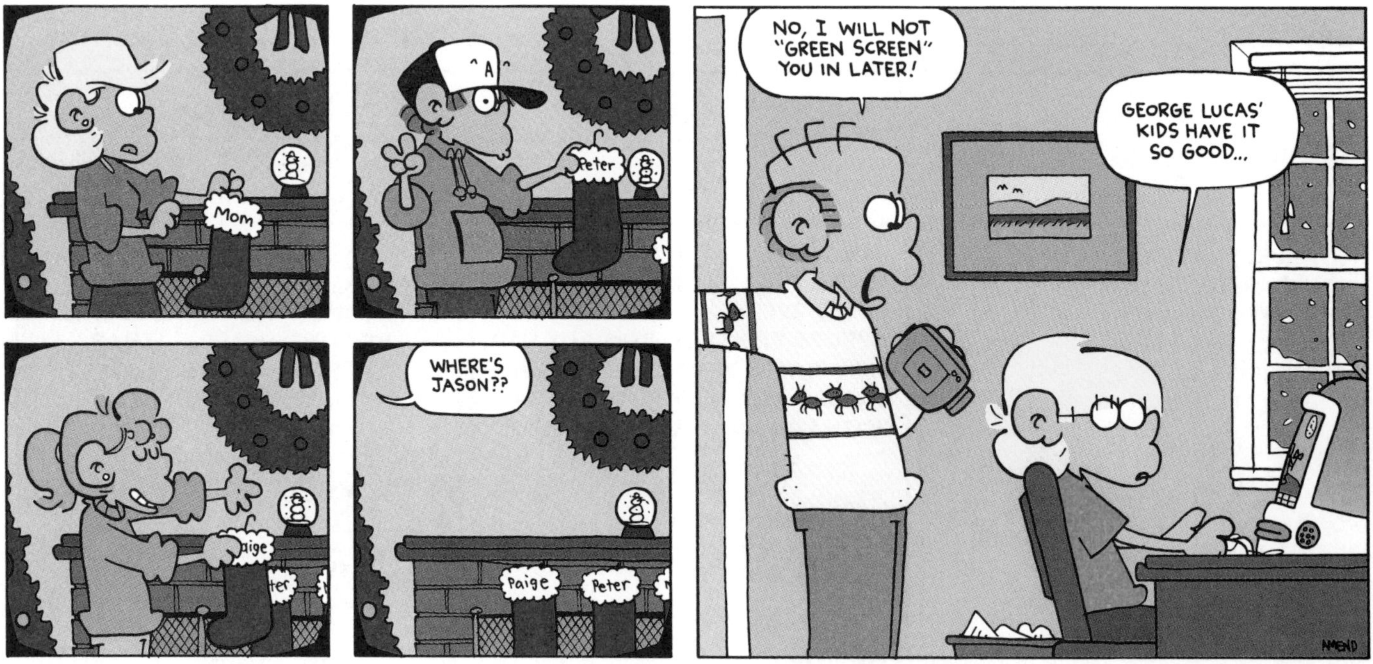
Mom
Peter
Paige
WHERE'S JASON??
Paige
Peter
NO, I WILL NOT "GREEN SCREEN" YOU IN LATER!
GEORGE LUCAS' KIDS HAVE IT SO GOOD...
AMEND

ERGO IPSO FACTO.
WHAT ARE YOU DOING?
SPEAKING LATIN. MY NEW YEAR'S RESOLUTION IS TO CEMENT MY REPUTATION AS A GENIUS, AND NOTHING CRIES OUT "INTELLECTUAL" MORE THAN SPEAKING LATIN.
AD HOC E PLURIBUS UNUM CARPE DIEM.
SEMPER FIDELIS PRIMA FACIE PER CAPITA.
A PRIORI QUOD ERAT DEMONST–
WILL YOU KNOCK IT OFF AND GET OUT OF MY ROOM?!?
YOU TOLD ME YOUR RESOLUTION WAS TO ANNOY US ALL IN NEW WAYS.
DID I SAY THAT? MEA CULPA.

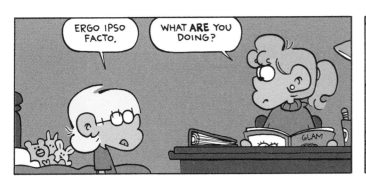

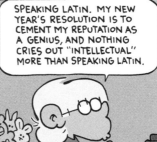

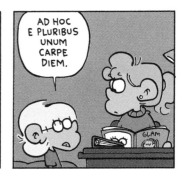

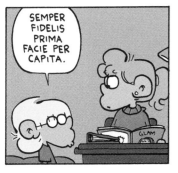

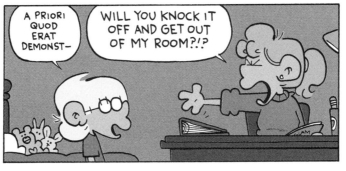

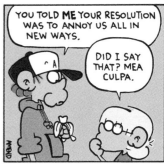